PREVENTING REGULATORY CAPTURE

When regulations (or lack thereof) seem to detract from the common good, critics often point to regulatory capture as a culprit. In some academic and policy circles, it seems to have assumed the status of an immutable law. Yet for all the ink spilled describing and decrying capture, the concept remains difficult to nail down in practice.

Is capture truly as powerful and unpreventable as the informed consensus seems to suggest? This edited volume brings together seventeen scholars from across the social sciences to address this question. Their work shows that capture is often misdiagnosed and may in fact be preventable and manageable. Focusing on the goal of prevention, the volume advances a more rigorous and empirical standard for diagnosing and measuring capture, paving the way for new lines of academic inquiry and more precise and nuanced reform.

Daniel Carpenter is the Allie S. Freed Professor of Government and Director of the Center for American Political Studies in the Faculty of Arts and Sciences at Harvard University. His first book, *The Forging of Bureaucratic Autonomy: Reputations, Networks and Policy Innovation in Executive Agencies, 1862–1928*, was awarded the American Political Science Association's Gladys Kammerer Prize, as well as the Charles Levine Prize of the International Political Science Association. His second book, *Reputation and Power: Organizational Image and Pharmaceutical Regulation at the FDA*, received the 2011 Allan Sharlin Memorial Award from the Social Science History Association.

Professor Carpenter has held fellowships from the John Simon Guggenheim Foundation, the Radcliffe Institute for Advanced Study, the Center for Advanced Study in the Behavioral Sciences, the Brookings Institution, and the Santa Fe Institute. He has received grants from the National Science Foundation, the National Endowment for the Humanities, the Robert Wood Johnson Foundation (Scholars in Health Policy 1998–2000, Investigator Award in Health Policy Research 2004–2007), the Alfred Sloan Foundation, the Russell Sage Foundation, and the Safra Center for Ethics.

David A. Moss is the John G. McLean Professor at Harvard Business School and the President of the Tobin Project, the nonprofit research organization that sponsored this volume. He has published numerous books and articles on economic policy and policy history, including *When All Else Fails: Government as the Ultimate Risk Manager*, which won the American Risk and Insurance Association's Annual Kulp-Wright Book Award for the "most influential text published on the economics of risk management and insurance." Other books include *Socializing Security: Progressive-Era Economists and the Origins of American Social Policy*, *A Concise Guide to Macroeconomics*, and *Government and Markets: Toward a New Theory of Regulation* (Cambridge University Press, 2010, coedited with Edward Balleisen).

Professor Moss is the recipient of numerous honors and awards, including the Robert F. Greenhill Award, the Editors' Prize from the *American Bankruptcy Law Journal*, and the Student Association Faculty Award for outstanding teaching at Harvard Business School.

Preventing Regulatory Capture

Special Interest Influence and How to Limit It

Edited by

DANIEL CARPENTER

Harvard University

DAVID A. MOSS

Harvard University

CAMBRIDGE
UNIVERSITY PRESS

CAMBRIDGE
UNIVERSITY PRESS

32 Avenue of the Americas, New York, NY 10013-2473, USA

Cambridge University Press is part of the University of Cambridge.

It furthers the University's mission by disseminating knowledge in the pursuit of
education, learning, and research at the highest international levels of excellence.

www.cambridge.org
Information on this title: www.cambridge.org/9781107646704

© The Tobin Project 2014

First published 2014

A catalog record for this publication is available from the British Library.

Library of Congress Cataloging in Publication Data
Preventing regulatory capture : special interest influence and how to limit it / [edited by] Daniel
Carpenter, Harvard University, David A. Moss, Harvard University.
pages cm
Includes index.
ISBN 978-1-107-03608-6 (hardback) – ISBN 978-1-107-64670-4 (pbk.)
1. Deregulation – United States.   2. Trade regulation – United States.   3. Interest groups –
United States.   I. Carpenter, Daniel P., 1967–   II. Moss, David A., 1964–
HD3616.U63P74   2013
338.973–dc23   2013008596

ISBN 978-1-107-03608-6 Hardback
ISBN 978-1-107-64670-4 Paperback

Contents

List of Figures

List of Tables

Editors

Daniel Carpenter is Allie S. Freed Professor of Government and Director of the Center for American Political Studies in the Faculty of Arts and Sciences at Harvard University. For the 2011–2012 academic year, he was a Walter Channing Cabot Faculty Fellow at Harvard and a visiting researcher at the Institut d'Études Politiques at the Université de Strasbourg in France. He graduated from Georgetown University in 1989 with distinction in Honors Government and received his doctorate in political science from the University of Chicago in 1996. He taught previously at Princeton University (1995–1998) and the University of Michigan (1998–2002). He joined the Harvard University faculty in 2002. Dr. Carpenter mixes theoretical, historical, statistical, and mathematical analyses to examine the development of political institutions, particularly in the United States. He focuses on public bureaucracies and government regulation, particularly regulation of health and financial products. His dissertation received the 1998 Harold D. Lasswell Award from the American Political Science Association (APSA) and as a book – *The Forging of Bureaucratic Autonomy: Reputations, Networks and Policy Innovation in Executive Agencies, 1862–1928* (Princeton: Princeton University Press, 2001) – was awarded the APSA's Gladys Kammerer Prize as well as the Charles Levine Prize of the International Political Science Association. His recently published book on pharmaceutical regulation in the United States, *Reputation and Power: Organizational Image and Pharmaceutical Regulation at the FDA* (Princeton: Princeton University Press, 2010), has received the 2011 Allan Sharlin Memorial Award from the Social Science History Association.

Professor Carpenter has held fellowships from the John Simon Guggenheim Foundation, the Radcliffe Institute for Advanced Study, the Center for Advanced Study in the Behavioral Sciences, the Brookings Institution, and the Santa Fe Institute. He has received grants from the National Endowment for the Humanities, the National Science Foundation, the Robert Wood

Johnson Foundation (Scholars in Health Policy 1998–2000, Investigator Award in Health Policy Research 2004–2007), the Alfred Sloan Foundation, the Russell Sage Foundation, and the Safra Center for Ethics. In the past few years, Professor Carpenter has been the winner of both the 2011 Herbert Simon Award of the Midwest Political Science Association for a scholar "who has made a significant career contribution to the scientific study of bureaucracy," as well as the 2011 David Collier Award of the American Political Science Association for career contributions to qualitative and multimethod research.

David A. Moss is the John G. McLean Professor at Harvard Business School, where he teaches in the Business, Government, and the International Economy (BGIE) unit. He earned his BA from Cornell University and his PhD from Yale. In 1992–1993, he served as a senior economist at Abt Associates. He joined the Harvard Business School faculty in July 1993. Professor Moss's research focuses on economic policy, especially the government's role as a risk manager. He has published three books on these subjects: *Socializing Security: Progressive-Era Economists and the Origins of American Social Policy* (Harvard University Press, 1996), which traces the intellectual and institutional origins of the American welfare state; *When All Else Fails: Government as the Ultimate Risk Manager* (Harvard University Press, 2002), which explores the government's pivotal role as a risk manager in policies ranging from limited liability law to federal disaster relief; and *A Concise Guide to Macroeconomics: What Managers, Executives, and Students Need to Know* (Harvard Business School Press, 2007), a primer on macroeconomics and macroeconomic policy. In addition to these books, Moss has coedited two volumes on economic regulation and has published numerous articles, book chapters, and case studies, mainly in the fields of institutional and policy history, financial history, political economy, and regulation. One recent article, "An Ounce of Prevention: Financial Regulation, Moral Hazard, and the End of 'Too Big to Fail'" (*Harvard Magazine*, September–October 2009), grew out of his research on financial regulation for the TARP Congressional Oversight Panel.

Professor Moss is the founder of the Tobin Project, a nonprofit research organization, and a member of the National Academy of Social Insurance. Recent honors include the Robert F. Greenhill Award, the Editors' Prize from the *American Bankruptcy Law Journal*, the Student Association Faculty Award for outstanding teaching at the Harvard Business School (seven times), and the American Risk and Insurance Association's Annual Kulp-Wright Book Award for the "most influential text published on the economics of risk management and insurance."

Contributors

Christopher Carrigan is an Assistant Professor in the Trachtenberg School of Public Policy and Public Administration at George Washington University, where he teaches courses on microeconomics and applied statistics. His research is focused on how political influences, social forces, and organizational characteristics interact to shape outcomes at government agencies. Currently, Professor Carrigan is analyzing the extent to which locating nonregulatory functions with regulators affects both behavior at and performance of these organizations. His work has been published or is forthcoming in the *Annual Review of Political Science* as well as edited volumes assessing regulatory capture and investigating disasters in regulated industries. Professor Carrigan holds a PhD in public policy from the Harvard Kennedy School, an MBA from the University of Chicago, and a BA in economics from Davidson College. He joined the Trachtenberg School from the University of Pennsylvania Law School, where he was the Regulation Fellow at the Penn Program on Regulation. Previously, Professor Carrigan worked as a director at two economic consulting firms and as a manager at a large financial services company.

Mariano-Florentino Cuéllar works at the intersection of law, public policy, and political science. A member of the Stanford Law School faculty since 2001, he has served in the Obama and Clinton administrations, testified before lawmakers, and has an extensive record of involvement in public service. His research and teaching focus on administrative law, executive power, and how organizations implement regulatory responsibilities involving public health and safety, migration, and international security in a changing world. He is the codirector of Stanford's university-wide Center for International Security and Cooperation. From early 2009 through the summer of 2010, he served as special assistant to President Obama for justice and regulatory policy at the White House. Among other issues, Cuéllar worked on stricter food safety standards, federal sentencing and law enforcement reform, civil rights policy, enhancing regulatory transparency, and strengthening border coordination and immigrant integration. Before working on the White House Domestic Policy Council staff, he cochaired the Obama-Biden Transition's Immigration Policy Working Group. During the second term of the Clinton administration, he worked at the U.S. Department of the Treasury as senior advisor to the Under Secretary for Enforcement. In July 2010, the president appointed him to the Council of the Administrative Conference of the United States, an independent agency charged with improving the efficiency and fairness of federal regulatory programs. He also serves on the Department of Education's National Commission on Educational Equity and Excellence, and the Department of State's Advisory Sub-Committee on Economic Sanctions. In addition, he is a board member of the Constitution Project, a nonprofit think tank that builds bipartisan consensus on constitutional and legal issues. After graduating from Calexico High School in California's Imperial Valley, he received an AB *magna cum laude* from Harvard, a JD from Yale Law School, and a PhD in political science from Stanford. He clerked for Chief Judge Mary M. Schroeder of the U.S. Court of Appeals for the Ninth Circuit and is a member of the American Law Institute and the Council on Foreign Relations.

Jonathan B. L. Decker is an associate in the Bankruptcy & Business Restructuring department of Ropes & Gray LLP. He graduated from Harvard College in 2003 and received his JD from Harvard Law School in 2007. His research in bankruptcy law focused on the surprising regional and debtor/creditor politics that shaped the U.S. Bankruptcy Act of 1898. He has also written about movie musicals and lifestyle magazines.

Sanford C. Gordon is Associate Professor of Politics at New York University. He received his BA from Cornell and his PhD from Princeton. Prior to his arrival at NYU, Professor Gordon taught at the Ohio State University from 1999–2002, and in 2005–2006, he was a Fellow-in-Residence at the Center for the Study of Democratic Politics at Princeton. Professor Gordon's work – spanning interest group influence in administrative and legislative politics, bureaucratic politicization, the political economy of criminal justice, and research methodology – has appeared in the *American Political Science Review*, the *American Journal of Political Science*, the *Journal of Politics*, the *Quarterly Journal of Political Science*, *Political Analysis*, the *Journal of Law,*

Economics, and Organization; and the *New England Journal of Medicine*, among other places.

Catherine Hafer is an Associate Professor of Politics at New York University. Her primary fields are political economy, applied game theory, and American politics. She received her BS in economics from the California Institute of Technology and PhD in political science from the University of Rochester. Her research focuses on the properties of incentives created by diverse social, legal, and political institutions and on the emergence and maintenance of such institutions in dynamic economic and political environments. Her recent work has focused on the emergence of property rights, authority, and the rule of law in weakly institutionalized settings, incentives for lobbying and campaign contributions, and determinants of informative argumentation in settings with diverse institutions of voting and debate. Her work has appeared in a number of leading political science and economics journals, including the *American Political Science Review, Review of Economic Studies, Journal of Politics, Quarterly Journal of Political Science*, and others.

James Kwak joined the faculty at the University of Connecticut School of Law in 2011 as an Associate Professor of Law. He has a wide range of interests, including business organizations, corporate governance, financial markets and regulation, and fiscal policy. He is an online columnist for *The Atlantic* and coauthor of The Baseline Scenario, a leading blog covering economics and public policy. His articles have appeared in many publications, including *Democracy, The American Prospect, The New York Times, The Washington Post,* and *The Los Angeles Times* and on the Web sites of *The Wall Street Journal, The Huffington Post, NPR, Foreign Policy,* and *The Financial Times*. He coauthored *13 Bankers: The Wall Street Takeover and the Next Financial Meltdown*, a 2010 *New York Times* bestseller chronicling the rise of the financial sector over the past three decades, and *White House Burning: The Founding Fathers, Our National Debt, and Why It Matters to You*, a *Wall Street Journal* business bestseller analyzing the history and politics of deficits and the national debt. Before going to law school, he worked as a management consultant at McKinsey and Company and cofounded Guidewire Software, a leading provider of core systems to property and casualty insurance companies. He lives in Amherst, Massachusetts, with his wife and two children.

Michael A. Livermore is the Executive Director of the Institute for Policy Integrity and an Associate Professor at NYU Law. He is the author, along with Richard L. Revesz, of *Retaking Rationality: How Cost-Benefit Analysis Can Better Protect the Environment and Our Health* (Oxford University Press, 2008). He is a frequent panelist at U.S. and international conferences on cost-benefit analysis, and his views and commentary have appeared in *BusinessWeek, Forbes, The Wall Street Journal, The Washington Post, The New Republic,* and *Time.* Livermore was a Postdoctoral Fellow at NYU's Law Center for Environmental and Land Use Law and served as a judicial clerk for the Honorable Harry T. Edwards at the U.S. Court of Appeals for the D.C. Circuit. Between 1995 and 2002, Livermore worked for the New York Public Interest Research Group (NYPIRG), where he was a leading voice of the state's environmental community. Livermore graduated *magna cum laude* from New York University School of Law, where he was a managing editor of the *NYU Law Review.* He has published legal scholarship on topics including cost-benefit analysis in the global context, regulatory ossification, water pollution control, judicial decisionmaking, and international food safety standards.

M. Elizabeth Magill was appointed the Richard E. Lang Professor of Law and Dean of Stanford Law School on September 1, 2012. She is the law school's thirteenth dean. Before coming to Stanford, she was on the faculty at the University of Virginia School of Law for fifteen years, serving most recently as vice dean, the Joseph Weintraub–Bank of America Distinguished Professor of Law, and the Elizabeth D. and Richard A. Merrill Professor. An expert in administrative law and constitutional structure, Dean Magill teaches administrative law, constitutional law, and food and drug law. Her scholarly articles have been published in leading law reviews, and she has won several awards for her scholarly contributions. She is a member of the American Law Institute and served as a Fellow in the Program in Law and Public Affairs at Princeton University; a visiting professor at Harvard Law School; and the Thomas Jefferson Visiting Fellow at Downing College, Cambridge University. After completing her BA in history at Yale University in 1988, Dean Magill served as a senior legislative assistant for energy and natural resources for U.S. Senator Kent Conrad, a position she held for four years. She left the Hill to attend the University of Virginia School of Law, where she was articles development editor of the *Virginia Law Review* and received several awards for academic and scholarly achievement. After graduating in 1995, Dean Magill clerked for Judge J. Harvie Wilkinson III of the U.S. Court of Appeals for the Fourth Circuit and then for U.S. Supreme Court Justice Ruth Bader Ginsburg.

Nolan McCarty is the Susan Dod Brown Professor of Politics and Public Affairs and Associate Dean at the Woodrow Wilson School of Public and

International Affairs. His research interests include U.S. politics, democratic political institutions, and political game theory. He is the coauthor of two books: *Political Game Theory* (2006, Cambridge University Press with Adam Meirowitz) and *Polarized America: The Dance of Ideology and Unequal Riches* (2006, MIT Press with Keith Poole and Howard Rosenthal). Other recent publications include *The Realignment of National Politics and the Income Distribution* (1997 with Keith Poole and Howard Rosenthal); "Does Gerrymandering Cause Polarization" (2009 with Keith Poole and Howard Rosenthal) in the *American Journal of Political Science*; "Presidential Vetoes in the Early Republic" (2004) in *Journal of Politics*; "Bureaucratic Capacity, Delegation, and Political Reform" (2004 with John Huber) in the *American Political Science Review*; "The Appointments Dilemma" (2004) in the *American Journal of Political Science*; "Political Resource Allocation: The Benefits and Costs of Voter Initiatives" (2001 with John G. Matsusaka) in the *Journal of Law, Economics, and Organization*; "The Hunt for Party Discipline" (2001 with Keith Poole and Howard Rosenthal) in the *American Political Science Review*; "Cabinet Decision Rules and Political Uncertainty in Parliamentary Bargaining" (2001 with John Huber) in the *American Political Science Review*; and "The Politics of Blame: Bargaining Before an Audience" (2000 with Timothy Groseclose) in the *American Journal of Political Science*. McCarty was the program cochair of the 2005 Midwest Political Association meetings and was a Fellow at the Center for Advanced Study in the Behavioral Sciences during the 2004–2005 academic year. During the 2007–2008 academic year, he was the acting dean of the Woodrow Wilson School. In 2010, he was elected a Fellow of the American Academy of Arts and Sciences. He blogs about American politics at http://www.nolanmccarty.com.

William J. Novak, an award-winning legal scholar and historian, joined the University of Michigan Law School faculty in fall 2009. Professor Novak came from the University of Chicago, where he had been an associate professor of history; a founding member of the university's Human Rights Program and Law, Letters, and Society Program; and director of its Center for Comparative Legal History. Since 2000, Novak has been a research professor at the American Bar Foundation. In 1996, he published *The People's Welfare: Law and Regulation in Nineteenth-Century America*, which won the American Historical Association's Littleton-Griswold Prize and was named Best Book in the History of Law and Society. A specialist on the legal, political, and intellectual history of the United States, Professor Novak earned his PhD in the history of American civilization from Brandeis University in 1991. He was a visiting faculty member at Michigan Law during fall 2007, when he taught courses in U.S. legal history and legislation. Professor Novak is currently at work on *The People's Government: Law and the Creation of the Modern American State*, a study of the transformation in American liberal governance around the turn of the twentieth century.

Judge Richard A. Posner clerked for Justice William F. Brennan Jr. following his graduation from Harvard Law School. From 1963 to 1965, he was assistant to Commissioner Philip Elman of the Federal Trade Commission. For the next two years he was assistant to the Solicitor General of the United States. Prior to going to Stanford Law School in 1968 as Associate Professor, Judge Posner served as general counsel of the President's Task Force on Communications Policy. He first came to the University of Chicago Law School in 1969 and was Lee and Brena Freeman Professor of Law prior to his appointment in 1981 as a judge of the U.S. Court of Appeals for the Seventh Circuit. He was the chief judge of the court from 1993 to 2000. Judge Posner has written a number of books, including *Economic Analysis of Law* (8th ed., 2011); *The Economics of Justice* (1981); *Law and Literature* (3rd ed., 2009); *The Problems of Jurisprudence* (1990); *Cardozo: A Study in Reputation* (1990); *The Essential Holmes* (1992); *Sex and Reason* (1992); *Overcoming Law* (1995); *The Federal Courts: Challenge and Reform* (1996); *Law and Legal Theory in England and America* (1996); *The Problematics of Moral and Legal Theory* (1999); *Antitrust Law* (2nd ed., 2001); *Law, Pragmatism, and Democracy* (2003); *Catastrophe: Risk and Response* (2004); *Preventing Surprise Attacks: Intelligence Reform in the Wake of 9/11* (2005); *How Judges Think* (2008); *A Failure of Capitalism: The Crisis of '08 and the Descent into Depression* (2009); and *The Crisis of Capitalist Democracy* (2010), as well as books on the Clinton impeachment and *Bush v. Gore* and many articles in legal and economic journals and book reviews in the popular press. He has taught administrative law, antitrust, economic analysis of law, history of legal thought, conflict of laws, regulated industries, law and literature, the legislative process, family law, primitive law, torts, civil procedure, evidence, health law and economics, law and science, and jurisprudence. He was the founding editor of the *Journal of Legal Studies* and (with Orley Ashenfelter) the *American Law and Economics Review*. He is an Honorary Bencher of the Inner Temple and a Corresponding Fellow of the British Academy, and he was the President of the American Law and Economics Association from 1995 to 1996 and the honorary President of the Bentham Club of University College London for 1998. He has received honorary degrees from leading American and foreign universities, along with a number of awards, including the Thomas Jefferson Memorial Foundation Award in Law from the University of Virginia in 1994, the Marshall-Wythe Medallion from the College of William and Mary in 1998, the 2003 Research Award from the Fellows of the American Bar Foundation, also in 2003 the John Sherman Award from the U.S. Department of Justice, the Learned Hand Medal for Excellence in Federal Jurisprudence from the Federal Bar Council in 2005, also in 2005 the Thomas C. Schelling Award from the John F. Kennedy School of Government at Harvard University, and the Ronald H. Coase Medal from the American Law and Economics Association in 2010.

Richard L. Revesz is one of the nation's leading voices in the fields of environmental and regulatory law and policy. He has published numerous books and more than fifty articles in major law reviews and journals. His work focuses on the use of cost-benefit analysis, the allocation of regulatory responsibility in a federal system, and the design of liability regimes. In 1994 and 2007, he received the American Bar Association's award for the best article or book on administrative law and regulatory practice published the previous year. Dean Revesz has actively participated in shaping environmental regulation and public policy. He currently serves on the National Academy of Sciences' Committee on Science, Technology, and Law, and is a public member of the Administrative Conference of the United States. He previously was a member of the Science Advisory Board of the U.S. Environmental Protection Agency, as well as a member of a committee of the National Research Council charged with studying the costs and benefits of U.S. energy production and use. Dean Revesz graduated *summa cum laude* from Princeton University, earned a master's degree in environmental engineering from the Massachusetts Institute of Technology, and received his law degree from Yale Law School, where he was editor-in-chief of the *Yale Law Journal*. Following clerkships with Chief Judge Wilfred Feinberg of the U.S. Court of Appeals for the Second Circuit and Justice Thurgood Marshall of the U.S. Supreme Court, Revesz joined the faculty of NYU School of Law in 1985 and became dean in 2002. He has been a visiting professor at Princeton's Woodrow Wilson School of Public and International Affairs, Harvard Law School, Yale Law School, and the Graduate Institute for International Studies in Geneva, Switzerland. Dean Revesz is a trustee of the American Museum of Natural History and a member of the Committee on Conscience of the United States Holocaust Memorial Museum. He is also a fellow of the American Academy of Arts and Sciences and a member of the Council on Foreign Relations and of the American Law Institute.

Daniel Schwarcz primarily focuses on consumer protection and regulation in property/casualty and health insurance markets. His articles have been published, or accepted for publication, in the *University of Chicago Law*

Review, Virginia Law Review, Minnesota Law Review, North Carolina Law Review, William and Mary Law Review, and *Tulane Law Review.* Additionally, he is the editor of a book entitled *The Law and Economics of Insurance* and recently joined the casebook *Abraham's Insurance Law and Regulation,* which has been used as the principal text in courses on insurance law in more than 100 American law schools. In 2011, his article "Reevaluating Standardized Insurance Policies" received the Liberty Mutual Prize for an exceptional article on insurance law and regulation. Professor Schwarcz teaches insurance law, health care regulation and finance, contract law, and commercial law. He was named the Stanley V. Kinyon Overall Teacher of the Year for 2011–2012 and the Stanley V. Kinyon Tenure-Track Teacher of the Year for 2007–2008. Additionally, he serves as a Funded Consumer Representative to the National Association of Insurance Commissioners and has served as an expert witness in multiple insurance-related disputes. Professor Schwarcz earned his AB, *magna cum laude,* from Amherst College and his JD, *magna cum laude,* from Harvard Law School. While in law school, he was an Articles Editor for the *Harvard Law Review* and a John M. Olin Fellow in Law and Economics. After law school, he clerked for Judge Sandra Lynch on the U.S. Court of Appeals for the First Circuit and practiced at the law firm Ropes & Gray, where he worked mainly on insurance law matters. He subsequently spent two years as a Climenko Fellow and Lecturer on Law at Harvard Law School.

Susan Webb Yackee is an Associate Professor of Public Affairs and Political Science. Her research and teaching interests include regulation, administrative law, interest groups, bureaucratic politics, and the policymaking process. Her work has been published in the *Journal of Politics, George Washington Law Review, Journal of Public Administration Research and Theory, British Journal of Political Science, Journal of Policy Analysis and Management, American Politics Research, Political Research Quarterly,* and *Policy Studies Journal.* Yackee won the 2008 Paul Volcker Endowment Junior Scholar Research Award from the American Political Science Association's Public Administration Section. She also received APSA's 2007 "Emerging Scholar Award" from its Political Parties and Organizations Section, and the Midwest Political Science Association honored her with the "Best Paper by an Emerging Scholar" Award in 2008. In 2010, she received a poster session award for "Excellent Research by New and Emerging Scholars" from the Association for Public Policy Analysis and Management. From 2003 to 2005, Dr. Yackee was a Robert Wood Johnson Foundation Scholar in Health Policy Research at the University of Michigan in Ann Arbor. She has served as a Smith Richardson Domestic Policy Fellow, a UW-Madison Vilas Associate Professor, and a Harry S. Truman Scholar. Before beginning her academic training, she worked as a legislative research assistant in the U.S. Senate.

Luigi Zingales joined the Chicago Booth faculty in 1992. His research interests range from corporate governance to financial development, from political economy to the economic effects of culture. Currently, he is involved in developing the best interventions to cope with the aftermath of the financial crisis. He also codeveloped the Financial Trust Index, which is designed to monitor the level of trust that Americans have toward their financial system. In addition to holding his position at Chicago Booth, Zingales is currently a Faculty Research Fellow for the National Bureau of Economic Research, a Research Fellow for the Center for Economic Policy Research, and a Fellow of the European Governance Institute. He is also the director of the American Finance Association and an editorialist for *Il Sole 24 Ore*, the Italian equivalent of the *Financial Times*. Zingales also serves on the Committee on Capital Markets Regulation, which has been examining the legislative, regulatory, and legal issues affecting how public companies function. His research has earned him the 2003 Bernácer Prize for the best young European financial economist, the 2002 NASDAQ award for best paper in capital formation, and a National Science Foundation grant in economics. His work has been published in the *Journal of Financial Economics*, the *Journal of Finance*, and the *American Economic Review*. Zingales received a bachelor's degree in economics *summa cum laude* from Università Bocconi in Italy in 1987 and a PhD in economics from the Massachusetts Institute of Technology in 1992. In addition to teaching and researching, Zingales enjoys cooking and spending time with his children.

Preface

In the wake of the global financial crisis of 2007–2009 and the Deep Water Horizon Oil Spill of 2010, regulatory capture has become at once a diagnosis and a source of discomfort. The word *capture* has been used by dozens upon dozens of authors – ranging from pundits and bloggers to journalists and leading scholars – as the telltale characterization of the regulatory failures that permitted these crises. In addition, critics who doubt whether regulatory reforms will be sufficient draw on capture as a source of widespread skepticism (if not despair). Seen this way, capture of regulation appears not only as a significant cause of these crises, but also as a constraint on any realistic solutions. Most of those solutions will, in this view, be watered down or dashed by captured regulators in the future.

Is capture truly as powerful and unpreventable as the informed consensus seems to suggest? When it prevails, does capture pose insurmountable obstacles to regulation, so much so that we ought to give up on regulation altogether? This edited volume brings together seventeen scholars from across disciplines whose contributions together question this logic and suggest that capture may, in fact, be preventable and manageable.

The volume is part of a broader project to re-imagine regulatory scholarship. In early 2008, a group of social scientists convened to consider the state of scholarship on regulation as part of a research initiative organized by the Tobin Project, an independent and nonprofit research organization based in Cambridge, Massachusetts. Although research on government failure had come a long way since the mid-twentieth century, scholarship on what distinguishes government success from failure had been less robust. It was as if medical researchers had spent decades identifying cases of medical error, without offering a complementary understanding of how (and when) doctors intervened successfully to improve patients' lives. A new focus was needed to better understand not only cases in which government failed, but also cases in which government succeeded, and the conditions under which each occurred. In 2010, this research effort produced a first edited volume – *Government & Markets: Toward a New Theory of Regulation* (eds. E. Balleisen & D. Moss, Cambridge University Press) – which explored both the promises and pitfalls of regulation and ultimately aimed to identify strategies for improving regulatory governance.

The financial crisis of 2007–2009 gave palpable urgency to this ongoing research initiative. As financial regulatory reform took center stage in Washington, D.C., policymakers were faced with a great range of complex issues, tasked with addressing the risks and benefits inherent in everything from derivatives markets to systemically significant financial institutions. To get up to speed on such highly specialized subjects, legislators and their staffs often turned to outside experts for input. At various points during the regulatory reform process, scholars involved in the Tobin Project's research efforts were asked to share their perspectives on the problems of financial regulation and to give advice on potential solutions.

As these conversations progressed, preventing capture emerged as an important issue for policymakers. Throughout 2009 and 2010, both the House of Representatives and the Senate were considering bills that would establish a new agency with independent authority to protect retail consumers of financial products, an idea initially developed by Professor (now Senator) Elizabeth Warren[1] and ultimately instituted as the new Consumer Financial Protection Bureau. At the same time, both houses of Congress were exploring options for how to manage systemic risk throughout the financial system, proposals that ultimately gave rise to the Financial Stability Oversight Council. With respect to both efforts, the question arose repeatedly: Was it possible to design agencies in ways that would protect or insulate them from capture?

In 2009, the Tobin Project convened many of our country's leading experts on regulation to take up this question of how to prevent regulatory capture. The inquiry quickly gained traction, and this volume is one of the products of that effort. In line with the mission of the Tobin Project, the chapters that follow aim to deepen our understanding of a truly important and consequential problem facing the nation. The Tobin Project is grateful to the authors who have contributed to this inquiry and hopeful that the

---

[1] See Elizabeth Warren. "Unsafe at Any Rate." *Democracy: A Journal of Ideas* 5 (2007): 8–19 (based on a working paper originally written for and presented at a 2007 Tobin Project working group meeting on risk policy).

volume will prove informative to scholars and policymakers alike and will inspire further rounds of research on regulatory capture – and how to prevent it – in the years ahead.

The Tobin Project
Cambridge, Massachusetts, 2013

Acknowledgments

This volume is the product of an ongoing process of collaboration and exchange at the Tobin Project, sustained by the energy, talents, and resources of numerous individuals.

We would first like to thank Steven Croley, of the University of Michigan Law School, for his vital input when the ideas for this project were still crystallizing, and Mitchell Weiss, the first executive director of the Tobin Project, who helped conceive of – and launch – the "preventing capture" effort. We are also deeply indebted to John Cisternino, the Tobin Project's Director of Research, who has played a large role in sparring over core ideas and moving the project forward, along with Melanie Wachtell Stinnett, the Tobin Project's Director of Policy and Communications.

From the genesis of the idea for this volume until the last round of revisions, and at every step in between, the tireless work of the Tobin staff has been simply invaluable, both intellectually and administratively. In addition to those already named, we would especially like to recognize Katie Nihill, Tim Lambert, Yousef Gharbieh, and Sage Trombulak for their outstanding contributions to the volume.

Many of the main ideas animating our research agenda on regulation originated during discussions with policymakers, whose work this volume aspires to illuminate and assist. We would like to thank all of those members of Congress and the administration who participated in a productive roundtable discussion on regulatory capture in the fall of 2011. We are also grateful to Senator Sheldon Whitehouse for his ongoing engagement with this project since 2011, and to Senator Whitehouse and Jim Leach, Chair of the National Endowment for the Humanities, for contributing the Afterword. Senator Whitehouse's staff members, including Steven Lilley and Ayo Griffin, have been instrumental in helping to facilitate and shape the

Afterword, and we are very much indebted to them for all of the superb work they put into this project.

At Cambridge University Press, Scott Parris and Kristin Purdy have been outstanding editors and intellectual partners, and we wish to thank both of them for their guidance, attentiveness, and patience. We are grateful as well to the anonymous reviewers of the manuscript, who devoted much time and energy to working through the draft chapters and offered excellent advice. We also would like to express our appreciation to the Center for American Political Studies at Harvard University, and its Assistant Director Lilia Halpern-Smith, which graciously hosted one of our early workshops on the volume.

Finally, none of this would have been possible without the committed leadership of the Tobin Project's Board of Directors, and the generosity of its financial supporters. Stephanie Khurana, current board member and former interim executive director of the Tobin Project, merits particular recognition for her exceptional guidance and support all along the way.

Introduction

Daniel Carpenter and David A. Moss

When markets or regulations fall short of our expectations, observers often point to regulatory capture as a culprit. Critics maintain that regulatory capture stunts competition and innovation, as firms able to capture their regulators effectively wield the regulatory power of the state and can use it as a weapon to block the entry or success of other firms. Some critics even blame regulatory capture for the outbreak of financial crises and other manmade disasters. Recent years provide no exception. In the wake of the global financial crisis of 2007–2009, and following catastrophes ranging from massive oil spills to mine explosions, observers seemed to find capture everywhere.

In explaining the financial crisis, for example, both left and right pounced on the reputed capture of state and federal regulatory agencies. *Forbes* columnist Daniel Kauffman maintained that "There are multiple causes of the financial crisis. But we cannot ignore the element of 'capture' in the systemic failures of oversight, regulation and disclosure in the financial sector." Chicago economist Gary Becker pointed to an "economically disastrous example of the capture theory," one "provided by the disgraceful regulation of the two mortgage housing behemoths, Fannie Mae and Freddie Mac, before and leading up to the financial crisis." After the *Deepwater Horizon* explosion and Gulf Oil spill of spring 2010, conservative columnist Gerald P. O'Driscoll wrote in the *Wall Street Journal* that, "Obviously, regulation failed. By all accounts, MMS operated as a rubber stamp for BP. It is a striking example of regulatory capture: Agencies tasked with protecting the public interest come to identify with the regulated industry and protect its interests against that of the public. The result: Government fails to protect the public."[1]

---

[1] Kauffman, "Corruption and the Global Financial Crisis," *Forbes* (January 27, 2009); Gary S. Becker, "'Capture' of Regulators by Fannie Mae and Freddie Mac-Becker,"

1

Capture has thus been alleged – perhaps quite plausibly – to figure significantly in the major human and environmental crises of our time. In the aftermath of these crises, capture has also been blamed for severely undercutting efforts at reform. The widespread belief that special interests capture regulation, and that neither the government nor the public can prevent this, understandably weakens public trust in government and contributes to a sense that our political system is not capable of meeting the challenges it faces.

Surely, no system will be able to meet every challenge it encounters, and even effective political solutions will often – perhaps always – appear imperfect, as they address multiple and conflicting goals. Just as surely, however, political and regulatory solutions have overcome significant challenges in the past, from increasing the safety of our food supply and the security of our bank accounts to cleaning our air and water and reducing hazards on the road.[2] Regulatory capture is not always and everywhere the devastating problem it is often made out to be. In some cases, good regulation does prevail, in spite of the special interests. But what exactly does this imply? If we know that capture doesn't affect all regulation equally, is it possible to translate this truism into a deeper understanding of capture – of how to prevent it before it occurs and how to detect and eliminate (or at least mitigate) it where it is found?

This volume represents a first step toward answering these questions. It brings together a set of authors from a range of disciplines who carefully examine contemporary regulation to gain a clearer grasp of what regulatory capture is, where and to what extent it occurs, what prevents it from occurring more fully and pervasively, and, finally, to distill lessons for policymakers and the public for how capture can be mitigated and the public

---

http://www.becker-posner-blog.com/2011/06/capture-of-regulators-by-fannie-mae-and-freddie-mac-becker.html (accessed July 21, 2011); Gerald P. O'Driscoll, Jr., "The Gulf Spill, the Financial Crisis and Government Failure," *Wall Street Journal* (June 12, 2010). See also James Surowiecki, "The Regulation Crisis," *New Yorker* (June 14, 2010).

[2] In fact, recent polling indicates strong support among Americans for regulation (and even for stricter regulation) in key areas. According to a 2011 Harris poll, "The strongest support for stricter regulation relates to food safety (73%), executive pay and bonuses (70%), the safety of pharmaceuticals (70%), banks and financial services (69%), air and water pollution (68%), consumer product safety (67%), and environmental safety (66%). Majorities also support more strict regulation of advertising claims (65%), big business (64%), and health and safety in the workplace (54%)." See "Do We Want More or Less Regulation of Business? It All Depends on What Is Being Regulated," The Harris Poll #76, June 10, 2010, accessed July 23, 2011, www.harrisinteractive.com/NewsRoom/HarrisPolls/tabid/447/ctl/ReadCustom%20Default/mid/1508/ArticleId/407/Default.aspx.

interest protected. Such a comprehensive approach is badly needed. Cries of regulatory capture, from all quarters, have been met with little more than murmurs from the academy for some time now.[3] A surfeit of claims has been neither demonstrated nor disproved. Although early models and stylized case studies greatly advanced our understanding of the danger, there has been relatively little follow-up in recent decades. Our conception of how capture works in practice, and what limits it, remains very far from complete. Indeed, no general volume on regulatory capture has been produced in more than three decades, since the 1981 publication of political scientist Paul Quirk's *Industry Influence in Regulatory Agencies.*[4]

The chapters in this volume suggest that regulatory capture is very commonly misdiagnosed and mistreated. *Misdiagnosed* because the study of regulatory capture, in both academic and policy circles, has grown stale and ever more detached from practice. All too often, observers are quick to see capture as the explanation for almost any regulatory problem, making large-scale inferences about agencies and their cultures without a careful look at the evidence. At the same time, there appears to be a great deal of fatalism – some of it strategic, no doubt – about the impossibility of ameliorating or preventing capture, virtually ensuring that the ailment is *mistreated* in many cases. Some or even much of this may be the product of

thesis

---

[3] As Rhode Island Senator Sheldon Whitehouse remarked on the Senate floor in June 2011, "regulatory capture isn't getting the attention it deserves." "Congressional Record – Senate, S4453" (July 7, 2011).

[4] There have, of course, been numerous synthetic publications and new treatments on regulation, most notably Ian Ayres and John Braithwaite's *Responsive Regulation: Transcending the Deregulation Debate* (New York: Oxford University Press, 1992); Cass R. Sunstein, *After the Rights Revolution: Reconceiving the Regulatory State* (Chicago: University of Chicago Press, 1990). More recent treatments include David Moss, *When All Else Fails: Government as the Ultimate Risk Manager* (Cambridge, MA: Harvard University Press, 2005); W. Kip Viscusi, John M. Vernon, and Joseph E. Harrington, Jr., *Economics of Regulation and Antitrust* (Cambridge, MA: MIT Press, 2005); Edward Balleisen and David Moss, eds., *Government and Markets: Toward a New Theory of Regulation* (New York: Cambridge University Press, 2012); Steven Croley, *Regulation and Public Interests: The Possibility of Good Regulatory Government* (Princeton: Princeton University Press, 2008); Marc Eisner, *Regulatory Politics in Transition* (Baltimore, MD: Johns Hopkins University Press, 2000); and Cary Coglianese, ed., *Regulatory Breakdown: The Crisis of Confidence in U.S. Regulation* (Philadelphia, PA: University of Pennsylvania Press, 2012).

The closest theoretical accounts in mathematical modeling occur in sections of Jean-Jacques Laffont and Jean Tirole's *A Theory of Incentives in Procurement and Regulation* (Cambridge, MA: MIT Press, 1992) and in Gene Grossman and Elhanan Helpman's *Special Interest Politics* (Cambridge, MA: MIT Press, 2003). Yet these books do not offer specific or general empirical tests of the theory, and the models have limited applicability to the kinds of regulatory capture that are most important for public policy discussions. We offer further critiques later.

highly simplified models – models in which the complete capture of regulators by incumbent firms is all but inevitable. Once such simplified models permeated policy discourse, it is perhaps not surprising that capture came to be seen as lurking nearly everywhere and that the range of options for treating capture became unduly narrowed (sometimes with deregulation being seen as the only viable option).

Consider a few recent "scandals" in the news: financial regulators missing investment fraud and toxic loans at the very time their staff was shuttling back and forth between Washington and Wall Street; energy regulators ignoring the risk of a catastrophic oil spill just as their inspectors and officials were cavorting with industry managers; a telecommunications regulator making a series of industry-friendly decisions, and just over a year later a prominent commissioner who was a pivotal vote in these decisions departing the agency to take a high-status vice-presidential position with a regulated company.[5] In all of these cases, capture certainly seems plausible.

Plausibility, however, lies quite a distance from proof. If residents of an apartment complex witnessed a bitter argument between a father and son just days before the father was murdered, investigators might reasonably be interested in the son as a potential suspect. Yet evidence of the argument, by itself, would hardly be grounds for conviction. Unfortunately, students of regulation are not always as disciplined about distinguishing plausibility from proof, and claims of capture proliferate so broadly that they are rarely tested or examined closely. Even when they are well supported, such claims

---

[5] See "Madoff Bragged about Profits to SEC while Advising on Oversight," *Huffington Post Business* (December 16, 2008), accessed October 20, 2012, http://www.huffingtonpost .com/2008/12/16/madoff-bragged-about-prof_n_151332.html; Eric Dash, "Post-Mortems Reveal Obvious Risk at Banks," *The New York Times* (November 18, 2009), accessed October 20, 2012, http://www.nytimes.com/2009/11/19/business/19risk.html? pagewanted=all&_r=0; Edward Wyatt, "Promises Made, and Remade, by Firms in S.E.C. Fraud Cases," *The New York Times* (November 7, 2011), accessed October 20, 2012, http://www.nytimes.com/2011/11/08/business/in-sec-fraud-cases-banks-make-and-break-promises.html?pagewanted=all&_r=0; Noelle Straub, "Interior Probe Finds Fraternizing, Porn and Drugs at MMS Office in La.," *The New York Times* (May 25, 2010), accessed October 20, 2012, http://www.nytimes.com/gwire/2010/05/25/25greenwire-interior-probe-finds-fraternizing-porn-and-dru-45260.html?pagewanted=all; Eric Lipton and John M. Broder, "Regulator Deferred to Oil Industry on Rig Safety," *The New York Times* (May 7, 2010), accessed October 20, 2012, http://www.nytimes.com/2010/05/08/us/08agency. html; David Hatch, "Baker Stuns with Abrupt Move from FCC to Comcast," *National Journal* (May 12, 2011), accessed October 20, 2012, http://www.nationaljournal.com/ tech/baker-stuns-with-abrupt-move-from-fcc-to-comcast-20110511; Edward Wyatt, "F.C.C. Commissioner Leaving to Join Comcast," *The New York Times Media Decoder Blog* (May 11, 2011), accessed October 20, 2012, http://mediadecoder.blogs.nytimes .com/2011/05/11/f-c-c-commissioner-to-join-comcast/.

are often extended far beyond the available evidence. All too frequently, moreover, casual claims of capture are associated with demands that the regulatory policy or agency in question be not merely reformed but abandoned. Observers of regulation are often quicker to yelp about the evils of capture than to think hard about how it might be prevented or mitigated, short of wholesale deregulation.

This fatalism is seen in the center, the left, and the right of political discourse. As recent polling suggests, "This fatalism has over time deeply influenced not just scholars and inside-the-beltway cynics, but the broad mass of the American electorate. Public trust in the Federal government has slid ever lower over the last forty years and as of this writing, stands at under 20%."[6] To the extent that assumptions about regulatory capture contribute to such fatalism, it is incumbent on us to move beyond simplified theories and carefully explore special interest influence with a closer eye on practice.

In this volume, we aspire to improve our understanding of capture, making it more rigorous, more thorough, and more practically useful to those who want to prevent capture. Capture is real and a genuine threat to regulation, we recognize, but regulation is also a fact of modern life and undoubtedly necessary in some circumstances to protect the public and stave off catastrophe. The critical question is whether capture, where it exists, can be mitigated or prevented. We believe the evidence strongly suggests that the answer is yes, and that better study of regulation and special interest influence can show us how to limit capture and make regulatory governance a more useful tool for accomplishing public ends.

CAPTURE AND THE ACADEMY

The principal problems with contemporary capture scholarship boil down to the link between theory and evidence. As the financial crisis of 2007–2009 unfolded, we began to notice some common features of the dozens (if not hundreds) of claims being made about captured regulatory agencies. The claims had the benefit of seeming to resonate with the unfolding story, yet a disturbing commonality among them was a lack of solid or thorough evidence. Unfortunately, much the same can be said about a large proportion of capture scholarship – that good stories, rooted in elegant models, too often take the place of rigorous evidence.

---

[6] "Public Trust in Government," Pew Research Center, April 18, 2012, accessed October 21, 2012, http://people-press.org/2010/04/18/public-trust-in-government-1958–2010/.

Some of the earliest claims of capture within the academy came from scholars who were reviewing the early history of government regulation, and even then there was a tendency to rely heavily on especially juicy tidbits from the historical record. In 1892, Richard Olney, a prominent corporate attorney and soon-to-be attorney general, advised Charles E. Perkins, a railroad president, against seeking the repeal of the Interstate Commerce Act, noting that:

The [Interstate Commerce] Commission, as its functions have now been limited by the courts, is, or can be made, of great use to the railroads. It satisfies the popular clamor for a government supervision of railroads, at the same time that that supervision is almost entirely nominal. Further, the older such a Commission gets to be, the more inclined it will be found to take the business and railroad view of things. It thus becomes a sort of barrier between the railroad corporations and the people and a sort of protection against hasty and crude legislation hostile to railroad interests.... The part of wisdom is not to destroy the Commission, but to utilize it.

Olney's remark has been repeatedly quoted and cited as evidence that even the earliest national regulatory agencies in the United States were captured. Its language inspired the work of Bernstein and Huntington, and it was rehearsed on the floor of the United States Senate.[7] It is critical to understand, however, that Olney's letter, although certainly powerful, provides no direct evidence that the Commission did in fact "take the business and railroad view of things." Rather, it reveals only that one potentially interested observer predicted that the Interstate Commerce Commission (ICC) would take such a view and that it could ultimately be harnessed by the railroads. Similarly, well before Stigler penned his famous essay, "The Theory of Economic Regulation," another economist later identified with the Chicago school, Ronald Coase, surveyed the early history of federal broadcast regulation and suggested it had been poorly designed and conceived. Although Coase's seminal paper on the Federal Communications Commission (FCC) did not claim that broadcast regulation had been captured, his analysis appears to have set the stage for many of his followers to diagnose

---

[7] Richard Olney to Charles E. Perkins, December 28, 1892, quoted in Marver Bernstein, *Regulating Business by Independent Commission* (Princeton: Princeton University Press, 1955), 265. For an early citation to this remark, consult Matthew Josephson, *The Politicos* (New York: Harcourt Brace, 1938), 526. For a review of the intellectual history of the uses to which Olney's letter has been put, among other claims, see Eduardo Federico Canedo, "The Rise of the Deregulation Movement in Modern America, 1957–1980" (PhD dissertation, Columbia University, 2008). Olney's letter constituted a core reference and piece of evidence for some of the founding scholars of capture theory, including Bernstein and Huntington.

capture rather too easily, in some cases after only a cursory look at the historical evidence.[8]

These older claims about capture have been succeeded by scholarly arguments that make vast inferences from statistical correlations. Having claimed to show by statistical association that the relative wage and profit effects of labor safety and environmental regulation fell more heavily on small firms and industries in Southern states, economists Ann Bartel and Lacy Glenn Thomas declared this to be a case of "predation by regulation": "We have shown that regulation has become a predatory device that indeed is utilized to enhance the wealth of predators and to reduce the wealth of rivals."[9] Thomas later claimed to show a similar impact for food and drug regulation.[10] Similarly, in examining the stability of the cotton dust standards implemented by the Occupational Safety and Health Administration (OSHA), economist W. Kip Viscusi wrote in 1992:

now that the large firms in the industry are in compliance, they no longer advocate changes in the regulation. Presumably, the reason is that the capital costs of achieving compliance represent a barrier to the entry of newcomers into the industry. This is simply one more illustration of the familiar point that surviving firms often have a strong vested interest in the continuation of a regulatory system.

[8] Ronald Coase, "The Federal Communications Commission," *Journal of Law and Economics* 2 (October 1959): 1–40. On later claims that broadcast regulation was captured from the beginning, see especially Thomas W. Hazlett, "The Rationality of U.S. Regulation of the Broadcast Spectrum," *Journal of Law and Economics* 33 (1990): 133–75, and Hazlett, "Assigning Property Rights to Radio Spectrum Users: Why Did FCC License Auctions Take 67 Years?" *Journal of Law and Economics* 41 (2) (October 1998): 529–76. For an evaluation of the evidence relating to the alleged capture of early broadcast regulation, see Chapter 8, "Capturing History," by Moss and Decker in this volume.

[9] In a revealing rhetorical defense of these conclusions, Bartel and Thomas argued that their statistical associations were due directly to congressional calculations of the time. "We recognize that public interest theorists will object to our characterization of OSHA and EPA as predatory. From the viewpoint of these scholars, regulations inevitably have heterogeneous effects, and indirect effects are entirely innocent by-products of the public pursuit of work-place safety and environmental quality. We explicitly reject any such defense of OSHA and EPA behavior.... [W]e ... find ample evidence of OSHA and EPA actions that unnecessarily exacerbate or even artificially create indirect effects for political purposes (what we call enforcement asymmetries). Furthermore, despite mounting evidence of the inefficiency of OSHA and EPA, Congress has continued to be uninterested in adequate monitoring of regulatory effect, much less in regulatory reform. All this suggests that indirect effects are far more than innocent by-products – indeed, they may well be the primary political concern." Ann P. Bartel and Lacy Glenn Thomas, "Predation through Regulation: The Wage and Profit Effects of the Occupational Safety and Health Administration and the Environmental Protection Agency," *Journal of Law and Economics* 30 (2) (October 1987): 239–64.

[10] Lacy Glenn Thomas, "Regulation and Firm Size: FDA Impacts on Innovation," *The RAND Journal of Economics* 21 (4) (Winter, 1990): 497–515.

The stability of any law or regulation, and the lack of opposition to these policies, could be due to capture, but also potentially to inertia, to the institutions in American politics (filibuster, bicameralism, presidential veto, the Administrative Procedures Act) that make policy change difficult, or to broad public support for the regulations. Yet Viscusi is quick to highlight a well-established capture argument – incentives for creating or preserving entry barriers to competitors – as the explanation. We believe that far more evidence is needed to make an accurate diagnosis of capture.[11]

In thinking this way, economists, legal scholars, and political scientists have been following the lead of George Stigler, who argued that empirical analyses of the operation and effect of regulation should be used to make inferences about the original purposes of its design:

The theory [of economic regulation] tells us to look, as precisely and carefully as we can, at who gains and who loses, and how much, when we seek to explain a regulatory policy.... It is of course true that the theory would be contradicted if, for a given regulatory policy, we found the group with larger benefits and lower costs of political action being dominated by another group with lesser benefits and higher cost of political action.... The first purpose of the empirical studies is to identify the purpose of the legislation! The announced goals of a policy are sometimes unrelated or perversely related to its actual effects, and *the truly intended effects should be deduced from the actual effects.*[12]

As Carpenter suggests in Chapter 3 (Detecting and Measuring Capture), Stigler's rather casual standard of causal inference has been uncritically embraced by a subsequent generation of economists. With little circumspection on the limits of drawing broad theoretical conclusions from observational data analysis, scholars have repeatedly proclaimed empirical triumphs for capture theory after data analysis of select cases or highly aggregated cross-national datasets. Roger Noll correctly wrote of "the lurking danger of tautology, i.e., of attributing causality to an inevitable consequence of any public policy action. It is impossible to imagine that regulation could be imposed without redistributing income. Hence, a look for winners in the process – and organizations that represent them – is virtually certain to succeed."[13]

---

[11] W. Kip Viscusi, *Fatal Tradeoffs* (New York: Oxford University Press, 1992), 177.

[12] George Stigler, "Supplementary Note on Economic Theories of Regulation," in *The Citizen and the State* (Chicago: University of Chicago Press, 1975), 140, emphasis in original.

[13] Roger G. Noll, "Economic Perspectives on the Politics of Regulation," in *Handbook of Industrial Organization*, vol. II, eds. Richard Schmalensee and Robert D. Willig (Amsterdam: North Holland, 1989), 1276–77. For a mathematical demonstration of the invalidity of Stigler's principle of inference, consult Daniel Carpenter, "Protection without Capture:

Perhaps the deepest problem with much of the research on regulatory capture is not merely its tendency to overstate the evidence for capture, but its lack of nuance in describing how and to what degree capture works in particular settings. As scholars in law, political science, economics, and other areas of policy have noted, sometimes almost in passing, capture often prevails in a matter of degrees, in some agencies or regulations more visibly and robustly, in others less so.[14] The regulatory world is one of shades of gray. Yet capture scholarship does not typically discriminate among these shades in ways that enable informed advice on the marginal value of regulatory (or deregulatory) policy options. Existing treatments of regulatory capture give us too little sense of the sources or patterns of variation in capture, and they fail to instruct readers as to how, given this variation, capture ought to be prevented or minimized.

All of this is not to say that capture scholarship has failed to progress beyond the seminal contribution of George Stigler in 1971.[15] Path-breaking work on capture preceded Stigler, and outstanding work has followed him as well.[16] In fact, economic models of interest group politics have evolved considerably since 1971, allowing for the interplay of multiple groups exerting influence on policymakers and multiple motivations on the part of policymakers themselves. However, the essential idea that policymakers are for sale, and that regulatory policy is largely purchased by those most interested and able to buy it, remains central to the literature.[17] And far too much of

---

Product Approval by a Politically Responsive, Learning Regulator," *American Political Science Review* (98) (4) (November 2004): 613–31.

[14] See especially Stephen Breyer, *Regulation and Its Reform* (Cambridge, MA: Harvard University Press, 1982).

[15] George Stigler, "The Theory of Economic Regulation," *Bell Journal of Economics and Management Science* 2 (1) (Spring 1971): 3–21.

[16] Several of the pioneering works include Samuel Huntington, "The Marasmus of the ICC: The Commission, the Railroads, and the Public Interest," *Yale Law Journal* 614 (1952): 467–509; Marver Bernstein, *Regulating Business*; and Gabriel Kolko, *The Triumph of Conservatism: A Reinterpretation of American History: 1900–1916* (New York: Free Press, 1963). Major contributions that built on – and extended – Stigler's model include Sam Peltzman, "Toward a More General Theory of Regulation," *Journal of Law and Economics* 19 (2) (August 1976): 211–40; Gary S. Becker, "A Theory of Competition among Pressure Groups for Political Influence," *Quarterly Journal of Economics* 98 (3) (August 1983): 371–400; and Gene M. Grossman and Elhanan Helpman, "Protection for Sale," *American Economic Review* 84 (4) (September 1994): 833–50. See also Jean-Jacques Laffont and Jean Tirole, "The Politics of Government Decision Making: A Theory of Regulatory Capture," *Quarterly Journal of Economics* 106 (4) (1991): 1089–127.

[17] See Ernesto Dal Bó and Rafael Di Tella, "Capture by Threat," *Journal of Political Economy* 111 (5) (2003): 1123–54; David Moss and Mary Oey, "The Paranoid Style in the Study of American Politics," in Balleisen and Moss, *Government and Markets*, 260.

the relevant empirical work has sought to confirm this thesis (often rather casually), rather than to test it or discover its limits.

Beyond this, arguments stipulating capture often carry policy prescriptions. They move quickly from "is" to "ought," and they are especially likely to recommend deregulation. This move – from the postulated fact of capture to strong arguments for the dismantling or avoidance of regulation – was a central stratagem of Stigler, and many specialists have since followed it. This is especially true of studies – such as the article "The Regulation of Entry" (2002) by former World Bank economist Simeon Djankov and coauthors – that posit two possible states of the world: "good" public interest regulation versus "bad" captured regulation. Notwithstanding the obvious fact that reality could fall anywhere between these two extremes, Djankov and coauthors proceeded from the premise that, if the empirical evidence on entry regulation appears consistent with the existence of the bad regulatory world, then such regulation must be bad worldwide. On the basis of aggregate-level data and the authors' starting premise, they concluded that the regulation of entry "does not yield visible social benefits," and that the "principal beneficiaries" of strict entry regulations "appear to be the politicians and bureaucrats themselves." If such regulations benefit the powerful few at the expense of the broader public, then it seems only a very short leap to the conclusion that the world would be better off without such regulation. Although no *explicit* leap of this sort was made within the article, Djankov's subsequent actions provide an especially revealing example of the move from analysis to advocacy. In the years following publication of "The Regulation of Entry," Djankov and his World Bank colleagues established a highly structured, Bank-funded deregulatory initiative that recommended and tracked reforms worldwide with the intent of easing barriers to the creation or launch of a new business.[18]

As a result of these trends in the literature, we now know much more about how regulation can fail due to capture than about the conditions under which regulation sometimes succeeds, or can be made to succeed, when capture is constrained. What is needed, we believe, is a new wave of

---

[18] Simeon Djankov, Rafael La Porta, Florencio Lopes-de-Silanes, and Andrei Shleifer, "The Regulation of Entry," *Quarterly Journal of Economics* 117 (1) (February 2002): 1–37, quotes from p. 35. More generally, see Andrei Shleifer and Robert Vishny, *The Grabbing Hand: Government Pathologies and Their Cures* (Cambridge, MA: Harvard University Press, 1999). The World Bank's Doing Business Project launched in 2002, the year of the Djankov et al. publication, and in addition to running deregulation seminars for policymakers in developing and industrialized countries, it also provides individualized national tracking of deregulatory reforms and even simulators for policymakers to examine the possible effects of deregulation (see http://www.doingbusiness.org, accessed July 28, 2011).

scholarship on regulatory capture, which aims to better understand what special interest influence actually looks like in practice, what mechanisms already exist for limiting such influence, and the circumstances under which these preventive measures work well or poorly. Careful research of this kind should ultimately help both scholars and practitioners to deepen their understanding of how capture manifests in the real world and, ideally, to improve on existing mechanisms for mitigating capture.

DEGREES OF CAPTURE: STRONG VS. WEAK   *intervention*

As a first step, we distinguish between *strong capture* and *weak capture*.[19] A central claim of this volume is that, to the extent capture exists, it prevails by degrees rather than by its presence or absence.[20] A critical corollary of this argument is that the existence of capture need not translate into a rationale for full-scale dismantling of regulation. Although a sufficiently high level of capture (what we call *strong capture*) can vitiate the purposes and rationale for regulation, much capture is likely of the weaker form, such that its existence can and does coincide with healthy regulatory functioning. This is not to deny that, where weaker capture exists, it would be better for the polity and the economy to reduce its severity. Yet reducing the severity of capture – or, to invoke the title of our volume, preventing capture – is a far cry from responding to the threat of capture through the wholesale purging of regulation.

definition

Strong capture violates the public interest to such an extent that the public would be better served by either (a) no regulation of the activity in question – because the benefits of regulation are outweighed by the costs of capture, or (b) comprehensive replacement of the policy and agency in question.[21] For example, if captured regulation reduced consumer welfare (on net) by completely blocking entry into an industry, this would be a case of strong capture – precisely the sort that Stigler and his disciples saw (and, to some extent, still see) as an inevitable fact of life in regulation, in both

---

[19] A general definition of capture appears shortly.

[20] We distinguish here between strong and weak capture by asking whether the degree of capture vitiates the public interest–serving characteristics of the regulatory policy. However, underlying this normative distinction is an empirical one – just how pervasive empirically is the capture described? Although we reference the *pervasive* versus *limited* distinction below, we focus here mainly on the *strong* versus *weak* distinction, both to retain simplicity in our introductory chapter and to focus on the policy implications of capture diagnoses.

[21] As we discuss later in this introduction, wholesale replacement of the existing regulatory order is an option when capture involved is not anticompetitive but "corrosive."

developed and developing economies. In Stigler's writings, the existence of
capture is enough to reject the public interest theory of regulation altogether.
This rejection not only means factually that democracy is not working
as advertised, but also that the proper policy response is to weaken or
fully remove regulation. It is of course possible that reform of strongly
captured regulation would be better than non-regulation, yet for purposes
of definition we assume that there might exist a form of capture so robust
and incorrigible that it cannot be reformed and hence that abandoning the
resulting regulation entirely would best serve the public interest.

Weak capture, by contrast, occurs when special interest influence compromises the capacity of regulation to enhance the public interest, but the public
is still being served by regulation, relative to the baseline of no regulation.[22]
In other words, weak capture prevails when the *net* social benefits of regulation are diminished as a result of special interest influence, but remain
positive overall.[23]

Our priors are that some amount of weak capture may well be fairly
ubiquitous, and the evidence collected in this volume partially corroborates
this view. In the chapters that follow, contributors carefully examine a
range of agencies (mostly in the American context), from the Food and
Drug Administration to the Department of Transportation, and find that
capture is far from complete in each of these cases – the result of numerous
limits and checks on industry influence. When capture exists, it appears
to be empirically *limited* rather than empirically *pervasive*. The picture that
emerges, therefore, is quite different from the one George Stigler envisioned,
in which capture by industry was virtually inevitable and complete. As a
result, the optimal policy responses may be quite different as well. When
capture is empirically limited, it is much less likely to vitiate the potential
benefits of regulation and is more likely, in our terms, to take the form of
weak capture than of strong.

[22] By the baseline of no regulation, we mean nonexistence of the captured regulation/
regulatory regime. So given an accurate diagnosis of weak capture, the proper comparison is between the weakly captured regulation as it is ("warts and all") and a state of
non-regulation.

[23] Our weak capture/strong capture distinction is meant to differentiate between (a) regulation influenced to a slight degree away from the regulator's best guess at the public
interest and (b) regulation that is largely or wholly in the service of the special interest.
As we have constructed the distinction here, it is possible for regulation to be motivated
wholly by service to the industry's interests and still be weakly captured, because we have
distinguished strong from weak capture based on the degree to which the public interest is
or is not served (partially served – weak, wholly not served – strong) instead of the degree
to which the regulator acts in the interest of industry.

DEFINING CAPTURE

Many of capture theory's problems boil down to the lack of a clear definition for the central concept. Capture is often equated with corruption, influence, and regulatory failure. It is also associated with distributive politics,[24] even though the two are quite distinct. Given the manifold problems in bringing conceptual structure to capture – and the more nuanced picture of capture that emerges in this volume (in which capture can be either strong or weak) – we begin our effort at definition by offering one that is both broad and flexible. As with any definition or model, numerous amendments must be (and will be) made in order to apply the term as we understand it. With that said, our definition is as follows:

Regulatory capture is the result or process by which regulation, in law or application, is consistently or repeatedly directed away from the public interest and toward the interests of the regulated industry, by the intent and action of the industry itself.

Our definition rests on several critical terms, especially *public interest, intent,* and *regulated industry,*[25] which we take up in turn:

Public Interest. To begin with, capture moves regulation away from the service of one goal (public interest) and toward another (industry interest).[26] Understanding capture thus requires an understanding of these two concepts or variables and when they diverge. Measuring the public interest is a thorny problem as old as democracy itself. Some would maintain that the repeated actions of democratic citizen majorities (or the repeated actions of the elected representatives of those citizens) constitute the most legitimate measure of the public interest.[27] Others would argue that calculations

---

[24] See Stigler, "The Theory of Economic Regulation"; Peltzman, "Toward a More General Theory of Regulation."

[25] As noted later in this introduction, and discussed at greater length by Carpenter in Chapter 3, it is possible for special interests other than the regulated industry to capture a regulation. For example, labor unions or certain activists might value some outcomes and goods (such as safety or the environment) more than does the public at large. We therefore use the term "regulated industry" not as a necessary condition of capture but rather as a convenient shorthand.

[26] These and other features of our definition cohere with general models of capture and industry influence in regulation, including Paul Quirk's *Industry Influence in Federal Regulatory Agencies* (Princeton: Princeton University Press, 1981), Stigler's foundational notion that "regulation is acquired by the industry and designed and operated primarily for its benefit," and Laffont and Tirole's model of producer protection in a multi-player political economy game (*A Theory of Incentives in Procurement and Regulation*, Chapter 11, and especially Propositions 11.1 and 11.2 and surrounding discussion, 485–93).

[27] Such an idea of repeated democratic expressions of the interest of the whole, as opposed to (a) near-term or short-run expressions of interest or (b) special interests, animates the

rooted in welfare economics should serve as the measure. We do not choose among these alternatives, but note that, in lieu of an ability to directly perceive and measure the public interest, we must build *defeasible models*[28] of the public interest for purposes of assessing whether a particular regulation is captured.

Intent. Under our definition, the fact that an industry is well served by regulation is deeply insufficient for a judgment of capture. Both intent and action on the part of the regulated industry are required. Unless the industry (or elements of it) actively and knowingly push regulation away from the public interest, there can be no capture. The fact that industry benefits from regulation is, by itself, insufficient because it could be alternately explained by bureaucratic drift, coincidence, or mistakes, or as a simple byproduct of public-serving regulation. We recognize that the high evidentiary bar associated with the necessity of showing intent, to meet our definition, may lead us to under-diagnose capture, but we believe that over-diagnosis is currently far more common and that our approach testifies to the robust empirical standards that are needed for scholarly analysis to move beyond journalistic descriptions and claims of capture.

Regulated Industry. Consistent with many of the earliest expressions of capture theory, from Huntington to Stigler, we have focused in our definition on cases in which *industry* captures regulation for its benefit. In principle, one could replace the word *industry* with *interest* in the definition, reflecting the fact that other regulated actors, such as labor unions, have the potential to twist regulation to serve their own interests at the expense of the broader public. Clearly, though, industry has a special position with respect to regulation, and it is no coincidence that early treatments of capture focused on business interests and their attempts to influence regulation. For the most part, we do the same in this volume.

---

idea of the public good in James Madison's *Federalist* #10, in which the celebrated concept of *faction* is defined as in opposition to the "permanent and aggregate interests of the community": "By a faction, I understand a number of citizens, whether amounting to a majority or a minority of the whole, who are united and actuated by some common impulse of passion, or of interest, adverse to the rights of other citizens, or to the permanent and aggregate interests of the community."

[28] By *defeasible* we mean to stress two different but complementary features of accounts of the public interest: First, they must be capable of being shown to be false (tautological or vacuous definitions are unacceptable). Second, we recognize that there is no certainty in making a value claim about the common good – interesting claims will be contestable and can be shown to be mistaken through persuasive argument. What matters is that an account of what is in the public interest be offered and defended so readers and future researchers can engage appropriately with the argument.

EVIDENCE

Our definition suggests a set of standards for making statements about whether capture has occurred in the case of a given regulation or agency. We offer a more detailed analysis of these empirical standards for detection and measurement (or what we more casually call *diagnosis*) in the third chapter of this volume. Yet three general empirical standards follow straightforwardly from our definition. To claim capture, an argument ought to:

- Provide a defeasible model of the public interest
- Show a policy shift away from the public interest and toward industry (special) interest
- Show action and intent by the industry (special interest) in pursuit of this policy shift sufficiently effective to have plausibly caused an appreciable part of the shift

If an argument that capture has occurred lacks one of these necessary components, then scholars making claims about capture should exhibit considerable circumspection about what exactly has been established. Showing all three components is, we believe, the gold standard for a diagnosis of capture.[29]

---

[29] In the American context, the case that would appear to come closest to this gold standard demonstration is probably air transport entry regulation as performed by the now defunct Civil Aeronautics Board (CAB), in which all three claims were advanced. In addition to widely advanced claims that the public interest was not served by airline regulation, it was claimed openly in congressional hearings in 1975 that the agency behaved in ways that reflected capture or "cartelism." As Donald Baker, then deputy assistant attorney general in the Department of Justice's Antitrust Division, remarked in calling for a fundamental change in statute, "the fault lies with the discretion the agency has and the use of it. Now this is not a unique situation with the CAB. In fact, the history of regulatory agencies generally has been that they have been granted 'broad discretion, they have generally been influenced heavily by the people they were supposed to regulate, and they have generally exercised the discretion in favor of the people who they were supposed to regulate." *Oversight of Civil Aeronautics Board: Practices and Procedures*, vol. 1 (Hearings before the Subcommittee on Administrative Practice and Procedure of the Committee on the Judiciary, United States Senate, February 14, 1975), 666, accessed December 4, 2012, http://archive.org/stream/ oversightofcivil01unit/oversightofcivil01unit_djvu.txt.

Even here, however, there is reason to question the empirical basis of this inference. It is easy, in light of the abolition of the CAB and the subsequent literature [including Thomas McCraw's famous *Prophets of Regulation: Charles Francis Adams, Louis D. Brandeis, James M. Landis, Alfred E. Kahn* (Cambridge, MA: Belknap Press of Harvard University Press, 1986)], to assume that the CAB was a case of strong capture. Yet as far as the empirical pervasiveness of the capture itself – "the requirement to show action and intent by the industry (special interest) in pursuit of this policy shift sufficiently powerful to have plausibly caused at least part of the shift" – the proof remains elusive.

Very often, claims of regulatory capture are silent on the third standard – action and intent – presumably because industry efforts to influence regulators against the public interest are not always easy to identify and document. In these cases, *motive* is sometimes seen as a legitimate substitute. However, indications that a regulated industry has a motive to twist regulation in its favor (and against the public interest) is not sufficient under our definition. Nor is *functionalist* evidence that a regulation happens to benefit some firms or interests at the expense of others.[30] As the novelist P. D. James once observed through a character, "Every death was a suspicious death if one looked only at motive."[31] To be sure, this creates a challenge. When a social scientist examines the writing of a rule, the passage of new legislation, or the enforcement of a policy, causal inference of the sort achieved in a randomized experiment in biology, medicine, or psychology is most often impossible. Yet this impossibility does not relieve scholars of the responsibility to examine their claims carefully, to distinguish between statistical association and causation, and to qualify whatever cause-and-effect claims they advance when important evidence is missing. Over the long run, greater care on the part of scholars is likely necessary for improving the accuracy of practical judgments, which will almost always need to be made on the basis of inconclusive data by citizens and policymakers alike.

CORROSIVE CAPTURE

Our definition does not, it is important to note, require that a captured policy process produce *more* rent-enhancing regulation, as Stigler and others imagined. A captured policy process can also result in *less* public interest– serving regulation, and (as a consequence) reduce or eliminate regulatory costs that fall on industry. Capture, in other words, can drive deregulation as readily as it drives regulation. We call this *corrosive capture*, which can dismantle regulation even in the absence of public support or a strong welfare rationale for doing so.

Corrosive capture occurs if organized firms render regulation less robust than intended in legislation or than what the public interest would recommend. By less robust we mean that the regulation is, in its formulation,

---

[30] For a mathematical model that examines and debunks some of these older functionalist claims, see Carpenter, "Protection without Capture." By functionalism we mean the kind of "actor-centered functionalism" described by Paul Pierson, whereby analysts observe the way an institution functions and then make the inference that strategic actors must have designed the institution to function in exactly this way. Paul Pierson, *Politics in Time: History, Institutions, and Social Analysis* (Princeton: Princeton University Press, 2004), 14, 104–27.

[31] Quoted in Moss and Oey, "Paranoid Style in the Study of American Politics."

application, or enforcement, rendered less stringent or less costly for regulated firms (again, relative to a world in which the public interest would be served by the regulation in question). The consequence of corrosive capture could potentially take the form of reduced entry,[32] but would far more commonly be observed in the reduction of costly rules and enforcement actions that cut into profits. Although corrosive capture can occur within either a legislative or an administrative context, it is quite plausible that deregulation through electorally sanctioned mechanisms would be less likely to meet our definition of capture than deregulation initiated by a regulator. This is because the "corrosion" of regulation within an administrative agency occurs not with the express sanction of voters in repeated elections, but rather – in many cases – as a result of increased independence of the regulator vis-à-vis the legislature and possibly reduced fidelity to its statutory obligations.

It is important to recognize that much if not most of the public and academic discussion of capture in recent decades has pertained to regulatory corrosion. Indeed, the types of capture that have triggered the most alarm over the recent period have rather little in common with the types that Huntington, Bernstein, and Stigler warned about in the middle of the twentieth century. Entry-barrier capture, which was their principal concern, was the process by which regulators intervened in markets with the effect of privileging one set of producers over another, incumbents over entrants and (as a consequence) producers over consumers. In these early models, it was the acquisition of regulation that marked capture, not the reduction or weakening of regulation.

By contrast, it is apparent that as far as plausible capture is concerned, something quite different has been going on over the past several decades. In some cases, it was capture evinced in the feeble application (or non-application) of regulatory tools. In other cases, it was the application of jurisdictional boundaries to prevent potentially aggressive agencies from regulating. Regulatory preemption – the move by which state and local regulations are invalidated by the imposition of national-level supremacy – became a favorite tool of officials in the George W. Bush Administration as means of achieving deregulation. In some cases, preemption of state regulation was asserted by regulatory agencies themselves, such as when the Office of Thrift Supervision and the Office of the Comptroller of the Currency issued rulings in the 1990s and early 2000s preempting the application of

---

[32] For an intriguing example, see Randall S. Krozner and Philip E. Strahan, "What Drives Deregulation? Economics and Politics of the Relaxation of Bank Branching Restrictions," *Quarterly Journal of Economics* 114 (1999): 1437–67.

state mortgage laws to federal thrifts and national banks.[33] Another form of boundary manipulation comes through regulatory arbitrage – for example, when banks choose their markets or institutional form so as to fit themselves to the least rigorous regulator. In each case, however, the result is *corrosive of existing regulation.*[34]

MECHANISMS OF CAPTURE

There are a range of different empirical and theoretical conditions under which capture of regulation prevails. We aim to provide greater clarity on the mechanisms already under consideration, as well as to subject new or understudied mechanisms to careful examination. In political science, economics, and law, there are models of implicit bribes or rent seeking (Laffont and Tirole;[35] Grossman and Helpman[36]). There are models by which a regulator might be inclined to pursue the public interest but is scared off from doing so by industry threats of political or legal retaliation, which are something different from an implicit bribe (Gordon and Hafer; Dal Bo and DiTella[37]). There are arguments about the cultural or social influence of repeated interaction with the regulated industry (as in Johnson and Kwak, *13 Bankers;*[38] and Kwak in this volume), such that the regulator begins to think like the regulated and cannot easily conceive another way of approaching its problems. In the case of cultural or social capture, the legislator or agency may not be fully conscious or aware of the extent to which its behavior has been captured. What is important about our conception of capture, including its strong and weak variants, is that it is not model-dependent or mechanism-dependent. Our definition is robust, in the sense that it can accommodate all the various models and mechanisms described

[33] Kathleen Engel and Patricia McCoy, *The Subprime Virus: Reckless Lending, Regulatory Failure, and Next Steps* (New York: Oxford University Press, 2011), 157–62.

[34] To preview one concern here, what would the existence of strong corrosive capture imply for policy? Strong capture is defined as that whose existence implies such a reduction in the benefits of the policy that deregulation would be suggested. Yet if corrosive capture is the problem, the "solution" may be less deregulation in the sense of removing regulatory constraints on the firm and more the wholesale replacement of the existing regulatory framework (the "blow it up and start over" paradigm) by one that better imposes the necessary constraints in fidelity to either statutory intent or the public interest.

[35] Laffont and Tirole, "The Politics of Government Decision Making."

[36] Grossman and Helpman, "Protection for Sale."

[37] Consider the paper by Gordon and Hafer, contributors to this volume, "Flexing Muscle: Corporate Political Expenditures as Signals to the Bureaucracy," *American Political Science Review* 99 (2) (May 2005): 245–61; or the essay of Dal Bo and DiTella, "Capture by Threat."

[38] Simon Johnson and James Kwak, *13 Bankers: The Wall Street Takeover and the Next Financial Meltdown* (New York: Pantheon, 2010).

in the preceding pages. It is also robust because it can accommodate both legislative capture[39] and administrative capture.[40]

CULTURAL CAPTURE

The plausible mechanisms of both traditional and corrosive capture are, to some degree, well known from the literature on capture in general. Firms and industries that want more or less regulation, relative to the preferences of the public or the regulatory aims expressed in statute, may rely on campaign contributions, pressure on politicians, and perhaps the "revolving door" to

[39] A principal mechanism by which regulation can come to serve the industry's interest rather than the public's interest is for the industry to acquire regulation in statute. The historical and statistical annals of legislative studies are filled with evidence for how business interests and other special interests (including labor unions) use their resources – voting blocs, campaign contributions, volunteer labor, networks, information, perhaps the (implicit or explicit) promise of future employment, and other tools – to induce politicians to bend. Stigler's classic examples of regulatory capture – state trucking weight limits and occupation licensing – were, on the whole, regulations passed by legislatures and less the result of state agency decisions based on statutory delegation from governors and state legislators. In some cases the outcomes of policy can be hardwired into statute, the most obvious case being entitlements. Even in those cases where outcomes depend on agency decisions, it is plausible to argue that once a statute has been tilted in favor of the industry's interest, it will be exceedingly difficult for other forces to direct the agency's administration of a statute toward the public interest. See Richard Hall and Alan Deardorff, "Lobbying as Legislative Subsidy," *American Political Science Review* 100 (2005): 69–84; James M. Snyder, Jr., "On Buying Legislatures," *Economics and Politics* 3 (1991): 93–109; Richard Hall and Frank Wayman, "Buying Time: Moneyed Interests and the Mobilization of Bias in Congressional Committees," *American Political Science Review* 84 (1990): 797–820. On the idea that various procedures in an agency's statute and in restrictions on rulemaking allow congressional majorities to "hardwire" administrative outcomes at the stage of rulemaking, see Mathew McCubbins, Roger Noll, and Barry Weingast (writing under the collective McNollgast), "Administrative Procedures as Instruments of Political Control," *Journal of Law, Economics, and Organization* 3 (2) (1987): 243–77. For another argument that statutes are strategically constructed so as to hardwire administrative outcomes, see John Huber and Charles Shipan, *Deliberate Discretion? The Institutional Foundations of Bureaucratic Autonomy* (New York: Cambridge University Press, 2002).

[40] The original focus of capture scholars, ranging from Gabriel Kolko to Sam Huntington and Marver Bernstein, concerned not regulatory capture by legislation, but instead the capture of administrative agencies. Following Bernstein, consider Olney's letter to Perkins. It counsels the (railroad-friendly) reader not to worry about the ICC because the Commission will eventually depart from its moorings in consumer protection and public interest and come to see the railroad's point of view. (There is a powerful gesture in this letter, written more than 120 years ago, to the concept of *cultural capture* as James Kwak defines it in Chapter 4 in this volume). Once the administrative agency does adopt the industry's way of viewing things, then most or all of the threat posed by the regulatory legislation will dissipate. Furthermore, because a regulatory organ exists, it will represent an important bulwark of legitimacy for the industry, which can always turn to its critics and point to the existence of a regulatory agency as a means by which the public is protected.

reduce their individual and collective regulatory burdens. As just suggested, however, another mechanism is available, one that is hard to prove but that seems to us increasingly relevant: what James Kwak, in Chapter 4 in this volume, terms *cultural capture*. It is conceivable that cultural capture, through the shaping of assumptions, lenses, and vocabularies, could be used to support more traditional forms of Stiglerian capture. Cultural capture, however, seems less likely to be deployed for the creation and maintenance of entry barriers than for deregulatory purposes, such as the weakening or dismantling of health, safety, or environmental regulations. It would seem easier for firms to coordinate on a single message of deregulation – the benefits of which could plausibly accrue to business across the board, in the form of lower costs, potentially at the expense of citizens or consumers more broadly – than to coordinate on a message of increased regulatory entry barriers, in which some firms win and other firms (even if they are weaker or smaller) lose.

Either way, the key questions that our definition raises for claims of cultural capture are (a) does the resulting regulation or deregulation advance firms' private interests at the expense of the public interest, and (b) did the firms that benefit intentionally and actively set out to achieve such an outcome ex ante? To be sure, shifts in the intellectual climate, which can occur for a whole host of reasons, have the power to influence the direction of regulation. Such shifts, however, cannot be considered products of capture, according to our definition, unless they can be shown to be deleterious to the public *and* stem from the deliberate efforts of firms to shape the intellectual climate for their own private benefit. Our definition, in other words, treats cultural capture no differently from corrosive capture or Stiglerian entry-barrier capture or any other form of capture, requiring the same tough evidentiary standards across the board.

THE PROMISE OF A NEW APPROACH

It is said that a little knowledge is a dangerous thing. With respect to regulatory capture, as we have seen, policy analysts are often quick to see capture whenever an interest group appears to benefit from regulation, or even when there is merely *motive* for capture. Many observers also – almost instinctively – conceive of capture in black-and-white terms when considering potential policy responses. Both steps are fraught with risk, and yet both are often seen as entirely legitimate, rooted not only in common sense but also (importantly) in powerful scholarly work on the subject. Although early research on capture – especially early modeling of the phenomenon – has taught us a great deal, it has somehow left the impression of an ailment so pervasive and so absolute that casual diagnosis and drastic remedies are entirely reasonable. Just as physicians once believed that the only effective way to treat infection was to cut it out surgically, it is commonplace today to believe that capture can only be treated by "amputating" the offending regulation. Fortunately, the evidence that emerges in this volume suggests that less drastic remedies may be equally if not more effective, and that some are already working – like the body's own immune system – almost invisibly behind the scenes.

And this presents an opportunity. Pushing forward with a new wave of research on regulatory capture, which is more empirical and more grounded in the realities of regulation and special interest influence, promises to give new purchase on an old problem. If some agencies are more or less captured than others, then naturally we need to understand why. Have some agencies developed defense mechanisms of various sorts that would be useful elsewhere? Are some types of regulation simply less vulnerable to capture than others? Are there institutional or cultural factors, whether inside or outside of the regulatory process itself, that enhance or attenuate the influence of special interests? These are the types of questions that need to be addressed in a new wave of capture scholarship – to deepen our understanding of the phenomenon and, ultimately, better inform regulatory practice.

To be sure, moving beyond an exclusive, and what today seems like a barbaric, reliance on surgery in treating infection required enormous advances in medical understanding – about the nature of infection, about the workings of the body's immune system, and about ways of supplementing the immune system (through antibiotics, for example). We believe that reaching a new level in the treatment of regulatory capture will require analogous advances in understanding – about the nature of capture itself and about mechanisms for mitigating it.

Our book thus advances three claims, one of which is critical in nature and the second and third of which are advanced as hypotheses. First, capture is often misdiagnosed, and these misdiagnoses are enabled by a kitbag of weak evidentiary standards that have arisen in economics, history, political science, and sociology for making inferences about capture in regulation. Second, although deregulation may sometimes be a very useful tool, it is no panacea for capture, and in fact deregulation may itself reflect the power of special interest influence through a process we call *corrosive capture*. Third, capture is, at least at the margins, preventable, and both analysis and advocacy of particular measures should focus on degrees of capture rather than on the unproductive and false binary of "pure" versus "captured" regulation. These three claims, we believe, bear large potential implications for how we think about tools of regulatory governance, including when and how to use them to best achieve the common good.

The volume is structured in four sections. The first section, entitled "Failures of Capture Scholarship," reconsiders capture theory, casting new light on the long history of special interest influence on regulation (Novak, Chapter 1), the evolution and role of capture theory since the mid-twentieth century (Posner, Chapter 2), and how more rigorous definition and evidentiary standards for diagnosing capture could yield better understanding of the problem and potential solutions (Carpenter, Chapter 3). The second section, entitled "New Conceptions of Capture: Mechanisms and Outcomes," suggests that regulated entities utilize a wider variety of means to influence regulation toward a wider variety of regulatory outcomes than typically recognized, ranging from cultural capture (Kwak, Chapter 4) and influence through expertise and information (McCarty, Chapter 5) to corrosive capture (Carpenter, Chapter 7) and even the capture of scholars in academia (Zingales, Chapter 6). Although traditional capture theory would predict regulatory capture to be pervasive, this volume's third section, entitled "Regulatory Case Studies," suggests that capture frequently has been over-diagnosed in the past (Moss/Decker, Gordon/Hafer, Carrigan, and Yackee, Chapters 8, 9, 10, and 11, respectively) and that internal mechanisms exist, within regulatory agencies and processes, for limiting the extent of industry influence (Yackee, Chapter 11, and Cuéllar, Chapter 12). Building on existing preventive mechanisms highlighted in Section III, the final section features essays discussing both existing and new ways to prevent capture (Schwarcz on consumer advocacy, Chapter 13; Magill on the courts, Chapter 14; and Livermore/Revesz on OIRA, Chapter 15).

Preventing capture will require conceptual clarity on what capture is, and evidentiary clarity on where, how, and to what extent capture is turning regulatory decision making against the public interest. In focusing on the goal of prevention, we have sought to identify gaps in scholarly understanding that require additional and rigorous study. This volume, we hope, marks a step toward building our understanding in ways that will allow better diagnosis and treatment of capture, so as to limit its scope, and even prevent it where possible, in the rough-and-tumble world of regulatory practice.

SECTION I

FAILURES OF CAPTURE SCHOLARSHIP

The chapters in this opening section offer new perspectives on the existing understanding of regulatory capture. Approaching the subject from three distinct disciplines (history, law, and political science), they illuminate how scholarship has yet to provide an explanation of capture that can adequately inform efforts to prevent it. Together, they provide a foundation for this volume's core inquiry into how capture manifests in practice and how it might best be mitigated going forward.

In an analysis of special interest influence over the course of U.S. history, William Novak uncovers the long history of American democracy's struggles with capture. Challenging the received wisdom – that capture emerged as a problem only with the rise of the administrative state beginning in the late nineteenth century – Novak argues that capture theory gave a new name to the longstanding (and long-recognized) problem of special interest influence in democratic decision making, going back to the dawn of the republic. He notes that the creation of the administrative state was to a large extent itself an attempt to *prevent* – or at least circumvent – undue influence within legislatures. With this longer history in view, Novak undercuts the belief that modern regulatory agencies are inherently the source of the problem. Noting that regulation has always been an important part of governance in America, he suggests that undue influence and its prevention are properly seen as a cat-and-mouse game, which has evolved over time, requiring persistent innovation to protect the common good.

Richard Posner assesses capture theory from its emergence in the mid-twentieth century to the present and finds that the explanatory power it once had has largely eroded. In an analysis that lends credence to Novak's picture of regulation and influence as co-evolving, Posner finds that academic models of capture that may have accurately described a large portion of regulation in the 1960s are no longer appropriate because of long-term changes in the structure of regulation. According to Posner, the concept of capture, as formalized by George Stigler in the 1970s, had considerable descriptive power at a time when specific industries were often regulated piecemeal by industry-specific agencies, such as the Civil Aeronautics Board (CAB). The trend in regulation since the 1970s, however, has been toward regulatory regimes that address not specific industries but practices across industries, as in the case of the Environmental Protection Agency (EPA). In Posner's view, these broader regulatory regimes "do not exhibit a general tendency to be captured by the regulated firms," at least not in the form (entry-barrier regulation) originally considered by the canonical capture scholarship. He therefore finds the very concept of capture unhelpful in a modern context.

Following these historical assessments, Daniel Carpenter endeavors to make the concept of capture more useful to understanding and improving policy. In "Detecting and Measuring Capture," Carpenter finds that "the evidentiary standards of the capture literature are rather low." He offers new standards for clarity and rigor of analysis and suggests that increased circumspection is warranted in interpreting empirical data. Toward this end, Carpenter presents a set of standards for diagnosing capture that help to clarify when and how capture is (and is not) suggested by the available evidence. If followed, Carpenter's guidance for detecting and measuring capture promises to facilitate greater consistency, comparability, and rigor in vital empirical work on the subject.

A Revisionist History of Regulatory Capture

William J. Novak

The idea of regulatory capture has controlled discussions of economic regulation and regulatory reform for more than two generations. Originating soon after World War II, the so-called capture thesis was an early harbinger of the more general critique of the American regulatory state that dominated the closing decades of the twentieth century. The political ramifications of that broad critique of government continue to be felt today both in the resilient influence of neoliberal policies such as deregulation and privatization as well as in the rise of more virulent and populist forms of anti-statism. Indeed, the capture thesis has so pervaded recent assessments of regulation that it has assumed something of the status of a ground norm – a taken-for-granted term of art and an all-purpose social-scientific explanation – that itself frequently escapes critical scrutiny or serious scholarly interrogation.

This chapter attempts to challenge this state of affairs by taking a critical look at the emergence of regulatory capture theory from the perspective of history. After introducing a brief account of the diverse intellectual roots of the capture idea, this chapter makes three interpretive moves. First, it suggests that, to a large extent, capture theory relies on a short and increasingly outmoded history of American regulation that is out of synch with the latest accounts of the development of the American regulatory and administrative state. Second, it questions just how "new" the insights of capture theory ever really were or are. Although earlier generations of American political thinkers and regulatory reformers did not use the language of "capture" per se, they were exceedingly well-versed in the general notion that democratic and republican institutions of government were prone to the corruptions of private interest. Finally, this chapter documents the degree to which progressive regulatory initiatives were themselves oriented toward the control of undue corporate and private influence in democratic and public life. It closes by suggesting that some of those original progressive explorations of the ongoing problem of private coercion in a democratic republic continue to provide a more satisfactory account than capture theory of the new configurations of public and private power that dominate early twenty-first century American life.

A BRIEF GENEALOGY OF THE CAPTURE THESIS

The basic outlines of the intellectual history of the regulatory capture thesis are fairly clear and broadly agreed on.[1] Indeed, one of the most surprising things about that genealogy is the extraordinary degree of consensus about regulatory capture across a broad spectrum of economists; historians; and scholars of law, politics, and public administration. Within legal and economics scholarship, it is customary to start discussions of capture theory with the Chicago School and George Stigler's pointed thesis in "The Theory of Economic Regulation" that "as a rule, regulation is acquired by the industry and is designed and operated primarily for its benefit."[2] However, there are a couple of other important earlier incarnations of the critique.

The capture thesis first originated not in law and economics but in the fields of political science and public administration. Indeed, the first essay to attempt to show systematically that "regulation is acquired by the industry" and operates "for its benefit" was a precocious bit of regulatory revisionism focused notably on the Interstate Commerce Commission (ICC) by a young Harvard government instructor named Samuel P. Huntington.[3] In "The Marasmus of the ICC," Huntington began by reflecting on the era of good feeling that had built up around the original federal independent regulatory commission: "During its sixty-five years of existence, the [Interstate Commerce] Commission developed an enviable reputation for honesty, impartiality, and expertness" that made it "the premier federal agency in the transportation field."[4] However, the bulk of his article was dedicated to

---

[1] See, for example, the strikingly similar accounts of Thomas W. Merrill, "Capture Theory and the Courts, 1967–1983," *Chicago-Kent Law Review* 72 (1996–1997): 1039, and John Shepard Wiley Jr., "A Capture Theory of Antitrust Federalism," *Harvard Law Review* 99 (1986): 713, 723–5.

[2] George J. Stigler, "The Theory of Economic Regulation," *Bell Journal of Economics and Management Science* 2 (1971): 3–21; Richard Posner, "Theories of Economic Regulation," *Bell Journal of Economics and Management Science* 4 (1974): 335–58; Sam Peltzman, "Toward a More General Theory of Regulation," *Journal of Law and Economics* 19 (1976): 211–20.

[3] Samuel P. Huntington, "The Marasmus of the ICC: The Commission, the Railroads, and the Public Interest," *Yale Law Journal* 61 (1952): 467.

[4] Huntington, "Marasmus," 468–9. Huntington could not help include as well the sarcastic assessment from conservative and anti–New Dealer James M. Beck, "The Commission has

a critique of that celebratory public administration orthodoxy. In contrast to the usual story of enlightened administrative regulation in the public interest, Huntington wrote a tale of trouble – a story of agency decline and what he polemically dubbed "marasmus": a biological pathology featuring a gradual and continuous wasting away of the body from a morbid cause. Morbid cause was key here, for it was not just time or desuetude or inertia that contributed to this peculiar regulatory disease. Rather, Huntington proffered a more distinct and direct cause, that is, the infectious influence of pervasive *railroad interest* in almost every aspect of ICC policymaking. Huntington ultimately proposed abolishing the ICC with a line of argumentation that would soon become a staple of formal capture theory: "The independence of a regulatory commission is based upon the premise that this independence will aid it in being objective and impartial. *When such a commission loses its objectivity and impartiality by becoming dependent upon the support of a single narrow interest group*, obviously the rationale for maintaining its independence has ceased to exist."[5]

Huntington's pointed critique of interest group influence on regulatory agencies did not remain confined to the ICC for very long. Three years later, in *Regulating Business by Independent Commission*, another politics scholar, Marver H. Bernstein, extended Huntington's analysis and capture perspective to six additional agencies: the Federal Trade Commission, Federal Power Commission, Civil Aeronautics Board, Federal Communications Commission, National Labor Relations Board, and the Securities and Exchange Commission.[6] Continuing Huntington's biological metaphor,[7] Bernstein examined the life cycle of commissions into a ripe "old age," where

become the sacred white elephant of our governmental system. Members of the Bar and even litigants may exercise their constitutional right, when the Supreme Court decides against them, to swear at the Court, but it seems to be a species of treason for any one to question the beneficence of the Interstate Commerce Commission." Beck's *Wonderland of Bureaucracy* (from which this quote was taken) was something of an antiregulatory screed, referring to "bureaucracy" generally as involving "the irrepressible war between the individual and the State" and a "wonderland of Socialist experiments in a government, whose constitution was intended to be a noble assertion of individualism." James Beck, *Our Wonderland of Bureaucracy* (New York: Macmillan, 1932), vii, x.

5 Huntington, "Marasmus," 467 (emphasis added).
6 Marver H. Bernstein, *Regulating Business by Independent Commission* (Westport, CT: Greenwood Press, 1955); Bernstein, "Independent Regulatory Agencies: A Perspective on Their Reform," *The Annals of the American Academy of Political and Social Science* 400 (1972): 14.
7 The return of biological metaphorical thinking about modern governmental institutions in these 1950s studies is a matter of concern given the earlier attempts of American social science to develop a more realistic and pragmatic approach to law and government that dispensed with just such naturalistic metaphors.

sclerotic relations with specific interest groups yielded agencies protecting the industries they were originally designed to regulate. Bernstein's resulting indictment of regulatory agencies exceeded Huntington's more focused critique and, in fact, outstripped the research bounds of his own investigation:

Commissions have proved to be *more* susceptible to private pressures, to manipulation for private purposes, and to administrative and public apathy than other types of governmental organization. They have *lacked* an affirmative concept of public interest; they have *failed* to meet the test of political responsibility in a democratic society; and they tend to define the interest of the regulated groups as the public interest.[8]

Two historical contexts are important in coming to terms with this original burst of capture theory in the 1950s. First, methodologically, Huntington and Bernstein were writing at the high tide of the influence of behavioralism in political science – an approach impatient with formal philosophical and juridical abstractions such as "the public interest" and eager to examine more "critically" and "scientifically" the real individual and group interests that were so frequently viewed as constituting and producing actual political behavior. Huntington relied explicitly on David B. Truman's *The Governmental Process: Political Interests and Public Opinion* (1951) – something of a culminating synthesis of the long methodological revolution begun by A. F. Bentley, Charles Merriam, Harold Lasswell, V. O. Key, Herbert Simon, and many others.[9] Second, coming as they did within a decade of the passage of the Administrative Procedure Act, Huntington's and Bernstein's critiques of the regulatory commission have to be read in the political context of a series of high-profile efforts to reorganize and control (if not exactly roll back) a maturing and sprawling administrative regulatory apparatus, including the persistent and contested efforts at executive reorganization advocated by the Brownlow Commission and the First and Second Hoover Commissions.[10] Like the First Hoover Commission that originally aired issues of undue industry influence as early as 1949,[11] Huntington recommended transferring the ICC's executive functions to the Secretary of Commerce. Bernstein

---

[8] Bernstein, *Regulating Business*, 296 (emphasis added).

[9] David B. Truman, *The Governmental Process: Political Interests and Public Opinion* (New York: Knopf, 1951). For a couple of useful summaries of the behavioral revolution, see Robert A. Dahl, "The Behavioral Approach in Political Science: Epitaph for a Monument to a Successful Protest," *The American Political Science Review* 55 (1961): 763–72; Bernard Crick, *The American Science of Politics* (Berkeley: University of California Press, 1959).

[10] For the best overarching history of these efforts, see Joanna Grisinger, *The Unwieldy American State: Administrative Politics since the New Deal* (New York: Cambridge University Press, 2012).

[11] Grisinger, 302–4.

even more explicitly linked the academic exercise of piercing the veil of commission independence to a policy prescription of increased political and executive supervision. With Eisenhower and Hoover guiding such recommendations, the links between the scholarly development of a capture thesis and the more general resurgence of interest in competition and private enterprise as countervailing forces to the rise of a bureaucratic state were already being forged.[12]

Despite these very specific intellectual and political contexts, however, over the next decade, this early political exploration of private influence in public regulation hardened into the prevailing wisdom known as *regulatory capture theory*. As Louis Jaffe put it in "The Limits of the Administrative Process" in 1954, "The phenomenon loosely and invidiously described as 'industry orientation' is much less a disease of certain administrations than a condition endemic in any agency or set of agencies which seek to perform such a [regulatory] task."[13] Undue influence (from malfeasance to *ex parte* approaches to "subtle but pervasive methods pursued by regulated industries to influence regulatory agencies by social favors, promises of later employment in the industry itself, and other similar means") was a major preoccupation of the 1960 Landis Report on Regulatory Agencies.[14] By the time the Chicago School began to focus seriously on the issue, Bernstein himself had already summarized that "The *most familiar charge* against independent commissions is that they develop an orientation toward the views and interests of their clientele and become ripe for *capture*."[15]

For the most part, early formulations of capture theory were mildly reformist in orientation – usually concluding with a call for something such as increased judicial review or enhanced executive supervision or a higher level of administrative formality in regulatory practice to rein in or counterbalance industry influence.[16] In the 1960s and 1970s, however, capture theory and social science investigations of regulatory agencies grew

---

[12] In a campaign speech in Seattle, Washington, on October 7, 1952, Eisenhower complained about certain "zealots" who urged a "whole-hog Federal Government" believing "that it must own and control just as many of our resources as it can lay its hands on – by fair means or foul." Quoted in Grisinger, 348–9. Also see Herbert Hoover, *The Challenge to Liberty* (New York: C. Scribner's Sons, 1934).

[13] Louis L. Jaffe, "Effective Limits of the Administrative Process," *Harvard Law Review* 67 (1953–1954), 1113. See also, Harold Seidman, *Politics, Position, and Power: The Dynamics of Federal Organization* (New York: Oxford University Press, 1970).

[14] James M. Landis, *Report on Regulatory Agencies to the President-Elect* (Washington, D.C.: U.S. Government Printing Office, December 1960), 12.

[15] Bernstein, "Independent Regulatory Agencies," 23 (emphasis added).

[16] Theodore J. Lowi, *The End of Liberalism* (New York: Norton, 1969); Kenneth Culp Davis, *Discretionary Justice: A Preliminary Inquiry* (Urbana: University of Illinois Press, 1969).

increasingly ideological, generating a much more thoroughgoing critique. And though the attack from the right and economics is most well-known, blood was drawn first on the left among an emerging generation of radical historians of American economic policy who produced what is known in the trade as the corporate liberal synthesis.

The corporate liberal synthesis originated in Gabriel Kolko's 1963 radical denunciation of progressive reform in the provocatively entitled *Triumph of Conservatism*. Like Huntington and Bernstein, Kolko was looking for an alternative to the public welfare, liberal consensus histories that too easily aligned economic regulation and the public good in a Whiggish morality play featuring the inevitable triumph of the democratic people over the special interests. However, Kolko took his cues from Veblen, Marx, and Weber rather than Merriam, Lasswell, and Truman. In a survey of the great episodes of Progressive-era regulation from the U.S. Industrial Commission to the Bureau of Corporations to the Food and Drug Administration and the Federal Trade Commission, Kolko redefined the entire progressive movement as an exemplar of capture theory writ large. He defined progressivism as "a movement that operated on the assumption that the general welfare of the community could be best served by satisfying the concrete needs of business." Consequently, Kolko contended, "Regulation itself was invariably controlled by leaders of the regulated industry, and directed toward ends they deemed acceptable or desirable."[17] James Weinstein and Martin Sklar continued in this vein, developing an overarching critical history of capture with more of a class-based edge than either the special-interest or rent-seeking theories of economists and political scientists. Weinstein explicitly disparaged the historical orthodoxy of the likes of Arthur Schlesinger, Jr. (whom he identified as "intellectual in residence of the Kennedys"), where "Liberalism in America" was self-understood as a progressive effort to "restrain the power of the business community." On the contrary, Weinstein argued, the liberal and regulatory reforms of the Progressive era were primarily "the product, consciously created, of the leaders of the giant corporations and financial institutions."[18]

---

[17] Gabriel Kolko, *The Triumph of Conservatism: A Reinterpretation of American History, 1900–1916* (Chicago: Quadrangle Books, 1963), 2–3.

[18] James Weinstein, *The Corporate Ideal in the Liberal State, 1900–1918* (Boston: Beacon Press, 1968), xv; Martin J. Sklar, *The Corporate Reconstruction of American Capitalism, 1890–1916: The Market, the Law, and Politics* (New York: Cambridge University Press, 1988). As Gerald Berk summarized this school of thought in an excellent review essay: "Corporate liberal scholarship, especially in its left-wing variant reintroduced class analysis into the study of twentieth-century politics, concluding that a powerful cadre of class-conscious corporate elites successfully used the state to stabilize modern capitalism and co-opt radical

In short, by the time George Stigler aimed his economic theories at the "idealistic view of public regulation," there seemed to be hardly any idealism left. Indeed, Stigler himself admitted that by 1971, denunciations of the ICC for "prorailroad policies" had become something of "a cliché of the literature." However, like their unlikely compatriots in history Kolko and Weinstein, the Chicago School economists were not particularly interested in the reform of regulatory processes or administrative procedures. Rather, the "capture thesis" was but an opening gambit in pursuit of a more total critique of the "basic logic of political life" that undergirded the regulatory impulse as a whole. Stigler bemoaned the many "victims" of the general and "pervasive use of the state's support of special groups." In addition, he encouraged economists to more aggressively establish a "license to practice," a "rational theory of political behavior." Until and unless that larger *economic* science of politics was produced, he concluded (rather imperiously and undemocratically), reformers were "ill equipped to use the state for their reforms."[19]

These were the intellectual roots of what Thomas Merrill dubbed "the public choice era," when capture theory's original skepticism about the behavior of a certain set of administrative institutions morphed into a more general and ideological "pessimism about the capacity of *any* governmental institution" to serve the "public interest."[20] Gary Becker foreshadowed this trend in an audacious five-page reflection on the slight topic of "Competition and Democracy" in the very first issue of the *Journal of Law and Economics* in 1958. He asked, "Does the existence of market imperfections justify government intervention?" He responded, "The answer would be 'no,' if the imperfections in government behavior were greater than those in the market." Capture theory was meant to demonstrate the pervasive "imperfections in government behavior" that called into question the general governmental regulatory impulse as a whole. As Becker concluded tellingly (challenging all the assumptions of progressive and liberal economic policymaking), "It may be preferable not to regulate economic monopolies and to suffer their bad effects, rather than to regulate them and suffer the effects of *political* imperfections."[21] Although public interest theories insisted upon the ultimate priority of democracy over economy,

policy demands from below." Gerald Berk, "Corporate Liberalism Reconsidered: A Review Essay," *Journal of Policy History* 3 (1991): 70–84, 70–71.

[19] Stigler, "The Theory of Economic Regulation," 18.

[20] Merrill, "Capture Theory and the Courts," 1053 (emphasis added).

[21] Gary S. Becker, "Competition and Democracy," *Journal of Law and Economics* 1 (1958), 105–9, 109 (emphasis added).

Becker's conclusion (and his title) began the process of putting competition back out front. It thus echoed perfectly Friedrich Hayek's original reasoning in *Freedom and the Economic System* (1939): "It is often said that democracy will not tolerate capitalism. If 'capitalism' here means a competitive society based on free disposal over private property, it is far more important to observe that only capitalism makes democracy possible."[22]

Caught in the middle of this triple (center-left-right; 50s-60s-70s) assault of politics, history, and economics, it is perhaps not surprising that the "public interest" or "public service" theory of regulation and administration has been treated by social scientists as something akin to a pipe dream since the heyday of the late New Deal.[23] Indeed, despite very different methodological and political contexts, the road from the public administration investigations of Huntington and Bernstein to the more formal law and economics theories of capture developed by Stigler and Peltzman runs fairly straight and narrow. En route, descriptions of a quite specific kind of regulatory pathology or misdevelopment gave way to a more general critique of public as compared with private ordering and a general preference for individual market as opposed to collective regulatory solutions. Moreover, this was an intellectual history with distinct policy ramifications, as progressive and New Deal initiatives in regulation, public utility, and social services were soon met with ubiquitous counter-reform proposals in the name of deregulation, privatization, and neoliberalism.

THE LONG (RATHER THAN SHORT) HISTORY OF ECONOMIC REGULATION IN AMERICA

Although the politics of capture theorists diverges significantly from Bernstein to Kolko to Stigler (creating something like a cacophony of consensus), one thing that remains common to the perspective as a whole is the historical point of departure. One thing that almost all capture narratives seem to agree on is that economic regulation in the United States began somewhere around 1887. For the historically adventurous, perhaps the state

[22] Friedrich A. von Hayek, *Freedom and the Economic System* (Chicago: University of Chicago Press, 1939), 28.

[23] Two classic statements of the public interest theory are Felix Frankfurter, *The Public and Its Government* (New Haven, CT: Yale University Press, 1930) and James M. Landis, *The Administrative Process* (New Haven, CT: Yale University Press, 1938). For some signs of a renewal of interest in "public interest," see Martha Minow, *Partners not Rivals: Privatization and the Public Good* (Boston: Beacon Press, 2002); and David A. Moss and Michael R. Fein, "Radio Regulation Revisited: Coase, the FCC, and the Public Interest," *Journal of Policy History* 15 (2003).

railroad commission movement might push the starting date back a decade or two. But otherwise, the founding of the federal independent regulatory commissions, especially the ICC, marks the genesis from which the capture story usually unfolds. From Huntington's marasmus to Kolko's railroad case study[24] to Stigler's cliché, capture theory embeds some strong assumptions about regulation and administration as comparatively recent developments in American history – modern departures from some original position of nineteenth century smaller government, competitive markets, perhaps even laissez-faire. For most capture theorists, in other words, the history of economic regulation in America is distinctly short. Indeed, it is sometimes so short that it can be seen as aberrational – something of a flawed experiment with governmental intervention in economic life primarily associated with the excesses of the Progressive and New Deal eras. Regulatory intervention is thus safely, historically confined to the "market-in-exile"[25] era between Herbert Spencer and Friedrich Hayek, when American liberal political economy went somewhat off the tracks. The capture thesis turns on a meta-narrative of exposing the short-term historical error in the interest of righting the wrong – returning policymaking to fundamental economic principles and restoring some kind of purer and lost original, natural, and classical order.

In "Why Have the Socialists Been Winning," Stigler made clear the political and ideological underpinnings of this kind of historical chronology, focusing directly on "the massive growth of governments in the twentieth century" – what he dubbed "the most conspicuous single change in the organization of social life – a growth so large and so pervasive that it would be as difficult to deny as the existence of the Pacific Ocean." For Stigler, this distinctly modern "growth of government" was the problem to be investigated – the thing to be explained, criticized, and ultimately repudiated. He ventured a hypothesis that explicitly linked this historical point about a novel departure in the scale and scope of regulatory power to the capture thesis point about the rising power of special interest groups. For as Stigler saw it, the unprecedented "growth of government" after 1887 was directly attributable to "the purposeful use of public power to increase the incomes of particular groups in society."[26] Political imperfections thus joined

---

[24] Gabriel Kolko, *Railroads and Regulation, 1877–1916* (Princeton: Princeton University Press, 1965).

[25] Cass R. Sunstein, *Radicals in Robes: Why Extreme Right-Wing Courts Are Wrong for America* (New York: Basic Books, 2006), 1 (on the "constitution-in-exile").

[26] George Stigler, "Why Have the Socialists Been Winning," in Kurt R. Leube and Thomas Gale Moore, eds., *The Essence of Stigler* (Stanford: Hoover Institution Press, Stanford

market imperfections to create something like the imperfect historical storm that yielded the modern regulatory state and the aberrational "growth of governments."

So, history is not peripheral to capture theory. Rather, temporal accounts and historical assumptions pervade the literature. Specific historical regulatory changes over time – particularly those of the Progressive and New Deal eras – seem to animate the entire inquiry. Unfortunately, however, the historical chronology of American regulation and administrative statecraft conventionally deployed by capture theory is flawed.

One of the most important developments in American political and legal historiography over the past decade or two has been a radical revision in commonly accepted notions of the lack of economic regulation or national administration in early American history.[27] Indeed, the overwhelming conclusion of a still rapidly expanding revisionist literature is that the history of economic regulation in America is distinctly long rather than short. Well before the founding of the Interstate Commerce Commission, the United States across all levels of government engaged in a huge number of regulatory and administrative activities. From the perspective of an emerging historical consensus, the growth of government is not a new deviation in American history; it is the historical norm. Economic regulation is a quite old rather than a relatively new phenomenon, found just as easily in the eighteenth and nineteenth centuries as in the twentieth and twenty-first centuries. Indeed, from the perspective of the overthrown Articles of Confederation, the growth of a stronger government, far from being a recent departure in the American political-economic tradition, is more like a founding *raison d'etre*. Administrative regulation in America was not invented in 1887 as a prelude to Progressive and New Deal reform; rather, it was a technique of governance with deep roots in the earliest political and economic practices of the American republic. Although it is still common for generalists to talk about American history in terms of a transition from nineteenth century laissez-faire to the twentieth century general welfare state, that political and ideological mythology has been under sustained attack from professional historians for almost half a century.

On the local and state level, a whole series of historical monographs have been written challenging the myth of nineteenth century laissez-faire by

University, 1986): 337–346. Although quite dissimilar in orientation, the corporate liberal theory of capture also focused on this distinctive expansion of governmental power – what Kolko dubbed a distinctly new form of "political capitalism."

[27] For an overview of just a small segment of this literature, see William J. Novak, "The Myth of the Weak American State," *The American Historical Review* 113 (2008), 752.

documenting a long history of market policing, public works, inspection laws, and health and safety regulations governing almost every aspect of social and economic life before the Civil War.[28] More importantly and more recently, at the national level, scholars such as Jerry Mashaw, Richard John, Gautham Rao, Nick Parrillo, and Max Edling have been making a powerful case that the story of national economic regulation and administrative governance needs to begin in 1787 not 1887.[29] As Mashaw's new book on "The Lost One Hundred Years of American Administrative Law" demonstrates clearly, the U.S. economy has developed in the shadow of almost constant and continuous scrutiny, investigation, promotion, protection, regulation, and redistribution by a cadre of public officers and national economic regulators.[30]

These are but few select examples from recent historical scholarship. A more comprehensive, but still quite selective list of scholars who have worked seriously and substantively on the long, distinctively non-aberrational history of regulation and administration in the United States includes a broad cross-section of the modern American social science community: Richard

[28] I am thinking here primarily of the so-called "commonwealth studies" of regulation in antebellum America – a literature on which I build in my own monograph, *The People's Welfare: Law and Regulation in Nineteenth-Century America* (Chapel Hill: University of North Carolina Press, 1996). An exhaustive bibliography of the commonwealth studies would make for a ridiculously long footnote. Here are the classics: Oscar and Mary Flug Handlin, *Commonwealth: A Study of the Role of Government in the American Economy: Massachusetts, 1774–1861*, rev. ed. (Cambridge, MA: Harvard University Press, 1969); Louis Hartz, *Economic Policy and Democratic Thought: Pennsylvania, 1776–1860* (New York: Cambridge University Press, 1948); Gerald D. Nash, *State Government and Economic Development: A History of Administrative Policies in California, 1849–1933* (Berkeley: University of California, 1964); and Carter Goodrich, *Government Promotion of American Canals and Railroads, 1800–1890* (New York: Columbia University Press, 1960). However, it is hard to get an idea of the full import of this school without also including the work of Harry Scheiber on the Ohio canal era, Milton Heath, Bray Hammond, James Neal Primm, George Miller, Paul Gates, and Edwin M. Dodd. For fuller bibliographical summaries and analysis see Robert A. Lively, "The American System: A Review Article," *Business History Review* 29 (1955): 91–6; and Harry N. Scheiber, "Government and the Economy: Studies of the 'Commonwealth' Policy in Nineteenth-Century America," *Journal of Interdisciplinary History* 3 (1972): 135–51.

[29] Jerry L. Mashaw, "Recovering American Administrative Law: Federalist Foundations, 1787–1801," *Yale Law Journal* 115 (2006): 1256–344; Max M. Edling, *A Revolution in Favor of Government: Origins of the U.S. Constitution and the Making of the American State* (New York: Oxford University Press, 2003); Richard R. John, *Spreading the News: The American Postal System from Franklin to Morse* (Cambridge, MA: Harvard University Press, 1995); John, "Governmental Institutions as Agents of Change: Rethinking American Political Development in the Early Republic, 1787–1835," *Studies in American Political Development* 11 (Fall 1997): 347–80.

[30] Jerry L. Mashaw, *Creating the Administrative Constitution: The Lost One Hundred Years of American Administrative Law* (New Haven: Yale University Press, 2012).

Bensel, Ed Berkowitz, Alan Brinkley, Elliot Brownlee, Daniel Carpenter, Michele Landis Dauber, Martha Derthick, Dan Ernst, Gary Gerstle, Otis Graham, Joanna Grisinger, Oscar and Mary Handlin, Louis Hartz, Ellis Hawley, Sam Hays, Christopher Howard, Barry Karl, Michael Katz, Ira Katznelson, Morton Keller, Jen Klein, John Larson, Robert Lieberman, David Mayhew, Tom McCraw, Ajay Mehrotra, Sid Milkis, David Moss, Karen Orren, Steve Sawyer, Harry Scheiber, Theda Skocpol, Stephen Skowronek, Bat Sparrow, Jim Sparrow, Mark Wilson, John Witt, Jim Wooten – the list goes on and on.

Yet the strange fact of the matter is that modern capture theory (focused directly as it is on trying to tell us something about patterns and tendencies of regulation in crucial eras of transition and transformation) rarely cites any of the authors or literatures listed previously. Somewhat curiously, capture theorists have been writing about and drawing bold conclusions from the history of the American regulatory state without actually consulting real histories of regulation. In consequence, the capture literature has been operating with a rather crimped and crabbed (if not outright fictional) portrait of the rise of the American regulatory state that no longer reflects the actual state of historical knowledge.

However, does a longer and more accurate historical chronology of the American regulatory state really matter – can it actually affect the way in which we substantively think about capture in regulatory processes more generally? Can the simple act of historical re-periodization really affect the analytics and interpretation? I think so. Indeed, even on the most general interpretive level, the vast range of extraordinarily diverse regulatory initiatives and practices currently being unearthed by historians as coincident with the earliest economic development of the United States simply resists easy, uniform categorization within a capture framework. The new histories provide an archive of new materials with which to investigate early national regulatory initiatives (e.g., the national steamboat inspection regime that dates from the late 1830s) as well as the habits and practices of the first real independent commissions (e.g., the Patent Office).[31] These histories also suggest that regulation is not something that originates historically outside of the development of a market economy (and at some later date for exogenous reasons), but is historically endemic to and constitutive of it. However, let me suggest another more specific way in which changing

---

[31] John G. Burke, "Bursting Boilers and the Federal Power," *Technology & Culture* 7 (1966): 1; Steven W. Usselman and Richard R. John, "Patent Politics: Intellectual Property, the Railroad Industry, and the Problem of Monopoly," *Journal of Policy History* 18 (2006): 96.

how we think about the history of regulation might lead to a reevaluation of capture, regulation, and public and private interest more generally.

CORRUPTION: THE ORIGINAL CAPTURE THEORY

Obviously, the first thing that the long history of American regulation opens up is a broader time horizon within which scholars must grapple with regulatory cause and effect, expectation and outcome, and success and failure. Lengthening the historical timeline greatly increases the range of factors behind the regulatory impulse and multiplies the social, political, and economic contexts out of which regulation emerged as a viable solution. This longer chronology thus disrupts some of the simple and politically freighted storylines that too often accompany the conventional eras that preoccupy capture theory: for example, Progressivism, the New Deal, or the new social regulation of the 1960s and 1970s. Looking at the formation of the ICC as an unsurprising mid-level development in a long regulatory history rather than as a sudden new point of departure (yet alone a violent rupture) in the American governmental tradition provides a different context from which to evaluate the interpretive implications of the capture narrative. More particularly, a longer chronology retrospectively highlights the nature of the special problems that regulation was responding to rather than the regulatory solution and the inevitable problems of implementation going forward. Capture theory all too often uses history like a rearview mirror, reading history backward from the present to the historical origin of a particular regulatory regime. In contrast, the long history of regulation in America recommends reading history forward starting with the specific historical reasons for the emergence of one set of regulatory policies over existing alternatives.

One thing highlighted by that longer historical perspective is the distinctive set of concerns articulated by reformers themselves in self-consciously redesigning the institutions of an existing American regulatory state at the turn of the twentieth century. In contrast to the caricature of regulatory reform frequently portrayed in the capture literature, progressives did not "invent" regulation, nor did they naively advocate regulatory solutions in the interest of some ill-specified and general "protection and benefit of the public at large."[32] Rather, the chief architects of progressive regulation and administration – people such as Frank Goodnow, Ernst Freund, Woodrow Wilson, Walton Hamilton, Felix Frankfurter, and Milton Handler – were

---

[32] Stigler, "The Theory of Economic Regulation," 1.

very serious and careful students of American (as well as European) political, regulatory, and economic history. They were under no illusions that the relationships of private and public interest or competition and democracy were simple matters (much less coverable in five pages in a new law and economics journal). And they were anything but unaware that businesses, corporations, unions, interest groups, private associations, professional societies, and lobbying organizations could and would influence regulatory policymaking. In contrast to the idealistic public-interestedness frequently attributed to them in the capture literature, progressive reformers in the regulatory field were sophisticated moderns – known explicitly for their pragmatism, positivism, empiricism, skepticism, and critical realism.[33] They helped professionalize the modern social sciences in the United States, and they were some of the shrewdest and most well-read and prolific students of law, politics, and economics in American intellectual history. Although the term *capture* might have been coined in the 1950s, 1960s, and 1970s, the economic and political phenomena it attempts to describe would hardly strike them as news.

Indeed, one of the central problems that progressive reformers were consciously attempting to remedy through regulation was something that itself looks very much like a version of the problem of "strong" capture delineated by Dan Carpenter and David Moss in the introduction to this volume.[34] The independent regulatory commissions were themselves designed to combat what progressives envisioned as a perennial problem in republican and democratic governance – that is, the tendency of private economic interests to capture the public political sphere. More particularly, they viewed late nineteenth century agglomerations of corporate wealth and power as producing a dangerous new form of the age-old threat of private interest trumping public democracy. Of course, they did not use the modern language (yet alone theory) of "capture" when they talked about this problem; rather in the vernacular of the time, they invoked the very old theme and problem of "corruption."

Although the capture thesis is frequently heralded as a new and distinctly contemporary economic theory, from the long perspective of history it looks more like old wine in new bottles. For there is simply no older theme in the Western legal and political tradition than the one highlighted by capture.

---

[33] See, for example, James T. Kloppenberg, *Uncertain Victory: Social Democracy and Progressivism in European and American Thought, 1870–1920* (New York: Oxford University Press, 1986); Daniel T. Rodgers, *Atlantic Crossings: Social Politics in a Progressive Age* (Cambridge, 1998).

[34] Daniel Carpenter and David Moss, "Introduction," *Preventing Capture*, 1–22.

In Plato's *Republic,* Socrates noted that "our aim in founding the State was not the disproportionate happiness of any one class, but the greatest happiness of the whole." In addition, he bemoaned "the corruption of society" whereby "the guardians of the laws and of the government are only seemingly and not real guardians" who "turn the State upside down" and ultimately destroy it.[35] Aristotle's *Politics* also decried the corrupting effects of private interest and private vice on the commonwealth noting, "The true forms of government, therefore, are those in which the one, or the few, or the many, govern with a view to the common interest; but governments which rule with a view to the private interest, whether of the one, the few, or the many, are perversions."[36]

As Gordon Wood, J. G. A. Pocock, and many other historians have convincingly argued, it was precisely this classical tradition from Aristotle to Montesquieu and its preoccupation with corruption and the private capture of the public sphere that structured the revolutionary political thinking of the original American founders. As Wood put it, "When the American Whigs described the English nation and government as eaten away by 'corruption,' they were in fact using a technical term of political science, rooted in the writings of classical antiquity, made famous by Machiavelli, developed by the classical republicans of seventeenth-century England, and carried into the eighteenth century by nearly everyone who laid claim to knowing anything about politics."[37] Anyone who knew anything about politics in the late eighteenth century was well aware of the dangers of "corruption" and the way the legislature and other branches could be turned from the public good by the force of private vice, group interest, and/or ministerial manipulation.

Two hundred years before the emergence of George Stigler, James Madison made a pretty compelling case for himself as the original American capture theorist in Federalist No. 10.[38] There, of course, Madison explicitly warned about the influence of faction in "public councils" and "public administrations" whereby the interests or passions of "a majority or a

---

35 Plato, *The Republic: The Complete and Unabridged Jowett Translation* (New York: Vintage Books, 1991), Book IV, 129–30. Socrates also offered a bit of wisdom on the priority of politics over economics: "Our opponent is thinking of peasants at a festival, who are enjoying a life of revelry, not of citizens who are doing their duty to the State."

36 Aristotle, *The Politics and The Constitution of Athens* (New York: Cambridge University Press, 1996), Book III, 71.

37 Gordon S. Wood, *The Creation of the American Republic, 1776–1787* (Chapel Hill: University of North Carolina Press, 1969), 32–3; J. G. A. Pocock, *The Machiavellian Moment: Florentine Political Thought in the Atlantic Republic Tradition* (Princeton: Princeton University Press, 1975).

38 James Madison, "The Federalist No. 10: The Utility of the Union as a Safeguard against Domestic Faction and Insurrection (continued)," *Daily Advertiser,* November 22, 1787.

minority of the whole" were pursued adversely to "the public good" or "the permanent and aggregate interests of the community." Madison concluded, moreover, that the causes and sources of factions, interests, and parties could not (and should not)[39] be stamped out or eliminated, for "the latent causes of faction are . . . sown in the nature of man." As he wisely noted, "It is in vain to say that enlightened statesmen will be able to adjust these clashing interests, and render them all subservient to the public good."

However, notably, and thankfully, Madison at this point did not put down his pen in pessimistic resignation about the prospects for legislation, regulation, or republican governance. Rather, the famous conclusion to which he was drawn was that although "the *causes* of faction cannot be removed," relief could still "be sought in the means of controlling its *effects*." In other words, the existence of faction, corruption, and capture was not fatal to the conceit of legislation and regulation in the public interest. Rather, they were prods to better public institutional design – the never-ending task of thinking through better plans of governance to control the noxious effects of all-too-human corruption: "factious tempers," "local prejudices," "sinister designs," and the "cabals of the few." In Federalist No. 10, Madison thought carefully through representation, voting, and the appropriate size of a body politic, because, as he put it, "The regulation of these various and interfering interests forms the principal task of modern legislation."

Long before the advent of the twentieth century, in other words, concern about private interests or factions capturing public governing institutions and bending them toward selfish ends rather than general benefits was a well-developed (indeed perhaps *the* central) trope in American political and economic commentary. In the Jacksonian era, just such a perspective dominated critiques of special incorporation via legislative charters. From Jackson's notorious fight with the Bank of the United States to calls for more general incorporation in states such as Massachusetts and Pennsylvania, reformers questioned the mixture of public/private motive and profit that guided the legislative distribution of monopoly privileges, land grants, rights-of-way, and other valuable statutory benefits. As the *Boston Daily Herald* complained in 1836, "They are not for the public good – in design or end. . . . They are for the aggrandizement of the stockholders – for the

---

[39] On the attempt to eliminate the causes of faction, Madison contended that the "remedy" would be "worse than the disease." As he put it, "Liberty is to faction what air is to fire, an aliment without which it instantly expires. But it could not be less folly to abolish liberty, which is essential to political life, because it nourishes faction, than it would be to wish the annihilation of air, which is essential to animal life, because it imparts to fire its destructive agency."

promotion of the interest of the few. . . . We wish to have public good and private speculation more distinctly separated."[40]

So, although seldom recognized by capture theory, it should come as no surprise that by the turn of the twentieth century, the problem of private interest in public governance was well understood. Indeed, the theme of public corruption was something of a leitmotif for progressive reform. Beyond the well-known exposes of the muckraking journalists Ida Tarbell, Lincoln Steffens, and Ray Stannard Baker who gathered around *McClure's Magazine*, progressive intellectuals and social scientists mounted a sustained attack on the corruptions of the so-called Gilded Age. So strong was the progressive preoccupation with private influence on public policy that historian Richard L. McCormick placed the "Discovery that Business Corrupts Politics" – the awakening of the people to illicit business influence in American public life – at the very origin point of progressivism itself.[41] Progressives used "corruption" in its classical sense indicating the despoiling of a distinctly collective public sphere (a republic supposedly devoted to *res publica* – the public things) by private and individual economic interests. They spent a great deal of time exposing the various frauds, thefts, bribes, extortions, and schemes that linked unvirtuous robber barons to corrupt politicos (to use Matthew Josephson's evocative terms).[42]

However, although concern about public corruption was as old as the republic, what was new at the turn of the twentieth century was an acute awareness of the unprecedented threat to the polity posed by the arrival of large-scale business and corporate interests in rail, oil, meatpacking, and insurance, whose corruptions were cataloged in a seemingly endless series of reports and even fictional portrayals from Charles and Henry Adams's *Chapters of Erie* (1871) to Frank Norris's *McTeague, The Octopus,* and *The Pit* (1899–1903).[43] "Laissez-faire constitutionalism" was understood as a

---

[40] Oscar Handlin and Mary Flug Handlin, *Commonwealth: A Study of the Role of Government in the American Economy, Massachusetts, 1774–1861* (New York: Cambridge University Press, 1969), 213; Louis Hartz, *Economic Policy and Democratic Thought: Pennsylvania, 1776–1860* (Cambridge: Harvard University Press, 1948); James Willard Hurst, *The Legitimacy of the Business Corporation* (Charlottesville: University Press of Virginia, 1970).

[41] Richard L. McCormick, "The Discovery that Business Corrupts Politics: A Reappraisal of the Origins of Progressivism," *American Historical Review* 86 (1981): 247–274.

[42] Matthew Josephson, *The Robber Barons: The Great American Capitalists, 1861–1901* (New York, 1934); Matthew Josephson, *The Politicos, 1865–1896* (New York: Harcourt Brace, 1938).

[43] Charles Francis Adams, Jr., and Henry Adams, *Chapters of Erie* (Boston: J.R. Osgood and Company, 1871); Frank Norris, *McTeague: A Story of San Francisco* (New York: Doubleday and McClure Co., 1899); Norris, *The Octopus: A Story of California* (New York: P.F. Collier, 1901); Norris, *The Pit: A Story of Chicago* (New York: Doubleday, Page, and Co., 1903).

corruption of the American rule of law in precisely this sense – as a usurpation (a capture) of the public law by private economic interests and philosophies. In "Business Principles in Law and Politics," Thorstein Veblen contended that "constitutional government has, in the main, become a department of the business organization and is guided by the advice of business men."[44] For just such sentiments, Veblen became something of a prophet for capture historians like Kolko, Weinstein, and Sklar.

However, the important point here is that there was nothing particularly unusual or prophetic in Veblen's perspective. Rather it was common wisdom – the baseline assumption from which much American constitutional development and almost all progressive reform proceeded.

In the economic regulatory field, the reformer who most clearly articulated the explicit relationship between regulation and corruption was Charles Francis Adams, Jr. It goes without saying that Adams was neither a wooly-headed idealist nor particularly naïve about the limits and possibilities of American politics. A lawyer, a historian, a regulator, a railroad executive, and a member of one of the most influential families in American politics and letters, Adams was well equipped to size up the problem of railroad economics in the late nineteenth century and its impact on the body politic. The picture he painted was not pretty, let alone rational. He talked about the railroad problem not in terms of market failure or externalities but as nothing less than a national "emergency."[45] In "A Chapter of Erie," he described the battle for control of the Erie Railroad between the Erie men – Jay Gould, Jim Fisk, and Daniel Drew – and Cornelius Vanderbilt as nothing less than the "Erie war."[46] Although capture theory's ex post analysis frequently draws attention to the "roads not taken," for example, competition or legislative regulation, Adams made clear ex ante that the starting point for regulatory reform was the explicit recognition that those "other roads were indeed taken" and found completely wanting. As Adams started his chapter on "The Government and the Railroad Corporations": "Neither competition nor legislation have proved themselves effective agents for the regulation of the railroad system." And so Montesquieu-like, Madison-like, he probed further: "What other and more effective [instrument] is there within the reach of the American people?"[47]

[44] Thorstein Veblen, *The Theory of Business Enterprise* (New York: A.M. Kelley, 1904), 287.

[45] Charles Francis Adams, Jr., "The Railroad System," in Charles Francis Adams, Jr., and Henry Adams, *Chapters of Erie and other Essays* (Boston: J.R. Osgood and Company, 1871), 333–429, 414.

[46] Charles Francis Adams, Jr., "A Chapter of Erie," in Adams and Adams, *Chapters of Erie*, 1–99, 6.

[47] Adams, "The Railroad System," 414.

Adams's other explicit starting point was capture – or as the progressives referred to it – corruption.[48] For Adams, the railroad problem involved not just the economic problem of expensive "natural monopolies" operating in an atmosphere of "ruinous competition" between states and localities (as Herbert Hovenkamp summarized the situation: "railroads seemed destined to be either filthy rich or perpetually broke").[49] Rather, anticipating Richard McCormick's analysis, Adams recognized that the railroad problem also involved the explicitly political problem of business corrupting the body politic – "the sturdy corporation beggars who infested the lobby" of state legislatures.[50] As Adams saw it, "Our legislatures are now universally becoming a species of irregular boards of railroad direction" creating persistent "scandal and alarm." "The effects upon political morality have been injurious," he suggested, adding that "many States in this country, and especially New York, New Jersey, Pennsylvania, and Maryland have now for years notoriously been controlled by their railroad corporations." Noting that "there is no power which can purify a corrupted legislature," Adams turned instead to the regulatory commission – independent, permanent, and competent tribunals that he analogized to courts.[51]

Now, at this critical juncture in the historical development of the modern regulatory commission, it must be noted that Charles Francis Adams was under no illusion that regulatory commissions would be somehow magically immune from private influence, economic interest, or other forms of group special pleading. On the contrary, he specifically anticipated the exact question of regulatory capture as early as 1871: "But it will be said, Who will guard the virtue of the tribunal? Why should the corporations not deal with [the commissions just] as [they did] with the legislatures?" Who would

---

[48] In *Prophets of Regulation*, Thomas K. McCraw draws attention to one of Adams's many classic depictions of Gilded Age corruption during the Erie war featuring an interrupted meeting of Daniel Drew in his New York office:

> They were speedily aroused from their real or affected tranquility by trustworthy intelligence that processes for contempt were already issued against them, and that their only chance of escape from incarceration lay in precipitate flight. At ten o'clock the astonished police saw a throng of panic-stricken railway directors – looking more like a frightened gang of thieves, disturbed in the division of their plunder, than like the wealthy representatives of a great corporation – rush headlong from the doors of the Erie office, and dash off in the direction of the Jersey ferry. In their hands were packages and files of papers, and their pockets were crammed with assets and securities. One individual bore away with him in a hackney-coach bales containing six millions of dollars in greenbacks.

McCraw, *Prophets of Regulation* (New York: Cambridge University Press, 1984), 16.

[49] Herbert Hovenkamp, *Enterprise and American Law, 1836–1937* (New York: Cambridge University Press, 1991), 148.

[50] Adams, "The Railroad System," 427.

[51] Ibid., 417–418.

guard the guardians? Adams's answer to this question was very important to the overarching goals and perspectives that animate this volume of essays on "Preventing Capture." For like Madison, Adams concluded that there was no final answer, no silver bullet, no complete economic theory or political model that would forever preclude the capture and corruption of any governmental institution in a democratic republic. Rather, the very nature and history of democracy suggested that the capture of public institutions by private interest was an ever-present weakness and danger. Vigilance was as necessary as it was eternal. The public virtue of the people themselves, of course, was perhaps the best line of defense against such corruption and capture, but as Madison famously observed long ago, "If men were angels, no government would be necessary. If angels were to govern men, neither external nor internal controls on government would be necessary."[52] No, Adams recognized that corruption and capture were endemic and historic problems in any truly popular form of government and that the only viable solution was the pragmatic, ongoing, never-ending Madisonian constitutional tradition of, as Adams marvelously phrased it, continually developing "all the checks and balances that human ingenuity can devise."[53] In the late nineteenth and early twentieth centuries, the independent regulatory commission offered a new, historical check and balance to offset private economic corruption and public legislative capture. Adams had no preconception that further checks and balances would not be necessary in a democratic American future.

So, progressive regulatory reformers were certainly not lacking basic awareness about the problem of capture. Quite the contrary, they explicitly emphasized the theme of corruption as a prelude to and a basis for their own reform proposals. The peak years of muckraking disclosure from 1904 to 1908 were accompanied by a wave of legislative activity specifically designed to curb the influence of private interest and private money in American politics, including federal and state corrupt practices, laws regulating campaign contributions and the solicitation of funds from corporations, laws regulating legislative lobbying, laws prohibiting free transportation passes, and political reforms such as direct primaries.[54] The development of the independent regulatory commissions (as well as economic

---

[52] James Madison, "The Federalist No. 51: The Structure of the Government Must Furnish the Proper Checks and Balances Between the Different Departments," *Independent Journal*, February 6, 1788.

[53] Ibid., 427 (emphasis added).

[54] McCormick, "Business Corrupts Politics," 266–7; Earl Ray Sikes, *State and Federal Corrupt Practices Legislation* (Durham: Duke University Press, 1928); Helen M. Rocca, *Corrupt Practices Legislation* (Washington: National League of Women Voters, 1928).

regulatory and police power measures) must be understood in this larger context of: (a) long American experience with regulatory and administrative techniques; and (b) a heightened concern about the susceptibility of existing democratic politics to capture by new organizations of private economic interest.

Viewing regulation and administration within this much longer arc of historical American regulatory practice (as opposed to exceptionalist departures from nonexistent traditions of laissez-faire) thus highlights a much more complex backdrop to regulatory change and innovation than suggested by the simple binary of public interest and private capture. Proponents of regulation were not unaware of the potential for corruption in state-directed activities – in fact, it was one of their main concerns about the *status quo ante*. Indeed, their original and almost obsessive focus on the undue influence of private economic interest on existing configurations of democratic politics eventually brought them to a more comprehensive reevaluation and critique of the new systemic forms of private coercion emerging from within the modern corporate economy. The problem of private "governing power" was not an oversight in the progressive theory of economic regulation; it was a driving force.

In the end, however, progressive reformers did not rest content with "corruption" analysis or some kind of incipient "capture" theory. Rather, their early inquiries into the influence of private economic actors on democratic politics soon gave way to a much more sophisticated concern with the role of "private coercion" more generally in American social and economic life. Beginning in the late nineteenth century and extending through to the early New Deal, a rather extraordinary group of legal, economic, and social science authors (some of whom Barbara Fried dubbed the "first law and economics movement") developed a deeper critique of the role of private economic power in modern societies.[55] Here organized business interest came to be seen as a threat not simply because of its secondary effects on the corruption of the polity, but as a primary concern in and of itself. The problem of organized private coercion – the creation of new forms of private

[55] Barbara H. Fried, *The Progressive Assault on Laissez Faire: Robert Hale and the First Law and Economics Movement* (Cambridge, MA: Harvard University Press, 1998). The list of key authors in this tradition (and I include a prototypical text for each) includes Henry Carter Adams ("Relation of the State to Industrial Action" and "Economics and Jurisprudence"), Thorstein Veblen (*Theory of Business Enterprise*), Richard T. Ely (*Property and Contract in their Relations to the Distribution of Wealth*), John R. Commons (*Legal Foundations of Capitalism*), John Maurice Clark (*Social Control of Business*), Bruce Wyman (*Control of the Market*), Samuel P. Orth (*Relation of Government to Property and Industry*), Robert Lee Hale (*Freedom Through Law*), Walton Hale Hamilton (*The Politics of Industry*), and Rexford G. Tugwell (*The Economic Basis of Public Interest*).

despotism in large and influential corporations and property holders (what Roscoe Pound once talked about as "the new feudalism") – supplemented earlier concerns about the corruptibility and capture of democratic power. The economic power of business came to be seen as problematic not simply for its undue influence on politics, but because of its implications for the imbalance and the concentration of power and wealth more generally in a supposedly free and democratic republic.

Robert Lee Hale's jurisprudential contribution (along with the work of Commons and Ely in economics and Pound and Morris Cohen in law) came when he detected in the new economic organizations of the late nineteenth and early twentieth centuries some of the attributes of "sovereignty" – unchecked social coercion and force. The problem of unprecedented private power in trusts, unions, corporations, and other large associations became the focus of legal-economic inquiry and experimentation in the first decades of the twentieth century precisely because such organizations seemed to operate beyond the jurisdiction of the traditional authority of state legislatures and common laws. The legal-governmental remedy in these analyses was not a series of political regulations insulating the polity from economic influence (yet alone a traditional reliance on common law litigation or ex post criminal prosecutions), but the development of new regulatory police powers and administrative agencies that envisioned an active state apparatus as a continuous, countervailing force to the organization of new forms of economic power in modern American life.

CONCLUSION

When looking at the history of economic regulation in the United States, capture theory frequently assumed that the main problem that regulation was attempting to solve was essentially an economic problem – for which a political solution was proposed. Theorists such as George Stigler and Gary Becker then went further and examined the political solution itself from the perspective of economic theory – that is, Stigler's promotion of an economic "license to practice on the rational theory of political behavior." From such an "economics all the way down" perspective, democratic political solutions were found to be (surprise, surprise) "inefficient." Consequently, regulatory policies almost always fared poorly when compared with some kind of ideal, theoretical market solution. In the process, democracy and government went from being viewed as the key political forums for the resolution of social and economic problems to being viewed, in Ronald Reagan's famous formulation, as part of (if not all of) the problem.

However, capture theory went somewhat astray in assuming that economic regulation was primarily motivated by an economic problem. As progressive theorists made perfectly clear in text after text, the problem of economic concentration at the turn of the century was viewed by and large as a political problem – both in terms of the unprecedented influence of large corporations on politics per se as well as the more subtle corrosive effects of an increasingly unequal distribution of wealth and power in an allegedly democratic regime. Political failure rather than market failure was the first priority of the reform tradition. And democracy came before competition.

In our own neoliberal era, it is a bit hard to fully comprehend this fundamentally political rather than economic perspective despite 2,000 years of development in the Western philosophical tradition and 200 years of experience with American constitutionalism. However, something of the continued salience of the priority of democracy over economy was suggested by Justice Oliver Wendell Holmes, Jr., when he opened the most famous dissenting opinion in American history with these words:

> This case is decided upon an economic theory which a large part of the country does not entertain. If it were a question whether I agree with that theory I should desire to study it further and longer before making up my mind. But I do not conceive that to be my duty, because I strongly believe that my agreement or disagreement has nothing to do with *the right of a majority to embody their opinions in law.*[56]

For Holmes, Herbert Spencer's *Social Statics* and late nineteenth century theories of laissez-faire prioritized economy over democracy and thus curiously elided or confused the basic principle undergirding the historic development of popular government in the Western world – the right of the people to embody their opinions in law. In many ways, late twentieth century capture theory made something of the same mistake.[57] Working with a foreshortened narrative of nineteenth century laissez-faire and twentieth century regulation, capture theorists missed the degree to which the problem of capture and corruption animated most previous American political, constitutional, and legislative (as well as regulatory) development – and indeed motivated the development of the regulatory commission in the first place. Thinking that the capture problem was peculiar to the regulatory form rather than endemic to democratic institutions in general, modern capture theory mistook the discovery of a general precondition for an immanent and incisive critique. Consequently, capture theory's traditional prescription – usually some form of deregulation or simply ending

---

[56] *Lochner v. New York*, 198 U.S. 45 (1905) (emphasis added).

[57] As Mark Twain observed, "History may not repeat itself, but it sometimes rhymes."

the regulation as we know it – ended up being as shortsighted as the myopic history that stood behind it. The Jacksonian critique of the role of special influence and interest in the Bank of the United States did not mean the end of central banking in American history. And the discovery of regulatory or agency capture does not signal the end of regulation in America.

For, as this chapter has attempted to demonstrate, the regulatory impulse itself is rooted in a much longer and wider historic American struggle with the problem of corruption – with the persistent threat that agglomerations of private interest continually pose to the aspirations of the commonwealth. As James Madison reminded us long ago, "It is of great importance in a republic, not only to guard the society against the oppression of its rulers; but to guard one part of the society against the injustice of the other part."[58] If history is any guide (or contemporary politics any indicator), the problems of faction, special interest, special privilege, and private coercion are not going away anytime soon in this still open and democratic society. And it is but a chimera to presume that a simple dismantling of an earlier era's checks and balances and regulatory institutions will somehow automatically and spontaneously vitiate the age-old problems of inequality, privilege, and private (as well as public) coercion. The problems of regulation and capture will not be solved by fleeing to some kind of imaginary laissez-faire past. No, the way forward involves neither ignoring the problems of corruption and capture, nor capitulating to the private interests that seek undue influence in the polity as well as the economy. Rather, a more sensible approach is recommended by both Western political tradition and American constitutional experience. The chapters in this volume build on the example of Montesquieu and Madison in embracing fresh thought on the question of institutional (as well as constitutional) design to prevent capture in new and uncertain times. And they continue the endless, vigilant democratic-republican project endorsed by Charles Francis Adams – the simultaneously mundane and heroic task of attempting to blunt the force of perennial public corruptions and private coercions by simply piling on "all the checks and balances that human ingenuity can devise."

[58] James Madison, "The Federalist No. 51: The Structure of the Government Must Furnish the Proper Checks and Balances Between the Different Departments," *Independent Journal*, February 6, 1788.

2

The Concept of Regulatory Capture

A Short, Inglorious History

Richard A. Posner[1]

The term *regulatory capture*, as I use it, refers to the subversion of regulatory agencies by the firms they regulate. This is to be distinguished from regulation that is intended by the legislative body that enacts it to serve the private interests of the regulated firms, for example by shielding them from new entry. Capture implies conflict, and regulatory capture implies that the regulated firms have, as it were, made war on the regulatory agency and won the war, turning the agency into their vassal. That at any rate is how I understand the concept.

The phenomenon of regulatory capture so understood must be as old as regulation itself – it was remarked for example by Woodrow Wilson in 1911[2] – but it first received sustained attention from political scientists, notably Marver Bernstein. In his book *Regulating Business by Independent Commission*, Bernstein proposed a "life cycle of regulatory commissions" having four phases: "gestation," "youth," "maturity: the process of devitalization," and "old age: debility and decline."[3] That misleadingly suggests an internal process, like the life cycle of a human being, who is born, grows, matures, declines, dies – all without having to be attacked and taken over. However, it turns out that Bernstein is describing regulatory capture and not merely regulatory juvenescence and senescence.

Gestation is the enactment of the regulatory statute after "a period of slowly mounting distress over a problem."[4] Because this period is apt to be

---

[1] Judge, U.S. Court of Appeals for the Seventh Circuit; Senior Lecturer, University of Chicago Law School. I thank Dan Carpenter, David Moss, and anonymous referees for their comments on an earlier draft.

[2] Woodrow Wilson, *The New Freedom: A Call for the Emancipation of the Generous Energies of a People* (New York: Doubleday, paperback ed. 2007 [1913]), 102.

[3] Marver H. Bernstein, *Regulating Business by Independent Commission*, ch. 3 (Westport, CT: Greenwood Press, 1955).

[4] Ibid., 74.

long and to involve a fierce struggle between opposing interests, the regulatory statute may well be out of date by the time it's enacted. Still, when finally created, the regulatory agency is likely to begin "its administrative career in an aggressive, crusading spirit."[5] That of course is the youth phase. It doesn't last long. The groups that fought *for* the regulatory program are tired; the diffuse support of the public is no match for the regulated firms, which form a cohesive group that seeks to make the agency its servant; the agency becomes embroiled in litigation with the regulated firms; the legislature that created the agency loses interest. The agency now enters its mature phase, in which it becomes part of the status quo and seeks both to protect its own existence and prerogatives and conciliate the regulated industry:

it is unlikely that the commission, in this period, will be able to extend regulation beyond the limits acceptable to the regulated groups... The commission loses vitality... Its goals become routine and accepted... Perhaps the most marked development in a mature commission is the growth of a passivity that borders on apathy. There is a desire to avoid conflicts and to enjoy good relations with the regulated groups.[6]

The period of maturity culminates in "the commission's surrender to the regulated... The commission finally becomes a captive of the regulated groups."[7] This would seem to be rock bottom, short of actual abolition – and deregulation wasn't in the cards when Bernstein wrote. However, for his regulatory take-off on Shakespeare's seven ages of man to be fully parallel to that illustrious precedent, Bernstein needs to add old age, which he calls the period of debility. However, it doesn't seem much different from maturity; it seems just more of the same.

Bernstein derived evidence for his life-cycle theory of regulation from the history of the major federal regulatory agencies of his time, such as the Interstate Commerce Commission (now abolished) and the Securities and Exchange Commission (still with us, but debilitated).

I think there is something to Bernstein's argument, but there is also a confusion between the life cycle of institutions in general and the distinctive life cycle (if there is one) of regulatory agencies. There is a tendency for institutions, both public and private, to ossify, especially if they are initially successful, because then they are reluctant to change; they may prefer the risk of a slow decline to the risk of the sudden disaster that a change of

[5] Ibid., 80.
[6] Ibid., 87–88.
[7] Ibid., 90.

course may precipitate. This has been a striking feature of the computer industry since the 1970s. Besides risk aversion, the institutional life cycle is affected by the fact that as an institution grows in size, as it will do if it is successful, entrepreneurship will give way to management, to bureaucracy (what Weber called the routinization of charisma), because bureaucratic practices are indispensable to the management of large organizations, public or private.

However, ossification and bureaucratization, key features of the institutional life cycle, need not imply capture. The deflection of an agency from its original goals may accompany the natural tendency of an institution to bureaucratization, but it is not entailed by it. Once one separates regulatory capture from the metaphor of aging, the former phenomenon is seen to be puzzling from a theoretical standpoint. If regulated firms have the political or organizational resources to take control of the regulators and turn them against their original mission, why couldn't they have shaped the regulatory scheme at the enactment stage? In addition, if they could not do this but could capture the regulatory agency after the agency began to age and weaken, why couldn't the intended beneficiaries of the regulation, who had had enough political muscle to obtain it in the first place, recapture the agency? Why wouldn't there be not a life cycle, which is not a cycle at all (death is not followed by rebirth), but a policy cycle?

It is to the credit of political scientists like Marver Bernstein that they were interested in regulatory agencies as organizations; economists in the era in which his book was published tended not to be. They were interested in regulation and critical of specific regulatory policies, but they did not study the causes of the regulatory policies they criticized; those policies were assumed to be the result of innocent mistakes that would have been avoided had regulators understood economics. Mainstream economists were preoccupied with market failures and saw efficient regulation as an essentially costless method of rectifying such failures; they did not consider the obstacles to efficient regulation. They saw market failures everywhere, but tended to be blind to government failures. They succumbed to what was called by conservative economists the "Nirvana fallacy."

Eventually a budding conservative economics movement centered on the University of Chicago began examining systemic characteristics of regulation that, rather than avoidable errors of design or implementation, might explain the common economic perversities of actual regulation. The economics of regulation thus became a domain for positive analysis, not just normative. George Stigler in an important article proposed a general, positive economic theory of regulation[8] – and ignored the political scientists, like Marver Bernstein, and with them regulatory capture in the sense in which the term had been used by them. Stigler's theory was that regulation is a product governed by the laws of supply and demand. The supplier is the legislature, or a regulatory agency if the legislature had delegated broad authority to an agency rather than specifying the regulatory program that the agency was to administer, and the demander is some group – presumably a consumer or business group – that anticipates benefits from the regulatory program. Stigler thought the demanders would usually be a business group rather than a consumer group because the benefits of a regulatory program to an individual consumer would usually be slight and the costs of organizing consumers into an effective pressure group high – and who would have an interest in bearing those costs? So the principal competition for regulation would be competing industries or segments of industry.

When Stigler wrote (the article was published in 1971), the principal regulatory programs were indeed industry-specific, and most seemed cartelizing in nature, notably the Interstate Commerce Commission, the Civil Aeronautics Board, the National Labor Relations Board (which fostered labor monopolies), the Securities and Exchange Commission (which enforced a cartel of brokers and stock exchanges), the Federal Communications Commission (which limited competition in broadcasting and telephony), the Federal Trade Commission (which protected retailers against competition from chain stores and discount houses, protected food brokers, protected producers of fur products against producers of cloth substitutes, and protected producers of domestic consumer goods against foreign producers – "made in Japan"), the bank-regulating agencies, the professional-licensure agencies, and even municipal regulators of taxicabs. However, Stigler's analysis, and virtually all (so far as I am aware) the subsequent literature expounding and elaborating the positive theory of economic regulation, were static (I discuss an exception later). A regulatory program was a commodity purchased by the regulated industry ("as a rule, regulation is acquired by the industry and is designed and operated primarily for its benefit"[9]), although in some analyses political pressure by a consumer

---

[8] George J. Stigler, "The Theory of Economic Regulation," *Bell Journal of Economics and Management Science* 3 (1971): 3. See also Gary S. Becker, "A Theory of Competition among Pressure Groups for Political Influence," *Quarterly Journal of Economics* 98 (1983): 171; Sam Peltzman, "Toward a More General Theory of Regulation," *Journal of Law and Economics* 19 (1976): 211; Richard A. Posner, "Theories of Economic Regulation," *Bell Journal of Economics* 5 (1974): 335.

[9] Stigler, note 8, at 3.

group was shown to have influenced the program.[10] The possibility that the program may not have had a protectionist, anticompetitive character at the outset, or that the program may have altered through time because of organizational factors such as bureaucratization, did not enter into the analyses.

The Stiglerian approach could have been assimilated to capture analysis by a change in focus from the regulatory agencies to Congress (or state legislatures in the case of state regulation). It was Congress that regulated industries had captured, and at their bidding Congress enacted regulatory programs that from their inception served the private interests of the regulated firms.

The deregulation movement altered the positive economic theory of regulation in one respect. Remember that Marver Bernstein had had difficulty in his "ages of man" theory of regulation with the final age, which should have been debility and death – but he wrote before agencies started dying (with a few special exceptions, such as the Federal Radio Commission, which gave way to the Federal Communications Commission, and some depression and wartime agencies). As a result of the deregulation movement, which began in the late 1970s mainly as a reaction to the economy's dismal performance in that decade, famous federal agencies, such as the Interstate Commerce Commission and the Civil Aeronautics Board, were abolished; others lost much of their authority, or became much less protectionist (the Securities and Exchange Commission, the Federal Trade Commission, and the bank regulatory agencies are notable examples). However, these were not changes from within, like biological aging, which was Bernstein's model of regulatory capture.

Meanwhile, as the traditional industry-specific regulation succumbed to deregulation, the regulation of practices that transcended specific industries, such as pollution and other environmental externalities, unsafe working conditions, unsafe or unhealthful products, exploitation of gullible consumers, and discrimination in employment, was increasing. New regulatory agencies were springing up to enforce these economy-wide or sector-wide regulatory programs, such as the Occupational Safety and Health Administration and the Equal Employment Opportunity Commission, and old agencies concerned with such problems were being strengthened, such as the Food and Drug Administration and the Federal Trade Commission. The FTC is an interesting case; created by legislation enacted in 1914, it

---

[10] See, for example, Richard A. Posner, "Taxation by Regulation," *Bell Journal of Economics and Management Science* 2 (1971): 22.

had never had an industry-specific charter – it had been intended to be an antitrust and consumer-protection agency – but in its protectionist phase, lasting from the 1920s to the 1960s, it had devoted most of its resources to limiting competition among sellers of consumer goods.

The surviving, and to some extent reformed, agencies have not succumbed to deregulation and on the whole seem not to have experienced Bernstein-like life cycles; they are in a continuous tug of war with the business and other institutions that engage in the activities these agencies regulate, but they do not exhibit a general tendency to be captured by the regulated firms. The surviving regulatory programs have considerable public support, and because the programs are not comprehensive regulations of the competitive activities of specific industries (regulations of price, entry, expansion, and service obligations), as in the common carrier and public utility regulation that provided the dominant model of the traditional regulatory agencies studied by Bernstein and Stigler, it is more difficult for the firms subject to the regulation to organize intense and focused efforts at capture.

Moreover, these newer forms of regulation are difficult to "capture" in the sense of being turned to the advantage of the regulated firms, to secure their monopolies or police their cartels. The goal of business in dealing with the newer forms of regulation is to weaken regulation, not to make it a servant of business. The term *regulatory capture* is sometimes used to describe successful efforts by regulated firms to weaken regulation,[11] but so used the term is misleading. The Interstate Commerce Act, which created the Interstate Commerce Commission, was enacted in 1887 at the behest of Western farmers. The Commission was captured first by railroads and used to limit competition among them, and later by truckers to limit competition from railroads. *That* is the authentic narrative of capture – a more interesting phenomenon than the often successful efforts of regulated firms to weaken regulation. What is true, however, is that because the top officials of federal regulatory agencies are presidential appointees, interest groups, whether they are industries, unions, or consumer or environmental groups, influence the regulatory agencies, and one can think of this influence as a kind of capture, although infiltration might be a better word for it.

Because of the deregulation of the older forms of regulation and the rise of newer forms that are less susceptible of being (fully) captured, regulatory

[11] For a useful catalog, see "Regulatory Capture," http://en.wikipedia.org/wiki/Regulatory_capture (accessed September 28, 2011).

capture is no longer at the forefront of analysis. In fact, it's almost been forgotten, other than by the editors of and contributors to this volume. This is shown rather dramatically by the chapter entitled "Regulatory Capture" in the massive (705 pages) Laffont-Tirole treatise on regulation.[12] The chapter has nothing on regulatory capture; the term is used to describe the static Stiglerian theory of regulation conceived of as a product from its inception of interest group pressures.[13] The chapter should have been entitled: "Who Owns Regulation?" A similar example is the excellent review article by Ernesto Dal Bó entitled "Regulatory Capture: A Review."[14]

The principal exception of which I'm aware in the modern literature on regulation is an article by David Martimort entitled "The Life Cycle of Regulatory Agencies: Dynamic Capture and Transaction Costs."[15] Notice the word "dynamic" – a necessary qualification because "regulatory capture" has become a static concept in the economics of regulation. Martimort's analysis is highly abstract; he does not apply it to any specific agencies; the article has no empirical dimension at all. Essentially he argues (so far as I am able to understand his argument – I fear I may have missed its subtleties) that regulators and regulatees collude to deceive the legislature that created the regulatory agency and that corresponds to the consumer in an analysis of cartels. Over time the agency and the regulated industry obtain enough information about each other to be able to exchange favors without excessive danger of being cheated by the other party to the collusive arrangement.

I shouldn't criticize Martimort's article because I doubt that I understand it adequately. It seems thin to me, but maybe I'm missing insights that could launch a fruitful research program on regulatory capture in its original and, what I regard as its precise and useful, sense. I am not optimistic that such a research program will emerge. (It hasn't, to my knowledge, yet emerged, although Martimort's article is more than a decade old.) Organization economists are interested in the rise and decline of institutions, but not, as far as I know, in regulatory agencies. Industrial-organization economists are interested in regulation, but to the extent that they have any interest at all in the life cycle of a regulatory agency, it is in the extreme end of the

---

[12] Jean-Jacques Laffont and Jean Tirole, *A Theory of Incentives in Procurement and Regulation*, ch. 11 (Cambridge, MA: MIT Press, 1993).

[13] A common usage: see, for example, Michael E. Levine and Jennifer L. Forrence, "Regulatory Capture, Public Interest, and the Public Agenda: Toward a Synthesis," *Journal of Law, Economics, and Organization: Special Issue* 6 (1990): 167.

[14] *Oxford Review of Economic Policy* 22 (2006): 203.

[15] *Review of Economic Studies* 66 (1999): 929.

cycle – the death phase (deregulation).[16] Dynamic analysis in economics is usually more difficult than static analysis, and the life of a regulatory agency may not be a sufficiently important subject to justify dynamic analysis of regulation. If so, then perhaps in the interest of clarity the term *regulatory capture* should be retired.

---

[16] Don't be fooled by the title of Ross D. Eckert's article "The Life Cycle of Regulatory Commissioners," *Journal of Law and Economics* 24 (1981): 113 – he's talking about commissioners – their "revolving door" behavior – rather than commissions.

3

Detecting and Measuring Capture

Daniel Carpenter

The plausible breadth of capture notwithstanding, scholars examining regulation and regulatory institutions face substantial difficulties demonstrating the existence and degree of capture. Several generations of research have
adduced quantitative or historical evidence that agency decisions or legislative outcomes have been partially associated or correlated with the wishes
of the regulated industry.[1] However, few of these analyses have been able to
demonstrate that the associations/correlations in question represent capture rather than other patterns – representation, differential (and rational)
weighting of other features of firms and industries, the possible coincidence
of public interest and industry interest in some dimensions of regulatory
policy, or something else.

In short, the evidentiary standards of the capture literature are rather
low, and the first aim of this essay will be to demonstrate this point and
to suggest that more circumspection is in order. A second aim of the essay
will be to examine possible inferential strategies, all of them involving
observational research using both quantitative and qualitative data, with
which qualified claims of capture might be made. A third aim is to encourage
scholars to point more concretely to different mechanisms by which capture
might operate. I elaborate these aims after a brief conceptual discussion of
capture.

---

[1] The literature here is large and well known, ranging from Samuel Huntington's "The
Marasmus of the ICC," *Yale Law Journal* 61 (1952) and Marver Bernstein's *Regulating
Business by Independent Commission* (Princeton, NJ: Princeton University Press, 1955),
through George J. Stigler's "The Theory of Economic Regulation," *Bell Journal of Economics and Management Science* 3 (1971) (much of which was taken up with empirical
demonstrations) and Richard A. Posner's "Theories of Economic Regulation," *Bell Journal
of Economics* 5 (1974) to a series of modern-day studies.

UNDERSTANDINGS OF CAPTURE

Let me begin with the observation that regulation scholars might learn something from recent advances in the study of "conflict of interest." In new writing and an intellectual initiative aimed at understanding "institutional corruption," Harvard scholar Lawrence Lessig has argued that institutional corruption is different from the kind of public corruption for which individuals and organizations are often found criminally liable. There may be nothing illegal – and for a long time, there has been nothing illegal – about the pattern of physicians prescribing a newer, more expensive drug to their patients (rather than an older and cheaper one with hypothetically equivalent quality) in part because they receive junkets and gifts from the company making the newer product. What is bothersome here is rather the way in which the "economy of influence" distorts the incentives or motivation of the physician to prescribe according to the best interest of the patient, rather than according to an alternative set of interests in which the gifts themselves figure into that interest.[2]

I take this starting point to say that *empirical studies of capture must have some notion of the public interest in mind as a counterfactual.* For one, some version of the public interest stands often as a compelling alternative explanation to capture for patterns observed in regulation and regulatory decision making. For another, it is only with reference to one or more measurable understandings of public interest that we can say, after empirical study, that capture has occurred in that one set of interests has been served instead of another set, with the counterfactual set of interests served being the public interest.

An empirical finding of capture requires the satisfaction of a *conjunction* of a set of claims. Each claim is individually necessary, but when taken together, the claims are jointly sufficient. I begin with the case of a regulation

---

[2] As Lessig describes the term in a *Boston Review* article, "Institutional corruption does not refer to the knowing violation of any law or ethical rule. This is not the problem of Rod Blagojevich, or, more generally, of bad souls acting badly. *It instead describes an influence, financial or otherwise, within an economy of influence, that weakens the effectiveness of an institution, especially by weakening public trust in that institution.* (An "economy of influence" rather than the simpler "system of influence" to emphasize the reciprocal character of such influence, often requiring little or no direct coordination.)" Lawrence Lessig "Democracy After Citizens' United," *Boston Review*, September/October 2010, http://bostonreview .net/BR35.5/lessig.php (accessed November 11, 2010; Emphasis added). Lessig's definition is of course differentiated from capture, but it is informative in the following way, namely that corruption in this sense can occur without "direct coordination" and that a critical result of corruption is reduced public trust in the institution itself.

Table 3.1. *A. The case of statutory capture*

A1. There exists an identifiable "general interest" or "public interest," or goal for which a regulation could, in theory, be created. Call this the people's welfare [W].

A2. There exists an identifiable interest or goal of the "industry" or "producers" in an industrial sector, or within an industry, there exists an interest of dominant or particular firms. Call this the industry interest (I).

A2a. There exists an identifiable "special interest" (S) outside of industry interest, such as the interests of labor unions or environmental groups that, although not the producers in question, value certain goods more highly than do the general public (the public good, in the republican sense, or the median voter in the social choice sense).

A3 [conflict of industry and public interest]: W and I conflict, or W and S conflict, in the minimally sufficient sense that for a set of possible laws created, the public interest or statutory obligations of the agency and the producer/special interest do not coincide.

A4 [capture mechanism]: There exists some mechanism of undue or disproportionate influence or capture (C) whereby the industry wishes to induce the legislature to choose I over W.

A5 [deterministic capture]: Given capture, the legislature repeatedly chooses I over W, or S over W, and the resulting statute or regulatory regime is enforced or implemented in way that preserves the dominance of I/S over W in the original legislation. Without capture, this pattern would not hold, as the legislature would choose W repeatedly over I or S.

A5 [probabilistic capture]: A weak probabilistic condition is that the legislature's choice of I/S comes with higher probability with capture than without. Hence

$$Pr[L = I \mid C] > Pr[L = I \mid {\sim}C] \text{ and/or } Pr[L = W \mid C] < Pr[L = W \mid {\sim}C]$$

---

that is captured before an administrator ever acts, the case of legislative or "statutory" capture (see Table 3.1).

It is important to recognize that an agency faithfully implementing a law that satisfied conditions A1 through A5 would be implementing a captured regulation, although doing so in a way that preserved the fidelity of delegation relations. Hence the existence of regulatory capture does not require that there exist a principal-agent problem between the legislature and the regulatory agency.

However, in many cases, scholars and policymakers are interested in a different kind of capture, one in which certain goals are expressed in legislation but where the achievement of these goals is distorted, corrupted, watered down, or otherwise turned to an industry's advantage. This is the case of agency capture, which is not exclusive of statutory capture and can coexist with it (see Table 3.2).

Table 3.2. *B. The case of agency capture*

B1. There exists an identifiable "general interest" or "public interest," or goal for which a regulation was created. Unlike a regime of statutory capture, we assume here that this public interest is embodied in the statute that delegates authority and resources to a regulator, which is charged with administering the regulation. Again, this public interest is embodied in the people's welfare (W).

B2. There exists an identifiable interest or goal of the "industry" (I) or "producers" in an industrial sector, or within an industry, there exists an interest of dominant or particular firms.

B2a. There exists an identifiable "special interest" (S) outside of industry interest, such as the interests of labor unions or environmental groups that, although not the producers in question, value certain goods more highly than do "the people" writ large.

B3 [conflict of industry and public interest]: W and I conflict, or W and S conflict, in the sense that in applications of regulation or enforcement, the public interest or statutory obligations of the agency and the producer/special interest do not coincide.

B4 [capture mechanism]: There exists some mechanism of undue or disproportionate influence [capture (C)] whereby the industry attempts to induce the regulator to choose I over W.

B5 [deterministic capture]: Given a pattern in which the agency's statute and case evidence directs it to choose W over either I or S, and given capture (C), the agency nonetheless repeatedly chooses I over W, or S over W. Under the same conditions but in the absence of capture, the agency would choose W repeatedly over I/S. To the extent that the agency's choice of producer/special interest over public interest is more ingrained or patterned, we say that the agency is *more* captured.

B5 [probabilistic capture]: A weak probabilistic condition is that the regulator's choice of I/S comes with higher probability with capture than without. Hence

$$\Pr[R = I \mid C] > \Pr[R = I \mid {\sim}C] \text{ and/or } \Pr[R = W \mid C] < \Pr[R = W \mid {\sim}C]$$

It should be clear that a major problem confronting any theoretical or empirical analysis of capture is that we do not know, and we should not presume to know, what W is. Scholars in political economy often take for granted what W is, such as when economists conclude that sector-specific or national protectionism is not in the public interest, because they assume that it has been well demonstrated elsewhere that the alternative policy of free trade does serve the public interest, and the particular interests served by protectionism (particular industries, sectors, companies, in particular locations) can be readily identified.[3]

The conception of regulatory capture used in this book offers some guidance. Capture is the result or process by which regulation (in law

---

[3] For example, Gene Grossman and Elhanan Helpman, "Protection for Sale," *American Economic Review* 84 (1994): 833–50.

or application) is, at least partially by intent and action of the industry regulated, consistently or repeatedly directed away from a defeasible model of the public interest and toward the interests of the regulated industry.

The empirical analysis of capture, given these criteria of necessity and joint sufficiency, must proceed with varying degrees of knowledge of W. Here are four possibilities, which do not in the aggregate necessarily exhaust the possibilities.

1. *We stipulate what W is* on the basis of accepted theory or a broad band of empirical evidence – examples might be a general preference toward free trade or a general preference to reduce as much as possible the prevalence of cigarette smoking.

2. *We take a republican approach to W*, whereby long-run judgments of democratically elected public officials or aggregated public opinion suggest that the people's judgment is superior to that of any other actor. Of course, special interests and industry will try to affect public opinion and the issuance of law from republican governments. Or a local or national public may be biased toward a certain conception of W (the benefit or income accruing to a certain industry or locality as opposed to the public at large).

3. *We take a technocratic or scientific approach to W*. In some cases, particularly in the area of medicine and public health where there is clearer evidence of the individual and public health harms or risk (tobacco), aggregated empirical studies from the scientific literature may give us partial or full information as to the content of the public interest in a policy domain. Of course, industrial special interests will try to shape science, and certain professions (attorneys, chemists and industrial chemists, economists, psychiatrists, toxicologists) may be subject to capture themselves. In addition, it is possible that certain scientific communities may be biased without having been captured.

4. We don't know what W is, and so *we look for capture procedurally*, by trying to (a) identify the special interests involved and (b) examine those institutions and outcomes that would seem consistent with their having been advantaged. What is often missing from these accounts is evidence of the mechanism by which the identified special interests are able to achieve the policy outcomes postulated.

We can think of these four possibilities as decreasing in the order of their reliance on theory and as increasing in the order of their reliance on empirics. In the first we take as a priori a given notion of the public interest, and in the second, we allow the aggregated and filtered judgments of the public to bequeath it to us through statutes and "super-statutes."[4] Republican notions of the public interest rely on theory (political philosophy or perhaps social choice theory) as well as the empirical content of the law and super-statutes. In the third we rely on particular fields of scientific expertise to inform, whatever theory or the law may or may not say, our conception of W. And in the fourth case we abandon any pretense of knowing the public interest and instead focus on "circumstantial evidence" consistent with a capture "story." Most all of the empirical literature claiming the existence or absence of capture takes the form of this fourth type of claim.

The process by which policy and institutions are directed away from the public interest and toward a special interest is crucial and often missing from analysis. One may properly ask whether we need intent in this definition. Is it necessary to have the industry wish for a tilt of policy toward its interests and away from those of the public?

My argument is that, yes, valid capture diagnoses require intent. There must, somewhere, be an attempt to lobby, an attempt to offer an implicit bribe or implicit contract, an attempt to stack the deck of an institutional process, or (as in cultural capture) an attempt to influence frames, assumptions, and worldviews of regulators or professionals involved in regulation. Causal and intentional action of industry is necessary because "bureaucratic drift" stands always as an alternative mechanism for administrative capture. So too, the fact that industry (or a particular subset thereof) is served well by the regulation is insufficient for a judgment of capture. It could be the happenstance of an otherwise neutral public policy process.[5] Or in a case in which cultural capture is claimed, a shift (not induced by industry) of the legislature and the regulatory agency toward a more deregulatory model – assuming for the sake of hypothesis that such was distinct from the public interest – would be more consistent with the idea of "false consciousness"

---

[4] I refer here to the celebrated notion of "small-c" constitutionalism laid out by William Eskridge and John Ferejohn, *A Republic of Statutes* (New Haven, CT: Yale University Press, 2010). In their theory, some statutes are more important than others and take on the properties, over time and through repeated ratification by legislatures and democratic publics, "super-statutes." Given the difficulties of amending the U.S. Constitution, Eskridge and Ferejohn argued, these super-statutes may express basic constitutional commitments – not only in the sense of a founding document, but in the sense of constitutive of society's basic principles – every bit as much as, if not more than, the "large-C" Constitution as amended. Examples in the United States would include the Civil Rights Act, the Social Security Act, the Clean Air Act, and others.

[5] Daniel P. Carpenter, "Protection without Capture: Product Approval by a Politically Responsive, Learning Regulator," *American Political Science Review* 98 (2004): 613–31; Daniel P. Carpenter and Michael M. Ting, "Regulatory Errors with Endogenous Agendas," *American Journal of Political Science* 51 (2007): 835–852.

than a conception of capture. In short, valid diagnoses of capture should be able to show that somewhere, the regulated industry was acting in a way so as to bring about the observed result.

We conclude then, that full diagnoses of capture need (a) to posit a defensible model of public interest, (b) to show action and intent by the regulated industry, and (c) to demonstrate that ultimate policy is shifted away from the public interest and toward industry interest. If a capture analysis (whatever its conclusions) is lacking in one or more of these demonstrations, then the analyst must accordingly be circumspect about what she or he has shown. To demonstrate all three of these conditions – preferably by a combination of quantitative and qualitative evidence in which various types of evidence corroborate one another – amounts to a gold standard of proof.

There are a range of different empirical and theoretical conditions under which capture of regulation prevails. In political science, economics, and law, there are models of implicit bribes or rent seeking.[6] There are models by which a regulator might be inclined to pursue the public interest but is scared off from doing so by industry threats of political or legal retaliation[7]; this is, strictly speaking, something different from an implicit bribe. There are arguments about the cultural or social influence of repeated interaction with the regulated industry,[8] such that the regulator begins to think like the regulated and cannot imagine another way of approaching its problems. In the case of cultural or social capture, the legislator or agency may not be fully conscious or aware of the extent to which its behavior has been captured. So what is important about the definitions offered previously is that they are not model dependent or mechanism dependent. There are, for instance, no preferences stated in the models, although the definitions could easily be stated in terms of preferences as a special case.

PROBLEMS WITH CAPTURE INFERENCES

It is common in the empirical and historical literature on regulation to claim that some degree of "capture," "industry influence," or "rent seeking" operated in regulation because of identified patterns of regulatory decision making. It may be that legislators' votes are found to be correlated

---

[6] Jean-Jacques Laffont and Jean Tirole, *A Theory of Incentives in Procurement and Regulation* (Cambridge, Massachusetts: MIT Press, 1993); Grossman and Helpman, "Protection for Sale," 833–50.

[7] Sanford Gordon and Catherine Hafer, "Flexing Muscle: Corporate Political Expenditures as Signals to the Bureaucracy," *American Political Science Review* 99 (2005): 245–61.

[8] As in Simon Johnson and James Kwak, *13 Bankers: The Wall Street Takeover and the Next Financial Crisis* (New York: Pantheon, 2010).

geo-graphically and over time with the presence or strength of measured industry interests.[9] It may be that a positive association is found between a measure of the industry's interest and regulatory decisions. Several decades of literature have exploited these kinds of partial correlations in an attempt to demonstrate the existence of rent seeking.

Let us first part ways with the very common pattern of claim making in policymaking and journalistic circles, but hardly absent from academic studies, that attributes capture to any regulation or regulatory outcome with which the writer does not agree. This is a common method of argumentation in medical and public health circles, as well as in environmental circles and in certain libertarian circles.[10] These claims fail, in essence, not merely because of their bias but because they do not distinguish between a plausible and counterfactual pattern of regulation based on the public interest (W) and that based on capture.

My concern is with something different, namely the claims made by scholars examining patterns of regulation, who claim from a certain kind of evidence base that a particular regulation or agency exhibits rent seeking, industry influence, or capture features. The empirical problems here are many, and they are almost uniformly ignored by published scholarship in economics, political science, sociology, public policy analysis, public administration, and other studies of regulatory agencies. I take three here.

- **Protection Without Capture.** If, for instance, we are able to show that a licensing agency acts in such a way that larger companies within an industry get their products licensed more quickly than smaller companies, we have not demonstrated capture per se. Such patterns can be observationally equivalent to a public interest explanation whereby the agency may rationally impose a risk premium on smaller companies because they tend to be newer or less experienced. In other words, *plausible demonstration of protection does not amount to proof of capture.* This protection without capture dynamic has been demonstrated formally and empirically for product approval and licensing decisions and is quite plausibly applicable to a range of other forms of entry regulation and quality regulation.[11]

---

[9] Joseph P. Kalt and Mark A. Zupan, "Capture and Ideology in the Economic Theory of Politics," *American Economic Review* 74 (3) (Jone 1984): 279–300.

[10] See for instance the claims made by critics such as Marcia Angell in *The Truth About the Drug Companies* (New York: Random House, 2004), or by critics of consumer financial regulation who claim that these regimes will inevitably serve the interests of mortgage lenders.

[11] For both decision- and game-theoretic models establishing this proposition, respectively, see Carpenter, "Protection without Capture: Product Approval by a Politically Responsive,

- **Measurement Error and Nonrandom Assignment.** If an analyst identifies a plausible and robust partial correlation between a measure of
industry influence or interest (I) and regulatory decision making (R),
there are all sorts of reasons that the correlation cannot be regarded
as causal, and the easiest way to approach this problem is to think
of the internal validity questions that one might pose of the claimed
correlation.

Take for instance Stigler's regressions[12] showing that professional licensing came earlier when (a) the size of the occupation relative to the labor
force was larger and (b) where urbanization of the occupation was greater.
As a number of critics have noted, this statistical exercise was far removed
from a demonstration of rent seeking. If licensing regulation were pursued for quality purposes (screening under asymmetric information for
experience goods or credence goods), then one would easily expect that it
would be pursued when the welfare effect of the screen was higher (a larger
market relative to the state's economy). It would also be pursued when a
larger number or greater share of consumers would be adversely affected
by information asymmetries, that is, in cases in which the services of the
occupation licensed were disproportionately available in larger concen-
trations of consumers (population). As economic historian Marc Law
has shown, it is in urbanizing economies that food quality regulation
was enacted, in part because of the separation between the production of
food (with concomitant inspection of quality) and the preparation and
consumption of meals.[13]

Or take Stigler's regressions[14] showing that that trucking weight limits
were positively correlated with trucks per 1,000 agricultural labor force,
with the idea that "the powerful agricultural interests would insist on
this." Of course, the presence of higher weight limits on roads that *already*
handle more trucks could easily be explained as a form of regulatory

---

Learning Regulator," and Carpenter and Ting, "Regulatory Errors with Endogenous Agendas." For a non-capture explanation of the pattern whereby earlier entrants to a market
receive more favorable licensing treatment than do later entrants and evidence supporting
this proposition in the case of pharmaceuticals, see Daniel Carpenter, Susan Moffitt, Colin
Moore, Ryan Rynbrandt, Michael Ting, Ian Yohai, and Evan James Zucker, "Early-Entrant
Protection in Approval Regulation: Theory and Evidence from FDA Drug Review," *Journal
of Law, Economics and Organization*, 26 (Fall 2010).

[12] George J. Stigler, *The Theory of Economic Regulation* (Chicago: University of Chicago
Press, 1971).

[13] Similar observations have been made with respect to choices about food quality in the
modern American obesity epidemic, as changes in technology (like the microwave) have
further separated the preparation from the consumption of food.

[14] Stigler, *The Citizen and the State*.

rationality – the safety limits might be responsive to experience with trucks on these roads. So too, states with more trucks per agricultural labor force might also house roads on which less passenger traffic per capita prevailed, presenting less of a safety risk for the heavier trucks. So too, if trucking weight limits were higher when average rail freight haul were higher, it might prevail not because railroads faced tougher competition on short-haul routes, but because states with a greater proportion of long-haul freight routes were also (rural) states in which there was less traffic congestion.

In these and other cases, then, Stigler's regressions suffered from the nonrandom assignment of industry interests or special interests (I/S) across states and the very plausible correlation of these variables with variables representing other factors and quite possibly variables measuring some form of the public welfare itself. It is easy and perhaps unfair to pick on Stigler here, but I do so because his regressions have become something of a commonly accepted method within different branches of economics, political science, and law. There have been few improvements on this dimension in the subsequent generation of Stigler-inspired research. It is difficult to find *any* study in the political economy of regulation that is fully immune from a critique based on nonrandom assignment, internal validity, or other well-established principles of causal inference.

Revolving Door Dynamics. It is now well known that the existence of revolving door dynamics does not, in and of itself, suggest capture. A purely informational account of regulation, whereby regulators invest in and acquire expertise, could account for revolving-door dynamics, especially if there are few other sources of expertise outside of the regulated industry. What is needed is something in the direction of William Gormley's famous study of Federal Communications Commission commissioners,[15] namely the demonstration that, conditioned on other variables, the rotators differed in their voting behavior from the nonrotators on the commission. Gormley found quite mixed evidence using this test, and it is deeply unfortunate that subsequent scholarship in law and economics, political science, and other fields has not followed upon his pioneering example with different methods.

- **Capture Versus Electorally Sanctioned Pro-Business Governance.** An otherwise neutral regulatory regime (statute) may be enforced by an appointee whose preferences align more with those of the regulated industry, as in the case of the Reagan Administration's governance of

---

[15] William T. Gormley, Jr., "A Test of the Revolving Door Hypothesis at the FCC," *American Journal of Political Science*, 23 (4) (November 1979): 665–683.

environmental policy and the Bush (II) Administration's governance of consumer protection agencies. Yet to show that the arrival of more conservative politicians is correlated with more business-friendly regulation is not, in my judgment, a sufficient demonstration of capture. Put differently, if the George W. Bush Administration were installed in power for the next forty years and regulatory enforcement withered over those decades, it would be difficult to describe the pattern as capture unless one had evidence that the electorate's preferences for stronger regulation (or for different regulation) were somehow being distorted by the electoral process. A better test of capture, it would appear, is that even when there are electoral majorities and political appointees in place who favor a more robust regulatory regime (more pursuit of W as opposed to I or S), the agency still, under conditions of capture, consistently chooses I/S over W in ways that are difficult for the electoral majority or political appointee to correct or penetrate.

TOWARD A BETTER PATTERN OF STUDY, CLAIMS, AND INFERENCES

What can be done to improve the pattern of inferences made by scholars, policymakers, and observers regarding the possible capture of regulation or regulatory institutions? Part of the solution, I think, rests in criticism itself. Scholars and observers should insist on clear standards of evidence and a solid counterfactual when receiving claims of regulatory capture.

As for questions about internal validity, I do not think that the answer lies in field or laboratory experiments. For the purposes of public policy and scholarly understanding, we must, in the end, identify which particular regimes and agencies are better described by capture dynamics and which are not. And the external validity problems of a field experiment in this kind of situation would seem to be imposing.

To be sure, the idea of using quasi-experimental techniques is important, whether these include "instruments" measuring plausible exogenous variation in industry interests or public welfare or refined statistical or econometric techniques such as panel analyses, differences-in-differences estimators with appropriate corrections, and nonparametric matching.

At the end of the day, causal inference techniques must be accompanied by two other research strategies.

1. **Measurement of public versus industry interest in regulatory studies.** Clear empirical identification of choices/outcomes that would, ex ante or ex post, serve a public welfare consideration as

opposed to an industry influence, and an empirical design that permits rejection of the hypothesis that both of these interests are served
in a pattern of decisions.

2. **Mechanisms.** If one is proceeding from a libertarian, antiregulation
perspective, then research strategy 1 is enough. Once we have found
a captured regulation, then we demonstrate that we are better off
without it (empirically and theoretically) and proceed to deregulate.
However, if the idea is to improve and not to abandon regulation,
then an understanding of the mechanisms of capture is critical. It
is critical for combating capture, and it is critical for the important
work of implementing mechanisms that would induce regulators to
proactively pursue their agency's statutory mission.

My brief chapter ends here. I take as a necessary subject of future research
the articulation of principles and methods by which analysts can more
rigorously test capture hypotheses. For now, I note that a larger literature
cited in this book[16] adduces methodological principles consistent with a
more rigorous approach to capture diagnoses.

---

[16] Ranging from David A. Moss and Mary Oey, "The Paranoid Style in the Study of Amer-
ican Politics," in *Government and Markets: Toward a New Theory of Regulation*, Edward
Balleisen and David Moss, eds. (New York: Cambridge University Press, 2009); David A.
Moss and Jonathan B.L. Decker, "Capturing History: The Case of the Federal Radio Com-
mission in 1927," in this volume; Gordon and Hafer, "Flexing Muscle: Corporate Political
Expenditures as Signals to the Bureaucracy"; Jason W. Yackee, and Susan W. Yackee, "A Bias
Towards Business? Assessing Interest Group Influence on the U.S. Bureaucracy," *Journal of
Politics*, 68 (2006): 128–39; Carpenter, "Protection without Capture: Product Approval by
a Politically Responsive, Learning Regulator," and Carpenter and Ting, "Regulatory Errors
with Endogenous Agendas."

SECTION II

NEW CONCEPTIONS OF CAPTURE –
MECHANISMS AND OUTCOMES

Understanding how regulatory capture occurs is essential for diagnosing capture where it exists, treating it appropriately when found, and designing new regulatory regimes that are resistant to it from the outset. The chapters in this section suggest that regulated entities and their representatives – in most cases, firms and industry organizations – employ a wider variety of mechanisms to influence regulation, and aim for a broader range of outcomes, than has generally been recognized. Achieving a deeper understanding of these mechanisms and outcomes is the first step toward better detection and mitigation of regulatory capture.

When considering mechanisms of capture, analysts frequently focus on crude incentives – such as the so-called revolving door – that provide industry with leverage over policy decisions by appealing to regulators' personal self-interest. In this section, James Kwak, Nolan McCarty, and Luigi Zingales each explore new mechanisms of capture. These include *cultural capture* – in which regulators are influenced, even unknowingly, by industry through a combination of social, cultural, and intellectual currents (Kwak, Chapter 4); *the provision of expertise by industry* – in which, as a result of heightened complexity, regulators come to rely on industry expertise in ways that tilt decision making toward industry interests (McCarty, Chapter 5); and, perhaps most subtly of all, *economists' capture* – in which industry influences and incentivizes scholars to favor an industry perspective in their work, thereby indirectly influencing regulators who rely on the scholars' judgment and expertise in making decisions (Zingales, Chapter 6). Taken together, these chapters suggest that efforts to diagnose and prevent capture must take into account a far wider range of actors and strategies than has been typical in the study of regulation in the past.

Just as capture can occur through pathways that tend to go overlooked, it can also push regulation toward outcomes different from those typically expected. Capture scholarship has long focused mainly on regulatory barriers to entry that increase incumbents' profits by reducing competition. As Judge Posner noted in Section I, however, much industry effort is aimed not at erecting new regulations, but at reducing regulatory requirements. Daniel Carpenter makes the case in Chapter 7 of this section that industry pressure for weaker regulation can also result in capture. Through an analysis of pharmaceutical industry attempts to influence the Food and Drug Administration (FDA), Carpenter illuminates the phenomenon of *corrosive capture*, which works not to build up new regulations, but rather to weaken current regulations and forestall new ones. Indeed, although deregulation promises to serve the public interest under certain circumstances, it may undermine the public interest in others due to corrosive capture. As a result, efforts to deregulate must be held to the same level of scrutiny as efforts to regulate in thinking about the potential costs and benefits for the public as a whole.

4

Cultural Capture and the Financial Crisis

James Kwak[1]

In 1992, Barbara Smiley, a resident of California, sued Citibank, alleging that it violated California law by charging late fees to her credit card account.[2] During the litigation, the Office of the Comptroller of the Currency (OCC) – the primary regulator for national banks such as Citibank – issued a proposed regulation specifying that late fees were "interest"[3]; under federal law,[4] this meant that Citibank was bound solely by the law of the state where its credit card subsidiary was situated – South Dakota.[5] When the case was appealed to the Supreme Court, twenty-five states and several consumer organizations signed onto briefs supporting Smiley; fifteen states, the American Bankers Association, and the OCC supported Citibank. The Supreme Court ruled for Citibank, deferring to the OCC.[6] The Court acknowledged but discarded the fact that the OCC seemed to have issued the regulation because of the ongoing litigation,[7] endorsing the ability of a federal agency to issue regulations to sway pending litigation in favor of the companies it supervised.

---

[1] Associate Professor, University of Connecticut School of Law. I would like to thank Christine Jolls, the other authors represented in this volume, and two anonymous reviewers for helpful suggestions.
[2] *Smiley v. Citi bank (South Dakota), N.A.*, 517 U.S. 735, 738 (1996).
[3] Office of the Comptroller of the Currency, "Interpretive Rulings," 60 Fed. Reg. 11924, 11929 (1995).
[4] Section 85 of the National Bank Act, 12 U.S.C. § 85, interpreted by *Marquette National Bank of Minneapolis v. First of Omaha Service Corp.*, 439 U.S. 299 (1978).
[5] Citibank located its credit card issuing bank in South Dakota because of favorable regulation offered by that state. Robin Stein, "The Ascendancy of the Credit Card Industry," *Frontline*, November 23, 2004. Available at http://www.pbs.org/wgbh/pages/frontline/shows/credit/more/rise.html.
[6] *Smiley*, 517 U.S. at 739.
[7] Ibid., 741.

The OCC's intervention in *Smiley v. Citibank* was just one part of a sweeping campaign to lift constraints on national banks, allowing them to enter new businesses while blocking efforts by states to rein them in.[8] The OCC, in turn, was just one of several federal agencies that spent most of the past two decades fulfilling the wishes of different segments of the financial sector. The Federal Reserve issued a series of decisions enabling banks to expand into the securities business[9] and later declined to enforce consumer protection statutes against the nonbank subsidiaries of bank holding companies.[10] All four major banking agencies (the Federal Reserve, the OCC, the Office of Thrift Supervision [OTS], and the Federal Deposit Insurance Corporation [FDIC]) relaxed the capital requirements governing structured financial products, enabling banks to ramp up their securitization businesses without setting aside large amounts of capital.[11] The Securities and Exchange Commission (SEC) allowed major investment banks to use their internal models to calculate their net capital, giving them greater flexibility to effectively increase their leverage;[12] in exchange, the banks gave the SEC new oversight powers that went essentially unused.[13] The OTS was perhaps the worst offender, seemingly engaging in blatant efforts to attract fee-paying regulatory "customers" with the promise of lax regulation.[14]

Several of these policies were vigorously contested at the time, as was the OCC's position in *Smiley*. In 2003, when the OCC issued two proposed rules that would expand federal preemption of state law, it received more than 2,700 comment letters. The vast majority of the non-form letters opposed the proposed rules, including a majority of letters from every category of

---

[8] Steven P. Croley, "Public Interested Regulation," *Florida State University Law Review* 28 (Fall 2000): 75–84; Adam J. Levitin, "Hydraulic Regulation: Regulating Credit Markets Upstream," *Yale Journal on Regulation* 26 (Summer 2009): 152–5.

[9] Simon Kwan, "Cracking the Glass-Steagall Barriers," *Federal Reserve Bank of San Francisco Economic Letter* 97–08, March 21, 1997.

[10] Binyamin Appelbaum, "Fed Held Back as Evidence Mounted on Subprime Loan Abuses," *Washington Post*, September 27, 2009. Available at http://www.washingtonpost.com/wp-dyn/content/article/2009/09/26/AR2009092602706.html.

[11] Corine Hegland, "Why It Failed," *National Journal*, April 11, 2009, 12–20.

[12] Securities and Exchange Commission, "Final Rule: Alternative Net Capital Requirements for Broker-Dealers That Are Part of Consolidated Supervised Entities," 69 Fed. Reg. 34428 (2004).

[13] SEC Office of Inspector General, *SEC's Oversight of Bear Stearns and Related Entities: The Consolidated Supervised Entity Program*, September 25, 2008.

[14] Binyamin Appelbaum and Ellen Nakashima, "Banking Regulator Played Advocate Over Enforcer," *Washington Post*, November 23, 2008. Available at http://www.washingtonpost.com/wp-dyn/content/article/2008/11/22/AR2008112202213.html.

respondent except "bank industry [other]."[15] The OCC made some changes in the final rule, but refused to budge on the core preemption issue.[16] Many of these policies also contributed to the financial crisis that began in 2007. Deregulation of financial markets enabled financial institutions to spawn new types of mortgages that fueled the housing bubble, manufacture enormous volumes of securities that became toxic when the bubble collapsed, magnify and concentrate risk through the use of customized derivatives, and lever up with short-term debt. Policies that were favored by the financial sector because they increased profits in the short run ended up making the financial system more fragile and imposing widespread losses on society.

CAPTURE?

At first glance, federal regulation of the financial system over the past two decades seems like a case of regulatory capture, in which agencies do the bidding of industry without regard for the public good. However, there is a problem with this picture, which can be identified by focusing on the definition of capture in this volume (slightly shortened): "a process by which regulation . . . is consistently or repeatedly directed away from the public interest and toward the interests of the regulated industry by the intent and action of the industry itself."

Most importantly, it is difficult to prove that the deregulatory policies pursued by these agencies were clearly not in the public interest as knowable at the time. In retrospect, given the economic and fiscal consequences of the financial crisis, it seems obvious that policies that increased the likelihood or severity of the crisis were not in the public interest. However, two defenses can be made against this indictment. First, bad outcomes are not proof of bad policy, because the outcomes of policies are probabilistic. It is theoretically possible that the recent financial crisis was a fluke accident[17] and that the true expected impact of these policies on the public interest was positive – just as a football team's failure to gain a first down on fourth-and-one does not mean that going for a first down was a bad decision.[18] Second, many agency

---

[15] Government Accountability Office, *OCC Preemption Rulemaking: Opportunities Existed to Enhance the Consultative Efforts and Better Document the Rulemaking Process*, October 2005, 30–6.

[16] Ibid., 36–40.

[17] For the record, I am highly skeptical of the "once-in-a-century flood" theory of the financial crisis.

[18] Indeed, Romer shows that teams should go for a first down on fourth-and-one regardless of field position, at least early in a game. David Romer, "Do Firms Maximize? Evidence from Professional Football," *Journal of Political Economy* 114, no. 2 (April 2006): 352–3.

policies that were controversial at the time (or have become controversial with hindsight) were within the range of plausible disagreement about the public interest. In *Smiley*, even if there are strong criticisms to be made of a credit card business model that relies on keeping people in debt and harvesting fees from them,[19] one can still argue that freeing banks from having to comply with fifty states' fee restrictions will increase efficiency and thereby reduce the cost of credit. In general, financial deregulation was justified by plausible arguments that unregulated markets would allocate capital more efficiently, both reducing the cost of credit and increasing its availability.[20]

Strong arguments can still be made that several of these deregulatory actions were in fact against the public interest. For example, the Federal Reserve's decision not to undertake consumer protection examinations of nonbank mortgage lenders seems to contradict the intent of the Home Ownership and Equity Protection Act of 1994, the scope of which is defined by the set of mortgages falling under its terms, not the set of institutions originating those mortgages.[21] Agencies' failures to enforce their own rules against institutions they regulated – even, in the case of the OTS, allowing IndyMac Bancorp to backdate its capital infusions to appear better capitalized than it actually was and avoid additional FDIC restrictions[22] – are also hard to defend as being in the public interest. However, it is difficult to make a blanket statement that the public interest was sufficiently well defined for financial deregulation to be categorically labeled as against the public interest.[23]

Even if we cannot unambiguously say that the financial sector captured its regulatory agencies, however, that should not end our inquiry. There is a range of possibilities ranging from a "bad" agency that consciously favors industry over a clearly identifiable public interest to a "good" agency that seeks only to identify and serve the general welfare. There is also a range of outcomes from strong capture, which produces regulation that harms the public interest, to weak capture, which reduces but does not eliminate the

---

[19] Ronald J. Mann, "Bankruptcy Reform and the 'Sweat Box' of Credit Card Debt," *University of Illinois Law Review* 375 (2007): 384–92.

[20] For example, the argument goes, unlimited late fees allow a bank to compensate itself for the specific risk of late payment; otherwise it would have to compensate itself by increasing the interest rate, which would affect all customers.

[21] Public Law 103–325 §§ 152, 156 (1994).

[22] Michael M. Phillips and Jessica Holzer, "Regulator Let IndyMac Backdate Infusion," *Wall Street Journal*, December 23, 2008. Available at http://online.wsj.com/article/SB122998621544328009.html.

[23] In some cases, it is also arguable that deregulatory policies were not the result of the "intent and action" of the financial sector. For example, returning to *Smiley*, the OCC might have reached its conclusion as a matter of pure statutory interpretation, leaving aside questions of the public interest.

benefits of regulation. Financial regulation, where different interest groups advance competing plausible conceptions of the public interest, is more likely to be the rule than the exception in regulatory policy. In this context, the key question is why agency policies generally ended up favoring the financial sector, with the outcomes we know too well – in other words, what mechanisms of influence enabled regulated industry to get its way.

MECHANISMS OF INFLUENCE

The motive force in traditional theories of capture is material self-interest.[24] According to Levine and Forrence,[25] capture exists when regulators[26] are motivated by self-interest and therefore select policies that would not gain the support of an informed public. Capture can be produced by several mechanisms in addition to bribes. Regulatory agencies may be dependent for funds on the firms they regulate; firms can provide support to legislators, who then apply pressure to agencies through oversight committees; or individual regulators may be attracted by higher paying jobs in the industry they oversee.

Traditional capture theory is almost certainly incomplete. In practice, general interests do sometimes win out over special interests.[27] Furthermore, it would be shocking if regulators did not sometimes attempt to advance their ideological interests – what they think is right – rather than their material self-interest. Even if regulators are not motivated solely by their conception of the public interest, regulatory discretion is still not traded for material gain in a transparent market. Instead, the complexities of politics imply that sometimes agencies are compelled to follow the general interest, sometimes industry exercises control over regulators, and sometimes regulators have the space to act on ideological grounds.[28] Croley[29] has argued that the structure of the administrative process makes it possible for

---

[24] For summaries, see Michael E. Levine and Jennifer L. Forrence, "Regulatory Capture, Public Interest, and the Public Agenda: Toward a Synthesis," *Journal of Law, Economics, and Organization* 6 (1990): 169–70; Steven P. Croley, "Public Interested Regulation," *Florida State University Law Review* 28 (Fall 2000): 9–15; and Nicholas Bagley and Richard L. Revesz, "Centralized Oversight of the Regulatory State," *Columbia Law Review* 106 (October 2006): 1284–85.

[25] Levine and Forrence, "Regulatory Capture, Public Interest, and the Public Agenda: Toward a Synthesis," 178.

[26] Although this chapter focuses on administrative agencies, the concepts discussed could also apply to other governmental actors.

[27] Levine and Forrence, "Regulatory Capture, Public Interest, and the Public Agenda," 172; Croley, "Public Interested Regulation," 4.

[28] Levine and Forrence, "Regulatory Capture, Public Interest, and the Public Agenda," 171–2.

[29] Croley, "Public Interested Regulation," 106.

regulators to escape the shadow of Congress or special interests and act in what they think is the public interest.[30]

So, it seems, regulators can either cash in or do what they think is right. However, this is still not a satisfying understanding of regulatory behavior and outcomes. There is a spectrum of behavior that ranges from outright corruption to nobly serving the public. People's actions are the product of many different factors, and mixes of motivations are certainly possible. In addition, to the extent that we believe that regulators act according to their ideological beliefs, this only raises the question of how those beliefs are formed – specifically, how the administrative process exposes regulators to a particular set of influences that can color their beliefs. Both the capture model and the public interest model of regulatory action assume that regulators are rational actors: either they maximize their material self-interest or they maximize their consciously held policy interests. However, there is another possibility: that regulators are susceptible to nonrational forms of influence, which interest groups can exploit to achieve the practical equivalent of capture – favorable policy outcomes.

It is uncontroversial that interest groups should attempt to convince regulators of their policy positions using the familiar tools of argument and evidence. Interest groups, however, have other channels of influence they can exploit to shape the way regulators think about the problems they are tasked with solving. Most fundamentally, regulators are human beings and are therefore subject to the same sets of cognitive shortcomings as other human beings. This implies that they make decisions for reasons other than their material self-interest or their consciously held policy beliefs. Even when they do act according to their policy beliefs, those beliefs depend on the peculiar ways in which people develop their ideological preferences. Policy outcomes, therefore, can depend not solely on regulators' material self-interest, their preexisting policy positions, and the process of rational debate, but also on the nonrational pressures that arise out of the administrative process.

This has been a growing area of inquiry as either a critique or an offshoot of capture theory.[31] Rachlinski and Farina[32] drew on cognitive psychology and behavioral economics to construct a model of governmental error that

---

[30] See also Levine and Forrence, "Regulatory Capture, Public Interest, and the Public Agenda," 185.

[31] In a sense, it is also a very old area of inquiry, dating back at least to Alexis de Tocqueville, who attributed America's "singular paucity of distinguished political characters" to the social pressures to conform to majority opinion. Alexis de Tocqueville, *Democracy in America*, Translated by Henry Reeve (New York: George Dearborn & Co., 1838), 244–7.

[32] Jeffrey J. Rachlinski and Cynthia R. Farina, "Cognitive Psychology and Optimal Government Design," *Cornell Law Review* 87 (January 2002): 571–82.

is opposed to the traditional capture model. Choi and Pritchard[33] similarly identified a set of behavioral biases that may partially explain the shortcomings of the SEC. In both cases, the authors suggested irrational decision-making processes rather than material self-interest as an explanation of suboptimal policies. At the same time, nonrational influences have also been framed as causes of capture. According to Hanson and Yosifon,[34] "[b]eneath the surface of behavior, the interior situation of relevant actors is also subject to capture."[35] More narrowly, Wagner[36] has identified "information capture," in which interest groups take advantage of administrative law – in particular, the requirement that agencies take all submissions into account – to inundate regulators with complex information to obtain favorable policy outcomes. An agency acting in good faith might "participate in a capture dynamic," according to Bagley, because "the agency might depend on information from the affected entities and lack the means or ability to review that information skeptically. Or the agency might come to see the world the way that its regulated entities do."[37] Davidoff has discussed "social capture," in which regulators' decisions are influenced by the composition of their social networks: "These men and women may believe they are doing their best, but their worldview is affected by the people they interact with."[38]

The recent financial crisis has provided new motivation for nonmaterialist accounts of capture. The financial sector (and the "Wall Street" investment banks and universal banks in particular) seems to have gained the cooperation of the federal regulatory agencies, not simply by appealing to material self-interest, but also by convincing them that financial

[33] Stephen J. Choi and A.C. Pritchard, "Behavioral Economics and the SEC," *Stanford Law Review* 56 (October 2003): 20–36.

[34] Jon D. Hanson and David G. Yosifon, "The Situation: An Introduction to the Situational Character, Critical Realism, Power Economics, and Deep Capture," *University of Pennsylvania Law Review* 152 (November 2003): 14.

[35] Hanson and Yosifon's concept of "deep capture" applies to society in general, not just government actors.

[36] Wendy Wagner, "Administrative Law, Filter Failure, and Information Capture," *Duke Law Journal* 59 (April 2010): 1321.

[37] Nicholas Bagley. "Agency Hygiene." *Texas Law Review See Also* 89 (November 20, 2010): 1–14. Available at http://www.texaslrev.com/seealso/vol/89/responses/bagley. See A.C. Pritchard, "The SEC at 70: Time for Retirement?" *Notre Dame Law Review* 80 (March 2005): 1073–1102. For example, Pritchard wrote (2005, p. 1089), "the financial services industry has considerable influence over the information that the SEC receives as it undertakes its rulemaking responsibilities. The result has been a system of securities regulation that largely benefits the big players in the securities industry."

[38] Steven M. Davidoff. "The Government's Elite and Regulatory Capture." DealBook, *New York Times*, June 11, 2010. Available at http://dealbook.nytimes.com/2010/06/11/the-governments-elite-and-regulatory-capture. See p. 39.

deregulation was in the public interest. This is not controversial in itself, but their positions were often contested at the time and, with hindsight, appear to have been catastrophically wrong. The question, then, is how regulators could have been so wrong, especially in the direction that favored the regulated industry. Joseph Stiglitz answered the question in terms of proximity: "I think that mindsets can be shaped by people you associate with, and you come to think that what's good for Wall Street is good for America."[39] Needham described cognitive biases as a potential contributor to the Federal Reserve's decision not to examine nonbank mortgage origi-nators during the housing bubble.[40] Buiter partially explained the response of the Federal Reserve to the growing panic of 2007–2008 by referring to "cognitive regulatory capture": "those in charge of the relevant state entity internalising, as if by osmosis, the objectives, interests and perception of reality of the vested interest they are meant to regulate."[41] Adair Turner,[42] chair of the U.K. Financial Services Authority, also used the phrase "cog-nitive capture" to describe the tendency of financial regulators to engage in "problem solving with the [regulated] institution" rather than enforcing existing rules. Baxter[43] has described the financial sector's influence over regulation as an example of the "deep capture" described by Hanson and Yosifon.[44] Johnson and I argued that the idea that unfettered financial activ-ity is always good for society became a form of "cultural capital" – an idea that people adopt in part because of the prestige it confers.[45]

There seems to be a widespread intuition that regulated industry can shape policy outcomes through influences other than material incentives and rational debate. This chapter discusses how and why this might happen:

[39] Jo Becker and Gretchen Morgenson, "Geithner, Member and Overseer of Finance Club," *New York Times*, April 26, 2009. Available at http://www.nytimes.com/2009/04/27/business/27geithner.html.

[40] Carol A. Needham. "Listening to Cassandra: The Difficult of Recognizing Risks and Taking Action." *Fordham Law Review* 78 (April 2010): 2347–2355.

[41] Willem Buiter. "Central Banks and Financial Crises." In *Maintaining Stability in a Changing Financial System* (proceedings of the Federal Reserve Bank of Kansas City Economic Policy Symposium, Jackson Hole, WY, August 21–23, 2008), 601.

[42] Adair Turner, interview with Financial Crisis Inquiry Commission Staff, November 30, 2010. Audiotape available at http://fcic.law.stanford.edu/interviews/view/102.

[43] Lawrence G. Baxter. "Capture in Financial Regulation: Can We Redirect It Toward the Common Good?" *Cornell Journal of Law and Public Policy* 21, no. 1 (Fall 2011): 175–200.

[44] In Baxter's view, "the language of regulation is shaped by the common backgrounds, edu-cation, experience and intermingling of the more powerful players in the policy formation process."

[45] Simon Johnson and James Kwak, *13 Bankers: The Wall Street Takeover and the Next Financial Meltdown* (New York: Pantheon, 2010), 104–5.

why regulators' perspectives and actions might be shaded by the nature of their interactions with interest groups, not just the substantive content of those interactions. In particular, I focus on three mechanisms of influence that are likely to operate in the regulatory context: group identification, status, and relationship networks.

I use the label *cultural capture* for this phenomenon: *cultural* because it operates through a set of shared but not explicitly stated understandings about the world; *capture* because it can produce the same outcome as traditional capture – regulatory actions that serve the ends of industry. Cultural capture, as I describe it, however, is not necessarily capture as strictly defined in this volume. It is one reason why capture can occur: an industry might consciously set out to induce its regulators to identify with industry members and their interests, and those regulators might make decisions because their conception of the public interest has been colonized by industry. The mechanisms of cultural capture, however, are also relevant in less clear-cut situations in which the industry position is arguably a plausible reading of the public interest. If we think of cultural capture as a strategy that interest groups can use to influence regulation, it is available both to sway regulators away from a clearly identifiable public interest and when there is a contest between multiple possible policies, none of which is clearly superior to any other for the public. In the terms used by Yackee in this volume (see Chapter 11), cultural capture may help an industry exert influence on agency actions, but that influence may fall short of being controlling. Cultural capture also implies that it is not enough from a public policy standpoint simply to prevent traditional capture based on material self-interest. The alternative to outright capture is not necessarily a world in which regulators follow the public interest, either in the abstract or as they perceive it. Instead, that perception is shaped by a host of nonrational factors, many of which can be manipulated by interest groups and not by the free competition of ideas and evidence.

Cultural capture, then, is a channel through which capture can occur in parallel to the traditional materialist channel. It contributes to the ongoing contest between rival ideological systems, which helps to shape the belief systems of governmental actors. Unfortunately, this means that in most cases it will be impossible to prove that cultural capture is the determining factor behind regulatory outcomes. Traditional capture is already hard enough to identify, because policymakers invariably cite some justifications other than self-interest for their actions. Cultural capture, if anything, is even harder to identify empirically, because there are always multiple explanations for why someone forms the beliefs she has; in practice, nonrational influences will ease the adoption and strengthen the grip of beliefs that have plausible rational justifications. In the psychology and economics literatures, the roles of different types of motivations can be isolated using laboratory or field experiments, but this is unlikely to be practical in the case of regulatory policy.

Still, cultural capture should not be written off on the grounds of nontestability. If we ignore the possibility that regulators hold beliefs or make decisions in part because of nonrational factors, we are both ignoring common sense and constraining the solution space for administrative policy.[46] That is, if the only problem we guard against is material self-interest, we will have a regulatory process protected from bribery but not from the other influences wielded by motivated interest groups. We should not doubt that sophisticated interest groups are doing what they can to achieve cultural capture wherever possible, because it is certainly in their interests. It is possible that our current practices are ideal – that we should have rules limiting bribery and its close relatives, but we should not worry about other forms of influence – but if so, that is a conclusion we should reach consciously, not by default.

HOW CULTURAL CAPTURE WORKS

In this section, I describe three mechanisms by which regulated industry is able to shape regulators' beliefs and actions – mechanisms that should not work if regulators are rational beings devoted to their self-interest or if they form their policy preferences rationally. They are:

- **Identity:** Regulators are more likely to adopt positions advanced by people whom they perceive as being in their in-group.
- **Status:** Regulators are more likely to adopt positions advanced by people whom they perceive to be of higher status in social, economic, intellectual, or other terms.
- **Relationships:** Regulators are more likely to adopt positions advanced by people who are in their social networks.

These mechanisms can overlap in practice, but they are conceptually distinct. For example, if I am an agency employee meeting with a lawyer who is representing a Wall Street investment bank, I may feel she is in my in-group because we went to the same law school, I may feel she is of higher status because she makes several times as much money as I do, and we

---

[46] In Rachlinski and Farina, "Cognitive Psychology and Optimal Government Design." 593–606, for example, Rachlinski and Farina argued that governmental decision-making processes should be informed by what we know about cognitive biases.

may send our children to the same schools and therefore be in the same social networks. However, each of these factors can also exist on its own. I might identify strongly as a civil servant and *against* the private interests she represents, but we might still send our children to the same schools, and I might see her regularly for those reasons. Furthermore, each type of influence relies on different psychological mechanisms and will therefore be important in different contexts. These are also factors that we should expect to be at work in interactions between regulators and regulated and that therefore have particular implications for administrative regulation.

Identity

Considerable psychological and economic research indicates that group identity matters, and not only because in helping my own group I help myself as a member of that group. Identification with a group has several effects on behavior that go beyond material self-interest. People seem to gain utility from behaving in conformity with their group identities. When multiple group identities are available to a person, her behavior will be influenced by the identity that she selects, whether that selection is conscious or unconscious.

A standard procedure in psychology or economics experiments is to sort participants into minimal groups, either randomly or based on some arbitrary or trivial attribute. Many such studies find that participants act more favorably toward in-group members even when there is no rational reason to do so. In one study, participants allocated more money to in-group members than out-group members and were more likely to reward and less likely to punish in-group members than out-group members.[47] Another study found that participants were more trusting of in-group members than of out-group members and were more trustworthy when dealing with in-group members.[48] The mere fact of group identification can make people not only more generous to in-group members but also more trusting and more willing to reciprocate favorably.[49] These effects also occur in experiments using real-world, randomly constituted groups.[50] In one study, participants in the

---

[47] Yan Chen and Sherry Xin Li, "Group Identity and Social Preferences," *American Economic Review* 99 (March 2009): 431–57.

[48] Shaun P. Hargreaves Heap and Daniel John Zizzo, "The Value of Groups," *American Economic Review* 99 (March 2009): 295–323.

[49] These group effects are also correlated with the salience of group membership to participants. See Gary Charness, Luca Rigotti, and Aldo Rustichini, "Individual Behavior and Group Membership," *American Economic Review* 97 (September 2007): 1340–52.

[50] Random assignment to groups is valuable because it isolates the effect of group membership from the effects of other characteristics that members of a group may share.

Joint Officer Training Program of the Swiss military were more trusting of and trustworthy to members of their own platoons than to members of other platoons.[51]

Group identification also induces people to conform to their expectations for the groups with which they identify. According to Akerlof and Kranton,[52] a person derives utility from her identity. That utility is a function of the social status of the group she identifies with, her similarity to the ideal type of that group, and the degree of conformity between her (and others') actions and her expectations of that group. For example, workers' effort depends on whether they identify as company insiders or as outsiders, not solely on their individual returns to effort, and, therefore, policies that encourage identification as insiders increase effort.[53] In some cases, people are able to choose the group with which they identify, by implication to maximize their utility.[54] This may be a choice within a single dimension such as gender (that is, identification as male or female is to some extent a matter of choice), or it may be a choice among the different group identifications that are available at any moment (that is, an Asian woman may choose to identify as Asian or as female in a given context). According to social identity theory, a person is simultaneously a member of several groups, and her thoughts and actions are influenced by the group affiliation that is most salient in a given context.[55] Experiments involving priming – by which participants are surreptitiously reminded of some aspect of their identity – show that behavior is even affected by unconscious selection among available identifications. For example, Asian-American female students' performance on a math test differed based on whether they were primed with their ethnic or their gender identity.[56]

---

[51] Lorenz Goette, David Huffman, and Stephan Meier, "The Impact of Group Membership on Cooperation and Norm Enforcement: Evidence Using Random Assignment to Real Social Groups," *American Economic Review* 96 (May 2006): 212–16. Donors are more likely to find a charity worthy if it is represented as serving people of the donor's race; see Christina M. Fong and Erzo F.P. Luttmer, "Do Fairness and Race Matter in Generosity? Evidence from a Nationally Representative Charity Experiment," *Journal of Public Economics* 95, no. 5–6 (June 2011): 372–94.

[52] George A. Akerlof and Rachel E. Kranton, "Economics and Identity," *Quarterly Journal of Economics* 115 (August 2000): 719.

[53] George A. Akerlof and Rechel E. Kranton, *Identity Economics: How Our Identities Shape Our Work, Wages and Well-Being* (Princeton: Princeton University Press, 2010).

[54] Akerlof and Kranton, "Economics and Identity," 719–20.

[55] Akerlof and Kranton, "Economics and Identity," 731 n. 30.

[56] Margaret Shih, Todd L. Pittinsky, and Nalini Ambady, "Stereotype Susceptibility: Identity Salience and Shifts in Quantitative Performance," *Psychological Science* 10 (January 1999): 80–3.

Key questions in the regulatory context, then, are what factors affect a regulator's choice of group identification and what that choice implies for policy. Two different types of identifications are relevant here. First, in a contest between two interest groups – say, credit card issuers and credit card customers – a regulator might identify with one group and not the other; the specific identification could be with the interest group itself (bankers or consumers) or with that group's representatives (bank lobbyists or consumer advocates). Although this may be unlikely to produce conscious favoritism, the regulator will be more inclined to trust the side with which she identifies more, which can affect her policy choices. Second, a regulator's actions might be influenced by her conception of her own role as a civil servant. Someone who identifies as an economically sophisticated steward of efficient financial markets will adopt different policy positions than someone who identifies as a defender of the "little guy" against large, faceless corporations, even if both share the ultimate objective of increasing the economic welfare of ordinary people. The steward of efficient markets would be more open to the argument that classifying late fees as interest would lower the overall cost of credit because it is more consistent with her self-conception – in Akerlof and Kranton's terms, she would gain greater utility from identity.

In the context of financial regulation, both of these effects appear more likely to favor regulated industry. On any significant issue, all interested parties are likely to send well-educated, articulate, well-dressed representatives to meet with agency officials. When it comes to financial regulation, however, industry has the advantage of the revolving door. From 2009 to mid-2010, for example, 148 former employees of financial regulatory agencies registered as lobbyists.[57] In this chapter, I do not consider the implications of the revolving door for regulators' material self-interest. However, the normalcy of moving from an administrative agency to the financial sector and the sheer number of people making the transition imply that the regulators and the representatives of financial institutions are really the same people, only at different points in their careers. Regulators are more likely to have personal connections with industry lobbyists or to envision themselves in their shoes. This may not directly affect their ideological sympathies or their assessment of the merits of an issue, but it could easily affect their identification – which side they consciously or unconsciously perceive as their in-group. And this will affect the degree to which they trust information or opinions provided by the financial sector.

---

[57] Eric Lichtblau, "Ex-Regulators Get Set to Lobby on New Financial Rules," *New York Times*, July 27, 2010. Available at http://www.nytimes.com/2010/07/28/business/28lobby.html.

The other industry advantage is that, until recently, few people came to Washington to protect ordinary people from banks. Before the recent financial crisis, banks faced four major federal regulators: the Federal Reserve, primarily responsible for stable economic growth and low inflation; the FDIC, responsible for the solvency of its insurance fund; and the OCC and the OTS, primarily responsible for the safety and soundness of banks and thrifts, respectively. Before the creation of the Consumer Financial Protection Bureau (CFPB) in the Dodd-Frank Act of 2010, no agency had the primary mandate of protecting consumers. Instead, the dominant theory was that consumers' interests would be best protected by free market competition. Because people rarely became bank regulators to protect consumers, it was more likely that regulators thought of themselves as stewards of an efficient financial system or, more simply, identified with the bankers. This attitude was on display in 2010 when members of the CFPB implementation team arrived for an on-site visit to a major financial institution. As people were meeting each other, a company executive who had flown in from another office introduced himself to someone he thought was from the CFPB. "No, I'm one of you," the person corrected him. "I'm from the [bank regulatory agency]."[58]

For both of these reasons, financial regulators tended to identify with the financial institutions that they regulated.[59] This perhaps contrasts with the Environmental Protection Agency (EPA), which is often cited as an agency that is not captured by the industries that it regulates[60] (and is sometimes criticized for being captured by environmental groups[61]). As Rachlinski and Farina[62] say, "Those who seek work at an agency charged with responsibility for the environment probably have strong views about the appropriate goals and means of environmental regulation." Their identity carries the expectation that they will protect the environment

---

[58] For large financial institutions, the primary regulator typically locates a group of agency employees on site – hence the identification with the institution itself and not with the outsiders from Washington.

[59] For example, discussing Eliot Spitzer's prominence in investigating financial industry scandals, Jonathan Macey wrote, "The SEC was fully acclimated to existing market practices and saw no urgent need to change them. The SEC staff identified with the market participants they were ostensibly regulating." Jonathan R. Macey, "State-Federal Relations Post-Eliot Spitzer," *Brooklyn Law Review* 70 (2004): 128.

[60] See Croley, "Public Interested Regulation," 55–66.

[61] For a summary and rebuttal of this criticism, see Bagley and Revesz, "Centralized Oversight of the Regulatory State," 1285–90.

[62] Rachlinski and Farina, "Cognitive Psychology and Optimal Government Design," 579–80.

(from, say, industrial companies), and that expectation conditions their actions.[63]

Status

Like group identification, status can have significant effects on behavior. On issues in which expertise is recognized to be important, laypeople tend to defer to people with specific status characteristics (e.g., a relevant advanced degree), which may seem reasonable. However, status can influence behavior in other ways not predicted by the rational actor model. Diffuse status characteristics, based on stereotypes rather than relevant qualifications, affect beliefs about social categories and thereby affect relationships between people.[64] As a result, people behave more favorably toward other people of high status. In addition, they are more likely to learn from or imitate people of high status, in part because they want to claim status themselves.

As with group identification, status can confer benefits even when it is assigned arbitrarily or based on seemingly irrelevant criteria. In one experiment, after people were classified as "stars" or "no-stars" based on their performance on a trivia quiz, stars were offered more money in an ultimatum game than no-stars.[65] In other experiments, high-status players obtained better market outcomes than low-status players, even when status assignment was transparently random.[66] Similar results are produced by preexisting indicators of social status. One study found that college students with higher social status received more money back in a trust game than students with lower status.[67] The common theme is that people behave

---

[63] Bagley and Revesz (p. 1301), however, argued that agency bureaucrats are motivated less by ideology and more by "career advancement, producing a quality work product, and abiding by professional and ethical norms."

[64] Catherine C. Eckel, Enrique Fatas, and Rick Wilson, "Cooperation and Status in Organizations," *Journal of Public Economic Theory* 12, no. 4 (2010): 740; Cecilia L. Ridgeway and Kristan Glasgow Erickson, "Creating and Spreading Status Beliefs," *American Journal of Sociology* 106 (November 2000): 580.

[65] Sheryl Ball and Catherine C. Eckel, "The Economic Value of Status," *Journal of Socio-Economics* 27, no. 4 (1998): 503–7. Participants thought that status was assigned based on the quiz, but the actual assignment was effectively random. It is theoretically possible that participants believed that people who are good at trivia quizzes either deserve more money or are more likely to reject low offers, but this would only demonstrate the tendency of status distinctions in one realm to affect behavior in generally unrelated realms.

[66] Ball and Eckel, "The Economic Value of Status," 507–10; Sheryl Ball, Catherine Eckel, Philip J. Grossman, and William Zame, "Status in Markets," *Quarterly Journal of Economics* 116 (February 2001): 161–88.

[67] Edward L. Glaeser, David I. Laibson, José A. Scheinkman, and Christine L. Soutter, "Measuring Trust," *Quarterly Journal of Economics* 115 (August 2000): 836–40.

more favorably toward people with high status even in contexts in which there is no obvious payoff from doing so. This happens in the real world as well, for example, when three star football players capitalized on their celebrity to raise money for their hedge funds – which then collapsed during the financial crisis.[68]

People are not only nicer to high-status people; they also are more likely to adopt their ideas and behaviors, even when not warranted by the source of their status.[69] In one culture, for example, "great turtle hunters are permitted to speak and are listened to more than others, despite the fact that their skill in hunting turtles gives no direct indication of their skill in public affairs or politics."[70] The influence of status is especially important in areas where it is difficult for individuals to learn on their own.[71] Anecdotally, it appears that a major charitable contribution by a high-status donor will lead to follow-on gifts by other donors.[72] Kumru and Vesterlund[73] confirmed experimentally that low-status participants are more likely to mimic high-status participants who donate first, whereas the converse is less likely to occur.[74] In another repeated-game experiment, participants were more likely to respond to a signal from a high-status than from a low-status counterparty.[75]

There are two plausible explanations for this behavior. One is deference to people with high status: we interpret their behavior as a command to behave accordingly, whether that means conceding in a negotiation or contributing to the same charity. Alternatively, we may want to obtain higher status or confirm our belief that we have that higher status. For Akerlof and Kranton,[76] higher status can provide utility directly. Empirically, we know

---

[68] Edward Robinson, "Winning Super Bowl Lets Montana Teammates Fumble Elite Investing," *Bloomberg Markets Magazine*, February 9, 2011. Available at http://www.bloomberg .com/news/2011–02–02/winning-super-bowls-lets-montana-teammates-fumble-handling-elite-investor.html.

[69] Joseph Henrich and Francisco J. Gil-White, "The Evolution of Prestige: Freely Conferred Deference as a Mechanism for Enhancing the Benefits of Cultural Transmission," *Evolution and Human Behavior* 22 (2001): 184–6.

[70] Ibid., 184.

[71] Ibid., 185.

[72] Cagri S. Kumru and Lise Vesterlund, "The Effect of Status on Charitable Giving," *Journal of Public Economic Theory* 12 (August 2010): 709–35.

[73] Ibid.

[74] See also Eckel, Fatas, and Wilson, "Cooperation and Status in Organizations," who found that participants in a voluntary contribution game are more likely to imitate a high-status player and are more responsive to punishment by a high-status player.

[75] Catherine C. Eckel and Rick K. Wilson, "Social Learning in Coordination Games: Does Status Matter?" *Experimental Economics* 10 (2007): 317–29.

[76] Akerlof and Kranton, "Economics and Identity," 719.

that people value status and will expend resources to gain it, even when it provides no material advantage. In one experiment, when output was publicly visible, people paid money to increase their own output or to reduce other participants' output even though it had no impact on their individual payoffs.[77] In another case, participants were willing to overinvest in seeking status, even though this reduced their expected payoffs.[78]

In the real world, where status is not determined in an experiment, we pursue status through signaling behaviors. According to social comparison theory, we can improve our self-image by emphasizing similarities with and connections to higher status people.[79] We like to behave in ways that are consistent with our idealized images of ourselves,[80] and so we adopt behaviors that we think are typical of high-status people. One example is conspicuous consumption, identified by Thorstein Veblen, but material wealth is only one indicator of status. According to Bourdieu,[81] cultural judgments are another means of establishing social prestige, with the advantage that taste cannot simply be bought and therefore serves as a lasting marker of class differentiation: "Social subjects ... distinguish themselves by the distinctions they make, between the beautiful and the ugly, the distinguished and the vulgar." In addition to pursuing status through consumption choices, people pursue status through cultural and intellectual choices.

In practice, status differentiations exist along many different dimensions. We look up to actors, athletes, firefighters, and hedge fund billionaires for different reasons. Several of these dimensions provide an advantage to financial institutions in the regulatory context. First, insofar as wealth and business success are sources of status, the financial sector has them in spades. Financial regulators living in Washington and New York saw firsthand the vast sums of money being made by Wall Street bankers and traders. In addition, with brief exceptions for the analyst and accounting scandals around 2001–2002, the financial sector was routinely lionized as both an exemplar of the knowledge economy and an engine of economic growth. Financial

---

[77] Gary Charness, David Masclet, and Marie-Claire Villeval, "Competitive Preferences and Status as an Incentive: Experimental Evidence," Working Paper 1016, Group d'Analyse et de Théorie Économique Lyon-St. Étienne, June 2010.

[78] Bernardo A. Huberman, Christoph H. Loch, and Ayse Onçuler, "Status as a Valued Resource," *Social Psychology Quarterly* 67 (2004): 103–14.

[79] Jerry Suls, René Martin, and Ladd Wheeler, "Social Comparison: Why, With Whom, and With What Effect?" *Current Directions in Psychological Science* 11 (October 2002): 159–63.

[80] Roy F. Baumeister, "A Self-Presentational View of Social Phenomena," *Psychological Bulletin* 91, no. 1 (1982): 3.

[81] Pierre Bourdieu, *Distinction: A Social Critique of the Judgment of Taste*, Translated by Richard Nice (Cambridge, MA: Harvard University Press, 1984), 6.

institutions and their captains also bought status through charitable work and contributions. For example, Sanford Weill, the creator of Citigroup, has donated several hundred million dollars to Cornell University (which named its medical school after him) and is chair of the board of Carnegie Hall.[82]

Second, finance itself became glamorous, thanks in part to its portrayal in major cultural works, beginning in the late 1980s with *The Bonfire of the Vanities, Wall Street*, and *Liar's Poker*. Despite the ambivalent light these works cast on modern finance, they popularized the image of the swash-buckling, individualistic, and very rich "master of the universe." For agency employees who never had a chance to become Hollywood stars or professional athletes, the banking lifestyle was perhaps the most glamorous one in their sphere of potential experience. At its peak, it seemed like finance was the most desirable job in the world, with financial institutions claiming 40 percent of the Princeton seniors who went to work directly after graduation.[83] The Wall Street recruiting machine, with its constant assertions that finance attracted the best and the brightest,[84] also ensured that anyone who went to a top college, business school, or law school was well aware of the prestige of banking. Insofar as status can exert any pull on regulators, then, the major financial institutions were likely to benefit from that pull.

Third, as the world of finance became more technical, its academic pedigree became more imposing. By the 1990s, financial economics was a branch of applied mathematics, and several of its leading figures were advocates of efficient markets and financial innovation, including multiple winners of the Nobel Prize in Economics. On an issue such as the use of value-at-risk statistical models for calculating capital requirements, regulators who might not understand the math had to choose between an old theory of the world that everyone knew was wrong (e.g., that all mortgages were exactly half as risky as all commercial loans[85]) and a new theory that, although not practically tested, was supported by famous economists. Academic endorsement may be a valid proxy for the correctness of a theory. However, subscribing

---

[82]　"*Slate* 60: Donor Bios," *Slate*, February 5, 2010. Steven Schwarzman, founder of Blackstone, has contributed $100 million to the New York Public Library (whose main building is named after him) and is chair of the board of the John F. Kennedy Center for the Performing Arts. "*Slate* 60: Donor Bios," *Slate*, January 23, 2009.

[83]　Cailey Hall, "Wall Street: Paradise Found?" *Daily Princetonian*, September 29, 2005. Available at http://www.dailyprincetonian.com/2005/09/29/13254/.

[84]　Karen Ho, *Liquidated: An Ethnography of Wall Street* (Durham, NC: Duke University Press, 2009), 42–55.

[85]　These were rules mandated by the Basel I Accord for calculating capital requirements.

to cutting-edge financial theories also provided perceived status benefits. These factors all enhanced the status of the financial sector, which could give financial regulators additional motivation to adopt its worldview and policy positions.

Relationships

On March 8, 2010, I attended a "blogger briefing" at the Treasury Department with Secretary Timothy Geithner and several other senior officials. Waldman said the following about a similar meeting the previous November:

Most corrupt acts don't take the form of clearly immoral choices. People fight those. Corruption thrives where there is a tension between institutional and interpersonal ethics. There is "the right thing" in abstract, but there are also very human impulses towards empathy, kindness, and reciprocity that result from relationships with flesh and blood people.... I was flattered and grateful for the meeting and left with more sympathy for the people I spoke to than I came in with. In other words, I have been corrupted, a little.[86]

(Note that Treasury did not pay the expenses of meeting attendees, whose only material benefit was cookies.)[87] This is the familiar effect of relationships: you are more favorably disposed toward someone you have shared cookies with, or at least it is harder for you to take some action that harms his or her interests. Relationships matter because we care about what other people think of us, in particular those people with whom we come into contact regularly. Relationship pressure is magnified both by visibility – the degree to which one party can observe the other's actions – and by the frequency with which people interact.

These familiar observations are borne out by research in psychology and economics. Because we care about what other people think about us, we engage in "self-presentation" that, according to Baumeister,[88] "is aimed at establishing, maintaining, or refining an image of the individual in the minds of others." One consequence is that "people conform more readily to the opinions and expectations of others when these others are watching than

---

[86] Steve Randy Waldman, "Sympathy for the Treasury," *Interfluidity*, November 5, 2009. Available at http://www.interfluidity.com/posts/1257407150.shtml.

[87] Cookies are no joking matter. In December 2010, as the Federal Communications Commission was setting rules for managing Internet traffic, AT&T sent the agency 1,530 cupcakes from Georgetown Cupcake. Edward Wyatt, "Arsenal of a Lobbyist: Hardball and Cupcakes," *New York Times*, March 26, 2011. Available at http://www.nytimes.com/2011/03/27/business/27phone.html.

[88] Baumeister, "A Self-Presentational View of Social Phenomena," 3.

when they are not"; deindividuation, where people's actions are not individually identifiable, has the effect of reducing conformity.[89] The importance of self-presentation has been borne out in economics experiments. In a trust game, participants were less likely to cooperate when their counterparties could not see their behavior and less likely to cooperate when it was not clear who was matched with whom.[90] Because participant pairs were randomly shuffled (and often anonymous), it is likely that people were motivated by what others thought about them and not by the material benefits of establishing a reputation.[91] In another experiment, players in two-person games behaved more aggressively before an audience of in-group members and more deferentially before an audience of out-group members.[92]

Similar behavior has been identified in the real world. A study of supermarket cashiers found that an individual cashier's productivity depended on the productivity of the cashiers immediately *behind* her – but not if her shifts had little overlap with theirs.[93] By implication, the individual cashier was motivated by what the people behind her (who could watch her working) thought about her, but only if she was likely to interact with them often in the future. As another example, when college students played a trust game, the amount that recipients returned to senders depended in part on the degree of social connection between them.[94]

In the regulatory context, relationship effects can be difficult to disentangle from revolving door effects. Traditional capture theory holds that regulators have a rational interest in doing favors for firms that can provide them future employment options. However, even an agency employee who is uninterested in higher paying private sector jobs is not immune to relationship pressures. In what Meidinger[95] called a "regulatory community," "members of the community frequently influence each other, act with reference to each other, and desire each other's respect." Or as Ayres and Braithwaite[96] put it, "One of the most plausible noneconomic theories

---

[89] Ibid., 8.

[90] Steven Tadelis, "The Power of Shame and the Rationality of Trust," *Working Paper*, March 2, 2011.

[91] Tadelis, "The Power of Shame and the Rationality of Trust," 14–15.

[92] Charness, Rigotti, and Rustichini, "Individual Behavior and Group Membership."

[93] Alexandre Mas and Enrico Moretti, "Peers at Work," *American Economic Review* 99 (March 2009): 112–45.

[94] Glaeser et al., "Measuring Trust," 834–86.

[95] Errol Meidinger, "Regulatory Culture: A Theoretical Outline," *Law & Policy* 9 (October 1987): 365.

[96] Ian Ayres and John Braithwaite, "Tripartism: Regulatory Capture and Empowerment," *Law & Social Inquiry* 16 (Summer 1991): 471.

of capture is the most mundane: regulators like to cooperate with firms because they seek a conflict-free work life."[97]

In principle, there is no reason why relationship pressures would necessarily favor one interest group over another, because administrative actions are equally visible to all sides (at least in theory), and regulatory policy is a repeat game in which the issues may change but the parties often remain the same. In practice, however, there are two reasons why relationship pressure is likely to favor regulated industry, at least in the case of financial regulation. First, for reasons discussed previously, financial regulators are likely to share more social networks with financial institutions and their lawyers and lobbyists than with competing interest groups such as consumers. Although group identification and relationship pressure are two conceptually distinct channels of influence, they are likely to occur in overlapping circumstances. The revolving door between government and industry, by creating social connections between people on opposite sides of the door, therefore has an influence even on people who are personally impervious to its attractions.[98] Similarly, Minerals Management Service (MMS) employees working in Lake Charles, Louisiana, shared social networks with industry personnel; as Carrigan notes in this volume (see Chapter 10), one MMS employee said, "Almost all of our inspectors have worked for oil companies out on these same platforms. They grew up in the same towns. . . . Some of these people, they've been friends with all their life."

Second, the importance of relationships exacerbates the collective action problem often identified as a cause of regulatory capture. According to the traditional account, small interest groups (in the sense that they have a small number of members, not that they are small economically) with a deep interest in the issue at hand are better able to coordinate their activities and buy favorable policy than large groups with diffuse interests; the former are typified by regulated industry, the latter by the public at large.[99] Croley[100] has criticized the collective action account for, among other things, assuming that politicians will necessarily be more responsive to small, well-financed

---

[97] Similarly, daily contact with agency staff can influence the positions held by agency heads, as described by Livermore and Revesz in this volume (see Chapter 15), reducing the potential impact of new political appointees on agency policies.

[98] One potential consequence, according to Baxter, is "a cognitive bias in which different views are not even perceived, let alone recognized and properly analyzed." Baxter, "Capture in Financial Regulation."

[99] See George J. Stigler, "The Theory of Economic Regulation," *Bell Journal of Economics and Management Science* 2 (Spring 1971): 10–13; Croley, "Public Interested Regulation," 13–15.

[100] Croley, "Public Interested Regulation," 18–21.

interest groups than to broad-based interest groups that represent large numbers of voters. However, even if broad-based groups can command attention at election time or when issues gain significant public attention, they are still likely to lack the organizational infrastructure and staying power to knock on regulators' doors month in, month out, on issue after issue.

For example, the congressional debate over financial regulatory reform in 2009–2010 attracted widespread media attention and the participation of broad-based, pro-reform groups such as Americans for Financial Reform (AFR), a coalition of hundreds of progressive organizations.[101] By contrast, when regulatory reform moved to the agencies for implementation, although AFR did not close up shop, representatives of financial institutions and large nonfinancial companies were much better able to fill the halls of the agencies. Early in 2011, CFTC chair Gary Gensler said, "Large institutions have a great deal more resources than the investor advocates. If you looked at those 475 meetings [in the past five months]... 90-plus percent are probably larger institutions or corporations."[102] In this case, industry representatives are better situated to build the long-term relationships that can shade regulators' perceptions of people and of the merits of policy issues. Similar distinctions can also occur within a single industry. For example, the Offshore Energy division of MMS chose to focus its attention on small, independent developers rather than the major energy companies in part because it was more familiar with the latter (see Chapter 10). Again, this apparent advantage for regulated industry might be contrasted with other regulatory domains such as certain types of environmental policy, in which major environmental organizations may occupy a more symmetric position to industry.

Regulators, like all human beings,[103] are susceptible to other cognitive biases beyond those discussed here, and this is not an exhaustive list of the ways in which interest groups can influence the process by which regulators

---

[101] This is an example of how "[t]he financial crisis and the national debate over financial regulation opened a social aperture in the realm of finance policy making." Daniel Carpenter, "The Contest of Lobbies and Disciplines: Financial Politics and Regulatory Reform in the Obama Administration," in Lawrence Jacobs and Theda Skocpol, eds., *Reaching for a New Deal: President Obama's Agenda and the Dynamics of U.S. Politics* (Russell Sage Foundation, 2011).

[102] Ben Protess and Mac William Bishop, "At Center of Derivatives Debate, a Gung-Ho Regulator," DealBook, *The New York Times*, February 10, 2011. Available at http://dealbook.nytimes.com/2011/02/10/at-center-of-debate-over-derivatives-a-gung-ho-regulator/.

[103] Or, at least, like most well-educated Americans. See Joseph Henrich, Steven J. Heine, and Ara Norenzayan, "The Weirdest People in the World?" *Behavioral and Brain Sciences* 33 (2010): 61–135.

form their beliefs and preferences.[104] The well-known set of cognitive limitations identified by behavioral psychology can provide inspiration for countless other lobbying tactics. Information capture as discussed by Wagner[105] works in part because human beings have limited processing capacity and therefore resort to useful but potentially misleading heuristics when dealing with large volumes of information. Filling up regulators' meeting schedules also affects regulators' ability to evaluate competing perspectives objectively. In general, the more complex and information-intensive an issue is and the less capacity the agency has to devote to the issue, the greater the potential importance of cultural capture. Faced with uncertainty deciding between competing theories of the world and the public interest, people are more likely to fall back on the signals communicated by identity, status, or relationships.

IMPLICATIONS

In the two decades leading up to the 2007–2009 financial crisis, the banking industry achieved the practical equivalent of capture, with federal regulatory agencies generally adopting its favored positions. Although several signs of traditional capture were present – notably a well-oiled revolving door between regulatory agencies and industry – the argument for capture in the strict sense is weakened by a plausible alternative explanation: that agency officials were genuinely persuaded by the argument that free financial markets were good for the public. In this light, the important question is why theories of the world that are wrong or at least widely contested gain broad acceptance in a specific community – here, the community of financial regulatory agencies. Where the underlying theories require highly specialized expertise (e.g., advanced degrees in financial economics) and are empirically contested, it would be naïve to expect policy debates to turn solely on the intellectual merits of the parties' positions. Cultural capture provides an alternative explanation of how policy is formed – neither through simple corruption nor through purely rational debate, but through the soft pressures that arise from the specific characteristics of the regulatory community.

---

[104] Rachlinski and Farina ("Cognitive Psychology and Optimal Government Design") discussed the general implications of several well-known cognitive biases for policymakers. Kuran and Sunstein discussed specific measures that could help executive agencies resist "availability cascades." Timur Kuran and Cass R. Sunstein, "Availability Cascades and Risk Regulation," *Stanford Law Review* 51 (April 1999): 754–8.

[105] Wagner, "Administrative Law, Filter Failure, and Information Capture."

Cultural capture need not operate alone, but can complement either a public interest theory of regulation or a materialist capture theory of regulation. On the one hand, the mechanisms of cultural capture can play an instrumental role in helping financial institutions convince regulators of the merits of their policy positions. Forced to evaluate opposing arguments that are difficult to compare and often based on incommensurate policy objectives (e.g., maximizing economic growth versus minimizing personal bankruptcies), regulators are more likely to resort to proxies such as their degree of trust in the people making those arguments or their academic pedigree. That reliance on proxies can be either conscious or unconscious and is shaped by regulators' susceptibility to the influences of identity, status, and relationships. On the other hand, cultural capture can also make it easier for regulators to pursue their material self-interest. Most regulators probably do not see themselves as trading influence for material gain. Instead, cultural capture provides additional motivations to adopt industry-friendly positions that are likely to be in their long-term material self-interest. According to the theory of cognitive dissonance, people choose their preferences or beliefs to make them consistent with their actions.[106] If a regulator sees her job as protecting ordinary people and believes that financial institutions harm consumers, then siding with industry will create psychological tension; if instead she believes that free markets are good for ordinary people, she will be able to adopt industry-friendly (and self-interest–maximizing) positions without suffering cognitive dissonance.

This is not to say that culture capture was the sole or primary reason for the dominance of deregulatory ideas in Washington during the past two decades. Modern academic finance, at least in its more popular interpretations, appeared to justify the ideology of free financial markets; that ideology also received the enthusiastic support of conservative think tanks and media outlets eager to make the case against government regulation in any form. Old-fashioned electoral politics gave deregulatory presidents, beginning with Ronald Reagan, the opportunity to appoint officials who explicitly favored relaxing constraints on financial institutions long before they arrived in Washington. Well-funded, plausibly rational ideas can certainly go a long way in shaping the policy beliefs of agency staffers, especially when they are championed by political appointees. However, cultural capture is likely to have lent a helping hand.

---

[106] See George A. Akerlof and William T. Dickens, "The Economic Consequences of Cognitive Dissonance," *American Economic Review* 72 (June 1982): 307–19.

Cultural capture is not a complete explanation of financial regulators' behavior in the run-up to the financial crisis for another reason: the mechanisms that produce cultural capture are basic features of human interactions and therefore predate the recent cycle of financial deregulation. Although the potential for cultural capture may be a constant, there are several reasons why its effects may have been more powerful in recent years. Rapid innovation in the financial sector pushed regulators to make decisions regarding new activities such as complex derivatives where neither existing statutes nor previous regulatory actions provided much guidance; the increasing complexity of finance made it more difficult for agency employees to evaluate proposals on their merits, increasing the importance of proxies; the growth in lobbying expenditures beginning in the 1970s exacerbated the asymmetry of influence between the financial industry and competing interest groups; and the rapid growth of financial industry compensation unmistakably widened the status gap between major banks and federal agencies. Together, these factors made cultural capture an increasingly important reason why regulators might be swayed in favor of industry positions.

This chapter has discussed cultural capture in the context of financial regulation. In general, however, some factors that should make cultural capture a particularly important channel of industry influence are a high degree of similarity between industry representatives and regulators; an industry with a notable social purpose with which regulators can identify; an industry with high social, cultural, or intellectual status; many social connections between industry and regulators; and technically complex issues, for which it is not clear how the benefits of policy alternatives are shared. To some extent, these same factors can also contribute to traditional capture based on material self-interest. If we think of material capture and cultural capture as alternative strategies for industry, then a major determinant of the importance of cultural capture might simply be the availability of material capture as an option. If bribes are legal, they are the simplest and surest way of achieving the desired outcome; insofar as bribes and their cousins become illegal, difficult, or subject to public scrutiny, then cultural capture will become more important.

The final question to ask about cultural capture is what we should do about it. In this context, it is important to remember that cultural capture is the unavoidable byproduct of necessary interactions between human beings. It is not feasible and probably not desirable to strip all interactions between regulated industry and regulatory agencies of their human elements. The close relationships and repeat interactions that help make cultural capture possible may also promote socially beneficial information sharing and cooperation.[107] Indeed, as McCarty shows in this volume (see Chapter 5), an agency's ability to gain useful information from firm behavior can depend on the proximity between its preferences and firm preferences. Countering cultural capture may also be particularly difficult: for example, how do you prevent regulators from being influenced by the desire to maintain decent social relationships with repeat players?

However, several policies designed to protect against traditional capture could potentially limit the importance of cultural capture: by weakening the underlying mechanisms of influence, by reducing the imbalance between regulated industry and other interest groups, or by raising the scientific or evidentiary standards for agency decision making. Tightening restrictions on the revolving door – for example, extending the period of time during which ex-regulators are prohibited from lobbying their former agencies – could attenuate the bonds of identification that link regulator and regulated. In the case of the recent financial crisis, criminal prosecution of bankers or their institutions (where warranted by the facts, of course) could go some way toward reducing the prestige of the financial sector. On balance, however, the mechanisms of cultural capture are likely to continue to favor financial institutions over competing interest groups such as consumer advocates.

Negotiated rulemaking, in which competing interest groups are invited to the agency's table to negotiate proposed rules, could reduce cultural capture by helping to equalize the influence of different interest groups and making relationships more explicit and less informal.[108] A conceptually related approach is tripartism, in which a nongovernment organization (NGO) is given full access to the regulatory process and standing to enforce violations after the fact; competition between NGOs should limit the risk of capture.[109] Another possibility is the appointment of an official public advocate to represent the public interest or consumers' interests

---

[107] See Errol Meidinger, "Regulatory Culture: A Theoretical Outline," *Law & Policy* 9 (October 1987): 366. A similar dynamic may exist in corporate boards of directors, where collegiality can produce higher productivity and performance but where social ties can lead some members to "develop a sense of 'in-group' bias that colors how they evaluate claims by others . . . that threaten one or more group members." Donald C. Langevoort, "The Human Nature of Corporate Boards: Law, Norms, and the Unintended Consequences of Independence and Accountability," *Georgetown Law Journal* 89 (April 2001): 810–11.

[108] Negotiated Rulemaking Act of 1990, codified at 5 U.S.C. §§ 561–570. For an overview of negotiated rulemaking and some critiques, see Jody Freeman, "Collaborative Governance in the Administrative State," *UCLA Law Review* 45 (October 1997): 33–40.

[109] Ayres and Braithwaite, "Tripartism: Regulatory Capture and Empowerment." On tripartism and financial regulation, see also Baxter, "Capture in Financial Regulation."

in agency proceedings.[110] Schwarcz in this volume (see Chapter 13) discusses the strengths and weaknesses of similar consumer empowerment programs in insurance regulation. In each of these cases, one goal is to provide a counterbalance to industry power and influence, whether material or cultural.

Another general approach to the problem of cultural capture is to create an external check on the information and analysis used to justify agency actions. One possible source of external review is the Office of Information and Regulatory Affairs (OIRA), which has issued guidelines governing data quality and the use of peer review by administrative agencies; Bagley and Revesz[111] regard "OIRA's standardization of agency science as a salutary development for the regulatory state," but argue that it could go further. OIRA's generalist scope and its role in harmonizing regulations among affected agencies, discussed by Livermore and Revesz in this volume (see Chapter 15), could also ensure that an agency's actions are reviewed by people with different group identifications and relationship networks. Another example is provided by the advisory boards convened by some agencies to review the data and methodologies that they use. Although OIRA enforcement could help reduce agencies' dependence on "bad science," the external academic community might do a better job of ensuring that agencies consider a diversity of relevant opinion and research. In the financial context, this might have meant paying more attention to research by people such as Robert Shiller showing that markets are not always efficient and housing bubbles can occur.[112] However, it would be unrealistic to expect academic criticism alone to solve the problem of cultural capture. In 2005, Raghuram Rajan, one of the world's leading finance scholars, chose the Federal Reserve's main policy conference to argue that financial liberalization was making the global financial system less rather than more stable. He was strongly criticized, both by Fed Vice Chair Donald Kohn and by former Treasury Secretary Larry Summers, and Federal Reserve policy did not budge.[113] And, of course, academics can also be captured, as shown by Zingales in this volume (see Chapter 6).

---

[110] Rachel E. Barkow, "Insulating Agencies: Avoiding Capture Through Regulatory Design," *Texas Law Review* 89 (November 2010): 62–4.

[111] Bagley and Revesz, "Centralized Oversight of the Regulatory State," 1316.

[112] For an overview of empirical attacks on the efficient markets hypothesis, see Justin Fox, *The Myth of the Rational Market: A History of Risk, Reward, and Delusion on Wall Street* (New York: Harper Business, 2009), 191–210.

[113] Justin Lahart, "Mr. Rajan Was Unpopular (But Prescient) at Greenspan Party." *Wall Street Journal*, January 2, 2009. Available at http://online.wsj.com/article/SB 123086154114948151.html.

Because cultural capture takes advantage of unconscious biases that regulators become subject to, another approach is to attempt to "debias" those regulators through procedures or substantive rules designed to counteract those biases.[114] A common debiasing strategy is to encourage or force people to consider disconfirming information or counterarguments.[115] One way to approach this goal could be through policies that explicitly increase the set of backgrounds from which regulators are drawn, thereby requiring a diversity of viewpoints.[116] A more aggressive step could be institutionalizing independent "devil's advocates" within agencies to represent contrarian viewpoints; by forcing regulators to justify their positions using evidence and reason, they could reduce the influence of unconscious biases and reliance on illegitimate proxies.[117]

In the end, however, cultural capture may simply be harder than traditional capture to protect against. In the traditional capture model, a regulator who sides with one interest group out of self-interest would still accept a better offer from another interest group. When groups or ideas attain prestige of their own, however, and when people identify with groups or adopt ideas in part because of the status they confer, it is considerably harder for those people to identify the sources of their choices. Those choices become sticky and are not vulnerable either to a higher offer or to rational argument about the public interest. And so, although cultural capture may be less reliable than the traditional kind, it can also provide a long-term source of advantage for regulated industries that are able to mobilize it.

---

[114] See Christine Jolls and Cass R. Sunstein, "Debiasing Through Law," *Journal of Legal Studies* 35 (January 2006): 201–2.

[115] For example, forcing (experimental) plaintiffs and defendants to consider and list the weaknesses in their respective cases eliminated self-serving bias on each side, making it easier to reach settlement. Linda Babcock, George Loewenstein, and Samuel Issacharoff, "Creating Convergence: Debiasing Biased Litigants," *Law and Social Inquiry* 22 (1997): 918–20.

[116] Steven M. Davidoff, "The Government's Elite and Regulatory Capture," DealBook, *New York Times*, June 11, 2010. Available at http://dealbook.nytimes.com/2010/06/11/the-governments-elite-and-regulatory-capture/.

[117] On regulatory devil's advocates in general, see Brett McDonnell and Daniel Schwarcz, "Regulatory Contrarians," *North Carolina Law Review* 89 (2011): 1629–79. Similarly, Troy Paredes has suggested that corporate boards should include a "chief naysayer" to counter CEO overconfidence. Troy A. Paredes, "Too Much Pay, Too Much Deference: Behavioral Corporate Finance, CEOs, and Corporate Governance," *Florida State University Law Review* 32 (Winter 2005): 740–7.

5

Complexity, Capacity, and Capture

Nolan McCarty[1]

INTRODUCTION

In the debates on financial market reform that followed the Financial Crisis of 2007 and the Great Recession, reformers advocated three distinct
approaches. Some argued that governments should act to fundamentally
restructure the financial sector. Large banks should be broken up. Investment and commercial banks should be separated as they had been under
the Glass-Steagall reforms of the 1930s (or at least the investment activity
of commercial banks should be drastically restricted). Limits on the types
of financial products that could be marketed and taxes on financial trans-
actions were promoted. Opponents of government intervention positioned
themselves at the opposite position. They argued that a government-led
reconstruction of the financial marketplace would be counterproductive,
if not futile. Such actions would impede financial innovation and restrict
credit and liquidity. At most, according to this view, reform should get the
taxpayer off the hook for the failure of financial firms. The middle ground
in this debate was held by those who argued that the basic structure of the
financial sector should remain intact but that the capacity and powers of
regulatory agencies should be enhanced to better monitor the sector for
systemic risks, financial fraud, and predatory lending practices. The middle
ground, reflected in the Dodd-Frank financial reform bill, appears to have
won out.

Although much of the debate centered on the economic trade-offs
embedded in this approach, the issue is essentially one of politics and public

[1] Professor of Politics and Public Affairs, Woodrow Wilson School, Princeton University.
This chapter has been deeply influenced by joint work on the politics of finance with Keith
Poole, Howard Rosenthal, and Tom Romer. I also wish to thank seminar participants at
the Stanford Graduate School of Business.

administration. Can the government effectively regulate a large, complex, and interconnected financial sector? If the answer is yes, then the middle ground of enhanced regulatory supervision seems promising. If the answer is no, then the more extreme approaches are more compelling.

Unfortunately, there are many reasons to believe the answer might indeed be no. Perhaps financial markets and products are so complex that out-gunned agencies lack the capacity to detect systemic risk and fraud. Regulators may be so extremely dependent on the industry for information, expertise, and talent that they are not able to exercise independent regulatory authority. At best, under such conditions, the financial industry will be highly influential and exercise "weak" capture of the agency. At worst, the capture may be of the "strong" form such that deregulation or bright-line rules would serve the public interest better than discretionary regulation. Importantly, these forms of capture can arise even if the agency is optimally pursuing the public interest.

Although bureaucratic capacity and capture in complex policy environments are particularity salient in financial reform, these issues manifest themselves in a very large number of policy domains ranging from rate and service regulation to product and workplace safety to the environment. Despite the centrality of these concerns, political scientists have been slow to develop theories and models of how complexity, capacity, and capture interact in the regulatory sphere and what policymaking trade-offs these interactions induce.

To be sure, political scientists have focused on the role of information and expertise in regulatory settings. Much of political science scholarship on the structure and development of the regulatory state focuses on the decision of elected politicians to delegate policymaking authority to better informed experts in the bureaucracy. Because legislators are policy generalists rather than experts, they may find it difficult to select good policies in uncertain environments. Consequently, they grant bureaucratic specialists wide discretion in policy choice.[2]

However, the informational approach to delegation downplays at least four issues that are important for understanding regulation in complex policy domains. The first is that the informational delegation literature

---

[2] The seminal works in this genre include David Epstein and Sharyn O'Halloran, *Delegating Powers: A Transaction Cost Politics Approach to Policy Making under Separate Powers* (New York: Cambridge University Press, 1999); John D. Huber and Charles R. Shipan, *Deliberate Discretion? The Institutional Foundations of Bureaucratic Autonomy* (New York: Cambridge University Press, 2002); and Jonathan Bendor and Adam Meirowitz, "Spatial Models of Delegation," *American Political Science Review* 98 (2004): 293–310.

does not problematize the source of bureaucratic expertise and information. Bureaucratic expertise is often taken as exogenous (bureaucrats are simply assumed to have it) or as the result of human capital investments (bureaucrats can pay to get it).[3] Likewise, information is something that the bureaucrat is assumed to obtain either exogenously or endogenously by paying some cost or exerting effort. In this regard, the approach in political science is quite different from that of regulatory economics, in which the regulator's extraction of information from the regulated firm is the central problem.[4]

Second, political scientists often model bureaucratic drift and regulatory capture as exogenous. The preference divergence between politicians and bureaucrats is taken as more or less fixed and is not influenced directly by the nature of the regulatory or policymaking environment.[5] Consequently, the legislative response to drift and capture is either to limit the bureaucrat's discretion through ex ante constraints and/or ex post oversight or to influence agency preferences through the politics of appointments.[6]

Third, much of the work on bureaucratic delegation assumes that bureaucrats efficiently and effectively implement their target policies. However, as Huber and McCarty[7] pointed out, imperfect implementation generates ex post control problems for political principals.[8] When there are errors in policy implementation, it is more difficult for political principals to detect agents who attempt to implement policies that the principals do not approve. This problem enhances the possibility of bureaucratic drift and capture.

[3] See Sean Gailmard and John W. Patty, "Slackers and Zealots: Civil Service Reform, Policy Discretion, and Bureaucratic Expertise," *American Journal of Political Science* 51 (2004): 873–89; Bendor and Meirowitz, "Spatial Models of Delegation."

[4] For a recent review of the economic literature on regulation and capture, see Ernesto Dal Bó, "Regulatory Capture: A Review," *Oxford Review of Economic Policy* 22 (2006): 203–25.

[5] Much of the empirical work on delegation in the United States assumes that bureaucratic preferences are derived from the preferences of the president; see for example, Epstein and O'Halloran, *Delegating Powers*, Bendor and Meirowitz, "Spatial Models of Delegation," and Nolan McCarty, "The Appointments Dilemma," *American Journal of Political Science* 48 (2004): 413–28, are exceptions in that they consider the optimal preference divergence between principals and agents.

[6] On the use of statutory discretion, see Epstein and O'Halloran, *Delegating Powers*, and Huber and Shipan, *Deliberate Discretion?* On appointments, see McCarty, "The Appointments Dilemma."

[7] John D. Huber and Nolan McCarty, "Bureaucratic Capacity, Delegation, and Political Reform," *American Political Science Review* 98 (2004): 481–94.

[8] For counter examples, see Huber and McCarty, "Bureaucratic Capacity, Delegation, and Political Reform"; Bendor and Meirowitz, "Spatial Models of Delegation."

Fourth, the literature often draws little distinction between information and knowledge. Expertise is treated as the obtainment of missing data that can be applied to a known model to generate some desired policy outcome. However, expertise also reflects knowledge of the underlying model. As I explain later, treating expertise as missing data can make inferences by nonexperts too easy, which in turn undermines the value of expertise. The more encompassing notion of expertise as both data and the knowledge of what to do with it makes deference to experts more likely.

In an attempt to fill in some of the gaps in our understanding of regulatory policymaking, I develop a simple model of policymaking in *complex* policy domains. By complex, I mean that bureaucrats find it very difficult to establish autonomous sources of information and expertise about the consequences of different policies. In such cases, regulators are highly dependent on the regulated industry for both policy-relevant information and expertise. Financial regulation fits these assumptions well. In a less complex regulatory environment, the government might mitigate any informational advantages of the regulated industry by hiring its own experts to serve on the staffs of legislative and regulatory agencies. However, in finance and other complex environments, the wage premium on expertise might be so large that the government cannot match the expertise of the industry. For example, Thomas Philippon and Ariell Reshef[9] have recently estimated that on the eve of the Financial Crisis, wages in the financial sector were 70 percent higher than those of comparably skilled and educated workers outside the sector. Governmental pay scales cannot compete with Wall Street for talent.[10]

Another aspect of complex environments is that the necessary expertise and training might be available only through the industry or in professional schools and training programs in which the curriculum is favorable to industry interests. In finance, there are few opportunities to acquire the necessary expertise about financial markets outside of the industry or from business schools. Consequently, financial regulators often share strong social ties to the industry and are more sympathetic on average to the industry's interests and viewpoints.[11]

[9] Thomas Philippon and Ariell Reshef, "Wages and Human Capital in the U.S. Financial Industry: 1909–2006," Working Paper 14644, National Bureau of Economic Research, January 2009.

[10] Ibid. Some financial regulatory agencies, such as the Federal Reserve, have higher pay schedules than those of the rest of the federal government. However, even these agencies pay much less than Wall Street does for similar job qualifications.

[11] For similar arguments and a review of the social, cultural, and psychological mechanisms that produce such effects, see James Kwak (Chapter 4 in this volume).

Together these features of complex policy environments invariably create trade-offs between expertise and capacity on one hand and autonomy on the other. In this chapter, I explore the implications of these trade-offs by developing a simple game theoretic model. In the model, a principal must decide whether to create a new agency (or delegate power to an existing one) to regulate the activities of a firm.[12] The policy domain is complex in that knowledge of the implications of different policy choices is embedded in the firm. Unless the agency is willing and able to commit significant resources to building its own expertise, it can learn about the policy environment only through monitoring the firm. This learning, however, is imperfect, and the information obtained from monitoring declines in the complexity of the policy environment.

The main result of the model is that as policy becomes more complex, regulatory outcomes are increasingly biased toward those preferred by the firm, consistent with this volume's notion of weak capture. This bias may become so severe that strong capture obtains, and the political principal prefers not to delegate power to the agency at all. If the outcomes are going to be those preferred by the firm anyway, the principal may prefer to economize on the fixed cost of regulation and let the firm go unregulated. Alternatively, if the outcomes associated with an unregulated firm are too unfavorable, the principal may decide either to ban the firm's activities or select some other bright-line rule that can be implemented by less expert bureaucrats. Importantly, capture may arise in the model even if the principal and agency have perfectly aligned preferences. Because of its expertise advantages, the firm may influence the agency without shifting its policy preferences. Moreover, the model suggests a rationale for why the principal may prefer that the agency have pro-firm preferences. Together these results suggest that preference divergence between the principal and agency is not an accurate indicator of the extent of capture.

THE MODEL

In this section, I sketch a model of the decision to regulate in a complex policy environment. I present the basic results and the underlying intuitions but leave most derivations and proofs to the appendix.

To simplify, I assume that there are just three relevant actors: a principal, denoted L; a regulatory agency, denoted A; and a firm, denoted F. For

---

[12] As discussed later, this principal may be a legislator, a president, or the public depending on the empirical or normative aims.

positive analyses of regulation, one might think of L as the majority legislative coalition or the president. However, it may also represent the "public interest" if one is interested in normative analyses.[13]

So that the model may be generalized across a large number of regulatory settings, I do not explicitly model the firm's production or the marketing of its output. Rather, I assume that each of the model's actors has preferences over *regulatory outcomes*. Let $X \quad R$ denote the set of outcomes. I interpret an outcome $x \quad X$ as the social cost imposed by the firm's activities, for a given level of social benefits. Because the firm internalizes social costs and benefits to a lesser degree than the principal, it is natural to assume that the principal prefers lower outcomes on this dimension than does the firm. To clarify this notion, consider an example from financial regulation. Suppose regulations are targeted at the degree of economic concentration in the financial sector. Concentration is presumed to have benefits in terms of economies of scale and costs in terms of increased systemic risk. One can think of x as reflecting a specific trade-off between the benefits of the economy of scale and the reduction of systemic risk. The principal might prefer low values of x where the economies of scale and the risks are small. The firm might prefer larger values because it captures more of the value of the scale economies and does not fully internalize the risk.[14]

So let l, a, and f be the ideal regulatory outcomes for L, A, and F, respectively. I assume that each player has quadratic preferences so that the utility of outcome x for player i is $\quad (x \quad i)^2$. Furthermore, I set $l = 0$ and $f = 1$. This specification of ideal outcomes is simply a normalization. All that matters is that L prefers less social costs per unit of social benefit than does the firm. In the analysis that follows, I consider a variety of assumptions about the preferences of the regulatory agency.

Following much of the literature on delegation to experts, I model expertise as the knowledge of how to obtain specific outcomes. However, as I discuss in the introduction, the required knowledge is not reducible to missing data as in previous models. Those models assume that outcomes are generated by a combination of policy choices and a random shock. Nonexperts know the relationship between the shock and the outcome, but

[13] Clearly, presidents and legislators can themselves be captured, but to keep things simple I focus only on the influence of the firm on administrative agents and not elected ones. For this reason, the empirical implications of the model may deviate from the normative ones – i.e., maximizing legislative utility may be different from pursuing the public interest.

[14] It is important to glean from this discussion that I intend to differentiate regulatory outcomes from ex post outcomes such as a financial crisis, nuclear meltdown, or offshore rig blowout. Rather, the regulatory outcomes might be thought of as probability distributions on the ultimate outcomes.

do not know the precise value of the shocks. Experts know the value of the random shock and are therefore able to choose policy to get a desired outcome.[15] Thus expertise is a simple question of missing data. However, in regulatory settings, regulators have ample opportunities to obtain data through regulatory reporting requirements and investigatory powers. What is more relevant is whether the agency knows what to do with the data. In other words, expertise also includes knowledge of the model that links policies and outcomes.

Recently, Steven Callander pointed out an important limitation of the standard model of expertise. Because it implies that the nonexpert need only observe one policy and one outcome to become an expert, the principal generally has an ex post incentive to renege on its delegation of policymaking authority and move policy toward its preferred outcome. Callander argued instead that the policy choices of experts should only reveal *local* information; that is, the principal should be able to make inferences about the effects of policies that are close to the one chosen by the expert but learn little about the effects of very distinct approaches.[16]

Callander's critique is extremely pertinent here, because I am precisely interested in those situations in which policy information is difficult to obtain. These criticisms are even more important in thinking about the informational asymmetry between the regulator and firm. One ought not assume that regulators are able to draw precise inferences about the consequences of policy choices simply by observing the firm's behavior.

So I develop a model of policy expertise with both of these considerations in mind.[17] First, I assume that any of the actors can become expert enough to implement a specific regulatory outcome by incurring a cost. Formally, if agent i selects regulatory outcome x and pays c_i, she can perfectly implement x. Returning to the example of financial regulation, suppose the regulator wanted to trade off economies of scale and systemic risk consistent with regulatory outcome x. At some cost (perhaps a prohibitive one), the regulator could hire sufficient numbers of economists to estimate the level of concentration that produces x and enough lawyers to write the regulations that enforce x. Because information obtained by paying these costs is acquired unilaterally and not through interaction with other agents, I label it

---

[15] Formally, the link between outcome x and policy p is given by $x = p + \omega$, where ω is a random variable observed by the regulator but not the principal policymaker.

[16] See Steven Callander, "A Theory of Policy Expertise," *Quarterly Journal of Political Science* 3 (2008): 123–40.

[17] Callander proposed a model similar to the one I pursue here. Unfortunately, his framework was not tractable for my purposes.

independent information. It is reasonable to assume that the costs of acquiring independent information are lower for the firm than for the regulatory agency and lower for the agency than the principal. For simplicity, I invoke an extreme form of this assumption and set $c_f = 0$, $c_a > 0$, and $c_l = \quad$.[18]

Second, I assume that the inferences other agents draw from observing the policy choices of others are limited and local. Therefore, the regulator cannot simply monitor the firm's actions that led to x and use that information to perfectly implement some other policy x. Although the agent can observe some of the firm's efforts to implement x, she does not know exactly how to modify them to get a distinct outcome. Formally, I assume that if any agent tries to implement *target outcome* x after only observing x, the *realized outcome* is $x + \omega$, where ω has mean zero and variance $|x \quad x|\sigma^2$. This setup captures the notion that it is easier to implement outcomes that are closer to existing outcomes because the variance term is close to zero when x is close to x. Moreover, the term σ^2 provides a handy index of complexity. When σ^2 is large, policymaking is complex in that moving from x to x is more fraught with uncertainty. I call information based on observing a policy choice *embedded*.

The assumptions about embedded information are presented in Figure 5.1. In this figure, regulatory outcome x was implemented by an expert agent. As there is no variance in this outcome, the frequency distribution is a spike at x. Now assume that nonexpert agents attempt to implement two distinct outcomes x and x with embedded information. The distributions of realized outcomes following these targets have positive variances. The solid black and gray lines denote the distribution of outcomes for targets x and x, respectively. Because the target outcome x is farther from x than x, the variation in the outcomes following its attempted implementation is much greater than that following x. The dashed lines represent the effects of increasing σ^2 as the variation in outcomes for both x and x increase.[19]

---

[18] Again, it is important to distinguish between what I call regulatory outcomes and ultimate outcomes. That the firm can implement a regulatory outcome with zero error does not imply that there is no risk associated with final outcomes. Indeed, the perfect implementation of a regulatory outcome desired by the firm may create substantial risks for society.

[19] My approach is also related to Alexander V. Hirsch and Kenneth W. Shotts, "Policy-Specific Information and Informal Agenda Power," *American Journal of Political Science* 56 no. 1 (2012): 67–83, and Jeffrey R. Lax and Charles M. Cameron, "Bargaining and Opinion Assignment on the U.S. Supreme Court," *Journal of Law, Economics, and Organization* 23 (2007): 276–302, who assumed that informed policymakers invest effort to produce higher quality policies (equivalent to low variance policies in my model). However, none of these investments in information or quality are expropriable by other agents; if the policy proposal is amended, the quality investment is lost. Alan Wiseman, "Delegation

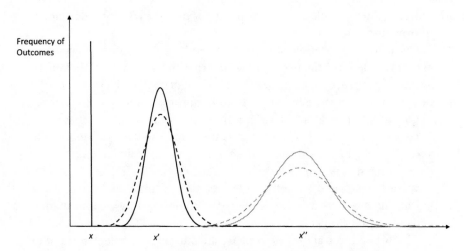

Figure 5.1. Regulatory Outcomes

To illustrate the assumptions of the model, consider another example from financial regulation. On May 6, 2010, the Dow Jones Industrial Average lost 900 points in a matter of minutes. The belief that this "flash crash" was caused or exacerbated by high-frequency trading led both regulators and the industry to consider new regulations, including circuit breakers that would stop trading securities whose price has fluctuated too much. The exchanges and their private regulator, the Financial Industry Regulatory Authority (FINRA), moved first to formulate rules for such circuit breakers. The Securities and Exchange Commission (SEC) therefore had the choice of accepting the FINRA standards, modifying them in various ways, or developing different ones from scratch. In my model, accepting the FINRA standards leads to the regulatory outcome targeted by the industry. However, modifying the proposal would lead to outcomes that are closer in expectation to the SEC's preferences, presumably a more aggressive set of circuit breakers. However, because of the SEC's limited expertise and capacity, changes in the target outcome may have unintended consequences. Requiring trading halts for smaller price changes may distort markets too much. So the SEC may be hesitant to change the FINRA proposal too drastically. Finally, my model assumes that the SEC would

and Positive-Sum Bureaucracies, *Journal of Politics* 71 (2009): 998–1014, also proposed a model of regulatory review in which adjusting rules set by agency experts is costly. However, in his model, the marginal cost of policy adjustment at the target policy is zero. Therefore, all agency rules are amended in equilibrium. In my model, however, the marginal cost of adjusting policy is always positive so that the agency may choose not to override the firm's decision.

only develop a completely new proposal if it paid the cost for independent information.[20]

Given my specification of preferences and the models of independent and embedded information, I now describe the sequence of actions of agents. These are represented graphically in Figure 5.2. In the first stage, the principal L chooses whether or not to allow the firm to engage in the activity in question. If L decides to ban the activity, the realized outcome has mean $q < 0$ and variance σ_q^2. Under this assumption, the ban is economically and politically inefficient. All of the actors in the model would prefer any target outcome $x < q$ to a ban were it known how to implement it with a variance less than σ_q^2. Another interpretation of this choice is that it is a bright-line rule that can be implemented with considerably less information and bureaucratic capacity.

Alternatively, if L allows the activity, she must choose whether or not to create an agency to regulate the firm. If the principal creates the agency, she pays a fixed cost κ. This cost reflects the resources of staffing and funding an agency. In the simplest version of the model, the ideal point of the new agency a is exogenous and known to the principal and the firm. I subsequently relax this assumption and allow the principal to directly influence the agency's preferences.[21] I label the three possible outcomes or regimes as *banned, regulated,* and *unregulated.*

In the unregulated regime, the firm implements a regulatory outcome and the game ends. Because $c_f = 0$, the firm perfectly implements the regulatory outcome of its choice. Clearly, F chooses $x_f = 1$. Consequently, F earns a payoff of 0 and L gets one equal to 1.

Outcomes in the regulated regime are the most interesting. In this regime, A observes F's policy choice x_f and then has two choices. First, A may choose to pay c_a to obtain independent policy information. With this information, A implements the policy outcome of its choice. Clearly, A implements outcome $x = a$. Therefore, the payoffs when the agency is independently informed are $u_a = c_a, u_l = a^2,$ and $u_f = (1 \quad a)^2.$

---

[20] In September 2010, the SEC adopted the FINRA rules. See "SEC Approves Rules Expanding Stock-by-Stock Circuit Breakers and Clarifying Process for Breaking Erroneous Trades," U.S. Securities and Exchange Commission, September 10, 2010. http://www.sec.gov/news/press/2010/2010-167.htm, accessed July 10, 2011.

[21] The exogenous agency preference model is most appropriate in one of two situations. First, it may reflect the effects of the separation of powers in which the legislature makes the decision of whether to create the agency, but the executive retains the authority for staffing the agency. See McCarty, "The Appointments Dilemma." Second, the assumption is consistent with the limiting case of perfect capture, in which the firm or some other outside interest controls the agency.

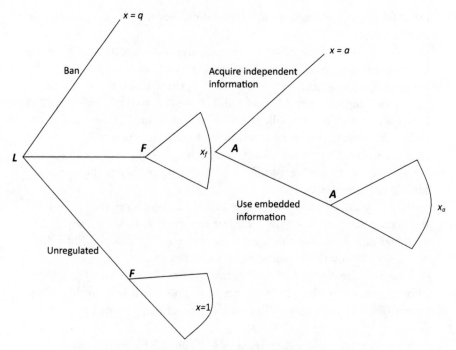

Figure 5.2. The Complex Policy Model

The agency's second option is to forgo the acquisition of independent information and target a different outcome based on embedded information. If the agency chooses to use embedded information, it understands that any attempt to implement a distinct target outcome $x = x_f$ leads to a random outcome with mean x and $|x - x^f|\sigma^2$.

Given these beliefs, the agency's optimal use of embedded information is to choose x_a to maximize its expected utility. This expected utility can be written as:[22]

$$(x_a - a)^2 - |x_f - x_a|\sigma^2.$$

In words, A faces a trade-off between increasing its utility from the target outcome and increasing the implementation variance. It can choose a target outcome x_a close to a to maximize its utility from the expected outcome (the first term in the expression). However, if doing so involves a policy

---

[22] This derivation uses the fact that $E[(a - x - \omega)^2] = E[(a - x)^2] + \text{var}(\omega)$; see Nolan McCarty and Adam Meirowitz, *Political Game Theory* (New York: Cambridge University Press, 2006).

target far from x_f, the uncertainty about the policy outcomes increases (the second term).

In the appendix, I show that A's optimal target outcome under embedded information is x_a, which is equal to the maximum of $a + \frac{\sigma^2}{2}$ and x_f. The first of these expressions, $x_a = a + \frac{\sigma^2}{2}$, is optimal when the firm's target x_f is much higher than A's ideal point. Here the agency uses embedded information to adjust the policy toward its ideal point. However, due to the uncertainty involved in using embedded information, the agency moves the target outcome only so far. It stops at exactly $a + \frac{\sigma^2}{2}$ so that the difference between the agency's ideal policy and the target policy is an increasing function of complexity σ^2.

If x_f is relatively close to the agency's ideal point so that $x_f < a + \frac{\sigma^2}{2}$, the agency does not have any incentive to move the outcome target. The marginal utility of any movement toward the agency's ideal point is outweighed by the marginal increase in policy variance.

Now that I have described how the agency uses (or fails to use) embedded information, I consider whether it has an incentive to acquire independent information. Here I consider the two cases described previously: $x_a = a + \frac{\sigma^2}{2}$ and $x_a = x_f$.

In the first case, the agency's payoffs from embedded information are:

$$\frac{\sigma^4}{4} \quad \left| x_f \quad a \quad \frac{\sigma^2}{2} \right| \sigma^2,$$

where the first term reflects the average policy distance from a, $\frac{\sigma^2}{2}$, and the second is the resulting policy variation. The payoffs to acquiring independent information (and implementing $x_a = a$) are $\quad c_a$. A simple comparison of these utilities reveals that A prefers independent information if and only if:

$$a + \frac{c_a}{\sigma^2} \quad \frac{\sigma^2}{2} \quad x_f.$$

This result reveals that the agency is more likely to choose independent information when the firm pursues an extreme policy, when its expertise costs c_a are low, or policy complexity σ^2 is high.

Now consider the second case. Here $x_a = x_f$ so that A compares a utility $(x_f \quad a)^2$ for embedded information with a utility of $\quad c_a$. So the agency prefers independent information if and only if $a + \quad \overline{c_a} < x_f$. In this case complexity plays no part in the calculus (because embedded information is not actually used). However, the effects of the firm's target outcome and the agency's expertise costs are the same as in the first case.

Having specified the agency's best response to the target outcome of the firm x_f, I now derive the firm's optimal target. Basically, the firm's choice boils down to three options. First, it could set a target so extreme that the agency decides to acquire independent information. Second, it could set a relatively extreme target that the agency might modify using embedded information. Or third, the firm might choose a policy that sufficiently accommodates the agency such that no regulatory revision is necessary.

It is easy to see that the first option is a losing proposition. Inducing the agency to acquire independent information results in an outcome of a, whereas I demonstrated earlier that the firm can always appease the agency by choosing a target strictly greater than a. Therefore, the firm will not provoke the agency sufficiently that it chooses to acquire independent information. That the second strategy never pays is just a little more subtle. Suppose the firm did choose some x_f in the expectation that the regulator would modify it to x_a. The expected outcome would be x_a, but there would be variation in the realized outcome equal to $|x_f \quad x_a|\sigma^2$. However, the firm could just as well have chosen x_a in the first place, which would not be modified and would produce no uncertainty in implementation. Clearly, the latter choice dominates the former.

So it is clear that the firm would like to deter the agency from using either embedded or independent information. Therefore, the firm's outcome choice must satisfy both $x_f < a + \frac{\sigma^2}{2}$ (else the agency uses embedded information) and $x_f < a + \quad \overline{c_a}$ (else the agency acquires independent information). Of course, the firm's best regulatory outcome that satisfies these constraints is the smaller of 1 and $a + \min\{ \quad \overline{c_a}, \frac{\sigma^2}{2} \}$.

To simplify the notation in what follows, let $\theta = \min\{ \quad \overline{c_a}, \frac{\sigma^2}{2} \}$ so that $x_f = \min\{1, a + \theta\}$. The new term θ has an important interpretation. It reflects the deviation in the final target outcome that can be attributed to the firm's informational and expertise advantages. So henceforward I refer to θ as the firm's *expertise rent*. It is important to note that this expertise rent is increasing in both the costs of independent information (reflected by c_a) and in the complexity of the policy (reflected by σ^2). Because the equilibrium policy target is $a + \theta$, the firm gains not only from the expertise rent but from a *preference rent* when the agency's ideal point is increased. Both sources of rent contribute to the firm's ability to capture the agency. An important implication of this result is that the preference rent is not necessary for a policy bias toward the firm. Even in the case of $a = 1 = 0$,

Table 5.1. *Payoffs and regulatory outcomes*

Regime	Principal	Firm	Agency	Target outcome
Banned	$-q^2 - \sigma_q^2$	$-(1-q)^2 - \sigma_q^2$	na	q
Unregulated	-1	0	na	1
Regulated – Independent Info	$-a^2 - \kappa$	$-(1-a)^2$	$-c_a$	a
Regulated – Embedded Info	$-(a+\theta)^2 - \kappa$	$-(1-a-\theta)^2$	$-\theta^2$	$a+\theta$

the equilibrium policy target remains $\theta > 0$. So better control of the agent by the principal will not alleviate capture (even in the normative benchmark where the principal is the public).[23]

Finally, I now back up to the first stage of the game and analyze the principal's decision to ban, regulate, or not regulate. Given that the regulatory regime produces $x_f = a + \theta$, the principal's utility from creating the regulatory regime is $-\kappa - (a+\theta)^2$. Recall that the payoffs from banned and unregulated firms are $-q^2 - \sigma_q^2$ and -1, respectively. Consequently, L prefers regulation to nonregulation if and only if $\sqrt{1-\kappa} > a + \theta$ and a regulatory regime to a ban if and only if $\sqrt{q^2 + \sigma_q^2 - \kappa} > a + \theta$. Therefore, two factors make regulation less attractive than the ban or unregulated outcome: preference divergence from the agency, a, and the size of the firm's expertise rent. When the sum of these terms is high, the capture induced by the preference and expertise rents is sufficiently strong that regulation is less attractive. Of course, regulation is also less likely to emerge when the fixed cost of creating the regulatory regime, κ, is large. If the regulatory approach is eschewed, the choice of a ban versus nonregulation depends exclusively on the comparison of the firm's ideal policy with the status quo outcome and variance. Clearly, if the ban is not too inefficient (q close to zero), the ban would be preferred. The same is true when the implications of the ban are well known so that σ_q^2 is low.

Table 5.1 summarizes the findings from the basic model by listing the payoffs to the actors as well as the final policy outcome for each of the regimes. For completeness, I include the payoffs and outcomes for regulation with independent information even though this situation does not occur on the equilibrium path.

---

[23] Although, as noted in the next section, the principal could eliminate capture in this baseline model by appointing an agent with extreme anti-firm preferences. However, in a more realistic extension of the model, this is not generally true.

PROXIMITY LEARNING

In the basic model described previously, the ideal point of the agency a is an exogenous feature of the political environment. However, in reality, the agency's preferences are influenced directly by both the principal and the firm. In the baseline model, the preferences of the principal and firm over the agency's ideal point are clear. L prefers $a = \theta$ so that the preference rent and the expertise rent cancel out and generate a policy outcome of zero. Therefore, absent any other consideration, the principal would like to delegate to an agency that is somewhat antagonistic to the firm. Conversely, the firm prefers a favorable agency with ideal point $a = 1$.[24]

However, these diametrically opposed preferences over the agency's ideal point depend on a key assumption: that the agency's ability to use embedded information is independent of its ideal point. There are several theoretical and empirical reasons to doubt such an assumption. On theoretical grounds, it runs counter to the basic findings of models of strategic communication that predict that more information can be communicated when there is less preference divergence between the sender and receiver.[25] Although my model departs from the strategic communication framework, it seems reasonable to relax the assumption that learning is independent of preference divergence. A second reason is empirical. In many regulatory settings (especially financial market regulation), the regulators may share social, educational, and professional ties to the industry that both cause the regulators to sympathize with the industry and make it easier for the regulators to extract embedded information.

To capture these effects, I consider an extension of the model in which the agency's ability to learn from the firm is a function of the preference distance of the agency from the firm. I capture this relationship by assuming that the variance associated with amending policy x with x (based on embedded information) is $h(|f - a|)|x - x|\sigma^2$, where $h(\cdot)$ is an increasing, convex function. I label this effect *proximity learning* because the agency learns more from the firm's actions the more proximate its preferences are to those of the firm's. This idea can be captured visually by returning to Figure 5.1. Now I assume that the solid curves represent the information about

---

[24] The firm's payoff is maximized at $u_f = 0$ for any agency preference such that $a > 1$ $min\{ \ \overline{c}_a, \frac{\sigma^2}{2} \}$.

[25] See Vincent Crawford and Joel Sobel, "Strategic Information Transmission," *Econometrica* 50 (1982): 1431–51, and Thomas W. Gilligan and Keith Krehbiel, "Collective Information and Standing Committees: An Informational Rationale for Restrictive Amendment Procedures," *Journal of Law, Economics, and Organization* 3 (1987): 287–335.

the consequences of policy change for an agent close to the firm and that the dashed curves represent the beliefs of an agency far from the firm. To simplify the analysis, I focus on the case in which the cost of independent information c_a is sufficiently high that the agency never chooses to acquire it.[26]

The agency's problem is solved exactly as before by maximizing its expected utility function that includes the negative of the sum of the expected outcome distance and the outcome variance. The agency's optimum is now:

$$x_a = min\left\{a + h(1 \quad a)\frac{\sigma^2}{2}, x_f\right\}.$$

Just as before, the firm has an incentive to deter a regulatory adjustment by choosing:

$$x_f = a + min\left\{h(1 \quad a)\frac{\sigma^2}{2}, 1 \quad a\right\}.$$

This solution is very similar to that presented earlier, only now the expertise rent is given by $h(1 \quad a)\frac{\sigma^2}{2}$. From the firm's perspective, a more sympathetic agency is something of a mixed bag. On one hand, the agency is more likely to tolerate outcomes close to the firm's ideal point. However, on the other hand, the firm's expertise rent is decreasing in a (because $h(\cdot)$ is an increasing function). In fact, if the marginal effect of preference proximity on the outcome variance is large enough, the firm gets a worse outcome when a moves toward its ideal point. The intuition is that under such circumstances, the expertise rent dissipates much faster than the agency's ideal point increases. However, beyond some point, the firm benefits unambiguously from a sympathetic agency as an agency close to its ideal point accepts $x_f = 1$. However, the firm is always weakly worse off with an agency whose ability to use embedded information increases with preference proximity to the firm.

The situation for the principal is just the opposite. By allowing A's preferences to move in the direction of the firm, the principal gains from dissipating the expertise rent at the loss of its own preference rent. So if the informational effect of preference proximity is large enough, the principal would prefer to create an agency closer to the firm's ideal point.

[26] Although I have only considered proximity learning effects related to embedded information, proximity effects of independent information can be modeled by allowing the expertise cost to decline with the proximity of the agency to the firm. The results of that model are qualitatively similar to those discussed here.

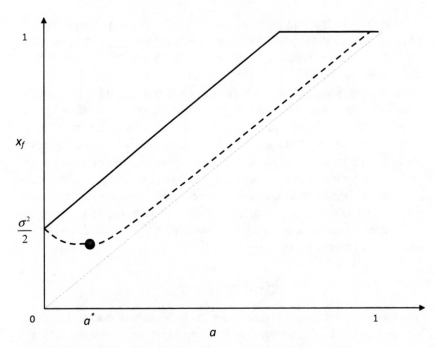

Figure 5.3. Policy Outcomes with Proximity Learning Effect

Figure 5.3 illustrates the policy outcomes for various assumptions about the proximity learning effect. The solid line represents the baseline case in which there is no proximity learning effect. In this case, the expertise rent is constant for all agency ideal points a (plotted on the horizontal axis). Therefore, the policy outcome (plotted on the vertical axis) is parallel to the 45 line (the thin line that represents $x_a = a$) until the policy reaches 1, where it remains for all higher values of a.

The thicker dashed line represents the policy when there is a proximity learning effect. The learning effect is represented by the decreasing gap between the dashed line and the 45 line. In this case, the information rent dissipates sufficiently fast for low values of a that policy moves toward the principal's ideal point. Clearly, the principal would prefer an agency located at a , the position corresponding to the minimum policy outcome (denoted by the black circle) to one located at her ideal point of 0. I should further note that proximity learning weakly advantages the principal for all values of a. Therefore, the existence of proximity learning effects makes it more likely that the L prefers a regulatory regime to a ban or the unregulated outcome.

That the principal may prefer an agency that leans toward the preferences of the firm has implications for our thinking about regulatory capture. An agency whose preferences are more aligned with the regulated firm than those of the legislative principal need not be evidence of capture. As noted previously, preference divergence is not necessary for capture. This proximity learning model implies that it need not be sufficient. In the case illustrated in Figure 5.3, the firm would be better off with the larger expertise rent that comes from $a = 0$ than it is when the agency is located at a . Therefore, in evaluating the extent of capture, it is important to distinguish optimal agency designs that distinguish the effects of complexity from more illicit forms of capture.[27] My results nicely complement those of Carpenter,[28] who argued that in the context of product approval, consumer welfare may be enhanced by a regulator who appears biased toward the incumbent firms in the industry.

INFLUENCE CAPTURE

The baseline model demonstrates how the firm's expertise advantage leads to pro-firm biases and capture. The proximity learning model shows that in some cases, the principal may wish to offset the expertise bias by increasing the pro-firm preference bias of the agency. However, clearly the firm often has incentives to increase the preference bias well beyond what the principal would tolerate. The firm may pressure the president to appoint an agency head sympathetic to the firm and oppose the confirmation of someone who is not. However, much of what firms do is to incentivize the agency to make policy choices that are more favorable to the firm without directly affecting the agency's policy preferences. So now I consider a simple extension of the model in which the firm may transfer resources to the agency in exchange for not interfering with the firm's policy choices. I call this a model of *influence capture*. Although it may be natural to think of these transfers as bribes, they can take many less questionable and more legal forms, such as the creation of expectations for future employment of the regulators and political support for the agency in the legislature.

[27] Frederick J. Boehmke, Sean Gailmard, and John Wiggs Patty, "Whose Ear to Bend? Information Sources and Venue Choice in Policy-Making," *Quarterly Journal of Political Science* 1 (2005): 139–69, also provided a rationale for delegating to an agent who is more sympathetic to the firm than is the principal. The underlying mechanism is quite different, however. In their model, the decision of the firm to lobby the legislature rather than a favorably biased agency sends a stronger signal that the state of the world is one in which the firm and legislature share policy goals.

[28] Daniel Carpenter, "Protection without Capture: Product Approval by a Politically Responsive, Learning Regulator," *American Political Science Review* 98 (2004): 613–31.

In this extension, the firm offers a transfer schedule $t(x_f)$ that specifies resources transferred to the agency if it accepts firm policy proposal x_f. I assume that the firm has all the power in this influence market so that it can make a take-it-or-leave-it offer. As I show in the appendix, the optimal transfer schedule is

$$t(x_f) = \begin{cases} 0 & \text{if } x_f \quad a+\theta \\ (x_f \quad a)^2 \quad (x_f \quad a)\sigma^2 + \frac{\sigma^4}{4} & \text{if } x_f > a+\theta \end{cases}.$$

This schedule assumes that if the agency rejects the offer and adjusts policy, it does so optimally by setting policy to $a + \theta$ based on embedded information. Now I consider whether the firm is willing to provide the required resources. Assuming that the firm maximizes its policy utility minus the transfers paid out, the firm's target policy is

$$x_f = \begin{cases} \frac{1+a+\theta}{2} & \text{if } 1 > a+\theta \\ 1 & \text{if } a+\theta \quad 1 \end{cases},$$

and the equilibrium level of transfers are

$$t(x_f) = \begin{cases} \frac{(1 \quad a+\theta)^2}{4} \quad \theta(1 \quad a) & \text{if } 1 > a+\theta \\ 0 & \text{if } a+\theta \quad 1 \end{cases}.$$

Two features of this equilibrium are noteworthy.[29] First, whenever the "no influence" outcome is $a + \theta$ implemented on embedded information, the firm uses transfers to move the outcome to $\frac{1+a+\theta}{2}$, which happens to be the midpoint between the firm's ideal points and the equilibrium policy in the game without transfers. Therefore, the overall regulatory outcome continues to be an increasing function of the expertise rent.[30] Second, the level of the transfer depends on the expertise rent. When the expertise rent is large, the payment is lower. The complexity of the policy benefits the firm through lower transfers and better policy outcomes. Therefore, this model suggests a strong link between the opportunity for expertise capture and influence capture.

A feature of the influence capture model is that the transfers are easy to detect by the principal. If the principal observes the agency's ideal point and the policy outcome, she can infer that a transfer occurred whenever $x > a + \theta$. So if the principal has sanctions at her disposal, the influence capture equilibrium may unravel. A more interesting scenario, therefore, involves the case in which the agency takes unobserved policy actions.

[29] Both of these results are proven in the appendix.
[30] It is important, however, to know that the distortion in regulatory policy caused by the transfers $\frac{1+a+\theta}{2}$ $(a+\theta)$ decreases in the expertise rent. This result is true precisely because the firm does so well in the model without transfers when this rent is large.

In such cases, the principal may not be able to perfectly detect influence capture, but can only draw inferences about whether it occurred from the realized outcomes.

A full analysis of the model when agency actions are unobservable to the principal is beyond the scope of this chapter. Instead I limit myself to a few observations about the effects of policy complexity on the ability of the principal to monitor the agent. Complexity makes monitoring for influence capture harder for two reasons. The first is that as σ gets larger, it is harder for the principal to discriminate between bad realizations of policy outcomes by a noncaptured agency and an extreme policy chosen to favor the industry.[31] In turn, the loss of this ability to discriminate means that the principal must cut the agency more slack, which in turn dulls the agency's incentives to avoid being influenced.

A second effect enhances the first. In the model, agency target policies close to x_f have lower outcome variation than more distant ones. This feature has the effect of reducing the likelihood of extreme outcomes when the agency caters to the firm. This provides extra insurance against the sorts of outcomes that might elicit suspicion and sanctions from the principal. In other words, the agency may be able to use embedded information to cover its tracks. Clearly, this incentive makes the agency more susceptible to influence capture.

In summary, policy complexity makes influence capture easier.

CONCLUSIONS

Dramatic outcomes such as the financial crash and the blowout of British Petroleum's *Deepwater Horizon* well have resurfaced perennial questions about the undue influence of economic interests over their regulators. However, as many chapters in this volume point out, "capture" is not a constant. Some agencies are clearly dominated by the interests they are supposed to regulate, whereas others pursue their mandate remarkably well in spite of well-organized opposition. A second theme of this volume is that industry influence and participation in the regulatory process are not always bad thing and do not always deserve the capture sobriquet.

In my chapter, I have explored both of these themes in relation to the role of expertise and complexity. The simple model of regulatory policymaking in complex environments should help us both understand when we should

---

[31] This variance effect is explored in more detail in Huber and McCarty, "Bureaucratic Capacity, Delegation, and Political Reform."

expect industry to be disproportionately influenced as well as the conditions under which industry influence can or cannot be justified in terms of democratic control of the agency.

My basic model highlights that the regulated firm may benefit from two sources of rent. The first is the preference rent in which an agency with preferences sympathetic to the firm tolerates the activities favored by the firm. The second is an expertise rent in which the agency's dependence on the firm for information forces it to tolerate policies that the firm finds advantageous.

Even in the baseline case, my model argues that policies in complex domains will be biased toward the preferences of the firm. However, an extension of the model also suggests that the legislative principal may have incentives to shift the preferences of the agency even more toward that of the firm if doing so raises the agency's ability to extract information. Consequently, substantial pro-firm biases may be part of an "optimal" regulatory design and be fully consistent with democratic control of the agency. Although these outcomes represent capture in the weak sense, regulation still may promote the public interest and be preferred to deregulation.

However, the greater worry is the one formulated in Section IV. The influence capture model suggests that complexity makes agencies more prone to influence capture. In the model in which agency policy targets are observable to the principal, complexity reduced the optimal transfer that a firm would pay to shift policy toward its preferences. In the unobservable target case, a variance effect combined with an insurance effect makes undue firm influence harder to detect by the principal. Of course, this effect provides additional slack for the agency to succumb to industry influence.

The model and straightforward extensions of its logic suggest several policy implications. The first and most obvious is that government should strive to reduce the expertise advantages of firms. The straightforward (but perhaps politically untenable) step would be to increase public sector salaries (at least in key areas) to rates that can better compete with the private sector. However, simply drawing talent out of the private sector may not be enough if the new regulators come with the social and cultural connections that lead to pro-firm biases.[32] Government agencies that regulate complex domains need to develop career paths and educational opportunities for their key

---

[32] See Kwak, Chapter 4 in this volume. One less desirable way to eliminate the public–private pay gap is through private contracting, public–private partnerships, and government-sponsored enterprises in which government functions are carried out by private sector employers. However, clearly these mechanisms are prone to even greater conflicts of interest.

personnel that are more autonomous from the regulated industry. These steps ought to reduce the expertise rent.[33]

Of course, it will be impossible and probably undesirable to build completely impermeable barriers between regulators and firms. To the extent to which additional resources and educational opportunities cannot eliminate the expertise gap, my arguments imply that good regulation may require staffing agencies with regulators who share the industry's preferences. The key in such situations will be to design personnel and ethics policies that prevent the excessive biases toward the industry and influence capture. The doors must revolve, but not too much.

Finally, although my model focuses on a firm with a monopoly on expertise, it could be extended straightforwardly to include multiple nongovernmental experts, including public interest groups. In such an extension, the option of a regulator to rely on the expertise of a public interest group will force the firm to make policy concessions that are much more favorable to the agency and principal. Therefore, permissive rules of standing and access for public interest groups can ameliorate the expertise rent (and allow the principal to correspondingly reduce the preference rent). The same benefit can be obtained from academic expertise so long as those experts are not themselves captured.[34]

APPENDIX

Proposition 1. *The unique subgame perfect Nash equilibrium to the regulation regime involves*

$$
x_f = \begin{cases} a + \theta & \text{if } a + \theta < 1 \\ 1 & \text{if } a + \theta \geq 1 \end{cases}
$$

where $\theta = min\{ \ \overline{c_a}, \frac{\sigma^2}{2} \}$. *A accepts this policy proposal.*

Proof. I begin with *A*'s best use of embedded information following x_f. Clearly, choosing $x_a > x_f$ is a dominated strategy. So *A* chooses x_a to maximize

$$
(x_a - a)^2 - |x_f - x_a|\sigma^2
$$

subject to $x_a \leq x_f$.

---

[33] For greater elaboration of many of these recommendations, see "The Changing Nature of Government Service," A Woodrow Wilson School Task Force Final Report, April 13, 2009. http://wws.princeton.edu/gstf/Volcker-Report.pdf.

[34] See Zingales, Chapter 6 in this volume.

The Kuhn-Tucker necessary conditions for this optimization problem are:

$$x_a = a + \frac{\sigma^2}{2} \quad \frac{\lambda}{2}$$
$$\lambda(x_f \quad x_a) = 0$$
$$\lambda \quad 0$$
$$x_a \quad x_f$$

where λ is the multiplier on the constraint. The only solution is

$$x_a(x_f) = \begin{cases} a + \frac{\sigma^2}{2} & \text{if } a + \frac{\sigma^2}{2} < x_f \\ x_f & \text{if } a + \frac{\sigma^2}{2} \quad x_f \end{cases}.$$

Because the objective function is strictly concave, the solution is a maximum.

Inserting this solution into A's utility function, one finds that the agency's payoffs from embedded information are

$$(x_f \quad a)^2 \quad \text{if } a + \frac{\sigma^2}{2} \quad x_f$$
$$\frac{\sigma^4}{4} \quad \left| x_f \quad a \quad \frac{\sigma^2}{2} \right| \sigma^2 \quad \text{if } a + \frac{\sigma^2}{2} < x_f.$$

Now consider the acquisition of independent information. Because the agency always targets its ideal outcome with independent information, its payoffs from independent information are c_a. Therefore, it prefers accepting the firm's target policy to acquiring independent information if $(a \quad x_f)^2 \quad c_a$ or $x_f \quad a + \sqrt{c_a}$. From earlier, we know that the agency prefers embedded information to both accepting x_f and acquiring independent information if $\frac{\sigma^4}{4} \quad |x_f \quad a \quad \frac{\sigma^2}{2}|\sigma^2 \quad c_a$ or $x_f \quad \frac{c_a}{\sigma^2} + \frac{\sigma^2}{4}$.

Summarizing these two conditions, the agency therefore prefers independent information if and only if

$$a + \frac{\sigma^2}{2} > x_f > a + \sqrt{c_a}$$
$$x_f > a + max\left\{ \frac{\sigma^2}{2}, \frac{c_a}{\sigma^2} + \frac{\sigma^2}{4} \right\}.$$

Now I turn to F's best response given $x_a(x_f)$. First, I argue that F never chooses x_f so that A uses embedded information. Suppose F chooses x_f such that $a + \frac{c_a}{\sigma^2} + \frac{\sigma^2}{4} > x_f > a + \frac{\sigma^2}{2}$ (the only case where embedded information would be used). Then A chooses $a + \frac{\sigma^2}{2}$ and F's payoff is $(1 - a - \frac{\sigma^2}{2})^2 - (x_f - a - \frac{\sigma^2}{2})\sigma^2$. This is lower than the utility of proposing $x_f = a + \frac{\sigma^2}{2}$, which is accepted and generates a payoff of $(1 - a - \frac{\sigma^2}{2})^2$.

Now I claim that the firm will not induce the agency to acquire independent information. There are two possible cases. First, suppose F chooses x_f such that $a + \frac{\sigma^2}{2} > x_f > a + \overline{c_a}$. This generates an outcome of a with certainty that generates a lower utility than $x_f = a + \overline{c_a}$, which is accepted by the agency with certainty. Second, suppose F chooses $x_f > a + max\{\frac{\sigma^2}{2}, \frac{c_a}{\sigma^2} + \frac{\sigma^2}{4}\}$. This results in a policy of a and is dominated by $x_f = a + max\{\frac{\sigma^2}{2}, \frac{c_a}{\sigma^2} + \frac{\sigma^2}{4}\}$, which is accepted with certainty.

Because the firm does not induce the agency to use either form of information, x_f must be lower than both $a + \overline{c_a}$ and $a + \frac{\sigma^2}{2}$ so that $x_f - a + \theta$, where $\theta = min\{\overline{c_a}, \frac{\sigma^2}{2}\}$. The optimality of x_f follows. □

Proposition 2. *With proximity learning, the unique subgame perfect Nash equilibrium to the regulation regime involves*

$$x_f = \begin{cases} a + \theta & \text{if } a + \theta < 1 \\ 1 & \text{if } a + \theta \quad 1 \end{cases},$$

where $\theta = h(1 - a)\frac{\sigma^2}{2}$. A accepts this policy proposal. The optimal location of the agency's ideal point from the perspective of L solves either $h (1 - a)\sigma^2 = 1$ or $a + h(1 - a)\sigma^2 = 0$.

Proof. With proximity learning, the outcome variance associated with embedded information has been rescaled by $h(1 - a)$. Because this term does not depend on x, all of the Kuhn-Tucker conditions are identical when $h(1 - a)\sigma^2$ replaces σ^2.

The principal would like to select the agency ideal point that sets x_f as close to zero as possible. There are two possible cases. First, assume that $a + h(1 - a)\sigma^2 \quad 0$ for some a. Then by continuity, there exists a such that $a + h(1 - a)\sigma^2 = 0$. The principal implements her ideal point by choosing this agency ideal point. Such a possibility would be ensured if the proximity learning effects were small such that $h(\cdot)\sigma^2 < 1$.

Now consider the case in which $a + h(1 - a)\sigma^2 > 0$ for all a. The principal's first order condition is $-2(a + h(1 - a)\sigma^2)(1 - h(1 - a)\sigma^2) = 0$. Because $h(\cdot)$ is strictly convex, $h(1 - a)\sigma^2 = 1$ defines a global maximum because $a + h(1 - a)\sigma^2 > 0$. □

Proposition 3. *In the capture model, the firm's target outcome is*

$$x_f = \begin{cases} \frac{1+a+\theta}{2} & \text{if } 1 > a+\theta \\ 1 & \text{if } a+\theta \geq 1 \end{cases},$$

and the equilibrium transfers are given by

$$t(x_f) = \begin{cases} \frac{(1-a+\theta)^2}{4} - \theta(1-a) & \text{if } 1 > a+\theta \\ 0 & \text{if } a+\theta \geq 1 \end{cases}.$$

Proof. I begin by computing the transfers necessary for the agency to accept a given firm policy outcome rather than amend the policy using embedded information. From earlier, we know that the firm's utility from using embedded information to amend x_f is given by $\frac{\sigma^4}{4} - |x_f - a| - \frac{\sigma^2}{2}|\sigma^2$. Therefore, the agency is willing to accept x_f and transfer $t(x_f)$ if $-(a-x_f)^2 + t(x_f) \geq \frac{\sigma^4}{4} - |x_f - a| - \frac{\sigma^2}{2}|\sigma^2$. This will hold whenever

$$t^*(x_f) = \begin{cases} 0 & \text{if } x_f \leq a+\theta \\ (x_f-a)^2 - (x_f-a)\sigma^2 + \frac{\sigma^4}{4} & \text{if } x_f > a+\theta \end{cases}.$$

Now we must compute the optimal policy target x_f given $t^*(x_f)$. The firm must maximize $-(1-x_f)^2 - t^*(x_f)$. In the case in which $a+\theta \geq 1$, $t^*(1) = 0$, so the firm's optimal is clearly $x_f = 1$. When $a+\theta < 1$, the firm maximizes $-(1-x_f)^2 - (x_f-a)^2 + (x_f-a)\sigma^2 + \frac{\sigma^4}{4}$. The first order condition is $2(1-x_f) - 2(x_f-a) - 2\theta = 0$. Therefore, the firm's optimal target outcome is $\frac{1+a+\theta}{2}$. □

6

Preventing Economists' Capture[1]

Luigi Zingales[2]

When economists talk about regulatory capture, we do not imply that regulators are corrupt or lack integrity. In fact, if regulatory capture were due solely to illegal behavior, it would be simpler to fight. Regulatory capture is so pervasive precisely because it is driven by standard economic incentives, which push even the most well-intentioned regulators to cater to the interests of the regulated. These incentives are built into their positions. Regulators depend on the regulated for much of the information they need to do their job properly, and this dependency encourages regulators to cater to the regulated. The regulated are also perhaps the primary audience of the regulators, as taxpayers and citizens more generally have much less incentive to monitor regulation, and generally remain ignorant. Hence the regulators will tend to perform their job with the regulated, rather than the public, in mind, further encouraging the regulators to cater to the interests of the regulated. Finally, career incentives play a big role. The regulators' human capital is highly industry-specific, and many of the best jobs available to them exist within the industries they regulate. Thus, the desire to preserve future career options makes it difficult for the regulator not to cater to the regulated.

If these are significant reasons regulators are captured, it is not clear why economists should not be similarly susceptible to capture. First, although not all data that economists use are proprietary, access to proprietary (that is, industry controlled) data provides a unique advantage in a highly competitive academic market. To obtain those data, academic economists generally

[1] I wish to thank Chiara Fratto for her research assistantship and the Center for Research on Security Prices, the George Stigler Center at the University of Chicago, and the Initiatives on Global Markets for financial support.
[2] University of Chicago, National Bureau of Economic Research, and Centre for Economic Policy Research.

have to maintain a reputation for treating their sources favorably. Therefore, there are incentives similar to those of regulators to cater to the industry or the political authority that controls the data. Second, outside of academia, the natural audience of economists' work consists of business people and government officials who would apply some of that knowledge. A piece of research, and the person who did it, will gain credibility by winning popularity and support among business people or the government. Even if no researcher purposefully caters to business or the government, this selection will tend to promote researchers who cater to business or the government. Finally, academic human capital is highly specific. Opportunities in consulting and other high-pay, high-status careers outside of academia are not equally distributed; economists who cater to business interests would seem to have a more lucrative set of opportunities.

Another more subtle source of bias arises from the publication process. In economics, authors cannot submit a paper to multiple journals contemporaneously, and manuscripts are subjected to many lengthy revisions. This extenuating process maximizes the power of the editor vis-à-vis the author. Thus, the capture of even a few editors can have magnified effects throughout the profession.

In sum, if economists face incentives very similar to those facing regulators, why shouldn't they be similarly susceptible to capture? In this chapter, I develop these arguments and provide some evidence consistent with the hypothesis that capture of economists by business interests exists, and is pervasive.

As with regulators, economists' capture is far from complete. There are numerous examples of academics at odds with industry wants, and even entire theories at odds with industry interests. For example, the Efficient Market theory is not very congenial to the finance industry.

What are some of the factors that limit capture in academia? One factor that can reduce capture is access to data that are independent from industry. Macroeconomists who rely on government-provided data or financial economists who rely on publicly available stock price data are less likely to be captured than researchers doing field experiments who have to obtain confidential data from companies. A second factor is the ability to speak to a broader audience. Economists who write for the larger public, such as Joseph Stiglitz and Paul Krugman, operate under fewer of the pressures that can lead economists to be captured by business. They might even suffer the opposite pressure: the high demand for economists who criticize business may risk introducing an antibusiness bias into some of these economists' work. Finally, some economists may be less attractive to an industry for reasons unrelated to their work itself, which in turn reduces for these economists the attractiveness of catering to that industry. For example, all other things being equal, an economist with a thick foreign accent might be less likely to be asked to be an expert witness or to find a job in a domestic industry, except in very quantitative (and generally not very lucrative) positions. We would expect such economists to be less likely to cater to business interests.

To help prevent capture, I propose several remedies. First, a reform of the publication process, allowing multiple contemporaneous submissions and restricting the outside activities of editors. Second, a data policy for field experiments and proprietary datasets that minimizes the ability of companies to influence the published results of this research. Third, a mechanism of shaming academic economists who take unjustifiable positions in the media or in expert testimony. Although academic writings are scrutinized during expert testimonies, expert testimonies are not scrutinized by the academic community. It is time for this to start.

Ultimately, the best way for economists to reduce and prevent capture is to promote awareness among ourselves that the risk of capture exists. Until we admit that we *can be* captured by vested interests in much the same ways that regulators can, we cannot hope to prevent capture. For this reason, the key first step is to start talking about this problem.

The rest of this chapter proceeds as follows. The first section reviews the forces that the literature has identified as leading to regulatory capture. The second section applies the same logic to economists, and also provides some empirical evidence in the context of the debate on executive compensations. The third section presents some mechanisms through which capture can be reduced.

THE FORCES THAT LEAD TO REGULATORY CAPTURE

Starting with Olson[3] and Stigler,[4] the economic literature on regulatory capture begins from two premises: regulators' opinions can be influenced, and not all groups have equal opportunities in influencing them. In this section I review the main reasons for regulatory capture as identified in this literature. This section does not claim any originality, but it is designed to set the stage for my analysis of how these same forces can theoretically lead to capture among economists.

[3] Mancur Olson, *The Logic of Collective Action* (Cambridge, MA: Harvard University Press, 1965).
[4] George Stigler, "Theory of Economic Regulation," *Bell Journal of Economics* 2 (1971): 3–21.

From bribes to threats, there are plenty of illegal ways to influence regulators.[5] I purposefully ignore these channels – not because they are unimportant – but because they are less interesting if we want to study how to prevent capture in the United States. Illegal methods are rare here and are easier to fight; admitting for a few exceptions, it is generally sufficient to enforce the law.

When we restrict our attention to legal means, there are three main channels through which regulators' opinions can be influenced: career concerns, information, and environmental pressure. I deal with each of these in turn.

Career Concerns

Outside interests can influence the career of a regulator by offering (implicitly or explicitly) better paid jobs to regulators outside of the regulatory arena. This channel only works when the typical wage prevailing in the outside organization is significantly higher than the one prevailing in the regulatory arena. This is not always the case. For example, nongovernmental organizations (NGOs) do not pay large salaries, preventing them from using this channel to influence the regulators.

This form of regulatory capture does not require an explicit quid pro quo between regulators and regulated, such as a job offer in exchange for a favorable decision. It can take a much more legitimate form, which can be quite pervasive. Industry players may hire former regulators because of the valuable skills they have accumulated as regulators. Given these skills, however, the industry employer will prefer former regulators whose record indicates they appreciate the employer's interests, and are more sympathetic to them. It is hard to imagine, for example, that an investment bank would hire a regulator who has expressed very negative views of the economic function of derivatives. Given these concerns, some regulators will try to signal their pro-industry view with decisions that favor the regulated.

Even if a regulator is not interested in getting a job outside of the regulatory arena, outside interests can affect her career inside the regulatory world. A key assumption in the economic theory of regulation is that large and dispersed constituencies remain poorly informed about regulatory issues. Because each individual is affected so little by regulatory decisions, it is not in his interest to invest in acquiring information on these issues. This rational ignorance theory[6] asserts that large and dispersed constituencies

---

[5] Ernesto Dal Bó and Rafael Di Tella, "Capture by Threat," *Journal of Political Economy* 111 (2003): 1123–54.

[6] Anthony Downs, *An Economic Theory of Democracy* (New York: Harper & Brothers, 1957).

are far less likely to follow regulatory decisions and thus do not provide much feedback on their actions. As a result, the main parties that provide outside feedback about the performance of a regulator are vested interests. This asymmetry of monitoring gives the vested interests greater influence. They can, for example, potentially undermine the career of a regulator by spreading false rumors about her level of competence.

If, as advanced by Hilton,[7] the main goal of a regulator is to avoid "squawking," or political complaints by the regulated firms, then regulators would as a rule be highly amenable to industry preferences. Yet a smart politician might read "squawking" by industry insiders as a sign of a regulator's effectiveness, and would therefore reward the regulator for doing precisely the opposite of what Hilton's model predicts. A more sophisticated model is provided by Leaver.[8] Leaver's model starts from the premise that regulators make mistakes. Regulators know, however, that when they make a mistake against the vested interests in their industry, these mistakes will be exposed as such and will have an impact on their reputation. By contrast, when regulators make mistakes that favor the industry, these mistakes will not be so easily exposed. Therefore, the model predicts that, when in doubt, regulators would rather err in favor of the regulated, rather than against them.

Furthermore, regulators may want to hedge against potential mistakes by routinely being more favorable to the industry they regulate. The industry will be less likely to expose a regulator's mistakes if the regulator has a reputation for being an industry ally.

Information

Regulators often require access to industry-specific information to do their job properly, and without this information they risk making embarrassing mistakes. Much of this information is possessed by the regulated firms. In the absence of an explicit disclosure requirement, the regulator must bargain with the regulated industry to obtain that information. This creates an easy opportunity for firms to "trade" information in exchange for favorable treatment. This quid pro quo is generally implicit. Regulators try to establish a cooperative environment with the regulated firms; to support this cooperation, regulators need to make certain concessions, and in turn

---

[7] George W. Hilton, "The Basic Behavior of Regulatory Commissions," *American Economic Review* 62 (1972): 47–54.

[8] Clare Leaver, "Bureaucratic Minimal Squawk Behavior: Theory and Evidence from Regulatory Agencies," *American Economic Review* 99 (2009): 572–607.

they expect the industry to cooperate by disclosing information. Both sides operate under the merely implicit threat of withdrawal from this cooperation.

An historical example of this kind of implicit bargain is provided by Mahony.[9] In drafting the 1933 and 1934 legislation, the Roosevelt administration needed a great deal of information in a short period of time. The traditional investment banks, already well connected politically, offered to provide this information. In exchange, Mahoney writes, the banks acquired some ability to influence legislation and were left largely untouched by the Pecora Committee investigations.

Environmental Pressure

Regulators do not operate in a vacuum. They generally possess industry-specific human capital, which has been accumulated through formal training and years of work in a specific industry. This specialized human capital tends to generate an interest in supporting activities that value this human capital. A person who specialized in derivative trading, for instance, is more likely than most to be impressed with the importance and value of derivatives, just as a nuclear engineer is more likely to think nuclear power is the energy source of the future. If most of the regulators were picked from among nuclear engineers, we might expect the country to more widely embrace nuclear energy. The example of France seems to demonstrate such an effect. As a result of complicated cultural reasons, an unusually large portion of the political and bureaucratic elite in France is trained in engineering at the Ecole Politechnique – and France derives more of its energy from nuclear power than any other nation.

Compounding the problem is the fact that regulators frequently rely on their network of trusted friends to gather information "from the outside." If everyone in that network is drawn from the same milieu, the information and ideas that flow to policymakers will be severely limited. A revealing anecdote comes from a Bush Treasury official, who noted that in the heat of the financial crisis, every time there was a phone call from Manhattan's 212 area code, the message was the same: "Buy the toxic assets." Such uniformity of advice makes it difficult for even the most intelligent or well-meaning policymakers not to be influenced.

---

[9] Paul G. Mahony, "The Political Economy of the Securities Act of 1933," *Journal of Legal Studies* 30 (2001): 1–31.

Asymmetries

All these potential sources of biases would not be very problematic if all the interests had equal ability to lobby and influence the regulators. The economic literature on regulatory capture relies on a fundamental asymmetry in the influence of various groups, because in a perfectly competitive world, competition among conflicting interests will lead to the efficient outcome.[10] The source of this imbalance of power has to be found in the small size (both in relative and in absolute terms) of many players. As Olson[11] argued, relatively small players capture a small fraction of the benefits of lobbying, whereas they have to pay the full cost. In a world in which coordination is costly, they will have fewer incentives to lobby than the large players, who internalize a significant fraction of the benefits of lobbying without having to pay any coordination costs. Besides the dispersion issue, a limited size is by itself an obstacle to lobbying. Lobbying has some fixed costs, which cannot be amortized if the market size is too small, even if the market is controlled by a monopolist. As a result, lobbying disproportionately increases along with the size of firms.[12]

Besides size, profitability is an important determinant of lobbying intensity. More profitable companies can afford to pay more to lobby, and they have more to protect. For example, public notaries in Italy (and in all French law countries) are limited in quantity and earn substantial rents. As a result, they have organized a powerful lobbying effort to justify the rationale of their position.[13] You do not see any similar effort in the United States, however, where public notaries are clerks and earn no rent.

HOW THESE FORCES CAPTURE ECONOMISTS

Now that I have reviewed the forces that can capture regulators, I can present and test the hypothesis that these forces can capture the economic profession as well. Because economic academic research spans many different fields, a generic captor does not exist. Both the captors and the degree of capture

---

[10] Gary Becker, "A Theory of Competition Among Pressure Groups for Political Influence," *Quarterly Journal of Finance* 98 (3) (1983): 371–400.

[11] Olson, *The Logic of Collective Action.*

[12] Deniz Igan, Prachi Mishra, and Thierry Tressel, "A Fistful of Dollars: Lobbying and the Financial Crisis," Working Paper 17076, National Bureau of Economic Research, May 2011.

[13] See, for example, XLI Congresso Nazionale del Notariato, "Civil law-Common law. Sviluppo Economico e certezza giuridica nel confront tra sistemi diversi," Pesaro, 2005.

vary across topics. To situate my ideas, I frame most of the examples in terms of the debate on executive compensation. I do not use this example because it is an example of uniform capture; to the contrary, many economists have written about the distortions in executive compensation caused by corporate governance problems.[14] I do not mean to suggest, therefore, that the profession is fully "captured," any more than I mean to suggest that all regulators are captured. What makes this topic particularly suitable is precisely the fact that the profession is not entirely aligned on one answer and that, at least in theory, you could argue successfully on both sides of the debate. One could argue that the market for executives is a competitive one, in which they get paid what their marginal productivity is, or one could argue that the market is distorted by corporate governance problems. It is precisely this variety that allows me to better identify the subtle biases that are present in the profession.

Career Concerns

As with regulators, vested interests can influence economists' careers along two dimensions. They can provide opportunities for employment (either full time or part time) outside of academia, and they can influence the career of a researcher inside academia.

Career Outside of Academia

Let us start with the easier channel: employment opportunities outside academia. Firms can hire academic economists for top-level positions, as a board member, or as a consultant. Regardless of the job they are hired for, it does not help to have taken a critical position on the level of executive compensation. One reason is that such a position might signal an antibusiness bias, which would be detrimental in any business job. It is also counterproductive if the economist ends up in the top position, because it might negatively affect his own compensation. Finally, it makes him less appealing to other CEOs who might want to have him on their board, because his presence on their board might spell trouble for them. For these reasons, if economists are interested in future outside appointments, they have incentives to take the position that the high level of executive compensation is justified.

---

[14] For example, Marianne Bertrand and Sendhil Mullainathan, "Are CEOs Rewarded for Luck? The Ones Without Principles Are," *Quarterly Journal of Economics* 116 (2001): 901–32.

Most economists, however, do not leave academia and are not appointed to any board. At most, they work as expert witnesses for various firms. Because there is not much litigation on this issue, it is not ideal to discuss the potential biases that arise from this activity (or from the desire to qualify for this activity). In addition, most economists will argue that the adversarial nature of the litigation process is the best guarantee that it will not lead to biases. For every plaintiff, there is a defendant, and thus expert witness positions should be able to offer an opportunity for everybody, on both sides of every issue.

Unfortunately, this is true only in principle. In most cases there is quite an imbalance between plaintiff and defendant. More often than not, plaintiffs are operating on a contingency basis, bearing the cost of all expenses. As a result, plaintiffs tend to be much more cautious than defendants in spending large amounts of money on expert witnesses. By construction, defendants are well endowed (if they were not, the plaintiff would not file suit against them). They tend to have a lot to lose and are therefore more willing to spend large sums of money to protect their interests in court. For this reason, consulting opportunities are not equally distributed across both sides of the same topic. It pays more to develop a reputation for being an apologist of powerful interests than to support plaintiffs' cases against those interests.

Furthermore, lawyers like consistency from the expert they use, because this minimizes the chances of a damaging cross-examination. Thus academics who want to play actively in this market have an interest in sticking to a very clear position in all their writing, including their academic writing, which is often read by the opposing counsel. This is the opposite of what the academic pursuit of truth would require.

Publish or Perish

A more challenging task is to establish a link between outside pressures and success in academic careers. An academic career is mostly determined by a person's ability to publish in peer reviewed journals and to have her articles cited.

Unlike in the law arena, in which top journals are edited by students, in economics and finance, major journals are peer reviewed. Hence the ability to publish is mostly determined by editors and referees. Editors have probably the greatest power in deciding whether to publish a paper or not. They choose the referees, who are generally very predictable in their taste, and reserve the right to overrule them. I am very confident that editors receive no form of direct pressure to publish articles that reflect more pro–business interests. Yet this does not mean that the publication process is free from biases and that academic careers are completely free of any outside influence.

The lack of bias in the publication process depends crucially on the lack of bias of the editors of major journals. Because there are multiple outlets, an author can shop around. Unlike in law, however, the search process is impaired by the prohibition on submitting the same paper to multiple outlets contemporaneously. Combined with the relatively long review time and the multiple rounds required, this process gives quite a bit of power to the editor to massage papers in the direction he or she prefers. If an assistant professor who is going up for review soon is asked at the last round of a long review process to modify slightly his conclusions to make them more palatable to a certain audience, would he refuse? It is easy to see why he might not. Such a compromise not only biases the conclusions of one paper, but also risks generating a perception that to publish in that journal one has to reach the "right conclusions." Hence researchers who want to publish in that journal may start tilting their conclusions in the "right" direction. In equilibrium, the editor does not have to exercise any arm twisting, because all the distortion takes place before the first submission, and is done voluntarily by the researchers to reduce the risk of seeing their paper rejected.

Even if impaired by the restriction on contemporaneous submission, competition across journals helps to reduce idiosyncratic biases among editors. It cannot help, however, when this bias is generalized among editors. Suppose, for instance, that all editors sit (or want to sit) on corporate boards. They might then all be biased in favor of papers that justify large compensation to executives and board members. Similarly, imagine a hypothetical paper showing that expert witnesses are for sale and bias their opinions for money. If most of the editors of the major journals do a significant amount of expert witness consulting, do you expect that they will be absolutely neutral in judging the paper?

An Empirical Analysis

All the analysis presented so far has been in the way of hypothesis. To test whether there is any bias of this nature in the publication process, I looked at publications in the area of executive compensation. One of the main problems in doing such an analysis is selecting the appropriate sample. On the one hand, to choose a sample that is not affected by the potential biases of editors, I cannot choose just published papers. On the other hand, if I do not have any measure of quality, the analysis is meaningless. For this

Table 6.1. *Variables' description*

Positive on level	Dummy equal to 1 if the paper supports current levels of compensation or it suggests to increase them, buying the optimal-contracting argument over the rent-seeking argument
Negative on level	Dummy equal to 1 if the paper proposes that the current levels of compensation are excessive and/or supports the rent-seeking argument
Greater slope	Dummy equal to 1 if the paper supports a higher weight given to the performance-based compensation
Smaller slope	Dummy equal to 1 if the paper supports a higher weight given to the performance-based compensation
Economic journal	Dummy equal to 1 if the paper is published in JPE, QJE, or AER
Financial journal	Dummy equal to 1 if the paper is published in the JF, JFE, or RFS
Managerial review	Dummy equal to 1 if the paper is published in a managerial review
Law review	Dummy equal to 1 if the paper is published in a law review
No business school	Dummy equal to 1 if no author is affiliated with a business school
Bebchuk dummy	Dummy equal to 1 if the author is Bebchuk
Citations in Google Scholar	Number of citations in Google Scholar as of 5/2/2011 – 5/5/2011
Downloads from SSRN	Number of downloads in SSRN as of 5/2/2011 – 5/5/2011

reason, I start from a sample of the 150 most downloaded papers from the Social Science Research Network (SSRN) before 2008 using the search key "executive compensation." SSRN downloads have the advantage of not being affected by editors. However, for published papers, they are highly correlated with citations and thus are a (noisy) proxy of quality. I chose pre-2008 articles to exclude the financial crisis and to give sufficient time for the papers to be published.

After dropping a few survey papers, I read all the abstracts and classified them on the basis of the conclusions I could draw from their results. I labeled as "positive on level" the papers that find that the current level of compensation is justified or even too low. For example, if an abstract concludes that "the evidence supports the optimal-contracting argument over the rent-seeking argument," (see Table 6.1). I classified the paper as positive on level. I labeled an article as "'negative on level" if it argues that the current level of CEOs' salaries is too high. For example, a paper that "explains how managerial influence might lead to substantially inefficient

Table 6.2. *Summary statistics*

Variable	Obs	Mean	Std. Dev.	Min	Max
Positive on level	144	0.146	0.354	0	1
Negative on level	144	0.208	0.408	0	1
Greater slope	144	0.125	0.332	0	1
Smaller slope	144	0.104	0.307	0	1
Economic journal	144	0.021	0.143	0	1
Financial journal	144	0.111	0.315	0	1
Managerial review	144	0.028	0.165	0	1
Law review	144	0.118	0.324	0	1
No business school	144	0.424	0.496	0	1
Bebchuk dummy	144	0.069	0.255	0	1
Citations in Google Scholar	141	83.021	144.535	0	793
Downloads from SSRN	144	1374.986	1061.984	580	7594

The sample is composed of the 150 most downloaded papers posted on SSRN as of 5/2/2011 – 5/5/2011 obtained using "executive compensation" as keywords. Variable definition is reported in Table 6.1.

arrangements that produce weak or even perverse incentives" is classified as negative. Overall, 15% of the papers fall in the first category and 21% in the second, whereas the rest are neutral (see Table 6.2). I did the same regarding the desired level of pay for performance sensitivity: 12% of the papers argue that the sensitivity should be higher, while 10% argue that the sensitivity should be lower. I consider a paper positive on the level of compensation and/or on the level of sensitivity as a more probusiness paper, whereas I consider one that advocates a lower level of compensation and/or a lower level of sensitivity as a more antibusiness paper.

In Table 6.3, I compare the probusiness and antibusiness biases of major outlets. Articles published in major economic journals (e.g., *Journal of Political Economy, Quarterly Journal of Economics,* and *American Economic Review*) tend to have a clear probusiness bias with respect to the rest of the sample: they have significantly more conclusions that are positive on the level of compensation, significantly less that are negative on the level, and significantly less that are negative on the sensitivity. Managerial reviews tend to publish fewer articles concluding that compensation should be lower and fewer articles suggesting that sensitivity should be lower. The finance journals and law reviews do not exhibit any significant bias. One possible explanation is that law reviews are edited by students and finance journals have a much faster turnaround, which reduces the ability of an editor to manipulate the content.

Table 6.3. *Probusiness and not probusiness content in different journals*

VARIABLES	(1) Positive on level	(2) Negative on level	(3) Greater slope	(4) Smaller slope
Economic journals	0.551*	0.183***	0.218	0.106***
	(0.279)	(0.0386)	(0.279)	(0.0307)
Finance journals	0.0721	0.130	0.00962	0.0433
	(0.104)	(0.124)	(0.0900)	(0.0688)
Managerial reviews	0.135	0.183***	0.115***	0.106***
	(0.223)	(0.0386)	(0.0319)	(0.0307)
Law reviews	0.0611	0.170	0.0611	0.0707
	(0.0994)	(0.124)	(0.0994)	(0.0990)
Constant	0.115***	0.183***	0.115***	0.106***
	(0.0319)	(0.0386)	(0.0319)	(0.0307)
Observations	144	144	144	144
R-squared	0.056	0.038	0.016	0.014

The sample is composed of the 150 most downloaded papers posted on SSRN as of 5/2/2011 – 5/5/2011 obtained using "executive compensation" as keywords. Variable definition is reported in Table 6.1. OLS coefficients reported. Robust standard errors in parentheses. ***$p < 0.01$, **$p < 0.05$, *$p < 0.1$.

Even if editors can capture economic research, why should they? And in what direction? Is it true that industry contacts bias researchers in a particular direction? To test whether people who sit on corporate boards have a disproportionately pro-management attitude, I looked at a new survey created by the University of Chicago Initiative on Global Markets (IGM), of which I am a director. The IGM asks a panel of expert economists – "senior faculty at the most elite research universities in the United States," as we say on our Web site, chosen "to be geographically diverse, and to include Democrats, Republicans and Independents as well as older and younger scholars" – two policy-related questions each week. (Because I am one of those experts, I omit my own responses to avoid contaminating the results.) It turned out that experts who served on a corporate board were four times more likely than those who did not to disagree with the statement, "The typical chief executive officer of a publicly traded corporation in the U.S. is paid more than his or her marginal contribution to the firm's value." Experts who served on a corporate board were also four times more likely than those who did not to disagree with the statement, "Mandating that U.S. publicly listed corporations must allow shareholders to cast a non-binding vote on executive compensation was a good idea."

Clearly, this correlation does not prove causation. It is possible, for instance, that the people who sit on corporate boards understand these issues better and are therefore more likely to disagree with both statements.

Table 6.4. *Citations as a function of content*

VARIABLES	(1) Citations Google Scholar	(2) Citations Google Scholar	(3) Citations Google Scholar	(4) Citations Google Scholar
Downloads from	0.0759***	0.0783***	0.0743***	0.0786***
SSRN	(0.0173)	(0.0173)	(0.0178)	(0.0178)
Positive on level	78.07**			
	(35.82)			
Negative on level		13.97		
		(30.93)		
Greater slope			59.95	
			(45.73)	
Smaller slope				41.24**
				(17.46)
Constant	33.86*	28.61	27.69	21.89
	(17.24)	(20.61)	(18.23)	(18.88)
Observations	141	141	141	141
R-squared	0.378	0.343	0.360	0.349

The sample is composed of the 150 most downloaded papers posted on SSRN as of 5/2/2011 – 5/5/2011 obtained using "executive compensation" as keywords. Time period: 1990–2007. The variable definition is reported in Table 6.1. OLS coefficients reported. Robust standard errors in parentheses. ***$p < 0.01$, **$p < 0.05$, *$p < 0.1$.

Since the survey asks respondents to state the confidence each one has in his own response, I can explore the validity of this hypothesis that people sitting on corporate boards know better. If this were the case, I would expect board members to exhibit greater confidence in their responses than the rest of the sample, but I find no evidence in favor of this hypothesis. Another possibility is that the direction of causality is reversed: it is not that joining corporate boards influences people's opinions, but that people with business-friendly views are likelier to be asked to join boards in the first place. Yet this would not absolve a regulator in an economist's eyes! If an economist were confronted with evidence that regulators with more pro-management beliefs had better career opportunities, she would conclude that, "on the margin," regulators had an incentive to tilt their beliefs in favor of management. Why should the conclusion be any different if the subject is an academic economist?

Academic success is not only driven by number of publications, but also by their impact. Therefore I want to see whether articles with more probusiness conclusions are more likely to be cited. Once again, I need to control for quality. As a measure of quality, I use the actual number of SSRN downloads because this number is not affected by editors' choices. Table 6.4

reports the results. Controlling for SSRN downloads, articles that are positive on the level of compensation receive more cites (measured as Google cites, but the results are the same if I use SSRN cites). Similarly, articles that suggest that sensitivity of pay to performance should be lower receive fewer cites.

Overall, these results suggest that the optimal strategy for a junior faculty member who works on executive compensation and wants to maximize her chances to get tenure is to write articles that show that the level of compensation is appropriate and the sensitivity to performance should be increased.

Biases at the Promotion Level

Thus far, I have only looked at the impact that editors' biases can have on a professional career. Promotion to tenure, however, is not just determined by the number of top publications and their cite count. Other factors play a role. Harvard Business School, for example, explicitly mentions impact on the world of business as one of the criteria to grant tenure. Other schools are not so explicit, yet "intangibles" clearly play a role. To what extent does probusiness bias help in promotions above and beyond what it contributes to getting papers published?

One potential source of bias comes from the fact that universities are major fundraisers. Fortunately, in the United States (but not necessarily in other countries), there are Chinese Walls to protect academic integrity from being corrupted by money. Donations cannot have constraints that impinge on academic freedom. A donor, for example, cannot name the holder of the chair he/she donated, nor indicate preferences for who should hold it. Similarly, a grant cannot be given with restrictions on the type of conclusions that need to be reached. Similar restrictions, however, apply to Political Action Committees, whose contributions cannot be tied to a particular position of the politicians. Nevertheless, we do think that political donations affect the politicians who appoint the regulators and that career-driven regulators take this bias into consideration when they make decisions. Why should it not be the case that donations influence deans, who in turn can influence promotions? If this is the case, why wouldn't faculty internalize this bias in their writing? The important difference is that, once tenured, faculty members are not subjected to this pressure any more, whereas regulators continue to be.

Documenting this bias is a very difficult empirical task, beyond the scope of this chapter. Nevertheless, I would like to provide a small piece of evidence consistent with this bias. Fundraising considerations are probably stronger in business schools than in other parts of academia. Hence, if this bias existed, it would be more pronounced among business school professors. Therefore, I can use the preceding sample of executive compensation articles to determine whether business school professors are more inclined to take pro-business positions in their articles. Because they are subjected to the same editors' biases, the difference between business school professors and other academics could be attributed either to business school promotions internalizing this bias, or to a pro-business selection bias among business schools.

Table 6.5 shows that when none of the authors of an article works at a business school, the article is significantly less likely to be positive on the level of executive compensation and significantly more likely to be negative. I find no effect on the pay-to-performance sensitivity.

Because Lucian Bebchuk, a law professor, has coauthored many articles that are critical of executive compensations and appear in the top 150 downloaded (7%), I want to make sure that the effect is not just a Bebchuk effect. To this purpose, in the second part of Table 6.5 I add a dummy equal to 1 if Bebchuk is a coauthor of the article. Not surprisingly, the Bebchuk dummy is highly significant with the expected sign. Although it reduces the significance of the non–business school dummy, it does not eliminate the effect.

This effect could just be a selection effect, if only probusiness people end up working in a business school. Once again, this is similar to the regulatory arena; more probusiness people end up in regulatory positions, because they have to work with business. Whether it is selection or actual distortion does not matter a great deal. Either way, industry can count on a faculty very attentive to its interest.

Economists Not Interested in Money
As I mentioned earlier, the biggest difference between academics and regulators is that academics have tenure. Thus the career concerns described thus far apply only before an academic has tenure. After earning tenure, academics might still have monetary considerations, but these may not be paramount. Although the idea of an economist not interested in money might sound like an oxymoron, such people do exist. Academics (even academic economists) are not motivated by money alone. In fact, one could argue that people who choose the academic career are selected among those who value other dimensions (like the ability to influence other people's ideas and fame) more than money. Yet this same exact counterargument applies to regulators. The choice of a regulatory career generally reflects an interest in the public good, more so than a career in business.

Table 6.5. *Content as a function of type of job of the authors*

VARIABLES	(1) Positive on level	(2) Negative on level	(3) Greater slope	(4) Smaller slope	(5) Positive on level	(6) Negative on level	(7) Greater slope	(8) Smaller slope
No business school Author	-0.111*	0.122*	0.0107	0.0468	-0.101*	0.0738	0.00443	0.0483
	(0.0561)	(0.0704)	(0.0565)	(0.0533)	(0.0566)	(0.0669)	(0.0552)	(0.0534)
Bebchuk dummy					-0.127***	0.614***	0.0793	-0.0188
					(0.0343)	(0.131)	(0.129)	(0.0980)
Constant	0.193***	0.157***	0.120***	0.0843***	0.197***	0.134***	0.118***	0.0850***
	(0.0436)	(0.0402)	(0.0360)	(0.0307)	(0.0441)	(0.0405)	(0.0368)	(0.0314)
Observations	144	144	144	144	144	144	144	144
R-squared	0.024	0.022	0.000	0.006	0.032	0.166	0.004	0.006

The sample is composed of the 150 most downloaded papers posted on SSRN as of 5/2/2011 – 5/5/2011 obtained using "executive compensation" as keywords. Variable definition is reported in Table 6.1. OLS coefficients reported. Robust standard errors in parentheses. ***p < 0.01, **p < 0.05, *p < 0.1.

As in the case of regulators, however, this argument does not exempt economists from the risk of capture. First of all, the fact that they have other motivations does not mean that money does not enter their utility function. *On the margin*, career concerns and monetary rewards should matter. Most importantly, even if economists are completely insensitive to monetary rewards and only motivated by fame and desire to influence the outside world, they can be captured by vested interests. It is enough for these interests to offer more influence and fame, which they can easily do.

Let's consider an example. Suppose that banks need to be regulated to curb the too-big-to-fail problem. Suppose there are two methods. One solves the problem completely, but it is very costly for banks. The other provides only a partial solution, but it is much less costly to banks. Which approach would an economist advocate who has no interest in money but is solely motivated by the desire to be famous? Obviously, the second one. By advocating the first one, she would be considered unrealistic. She would not be invited to major conferences sponsored by banks or by regulators who are in cahoots with banks, and her papers would probably be rejected from the major economic journal where economists who are more attuned with the industry needs will referee her paper and publish their "more realistic" schemes. When some version of the inferior scheme is approved, the academic economists first proposing it will receive fame and glory, whereas the advocate of the effective scheme will be ignored. When the scheme, many years later, will show its shortcomings, the fault will all be attributed to the politicians who implemented it wrongly. The academic supporters will still enjoy the reputation of "having done something."

In fact, these concerns start to be internalized in the economic discussion, in the form of political economy constraints. Academic analysis of policy issues is not satisfactory if it does not incorporate the political constraints imposed by lobbying. In other words, models that do not consider sufficiently the power of vested interests are not acceptable. In a Brookings Papers meeting, I was criticized for my political naiveté, because "to take public positions on important policy issues without knowledge of the political process is a big mistake,"[15] where "political process" should be read as political constraints imposed by lobbying.

Information Needs

A late colleague of mine used to say that because entomologists do not have to socialize with bugs, he did not have to socialize with business people.

[15] "Brookings Papers on Economic Activity," The Brookings Institute, Spring 2009, 76.

Entomologists, however, cannot socialize with bugs. If they could, are we sure they would not? The entomologists who socialize would be able to understand better the world of insects, collect better data, and, most likely, write better papers. I suspect that if socialization with bugs were possible, academic competition would lead entomologists to spend a lot of time with bugs. The real question is whether the bugs would want to socialize with entomologists. Bugs do not have much choice, but business people do. Why would business people spend some of their very valuable time with us? We would like to believe that it is because they learn a lot from us. It could be the other way around: we learn from them and they know it and take advantage of it to influence us.

Researchers need data. Often a proprietary dataset can make a researcher's career. What are the incentives for a business to share these data? Generally, the first concern is not to damage the business in any possible way. Thus any business protects itself with some right of refusal, in case the data amount to some evidence that could harm the business. Researchers, anticipating that the company that provided the data may prevent controversial evidence from being published, will prefer to focus on either noncontroversial topics or topics for which the results are likely to cast the company in good light. This implicit agreement is not unique to academic economists. Biographers know that to have access to confidential information about their subjects, which enhances the quality of their work, they must develop a reputation for slanting biographies positively. If a biographer writes a negative or critical biography, then future potential subjects will be more likely to refuse him or her access.

The easiest place to see the importance of this quid pro quo is with Harvard case studies. The most typical cases are field cases, based in part on private information provided by the company to the Harvard professor who is writing the case. The explicit quid pro quo is that field cases require approval by the company before release. As we described in Dyck and Zingales,[16] some companies actively manage their information release to shape the cases. Recalls HBS professor Louis Wells:

I learned that Enron was upset with my public-source case on the conflict surrounding the company's investment in India. After the second time the case was taught, someone from the administration approached me, told me of the company's concerns, and asked if anything could be done about it. Another faculty member was, I was told, writing a field-based case on the same subject. It was suggested that I might

---

[16] Alexander Dyck and Luigi Zingales, "The Bubble and the Media," in *Corporate Governance and Capital Flows in a Global Economy*, eds. Peter Cornelius and Bruce Kogut (New York: Oxford University Press, 2003).

consider teaching the more rich field case, if it fit my teaching objectives. Meanwhile, I sent my public-source case to Enron for comment. In the end, I removed the public source case from the system and adopted a shortened version of the field case, which was indeed richer in information and enabled me to accomplish the original teaching objectives.[17]

Interestingly, the case in question – the shortened field case – was taught for many years at HBS, and it ended up provoking bitter complaints from Enron. The fact that the case continued to be taught despite these complaints suggests that a company's ability to manage the process only goes so far. Nevertheless, there's no denying that firms can potentially exert non-trivial influence over the cases that are written about them.

An implicit quid pro quo takes place even in academic research, and it is much more pernicious as the importance of field experiments increases, because the power of companies over researchers increases. A younger colleague, for example, was offered the opportunity to conduct a field study with a payday loan company. She was offered this option because she had written a paper with a very positive view of payday loans. Although the company had no say in the conclusions of the paper, they had to approve the study. Most importantly, if the study had found some embarrassing result and this result was properly emphasized in the paper resulting from this study, my colleague's chances to continue collaborating with the payday loan company (or for that matter, any payday loan company) would have been seriously in doubt. Nobody is doing anything improper; still, it is unlikely that any similar studies will cast payday loans in a negative light.

Environmental Pressure

Akerlof and Kranton[18] highlighted that people are not only motivated by monetary incentives. They can exert a great deal of effort when they identify with the values and the culture of an organization or a subgroup (see Kwak, Chapter 4). Thus capture can take place not just through monetary payoff, but also through the desire to belong to a certain group with which a person identifies. The more homogeneous business elites are, the more severe this problem is, because the pressure to conform becomes greater.

Many academic economists, and business professors in particular, have a form of admiration for and envy of successful business leaders. Just as military strategists who never fought a war seek credibility and support from

---

[17] Dyck and Zingales, "The Bubble and the Media."
[18] George Akerlof and Rachel Kranton, *Identity Economics* (Princeton: Princeton University Press, 2010).

generals who won important battles, academic economists seek validation from business leaders.

Asymmetries

As for regulators, all these potential biases would be irrelevant if all the interests involved had the same power to influence. Unfortunately, for economists this is very unlikely to be the case. To the extent that economists are influenced by potential future employment or board opportunities, bigger companies are disproportionately more powerful, because they can provide more prestigious positions and better paid ones (salaries are highly correlated with size). To the extent that economists are influenced by future consulting opportunities, bigger companies have disproportionately more difficult (and interesting) problems to resolve[19] and they can afford to pay more, because any solution can be applied on a much broader basis. The same is true if the attractive career prospects are in the expert witness business. Bigger companies have more at stake and are therefore willing to pay more to defend their interests. If a source of economists' capture derives from the information the industry has, bigger players have more and more valuable information and are better able to deliver it.

Thus, as is the case for regulators, the types of pressures economists receive are unbalanced.

PREVENTING ECONOMISTS' CAPTURE

Given the similarity of the mechanisms that lead regulators and economists to be captured, some general remedies can work for both. I briefly mention these, while focusing most of my attention on the mechanisms specific to the academic market.

General Measures

The Power of the Media
The reason why small vested interests dominate the political agenda is that it is frequently rational for the public at large not to become informed. When a new bankruptcy law is considered, most voters do not pay attention. The probability that it will affect them personally is very low. Hence it is not

---

[19]   Luis Garicano, "Hierarchies and the Organization of Knowledge in Production," *Journal of Political Economy* 108 (2000): 874–904.

worth their time to become informed on what the issues are. If voters remain ignorant about their own interests, moreover, it does not pay for politicians to try to protect them.

The press, however, reduces the cost of getting informed by collecting, verifying, and summarizing the facts.[20] By repackaging information in a way that makes it entertaining, news media are also able to overcome the private cost that individuals face in learning the gathered information. Even if it is not in each individual's monetary interest to become informed, the utility benefit provided by the entertainment component can overcome the cost of the time spent in absorbing the information.

Making citizens informed not only changes the incentives of politicians, but could also change the behavior of the chief executive officers of the firms lobbying the regulators. Why did U.S. producers of canned tuna choose, at very significant cost, to change the way they fished for tuna to protect the dolphins? Why is Nike so careful in avoiding the use of child labor when it manufactures its products abroad? In both cases, intense media coverage compelled these companies to change course.[21]

Most CEOs care about their public image. At the very least, they would like to avoid being labeled "dolphin killer" or to be considered responsible for child exploitation. It tarnishes not only their image but the brand image of their company, which they spend so much money to create and maintain. For this reason, they are willing to pay attention to citizens' concerns, even if these concerns do not immediately affect the demand for their products. In the same way, they could be shamed if found to influence regulators or academics too much.

News media can also reduce the capture of economists. Academics, as a group, tend to be very sensitive to their public image. For those who are motivated by fame and impact, a negative public image is extremely costly. Thus media inquiries of the academic world, like the one done in the movie "*Inside Job*," can be extremely useful in curbing the potential effects of capture.

---

[20] Alexander Dyck, David Moss, and Luigi Zingales, "Media vs. Special Interests," Working Paper 14360, National Bureau of Economic Research, September 2008.

[21] On March 8, 1988, all the major U.S. networks broadcast a tape of a Panamanian tuna boat, the *Maria Luisa*, killing hundreds of dolphins while fishing for tuna. Building on public outrage, the Earth Island Institute, Greenpeace, and the Humane Society launched a boycott of tuna. Restaurant chains took tuna off the menu and school boards across the country stopped using tuna until it was "dolphin safe." On April 12, 1990, Heinz announced that it would only sell dolphin-safe tuna. Within hours the two other largest tuna producers made a similar commitment. A similar story applies to Nike after the June 1996 issue of *Life* magazine carried an article about the use of child labor in Pakistan to produce Nike's soccer balls.

Indirect Benefits of Antitrust Enforcement

As mentioned previously, that business interests can have an impact on academic research does not, in itself, present a problem; rather, the problem is that in this influence game the playing field is uneven and some interests are much more powerful than others. Disparities in power arise from disparities in size and concentration, two variables that antitrust policy can address. Strong antitrust enforcement has two indirect benefits. First, by reducing size and concentration, it can level the playing field in the influence game. Second, by breaking up monopolies it divides the homogeneity of interests, creating some competition among conflicting lobbies.

Specific Measures

Besides general measures, there are several remedies that can be applied specifically to the academic market.

Shaming Economists Without Principles

A very useful self-defense against lobbying pressure is adherence to principles. Principles force economists to be coherent through time and through situations. Although not all economists adhere to the same principles and we certainly cannot expect that they will, adherence to some set of shared principles, whatever they might be, would be useful. Judges, for example, motivate their decisions on the basis of legal principles and precedents. Although they have the flexibility to adapt these principles and precedents to particular circumstances, legal principles and precedents nevertheless limit the available options in any decision.

In the same way, if economists had to justify on the basis of principles and data all their major public policy statements as well as their expert testimony, they would be less malleable to industry pressure. This defense would be enhanced if they could be shamed by colleagues for violating these principles. For example, an economist who always opposes government intervention but makes an exception when the government bails out a certain industry in which he has a direct interest could be easily exposed to professional disapprobation and public ridicule.

Unfortunately, shaming is a public good, at least as far as shaming aimed at keeping people honest is concerned. When it involves politicians and celebrities, it can pay off commercially; the program "Keeping Them Honest," run by CNN, presents a case in point. When it comes to economists, however, this hardly seems a viable commercial enterprise. For this reason, this "wall of shame" should be organized by a professional association or some public interest NGO.

Ideally, this "wall of shame" would also penalize economists who have compromised their principles for money or have made major mistakes. For example, in years past, many famous economists wrote papers commissioned by Fannie Mae and Freddie Mac. In some of these papers, they went so far as to say, "This analysis shows that, based on historical data, the probability of a shock as severe as embodied in the risk-based capital standard is substantially less than one in 500,000 – and may be smaller than one in three million."[22] Still, the authors do not seem to have suffered any consequences from these patently incorrect conclusions. In fact, one of these authors was promoted to director of the Office of Management and Budget and later hired as vice chairman of Global Banking at Citigroup.

Mandatory Disclosure of Expert Witnesses
To facilitate public shaming and to make the capture of economists more difficult, it will be useful to mandate the disclosure (possibly with a delay) of expert witness testimonies, even when a case settled. If economists know that their testimony will be read by colleagues and checked by students, the reputational cost of lying will increase. The possible delay will protect the expertise of the academic from being immediately diffused, but it will not undermine the reputational cost of defending positions most academics would consider untenable.

A Data Code
The beauty of empirical research is that you never know what you find. In fact, the surprising results are the most interesting ones. But some interesting results might reflect poorly on a company. And this is a risk companies do not want to face. Thus, when they disclose data, they generally disclose it with some strings attached. One common string is that they reserve the right to prevent publication of the research if the results are damaging to the company. Even if there is no explicit agreement of this type, the company and the researcher often have an implicit agreement to the same effect. Hoping to avoid having their work buried, researchers tend not to look where they may unearth potential problems. In effect, they only look for certain results.

[22] Joseph E. Stiglitz, Jonathan M. Orszag, and Peter R. Orszag, "Implications of the New Fannie Mae and Freddie Mac Risk-Based Capital Standard," in *Fannie Mae Papers*, 1 (2) (March 2002), 6.

If everybody understands this limitation and is able to place it in context, it will still be possible to draw appropriate inferences from the research. If I can only report when a coin flip yields a tail, others can easily infer when it yielded a head, as long as they know how many times I flipped the coin. On the other hand, if only tails are reported and published, but not how many coin flips have taken place, then readers will find it much more difficult to infer the proper picture of the underlying phenomenon – especially when some economists will dare to say that "tail" is an established fact because all the published papers agree that coin flips yield tails.

How can the profession avoid this severe distortion? One solution is to impose two disclosure requirements at the submission stage. The first is a disclosure of the type of agreement with the company that provided the data at the time the access, or the permission to conduct the field study, was granted. Although the disclosure of explicit agreements cannot prevent implicit agreements to the contrary, a proper formulation of the contract can make them more difficult.

The second disclosure is the number of related studies that were conducted and have not been published. This is tantamount to disclosing the total number of coin flips, so that other researchers can correctly infer how many times the coin came up "heads."

Another way to reduce this potential distortion is to increase the disclosure requirements and to create more public datasets. It is probably not a coincidence that the emergence of the Efficient Market theory in finance, which was strongly at odds with the interest of the financial industry, coincides with the creation of the Center of Research on Security Prices at the University of Chicago, which gave access to data to all researchers.[23]

A New Governance of the Publishing Market

In economic and financial journals, editors hold significant power vis-à-vis authors, especially untenured authors. A rejection of a paper after three rounds can easily make a difference between receiving a promotion and being passed over. Most editors do not abuse this power. Nevertheless, it creates a dangerous scope of abuses because editors are more likely to have interests outside of academia. Suppose I am advising Microsoft in its antitrust litigation – how likely am I to publish a paper that shows that Microsoft abuses its dominant position in the operating system market? One could argue that a smart researcher will know of this potential bias and

---

[23] As my initial footnote reveals, Center for Research on Security Prices funds my research; so I may be accused of a conflict of interest here.

submit the paper to another journal. Yet this information is not publicly disclosed, and only people "in the know" might find out.

Even if the editor is a very honest person and will give the paper a fair chance, he or she is likely to shape it in a way that downplays disturbing results. Editors' advice at the last round is rarely ignored by authors, especially young, untenured ones. For most it is just too costly and risky to start from scratch.

To eliminate this potential distorting power, I suggest a few reforms in the governance of the publication process. First, economic journals should open up to competition, as law journals do. It is ironic that the economics profession, which touts the benefits of competition, limits it when it comes to its own research submission process. Contemporaneous submissions will reduce the power of the editors, to the advantage of the authors. This is the reason why it is unlikely that this reform will start from the journals themselves.

The second element of the reform consists in allowing the authors to post their signed rejection letters. Journals insist that rejection letters are their sole property and they are sent to authors for their eyes only. Authors do not own the copyright. If rejection letters are kept confidential, then editors' reputations are unaffected, even when they make egregious rejection mistakes. If authors can post rejection letters, they can embarrass the editors when they make mistakes, especially when these mistakes seem to be driven by outside interests.

The last element of my reform will impose more rigid restrictions for editors. They should receive higher compensation from the journal, but commit not to do any other job outside of teaching. This restriction should hold not just for the period of their editorship, but also for two years after. Although imperfect, this revolving door policy can limit the most egregious cases of conflicts of interest.

The Importance of Being Nerds

In the 1950s and 1960s, Harvard Business School (HBS) was recruiting its faculty among the most talented, more analytical MBA students. Starting in the 1970s, the rise of big consulting companies and their competition for talents started to deprive HBS of its natural pool: analytical MBAs with high social skills. As a result, they started to recruit among PhDs from other institutions. There are generally two characteristics of PhDs: they are smart and they tend to have some social issues. They are smart, because otherwise they would never be permitted to enter a PhD program. They have social issues, because otherwise they would never *choose* to enter a PhD program:

smart and socially skillful people make much more money in the industry. When they ran out of talented American PhDs (because many moved to the industry), HBS and many other schools started recruiting foreigners.

There are several ways in which diversity in backgrounds and the presence of faculty with social handicaps help reduce the degree of capture. Social handicaps make a person less suitable to an industry job, reducing the value of what businesses have to offer down the line and thus reducing a possible channel of capture.

Similarly, diversity of backgrounds can be beneficial in several ways. First, diversity forces people to challenge the conventional wisdom and gives them a broader perspective, making social pressure and environmental capture less likely. Second, diversity implies that at least some faculty are not easily employable, reducing this channel of capture. Third, people with double nationality and backgrounds have two communities in which they can be captured. If the interests of these two communities are not perfectly aligned, then this multiple potential capture can generate competition, reducing the power of each individual captor.

In this respect, the internationalization of the academic market is very positive because it facilitates the debate among academic groups influenced by different interests. Once again, competition among these different groups leads to a more efficient outcome, in the spirit of Becker.[24]

Awareness

Shortly after the Greek debt crisis in May 2010, I spoke with a high-level official of the European Central Bank (ECB) who was in charge of monitoring the market. We discussed the potential cost of letting Greece fail. The crucial question was how the debt holders of other sovereign debt would have reacted to a default of Greece. I agreed that that was the crucial question, but I raised the doubt that some market makers had a vested interest in spreading the perception that the consequences would be disastrous, so that the ECB would intervene, reducing their losses. "I am aware of this bias," said the ECB official, "and every day when I talk to market participants I try to undo it. Whether I am successful in fully undoing this bias, it remains an open question."

Awareness of the risk of capture is the first line of defense. It might not be sufficient protection, but it is certainly a necessary one. Without this awareness, any other initiative is hopeless. Unfortunately, my experience talking with colleagues suggests that this sense of awareness is missing.

---

[24] Becker, "A Theory of Competition Among Pressure Groups for Political Influence."

There is a diffuse perception that we are different. Even though a simple application of economic principles, as I have done in this chapter, shows that we should be no different from regulators in our susceptibility to capture, we are unwilling to admit it. Until we are ready to do so, any other mechanism to prevent capture will be useless.

CONCLUSIONS

Most academic economists are very honest people who chose their career because they were motivated by noble goals, such as the quest for truth and "making the world a better place." The same, however, can be said for regulators. So why do academic economists think that regulators are generally captured, whereas they cannot stand even the thought that this might happen to one of them? How can it be that this time *we are different*?

The purpose of this chapter is to highlight parallels between the forces that we use to explain regulatory capture and the forces that can capture economists. Unless we economists are made of a different fabric from the regulators, I do not see why we should not be subjected to the same kind of pressures.

Based on the analysis of these forces, I discuss several mechanisms to help prevent (or reduce the effects of) capture: a reform of the publication process, an enhanced data disclosure, a stronger theoretical foundation, and a mechanism of peer pressure. Ultimately, however, the most important remedy is awareness of the problem – an awareness most economists still do not have.

7

Corrosive Capture? The Dueling Forces of Autonomy and Industry Influence in FDA Pharmaceutical Regulation

Daniel Carpenter

Modern government offers few if any agencies more powerful, more watched, or more pressured than the U.S. Food and Drug Administration (FDA). Rough estimates suggest that the FDA regulates more than one quarter of U.S. gross domestic product, with primary responsibilities for food, pharmaceuticals and medical devices, cosmetics, and, since 2009, tobacco products. Over a wide range of these products – drugs, medical devices, food additives, and certain tobacco products – the FDA has expansive gate-keeping power: the congressionally mandated task of deciding whether the products in question can be marketed at all. Gatekeeping power has many facets. Gatekeeping can be used to protect the public or provide it with false confidence; create market-wide confidence in new products; enhance or stifle innovation (often both); snow and guile consumers into thinking that poor, unsafe products are safer and better than they are; and hone the production, dosage, and information about drugs to help doctors and patients optimize their use.

If ever there were a plausible prima facie case for capture, a gatekeeping regulator like the FDA would seem to provide it. In its governance of pharmaceuticals, the FDA regulates a vast industry, one that supplies a global market approaching $1 trillion in size. Given its size and its historical connections to science and technology, this industry possesses broad economic, political, and cultural power. When Samuel Huntington[1] and Marver Bernstein[2] wrote about the potential capture of regulatory agencies in the 1950s and 1960s, it was with just such an agency-industry

---

[1] Samuel P. Huntington, "The Marasmus of the ICC: The Commission, the Railroads and the Public Interest," *Yale Law Journal* 61 (1953): 467–509.

[2] Marver H. Bernstein, *Regulating Business by Independent Commission* (Princeton: Princeton University Press, 1955).

relationship in mind (although neither wrote about the FDA). Large industries like these would seem to be primed to limit entry and preserve market access for themselves. And when George Stigler[3] looked for examples of when "regulation is acquired by the industry," he found his examples among entry-limiting regulation: weight limits for trucks (shaped by the lobbying of railroads and farmers) and occupational licensing (in which those with market power limit the entry of their potential competitors, restraining supply and inflating equilibrium price).

In this chapter I elaborate on the possibility of regulatory capture at the FDA and its potential mechanisms. Using traditional definitions of, and evidence for, capture as Huntington, Bernstein, and Stigler and their successors wrote about it, I conclude that until the late 1990s, there was little strong evidence of systematic or widespread capture of the FDA by the American or global pharmaceutical industry. There is, to put it simply, abundant evidence against the idea that American pharmaceutical regulation has been built through the attempts of drug companies to limit entry and preserve market power. Examining the prospect of capture through other mechanisms, however, suggests a possibly different conclusion. A degree of cultural capture of the FDA may have occurred, but the hypothesis needs further refinement and investigation. If this capture occurred, it is not of the entry-barrier form, but is rather of the *corrosive form*, whereby deregulation is accomplished not through republican mechanisms but through cultural capture of regulatory institutions. In addition, under no circumstances does the evidence support the strong capture welfare hypothesis that the FDA is so captured that the public would be better off without this form of regulation.

Before turning to a review of the historical and statistical evidence on FDA capture, I examine the idea of corrosive capture and how it might be applied to deregulatory efforts in pharmaceutical regulation and other realms of regulation.

THE IDEA OF CORROSIVE CAPTURE

Special interests and regulated industries can shape policies in different ways, and they can push policies in several directions. The Stiglerian account of capture predicts that captured regulation will be *stronger* in the sense of imposing more rigid and less permeable entry barriers to the market. If

[3] George J. Stigler, *The Citizen and the State: Essays on Regulation* (Chicago: University of Chicago Press, 1975).

the industry is using regulation to form a cartel and restrict supply and/or entry, in other words, then captured regulation will be *more effective* in terms of achieving these aims to the extent that the entry barriers are strong. If physicians seek to limit the supply of their services and thereby raise their pay, then licensing needs to present higher hurdles to qualification and entry for prospective doctors.

Corrosive capture, however, occurs if clearly organized firms push the regulatory process in a "weaker" direction, not with the aim of reducing entry, but with the aim of reducing costly rules and enforcement actions that reduce firm profits. This is a form of deregulation, of course, but it is quite plausible that deregulation through electorally sanctioned mechanisms would not present as much of a policy problem as deregulation by cultural capture. The corrosion of regulation occurs not with the express sanction of voters in repeated elections, but in the weakening of regulatory independence – and the fidelity of regulators to their statutory obligations – through various forms of capture.

It is important to recognize that much if not most of the public and academic discussion about capture in recent decades is about regulatory corrosion. Hence the capture and regulatory failure of the past few decades are distinct from the kind that Huntington, Bernstein, and Stigler were concerned with in the mid-twentieth century. Entry-barrier capture was the process by which regulators intervened in markets with the effect of privileging one set of producers over another (the railroads and trucking regulation, the Civil Aeronautics Board) and often producers over consumers altogether. However, in these early models, it was the application of regulation directly to markets and firms that marked capture, not the application of deregulation or weak regulation.

By contrast, it is apparent that as far as plausible capture is concerned, something quite different was going on over the past several decades. It was capture evinced in the weak application (or nonapplication) of regulatory tools. In other cases, it was the application of jurisdictional boundaries to prevent other agencies from regulating. Regulatory preemption – the move by which state and local regulations are invalidated by the imposition of national-level supremacy – became a favorite tool of officials in the George W. Bush Administration as a means of achieving deregulation. In some cases, preemption of state regulation was asserted by regulatory agencies themselves, such as when the Office of Thrift Supervision (OTS) and the Office of the Comptroller of the Currency (OCC) issued rulings in the 1990s and early 2000s preempting the application of state mortgage laws to federal thrifts and national banks.[4] Another form of boundary manipulation comes in regulatory arbitrage, or when banks choose their markets or institutional form so as to fit themselves to the least rigorous regulator.

The plausible mechanisms of corrosive capture are, to some degree, well known from the literature on capture in general. Firms and industries that want lower regulation, relative to the preferences of the public and/or the regulatory aims expressed in statute, will rely on campaign contributions, pressure on politicians, and perhaps the "revolving door" to reduce their individual and collective regulatory burdens. Yet another mechanism is available – one hard to prove, but one that seems to me increasingly relevant: what James Kwak, in Chapter 4 of this volume, terms *cultural capture*. It is always possible that cultural capture, through the shaping of assumptions, lenses, and vocabularies, can be used to support more traditional forms of Stiglerian capture. Yet cultural capture seems less likely to be deployed for the erection and maintenance of entry barriers than for deregulatory purposes. It would seem easier for industry to coordinate on a single message to reduce regulation – the benefits are industry-wide and the losers in this process are probably consumers – than to coordinate on a message in which some firms win and other firms (even if they are weaker or smaller) lose. So too, the innovation and laissez-faire ideologies that have shaped regulation in the past thirty to forty years have been deregulatory in their aim, and the existing accounts of cultural capture emphasize these ideological framings as central to recent developments in financial regulation.

PHARMACEUTICAL REGULATION: A REVIEW OF INSTITUTIONAL DEVELOPMENT

The Food, Drug and Cosmetic Act of 1938

The idea of regulatory entry barriers as a function of capture is one that invokes (implicitly or explicitly) a model of regulatory legislation. When regulation limits entry, then the benefitting firms are likely to have bought this protection through inducements to legislators.[5] If such a stratagem had worked to secure entry barriers for the larger and better established pharmaceutical firms of the early twentieth century, then the focus of

---

[4] Kathleen Engel and Patricia McCoy, *The Subprime Virus: Reckless Lending, Regulatory Failure and Next Steps* (New York: Oxford University Press, 2011), 157–62.

[5] Gene Grossman and Elhanan Helpman, *Special Interest Politics* (Cambridge, MA: MIT Press, 2003).

analysis should be on the Food, Drug and Cosmetic Act of 1938, which established FDA pre-market review authority.[6]

The agenda-setting process for the 1938 Act came from various calls for a revision of the FDA's original enabling statute, the 1906 Pure Food and Drugs Act. As historians have documented, two forces – the FDA itself and organized women's groups – exercised strong leverage in pressing for changes to the 1906 law.[7] FDA officials had long been disappointed with the operation of the 1906 Act. The first bill addressing these problems was authored by FDA personnel, was sponsored by New York Senator Royal Copeland, and was titled "S. 2800." Along with its successors "S. 5" and "S. 1944," S. 2800 attempted to rein in the patent medicine industry. One might temptingly interpret this bill, and its successors, as plausible candidates for placing competitive and entry barriers on the primary competitors of established pharmaceutical operations. The patent medicine industry was, after all, a multimillion-dollar market in the early twentieth century. The S. 2800 bill required disclosure of ingredients on labels (something that established drug companies such as Abbott, Pfizer, and Parke-Davis did, but that patent medicine companies did not), and removed the 1906 Act's condition that the FDA had to prove intent to defraud to seize commodity shipments. It also gave the FDA power to seize multiple shipments of "misbranded" goods and rendered advertisers and manufacturers alike legally liable for fraudulent claims. S. 2800 also empowered the FDA with new tools to govern pharmaceutical advertising. S. 5 weakened a number of these provisions, but remained a strong entry-constraining bill for the patent medicine industry and for many fledgling outfits in pharmaceuticals.

To advance these bills on the congressional and national agendas, the FDA launched a publicity initiative aimed at demonstrating the hazards of adulterated food and medicines to the nation's press. The FDA had been prevented from direct lobbying and publicity efforts by the Deficiency

---

[6] This section draws on both older and newer literatures on the 1938 Act. Charles O. Jackson, *Food and Drug Legislation in the New Deal* (Princeton: Princeton University Press, 1970); James Harvey Young, *The Medical Messiahs: A Social History of Health Quackery in Twentieth-Century America* (Princeton: Princeton University Press, 1967); Daniel Carpenter and Gisela Sin, "Policy Tragedy and the Emergence of Regulation: The Food, Drug and Cosmetic Act of 1938," *Studies in American Political Development* 21 (2007): 149–80; Daniel Carpenter, *Reputation and Power: Organizational Image and Pharmaceutical Regulation at the FDA* (Princeton: Princeton University Press, 2010), Chapter 2.

[7] Oscar E. Anderson, *The Health of a Nation: Harvey W. Wiley and the Fight for Pure Food* (Chicago: University of Chicago Press, 1958); James Harvey Young, *Pure Food* (Princeton: Princeton University Press, 1990); Daniel Carpenter, *The Forging of Bureaucratic Autonomy: Reputations, Networks and Policy Innovation in Executive Agencies, 1862–1928* (Princeton: Princeton University Press, 2001), 8.

Appropriations Act of 1919, yet the agency circumvented this constraint, distributing pamphlets such as *Why We Need a New Pure Food Law* and allowing its officials to make radio addresses on S. 2800. FDA Information Officer Ruth Lamb successfully invited press outlets to cover Copeland's first Senate bill (S. 1944), and she used her own time and money to author a popular book on the hazards of patent medicines entitled *The American Chamber of Horrors* (1936).[8]

FDA officials also drew strength from their decades-old alliances with women's groups and organized consumer unions. Two women's groups – the General Federation of Women's Clubs (GFWC) and the Women's Christian Temperance Union (WCTU), two of the most powerful lobbies of their time – almost single-handedly waged successful campaigns for mothers' pensions and child-labor laws. With FDA facilitation, these two groups had been instrumental in lobbying for the 1906 Act. In the 1930s debates, they were joined by Consumers' Research (CR). CR was founded in 1929 with 1,000 members and by 1933 had ballooned to 45,000 members. As historian Charles Jackson described the union, "CR's influence and significance far exceeded its actual membership. The organization served as a coordinating body for Congressional and other sympathizers of consumer legislation." Rexford Tugwell found "astounding" the "receptive attitude of the general public" toward CR.[9]

Despite what might seem like favorable circumstances in the early New Deal – an overwhelming Democratic majority in Congress with proregulation impulses, a Democratic president, supportive women's groups, and a well-coordinated rhetorical campaign – several factors combined to blunt the FDA's initiative for food and drug law reform. The most salient was well-organized and well-represented opposition from the affected industries. As Jackson described the rise of opposition, "Many existing trade bodies were turned almost immediately into vehicles of resistance. Especially militant were the Proprietary Association [PA] and the United Medicine Manufacturers of America [UMMA]." The PA and UMMA sponsored protest gatherings, radio advertisements, and coordinated petition campaigns against FDA-strengthening bills. The manufacturers found able legislative defenders such as Senators Josiah Bailey of Tennessee and Arthur Vandenberg of

---

[8] Gwen Kay, "Healthy Public Relations: The FDA's 1930s Legislative Campaign," *Bulletin of the History of Medicine* 75 (2001): 446–87.

[9] Carpenter, *The Forging of Bureaucratic Autonomy*, Chapter 8; Theda Skocpol, *Protecting Soldiers and Mothers* (Cambridge, MA: Harvard University Press, 1992); Elizabeth S. Clemens, *The People's Lobby* (Chicago: University of Chicago Press, 1998); Jackson, *Food and Drug Legislation in the New Deal*, 20–21.

Michigan. Two of the legislation's sponsors – Senator Copeland himself and Rexford Tugwell – also had the disadvantage of having well-ensconced political enemies, with FDR himself displeased with Copeland and many New Deal opponents hammering Tugwell as a symbol of what they perceived as the Roosevelt Administration's new liberal arrogance.[10]

Reform opponents landed an apparent deathblow in 1935, when the Senate passed Copeland's S. 5, but only after attaching the infamous "Bailey Amendment," which vitiated the measure. The Bailey Amendment prohibited the FDA from regulating any aspect of pharmaceutical advertising and would have given all such control to the Federal Trade Commission (FTC). From the vantage of the 1906 law, in which the FDA had control over fraudulent advertising, this was a step backward for the FDA. Once the Bailey Amendment was approved, S. 5 passed the Senate but was doomed by criticisms from the left and the right. S. 5 then died in the House by a substantial 190–70 vote.

Roll call votes are available for three crucial votes on the Senate measure in the seventy-fourth Congress (1935–1936), and these votes can be examined to test for the impact of observed ideology, party, region, and organized interests. The first two votes were on procedural measures to reconsider an amendment that had been attached to S. 5 during committee. Those who favored a stronger FDA wanted to revisit the committee's decisions and voted yes on this measure. The third vote was a vote on the Bailey Amendment prohibiting the FDA from regulating pharmaceutical advertising. Proponents of reform voted no on this measure, whereas most opponents of reform voted to pass it.

Probit regression analyses of these three votes in the seventy-fourth Congress were conducted, and coefficient estimates appear in Table 7.1. The control variables are chosen to unearth patterns of support for FDA-strengthening regulation before the sulfanilamide disaster. The most important of these controls are two general measures of ideology or voting propensity, namely first- and second-dimension D-NOMINATE scores. Also included are the senator's party (1 if Democrat) and the underlying Democratic strength of his constituency, measured by the percentage of votes for FDR in the 1932 election, and a variable measuring the shift in voter support for FDR from 1932 to 1936 as a way of measuring political trends within each state. To these political covariates are added demographic and economic variables measuring the state's rate of unemployment in 1930, the percentage of its residents aged 18–20 in school, the percentage of its

---

[10] Jackson, *Food and Drug Legislation in the New Deal*, 38–39.

Table 7.1. *Probit analyses of three votes on S. 5. [Senate Votes, 74th Congress]*

Variable	S. 5 amendment reconsideration [4/1/1935]	S. 5 amendment reconsideration [4/2/1935]	Bailey Amendment [4/8/1935]
Constant	1.8371	3.8839	1.7690
	(1.5636)	(1.8262)	(1.4917)
D-NOMINATE 1-D	2.0944	2.6960	1.8166
	(0.8531)	(1.0643)	(0.8019)
D-NOMINATE 2-D	1.3916	0.3583	0.3844
	(0.8194)	(1.1096)	(0.8613)
Party (Democrat = 1)	0.7572	1.3627	1.0947
	(0.6857)	(0.8369)	(0.6750)
Percentage of State Vote for FDR, 1932	0.0041	0.0169	0.0081
	(0.0206)	(0.0250)	(0.0185)
Change in % of State for FDR, 1932 1936	0.0103	0.0471	0.0177
	(0.0321)	(0.0386)	(0.0250)
% of State Population African American	0.0445	0.0429	0.0153
	(0.0396)	(0.0492)	(0.0377)
% of State Population Illiterate	0.1166	0.2109	0.1061
	(0.0790)	(0.0924)	(0.0818)
% of State Population Educated	0.0879	0.2119	0.0370
	(0.0494)	(0.0683)	(0.0469)
% of State "Gainful Workers" Unemployed	0.4181	0.5893	0.0815
	(0.1327)	(0.1736)	(0.1134)
Retail sales as % of Wholesale	0.0010	0.0009	0.0007
	(0.0026)	(0.0028)	(0.0025)
South	2.1259	1.1556	0.8767
	(0.9639)	(1.5649)	(0.8770)
Number of Proprietary Association firms in state	0.0375	0.0311	0.0179
	(0.0215)	(0.0245)	(0.0178)
Number of UMMA firms in state	0.2596	0.2888	0.0882
	(0.0829)	(0.0929)	(0.0541)
N (df)	83 (69)	75 (61)	81 (67)
LLF	43.512	33.796	49.307
Pseudo-R^2	0.2417	0.3396	0.1139

Notes: Asymptotic standard errors in parentheses. Bold coefficient estimate implies statistical significance at $p < 0.05$ (two-tailed test). UMMA firms and PA firms variables correlated at 0.5598. Removal of UMMA firms variable results in negative but insignificant estimate on PA firms variable.

residents who were illiterate as defined by the Census, and the percentage of its residents who were African American.[11]

[11] On NOMINATE-based methods and their application to American political history, see Keith Poole and Howard Rosenthal, *Congress: A Political-Economic History of Roll-Call Voting* (New York: Oxford University Press, 1998).

Two variables measuring the presence of organized patent medicine and pharmaceutical manufacturers in a state are included to test industry capture and rent-seeking hypotheses. The first measures the number of industry members of the Proprietary Association whose headquarters were in a state. The second measures the number of primary (above associate) members of the United Medicine Manufacturers' Association (UMMA) whose headquarters were in a state.

A key result from the Table 7.1 regressions is that rent-seeking hypotheses are strongly rejected. The variable measuring UMMA firms headquartered in a state is negatively associated with "yes" votes for the first two reconsideration measures and positively associated with votes for the Bailey Amendment. In other words, pharmaceutical interests aligned themselves against the entry-constraining legislation, and their legislative representatives followed suit.[12] In addition, senators from states with higher unemployment rates were more likely to support the reconsideration measure, which may reflect anticipated effects of tighter regulation on proprietary manufacturers in the state. This result is not, however, predicted by a rent-seeking perspective.[13]

Rent-seeking and industry capture explanations are not, then, supported by these analyses of legislative votes on entry-constraining regulation. Indeed, a hypothesis that runs *counter* to the capture perspective receives strong support. Affected industries, particularly the organized pharmaceutical firms that would have benefited from reduced proprietary competition,

---

[12] The variable measuring state-level presence of proprietary manufacturers is insignificant at the $p < 0.05$ level in all regressions. The coefficient estimate for the PA measure does achieve significance at the $p < 0.10$ level in the model for the first reconsideration vote, but this is due to the fact that this measure is highly correlated (rho = 0.5598) with the UMMA measure. Once the UMMA measure is removed, the coefficient estimate for the PA measure in this model switches sign and becomes insignificant ($b = 0.00029; z = 0.019$). This is not true for the UMMA measure, which remains negative and statistically significant in the first two models and positive and statistically significant in the third model when the PA measure is removed.

[13] The control variables are not particularly notable for their estimates, as they support standard legislative politics accounts of voting on these issues. The first dimension D-NOMINATE score (measuring left-right "economic ideology," roughly) has a negative coefficient estimate in the first two regressions and a positive estimate in the third. Because higher scores indicate more conservative members, this result implies that more liberal senators were more likely to vote for the first two measures and less likely to vote for the third. Conditioning on this effect, Democrats appear to be slightly more likely to vote against FDA-strengthening legislation, but these coefficient estimates are statistically indistinguishable from zero. The variables measuring support for FDR are also insignificant, suggesting that underlying Democratic support in one's constituency did not, net of other factors, induce more or less support for reform.

nonetheless fought the legislation, and their representatives were more likely to vote against FDA-strengthening measures.

In the end, the Food, Drug and Cosmetic Act of 1938 would pass, with even stronger gatekeeping provisions than envisioned in the earlier bills. In the wake of the sulfanilamide tragedy of 1937 and 1938, when an otherwise common sulfanilamide ingredient was suspended in a highly toxic elixir and more than 100 Americans died, Congress acted quickly to give FDA officials the gatekeeping power that they had long sought and that they viewed as particularly necessary in light of the tragedy.[14] The legislation defined the concept of a new drug and stipulated that any new drug must be approved by the FDA on the basis of its demonstrated safety.

POST-1938 DEVELOPMENTS

The tale of the FDA's enabling legislation in pharmaceutical regulation – the law that gave the agency gatekeeping power over the new drug marketplace – offers a stark rejection of capture-based hypotheses. This was a law passed largely through consumer pressure, pressure that had become incredibly amplified in the wake of a tragedy, and its gatekeeping provisions were resisted by the very companies that would benefit from them.[15] A similar inference can be drawn from developments in the 1940s and 1950s, when the FDA began to flesh out its regulatory power by establishing precedents through operations, decisions, and enforcement. The predominant influence on the agency during this period came from a set of multiple constituencies and audiences at the nexus of academic pharmacology, government and university scientists, and industry. There was industry participation in the process, to be sure, and drug companies and their political representatives had occasional successes in resisting regulatory expansion. Yet the development of the new drug application and the emergence of drug efficacy standards (whereby the FDA would assess drugs not only for their toxicity but also for their therapeutic results) happened far more outside of industry circles and influence than within them. By the time that another policy tragedy – the thalidomide crisis of the early 1960s, in which a commonly used sedative induced thousands upon thousands of

[14] Carpenter and Sin, "Policy Tragedy and the Emergence of Regulation."
[15] It should be clear that drug companies in the New Deal and in the early 1960s likely perceived that there would be other costs – such as increased regulatory scrutiny of their research and development processes, their products, and their marketing operations – that would outweigh whatever supply restriction benefits they derived from these new laws and regulations; Carpenter, *Reputation and Power*, Chapters 2 through 4.

birth defects – came along, the FDA was already regulating efficacy in new drug applications and imposing a scientific and procedural stringency that had alarmed the industry. Much of this stringency was codified and further elaborated in the Drug Amendments of 1962 that followed the thalidomide crisis. It was from the rulemaking following this statute (the Investigational New Drug [IND] rules of 1963) that the three-phase system of testing that governs global pharmaceutical development was hatched and codified. In these critical developments, the organized pharmaceutical industry largely played the role of an observer.[16]

There were more successful industry attempts in the years following the 1962 Amendments to shape the dialogue on regulation. Through a series of articles and books partially sponsored by industry and supported and often hosted and published by the conservative American Enterprise Institute (AEI) in Washington, D.C., clinical pharmacologists and industrial organization economists began to question the effect of FDA governance on a new watchword: "pharmaceutical innovation." These arguments were led by clinical pharmacologists Louis Lasagna and William Wardell and economists Sam Peltzman, Henry Grabowski, and John Vernon, among others. In addition to the focus of attention on the broad concept of innovation, these scholars coined a term – the "drug lag" – that refocused the international comparison on how quickly drugs reached the market in the United States versus comparator nations, especially Great Britain. The conclusions of these analyses were generally that the FDA's regulatory stringency had the effect of depriving American doctors and their patients of the latest advances in the pharmaceutical armamentarium. The critiques were highly effective, so much so that the FDA internally began tabbing some of its drug applications as "drug lag drugs" once another country had approved them and also began approving many drugs at the end of the year (a so-called December effect).[17]

To the extent that a deregulatory trend has shaped the FDA, it came as much from unlikely capture sources – organized patient advocates and

[16] Carpenter, *Reputation and Power*, Chapters 3 and 4; see also Philip Hilts, *Protecting America's Health: The FDA, Business and One Hundred Years of Regulation* (New York: Knopf, 2003). The National Cancer Institute (NCI) also played an important role in the development of phased clinical trials, yet the available evidence suggests that the idea of sequenced studies for examining toxicity and effectiveness was one that emerged from the U.S. Department of Agriculture and the FDA, and it pre-dated the concrete notions of phased studies in the NCI.

[17] Carpenter, *Reputation and Power*, Chapters 5, 7, and 12; Hilts, *Protecting America's Health*, "The Drug Lag."

government health officials – as from drug companies and their political organizations. Beginning with critiques about the drug lag and crystallizing in battles over cancer therapeutics and AIDS medicines, the FDA began to demonstrate greater flexibility in its drug development rules and its approval decisions. The transformation occurred first in the FDA's governance of cancer drugs, not least because forceful voices in oncology circles had begun to complain loudly about FDA interference in their clinical experiments, and because the National Cancer Institute (the largest and most powerful arm of the National Institutes of Health [NIH]) had begun to legitimate these complaints. In the late 1970s and early- to mid-1980s, before the AIDS crisis began to occupy health officials and drug development experts, the FDA moderated its stance and introduced more flexibility to its clinical development guidelines for cancer.[18]

When the AIDS crisis hit, other government health agencies such as the NIH and the Public Health Service (PHS) initially launched into action to identify the pathogenesis of the disorder and to isolate potential molecular treatments. It was not until after the first AIDS drug approval (azidothymidine [AZT]) that AIDS patients and gay men's groups began to coalesce around an agenda of FDA reform. AIDS activists did this cautiously, wary of alliances with the pharmaceutical industry. Yet this moment, and the overwhelming public and professional anxiety induced by the globalizing AIDS epidemic, saw industry-backed lobbyists and conservative voices seize an opportunity to create a strange-bedfellows coalition in support of FDA transformation. The longer term result was the Prescription Drug User Fee Act (PDUFA) of 1992, which levied per-application taxes on drug companies in return for greater industry voices in FDA management and FDA observance of deadlines in new drug review. PDUFA is widely acknowledged to have accelerated the agency's review of new drug applications.

Many agency observers and critics have argued that the user-fee law represents a form of agency capture, insofar as the FDA depends for its funding on the industry it regulates. This interpretation is plausible but lacks solid evidence and, in the most simplistic of cases,[19] rests on a misunderstanding of PDUFA's history. The user-fee act was a compromise between liberal Democrats (headed by the late Senator Edward Kennedy of Massachusetts) and conservative Republicans (represented by Senator Orrin Hatch of Utah). Kennedy and Hatch cosponsored the bill, and it passed the

[18] Carpenter, *Reputation and Power*, Chapter 6.
[19] Marcia Angell, "FDA: This Agency Can Be Dangerous," *The New York Review of Books*, September 2010.

U.S. Senate unanimously; few if any of its sponsors at the time saw it as a deregulatory measure. If corrosive capture was the result of PDUFA, it cannot be said to have been an intended result.

The problem with representing PDUFA as a cause of agency capture – clearly the critics have in mind the corrosive form – is that its emergence coincides with a number of other plausible explanations. These include the following:

- The more conservative and antiregulatory climate of the 1980s and 1990s, one that was reinforced in presidential elections and congressional policymaking
- The AIDS crisis itself and its related calls for acceleration of the FDA approval process
- The information technology revolution occurring in society, whereby new drug applications and a host of other government functions have been completed more quickly
- The increasing staff totals at the FDA, which permitted quicker new drug reviews and which began at least five years before the user-fee act was struck into law[20]

Any claim that the user-fee act is the proximate cause of corrosive capture, or even that capture has occurred in the past fifteen to twenty years of American pharmaceutical regulation, must contend with these alternative explanations. Simply put, those claiming that capture has occurred have failed to provide anything but anecdotal evidence and policy testimonials.

Perhaps the most plausible mechanism for capture to have occurred is that of cultural capture. The revolving door hypothesis is unlikely to explain recent changes, insofar as some of the FDA's most long-serving members (Robert Temple, Janet Woodcock, John Jenkins) have become, in recent years, more receptive to some industry arguments about drug innovation and the regulation of safety. Because these members have not left for the cozy pastures of the pharmaceutical industry (and they long ago could have), and because these members have been important catalysts in the agency's changes, it is unlikely that the revolving door accounts for the change. What is more likely, if corrosive capture is involved, is that the political organizations of the global pharmaceutical industry have come to shape the conversation about how drugs ought to be regulated. Chief among these developments is the notion that there is a direct trade-off between

---

[20] Daniel Carpenter, Dean Smith, Michael Chernew, and A. Mark Fendrick, "Approval Times for New Drugs: Does the Source of Funding for FDA Staff Matter?" *Health Affairs*, Web Exclusive, December 17, 2003, W3-618-624.

drug safety and drug innovation and that these values (and not market confidence or scientific improvements in drug quality per se) are the main variables to be considered in examining this regime of regulation.[21]

To the extent that cultural capture embodies a change in regulatory cognition, there are seasoned observers of American pharmaceutical regulation who believe that it has occurred. In January 2010, Jim Dickinson, editor of *FDA Webview* and a long-time columnist and consultant on matters in the pharmaceutical sphere, remarked that the FDA was more "pro-industry" than at any time in the previous thirty-five years, and that new Obama Administration appointees Margaret Hamburg (commissioner) and Joshua Sharfstein (then principal deputy commissioner) could do little to change this fact, because the mechanism was embedded in agency culture. In a widely read post on his Web log in 2010, Dickinson wrote that:

It has taken almost a generation, but by now, the pro-industry infiltration of FDA's culture is firmly entrenched. Not only is collaboration in product reviews officially encouraged, but good relationships across the regulatory fence hold the prospect of a possible future career in a well-paid industry job – a connection that is less likely to be publicly noticed in news media that now have to line up for information that has been filtered through agency press offices. The arm's-length relationship that formerly ruled every contact between agency and industry has become a fading memory.

According to health care journalist Merrill Goozner, Dickinson argued that "the shift in culture accelerated after the 1992 passage of the Prescription Drug User Fee Act, which made the agency dependent on industry funding." He concluded that "there's nothing that Margaret Hamburg, the new commissioner, and Joshua Sharfstein, her deputy, can do about it." Dickinson then quoted a former FDA chief of enforcement, who wrote that: "User fees at FDA are the primary villain, because they allowed the industry to dictate the changes at the FDA in programs, procedures and practices. It will be impossible for the Obama administration to reverse the trend because as long as the user fees are in place the industry has the upper hand."[22]

---

[21] It is here where I must myself offer something of a *mea culpa*, as some of my own early work on FDA pharmaceutical regulation contributed to the reification of this trade-off. Daniel Carpenter, "Groups, the Media, Agency Waiting Costs, and FDA Drug Approval," *American Journal of Political Science* 46 (2) (July 2002): 490–505; Daniel Carpenter, "The Political Economy of FDA Drug Approval: Processing, Politics and Implications for Policy," *Health Affairs* 23 (1) (January/February 2004): 52–63. In more recent writings – *Reputation and Power* (2010) – I have tried to incorporate other variables that have eluded much of the public and academic conversation.

[22] The Dickinson language, reproduced in a Health Care blog column by Goozner, accessed July 16, 2011, http://www.reducedrugprices.org/read.asp?news=4978.

Coming from an observer with knowledge of Dickinson, these are strong words and even stronger quotations. They certainly compel us to entertain the possibility of regulatory corrosion through cultural capture. Yet as plausible as that case may be, plausibility lies a far distance from proof. This distance, in general, is a problem with cultural capture accounts; not unlike the kind of hegemony postulated by the Italian theorist Antonio Gramsci, it is difficult to follow the train of concepts and thoughts from their source in industry to their realization in the minds and actions of regulatory officials. It is also difficult to evaluate the necessary counterfactuals – in the absence of cultural capture, would capture have occurred anyway? Would regulatory officials have come to these conclusions in the absence of industry pressure and dialogue? – in these claims. Still, one lesson from recent evidence, including the plausibility of cultural capture of the FDA, is clear; the capture being entertained is not of the Huntington-Bernstein-Stigler sort of constructed entry barriers, but of the corrosive sort, whereby deregulation is plausibly being accomplished through nonlegislative means.

PHARMACEUTICAL REGULATION: A REVIEW OF STATISTICAL EVIDENCE

Although the historical evidence offers a clear rejection of industry capture hypotheses for American pharmaceutical regulation, it is important to consider aggregate statistical evidence from regulatory operations. Here, too, the evidence allows for strong rejection of Stiglerian capture hypotheses, even as we observe some correlations that, initially, would seem to cohere with capture accounts.

Firm Sales Regressions

One illuminating test of entry-barrier capture for a regulatory agency such as the FDA can be applied to its approval decisions. Because regulatory approval is required for market entry, one might surmise that larger firms are likely to pass through this process more quickly than smaller firms, especially if the regime is rigged against smaller and newer competitors. An important operationalization of this hypothesis is that larger and wealthier firms should receive quicker review times. The data for the present analysis of this hypothesis consist of 447 new molecular entities (NMEs) submitted to the FDA over the period 1979–2000 (see Table 7.2).[23] A larger set of

---

[23] Some of the analysis conducted here was conducted for a broader, not yet published paper entitled "Why Do Bigger Firms Receive Faster Drug Approvals?" coauthored with Colin Moore, Marc Turenne, Ian Yohai, and Evan James Zucker.

Table 7.2. *Duration regressions for new molecular entities, 1979–2000 [Negative coefficients imply association with faster reviews.]*

(Model)	(1) No fixed effects	(2) Firm fixed effects	(3) No fixed effects	(4) Firm fixed effects
VARIABLES				
ln (firm sales)	0.0757	0.0511	0.0587	0.0203
	(0.0147)	(0.0213)	(0.0181)	(0.0216)
ln (firm submissions)			0.0728	**0.3705**
			(0.0458)	(0.0746)
Constant	3.4623	3.4518	3.4434	3.4746
	(0.1263)	(0.1283)	(0.1263)	(0.1247)
NDAs	447	447	447	447
Number of disease-based random effects	149	149	149	149

Log-normal duration regressions of FDA review time on firm sales and firm previous submissions at time of submission. Standard errors in parentheses; all tests are two-tailed.

drugs was submitted, but the sample here contains verifiable review time data and available firm data such as submission histories, sales, and the like. During this period, the FDA reported that approximately 25 percent of all NDAs are not (eventually) approved (FDA 1988), so the present sample may over-sample or under-sample nonapproved drugs, depending on the analysis.[24] All NMEs in our analysis were considered under the FDA's new drug application (NDA) procedures, but not all NDAs during this period are included in our sample. In particular, generic drug applications, supplemental indication submissions that occur when a company seeks to market its drug for a disease other than the one for which it was originally submitted, and abbreviated new drug applications are excluded from analysis. The dependent variable is the review time, in months, from the NDA submission date to the NDA approval date (if approval occurred).

Any number of pharmaceutical firms may combine to develop and market a drug. One firm may discover the chemical entity, another may license it for clinical development in return for up-front and "milestone"

---

[24] Acquiring complete data for nonapproved drugs is a very difficult undertaking. The essential dilemma is that any and all information concerning an NDA that is not yet approved is considered proprietary under FDA regulations and is excluded from availability under the Freedom of Information Act. In fact, the FDA is legally proscribed from acknowledging the *existence* of a pending NDA until (and only if) the application is approved. In the 1960s, medical reporters reported that approximately "30% of all applications are withdrawn or die as incomplete. Formal rejection is rare." "Safety and Skepticism: Thalidomide," *Modern Medicine* (October 15, 1962): 28.

payments, and then the drug may be marketed by yet a third company. Almost invariably only one of these firms sponsors a new drug application to the FDA. All of the firm-level measures used here are keyed to the *submitting firm*. In most cases, the submitting firm has played an important role in the clinical development of the drug (funding clinical trials, for example) even if the firm in question did not discover the chemical entity.[25]

Measuring Firm Size

I use several indices to measure the size of firms. I first use world sales in the year of the drug's submission. World sales are preferable to U.S. sales because pharmaceutical revenues can come from a variety of national markets. I calibrate each firm's sales to a common index (U.S. dollars) using average yearly exchange rates, then deflate the dollar aggregates using implicit gross domestic product price deflators. Occasionally, I also use firm-specific employment aggregates, as larger firms will customarily employ more workers. These workers may represent a political constituency – for example, the "Pill Belt" commonly understood to comprise New Jersey, Eastern Pennsylvania, Delaware, and Maryland – that politicians may seek to satisfy by lobbying the FDA.

Measuring Familiarity: Submissions and Mergers

For each drug submitted, I tabulate the number of previous submissions that the submitting firm has at the date of NDA submission. Because the sample may not capture all nonapproved drugs, my measure probably underrepresents firm submissions. For firms that merged during our sample period, we restart this counter but also code for the merger with a dummy variable and a separate variable tabulating the years since the firm's most recent merger. Mergers may lead to greater FDA uncertainty over firm attributes; they combine the experience of two or more firms but also generate a "matching" effect about which the agency must learn.

U.S. versus non-U.S. firms

Rent seeking would predict that domestic firms will be privileged over foreign ones, or at the very least not disadvantaged relative to foreign firms. One would particularly expect this pattern in U.S. pharmaceutical

---

[25] Carpenter, *Reputation and Power*, Chapter 10.

Table 7.3. *Duration regressions for new molecular entities,
1979–2000: analysis of foreign versus domestic firm effects
[Negative coefficients imply association with faster reviews.]*

(Model) VARIABLES	(1)	(2)
ln (firm sales)	0.0447	0.0381
	(0.0202)	(0.0201)
ln (firm submissions)	0.0945	0.1071
	(0.0485)	(0.0510)
Foreign Firm	0.1508	0.1296
	(0.0855)	(0.0861)
Merged Firm		0.3475
		(0.2081)
ln (submissions) * merged		0.1027
		(0.1067)
Constant	3.4449	3.4351
	(0.1294)	(0.1291)
NDAs	439	439
Number of disease-based random effects	148	148

Log-normal duration regressions of FDA review time on firm sales and firm
previous submissions at time of submission. Standard errors in parentheses;
all tests are two-tailed.

regulation, given the FDA's putative history of being more danger-averse
than regulators overseas[26] and the cohesive political organization of
pharmaceutical manufacturers here. Yet the estimates show that, in the
aggregate, it is foreign firms who pass more quickly through the FDA's drug
review process in the 1979–2000 period (see Table 7.3). This is a direct and
strong refutation of Stiglerian capture theory.

The rejection of rent-seeking and capture hypotheses may seem odd,
given that wealthier and larger firms do seem to bear approval time advantages. Yet when one turns to explain large-firm advantage at the FDA, the
results here are remarkably inconsistent with the most basic predictions of
rent-seeking theory. Domestic firms do much worse than foreign firms in
FDA regulation, and older firms do worse than younger ones. Analyses of
lobbying contributions, moreover, show inconsistent results that disappear
once other covariates are added to the estimation.

The analyses show that, once the effect of mergers is accounted for, the
simple advantage of being better known to the agency accounts for as much

[26] Henry G. Grabowski and John M. Vernon, *The Regulation of Pharmaceuticals* (Washington,
D.C.: AEI Press, 1983).

as 55 percent of estimated large-firm advantage in NDA approval times. Adding this variable and controlling for firm fixed effects are enough to make the estimated effect "disappear" in the sense of falling below conventional levels of statistical significance.

In related analyses of review times,[27] the relationship between order of entry into a market niche (the particular disease being treated by the drug) and review times was examined. Again, entry-barrier capture accounts such as the Huntington-Bernstein-Stigler synthesis suggest that earlier entrants to a market niche should receive quicker and steadier regulatory approval. This relationship was indeed discovered, yet analysis of the data (tied to mathematical modeling) suggests that the reason for "early-entrant protection" in FDA drug review was not industry capture, but patient advocacy. Once the first few drugs for a disease had been introduced on the market, the pressure for additional approvals fell sharply, as patients and their advocates become politically "satisfied" with the supply of new drugs available and their propensity to lobby for more approvals falls.

One must acknowledge, in presenting and reviewing this evidence, the very real possibility that capture and rent seeking may express themselves in other venues, namely the ability of the FDA to induce pre-NDA product abandonment through rulemaking and expectations of delay at the NDA review stage. These hypotheses remain untested, and the proper framework for doing so remains one for which submissions are endogenous to the review process, both theoretically[28] and empirically, through joint estimation of a submission equation and an approval equation. The present chapter, we hope, has clarified what the sample ought to look like (it needs to include nonapproved drugs), has elucidated the importance of firm reputations and disease politics, and has clarified the behavior of the FDA, the last mover in the complicated game of drug development.

RELATED CONSIDERATIONS AND CONCLUSION

Although the present analysis has been focused on pharmaceuticals, it is useful to consider related commodities for which the FDA and the U.S. government have been slow to assert their authority. Consider the following two

---

[27] Daniel Carpenter, Susan Moffitt, Colin Moore, Ryan Rynbrandt, Michael Ting, Ian Yohai, and Evan James Zucker, "Early-Entrant Protection in Approval Regulation: Theory and Evidence from FDA Drug Review," *Journal of Law, Economics and Organization*, 26 (2) (Fall 2010). doi: 10.1093/jleo/ewp002.

[28] Daniel P. Carpenter and Michael M. Ting, "Regulatory Errors with Endogenous Agendas," *American Journal of Political Science* 51 (October 2007): 835–52.

product types, both of which deserve more academic study, but where a cursory look at their regulation suggests a clear rejection of rent-seeking capture hypotheses with perhaps the plausibility of corrosive capture hypotheses.

- **Nutritional supplements and dietary supplements:** Public health advocates and some FDA officials have long tried to regulate dietary supplements, which by their classification as foods have escaped the gatekeeping provisions of the 1938 and 1962 legislation governing new drugs. An entry-barrier approach to capture would suggest that the pharmaceutical industry would attempt to get these drugs regulated, as their relatively large market likely substitutes for a considerable amount of pharmaceutical utilization and sales. Yet repeated attempts by the FDA and Congress to regulate the dietary supplements industry have failed; in some cases (as with the Proxmire Amendment of 1976 and the Dietary Supplement Health and Education Act of 1994), these attempts have been so heavily rebuffed that the FDA's authority over these products has been rigidly delimited or even prohibited.

- **Medical devices:** Given that the pharmaceutical industry has a longer history than the medical device industry, and that surgical procedures and medical devices compete with pharmaceuticals for the treatment of disease, one would plausibly expect, under an entry-barrier capture account, that drug companies would use the approval process to erect barriers to entry among devices. Yet most observers of the medical device industry and the pharmaceutical industry over the past thirty years would argue that it is the medical device industry that is more lightly regulated regarding approval, which is the reverse of what an entry-barrier capture perspective would suggest. Some of these apparent differences concern FDA behavior, whereas others derive from legislative sources such as the Medical Device Amendments Act of 1976 and related rulemaking.

The strongest conclusion that can be drawn from the historical and statistical evidence is that entry-barrier capture of the sort theorized by Huntington, Bernstein, and Stigler is not a solid or powerful explanation for the development or operation of American pharmaceutical regulation. If anything, the capture that has plausibly occurred has been of the corrosive, deregulatory kind, and this raises larger questions about the limits of existing capture theory.

To the extent that capture exists in American pharmaceutical regulation, it is certainly weak capture and not strong capture as we have defined it in this volume. Some corrosion may have occurred – although the evidence supporting these vague claims is impressionistic and far from robust – and yet, the plausible corrosion functions much like the exception that proves the rule. The decline in trust in the FDA has corresponded with a decline in trust in the pharmaceutical industry and its new products,[29] and this relationship underscores the critically valuable confidence benefits that approval regulation of new drug treatments brings. Both capture analyses and economic analyses of regulation will need to take into account these benefits in order for a fuller calculus (political and economic) of pharmaceutical regulation to hold.

---

[29] Carpenter, *Reputation and Power*, Chapter 12, and Alex Berenson, "Big Drug Makers See Sales Decline with Their Image," *The New York Times* (November 14, 2005).

SECTION III

REGULATORY CASE STUDIES

The chapters in this section examine actual cases of regulation and, in so doing, illuminate capture in ways that may foster its prevention. The cases, ranging in time from the 1920s to the present, cover a spectrum of domains regulated by government, from the airwaves and highways to deep-water drilling and public health. Although consistent with our hypothesis that *weak* capture may be widespread,[1] these chapters consider a range of cases in which regulators succeeded, despite entrenched interests, and in which regulation failed for reasons only partly related to capture. These cases make clear that capture is neither a constant barrier to regulatory success, nor the sole cause of regulatory failure. They suggest that, in addition to model building, in-depth investigation of real-world regulation is necessary to better understand both the ways capture manifests in practice and how (and under what conditions) the public interest can be advanced through contemporary regulation.

David Moss and Jonathan B.L. Decker's historical analysis in Chapter 8 demonstrates the folly of inferring capture from the mere fact that a regulatory decision seems to benefit a particular interest group. The Federal Radio Commission's 1927 decision against expanding the broadcast spectrum has long been viewed as a classic case of capture, in which incumbent

---

[1] See Introduction, 12–14.

broadcasters benefited at the expense of the broader public. However, Moss and Decker find that the FRC's decision was supported by *all* of the relevant interest groups at the time, from radio manufacturers to radio listeners, and that the incumbent broadcasters alleged to have captured the decision were in fact among the least unified on the issue. The authors find no basis for the consensus judgment that the decision was captured, and they encourage more rigorous historical inquiry to avoid such misdiagnoses in the future.

Although it is striking that Moss and Decker find no evidence of capture in the decision they studied, many regulatory decisions are subject to some degree of undue influence, or weak capture by our definition.[2] Even when evidence of undue influence is present, however, careful study is needed to assess the extent to which capture has contributed to any particular bad outcome. Christopher Carrigan's examination of the Minerals Management Service (MMS) and its deepwater drilling safety regulations at the time of the BP *Deepwater Horizon* catastrophe (Chapter 10) is illustrative. With the largest oil spill in U.S. history having occurred under the supervision of an agency now infamous for its improper links with industry, it is understandable that commentators quickly jumped to the conclusion that capture was the principal cause of regulatory failure. Yet Carrigan finds that most stakeholders, including a majority of the public, favored trading off precaution for expedited development of deepwater wells in advance of the disaster and that this contributed significantly to the regulatory climate in which the accident occurred. Although fixating on capture makes for easy scapegoats, Carrigan argues that it also masks the true source of the problem in the case of the MMS, which in turn undermines the potential for effective reform.

Careful empirical analysis enables Sanford Gordon and Catherine Hafer to demonstrate in Chapter 9 that industry influence is but one factor among many that shape enforcement decisions at the Mining Safety and Health Administration. Gordon and Hafer find that both the political leanings of administration leadership and media coverage of mining disasters shape enforcement regimes in ways that defy a simple capture-based explanation. Indeed, they find strong evidence that political leaders "succeed in exercising influence on agency affairs separate from that exercised by the industry." Based on these findings, Gordon and Hafer recommend extending their modes of analysis to other regulatory contexts, and they urge scholars to

---

[2] As discussed in the Introduction, weak capture can be diagnosed when an agency is subject to the undue influence of industry but not to such an extent that it renders the regulation contrary to the public interest.

look beyond simple capture hypotheses to understand the complex and dynamic ways in which influence is exerted on regulation.

Similarly sensitive to the process of regulation, Susan Webb Yackee finds in Chapter 11 that structural features of administrative procedure – and especially the involvement of state- and local-level government officials – can mitigate undue influence over federal regulation. In an innovative empirical study of the role of influence in the notice and comment period at the Department of Transportation, Yackee demonstrates that business interests are both the most active and the most influential participants. Yet she also finds that industry influence is mitigated by the active role of state and local transportation officials engaged in the federal process, highlighting an intriguing capture-prevention strategy. Indeed, Yackee's study suggests that where state and local level officials can provide alternative sources of information and expertise to federal regulators, the influence of industry interests can be reduced.

In Chapter 12, Mariano-Florentino Cuéllar examines cases in which the public interest was apparently served by three federal agencies – the Centers for Disease Control and Prevention, the Food and Drug Administration, and the United States Department of Agriculture – despite organized industry opposition. Although traditional capture theory would heavily discount the possibility of successful (public interest) regulation under such conditions, Cuéllar details how the agencies were able to succeed in part by building alliances outside government and by relying on the independent expertise and reputation of agency staff. These possibilities suggest that while special interest influence matters in regulation, it can be overcome. They also give reason to believe that further research, sensitive to the actual conditions in which regulatory policy is made, could inform how capture might be prevented and the public interest more fully achieved in the future.

8

Capturing History

The Case of the Federal Radio Commission in 1927

David A. Moss and Jonathan B.L. Decker

INTRODUCTION

What is the role of history in the study of political economy? Perhaps its most important role in this context is as a test of theory and a source of new hypotheses. Ronald Coase, for example, famously challenged our understanding of public goods by exposing the hidden history of private lighthouses when theory had imagined only public ownership.[1]

History can also be informed by theory. With respect to regulatory capture, George Stigler once observed that important historical inferences about policy intent could be drawn from the economic theory of regulation. Noting that the "theory tells us to look... at who gains and who loses, and how much, when we seek to explain a regulatory policy," he suggested that "*the truly intended effects* [of a policy] *should be deduced from the actual effects.*"[2] Indeed, inferences of this sort have become common in the study of regulation.[3]

One significant danger is that these two strategies may become intertwined – that historical inferences *from* theory may somehow make their way into historical tests *of* theory. Surely, such inferences cannot legitimately be adduced as evidence for the theory that generated them. To the extent

---

[1] Ronald H. Coase, "The Lighthouse in Economics," *Journal of Law and Economics* 357 (1974): 357–76.

[2] George Stigler, *The Citizen and the State* (Chicago: University of Chicago Press, 1975), "Supplementary Note on Economic Theories of Regulation," 140, emphasis in the original.

[3] However, Roger Noll warns of "the lurking danger of tautology, i.e., of attributing causality to an inevitable consequence of any public policy action. It is impossible to imagine that regulation could be imposed without redistributing income. Hence, a look for winners in the process – and organizations that represent them – is virtually certain to succeed." See Roger G. Noll, "Economic Perspectives on the Politics of Regulation," in *Handbook of Industrial Organization*, Vol. II, eds. Richard Schmalensee and Robert D. Willig (Amsterdam: North-Holland, 1989), 1276–77.

that historical cases are regarded as support for a theory, they must be based on hard evidence, not on inference from the theory itself.

Avoiding this trap is anything but easy in the study of regulation, particularly given the powerful hold that the economic theory of regulation has within the field. When we see an interest group benefit from a regulation, it is now almost instinctive to conclude that this was the intended result and that the interest that benefited must have been at least partly – and perhaps wholly – responsible for securing the regulation in the first place (through lobbying, etc.).[4]

One unfortunate consequence with respect to historical inquiry is that researchers may be tempted to scratch around in the documentary record to find what they were looking for – to find what they knew in advance, based on theory, *had* to be there. To avoid this trap, it is imperative that the use of history as a test of theory always involve a vigorous search not only for confirming evidence, but for disconfirming evidence as well. Good scholarship requires nothing less.

In this chapter, we take up the challenge of using history to test theory by focusing on a single well-known case: the Federal Radio Commission's (FRC's) 1927 decision not to expand the broadcast radio band.

The most widely cited study of this decision was conducted by Thomas Hazlett, who concluded that incumbent broadcasters had succeeded in capturing the FRC. Drawing especially on a primary historical source, the magazine *Radio Broadcast*, Hazlett found that incumbent radio broadcasters – who presumably would have suffered from additional competition on an expanded broadcast band – strongly opposed the expansion proposal in 1927.[5] He also took for granted that the listening public would have benefited from expansion of the band, because it would have gained more choice with respect to broadcasting stations.[6] The FRC's rejection of the expansion proposal thus represented "a classic regulatory capture, creating significant

---

[4] For example, Thomas Hazlett and Matthew Spitzer wrote, "One need not assume perfect foresight nor abstract from the transactional difficulties in a political world to conclude that when interests with substantial rents at stake appear to secure optimal regulatory outcomes they were more than lucky. Indeed, George Stigler long held that it made sense to infer backwards . . . " Thomas W. Hazlett and Matthew L. Spitzer, "Digital Television and the Quid Pro Quo," *Business and Politics* 2 (2000): 115–59.

[5] See Thomas W. Hazlett, "The Rationality of U.S. Regulation of the Broadcast Spectrum," *Journal of Law and Economics* 133 (1990): 154–58. See also Thomas W. Hazlett, "Physical Scarcity, Rent-Seeking and the First Amendment," *Columbia Law Review* 905 (1997): 918–19; Thomas W. Hazlett, "Underregulation: The Case of the Radio Spectrum," in *The Regulators' Revenge*, ed. Thomas W. Bell (Washington, D.C.: Cato Institute, 1998), 92.

[6] Hazlett, "The Rationality of U.S. Regulation," 155–56.

industry rents that were shared with political constituencies in proportion to their effective influence over policy."[7]

The fact that a powerful interest group favored a regulatory result that appears ultimately to have benefited it stands as a notable piece of confirming evidence for a capture interpretation. It is also necessary, however, to consider what sorts of historical evidence would contradict this interpretation and whether any such evidence exists.

In undertaking this exercise with regard to the FRC's 1927 decision, we conceived of three potential categories of disconfirming evidence: (1) evidence that a broad range of groups, in addition to broadcasters, opposed expansion of the broadcast band; (2) evidence that at least some incumbent broadcasters did not oppose expansion; and (3) evidence that incumbent broadcasters did not in fact expect to benefit from an FRC decision to retain the existing band.

Our review of the historical record, including examination of previously unutilized transcripts of the relevant FRC hearings, produced strong disconfirming evidence in category 1 (in short, that *every* major interest group, not just radio broadcasters, publicly opposed expansion of the band in 1927); weak disconfirming evidence in category 2 (namely, that the broadcasters who testified at the FRC hearings were about evenly divided between opposition and support for the expansion proposal); and some interesting, but ultimately inconclusive, evidence in category 3 (highlighting the relatively bleak expectations about the long-term profitability of commercial radio as of early 1927).

We also searched for additional confirming evidence of a capture interpretation, particularly for direct evidence of attempts by incumbent radio broadcasters to influence FRC commissioners, but found very little evidence of this type.

Overall, we conclude that the disconfirming evidence outweighs the confirming evidence in this case and thus that the 1927 episode cannot reasonably be regarded as a case of regulatory capture.

The remainder of this chapter proceeds as follows: first, we summarize the logic and evidence behind the traditional argument that the FRC's expansion decision was captured by incumbent broadcasters; second, we provide a brief overview of our argument and key historical findings, most of which run contrary to the capture interpretation; and third, in three consecutive sections that comprise the bulk of the chapter, we review the relevant historical evidence in detail. Finally, in the conclusion, we discuss

---

[7] Hazlett, "Physical Scarcity," 918–19.

the implications of our findings and offer some additional thoughts about the proper role of history in the study of regulatory capture and political economy more generally.

THE TRADITIONAL STORY:
CAPTURE OF THE EXPANSION DECISION

The story of the expansion decision culminates on April 5, 1927, when the FRC rejected a proposal that would have expanded the ninety-six-channel radio broadcast band to include the fifty adjacent higher frequency channels, enlarging the 550- to 1,500-kHz band to include the 1,500- to 2,000-kHz band. At the time, nearly all observers believed that the airwaves were overcrowded. More than 700 stations across the country were broadcasting simultaneously on the allotted ninety-six channels, resulting in significant interference. Enlarging the broadcast band ideally would have allowed the retention of existing stations while also providing room for new broadcasters looking for a share of the radio spectrum. Hazlett argued that by rejecting the expansion proposal, the FRC displayed a clear preference for the anticompetitive interests of incumbent broadcasters over the interest of consumers (listeners) in a larger choice of stations.

In Hazlett's view, no reasonable, impartial regulator could have made such a decision: "If regulators had made a good-faith, even if analytically unsophisticated, attempt to deal straightforwardly with overcrowding of the airwaves, their first step should have been to allow for an expansion of available broadcasting frequencies."[8] Hazlett maintained that no technological barrier blocked the use of those channels. In fact, a band sixty times larger than that assigned to broadcasters was "known to be potentially available given then current technology," having already been assigned for other communications uses.[9]

The "radio industry's argument" for artificially limiting this nearly boundless terrain was that expansion would harm consumers with first-generation radios, by forcing them to buy new receivers. This "transparently false" argument, as Hazlett characterized it, misrepresented the gains from expansion: "Clearly, consumers would be better off having a choice between listening to an uncluttered one-MHz band on an existing radio and purchasing a broader-band receiver so as to enjoy enhanced program selection, than in being given only the first alternative."[10]

---

[8] Hazlett, "The Rationality of U.S. Regulation," 155–56.
[9] Ibid.
[10] Ibid.

Hazlett offered evidence for the broadcasters' position on spectrum expansion by quoting from the "trade journal" *Radio Broadcast*.[11] He observed that "the industry was most concerned about how the FRC would deal with 'such dangerous propositions as the pressure to extend the broadcast band . . . ; the fatuous claims of the more recently licensed stations to a place in the ether; and the uneconomic proposals to split time on the air rather than eliminate excess stations wholesale . . . ,' as one trade journal forthrightly summarized." He quoted from the same journal to highlight the broadcasters' relief and satisfaction once the commission had rendered its decision: "'Broadening of the band was disposed of with a finality which leaves little hope for the revival of that pernicious proposition; . . . the commissioners were convinced that less [sic.] stations was the only answer.'"[12]

A NEW LOOK AT THE HISTORICAL RECORD: THE PRESENCE OF *DISCONFIRMING* EVIDENCE

Although the traditional story of why the FRC rejected the proposal to expand the broadcast band in 1927 seems logical (and fully consistent with the economic theory of regulation), a thorough review of the available documents – including newly discovered transcripts of the FRC's hearings on the subject in late March and early April of 1927 – reveals a surprising amount of disconfirming evidence not previously presented.

A Broad Coalition Against the Expansion Proposal

To begin with, radio broadcasters were neither the only, nor the staunchest, opponents of expansion. In fact, almost every interest group represented at the hearings opposed expansion, leading the *Washington Post* to run a story under the headline, "Radio Witnesses Unanimous Against Wider Wave Bands."[13] These opponents included not only radio broadcasters,

[11] Ibid., 154.
[12] Ibid., 155.
[13] "Radio Witnesses Unanimous Against Wider Wave Bands," *Washington Post* (March 30, 1927): 4. In a *Columbia Law Review* article, Hazlett reaffirmed his claim that "[r]adio broadcast interests bitterly opposed" the proposal to expand the broadcast band by citing the FRC's 1927 annual report, which "noted that '[u]nited opposition to widening the broadcasting band in order to accommodate more stations was expressed at the hearings by representatives of the radio art, science, and industry . . . '" (Hazlett, "Physical Scarcity," 918–19). Clearly, though, in using the phrase "representatives of the radio art, science, and industry," the commission meant to cover multiple interests associated with radio (engineers, amateurs, manufacturers, etc.), not just broadcasters.

but also radio engineers (who claimed that the proposed frequencies were inferior for broadcasting and that designing new radios to receive those frequencies would prove complicated and costly), radio manufacturers (who shared the engineers' concerns and expressed an unwillingness to antagonize their customers by supporting a decision that would render existing radios obsolete), amateur radio operators and inventors (who did not want to lose access to the proposed frequencies, in part because they believed their early experimentation with television had to take place on those frequencies), and representatives of radio listeners' organizations (which echoed concerns about higher cost radios and lower quality reception associated with the expanded band and which apparently preferred a smaller number of high-quality stations to a larger number of low-quality ones).[14] Given the broad alignment of interests against the proposal to expand the band, it would have been shocking indeed had the FRC decided in favor of it.[15]

[14] Although some speakers at the 1927 hearings referred to having received "invitations," Herbert Hoover's assistant observed in a letter at the time that "the Radio Commission has sent out a blanket invitation to all people in the country who desire either to appear in person or to submit their recommendations in writing. I do not understand that the Commission has sent for any particular individuals, however" [Letter from George Akerson, assistant to Sec. Hoover, to Mrs. James T. Rourke, Box 497, Commerce Period Papers, Herbert Hoover Presidential Library (March 29, 1927)].

[15] In documenting this consensus opinion against expansion, we focus mainly on the views expressed by the various interests (manufacturers, broadcasters, amateurs, listeners, etc.) *prior* to the announcement of the FRC decision. However, we also reviewed coverage in six major newspapers (the *Atlanta Constitution*, the *Chicago Tribune*, the *Los Angeles Times*, the *New York Times*, the *Wall Street Journal*, and the *Washington Post*) in the month following the decision. Significantly, none of these papers expressed opposition – or reported on any opposition – to the decision during this period. For example, a *New York Times* editorial on ways to deal with the interference problem did not object to limiting the band. Instead it repeated, without comment, the arguments that to widen it would encroach on "necessary forms of radio communication" and would force "millions of radio sets" to be rebuilt ["The Radio Dilemma," *The New York Times* (April 4, 1927): 22]. Another article equated widening the band with "invading air channels now used by amateurs" ["Asks City Control of Broadcasting," *The New York Times* (April 5, 1927): 32]. A later article in the *Times* reiterated the fears of "junking . . . millions of dollars' worth of radio receiving sets built to operate on the present broadcasting band" and added that setting the band aside for experimentation was intended to "encourage radio development and with a view to effecting television" ["Wave Band Taken to Aid Television," *The New York Times* (April 6, 1927): 1]. Other newspapers produced similar coverage. See e.g. "Amateurs of Radio to Protect Wider Wave-Length Band," *Washington Post* (March 27, 1927): 15; Alfred P. Reck, "Radio Men Hear Simple Remedy," *Atlanta Constitution* (March 29, 1927): 1; Frank Hinman, *Chicago Daily Tribune* (March 30, 1927): 16; "Hearings to End Chaos," *Los Angeles Times* (March 30, 1927): 1; "Air Rights of Way," *Los Angeles Times* (April 6, 1927).

Broadcasters Were Divided

Perhaps most surprising of all, the group that was weakest in its opposition to expanding the broadcast band – or at least expressed the most ambivalence about the outcome – comprised the broadcasters themselves. Although one might dismiss such ambivalence as merely a clever exercise in positioning, allowing the broadcasters to hide their true motives from the public, there is reason to believe that their ambivalence was sincere. The biggest player in the broadcasting business, NBC, owned relatively few stations itself and received a significant part of its revenue from selling network programming to other stations. For NBC, therefore, a broader band – and thus more stations – could potentially have meant increased demand for its primary product.

Hazlett, it turns out, may have inadvertently mischaracterized the intensity of the broadcasters' position by misinterpreting a critical source. Specifically, the "trade journal" that he cited in characterizing the position of the broadcasters – *Radio Broadcast* – was not in fact a broadcasters' trade journal in 1926–1927, but rather a radio enthusiasts' and listeners' magazine. In October 1926, the publication referred to its own typical reader as "Mr. Average Radio Enthusiast" and "Mr. Average Listener."[16] The passages that Hazlett quoted from the publication thus reflect not broadcaster opposition, but rather (if anything) listener opposition to spectrum expansion.[17]

Expected Broadcaster Rents May Have Been Smaller than Assumed

Another possible explanation for the ambivalence of certain incumbent broadcasters is that less may have been at stake than is now commonly believed. In early 1927, radio advertising was still in its infancy, and broadcasting was not yet viewed as a particularly profitable endeavor (and, in a great many cases, it was even seen as a loss-making endeavor). As a result, the rents that incumbent broadcasters are thought to have been seeking at the time may not have provided them with as strong a motivation to oppose expansion as one might assume in retrospect (i.e., based on a current understanding of the profitability of broadcasting).

[16] See Kingsley Welles, "Meet Mr. Average Radio Enthusiast," *Radio Broadcast* 531 (October 1926).

[17] For a detailed assessment of *Radio Broadcast* and its readership, see David Moss and Jonathan B.L. Decker, "Rethinking the Role of History in Law and Economics: The Case of the Federal Radio Commission in 1927" (Harvard Business School Working Paper No. 09-008, July 13, 2008), "Appendix: Reassessing a Critical Source," 32–36.

What Comes Next: A Detailed Review of the Evidence

The next three sections of this chapter present this new evidence in detail. We begin with a brief portrait of the FRC, including the origins of the commission and the context for the expansion proposal. We then review the positions of each of the major groups with an interest in the broadcast band and survey the state of broadcast advertising as of 1927. Finally, in the conclusion, we offer an overall assessment of the evidence as well as some general observations about the use of qualitative history in hypothesis testing and the importance of vigorously searching for disconfirming – as well as confirming – evidence in the historical record.

Although the historical evidence presented in the pages that follow is offered in considerably greater depth than is typical outside of a history journal, we believe such granularity (and attention to primary sources) is essential if history is to be used credibly as a test of theory. As almost any criminal lawyer will attest, critical details can easily be misinterpreted from a distance – with bias and presumption gradually replacing true observation as distance increases. It is for this reason that, after having summarized the argument and evidence, we now move on to take a much closer look at the evidence (and the surrounding historical context) in the sections that follow.

THE FEDERAL RADIO COMMISSION

The FRC itself was created under the Radio Act of 1927 and succeeded the Commerce Department, which had previously exercised authority over radio based on the Radio Act of 1912. Although the 1912 Act did not explicitly cover broadcasting, the department assumed that it had the authority to grant broadcast licenses and continued to believe this through 1926. Having convened a series of National Radio Conferences from 1922 to 1925, the Commerce Department followed the resulting recommendations in (a) limiting broadcasting to the 550–1,500 kHz band, (b) separating broadcast stations by at least 10 kHz, (c) preferring high-power national stations to local low-power ones, and (d) awarding a limited number of free licenses to stations on the grounds of service to the public interest – all prominent features of what would become the FRC regime.[18]

The year 1920 saw what was arguably the first regular broadcast station, Pittsburgh station KDKA, broadcasting news of Warren G. Harding's

[18] Christopher N. Sterling and John Michael Kittross, *Stay Tuned*, 3rd ed. (New York: Routledge, 2002), 97.

victory in the presidential election on its 100-watt set from six o'clock in the evening until noon the next day.[19] More than a thousand broadcasters entered the field over the next six-and-a-half years, such that by the time the FRC was formed in 1927, there were 733 stations vying for the ninety-six channels between 550 and 1500 kilohertz.[20]

A period of "chaos" began when Commerce denied the Zenith Radio Corporation the right to broadcast on the 910-kHz channel. Unhappy with the crowded 930-kHz channel that it had been allotted, Zenith ignored Commerce and "jumped" to the 910 channel in December 1925. The courts ruled that Commerce had no power to refuse requests for broadcast frequencies. Apparently acting on advice from the Attorney General, who concurred that the 1912 Act "provided no criteria for licensing," the department chose not to appeal.[21]

Hundreds of incumbent stations proceeded to jostle for better frequencies and time assignments, and hundreds of new stations entered on existing and intermediate channels. This caused considerable interference – far worse than the typical static that today's AM listeners still hear. Radio Commissioner Orestes Caldwell subsequently described the interference as being "so bad at many points on the dial that the listener might suppose instead of a receiving set he had a peanut roaster with assorted whistles."[22] The outbreak of chaos on the airwaves provoked Congress to pass the 1927 Radio Act in February 1927.[23]

The new Radio Act created an independent commission, the FRC, with the authority to regulate the radio spectrum and to license broadcasters. It asserted federal control over radio frequencies, to be dispensed on a temporary basis according to "public convenience, interest, or necessity."[24] Although the original 1927 legislation established the commission for only one year, to clear up the "chaos," the FRC was renewed annually until the 1934 Communications Act replaced it with the permanent Federal Communications Commission.

---

[19] Sterling and Kittross, *Stay Tuned*.

[20] Lawrence Frederick Schmeckebier, *The Federal Radio Commission* (Washington, D.C.: Brookings Institution, 1932). Six of these channels had, by agreement, been reserved for Canadian broadcasters.

[21] Robert W. McChesney, *Telecommunications, Mass Media, and Democracy* (New York: Oxford University Press), 16.

[22] "Annual Report of the Federal Radio Commission for the Fiscal Year Ended June 30, 1927," (Washington, D.C.: United States Government Printing Office, 1927). [Hereafter "FRC 1927 Annual Report"].

[23] Marvin R. Bensman, *The Beginning of Broadcast Regulation in the Twentieth Century* (Jefferson, NC: McFarland, 2000), 208.

[24] Radio Act of 1927, 47 U.S.C. §4 and preamble (repealed 1934).

In passing the 1927 Act, Congress had worried a great deal about the threat of concentrated control over the broadcasting spectrum, especially given the extraordinary political significance of radio.[25] Presumably, its decision to vest control of all frequencies with the federal government (and to prohibit private ownership of the spectrum) was seen as a sufficient response to that threat, preventing any individual or group from buying up a large number of stations and thus obtaining (and exercising) undue political influence. Having taken control of the spectrum, however, the federal government simultaneously assumed responsibility for managing it. And this is where the FRC came in.

By all accounts, the commission's primary mission was to clean up the airwaves – to make order out of the chaos. Chairman Eugene Sykes told the House that "the commission understands, under the law, that the dominant intent and purpose of that law, so far as the broadcasting situation is concerned, which we understood was the most acute problem then confronting the commission, it is [sic.] our duty to try and ensure good radio reception to the listening public."[26] Henry Bellows, another commissioner, was just as explicit during the first public hearings, saying: "You all know what the immediate problem before the Commission is – the problem of reallocating and re-arranging the wave lengths within the broadcasting band so as to eliminate, or at any rate greatly reduce, the amount of interference between stations."[27]

To that end, the FRC called public hearings from March 29 to April 1 of 1927 to solicit and evaluate ideas for how best to manage the broadcasting spectrum. As Commissioner Bellows explained at the outset of the initial session, a proposal for "widening of the broadcast band" was taken up first

because, obviously, in working out the policies of the Commission it is going to be necessary to determine first of all whether the only channels available for broadcasting are the channels now assigned to this service, or whether, from the standpoint of the listener, the broadcaster, the manufacturer, and the users of other types of radio transmission it is going to be better at this time to make a change in the broadcasting band.[28]

[25] David A. Moss and Michael R. Fein, "Radio Regulation Revisited: Coase, the FCC, and the Public Interest," *Journal of Policy History* 15 (2003): 389–416.

[26] Jurisdiction of Radio Commission, Hearing before the House of Representatives, Committee on the Merchant Marine and Fisheries, January 26, 1928.

[27] Minutes (March 29, 1927), 39. A third commissioner, Orestes Caldwell, bemoaned interference as the issue "on which is based the whole problem of allocation of stations all sharing the wave lengths" (ibid., 97). Caldwell said the commissioners intended to found a "listeners' paradise," and their interpretation of the listener's interest was clearly the promotion of interference-free broadcasting [Hugh R. Slotten, *Radio and Television Regulation* (Baltimore, MD: Johns Hopkins University Press, 2000)].

[28] Minutes (March 29, 1927), 3.

EXPANDING THE BROADCASTING BAND:
A DECIDEDLY UNPOPULAR PROPOSAL

Although the proposal to expand the broadcast band became the first topic of discussion at the FRC hearings, it is not entirely clear where the proposal originated. Commissioner Bellows noted early on in the first session that "a great many of those who have written to us have very strongly urged this change."[29] However, he seemed to contradict himself on this point the very next day when he announced that more than 3,000 letters had been analyzed so far and that on "the subject . . . of widening the broadcast band, it is quite extraordinary how few letters have come into the Commission advocating a change in the broadcast band."[30]

In any case, the main proposal on the table would have enlarged the existing ninety-six-channel 550–1,500 kHz (545 to 200 meters) band to include fifty more channels on the 1,500–2,000 kHz (200–150 meters) portion of the spectrum.[31] Participants at the hearings appeared to view the expansion proposal primarily as an option for reducing interference by moving some existing stations to the new band, although they also recognized that the new broadcasting spectrum would likely spur new broadcasting entrants as well.[32]

Opposition to this proposal was nearly universal at the hearings. In fact, the opposition was so strong and so widespread that it seemed to catch the commissioners by surprise, leading them to ask whether "there are any persons present who do advocate the increase of the broadcasting band. . . . "[33]

Before moving on to each of the groups that testified at the hearings, it is worth noting that our assessment is based to a very significant extent on historical records that have remained largely unexamined until now – namely,

---

[29] Minutes (March 29, 1927), 32.

[30] Minutes (March 30, 1927), 165. Unfortunately, we were unable to locate any of these letters, or the analysis that Bellows described, in either the National Archives or the Herbert Hoover Presidential Library.

[31] There apparently had been some interest in expanding in the other direction, below 550 kHz (above 545 meters), but this proposal received less serious attention at the hearings, presumably because it would have impinged on existing maritime frequencies.

[32] Although broadcaster Ira Nelson opposed expansion because of the procompetitive effect of new entrants on the industry [Minutes (March 31, 1927), 284–86], broadcaster H.V. Hough saw it as the clear answer to the problem of accommodating the large number of existing stations [Minutes (March 31, 1927), 325–27], and NBC representative Alfred Goldsmith also offered it as one (rather poor) solution to the congestion problem caused by the many existing stations all attempting to broadcast [Minutes (March 29, 1927), 22–23]. See infra.

[33] Minutes (March 29, 1927), 32.

the transcripts of the FRC's first public hearings. These transcripts, which we obtained from the Herbert Hoover Presidential Library after being informed that they could not be located at the National Archives, represent the most exhaustive available record of debate and testimony on the expansion issue. A great many individuals representing the full gamut of radio interest groups made their case to the Commission over several days of hearings. Perhaps the most remarkable fact to emerge from their testimony – and the one that most starkly contrasts with the prevailing view within the literature – is that nearly all of the interest groups represented at the hearing agreed on the inadvisability of the expansion proposal. Far from standing alone on the issue, broadcasters who objected to expansion joined engineers, manufacturers, amateur operators, and listeners in opposing the plan to add new frequencies to the broadcast band.

Radio Engineers

The strongest arguments against expansion were generally articulated by radio engineers, who questioned whether the substantial technical challenges and difficulties associated with the proposal could be justified. Specifically, the engineers emphasized that the new wavelengths would not be conducive to reliable broadcasting; that transmissions on the additional frequencies would face harmonic interference from high-powered stations on the existing frequencies; and that new radios covering the expanded band would be difficult to design, would offer poorer performance, and would be considerably more expensive.

Professor Louis Hazeltine, inventor of the Neutrodyne receiver and a member of the board of the Hazeltine Corporation, a radio manufacturer, explained in a letter to the commission that "the designing engineer well knows that to increase the frequency covered by radio receivers will either make its performance poorer at each frequency which it covers or else will make it considerably more expensive, or more likely of all, will both impair its performance and increase its cost." He suggested that although

the present frequency band was allotted to broadcasting largely by reason of special circumstances . . . it is . . . just the band that the designing engineer would pick out as the most suitable. . . . The reason is that the natural selectivity [the ability to tune in just one station] of ordinary tuned circuits in the present frequency band is just about right to give the desired fidelity [the ability to hear broadcasts clearly] . . . by covering the side bands [the 5 kHz on either side of the broadcasting frequency] and no more.

Finally, he warned that "at higher frequencies, shorter waves, the selectivity would naturally be poorer than is necessary to secure fidelity."[34]

R. H. Langley, an engineer associated with the Crosley Radio Corporation, placed particular emphasis on the problem of interference:

In the present band of frequencies from 750 kilocycles [kHz] down, it is possible to receive the second harmonic of each broadcasting station on an ordinary broadcast receiver. This means that if the local station which you are anxious to avoid is at 750 kilocycles or below, he is in shadow in the upper range of your receiver, and if he is loud enough, you are quite likely to get him in two places. If the band was widened down to 150 meters [2000 kHz], then 71 of the 146 channels would have this second harmonic reflection point and would be received at two points on the receiver, if you were near enough to them, and the signal were sufficiently powerful.... That difficulty... of the harmonics, would mean that all of the new channels would be open to that difficulty....[35]

Making implicit reference to the extension of the broadcast band from 1,350 to 1,500 kHz in 1924, Langley also observed that there were actually very few receivers on the market that went all the way up to the then-allowable 1,500 kHz.[36] "Many of the circuits now in use are extremely difficult to stabilize," he explained, "especially the upper frequency. Some of the circuits now in use... would be impossible to stabilize at very much higher than 1,500 kilocycles, and some new means would have to be provided to get a suitable amplification at the higher frequencies." Like Hazeltine, he predicted that to "build a receiver which would be as satisfactory as the better receivers are today would make it cost considerably more."[37]

Dr. Alfred N. Goldsmith, chairman of the board of consulting engineers for NBC and a luminary in the field of radio engineering, began his comments by acknowledging the problem that expansion of the band was

[34] Minutes (March 29, 1927), 8–9.

[35] Minutes (March 29, 1927), 14–15.

[36] The October 1924 National Radio Conference recommended raising the upper broadcasting frequency from 1,350 kHz to 1,500 kHz. The primary objective of this expansion was to provide a band for "all broadcasting stations which use less than 100 watts power" and thus to grant "great improvement" to higher-power stations, which would then be "relatively free from local interference produced by the stations of very small power which, on the average, furnish a grade of program which is of only local and limited interest" [Recommendations for Regulation of Radio Adopted by the Third National Radio Conference (1924)]. The recommendation was apparently adopted: as late as mid-1927, the average power of a station in the 550–590 band was more than 1,000 watts, whereas in the 1,460–1,500 band it was only 75 watts [Commerce, Radio Stations]. Ironically, then, the proposal to expand the broadcast band – which Hazlett and others believe ran contrary to the interests of incumbent broadcasters in 1927 – may actually have been used to *advance* the interests of major incumbent broadcasters in 1924.

[37] Minutes (March 29, 1927), 16–17.

intended to solve. The existing broadcasting band (from 550 to 1,500 kHz) provided ninety-five channels,[38] six of which had been allotted to Canada. The remaining eighty-nine "American channels are now called upon to accommodate more than 730 existing broadcasting stations. The congestion is, therefore, extreme and the interference correspondingly great." For this reason, expansion of the band had to be considered. "In the abstract," Goldsmith declared, "there can be no objection to the widening of the frequency bands . . . provided the additional frequencies . . . are suitable for broadcasting. . . . It must be recognized, however, that the usefulness of such frequencies for this purpose has not been demonstrated by large scale experiments up to the present time."[39]

Although most of the engineers who testified on the expansion issue at the FRC hearings were affiliated with either a broadcasting company or (more commonly) a radio manufacturer, there were others present who were not so affiliated. John Dellinger, chief of the Bureau of Standards' Radio Section in 1927, had been president of the Institute of Radio Engineers (IRE) in 1925 and director from 1924–1927. (He subsequently served as chief engineer for the FRC from 1928–1929 and, in 1938, was awarded the IRE Medal of Honor.) Although Dellinger did not explicitly comment on expansion at the FRC hearings, he did speak at great length about the problem of heterodyne interference, which he characterized as "probably the worst thing we have to combat in the radio broadcasting allocation today."[40]

In addition, the Radio Broadcast Committee of the American Engineering Council issued a report, which was presented to the FRC at the March 30 hearing, offering a "compilation of engineering principles and facts believed to affect the duties of the Federal Radio Commission."[41] Among other things, the report concluded that the proposal to widen the broadcast band "is not now practicable" because such widening would impinge on "other useful radio services," would render millions of existing sets obsolete, would

---

[38] Although most authorities on the subject, including the Commission itself, spoke of ninety-six channels (six of which being reserved for Canadian stations), some – including Goldsmith – spoke of ninety-five.

[39] Minutes (March 29, 1927), 22–23.

[40] Minutes (March 30, 1927), 116. Three years later, Dellinger published an article noting that although the notion of expanding the broadcast band "has been a major issue at every national and international radio conference since 1924," these conferences had "uniformly concluded that extension of the broadcast range of frequencies is impracticable for several reasons" [John H. Dellinger, "The Broadcasting Band," in *Radio and Its Future*, ed. Martin Codel (New York and London: Harper and Brothers Publishers, 1930), 293].

[41] Minutes (March 30, 1927), 200.

require more complicated and more expensive radio receivers, and would "increase the number of stations open to interference from harmonics or other broadcasting stations."[42]

Radio Manufacturers

To a large extent, the position of radio manufacturers on the question of widening the spectrum has already been presented, because many of the engineers just quoted were affiliated with manufacturing companies and were specifically lined up to speak at the FRC hearings by the Radio Manufacturers' Association.[43] In his letter to the commission, Louis Hazeltine quoted a recent resolution in which "engineers associated with the Independent Radio Manufacturers, Inc., and with the Hazeltine Corporation, assembled in conference on March 17, 1927," unanimously resolved "that in the present state of the radio art, it would be against the best interests of the broadcast listening public to increase the frequency band. . . ."[44]

An intriguing question – especially for students of the economic theory of regulation – is why radio manufacturers would oppose expansion of the broadcasting band in the first place, because one might assume they would stand to benefit from increased demand for new radios. By the beginning of 1927, the number of American homes with radio receivers had reached 6.5 million. Since 1922, when only 60,000 homes had radio sets, the increase in radio penetration had been about 1 to 1.5 million homes per year.[45] Given this, one might think manufacturers would have found the prospect of obsolescing a large part of the existing stock to be absolutely tantalizing. They apparently had other concerns, however.

One possible explanation that deserves consideration is that the manufacturers opposed widening the band because they owned a large number of

---

[42] Minutes (March 30, 1927), 202–203. The committee comprised both affiliated engineers (e.g., Calvert Townley, assistant to the president of the Westinghouse Electric and Manufacturing Company, Alfred Goldsmith of NBC, David Sarnoff of RCA, and L.E. Whittemore of ATT) and unaffiliated engineers (e.g., John Dellinger of the Bureau of Standards and C. Moreau Jansky Jr., Assistant Professor of Radio Engineering at the University of Minnesota). See "Will Survey Radio Needs: Engineering Council Names Committee to Suggest Control Legislation," *New York Times* (January 14, 1927): 10. Note that Jansky, characterized in his obituary as a "pioneer in radio broadcasting," subsequently was "co-founder and chairman of Jansky & Bailey, a consulting engineering company formed in 1930 . . ." ["C. Moreau Jansky Jr., 79, Pioneer in Radio Broadcast," *The New York Times* (March 27, 1975): 28].

[43] Minutes (March 29, 1927), 5–6.

[44] Minutes (March 29, 1927), 7–8.

[45] O.H. Caldwell, "The Radio Market," in *Radio and Its Future*, 206.

radio stations, which they wanted to protect against competition. One problem here is that most manufacturers at the time had a much larger stake in radio manufacturing than in radio broadcasting, particularly because most broadcasters were still making little if any money, and annual radio sales remained exceedingly large. Another problem is that the opposition to widening expressed at the hearings was voiced at least as strongly, if not more strongly, by manufacturers with no discernible connection to broadcasting, such as Jack Binns, treasurer of the Hazeltine Corporation, and L. P. F. Raycroft of the Electric Storage Battery Company.[46]

Indeed, Raycroft himself insisted that the reason he and his fellow manufacturers opposed widening the band was that it would harm them by harming their customers, the nation's radio listeners. "The radio broadcast listeners are by all means our customers and our customers must be satisfied," he said.[47] Raycroft was speaking on behalf of the radio division of the National Electrical Manufacturers Association, the members of which, he claimed, accounted for more than three-quarters of radio production in the United States.[48] The main problem, as he saw it, was that widening the band would render existing radios obsolete. And this was no small matter: he estimated that the average radio cost about $100 in 1927,[49] which was more than 10 percent of per capita gross domestic product at the time (the equivalent of more than $4,500 today). "Gentleman," he declared at the hearings,

I want to tell you this; when we appeared before the Congress in the strongest sort of support for the legislation [the Radio Act of 1927] which is now made effective, and we did so as radio manufacturers trying to protect our interests and the interests of the radio broadcast listener at large, our customers, we never conceived for one moment that we would come before any established commission and ask that it take any steps which would make practically the entire number of sets in the country obsolete, either in whole or in part, and we refuse to take that position today. *As radio manufacturers, we cannot afford, in accordance of our own ethics, to appear in support of that proposition.*[50]

Whether the radio manufacturers were truly motivated by an unwillingness to anger their customers (more than 1.5 million of whom had bought new

---

[46] Neither of these corporations is listed as a station owner in the 1927 *Radio Stations of the United States*. Two of the radio engineers who testified at the hearings and who worked for manufacturers that also owned broadcasters were R. H. Langley of the Crosley Radio Corporation (which operated WLW) and Ray Manson of the Stromberg-Carlson Company (which operated WHAM).

[47] Minutes (March 29, 1927), 52.

[48] Minutes (March 29, 1927), 50–51.

[49] Minutes (March 29, 1927), 57.

[50] Minutes (March 29, 1927), 58, emphasis added.

sets in just the last year alone) or perhaps by some other fear or objective, is impossible to say with certainty. Patent holders may have worried that their patents would be rendered obsolete by the change. Or, alternatively, smaller producers may have worried that the giants, like RCA, would gain even greater control over the industry as a result of their superior research capabilities. In fact, there are many possible explanations. Unfortunately, we were unable to find appropriate and compelling evidence that distinguishes between them.

Still, the position of manufacturers at the hearings was clear. Langley (of the Crosley Radio Corporation) observed that if the broadcasting band were widened, it would "immediately obsolete not only the receivers which broadcast listeners have already purchased, but also the receivers which are now on the shelves in dealers' stores, and also the receivers which are now in the process of being put into production in factories of the manufacturers."[51] What is more, "there would be a period of three, four or five months during which all the manufacturers would have to work under intense pressure to develop some new form of receiver that would cover the band." Although he insisted that he personally was "not a bit loathe to undertake that work for myself and my group of engineers" (because it would be "a very interesting engineering problem"), he simply could "see . . . no great advantage to the listening public or to the radio manufacturers in any extension of the broadcast band."[52]

Amateur Radio Operators and Experimenters

The proposal to expand the broadcast band provoked a particularly fierce response from amateur radio operators. This was mostly because the wavelengths under consideration had, for some time, been the domain of the amateurs. From the perspective of the amateur operator, commercial broadcasting from 1,500 to 2,000 kHz would amount to criminal trespass on his own precious real estate.

On the very first day of the hearings, Secretary K. B. Warner of the American Radio Relay League (ARRL)[53] dismissed claims that amateurs were no longer interested in the 1,500–2,000-kHz band, emphasizing that only this band could be used for voice communications: "This is the only amateur

[51] Minutes (March 29, 1927), 18.

[52] Ibid. At the conclusion of his statement, Langley noted that in making his statement he was representing the Amrad Corporation as well as the Crosely Radio Corporation.

[53] The ARRL continues to operate to this day as the country's premier amateur radio organization.

band in which really successful amateur telephony is possible, because all of our shorter waves [higher frequencies] are subject to technical difficulties such as audio-frequency fading which, while they do not adversely affect telegraphy, do make it extremely difficult to carry on successful telephony."[54] If there were to be any significant advances made in voice transmission, he argued, it would need to take place in the 1,500–2,000-kHz band.

The commissioners had good reason to take the amateurs seriously. Many radio amateurs began as military radio operators during the war, and amateur use allowed them to continue to hone their skills. Furthermore, amateurs had historically been at the forefront of radio innovation, having shown not only that frequencies above 1,500 kHz could be used, but also that they propagated to far greater range than those below. Confined to the so-called trash wavelengths, early radio amateurs took great pride in their successful trans-continental and trans-oceanic communications.[55] According to the 1930 president of the ARRL, "the success of the amateur with his short waves naturally stimulated all manner of commercial aspiration." As the broadcast spectrum crowded, the ARRL feared this meant "ejecting the amateurs from some of the territory that they had done so much to pioneer."[56]

Another speaker, C. Francis Jenkins, was even more adamant about what could be lost to society if amateurs were deprived of the frequencies above 1,500 kHz. An inventor and amateur lab operator experimenting with the broadcast of still images (or "radiofacsimile"), Jenkins urged that "this band below 200 meters [above 1500 kHz] should be kept more or less virgin field for the amateurs who have no particular object other than that of developing useful applications of radio."[57] He no doubt captured the attention – and the imagination – of the commissioners when he began speculating about the possibility of broadcasting *moving* pictures over the airwaves:

Presently, when what we call still pictures are considered fairly well launched on their useful career, we want to take up a still further development, which has been shown by experiment to be perfectly feasible with the apparatus that we have today, and that is radio vision, the ability to see on a small white screen, if you like, what is happening at a distant place.[58]

The one catch, he suggested, was that experiments of this sort would have to take place in precisely the same part of the spectrum that the commission

[54] Minutes (March 29, 1927), 29.
[55] Hiram Percy Maxim, "The Radio Amateur," in *Radio and Its Future*, 149.
[56] Ibid., 155.
[57] Minutes (March 29, 1927), 35.
[58] Minutes (March 29, 1927), 34.

was considering giving away to radio broadcasters: "[B]ecause we need electrical pulsations to make up radio vision, electrical pulsations of such high frequency, we rather expect that it is in the amateur band only that radio vision is possible."[59]

Apparently tantalized by the specter that Jenkins had conjured up, the commissioners ultimately relied heavily on the promise of experimentation in justifying their decision not to expand the broadcast band. According to the FRC's General Order no. 4, "the band between 1,500 and 2,000 kilocycles (199.9 to 149.9 meters) should, so far as may be practicable, be held open for experimental work in broadcasting and allied forms of radio service, to the end that, with the further development of the art, this band may be eventually made available for broadcasting, whether for the ear or the eye."[60]

Although "radiofacsimile" never took off, the FRC did make good on its promise that the frequencies near to the existing band be used for experimentation with new forms of broadcasting. Jenkins himself received the very first license for an experimental 1927 television station, W3XK, in the adjacent 2,000–2,100-kHz band.[61] Furthermore, throughout the 1930s, several high-fidelity AM stations operated with experimental licenses between 1,500 and 1,600 kHz, each occupying 20 kHz of bandwidth.[62] In 1936, W2XR famously received an experimental license for high-fidelity stereo broadcasting.[63] When regulators officially expanded the broadcasting spectrum to 1,600 kHz in 1941, W2XR began operation as WQXR, which continues to operate to this day (on FM) as one of New York's most popular classical stations.

Radio Listeners

As the commissioners themselves repeatedly noted, listeners were the commission's most important constituents. To quote Commissioner Bellows, "[I]t is the radio listener we must consider above everybody else."[64] The problem, of course, is that listeners were not as well organized as most of

---

[59] Minutes (March 29, 1927), 34.
[60] FRC 1927 Annual Report, 13.
[61] R.W. Burns, *British Television: The Formative Years* (London: Peter Peregrinus, 1986), 116–17.
[62] Sterling and Kittross, *Stay Tuned*, 109.
[63] The number after the "W" indicates an amateur or experimental license.
[64] Minutes (March 29, 1927), 40.

the other interests. Consequently, listener representation at the FRC hearings was not very strong, but neither was it missing altogether.

According to those who claimed to represent them, listeners preferred a smaller number of good stations to a larger number of poor and overlapping ones.[65] Francis St. Austell, president of the Iowa Radio Listeners' League, exclaimed on the second day of the hearings:

The broadcaster at the present time has brought about a great deal of confusion for the simple reason that there are so many stations on the air that the ordinary listener, with a $150 set is practically incompetent to get anything....

Damn it, I don't want to listen to a lot of rotten stuff over the air, but I want to listen to something good, to a good concert, for instance, and feel that the broadcaster is a friend of mine, and that he is not an enemy of the other broadcasters....

... We do not want 733, or whatever the number is, on the air; we want to get good broadcasting....[66]

L. P. F. Raycroft, a manufacturer, agreed:

I could say 90% easily, of all the broadcast listeners with whom I have spoken, have stated in regard to the question as to the number of broadcast stations that should be allowed upon the air, that they did not care how few they were if they could have such and such a station left, and in some localities it was WJZ, and in others WEAF, and in others other stations.

Raycroft added that the days of listeners trying to hear every last station – "and add those scalps to their belt" – were basically gone. What the listeners had come to want "was good substantial broadcasting of a quality character, and ... they are willing to hook up pretty well to one, or a small number of large stations, or nearby stations to satisfy that desire on their part."[67]

Interestingly, Raycroft also reported on some correspondence he had had with the Broadcast Listeners' Association of Minneapolis – specifically regarding one of the association's resolutions that seemed to favor broadening of the broadcast band. When he wrote to the association on "January

---

[65] In addition to the statements at the hearings cited later, see also "Radio Freedom of Speech Impossible," *Radio Broadcast* 11 (April 1927): 138–39, reporting in general terms on the results of their questionnaire to readers (listeners). For example, the magazine's editors declared, "We are in favor of eliminating a great number of small stations so that we may have more great stations. This is our stand because it is sound common sense and because it is the expressed wish of a majority of our readers" (ibid., 139).

[66] Minutes (March 30, 1927), 144–46.

[67] Minutes (March 29, 1927), 57.

7th and called their attention to some of the difficulties involved in their suggestion on the basis of good engineering advice," their response was telling:

You will note from a careful reading [of the resolution] that we do not urge this change but that we suggested that Congress encourage a study of the matter by competent engineers.... We are not sure that this would be a good thing for radio but hold our minds open for competent advice in these matters so the real purpose of that recommendation was to accomplish the result that has been brought about, namely, an intelligent discussion both for and against the proposal ... and therefore, we are not urging the change unless it should be found entirely practicable and an advantage to the advancement of radio.[68]

Willing to entertain widening of the band so long as it was "entirely practicable," the Broadcast Listeners' Association of Minneapolis appears to have taken a position remarkably similar to that of Goldsmith at NBC.

On the final day of the hearings, P. A. Green of the United States Radio Society, a national radio listeners' organization, reinforced the notion that the costs of widening the band likely outweighed the benefits. "Although the opinions of the radio listeners of the United States have not been presented on this particular subject," he remarked, "I am of the opinion that to widen the band at this time would possibly work a hardship on the present users of radio receiving sets. Therefore the society recommends that the broadcasting stations be assigned frequencies within the now existing bands."[69] Apparently, the threat of having their radios rendered obsolete – or, at least, no longer complete – was a real concern to listeners.[70]

At least one prominent radio enthusiasts' and listeners' magazine, moreover, staunchly opposed widening the band, both in contemporary articles and through its representative who spoke at the hearings, offering further evidence of where listeners stood on this issue. The magazine was none other

[68] Quoted in Minutes (March 29, 1927), 55–56.

[69] Minutes (April 1, 1927), 352.

[70] Interestingly, another major concern, according to Green, related to direct advertising (which today would simply be called "advertising," as opposed to indirect advertising, or sponsorship). "The United States Radio Society has received many communications of protest against the use of the air as a means of direct advertising. The opposition to this type of broadcasting has been so strong that the society has recently started a campaign against this evil ... " [Minutes (April 1, 1927), 354]. Significantly, Francis St. Austell of the Iowa Radio Listeners' League, quoted previously, took the same position about a year later. According to the *New York Times*, Austell's Listener's League was circulating petitions to make the practice of direct selling over radio illegal. "The petitions," noted the *Times*, "brand direct selling as unfair competition and a menace to the retail business structure of the country" ["Selling by Radio Opposed," *New York Times* (February 1, 1928): 20].

than *Radio Broadcast*.[71] Its editors certainly minced no words, urging the commission "to dispose of such dangerous propositions as the pressure to extend the broadcast band downward, brought by short-sighted would-be broadcasters and selfish set manufacturers, seeking to create an artificial market for short-wave receivers.... "[72] Like some of the other listeners' representatives already quoted, the magazine subscribed to the notion that less was more, as far as radio listeners were concerned, because interference compromised reception: "The principle must be recognized that the fewer broadcasting stations there are on the air, the more stations the listener can enjoy."[73] Expansion of the broadcasting band was decidedly not the answer.

Radio Broadcasters

In some ways, the position of the broadcasters on the proposal to widen the band paralleled that of the manufacturers. In fact, the very same person who lined up speakers for the Radio Manufactures' Association also lined up speakers for the National Association of Broadcasters. Frank D. Scott, a former congressman from Michigan, represented both organizations at the hearings and put together a combined slate of speakers, who spoke at the outset of the first session.[74]

Without question, one can find statements of naked self-interest on the part of some broadcasters, just as one might expect from incumbents trying to protect their competitive positions. Ira Nelson of WAAM in Newark, for example, announced on the third day of hearings that the central question was: "Who shall broadcast?"[75] In answering this question, he cautioned that "[i]t should not be our attitude to foster the inauguration of many stations, realizing that most of them will find it well-nigh impossible to earn three squares a day." New entrants were continually coming into broadcasting, he lamented, despite "a great many warnings of deep water ahead to our new brethren.... The increased number of broadcasting stations has worked a great hardship upon already established commercial organization[s] who have for years been building up audiences and services so that they might

[71] See earlier discussion on the mischaracterization of *Radio Broadcast* as a trade journal. It was in fact a radio listeners' journal.
[72] "Welcome to the Radio Commission," *Radio Broadcast* (April 1927): 555.
[73] "Welcome to the Radio Commission."
[74] Minutes (March 29, 1927), 5, 6–25. The lineup that Scott put together included Jack Binns of the Hazeltine Corporation (who also read a letter from Louis Hazeltine), R. H. Langley of the Crosley Radio Corporation, F. A. Kolster of the Federal Telegraph Company, and Arthur Goldsmith of NBC.
[75] Minutes (March 31, 1927), 281.

have something to sell...."[76] What was necessary, he believed, was not for the commission "to open any more broadcasting channels" but for it to weed out weak stations, based on "their respective incomes in payment of their services, and the degree of satisfaction they have produced for their clients."[77] Ultimately, the commission would have to decide "who shall stay, taking into consideration only one class. Commercial stations who have a previous record of faithful service, should be retained."[78]

In spite of the comments of Nelson and others, what is most striking about the commercial broadcasters is that they were – if anything – less unified and less vehement in their opposition to the proposal for widening the broadcast band than were most other groups represented at the hearings. In fact, at least as many broadcasters spoke for the proposal as spoke against it.[79] Ira Nelson, it turns out, did not represent all of his brethren in the broadcasting industry.

As we have seen (in the section on engineers), Alfred Goldsmith expressed ambivalence about the proposal to widen the band, even though he was chairman of the board of consulting engineers of NBC, which was the dominant radio network at the time and whose parent companies owned ten of the country's largest and oldest broadcasting stations. In fact, when Goldsmith finally summarized the position of NBC on the issue, it fell somewhere between weak support and weak opposition. "The . . . National Broadcasting Company," he maintained, "is not opposed to widening the wave band whenever it is demonstrated to be technically feasible, and when this could be done without interference with other established radio services."[80]

Even more remarkable were the comments of another broadcaster, H. V. Hough of WBAP in Texas, who tried – on the third day of the FRC hearings – to resurrect the proposal for widening the band, which already appeared dead by the end of the first day due to lack of support. Hough had been operating WBAP for five years, and by 1927 was licensed for the very desirable 600-kHz frequency and a substantial 1,500 watts of power.[81] By almost any definition, he was an incumbent broadcaster. Yet after sitting through the hearings and listening to attacks on one proposal after another

---

[76] Minutes (March 31, 1927), 284–285.

[77] Minutes (March 31, 1927), 284, 285–286.

[78] Minutes (March 31, 1927), 286.

[79] For opposition from commercial broadcasters to the proposal to expand the broadcast band, see testimony of A. H. Grebe, Ray H. Manson, and Ira N. Nelson (Minutes). For support from commercial broadcasters for the proposal, see testimony of H. V. Hough, John S. Cohen, and Landen Kay (Minutes).

[80] Minutes (March 29, 1927), 25.

[81] Department of Commerce, *Commercial and Government Radio Stations of the United States* (Washington, D.C.: U.S. Government Printing Office, 1927), 77.

for dealing with the interference problem, he began to think that the original proposal to widen the band might not be so bad after all:

We have had quite a bit of discussion, and what we want to do, I believe, is to eliminate stations or eliminate interference, one or the other. One goes with the other. It just occurs to me that when we got up on our feet and told the Commission that we did not think it was a good idea to open up those lower wave bands we were traveling around in a pasture that was a good deal greener than we thought it was. . . .

Some folks say that it would not be very profitable down there. I certainly would like to have a wave band for myself down about 200 meters, and in two years from now it would be as important as any other place. When they moved us from 360 to 400 they said that nobody would listen, and then later on they moved us again, and the same thing was said. It would be a sporting proposition for a man to go down there and get something that the other fellow has not got, and then the next day the next man would be getting it, too, because each man wishes to be as well posted as his neighbor.

We have looked around in these pastures and we are right back in a circle. The proposition you submitted in reference to opening up the lower wave bands may be, after all, the solution, and we have not been able to locate it.[82]

Here was a "sporting proposition" indeed – coming from an incumbent broadcaster – for some new competition in the outer reaches of an expanded band!

Ironically, it was not a commercial broadcaster but rather a nonprofit broadcaster who articulated perhaps the clearest and most unequivocal statement of opposition to expansion on the third day of the hearings. When another speaker proposed that educational stations should be allocated the 1,500–1,600 kHz frequencies, for which special educational band radios could be produced, C. A. Culver, president of the Association of College and University Broadcasting Stations, responded resolutely. University broadcasters, Culver insisted, sought to provide more general cultural services in addition to straightforward education, and they would find this new fragment of spectrum "practically prohibitive, because the listeners would have to have special receiving sets, and that would practically inhibit the service that they want to give in those regions." Repeating his key point as he concluded his remarks, he again warned that "to take a band at this extreme end down below all the other broadcasting would be practically prohibitive and would cut [the stations that were moved there] out from the service they are certainly rendering now."[83]

---

[82] Minutes (March 31, 1927), 325–27.
[83] Minutes (March 31, 1927), 277.

Nonprofits did not want to risk being reassigned to a lower wave band (higher frequency), which would be of lower quality and would force their listeners to purchase new and potentially more expensive equipment to hear their programs. In fact, it may be that Hough of WBAP was willing to entertain the opening of new wavelengths to broadcasting precisely because he knew there was little or no risk of his five-year-old commercial station ending up there.

Overall, by our count, the broadcasters who spoke at the hearings divided about evenly between support and opposition. H. V. Hough of WBAP ended up concluding it was probably the best way of addressing the interference problem; at least two other broadcasters weakly supported the idea; and Alfred Goldsmith of NBC expressed ambivalence. Three other broadcasters (including C. A. Culver) opposed the expansion proposal at the hearings, two strongly and one weakly.

There is no way to know for sure whether the broadcasters who testified were representative of broadcasters more generally and, if so, why they were not more unified in their opposition to the expansion proposal. Still, a few possible explanations for their lack of unity on the issue are worth considering. Because it was widely believed among radio engineers at the time that the frequencies above 1,500 kHz were inferior as far as broadcasting was concerned, incumbent broadcasters with the requisite technical expertise may not have felt particularly threatened by the prospect of new competitors broadcasting on those upper frequencies. In fact, expansion could well have been regarded – as it was when the edge of the band was shifted from 1,350 to 1,500 kHz in 1924[84] – as a way of clearing out the good frequencies, by moving the weak (some would say, bothersome) stations off to the periphery. From NBC's perspective, moreover, additional room for more broadcasters was not necessarily a net negative, since the added stations could create additional demand both for one of its primary products (radio programs sold to affiliate stations) and for one of the primary products of its parent company (radio receivers). Finally, because radio advertising remained rather primitive by today's standards and because relatively few stations were making much money, the rents that incumbents might have sought to protect may not have appeared nearly as large or as promising back then as they would to us now, biased as we are by today's far more lucrative radio environment.[85]

---

[84] Recommendations for Regulation of Radio Adopted by the Third National Radio Conference (1924).

[85] Another possibility is that it was all an act. Perhaps, behind the scenes, all of the broadcasters fiercely opposed expansion and were conspiring with the commissioners to kill the proposal, but did their best to hide this from the public by taking a more moderate

MISUNDERSTOOD MOTIVES:
THE ROLE OF ADVERTISING IN EARLY RADIO

As late as the mid 1920s, even the most thoughtful scholars and journalists were unable to predict the dominant role that advertising would play in radio broadcasting by the start of the next decade. In fact, throughout much of the 1920s, there was no consensus that broadcasters would be able to sustain their operations without outside support.

Hiram Jome's extensive 1925 study, *Economics of the Radio Industry*, repeatedly returns to "the 'who shall pay' problem."[86] Jome estimated that radio broadcasting was bound to be unprofitable because the "few sources of income, such as paid advertising," would be unlikely to cover the considerable expenses of a commercial station (including normal operating expenses, royalties, and so forth).[87] The discrepancy seemed so obvious that Jome proposed a tax on radio manufacturers' sales to make up the difference.[88]

However, if the average radio station was not expected to pay for itself, then why were so many stations established in the 1920s? Some owners, presumably, expected to beat the average. Others, perhaps, were not primarily interested in making money. By our count, one-quarter of stations in 1927 were nonprofits, ranging from religious stations to agricultural information stations to university stations.[89]

Many for-profit owners, meanwhile, sought to make money only indirectly. According to *Radio Broadcast*, these included "individual publicity stations operated by department stores, newspapers, radio companies, and

---

position at the hearings. Although this explanation is possible, we were unable to find any evidence in support of it.

[86] Hiram Jome, *Economics of the Radio Industry* (Chicago: A. W. Shaw & Co., 1925). See also Susan Smulyan, *Selling of Radio: The Commercialization of American Broadcasting 1920–1934* (Washington, D.C.: Smithsonian Institution Press, 1994), especially Chapter 3.

[87] Jome, *Economics of the Radio Industry*, 253–54.

[88] Jome, *Economics of the Radio Industry*, 254–55. Also reflecting concern about radio's financial future, *Radio Broadcast* offered a $500 prize in March 1925 to the best plan for funding broadcasting. The winning idea was a proposal for a receiver tax reminiscent of the BBC's. David Sarnoff himself advocated "philanthropic donations to support radio" in 1926, the same year that a GE spokesman predicted that broadcasting would eventually be supported by either "voluntary contributions or receiver licenses," according to Sterling and Kittross, *Stay Tuned*, 80.

[89] To produce our estimate of the proportion of nonprofit stations, we looked at the names of station owners listed in the Commerce Department's guide to U.S. radio stations for 1927. Assuming stations owned by such organizations as the First Baptist Church of Shreveport, Louisiana, or the South Dakota State College were nonprofits, we counted 170 nonprofits out of a total of 694 stations listed. See Department of Commerce, *Commercial and Government Radio Stations of the United States*, 72–92.

other commercial institutions for the purpose of building good will for the owner, but not accepting outside pay for broadcasting."[90] In fact, the first (and probably most prominent) station owners during the 1920s were radio manufacturers, who initially entered broadcasting to boost demand for their receivers.[91]

Perhaps most striking of all from a modern vantage point, paid advertising as we know it today was not originally regarded as an ideal or dominant financing mechanism for broadcasting. In fact, direct advertising over the airwaves was practically an afterthought in the minds of many broadcasters. When Jome asked a sample of sixty-nine broadcasters in 1925 their purpose in broadcasting, only two responded that even their secondary purpose was "to profit by direct sale of advertising time."[92] Part of the reason for this may have been that direct advertising – the explicit discussion of products that we recognize as advertising today – was often viewed by the public as distasteful in the 1920s. The 1925 National Radio Conference, organized by Herbert Hoover, held that "both direct and mixed advertising were objectionable to the listening public."[93] In 1927, a representative of the United States Radio Society, which identified itself as a listeners' organization, told the FRC that it had "received many communications of protest against the use of the air as a means of direct advertising. The opposition to this type of broadcasting has been so strong that the society has recently started a campaign against this evil."[94]

---

[90] Austin C. Lescarboura, "How Much It Costs to Broadcast," *Radio Broadcast* (1926): 367–71.

[91] As RCA's David Sarnoff wrote, "When the radio industry outgrew its first customer – the radio amateur – the electrical industry of the United States undertook to create a listening public" [David Sarnoff, "Art and Industry," in *Radio and Its Future* (1930)]. Similarly, the *Wall Street Journal* announced to its readers in November 1926 that RCA, "with its subsidiary company, the National Broadcasting Co., is preparing better and bigger programs, and this is the key to increased sales of radio sets" ["Radio Having Biggest Year," *Wall Street Journal* (November 2, 1926): 9]. Not everyone agreed, however, that increased radio sales would be sufficient to support broadcasting. One contemporary radio commentator declared in September of 1926 that "no manufacturer and not even a group of manufacturers could afford to broadcast throughout the entire country day in and day out in return for the sale of radio receivers and radio accessories" (Lescarboura, "How Much It Costs").

[92] Jome, *Economics of the Radio Industry*, 168.

[93] *Proceedings of the Fourth National Radio Conference and Recommendations for Regulation of Radio, November 9–11, 1925*, issued by the Government Printing Office in Washington, D.C., for the Department of Commerce (1925).

[94] Minutes (April 1, 1927), 354. In a review of listeners' organizations in its July 1927 issue, *Radio Broadcast* characterized the United States Radio Society as the "most promising [listeners'] organization from which we have heard" ["Where Are the Listeners' Organizations," *Radio Broadcast* (July 1927): 141]. Although RCA's Alfred Goldsmith had determined by 1925 that "there is no way in which the Radio Corporation could secure

An alternative form of advertising involved indirect or "good will" advertising, similar to today's PBS underwriting, in which the sponsor's name would appear in the program's title – the Everready and Atwater Kent Hours were prominent examples – or in a brief mention at the end of the program. The sponsors' products were also likely to figure in the programs themselves.[95] Although listeners came to accept these indirect advertisements, even this was only grudgingly conceded in many cases.[96]

What little we know of radio finances in the 1920s only reinforces this picture of financial uncertainty.[97] Even by our most conservative estimate, regular operating costs in broadcasting in 1927 exceeded total advertising revenues, which have been estimated at $4.8 million that year.[98] In a February 1927 speech, RCA president James G. Harbord told the company's trustees, "We are breaking even in our national broadcasting proposition.

such financial returns [as AT&T] outside of the advertising business," he expressed concerns that advertising would mean that "the good will of the broadcast listener . . . might be jeopardized," hurting the company's radio sales. A. Michael McMahon, *The Making of a Profession: A Century of Electrical Engineering in America* (New York: IEEE Press, 1984).

[95] Sterling and Kittross, *Stay Tuned*, 80; Smulyan, *Selling of Radio*, especially Chapter 3. Interestingly, corporate underwriting of this sort – though clearly the dominant form of radio advertising at the time – was only part of what Austin Lescarboura, a writer for *Radio Broadcast*, had in mind when he announced in 1926 that "the sponsored program is the solution to the old, old question, 'Who will pay for broadcasting?'" Whether it was the First Baptist Church or RCA or Everready, someone was always willing to pay. "[T]hey have one point in common," Lescarboura observed, "they are all bent on selling something, whether it be a product or a religion, agricultural ideas or interest in economics, better voice transmission, or the name of the owner" (Lescarboura, "How Much it Costs"). Such an expansive notion of sponsorship – which sounds so quaint today – accurately reflects the still-primitive state of radio advertising just one year before the establishment of the FRC.

[96] In a morbidly comic cartoon from 1928, a listener subject to too many sponsor announcements bombs his local radio station. "The Events Leading Up to the Tragedy," *New York World* (September 19, 1928), reprinted in Smulyan, *Selling of Radio*.

[97] A monograph on radio advertising written in 1934 found that a full tally of profits was only possible beginning in 1931, adding in a footnote that "an attempt to do this [before 1931] was abandoned upon advice of experts, because of the chaotic state of many station books even in recent years, and because the turnover of station ownership further complicated the matter" [Herman S. Hettinger, *A Decade of Radio Advertising* (Chicago: University of Chicago Press, 1934)].

[98] The 1951 Yearbook issue of *Broadcasting* magazine estimated that, for the entirety of 1927, advertising expenditure on radio totaled $4.8 million, with $3.8 million of that going to national networks. To put this figure in some perspective, it is worth noting that sales of radio sets were widely estimated to have totaled $168 million that year [Caldwell, "The Radio Market"]. Our rough estimate of total operating costs for broadcasting in 1927 ranges from $5.7 million to $18.3 million; it is based on Jome's 1924 survey of broadcasters, at 174–175, suggesting that average annual costs ranged from a lower bound of $7,800 to an upper bound of $24,900 that year (not including installation expenses) and the fact that there were 733 stations in operation in 1927.

We had no thought of making money in this venture, but we wanted to give the public the best possible radio program and I think we have succeeded in doing this. If we continue to break even I will be more than satisfied."[99]

In retrospect, it seems that this environment was beginning to change in 1927, at least with respect to radio advertising. In a July 8, 1928, speech at the International Advertising Convention, NBC's Frank Arnold declared that just eighteen months before (i.e., in early 1927), "the attitude of the advertising agents of the country toward Broadcast Advertising was either negative or indifferent.... Nowhere along the agency line was there any marked enthusiasm, to say nothing of general acceptance."[100] However, according to Arnold, that indifference had finally given way to genuine interest roughly six months later – in mid–1927 – when "Radio Broadcasting was recognized as an advertising medium by the International Advertising Association."[101] Similarly, Sterling and Kittross suggested that "it was not until 1928 that broadcast advertising clearly became the breadwinner for American radio broadcasting"[102] – one year *after* passage of the Federal Radio Act on February 23, 1927.[103]

On the eve of broadcast regulation, therefore, the radio landscape and the financing of radio both dramatically differed from what we might expect, given our current assumptions about the economics of broadcasting. Back in 1927, networks were still relatively new and immature. Direct advertising (now practically the universal mode of financing radio) had few supporters. There was no consensus about how, or whether, broadcasting would ever be profitable. Thus, in considering the incentives of various radio interest groups at the dawn of the Radio Commission, it may not be appropriate to assume that commercial broadcasters anticipated the sort of rents that would later accrue to them as advertising matured.

CONCLUSION

This chapter has examined the proposition that, in refusing to expand the broadcast band in 1927, the FRC was responding to the appeals of incumbent broadcasters to advance their own special interest at the expense of

---

[99] "Promising Radio Year Predicted by Harbord," *Wall Street Journal* (February 7, 1927): 16.

[100] Frank A. Arnold, *Popular Reactions to Radio Broadcasting* (New York: National Broadcasting Company, 1928).

[101] Arnold, *Popular Reactions to Radio Broadcasting*, 5.

[102] Sterling and Kittross, *Stay Tuned*, 80.

[103] Jome signed and dated his preface on August 18, 1925. Jome, *Economics of the Radio Industry*, vii.

the public interest – that this FRC decision was, in short, captured by the broadcasters. Prior studies have highlighted evidence consistent with this proposition: namely, the opposition of incumbent broadcasters to the expansion proposal. However, on further review of the record, we found little in the way of additional confirming evidence. We also found powerful disconfirming evidence, which we believe outweighs the available supporting evidence in this case.

Most notably, we found that every major interest group – not just broadcasters – opposed the expansion proposal. This is significant because it suggests that the FRC commissioners had no reason to believe that maintaining the existing band would violate the public interest in the service of any particular special interest. This in turn appears to place the episode well outside the definition of regulatory capture provided in the introduction to this volume, because the definition requires that captured regulation is "directed away from the public interest." The broad consensus against the expansion proposal also raises the question of why incumbent broadcasters would have needed to expend resources to "capture" a decision that, given the position of other interests, was nearly a foregone conclusion in any case.

We also were surprised to discover that the broadcasters who testified at the FRC hearings were themselves divided on the issue, with some opposing expansion and others apparently willing to support it. Admittedly, only a small number of broadcasters testified at the hearings, and there is no reason to believe that they necessarily constituted a representative sample. Yet until additional documents shedding light on the broadcaster position are uncovered, this is the best indication we have. (Recall that prior "evidence" of intense – and presumably unified – broadcaster opposition to the expansion proposal was mistakenly based on quotes from a radio listeners' journal, rather than a broadcasters' journal.[104])

Finally, the historical record suggests that in early 1927, there was still little agreement whether radio broadcasting would ever be profitable. Thus it seems likely that the rents that could have accrued from limiting entry might have appeared less impressive (and perhaps *far* less impressive) to broadcasters at the time – that is, prospectively – than they do retrospectively today. Although we do not doubt that incumbent broadcasters ultimately may have benefited from the FRC's decision not to expand the band, we simply suggest that the broadcasters themselves may not have fully anticipated the potential gains at the time.

---

[104] See subheading "Broadcasters Were Divided" in the section on "A Broad Coalition Against the Expansion Proposal" in this chapter and note 17 above.

Of course, none of these findings contradict the economic theory of regulation itself because we would expect, based on the theory, that a regulatory proposal opposed by all major interest groups would ultimately be rejected by regulators. The evidence presented here is inconsistent only with a capture interpretation of the episode. This is significant, however, because it means that we cannot use the episode to discriminate in favor of the economic theory of regulation on the one hand as compared with a public interest interpretation on the other.

For a case to contradict the economic theory of regulation outright, it would have to involve the converse of capture. As Stigler himself once suggested, "the theory would be contradicted if, for a given regulatory policy, we found the group with larger benefits and lower costs of political action being dominated by another group with lesser benefits and higher cost of political action."[105] Students of regulation, as good scholars, should look hard for examples of this sort – precisely because the theory predicts that "[t]emporary accidents aside, such cases simply will not arise. . . . "[106]

Medicare's enactment in 1965 might conceivably constitute such a case, because the most powerful and well-organized interest group involved, the American Medical Association (which represented individuals with arguably the most at stake – physicians), failed in its very determined and well-funded effort to stop the legislation.[107] It has also been suggested that the passage of anti-gouging laws may contradict a capture interpretation: "The affected firms lose money, and the 'winners' (namely the consumers that end up paying lower prices) are quite scattered. Indeed, it is difficult to know [in advance] which consumer will win by paying a low price and which consumer will lose by being rationed."[108]

Further historical research would naturally be required to determine if either of these cases, or if other historical cases, are consistent or inconsistent with the economic theory of regulation. This is precisely the point, however. Further (and finer grained) historical research is needed if we wish to test

---

[105] Stigler, "Supplementary Note," 140.

[106] Ibid.

[107] See David Moss and Mary Oey, "The Paranoid Style in the Study of American Politics," in *Government and Markets: Toward a New Theory of Regulation,* eds. Edward Balleisen and David Moss (Cambridge, MA: Cambridge University Press, 2010).

[108] Julio J. Rotemberg, "Behavior Aspects of Price Setting, and Their Policy Implications" (unpublished draft paper, July 19, 2007), 25. This paper was subsequently revised and published as Julio J. Rotemberg, "Behavioral Aspects of Price Setting and Their Policy Implications," in Christopher L. Foote, Lorenz Goette, and Stephan Meier, eds., *Policymaking Insights from Behavioral Economics* (Boston: Federal Reserve Bank of Boston, 2009), chapter 2, pp. 51–98; see esp. pp. 75–76.

the economic theory of regulation and enhance our understanding of the conditions under which it does (and does not) apply. Quick-and-dirty history is not only not sufficient, it is also potentially dangerous because it may lead researchers to false conclusions and provide false confidence in their prior assumptions.

It is certainly reasonable, as George Stigler suggested more than thirty years ago, to derive historical inferences from a compelling theory. However, history should also be used as an *independent* test of theory, and this must involve more than merely a search for confirming evidence (which, by itself, represents the historical equivalent of data mining). What might be called history-by-inference is never a legitimate test. Perusing the historical record for evidence that seems to support a favorite theory may provide some emotional comfort, but it is decidedly not the stuff of good scholarship. Rather, good scholarship requires that we search vigorously for disconfirming evidence as well – the goal being always to challenge the prevailing theory, to find its limits, to move beyond it, and never simply to protect it for its own sake.

9

Conditional Forbearance as an Alternative to Capture

Evidence From Coal Mine Safety Regulation

Sanford C. Gordon and Catherine Hafer[1]

INTRODUCTION

Regulatory agencies are often accused of offering forbearance to powerful actors within the industries they are charged with overseeing, possibly in violation of their statutory mandates and to the potential detriment of the broader public. The term *bureaucratic capture* is often employed as a short-hand for this phenomenon. Any attempt to construct a coherent analytical framework for understanding it, and to assess its empirical referents, however, must confront the interaction between two broad forces shaping the context in which regulators act: efforts by firms within the industry to protect and promote their economic interests and the actions of the regulators' political superordinates.

Regulatory agencies are fundamentally complex hierarchies – chains of principal–agent relationships[2] – consisting of many tiers of civil servants overseen by a leadership appointed by, and ultimately (more or less, depending on the extent of agency independence) responsive to, elected public officials (and, by extension, the public). At all levels of an agency's hierarchy, occupants are, to some extent, responsive to the incentives created for them by their administrative or political superordinates. To the extent that the goals of those superordinates may change, whether because the superordinates themselves have been replaced or because they have revised their regulatory goals, one may expect commensurate changes in the behavior of regulators.

However, regulated interests have a variety of means at their disposal to influence regulators and may be expected to use them to protect their

---

[1] Department of Politics, New York University.

[2] E.g., Terry M. Moe, "The New Economics of Organization," *American Journal of Political Science* 28 (1984): 739–77.

own profitability. These means fall under the broad rubric of agency *capture*. Some accounts stress an implicit exchange in which leniency is exchanged for political or financial support or the promise of future employment, whereas others stress that regulators drawn from industry will prove inherently sympathetic to their former employers. In either case, the operative notion of capture presupposes a principal–agent relationship in which an agency's effective principal is the industry itself.

The existence of these two influences on regulators naturally raises the question of how they interact. Capture in its purest form could correspond to a situation in which the agency's allegiance to the industry completely dominates its accountability to political principals (who may be relatively unsympathetic to industry interests, but powerless to act on their conception of the public interest). Alternatively, it could imply that the political principals are, themselves, captured by industry. In both situations, the preferences of the agency's personnel would be fundamentally and inalterably shaped by those of the industry.

Alternatively, consider a situation in which the agency's allegiance to industry is not complete, but instead shifts according to the preferences of elected officials and/or their constituents. Although we may still see responsiveness to industry interests in this circumstance, it would correspond to an altogether different account of industry–agency relations: one in which the degree of regulatory *forbearance* (defined as a reduction in the stringency with which regulations are enforced) is *conditional* on the identity of the agency's political principals and/or the salience of the policy area falling in its jurisdiction.

In this chapter, we consider the possibility of conditional forbearance in the context of the regulation of coal mining by the U.S. Mine Safety and Health Administration (MSHA). Coal mining represents an interesting case for scholars of regulation: historically, the mining industry has enjoyed substantial political strength at the national[3] and, particularly, the state and local[4] levels. At the same time, the history of mining regulation suggests a pattern in which tragic accidents lead to mine safety legislation, often over the objections of industry. In fact, a familiar adage in mining communities holds that "safety laws are written in miners' blood." Moreover, Congress placed MSHA in the Department of Labor in large part because critics of

---

[3] Bruce A. Ackerman and William T. Hassler, *Clean Coal/Dirty Air* (New Haven, CT: Yale University Press, 1981).

[4] John Bartlow Martin, "The Blast in Centralia No. 5: A Mine Disaster No One Stopped," *Harper's* (March, 1948): 193–220; John Gaventa, *Power and Powerlessness: Quiescence and Rebellion in an Appalachian Valley* (Champaign, IL: University of Illinois Press, 1980).

its predecessor in the Department of Interior were seen as too beholden to industry interests.

At the same time, the case of coal mining departs in an important sense from canonical accounts of agency capture: according to those accounts, the interests of industry that motivate it to shape agency behavior are arrayed against the interests of a diffuse and typically unorganized public. Much of the development of mine safety regulation in the United States, by contrast, has taken place against the backdrop of conflict between two organized interests: mining companies and labor unions, most prominently the United Mine Workers of America.

In Chapter 3 of this volume on "Detecting and Measuring Capture," Carpenter offers much-needed clarity with respect to some of the conceptual challenges associated with diagnosing bureaucratic capture. Most importantly, he argues that several evidentiary standards must be met to sustain such a finding. First and foremost is the ability to articulate some notion of the public interest as a counterfactual. Doing so is rather tricky in the field of mine safety regulation, given the conflict of interests that lies at its heart, and given the close association of mining companies and labor unions with, respectively, the Republican and Democratic parties in contemporary U.S. politics. Each of these groups of actors has a different – and often plausible – conception of the public interest in mind, which weighs the inherent trade-offs associated with more and less stringent regulation of the industry differently. These trade-offs involve, inter alia, miner safety, miner employment, regional development, energy independence, and environmental degradation.

Moreover, although even the most zealous advocate of the industry would surely agree that an accident that resulted in miners' deaths is not itself "in the public interest," this cannot be taken as evidence that the public interest is unfailingly synonymous with maximally stringent regulations to reduce the risk of accidents to negligible levels. Indeed, we would expect the miners themselves to chafe under such restrictions – particularly if they led to the miners' unemployment. By the same token, a radical environmentalist might take the mere *existence* of the mining industry to be a net public harm; if this is stipulated, then any government activity that permits the industry to continue functioning at all is synonymous with capture.

Carpenter suggests, further, that scholars often conflate capture and what he refers to as "electorally sanctioned pro-business governance." One may take our theory of conditional forbearance as fleshing out the details of this alternative mechanism, which we believe often provides a more compelling account of industry influence in government than that of pure capture, and particularly so in the case of MSHA.[5]

Assessing conditional regulatory forbearance empirically faces two challenges. First, changes in agency incentives commensurate with changes in political principals or policy salience may induce behavioral change not only in the *agency*'s behavior, but also in the *industry*'s behavior. Strategic adjustment by the industry, as we explain in greater detail later, can make evidence of variation in the degree of agency forbearance difficult to document. To address this issue, we examine the effects of mining accidents on subsequent agency behavior. In the short run, we argue, MSHA can alter its enforcement of safety standards before strategic adjustment by the industry has a chance to occur. By focusing our attention on mining accidents occurring in different political climates, we can assess whether, in fact, agency deference to industry influence is mediated by deference to its political principals.

Second, it is possible that the changes in agency behavior following an accident are purely cosmetic and designed to squelch public outcry and prevent meaningful reform. Our empirical strategy for addressing this concern involves comparing MSHA's response across accidents receiving different levels of publicity within the same administration and comparing similarly publicized accidents across administrations.[6] As we explain in greater detail later, the conditional forbearance account is supported if the first comparison suggests greater responsiveness in the more highly publicized case, and the second implies changes in agency behavior imposing a direct, material cost to industry and more protests from industry.

In fact, we observe precisely this pattern in the data. We document no significant change in agency behavior following a little-publicized disaster occurring shortly after September 11, 2001, but substantial changes following the highly visible Sago mine disaster in 2006. Increases in enforcement activity similar to those following the Sago tragedy followed the Upper Big Branch Disaster in 2010; however, following the latter accident, average penalties increased, and agency action was met with more resistance from industry.

---

[5] Of course, mining regulation is just one of many policies over which elected officials have responsibilities, a fact that may contribute to agency loss between the typical voter and the elected official. Thus we do not take "electorally sanctioned" to imply "ideal from the perspective of the median voter."

[6] For a related treatment of the media's effects on agency behavior, see Daniel P. Carpenter, "Groups, the Media, and Agency Waiting Costs: The Political Economy of FDA Drug Approval," *American Journal of Political Science* 46 (2002): 490–505.

The remainder of the chapter proceeds as follows. In the first section following this introduction, we provide a brief background on the evolution of federal mine safety laws in the United States and describe the MSHA enforcement process. We then provide a simple heuristic model, outline our empirical strategy, and describe our empirical expectations. The next section describes data and measures used in our analysis. We then present our empirical results and interpret them in the context of the conditional forbearance account. We conclude by discussing the implications of our findings for the empirical analysis of industry influence in regulatory policy more generally.

BACKGROUND

The Coal Industry: Technology and Safety

Coal has long played a substantial role in the nation's profile of energy sources and thus its economy, fluctuating between 20 and 40 percent of total energy production in the last sixty years.[7] As of June 2012, the industry employed about 84,000 workers,[8] a steep decline from the industry's peak in the 1920s, when bituminous and anthracite coal mining employed more than 860,000 workers nationwide.[9]

The historical development of coal mining in the past century has been characterized by remarkable changes in technology of extraction. In the nineteenth century, miners – drawn increasingly from the ranks of Eastern European immigrants – would descend below ground with kerosene lamps attached to their helmets, armed with pick axes, shovels, drills, and/or explosives. In the case of soft, bituminous coal, miners would manually cut the coal from the exposed face of a seam. In the case of harder, anthracite coal (a once-common domestic heating fuel), a carefully placed explosive shot – first black powder, and later dynamite – would, on detonation, release a significant quantity of coal from a seam onto the mine floor, whereupon the miner would shovel the coal either into a cart or onto a conveyor for removal and subsequent processing. Mules typically drew carts, but electric

---

[7] U.S. Department of Energy, *Annual Energy Review 2009* (Washington, DC: Energy Information Administration, Department of Energy, 2010).

[8] U.S. Bureau of Labor Statistics, *The Employment Situation: June 2012* (Washington, DC: Bureau of Labor Statistics, Department of Labor, 2012).

[9] Susan B. Carter, Scott Sigmund Gartner, Michael R. Haines, Alan L. Olmstead, Richard Sutch, and Gavin Wright, eds., *Historical Statistics of the United States: Millennial Edition* (New York: Cambridge University Press, 2006).

locomotives replaced these draught animals by the early twentieth century. These locomotives were initially powered by exposed high-voltage copper wires running the length of mine tunnels, posing a substantial electrocution risk to the miners (as well as the remaining mules). Later, battery-powered locomotives reduced that risk. Kerosene illumination gave way to carbide and then battery-powered lamps. Hand-cranked drills gave way to electrical ones and then (to reduce the risk of sparking) drills powered by compressed air.

Over the twentieth century, the process of underground coal mining became increasingly mechanized, with teams of miners operating heavy machinery to remove ever-larger quantities of coal from a seam. Conventional mining, which employs techniques evolved from those described previously, now accounts for less than 3 percent of all underground coal production in the United States.[10] Like conventional mining, continuous mining employs a "room and pillar" approach in which a grid of tunnels is excavated, leaving sufficient quantities of the mined materials to support the millions of tons of "overburden" material overhead. However, continuous mining replaces manual techniques with a tungsten carbide-toothed cutting machine capable of a far more rapid rate of recovery. The most common modern technique in the United States is long-wall mining, in which a coal-shearing machine moves on a conveyor to dislodge coal from a single "panel" that may be more than a mile long and 800 feet wide.[11]

NB

These developments have been accompanied by the development of surface mining techniques to harvest shallow coal deposits. In strip mining, overburden material – sand, rock, gravel, and dirt – is removed (e.g., by enormous excavators) and coal seams are accessed directly. Mountaintop removal mining is exactly that: explosives blast the overburden off of mountains, exposing the coal seams beneath.[12]

Mining is one of the most hazardous jobs in the United States.[13] Added to the host of industrial accidents that may occur in any environment where heavy equipment is operated, a spark from the equipment can ignite accumulated flammable gases or coal dust if insufficient safeguards are

---

[10] U.S. Department of Energy, *Annual Coal Report* (Washington, DC: Energy Information Administration, Department of Energy, 2009).

[11] U.S. Department of Energy, *Longwall Mining* (Washington, DC: Energy Information Administration, Department of Energy, 1995).

[12] Note that these techniques are controversial primarily for their deleterious environmental effects, an important topic that is, unfortunately, beyond the scope of the current inquiry.

[13] U.S. Bureau of Labor Statistics, *The Employment Situation: June 2012* (Washington, DC: Bureau of Labor Statistics, Department of Labor, 2012).

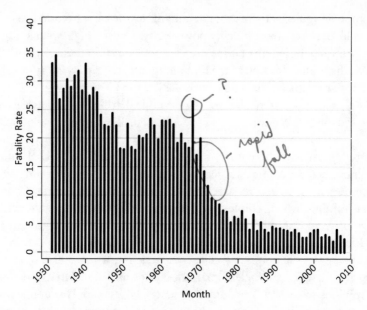

Figure 9.1. Miner Deaths per 10,000 Full-Time Equivalent Workers, 1931–2008. *Source:* MSHA.

employed or if the mine is insufficiently ventilated, causing a deadly explosion. Asphyxiation and drowning are threats in some mines. In addition, cave-ins or collapses are also possible at any point in the mining process, but particularly in the case of "retreat" mining, where the pillar material in a room and pillar site is harvested in the final phases of a mine's operational lifetime.

Despite these risks, the twentieth century witnessed a remarkable decline in the incidence of mining-related fatalities. Three thousand coal miners lost their lives in 1907; by 2010 – a year that experienced the worst single disaster since the 1970s – that number had fallen to fewer than fifty. Figure 9.1 displays historical data on miner deaths per 10,000 full-time equivalent workers. In 1931 (the first year in the time series), 1,463 miners lost their lives on the job; the figure displays that a massive reduction in fatalities has occurred even once one accounts for the roughly 70 percent reduction in total employee hours worked that occurred over the same period. Although supporters of stringent mining regulation attribute this success to the evolution of the regulatory regime itself,[14] critics suggest that

[14] For example, Michael S. Lewis-Beck and John R. Alford, "Can Government Regulate Safety? The Coal Mine Example," *American Political Science Review* 74 (1980): 745–56;

regulation is not cost effective[15] and that technological change would have led to similar reductions even in the absence of regulation. Others have attributed improvements in safety to unionization,[16] although the empirical evidence for this has been mixed.[17]

Federal Mine Safety Regulation in the United States

The historical development of a federal presence in the arena of mine safety and health regulation has followed a remarkably consistent, if depressing, pattern since its rather meager beginnings in the late nineteenth century. Typically, a catastrophic mining accident or series of accidents revulses public sentiment and produces accusations, either from unions or progressive elites, that gross inadequacies in the existing landscape of state and federal laws and regulations led to the accident and that regulatory agencies are captured by mining companies (whether through pro-industry appointments, intimidation, or outright bribery). Congress subsequently responds accordingly with more stringent legislation – in some cases cosmetic, but in others dramatically increasing the scope of federal regulatory authority.

For example, in 1891, an explosion at the Mammoth Mine in Mount Pleasant Township, Pennsylvania, killed 107 miners.[18] Several months later, Congress responded with the first federal law governing coal mining. As its name suggested, "An Act for the Protection of the Lives of Miners in the Territories" only covered mines in U.S. territories, but it established

John Braithwaite, *To Punish or Persuade: Enforcement of Coal Mine Safety* (Albany, NY: State University of New York Press, 1985).

[15] For example, Thomas J. Kniesner and John D. Leeth, "Data Mining Mining Data: MSHA Enforcement Efforts, Underground Coal Mine Safety, and New Health Policy Implications," *Journal of Risk and Uncertainty* 29 (2004): 83–111.

[16] William Graebner, *Coal-Mining Safety in the Progressive Period: The Political Economy of Reform* (Lexington, KY: University Press of Kentucky, 1976), 139.

[17] For example, William C. Appleton and Joe G. Baker, "The Effect of Unionization on Safety in Bituminous Deep Mines," *Journal of Labor Research* 4 (1984): 139–47; Price V. Fishback, "Workplace Safety During the Progressive Era: Fatal Accidents in Bituminous Coal Mining, 1912–1923," *Explorations in Economic History* 23 (1986): 269–98; Alison Morantz, "The Elusive Union Safety Effect: Towards a New Empirical Research Agenda," *Proceedings of the 61st Annual Meeting of the Labor and Employment Relations Association* (Champaign, IL: Labor and Employment Relations Association, 2009), 130–46; Alison Morantz, "Coal Mine Safety: Do Unions Make a Difference?" *Industrial and Labor Relations Review*, forthcoming.

[18] Much of the information contained in this summary, unless otherwise noted, is drawn from MSHA's own History of Mine Safety and Health Regulation and its list of fatal mining disasters, available on its Web site. U.S. Mine Safety and Health Administration, "History of Mine Safety and Health Regulation," available at www.msha.gov/mshainfo/mshainf2 .htm; U.S. Mine Safety and Health Administration, "Historical Data on Mine Disasters in the United States," available at www.msha.gov/mshainfo/factsheets/mshafct8.htm.

the first federal safety standards for mines in U.S. history and permitted the president to appoint a corps of territorial mine inspectors in the Department of Interior.[19]

In 1907, the largest mining disaster in U.S. history, an explosion in the Monongah Nos. 6 and 8 Coal Mines in Monongah, West Virginia, took the lives of 362 miners. Two years later, 259 miners were killed in a fire at the Cherry Mine in Cherry, Illinois. In fact, the period 1909–1910 experienced more separate coal mine disasters than any other two-year period in American history: thirty-nine.[20] In response, Congress created the U.S. Bureau of Mines (USBM) in 1910. Located within the Department of Interior, the Bureau initially conducted research into mine safety, but had no regulatory authority. In 1940, an explosion in the Willow Grove Mine in St. Clairsvill, Ohio, killed seventy-two miners; in 1941, Congress granted federal USBM inspectors the authority to enter mines. In 1947, a blast in the Centralia No. 5 Mine in Centralia, Illinois, killed 111 miners; Congress responded by granting rulemaking authority to USBM. In 1951, an explosion at the Orient No. 2 Mine in West Frankfort, Illinois, killed 119 miners; the following year, Congress granted limited penalty authority to the Bureau and annual inspections of some underground mines. The 1952 legislation was amended to cover all coal mines in 1966. That year, Congress also granted limited rulemaking and enforcement authority to the USBM for metal and nonmetal mines.

Following an explosion that killed seventy-eight miners at Consol No. 9 in Farmington, West Virginia, the previous year, Congress passed the Federal Coal Mine Health and Safety Act of 1969 (popularly known as the Coal Act). The act mandated inspections at underground and surface coal operations, created a regime of civil and criminal monetary penalties, and contained agency-forcing language for the promulgation of health and safety standards. The Coal Act was in force in 1972 when a fire at the Sunshine Mine in Kellogg, Idaho, killed ninety-one miners. The following year, Nixon Interior Secretary Rogers C.B. Morton split the enforcement and rulemaking functions from the USBM into a new agency in Interior, the Mine Enforcement and Safety Administration (MESA).

---

[19] Anne T. Nichting, Laura E. Beverage, and Karen L. Johnston, "Mine Safety and Health Law," in *Industrial Minerals and Rocks: Commodities, Markets, and Uses*, 7th ed., eds. Jessica Elzea Kogel, Nikhil C. Trivedi, James M. Barker, and Stanley T. Krukowski (Littleton, CO: Society for Mining, Metallurgy, and Exploration, 2006), 109–19.

[20] U.S. Bureau of Mines, "Historical Summary of Coal-Mine Explosions in the United States, 1810–1958" (Bulletin 586, 1960).

1977 saw the creation of the current statutory structure for mine safety and health regulation: the Federal Mine Safety and Health Act (popularly known as the Mine Act). The Mine Act consolidated regulatory procedures for coal and metal/nonmetal mines, detailed procedures for miners to report violations and accompany regulators on inspections, and implemented protections for those workers against retaliation from employers. Most importantly, the Mine Act transformed MESA into a new agency, called the Mine Safety and Health Administration (MSHA), in the Department of Labor. This transfer represented a major victory for labor: union representatives argued that the Department of Interior frequently sided with management against them and anticipated, based on their experience with the Occupational Safety and Health Administration, a more favorable agency in Labor. Management, for their part, argued vociferously against the transfer;[21] however, several amendments offered by western members of Congress to block the move failed to garner a majority in either chamber.[22] Management did win a concession in the form of a Mine Safety and Health Review Commission, staffed by presidential appointees and Administrative Law Judges, to hear appeals of citations and orders issued by MSHA.

Similar legislation had failed to garner the necessary support in the previous Congress,[23] but with comparable Democratic majorities in place and a Democrat in the White House, the Mine Act passed easily in July 1977. The structural changes represented by the Mine Act follow a familiar pattern to students of regulatory agency design:[24] a statute's enacting coalition, concerned that its majority status may be temporary, seeks to place statutory functions in a friendly executive department.[25] Its opponents, however, succeed in introducing appellate procedures that permit them to delay agency action or limit its effect.

[21] U.S. House of Representatives, *Federal Mine Safety and Health Act of 1977: Report No. 95–312* (Washington, DC: U.S. House of Representatives, 95th Congress, First Session, 1977).

[22] "Senate Clears Bill That Toughens Mine-Safety Law," *Wall Street Journal* (June 22, 1977): 14.

[23] "Tighter Mine Safety, Power Shift Voted," *Washington Post* (July 29, 1976): A2.

[24] See, especially, Terry M. Moe, "The Politics of Bureaucratic Structure," in *Can the Government Govern?* eds. John E. Chubb and Paul E. Peterson (Washington, DC: Brookings Institution Press, 1989), 267–329.

[25] See also the discussion of the Forest Reserve Transfer Act, which moved management responsibilities for U.S. Forests from the Department of Interior to Agriculture, in Herbert Kaufman, *The Forest Ranger* (Washington, DC: Resources for the Future, 1960), and Daniel P. Carpenter, *The Forging of Bureaucratic Autonomy* (Princeton, NJ: Princeton University Press, 2001).

While the Mine Act continues to be in force, it was strengthened in 2006 with the Mine Improvement and New Emergency Response Act, or MINER Act. This legislation had its origins in two mine disasters that same year: an explosion in the Sago Mine in Sago, West Virginia, killed twelve in January of that year, and an explosion in Darby Mine No. 1 in Darby, Kentucky, killed five. The MINER Act requires operators to establish emergency response plans specific to each mine and increases civil and criminal penalties. Pursuant to the Act, a new penalty regime went into effect in April 2007, yielding sharply higher penalties (and, at the outset, greater rates of contested penalties).

The MSHA Enforcement Process

MSHA is charged with regulating almost 15,000 coal, metal, and nonmetal (e.g., sand and gravel pit) mines and processing facilities in the United States. Inspection operations, the issuance of citations, and negotiations over remediation and penalties are largely conducted by the Administration's eleven district offices. MSHA inspectors visit surface operations at least twice yearly and underground operations at least four times a year. However, there is enormous variation in the intensity of individual inspections: the shortest inspections may involve one individual visiting a site for fifteen minutes. By contrast, the most intensive single inspection in the last decade involved eighty-eight inspectors and more than 16,000 inspector-hours over four months at Massey Energy's Upper Big Branch Mine in Montcoal, West Virginia, following an explosion on April 5, 2010, that killed twenty-nine miners.

At a visit to a mine, inspectors document health and safety violations. The Mine Act mandates that management and labor representatives may accompany inspectors as they make their way around the mine. An MSHA inspector can issue a citation or order for detected violations; in consultation with the agency's Office of Assessments, these may be accompanied by civil penalties. Although the penalty associated with an individual citation is typically small (currently $60 for a violation that does not constitute an immediate risk of injury), inspectors typically document numerous violations on a given visit: conditional on detecting any violations, the mean number of violations detected per visit was thirteen over the course of the last decade. For more serious infractions (e.g., so-called "S&S" – significant and substantial – violations), civil penalties can be quite severe: under the agency's penalty policy promulgated under the 2006 MINER Act, penalties for flagrant violations can reach $220,000. The operating company then has thirty days to respond to the citation(s) and to inform the district office whether it intends to contest the findings. Depending on the nature of the citation, initial appeals may be heard by an Administrative Law Judge and then subsequently by the Mine Safety and Health Review Commission and, finally, in the federal courts.

Accusations of Agency Capture

The history of federal mine safety regulation in the United States may be characterized as a steadily increasing array of regulatory requirements and a decreasing frequency of fatal mining accidents. Nonetheless, critics of MSHA complain that the mining industry exercises disproportionate and unwarranted influence over the agency's activities. Immediately following the Sago disaster in 2006, a *Washington Post* editorial opined that "the MSHA has in the past several years formed a series of 'partnerships' with mining industry groups. In principle, such partnerships might help make mines safer. In practice, they might have allowed the agency to become too friendly with the businesses it regulates".[26] And following 2010's horrendous accident at the Upper Big Branch Mine, Representative George Miller (D-CA) argued that, following accidents, "everyone pledges to make it safer. But the mine owners, they just wait and let time work and let time erode emotion, and then they come to Washington. They tell members they can't do business [under more stringent regulation]".[27]

At the level of enforcement, the most frequent complaint concerning the undue influence of mining companies concerns the ability of companies to tie up agency resources by contesting MSHA inspectors' determinations of noncompliance. Because a case may take months or even years to pass through the agency's appellate procedure to the Mine Safety and Health Review Commission, MSHA officials face a strong incentive to settle for penalties smaller than those initially proposed.

In addition to reduced penalties, contesting citations may confer two additional benefits to mine operators: first, it may allow them to defer additional compliance expenditures associated with the cited violation. Second, it may prevent the official tally of S&S violations from reaching a critical threshold. Section 104(e) of the federal Mine Act affords MSHA discretion

[26] "A Mining Disaster," *Washington Post* (January 4, 2006): Editorial, A16.
[27] Kimberly Kindy, "Longtime Tug of War on Mine Safety," *Washington Post* (January 4, 2011): A1.

to confer a dreaded "pattern of violations" (POV) designation on a mine in the event of recurrent S&S violations. In theory, POV status can economically cripple a mine: it gives MSHA personnel the right to withdraw miners from the area of a mine affected by any subsequent S&S violation for ninety days. Until it did so for two mines in April 2011, however, MSHA had never conferred POV status on any mine.

Despite the apparent benefits to contestation, different mining companies have availed themselves of the opportunity to contest citations at substantially different rates. For example, in 2008, Murray Energy contested 1,806 of 3,091 cited violations at thirteen mines, or 58 percent. By contrast, Alpha Natural Resources (which acquired Upper Big Branch operator Massey Energy in 2011) contested 59 of 745 citations, or just over 9 percent.[28]

Critics have also raised the specter of a "revolving door" at MSHA, pointing specifically to the industry experience of George W. Bush's two MSHA heads: Dave Lauriski and Richard E. Stickler. In addition, research by two reporters for the *Washington Post* revealed "nearly a dozen" district directors who recently took jobs at Massey or Murray Energy.[29] What is notable about the latter finding is that unlike the MSHA administrator, district directors are not political appointees.

EMPIRICAL STRATEGY: CHALLENGES TO IDENTIFICATION AND INTERPRETATION

Consider the following simple heuristic model of the relationship between a regulatory agency and a mining firm. The agency chooses a level of monitoring m, lying between 0 and 1, while the firm chooses a level of compliance investment c, also lying between 0 and 1.

Investment at level c yields a fraction $(1 - c)$ safety violations unremedied, and monitoring at level m yields a fraction $(1 - m)$ unremedied violations undetected. The probability of a fatal accident, then, is increasing in the quantity $(1 - m)(1 - c)$; for simplicity, we assume that the probability is equal to that quantity. Both the agency and the firm suffer a cost from a fatal accident, denoted by q_a for the agency and q_f for the firm. Additionally, the firm pays a sanction for detected violations, with the marginal sanction equal to s.[30] Finally, for simplicity, we give the agency and firm quadratic

---

[28] That year, Massey contested 2,379 violations, a third of its 7,179 total citations.

[29] Kimberley Kindy and Dan Eggen, "Revolving Door Is Used by Many: West Virginia Disaster Highlights Industry–Government Ties," *Washington Post* (April 18, 2010): A1.

[30] The model could be extended by also permitting the agency to benefit from detecting violations as well as preventing accidents; this will not affect the intuition here.

costs: in particular, the cost to the agency of monitoring at level m is given by $\mu m^2 / 2$, and the cost to the firm of investing at level c is $\kappa c^2 / 2$, where $\mu > 0$ and $\kappa > 0$ are parameters scaling the cost.

In a Nash equilibrium, each player will correctly anticipate the strategy of the other player. The expected utility to the agency is given by

$$E[u_a(m, c; \mu, q_a)] = (1 - m)(1 - c)q_a - \frac{\mu}{2}m^2,$$

and the expected utility to the firm is given by

$$E[u_f(c, m; \kappa, q_f, s)] = -m(1 - c)s - (1 - m)(1 - c)q_f - \frac{\kappa}{2}c^2.$$

Label the agency's best response to firm investment $m(c)$. It is straightforward to demonstrate that this is given by

$$m(c; \mu, q_a) = \frac{(1 - c)q_a}{\mu}. \tag{1}$$

Unsurprisingly, the agency's optimal level of monitoring is decreasing in the level of firm investment: firm compliance is a substitute for agency activity in the agency's objective function.

Next, label the firm's best response to agency monitoring $c(m)$. This is given by

$$c(m; \gamma, q_f, s) = \frac{q_f + (s - q_f)m}{\kappa}. \tag{2}$$

Note that whether the firm's optimal level of investment is increasing or decreasing in the level of agency scrutiny depends on the sign of the quantity $s - q_f$. If sanctions are sufficiently high ($s > q_f$), then firm compliance is increasing in oversight; the actions of the firm and agency are complements in the firm's objective function. If, however, sanctions are low ($s < q_f$), then firm compliance is *decreasing* in oversight: agency and firm behavior in that instance are substitutes in the firm's objective.

Consider the case in which the firm's compliance is increasing in the degree of scrutiny. The logic of the equilibrium to the game is displayed graphically in Figure 9.2. The upward sloping curves labeled C_1 and C_2 correspond to the firm's best response correspondences for different parameter values, and the downward sloping curves labeled M_1 and M_2 correspond to hypothetical best response correspondences for the agency. Equilibrium levels of monitoring and compliance may be found at the intersections of the curves.

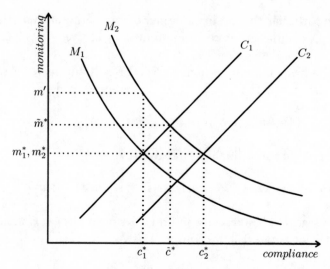

Figure 9.2. Equilibrium in the Regulatory Enforcement Game and the Identification Problem.

At first glance, a natural empirical strategy for adjudicating between a strong capture account, in which the industry effectively directs MSHA behavior irrespective of elected officials, and our conditional forbearance account, in which the agency adjusts the intensity of oversight in response to changes in the political environment, would involve comparing agency behavior across administrations. To understand the challenges associated with this approach, consider a stable equilibrium at the intersection of C_1 and M_1, given by the strategy pair (c_1, m_1). Now suppose the agency's incentives change – perhaps a new administration with fewer ties to the regulated interest group comes to power, resulting in a reduction in the cost parameter μ for the agency. This shifts the agency's best response correspondence from M_1 to M_2. In equilibrium, this shift produces a change not only in monitoring, but also in compliance. The increase in compliance, in turn, induces the agency to invest less in monitoring than it would had the firm's behavior been completely unresponsive to changes in monitoring. In the figure, this implies the new equilibrium is at c , m rather than at c_1, m . The net effect would be to obscure or weaken the observed effect of the change in the preferences of the political principal on the agency's behavior. In other words, compensating behavior by regulated parties exerts a downward bias on our ability to recover an estimate of the agency's response to the change in administration.

From the perspective of the analyst, matters are worse if the change in the environment affects the incentives of both the agency and the firm simultaneously. Suppose, for example, that the change in administration yields a reduction in monitoring costs to the agency (because of the change in the political environment) and a reduction in compliance costs for firms (e.g., because the new administration facilitates a low-interest loan program for compliance technology upgrades). This situation would correspond to a shift both from M_1 to M_2 and from C_1 to C_2. In the example given in the figure, the effects are completely offsetting the level of monitoring intensity – the new equilibrium monitoring level m_2 is the same as the old. All of the action comes in the form of increased compliance – something that is much more difficult for the analyst to observe.

Our response to this challenge is to examine changes in MSHA's enforcement behavior immediately following mining accidents. Mining accidents, unlike changes of administrations, are highly stochastic, (unfortunately) recurrent incidents that may exogenously shock the preferences of the agency, as well as those of industry players.[31] In the aftermath of a lethal tragedy, MSHA can take steps to immediately increase the intensity of regulation: starting new spot inspections, employing a lower threshold for labeling violations S&S, or issuing citations with accompanying penalties instead of warnings. It can also identify a POV at a mine and suspend operations until compliance problems are addressed.

Such incidents are likely to reveal information about aspects of the unlucky firm's regulatory compliance that are otherwise difficult for the agency to observe. Thus, although firms make calculated decisions about how much to invest into rectifying more easily observed violations as a function of the stringency of the regulatory regime, accidents are likely to expose vulnerabilities that are less affected by compensatory strategic behavior by the firm, at least in the short term. In the figure, this short-term adjustment by the agency corresponds to a shift from m_1 to m . We use the difference in agency behavior immediately before and immediately after such incidents as a measure of agency responsiveness and compare this measure across administrations to assess the conditional forbearance account.

Although the agency does have a "first mover" advantage over industry following an unanticipated tragedy, industry is likely to adjust to changes in regulatory zeal in the medium to long term. As we note previously,

---

[31] Examples of similar shocks in other regulated industries include food-borne pathogen scares, plane crashes, and periodic nuclear reactor shutdowns.

this response may itself feed back into the behavior of regulators. The empirical implication of this dynamic is that momentary increases in observable metrics of regulatory enforcement intensity in response to unanticipated shocks are likely to be transient. Of course, it is also possible that the agency's incentives return to pre-accident levels, which would also yield a gradual diminishment in the level of monitoring intensity. However, a return to long-run steady-state levels of enforcement need *not* signify the "business as usual" of a captured agency, as it could be consistent with a new equilibrium reflecting a more stringent regulatory regime.

The second methodological challenge in distinguishing the conditional forbearance from strong capture stems from the possibility that a fully captured agency might behave strategically to *appear* responsive to accidents. Suppose, for example, a mining accident occurs and pressure mounts for new mine safety laws. Under such circumstances, industry (and a hypothetically captured agency in its thrall) might find it beneficial to stave off the legislation by making a show of increased regulatory scrutiny under the existing statutory framework. In such circumstances, we would be unable to distinguish between conditional forbearance, in which a pro-industry president, in line with his preexisting preferences, directs such a show, and a strong capture account, in which the industry calls the shots directly.

Our approach for addressing this issue is to compare agency responses to different disasters. First, we compare MSHA's response to two disasters that occurred *in the same administration,* but that invited different levels of public scrutiny. Specifically, we look at changes in MSHA behavior following three George W. Bush-era tragedies: the Jim Walter Resources No. 5 accident, which, because of its proximity to September 11, 2001, received very little press coverage, and the Sago and Crandall canyon disasters in 2006 and 2007, each of which received extensive publicity. Second, we compare MSHA's response to disasters occurring *in different administrations,* but that invited similar levels of public scrutiny. In particular, we compare MSHA's response to Sago and Crandall Canyon to its response to the Upper Big Branch disaster in 2010, during the presidency of Barack Obama. There are four possible conjunctions of findings to consider.

First, the agency may be equally responsive to high- and low-publicity events and equally responsive across administrations. If we observe this, one cannot rule out either the possibility of agencies being fully insulated from political and industry pressures, or being fully captured by an industry that perceives no danger from greater public salience.

Second, the agency may be more responsive to high- than to low-publicity events in the same administration, but equally responsive across administrations. Such evidence would be consistent with two accounts: the first is a strong capture account in which, in the face of public outcry, the industry compels the agency to impose costs on it in the short run to prevent the imposition of still greater costs that would come about through legislative reform. The alternative interpretation is that the preferences of the two administrations are, with respect to the desirability of regulatory action and responsiveness to public scrutiny, so similar *independent of industry influence* as to induce equality in responses.

Third, it may be equally responsive to high- and low-publicity events in the same administration, but more responsive in one administration than the other. This would be consistent with an account of conditional forbearance in which the agency is somewhat insulated from the public opinion pressures regarding the regulatory action driven by the accidents themselves, but is sensitive to changes in the preferences of its political principals.

Finally, MSHA may be both more responsive to high-publicity than low-publicity events in the same administration and more responsive in one administration than the other. Such a conjunction of findings would be consistent with two accounts. The first is a relatively reassuring picture in which the elected official treats the public's attention to the event as an indicator of the public will, and influences the agency's behavior accordingly. A more disturbing possibility is that the official wishes to create a public impression of the administration's regulatory stance that is at odds with its true, effective position. In *either* case, though, the difference across administrations would be consistent with hierarchical political control and thus conditional forbearance.

Moreover, we can make additional inferences about the extent to which the agency's response is real or symbolic by looking closely at the *kinds* of changes that occur in the wake of an accident. First, we distinguish between changes in agency behavior that impose specific, direct costs on the agency and those that are as likely to be symbolic as to impose costs. If the agency is strongly captured but sensitive to public perceptions, we might expect to observe increases in the number of inspections or violations, but not in, for example, the penalties associated with a violation. Second, we look at the rate at which the industry challenges increases in scrutiny following a tragedy. If the agency is putting on a show for the public on behalf of the industry, it is less likely that the industry will seek to undermine the demonstration by challenging the agency's behavior. If, however, the agency is indeed cracking down contrary to the desires of industry executives, we should see evidence of that dissatisfaction in greater rates of contestation.

To be sure, public salience may be both an antecedent and a consequence of agency behavior, and, consequently, one may worry that efforts to assess the effect of the former on the latter empirically may suffer from bias unless an exogenous source of variation in salience can be found. Our response to this concern is two-fold. First, our focus on the accidents – as we noted earlier, a plausible source of exogenous variation – significantly mitigates this concern. Such events are typically followed by media coverage and accusations of regulators "asleep at the switch." This coverage and the resulting scrutiny of agency behavior then gradually subside until the next such event begins the cycle again. Second, our measures of low versus high salience are themselves functions of exogenous events: the background news stories that had been the focus of media outlets. Thus we compare a mining accident that took place in the wake of 9/11 and received very little media coverage with an accident that took place at a "slow news" period and was, consequently, widely publicized.

DATA

To examine the effect of unanticipated accidents on MSHA enforcement behavior, we assembled a dataset consisting of weekly indicators of regulatory performance from 2000 to 2010. The dataset was compiled from raw data from the Mine Data Retrieval System, which contains detailed information on more than 240,000 inspections of active coal mines and almost 800,000 documented violations during this period. We look at six indicators of agency performance and how they react to accidents:

The first of these is the *number of new inspection starts* in a particular week. The second two concern the number of documented violations in active coal mines. Depending on the applicable portion of the Mine Act, MSHA inspectors can hand out citations, orders, or safeguards on detecting regulatory violations. Safeguards do not carry penalties with them, but citations and orders may. We examine the number of *documented violations with proposed penalties* and the number of *documented violations with no proposed penalties*. We also look at the *average proposed penalty per violation*, as well as the *fraction of penalties ultimately assessed* to determine whether MSHA is generous with its eventual settlements. We also look at the *contestation rate* – the fraction of proposed penalty dollars contested by mining companies – to ascertain whether they adjust dynamically to any changes in enforcement stringency.

Table 9.1. *Summary statistics for measures employed in the analysis*

Variable	Mean	Std. dev.	Min	Max
New inspection starts	420.67	159.61	149	1180
Documented violations with penalties	1304.3	446.7	273	2695
Documented violations with no penalties	43.54	26.84	8	204
Averaged proposed penalty per violation				
– Before 2007 policy change	261.97	150.25	125.11	1665.81
– After 2007 policy change	1048.5	296.47	527.29	1833.89
Fraction of penalties ultimately assessed	0.9	0.09	0.32	1
Contestation rate (dollar-weighted)	0.14	0.11	0	0.37

Summary statistics for these measures appear in Table 9.1. Note that we report two figures for the average proposed penalty measure: before and after April 23, 2007, the date in which MSHA's new penalty policy went into effect (pursuant to the 2006 MINER Act). As the summary data indicate, the change in policy led to a near quadrupling of the average proposed penalty.

RESULTS

Preliminary Results: Public Awareness and Company Performance

Before proceeding with our main analysis, we examine the effect of mine disasters on media coverage of MSHA and on the stock performance of directly affected mine companies. Figure 9.3 shows the number of U.S. newspaper and wire stories mentioning the agency from 1999 through 2010 (source: compiled by authors from Lexis-Nexis). Six events are labeled in the graph: the Jim Walter Resources No. 5, Sago, Darby, Crandall Canyon, and Upper Big Branch disasters, and, for purposes of comparison, an accident with a happy outcome: the successful rescue of nine trapped miners from the Quecreek mine following the accidental breach of an adjacent flooded abandoned mine in July 2002. As the chart indicates, mining tragedies typically generate a spike of news coverage for the agency, although the extent of that coverage varies considerably across accidents. For example, the worst mine disaster in the last two decades, at Upper Big Branch, actually generated less coverage for MSHA than the Sago and Crandall Canyon disasters. By contrast, the accident at the Jim Walter Resources No. 5 mine in Brookwood, Alabama, generated almost no additional coverage for the agency, presumably because it took place less than two weeks after September 11, 2001. In the first nine months of 2004, a year with relatively

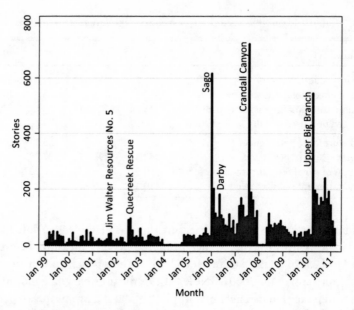

Figure 9.3. U.S. Newspaper and Wire Stories Mentioning the Mine Safety and Health Administration, by Month, 1999–2010.

few mining accidents and injuries, there was just one story mentioning MSHA.

To assess the impact of mine disasters on the mining companies themselves, we next consider changes in the stock prices of mining companies accompanying accidents. Because not all mining companies are publicly traded, we restrict attention to three cases: Walter Resources (the ultimate owner of the Jim Walter No. 5 Mine), International Coal Group (ICG; ultimate owner of Sago), and Massey Energy (ultimate owner of Upper Big Branch). Despite the occurrence of accidents in mines under their purview, neither Walter nor ICG experienced significant short-term changes in their companies' returns when compared against the S&P 500. By contrast, Massey experienced a more than 10 percent decline in share price immediately following the Upper Big Branch disaster and abnormally low (though falling just short of statistical significance) returns relative to the S&P for the subsequent two-month period. Insofar as Upper Big Branch represented only about 1 percent of Massey's total coal output, it is reasonable to infer that the threat of regulatory response (as well as litigation) contributed to the drop.

We also examined changes in the stock prices of Arch Coal, a large rival coal company that did not experience any major incidents during the period under consideration. An accident for producer A may have several different, potentially offsetting effects on producer B's prices. First, there may be a direct substitution effect, wherein coal buyers shift their purchases away from A and toward B, driving up B's returns. Second, there may be an indirect, regulatory substitution effect, in which MSHA reduces its regulatory burden on B to focus its resources on the less fortunate rival, to B's benefit. Finally, there may be a regulatory externality, wherein MSHA increases its regulatory burden at the mines of both producer A and producer B: this could drive down the share prices of producer B. We find that the Jim Walter Resources, Sago, and Upper Big Branch Mine disasters had no effect on the returns of Arch Coal relative to the S&P. The Crandall Canyon disaster, however, did increase relative returns by a bit less than one percentage point in the two months following that incident, although the effect just misses being statistically significant at conventional levels.

Main Results

Jim Walter Resources No. 5. The first disaster whose effect on MSHA enforcement we consider occurred on September 23, 2001, in Brookwood, Alabama, less than two weeks after the September 11 attacks on the World Trade Center and Pentagon. A cave-in at the mine led to the release of methane; the subsequent explosions killed thirteen miners. As noted previously, the disaster generated negligible coverage in the press and had no impact on Walter Resources' stock returns.

Figure 9.4 displays scatterplots of the measures of regulatory performance detailed earlier. Overlaid on each scatterplot are smoothed, local linear regression curves and their associated 95 percent confidence intervals. Two curves are fit for each plot: one corresponding to the subsample of data from before the accident and one for the subsample occurring after. The date of the accident is depicted by the vertical black line.[32]

An immediate effect on MSHA enforcement activities attributable to the accident would be indicated by a sharp break in the smoothed curves around the boundary. However, we observe no such effect in any of the figures. Nor do the data appear to indicate any substantial intermediate-term changes in agency behavior; the one possible exception being that a mild increase

---

[32] Bandwidths are calculated using the procedure described in Guido Imbens and Karthik Kalyanaraman, "Optimal Bandwidth Choice for the Regression Discontinuity Estimator" (NBER Working Paper, 2009).

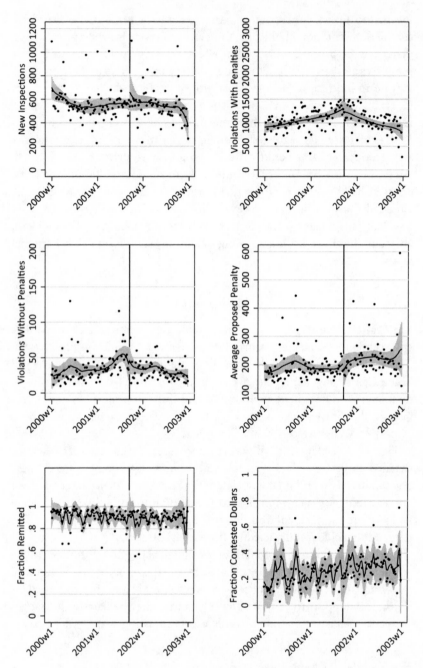

Figure 9.4. The Effect of the Jim Walter Resources No. 5 Mine Disaster on MSHA Enforcement: Interrupted Time Series Analysis

occurring in the number of violations assessed appears to reverse itself following the accident.

Sago. An explosion in the Sago Mine on January 2, 2006, trapped thirteen miners. The ensuing rescue attempt garnered major media attention and subsequent outrage when media outlets erroneously reported that all of the miners had been rescued when in fact only one had been. Ultimately, only one of the trapped miners was saved. Our analysis uses a breakpoint of January 4, the day on which the full scope of the tragedy was recognized. Figure 9.5 reports the interrupted time series results for the Sago event.

A different pattern from the one observed around the Brookwood tragedy emerges: in particular, following the Sago event, MSHA almost doubled the number of new inspection starts from the preceding weeks, from around 200 to 400. We also observe a statistically significant immediate increase in the number of violations issued with penalties, as well as a slightly delayed bump in the number of violations issued without penalties. However, if one looks at the average proposed penalty, there is no significant immediate effect, although a slight rise does occur over the period in question.

As in the Walter Resources disaster, there appears to be no significant effect of the disaster on the fraction of penalties remitted or the rate at which the industry contested penalties.

Crandall Canyon. The Crandall Canyon disaster occurred on August 6, 2007, in Emery County, Utah. A collapse trapped and killed six miners; three rescue workers were also killed. Results for the analysis of the Crandall Canyon disaster appear in Figure 9.6. In addition to the black vertical line corresponding to the occurrence of the accident, the figure also displays a dashed line corresponding to the date on which MSHA's new penalty policy went into effect.

The most striking feature of the figure comes in the form of the sharp increase in average proposed penalties preceding the disaster; closer inspection, however, reveals that this is entirely attributable to the change in MSHA's penalty policy occurring in late April, 2007. Interestingly, the data document a *decline* in the average proposed penalty per violation in the months following the disaster.

The only significantly difference observable in the data is an increase in the number of violations issued with no penalties. A similar increase in violations with associated penalties is not statistically significant. Unlike Sago, the Crandall Canyon disaster did not lead to any discernible increase in the rate of inspection starts.

Upper Big Branch. The fourth disaster whose effect we consider is the recent tragedy at the Upper Big Branch Mine at Montcoal, West Virginia.

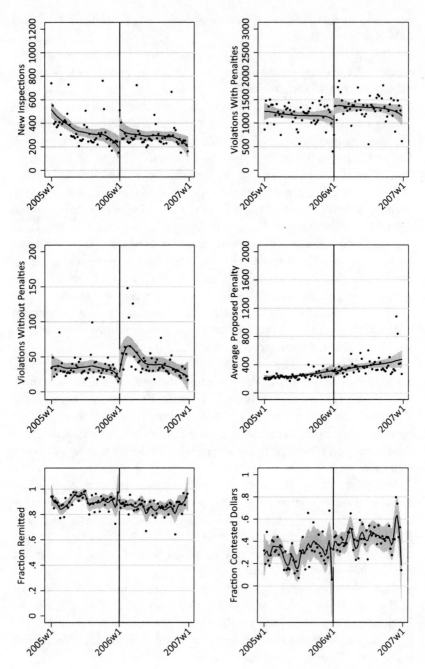

Figure 9.5. The Effect of the Sago Mine Disaster on MSHA Enforcement: Interrupted Time Series Analysis

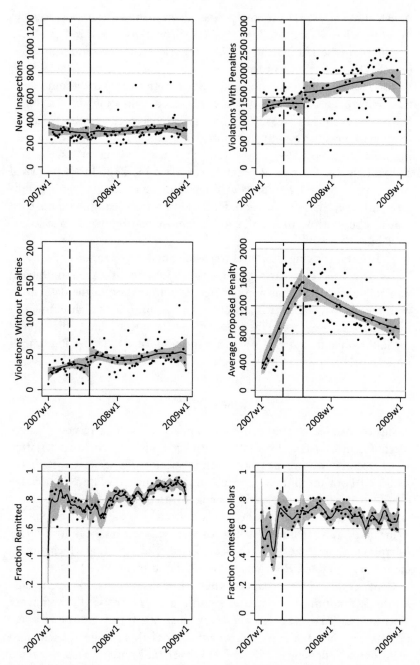

Figure 9.6. The Effect of the Crandall Canyon Mine Disaster on MSHA Enforcement: Interrupted Time Series Analysis

A methane explosion killed twenty-nine miners in the worst mining accident in decades. Results for the Upper Big Branch analysis appear in Figure 9.7.

Patterns in the data indicate that Upper Big Branch had a significant effect on MSHA's pattern of enforcement. The data indicate a highly significant increase in the number of violations issued, both with and without penalties. Unlike Sago, the average proposed penalty per violation jumped almost 50 percent, or more than $400. Regulatory intransigence, as indicated by the fraction of penalties eventually remitted, appears to have increased as well, increasing to almost 100 percent in the months following the tragedy. Not surprisingly, the fraction of penalties contested by the industry increased in response to the large jump in the size of penalties. The graph indicates, however, that this fraction declines following the initial bump, such that by the end of 2010 it was lower than it had been previous to the accident.

The most intriguing result for this part of our analysis concerns the number of new inspection starts. Contrary to expectation, the data indicate an immediate *decline* in that number. Closer examination of the data, however, reveals that the shift is attributable to an unusually high number of inspections taking place in the week prior to the tragedy and to the deployment of a large fraction of MSHA's inspection force to Upper Big Branch immediately following the explosion.

DISCUSSION

A suggestive picture emerges from comparing MSHA's response across the different disasters. First, after the Upper Big Branch Mine Disaster, which occurred during the Obama administration, the agency substantially increased both the number of violations with penalties and the average proposed penalty per violation. Coupled with a higher fraction remitted (approaching 1 after the disaster), this suggests that the agency responded to the disaster in a manner that directly imposed costs on the industry. This interpretation is borne out by the sharp increase in the rate at which mining companies contested violations following the accident.

Contrast this with Sago, a highly publicized disaster that took place during the Bush administration. After Sago, the agency increased the number of violations issued with penalties and very substantially increased new inspection starts. However, the average penalty per violation remained unchanged in the period following the disaster; moreover, the remittance rate remained unaffected, as did the rate at which mining companies contested violations.

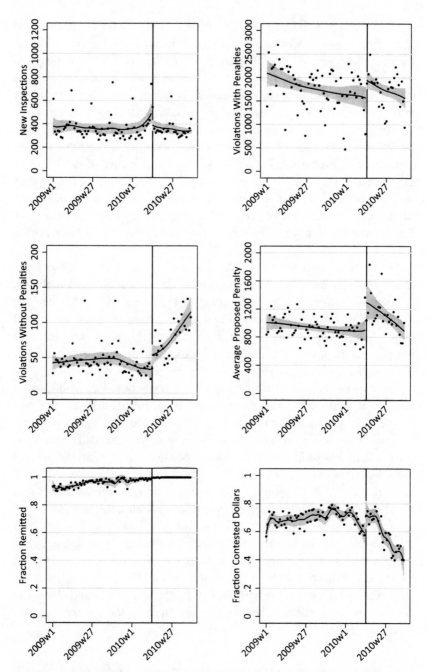

Figure 9.7. The Effect of the Upper Big Branch Mine Disaster on MSHA Enforcement: Interrupted Time Series Analysis

A comparison of MSHA's enforcement response to Upper Big Branch and Sago, then, suggests a more vigorous response by the Obama-era MSHA than the Bush-era MSHA. This interpretation is further borne out by a comparison with the Crandall Canyon disaster, in which the only observed statistically significant change in agency behavior is the increase in the number of violations issued without any penalties attached. Together, these findings suggest the importance of hierarchical political control, and thus conditional forbearance, at odds with a strong capture account. Note, however, that this assessment cannot be said to be definitive. Because Upper Big Branch took more lives (twenty-nine fatalities, compared with thirteen at Sago and nine at Crandall Canyon), we cannot dismiss the possibility that an accident of comparable magnitude occurring under the Bush administration would have fueled public appetite for a similar agency response.

The comparison between MSHA's response to Sago and to the comparatively little-publicized Jim Walter Resources No. 5 in Brookwood, Alabama, is instructive with respect to the effect of media coverage: although the change in agency behavior following Sago may have been less substantial than following Upper Big Branch, it was inarguably far greater than the response to the much less-publicized Brookwood tragedy, after which we observe effectively no change in agency behavior.

In terms of the effect of publicity on agency action, Crandall Canyon stands out as something of an anomaly: as indicated in Figure 9.3, this disaster had the most media coverage of all of the four disasters whose effects we examine.[33] However, the agency response to Crandall Canyon was considerably less pronounced than its response to the similarly publicized Sago disaster a year earlier. There are two plausible explanations for this. First, the Crandall Canyon disaster occurred shortly after MSHA's new penalty policy went into effect. As Figure 9.6 indicates, the new policy had a substantial effect on agency enforcement practices, and this may have muffled the subsequent effect of the Crandall disaster. Second, the agency may have faced stronger incentives to appear effective and adversarial toward the industry at the time of the Sago disaster because MSHA faced a legislative challenge in the form of the MINER Act. By the time the Crandall Canyon disaster occurred, the new law was already on the books, as was the new penalty policy.

---

[33] We did not examine the Darby disaster owing to its proximity to a potentially confounding event: the passage of the MINER Act.

CONCLUSION

Regulators face multiple, overlapping sets of incentives and constraints brought about by their strategic interaction with regulated interests and their positions as agents in political hierarchies. Too blunt an account of the influence of regulated interests on agency behavior risks neglecting the different mechanisms by which those regulated interests might exercise influence in regulatory decision making, as well as the extent to which placement in a political hierarchy can mediate the extent of influence.

In this chapter, we describe a more subtle account of industry influence, in which the broader political context of regulatory action determines the extent to which regulators offer forbearance to regulated industries. The pure capture and conditional forbearance accounts yield distinct predictions about regulatory enforcement, which we examine in the empirical context of mine safety and health regulation. To overcome an empirical challenge associated with strategic behavior by regulated parties, we examine the effect of exogenous shocks to the political environment of MSHA on subsequent agency behavior. Our examination of MSHA's response to different disasters, each of which occurred in a different political climate, bolsters support for the conditional forbearance account.

In particular, the data indicate that the Bush administration responded forcefully to the highly publicized Sago mine disaster, relative to the Jim Walter Resources disaster, which occurred shortly after September 11, 2001, and to the Crandall Canyon disaster, which, although highly publicized, occurred just after a new mine safety legislation and pursuant regulations had gone into effect. The data also indicate a more aggressive regulatory response by the Obama administration following a major disaster that occurred on its watch. Taken together, these findings suggest that MSHA's political principals do succeed in exercising influence on agency affairs separate from that exercised by the industry. Moreover, although the fact of a stronger response under Obama than under Bush may seem consistent with a common understanding of the ideological leanings of both administrations, it is important to note that *any* increase in regulatory scrutiny under Obama following the accident would imply, ipso facto, that the administration did not completely disregard management concerns *before* the accident.

We conclude by noting that posing broader questions about the determinants of regulatory behavior, rather than focusing more narrowly on regulatory capture, may illuminate our understanding of the mechanisms by which regulated interests influence implemented policy. With a more complete picture of the avenues through which interests influence policy, we will be better able to assess the legitimacy of particular outcomes. While MSHA represents a particularly interesting case for scholars of interest group influence in regulatory behavior, our approach can be applied in a host of policy areas, such as food and drug, nuclear power, and airline safety regulation. In all cases, regulators face complex incentives in strategic interactions with political superordinates and regulated interests. And although the particulars of the political environment may differ in each case, the basic principle of using exogenous shocks to agency preferences represents a promising avenue for fleshing out a more textured account of regulatory politics.

10

Captured by Disaster? Reinterpreting Regulatory Behavior in the Shadow of the Gulf Oil Spill

Christopher Carrigan[1]

As this volume aptly illustrates, regulatory capture – which Daniel Carpenter and David Moss describe in the Introduction as a condition whereby regulation is applied for the benefit of the regulated entities as opposed to the public interest – has occupied the fascination of researchers from a wide variety of academic fields for a long time.[2] However, in terms of salient examples, at first glance the plight of the Minerals Management Service (MMS), a defunct agency of the Department of the Interior (Interior) that employed roughly 1,600 federal workers,[3] presents perhaps the clearest case of capture in recent history. Not only did behavior at the agency provide rare public confirmation of the types of activities including bribery and excessive gift exchange that theorists have predicted do occur with captured regulatory relationships, drug use and sexual misconduct involving MMS employees and their industry counterparts revealed evidence of actions that extend beyond those that even captured agencies typically display. Support for MMS's failure was tangible given its association with the

[1] George Washington University, Trachtenberg School of Public Policy and Public Administration. I am grateful to Dan Carpenter, Cary Coglianese, Steve Kelman, and Dennis Yao as well as participants in the Tobin Project's November 2010 and April 2011 *Preventing Capture* conferences for helpful conversations regarding this chapter. I have also benefited from the research assistance of Ben Meltzer, Ellen Qualey, and Tim Von Dulm throughout.

[2] Samuel P. Huntington, "The Marasmus of the ICC: The Commission, the Railroads, and the Public Interest," *Yale Law Journal* 61 (4) (1952): 467–509; Marver H. Bernstein, *Regulating Business by Independent Commission* (Princeton: Princeton University Press, 1955); George J. Stigler, "The Theory of Economic Regulation," *Bell Journal of Economics and Management Science* 2 (1971): 3–21; Sam Peltzman, "Toward a More General Theory of Regulation," *Journal of Law and Economics* 19 (2) (1976): 211–40; Michael E. Levine and Jennifer L. Forrence, "Regulatory Capture, Public Interest, and the Public Agenda: Toward a Synthesis," *Journal of Law, Economics, and Organization* 6 (1990): 167–98.

[3] Minerals Management Service (MMS), "United States Department of the Interior Budget Justification, F.Y. 2011" (U.S. Department of the Interior, 2010).

April 2010 *Deepwater Horizon* oil rig fire and subsequent spill that deposited roughly 4.9 million barrels of oil into the Gulf of Mexico and had historians debating its place on the list of worst environmental disasters in U.S. history.[4]

With these facts in hand, it is not surprising that a large number of observers regarded capture as central to explaining the oil spill and MMS's role in facilitating it. For this reason, most attention focused on why MMS was captured and what should be done about it, relative to serious consideration of both the extent to which the agency was captured and how important this factor was in understanding why the spill might have occurred. Two popular theories surfaced to explain the apparent failure of MMS, one emphasizing the role of the agency's outwardly conflicting missions and the other focusing on the collaborative stance adopted by the agency toward its regulated industry. In fact, similar thinking contributed to Secretary of the Interior Ken Salazar's announcement on May 19, 2010, to disband the agency, only one month after the initial explosion on the BP-leased *Deepwater Horizon* drill ship. Citing conflicts of interest in fulfilling its functions to collect revenue, provide regulatory oversight, and facilitate energy development, the Secretary outlined a plan to disseminate MMS's functions among three discrete organizations within Interior.[5]

Still, closer examination of the organizational and political development of MMS raises questions that force us to be precise about how the mechanisms commonly cited contributed to the oil and gas industry's capture of MMS. In contrast to initial impressions, a review of the historical evidence indicates that the importance of capture to explaining the Gulf oil spill may be overstated. More careful study likewise suggests that inquiry into the degree to which MMS was in fact captured is worthwhile. This does not suggest that one should discount the obvious evidence of inappropriate and unethical activity by some MMS employees. Such behavior is clearly wrong and, if it promotes agency actions that favor the regulated industry, can be associated with capture.

However, inspection of MMS's development reveals the need to be careful in focusing only on the set of newsworthy events to characterize the behavior of the entire organization, both at the time the events occurred and historically. Furthermore, as the analysis in this case demonstrates, overemphasizing capture and the vague connotations traditionally associated with

---

[4] David A. Fahrenthold and Ylan Q. Mui, "Historians Debate Designation of 'Worst Environmental Disaster' in U.S.," *Washington Post* (June 22, 2010): A6; United States Geological Survey, "Deepwater Horizon MC252 Gulf Incident Oil Budget, Government Estimates – Through August 01 (Day 104)," 2010, http://www.usgs.gov/foia/budget/08–02–2010 . . . Deepwater%20Horizon%20Oil%20Budget.pdf.

[5] Department of the Interior, "Reorganization of the Minerals Management Service" (Implementation Report, U.S. Department of the Interior, 2010).

the concept underscores the potential for such overarching claims to obscure plausible alternative explanations. Such a failure can lead to potentially misguided policy responses that do not correct existing problems. In addition, these solutions may not properly account for unintended side effects associated with their implementation – side effects that may explain why an agency like MMS was created so as to combine seemingly incompatible roles. In short, focusing on organizational characteristics such as MMS's conflicting functions and cooperative regulatory approach solely from the perspective of capture precludes the possibility that such characteristics may have cause and effect relationships quite unrelated to it. Although it may well explain some portion of what precipitated the Gulf oil spill, focusing solely on capture certainly does not reveal the whole story.

After first reviewing the evidence and arguments for MMS's capture, the remainder of the chapter focuses on analyzing the political and operational history of MMS. The discussion begins with MMS's creation in 1982 and follows its development through the beginning of 2010 before the disaster. Even so, the study is centered less on the progression of MMS over time and more on its evolution with regard to several broad themes. These include recognizing that MMS was (a) created in response to perceived failures among existing Interior agencies to adequately manage governmental oil and gas functions; (b) organized by separating its core missions, revenue collection and offshore energy management, into two independent units; (c) embroiled from its inception in revenue collection difficulties that were matched by curious agency funding decisions; (d) facing a broad shift in political and public policy preferences toward greater emphasis on energy production relative to environmental protection; and (e) operating in a radically changing offshore environment with emerging technologies. Collectively, these themes reveal that MMS's original organizational design had a purpose, that MMS's mixed mission may have played less of a role in its capture than originally thought, and that, even to the extent MMS was captured, this feature may not be of fundamental importance to understanding the historical progression of U.S. offshore oil and gas policy. Given that the goal of MMS's disbanding was to overcome its perceived organizational inadequacies, this analysis also raises questions about the wisdom of that choice.

THE BASIS FOR THE OIL AND GAS INDUSTRY'S CAPTURE OF MMS

The primary and most direct evidence for the oil and gas industry's capture of MMS is derived from two Department of the Interior Office of Inspector General (OIG) communications released in September 2008 and

May 2010, respectively.[6] The first, summarizing the results of three separate investigations, focused primarily on the activities between 2002 and 2006 of members of the Royalty in Kind (RIK) Program within MMS's Minerals Revenue Management (Revenue Management) division. The RIK Program was an initiative designed to allow MMS to receive royalty revenue from industry by taking possession of a portion of the oil and gas produced rather than the monetary equivalent and subsequently selling that oil on the open market.[7] The memorandum and associated investigative reports detail the extent to which nine of the nineteen implicated employees accepted industry gifts in the form of unreimbursed meals, parties, trips, and attendance at events such as golf tournaments. Although OIG noted that no gifts were individually large, these individuals received gifts frequently and often did not report them internally.[8] Furthermore, two of the cited employees admitted to "brief sexual relationships" with industry contacts and confided that industry events often included alcohol consumption.[9] OIG also uncovered evidence of drug abuse by some members of the group as well as outside employment that was not reported on internal disclosure forms. In one case, the individual appears to have deliberately withheld his involvement in a firm that consulted to oil and gas companies interacting with the RIK Program.[10] Finally, although not necessarily evidence of capture but still unethical, one report describes how three senior officials in the Revenue Management division "remained calculatedly ignorant of the rules governing post-employment restrictions, conflicts of interest and Federal Acquisition Regulations" in awarding two consulting contracts to two of these employees after they retired from MMS.[11]

The other memorandum from May 2010 summarized the results of an investigation of the Lake Charles, Louisiana, district office, one of five offices

---

[6] Earl E. Devaney, "OIG Investigations of MMS Employees" (Memorandum, Office of the Inspector General, U.S. Department of the Interior, 2008); Mary L. Kendall, "Investigative Report – Island Operating Company, et al." (Memorandum, Office of the Inspector General, U.S. Department of the Interior, 2010).

[7] Devaney, "OIG Investigations of MMS Employees"; Office of the Inspector General, "Investigative Report: MMS Oil Marketing Group – Lakewood" (Office of the Inspector General, U.S. Department of the Interior, 2008), 2.

[8] Devaney, "OIG Investigations of MMS Employees," 2; Office of the Inspector General, "Investigative Report: MMS Oil Marketing Group," 5.

[9] Office of the Inspector General, "Investigative Report: MMS Oil Marketing Group," 8.

[10] Office of the Inspector General, "Investigative Report: Gregory W. Smith" (Office of the Inspector General, U.S. Department of the Interior, 2008).

[11] Devaney, "OIG Investigations of MMS Employees," 2; Office of the Inspector General, "Investigative Report: Federal Business Solutions Contracts" (Office of the Inspector General, U.S. Department of the Interior, 2008).

charged with overseeing oil and gas operations in the Gulf of Mexico.[12] The communication and associated report described the extent to which MMS employees in the office accepted gifts from offshore operators. These gifts included lunches and admission to sporting events in addition to participation in activities with industry personnel such as golf outings, hunting and fishing trips, and skeet-shooting contests.[13] When asked about the events, one employee noted, "Almost all of our inspectors have worked for oil companies out on these same platforms. They grew up in the same towns... Some of these people, they've been friends with all their life."[14] Although the earliest reference to such activities was in 2000, they ceased in 2007 after MMS's regional director for the Gulf in New Orleans alleged that the regional supervisor had accepted fishing and hunting trips from an offshore drilling operator. These gifts prompted the supervisor to issue a letter supporting a $90 million insurance claim by the company for a drilling rig that sunk during Hurricane Rita.[15] In addition to accepting gifts, although OIG examined a number of reports and did not find evidence to support the allegation, a confidential source accused some MMS inspectors of allowing companies to fill out inspection forms.[16] Finally, the report chronicled a series of e-mail exchanges between a former inspector and an employee of an offshore operator discussing his potential employment at the company. During this period, the inspector was responsible for overseeing operations of this firm, a conflict that appears to have affected the extent to which he was willing to cite the company for noncompliance.[17]

In addition to the OIG investigations, within weeks of the initial explosion and fire on *Deepwater Horizon*, allegations that agency scientists were not able to exert enough influence over some recent MMS decisions to lease offshore properties began to surface as well.[18] Although similar accusations

---

[12] Kendall, "Investigative Report."

[13] Kendall, "Investigative Report"; Office of the Inspector General, "Investigative Report: Island Operating Company et al." (Office of the Inspector General, U.S. Department of the Interior, 2010).

[14] Office of the Inspector General, "Investigative Report: Island Operating Company et al.," 3.

[15] Office of the Inspector General, "Investigative Report: Donald C. Howard" (Office of the Inspector General, U.S. Department of the Interior, 2010); Office of the Inspector General, "Investigative Report: Island Operating Company et al."

[16] Office of the Inspector General, "Investigative Report: Island Operating Company et al.," 7.

[17] Ibid.

[18] Juliet Eilperin, "U.S. Oil Drilling Regulator Ignored Experts' Red Flags on Environmental Risks," *Washington Post* (May 25, 2010), http://www.washingtonpost.com/wp-dyn/

were levied at Interior more broadly, MMS was singled out in particular as an agency in which such decisions lacked adequate consideration of possible environmental impacts. As Deputy Interior Secretary Hayes indicated in an interview, "There are certainly historical issues there [at MMS] that we're interested in addressing and reforming. I think we're in the process of getting a cultural change in the scientific part of MMS. We're making sure the science is not a means to an end, but an independent input to the process."[19] Furthermore, one news article reported that some current and former staff scientists, on condition of anonymity, contended that MMS managers "routinely" overruled them when their studies highlighted environmental risks.[20] As one scientist suggested, "You simply are not allowed to conclude that the drilling will have an impact."[21]

Given the nature of these and the OIG findings, it is not surprising that many observers derided MMS as a clear case of a captured agency. Furthermore, these assertions originated from a broad set of commentators. Media outlets including the *New York Times* and *Washington Post* chronicled the exploits of MMS, citing its "partnership" and overly "cozy ties to industry" as important factors in explaining MMS's inadequate performance of its regulatory duties.[22] Referencing these stories, research institutions as ideologically varied as the Center for Progressive Reform and CATO, although offering substantially different remedies for the problem, nonetheless agreed that MMS presented a clear example of a captured agency.[23] Political opinions were similarly unified in their view of MMS. This is exemplified in President Barack Obama's remark during his May 2010 press conference temporarily halting deep water drilling that "the oil industry's cozy and

content/article/2010/05/24/AR2010052401974.html; Ian Urbina, "U.S. Said to Allow Drilling without Needed Permits," *The New York Times* (May 13, 2010): A1.

[19] Eilperin, "U.S. Oil Drilling Regulator Ignored Experts' Red Flags."

[20] Urbina, "U.S. Said to Allow Drilling without Needed Permits."

[21] Ibid.

[22] Juliet Eilperin and Scott Higham, "How the Minerals Management Service's Partnership with Industry Led to Failure," *Washington Post* (August 24, 2010), http://www.washingtonpost.com/wp-dyn/content/article/2010/08/24/AR2010082406754.html; Ian Urbina, "Inspector General's Inquiry Faults Regulators," *The New York Times* (May 24, 2010), http://www.nytimes.com/2010/05/25/us/25mms.html.

[23] Cato Institute, *MMS 'Captured' by Industry* (Washington, D.C.: Cato Institute, 2010), http://www.downsizinggovernment.org/mms-%E2%80%98captured%E2%80%99-in dustry; Alyson Flournoy, William Andreen, Rebecca Bratspies, Holly Doremus, Victor Flatt, Robert Glicksman, Joel Mintz, Daniel Rohlf, Amy Sinden, Rena Steinzor, Joseph Tomain, Sandra Zellmer, and James Goodwin, "Regulatory Blowout: How Regulatory Failures Made the BP Disaster Possible, And How the System Can Be Fixed to Avoid a Recurrence" (Center for Progressive Reform White Paper 1007, Center for Progressive Reform, 2010).

sometimes corrupt relationship with government regulators meant little or no regulation at all."[24] In addition to the literally dozens of House and Senate hearings evaluating the role of MMS in the disaster, the OIG allegations even prompted the Senate Judiciary Committee to hold a hearing directly addressing capture, entitled "Protecting the Public Interest: Understanding the Threat of Agency Capture."[25]

The many commissions tasked to investigate the accident also often reached the same conclusion. When asked to comment on the Interior's reorganization plan for the agency, a cochair of the National Commission on the BP Deepwater Horizon Oil Spill and Offshore Drilling (National Commission) responded that MMS was "overly susceptible to industry influence, certainly outgunned and possibly captured."[26] Perhaps even more telling, during hearings conducted by the National Commission, former MMS Director Elizabeth Birnbaum described the "close connection" that existed between the agency's inspectors and oil and gas industry employees.[27] Secretary Salazar echoed Birnbaum's comments in reacting to the aforementioned OIG report on activities at the Lake Charles office, suggesting it was "further evidence of the cozy relationship between some elements of MMS and the oil and gas industry."[28]

Given the degree of consensus associated with the notion that the oil and gas industry captured MMS, commentators turned their attention to identifying why MMS was susceptible to capture. These investigations tended to focus on two aspects of MMS's operations that contributed to its failure as a regulator. The first relates to MMS's collaborative stance toward regulatory enforcement. Critics suggested that the fact that MMS engaged the industry to jointly develop standards for offshore operations positioned it as an industry partner rather than a regulator with its own independently

[24] Barack Obama, "Remarks by the President on the Gulf Oil Spill" (The White House, Office of the Press Secretary, 2010).

[25] Subcommittee on Administrative Oversight and the Courts of the Committee on the Judiciary, U.S. Senate, "Protecting the Public Interest: Understanding the Threat of Agency Capture" (Hearing, 111th Congress, 2010).

[26] Katherine M. Peters, "Reorganization of Minerals Management Service Raises Doubts," Government Executive.com, 2010, http://www.govexec.com/oversight/2010/09/reorga nization-of-minerals-management-service-raises-doubts/32425/.

[27] S.E. Birnbaum, "Statement of S. Elizabeth Birnbaum, Director, Minerals Management Service, Department of the Interior, before the Subcommittee on Energy and Environment, Committee on Energy and Commerce" (U.S. House of Representatives, 2010).

[28] Office of the Secretary of the Interior, "Salazar: IG Report on Abuses in MMS Is 'Yet Another Reason to Clean House'" (Press Release, Office of the Secretary, U.S. Department of the Interior, 2010).

informed views.[29] This position is crystallized in Congressman Henry Waxman's reference to the limited role of President Obama's reforms in changing "the laissez-faire approach of MMS in regulating the BP well."[30] MMS's laissez-faire style was also a fundamental concern for those who bemoaned the fact that the agency left some of its standards voluntary, undercutting their effectiveness.[31] For example, although it began discussions in 1991 with the oil and gas industry over the need for operators to have management systems in place to direct various operational activities, the resulting American Petroleum Institute Recommended Practice 75 was only made mandatory after the agency's breakup in 2010.[32]

Many viewed such examples of MMS's collaborative approach to regulating as a precursor to its capture. At some point, this stance caused the agency to become captive to its regulated entities rather than their overseer. Although the direction of causation – whether collaboration caused capture or vice versa – is somewhat unclear, the implication remains that a more adversarial regulatory body would have limited the potential for a spill such as that associated with the *Deepwater Horizon* explosion.[33] At a 2011 talk at the International Offshore Oil and Gas Law Conference, Bureau of Ocean Energy Management, Regulation and Enforcement (BOEMRE) Director Michael Bromwich stressed the need for the successor to MMS to "strike a new balance that fully involves industry in the regulatory process but that recognizes the need . . . to exercise independent judgment."[34]

[29] Eilperin and Higham, "How the Minerals Management Service's Partnership with Industry Led to Failure."

[30] Henry A. Waxman, "The Role of the Interior Department in the Deepwater Horizon Disaster," Statement of Rep. Henry A. Waxman, Chairman, Committee on Energy and Commerce (Subcommittee on Oversight and Investigations and the Subcommittee on Energy and Environment, U.S. House of Representatives, 2010).

[31] National Commission on the BP Deepwater Horizon Oil Spill and Offshore Drilling, "Deep Water: The Gulf Oil Disaster and the Future of Offshore Drilling," Report to the President (National Commission on the BP Deepwater Horizon Oil Spill and Offshore Drilling, 2011), 71–72.

[32] Walt Rosenbusch, "Meeting the Challenge at the Minerals Management Service," in *Fifty-Second Annual Institute on Oil and Gas Law and Taxation* (New York: Matthew Bender, 2001); Office of Public Affairs, "BOEMRE Director Makes Case for Regulatory Reform at Oil and Gas Law Conference" (Press Release, Bureau of Ocean Management, Regulation and Enforcement, Office of Public Affairs, 2010).

[33] Eilperin and Higham, "How the Minerals Management Service's Partnership with Industry Led to Failure"; K.A. Neill and J.C. Morris, "Examining Agency Capture through a Principal-Agent Lens: The Case of the Deepwater Horizon Oil Spill" (Working Paper, 2011).

[34] Office of Public Affairs, "BOEMRE Director Makes Case for Regulatory Reform."

excellent

The second explanation for MMS's capture centered on its charge to fulfill multiple and what were generally regarded as conflicting functions.[35] When it was created in 1982 by then Secretary of the Interior James Watt, MMS was tasked with the role of collecting and distributing the revenue generated through onshore and offshore leases of federal property to companies who used the lands to extract oil and natural gas for private sale.[36] However, Secretary Watt simultaneously entrusted the agency with overseeing the orderly development and regulation of offshore oil and gas production on the Outer Continental Shelf (OCS), which included the Atlantic and Pacific coasts as well as the waters of the Gulf and those surrounding Alaska.[37]

design

Many commentators pointed to this design issue as one that laid the foundation for MMS's capture.[38] Specifically, by structuring the agency such that it was tasked to collect revenue – and given that revenue could not be collected without production – the decision to place both functions with MMS made it difficult for the agency to fulfill its role as regulator, as doing so effectively would limit offshore development and resulting production. Thus, in restricting MMS's ability from the outset to regulate effectively, the agency readily became captured by the industry, as the two were never really at cross-purposes anyway.[39] However, to make matters worse, the agency was also allowed to offset a substantial portion of its budget appropriations using the revenue it collected from oil and gas production on federal lands.[40] As a result, to the extent that it accomplished its mission as regulator, it limited its own budget. However, conflict was not only present between the offshore management and revenue collection groups. It could also be identified within the management group as well. Divided into leasing and offshore operations, the first would oversee development and the second regulation. In the same way that revenue collection stymied regulation,

---

[35] Nicholas Bagley, "Subcommittee on Administrative Oversight and the Courts of the Committee on the Judiciary, U.S. Senate, Protecting the Public Interest: Understanding the Threat of Agency Capture" (Submission for the Record, Hearing, 111th Congress, 2010), 38–45.

[36] Robert F. Durant, *The Administrative Presidency Revisited: Public Lands, the BLM, and the Reagan Revolution* (Albany, NY: State University of New York Press, 1992).

[37] Durant, *The Administrative Presidency Revisited.*

[38] Flournoy et al., "Regulatory Blowout"; Robert Forbis, Jr., "Sex, Drugs, and Oil and Gas: An Analysis of How the Energy Industry Captured the Minerals Management Service" (Working Paper, 2011); Peter J. Honigsberg, "Conflict of Interest that Led to the Gulf Oil Disaster" (Working Paper, 2011).

[39] Honigsberg, "Conflict of Interest."

[40] Flournoy et al., "Regulatory Blowout."

having MMS manage offshore development further weakened its impetus to engage in effective regulation of offshore oil and gas activities.

In addition to its theoretical relevance, this view of MMS propelled important reforms as well. As described, it prompted Secretary Salazar's Order 3299, which separated the components of MMS into three agencies, one focused only on collecting revenue, another on offshore management, and the third on safety and environmental protection.[41] Accompanying the change, Salazar noted that MMS "has three distinct and conflicting missions that – for the benefit of effective enforcement, energy development, and revenue collection – must be divided."[42] Even so, some did not regard such reforms as enough, advocating more radical reorganizations, including moving revenue collection to a separate department and dividing the tasks of MMS even more finely to create additional independent bureaucratic units.[43]

DEPARTMENT OF THE INTERIOR DEFICIENCIES AND MMS'S ORGANIZATIONAL DEVELOPMENT

Having described the foundation for and evidence supporting its disbanding in 2010, the discussion now shifts to an examination of MMS's creation in 1982 and subsequent organizational, operational, and political development up to the point of that 2010 decision. MMS was formed primarily as a result of the recommendations of the Commission on Fiscal Accountability of the Nation's Energy Resources, otherwise known as the Linowes Commission.[44] The Commission was an independent panel formed in 1981 to investigate the performance of the U.S. Geological Survey (USGS) as Interior minerals revenue collector. USGS, authorized by Congress in 1926 to supervise performance of leases and royalty collection, was repeatedly criticized beginning in the late 1950s by the Government Accountability Office (GAO) as well as OIG for its inability to perform these roles adequately.[45]

---

[41] Ken Salazar, "Establishment of the Bureau of Ocean Management, the Bureau of Safety and Environmental Enforcement, and the Office of Natural Resources Revenue" (Order No. 3299, Secretary of the Interior, U.S. Department of the Interior).

[42] Office of the Secretary of the Interior, "Salazar Divides MMS's Three Conflicting Missions" (Press Release, Office of the Secretary, U.S. Department of the Interior, 2010).

[43] Flournoy et al., "Regulatory Blowout."

[44] David F. Linowes, *Creating Public Policy: The Chairman's Memoirs of Four Presidential Commissions* (Westport, CT: Praeger, 1998); Henry B. Hogue, "Reorganization of the Minerals Management Service in the Aftermath of the Deepwater Horizon Oil Spill" (CRS Report for Congress 7-5700, Congressional Research Service, 2010).

[45] Commission on Fiscal Accountability of the Nation's Energy Resources, *Fiscal Accountability of the Nation's Energy Resources* (Washington, D.C.: Commission on Fiscal

At the core of the problem was the structure of the revenue management function within USGS, which was decentralized in its eleven regional offices. According to the Commission, USGS's failure, including its chronic inadequate collection of royalties as well as its inability to prevent oil companies from physically taking oil from oil fields without reporting it for tax purposes, was costing the federal government several hundred million dollars per year in lost revenue. In particular, the scientific focus of USGS was just not consistent with its mission to collect revenue and supervise leasing operations. Specifically, among its sixty recommendations, the Commission called for the creation of an independent agency focused on royalty collection and lease management and staffed with financial professionals to develop a centralized accounting system.[46]

This call was reinforced by the Federal Oil and Gas Royalty Management Act (FOGRMA), enacted in January 1983 as a result of a bill introduced by Representative Edward Markey of Massachusetts in December 1981.[47] In it, Congress reiterated the need for the Secretary of the Interior to "establish a comprehensive inspection, collection and fiscal and production accounting and auditing system to provide the capability to accurately determine oil and gas royalties, interest, fines, penalties, fees, deposits, and other payments owed and account for such amounts in a timely manner."[48] Furthermore, FOGRMA required yearly inspections of those leases producing "significant quantities of oil or gas in any year" or having "a history of noncompliance."[49]

Against this troubled backdrop, Secretary Watt established MMS in January 1982 through the first of a series of Secretarial Orders and Amendments during 1982 and the beginning of 1983, moving royalty collection from the Conservation Division of USGS to the new organization.[50] Later in 1982, the secretary further transitioned all offshore preleasing and lease management responsibilities to MMS from the Bureau of Land Management (BLM) and USGS, respectively, which, at the time, had split these duties.[51] Through

Accountability of the Nation's Energy Resources, 1982); Minerals Management Service, "United States Department of the Interior Budget Justifications, F.Y. 1996" (U.S. Department of the Interior, 1995).

[46] Commission on Fiscal Accountability of the Nation's Energy Resources, *Fiscal Accountability.*

[47] Congressional Research Service, "Bill Summary and Status" (CRS Summary, H.R. 5121, 97th Congress, 1982).

[48] Federal Oil and Gas Royalty Management Act of 1982, Pub. L. No. 97-451, §101 (1983).

[49] Federal Oil and Gas Royalty Management Act of 1982, §101.

[50] Department of the Interior, *Departmental Manual* (Washington, D.C.: Minerals Management Service, 2008).

[51] Department of the Interior, *Departmental Manual*; Hogue, "Reorganization of the Minerals Management Service in the Aftermath of the Deepwater Horizon Oil Spill."

his final Order and Amendment, Secretary Watt shifted onshore management to BLM.[52] The end result was that BLM assumed the duties associated with onshore development, leasing, and regulation, whereas MMS became responsible for the same components for offshore energy as well as revenue collection for both onshore and offshore leases.[53]

Although not directly referenced in the Linowes Commission report, consolidation of offshore functions at MMS was actually in the spirit of what the Commission had been seeking.[54] In addition, GAO, which had also been investigating the performance of the minerals management program, went even further in its recommendations. In a statement before the Interior Subcommittee of the House Appropriations Committee after the initial Secretarial Order, the Special Assistant to the Comptroller General stated:

As we understand it, the responsibilities of the Minerals Management Service may eventually go beyond accounting and collecting of oil and gas royalties, and may address the entire mineral management area. We have previously recommended that Interior evaluate the need to consolidate mineral management responsibilities. Establishment of the Minerals Management Service is consistent with this recommendation.[55]

The fact that BLM had managed offshore pre-lease activities as well as initial sales whereas USGS had maintained authority over lease management and revenue collection had created jurisdictional disputes and delays. These issues resulted in application backlogs and facilitated the oil thefts discussed in the Linowes Commission report. Thus it is not surprising that the House Appropriations Committee supported the MMS reorganization, indicating in its report:

The reorganization was the result of the underreporting of oil and gas production from Federal and Indian lands, theft of oil from those lands, and underpayment and inadequate collection of royalties owed to the United States . . . The bulk of the appropriation . . . is associated with the . . . evaluation of resources, regulations, and activities associated with Federal and Indian lands. These are functions formerly divided between the Geological Survey and the Bureau of Land Management. That

[52] Department of the Interior, *Departmental Manual*.
[53] Durant, *The Administrative Presidency Revisited*.
[54] Ibid.
[55] Milton J. Socolar, "Statement of Milton J. Socolar, Special Assistant to the Comptroller General, before the Chairman, Subcommittee on Interior of the House Committee on Appropriations on the Report of the Commission on Fiscal Accountability of the Nation's Energy Resources" (U.S. House of Representatives, 1982), 6.

division of function often caused problems of neglect, duplication, and turf wars. The Committee agrees with the consolidation.[56]

Aside from centralizing some of the agency's general administrative functions, to implement its dual charge to collect revenue and manage offshore development, MMS was organized specifically around these two functions from the beginning.[57] Under the broad activity Royalty Management, later renamed Minerals Revenue Management (Revenue Management), MMS housed its Royalty Collections, Royalty Compliance, and Systems Development subactivities.[58] These functions were collectively charged with implementing FOGRMA, which had attempted to set a course for improved oil and gas revenue collection. Although it maintained field offices in Dallas, Houston, and Tulsa to conduct agency audits, the bulk of Revenue Management's operations were centralized in its Lakewood office located outside of Denver in an effort to "provide efficiency and economies of scale in the financial and data collection process and to ensure consistent guidance to lessees and operators."[59]

The second function, labeled Outer Continental Shelf Lands and later renamed Offshore Energy and Minerals Management (Offshore Energy), included MMS's Resource Evaluation, Leasing and Environmental, and Regulatory programs.[60] Although each had a different responsibility in the sequential process of preparing offshore properties for oil and gas exploration and development, these three subactivities were held tightly together by their respective roles in carrying out the Outer Continental Shelf Lands Act of 1953 (OCSLA). The Act established federal jurisdiction over submerged lands and set out basic procedures for leasing these lands.[61] Moreover, the Act described the need to balance the objectives of development to support national economic and energy policy goals while providing for the protection of human, marine, and coastal environments. As a result of their joint charge to carry out the OCSLA, groups within Offshore Energy

---

[56] Committee on Appropriations, "Department of the Interior and Related Agencies Appropriation Bill, 1983" (House Report 97-942, U.S. House of Representatives, 1982), 40.

[57] Minerals Management Service, "United States Department of the Interior Budget Justifications, F.Y. 1985" (U.S. Department of the Interior, 1984); W. Bonora and T. Gallagher, "Retrospective: MMS in the 1990s," *MMS Today* Winter (2001): 1–4, 9, 13.

[58] Minerals Management Service, "United States Department of the Interior Budget Justifications, F.Y. 1985."

[59] Minerals Management Service, "United States Department of the Interior Budget Justifications, F.Y. 1994" (U.S. Department of the Interior, 1993), 108.

[60] Minerals Management Service, "United States Department of the Interior Budget Justifications, F.Y. 1985."

[61] Outer Continental Shelf Lands Act, 1953, 43 U.S.C. 1331, et seq.

operated with a substantial degree of overlap, where, for example, an environmental study could support evaluation, leasing, and regulatory decisions simultaneously. Furthermore, although resource evaluation–related activities were most closely associated with planning efforts to identify areas for oil and gas development, the program was also "involved in all phases of OCS program activities," even assisting "regulatory personnel to ensure that discoveries [were] developed and produced in accordance with the goals and priorities of the OCSLA."[62]

To the extent that federal offshore lands included the Atlantic and Pacific coasts as well as Alaska and the Gulf of Mexico, Offshore Energy maintained offices in all locations. Even so, in addition to housing a number of administrative personnel in Herndon, Virginia, most of the core Offshore Energy staff were situated in either the New Orleans office or one of the other district offices situated along the Gulf. This concentration of staff was further intensified by the decision to close the Atlantic office following President George H. W. Bush's 1990 declaration of a moratorium on drilling in the region after the Exxon Valdez oil spill.[63]

In many ways, MMS's organizational design represented a complete reversal of what had preceded and failed before it. Rather than maintain separation between evaluation and leasing decisions and ongoing operations, as was the case when BLM and USGS split these functions, at MMS, these were joined together into one broad group. In addition, although USGS located royalty collection and leasing oversight in the same office for each region, MMS maintained a firm division between the two. Moreover, the separation between the Revenue Management and Offshore Energy groups was not something that simply characterized MMS's initial creation. As Table 10.1 suggests, a strong correlation between geographical location and function still characterized MMS in 2008, two years before its breakup. Even using broad employment categories, science and engineering functions – associated specifically with Offshore Energy – were predominantly carried out by employees located in Louisiana. However, accounting and business roles remained centrally focused with Revenue Management in Colorado. These figures present a stark contrast to general administration and technology, which, as would be expected, was needed in both locations.

In addition to pointing out the geographical separation of the two groups, Table 10.1 further highlights how different the core functions associated

---

[62] Minerals Management Service, "United States Department of the Interior Budget Justification, F.Y. 2005" (U.S. Department of the Interior, 2004), 108.
[63] Minerals Management Service, "United States Department of the Interior Budget Justifications, F.Y. 1996."

Table 10.1. *Percentage of MMS employees by category in Colorado and Louisiana in September 2008*

Employment category	Colorado	Louisiana
Biological, physical, and social sciences	4.0%	62.5%
Engineering and investigation	4.9%	69.3%
Accounting and budget	56.3%	0.4%
Business and industry	73.5%	3.7%
Administration and technology	18.6%	31.9%
Total	27.4%	33.8%

Notes: Percentages do not sum horizontally to 100 percent because MMS maintained offices in other locations as well, most notably Virginia and Washington, D.C. Each figure reflects the percentage of total MMS employees in that employment category who were stationed in Colorado or Louisiana in September 2008. *Source:* Office of Personnel Management's FedScope data.

with the two entities within MMS were. In fact, the fundamental reason that the Linowes Commission recommended the removal of the royalty function from USGS was that the "scientifically oriented" agency was never "able to supply the active sophisticated management that [was] needed."[64] In implementing the recommendation that properly collecting royalties required "top quality financial managers,"[65] Revenue Management built its group by hiring candidates with accounting and audit experience. However, Offshore Energy employed individuals with science backgrounds such as oceanographers and biologists in addition to engineers and those with experience on oil and gas platforms to fill its inspector roles. Even a cursory review of 2010 job openings confirms the extent to which the functions of the two programs differed. As one might expect, whereas auditing and accounting positions in Lakewood required significant prior experience in accounting and a CPA or Certified Internal Auditor certificate, undergraduate and graduate degree requirements for those applying for positions on the OCS specified chemistry, engineering, biology, geology, and related fields.[66]

---

[64] Commission on Fiscal Accountability of the Nation's Energy Resources, *Fiscal Accountability*, xvi.

[65] Socolar, Milton J., and United States. General Accounting Office, *Inspector General Act Amendments of 1988: Statement of Milton J. Socolar, Special Assistant to the Comptroller General, Before the Subcommittee On Legislation and National Security of the House Committee On Government Operations* [Washington, D.C.]: U.S. General Accounting Office, 1988.

[66] Bureau of Ocean Energy Management, Regulation and Enforcement, "Biologist: Job Advertisement," U.S. Department of the Interior, 2011, USAJobs.com; Bureau of Ocean Energy Management, Regulation and Enforcement, "Inspector (Offshore Operations & Safety): Job Advertisement," U.S. Department of the Interior, 2011, USAJobs.com; Bureau of

Given the vast differences between the two groups' operations personnel with respect to functions and backgrounds as well as their geographical dispersion, it is not surprising that they had difficulty coordinating their activities to the extent required. A December 2007 report of the Subcommittee on Royalty Management, a committee appointed by the Secretary of the Interior to study minerals revenue collection following an OIG investigation of the audit and compliance program, suggests the difficulties MMS had in this regard.[67] In prospectively recommending improvements to increase the efficacy of minerals collections, the Subcommittee noted the particular complications associated with having three bureaus involved in onshore minerals revenue collection. As both the Bureau of Indian Affairs (BIA) and BLM were responsible for relaying data on onshore production to the Revenue Management group, the Subcommittee was able to identify numerous instances in which the information was either incomplete or incorrect, resulting in excess costs, delays, and errors. However, beyond emphasizing the need to improve coordination among the three agencies, the subcommittee also noted that procedures needed to be established for "intra-Bureau coordination" as well.[68] In examining the systems used for sharing information between BLM and Revenue Management, the report documented that manual and paper-based transmissions between the two bureaus were "a major impediment to efficient royalty collection operations."[69] Somewhat surprisingly, the Subcommittee also described how the transmission of data between the Offshore Energy and Revenue Management functions encountered similar problems, as computer systems were not completely linked within MMS. The report went on to conclude, "Increased sharing of electronic information between BLM and MRM [Revenue Management], as well as between OMM [Offshore Energy] and MRM, would dramatically increase the consistency of Federal lease status and production information across these agencies."[70]

Ocean Energy Management, Regulation and Enforcement, "Oceanographer: Job Advertisement," U.S. Department of the Interior, 2011, USAJobs.com; Bureau of Ocean Energy Management, Regulation and Enforcement, "Petroleum Engineer: Job Advertisement," U.S. Department of the Interior, 2011, USAJobs.com; Office of the Secretary of the Interior, "Accountant: Job Advertisement," U.S. Department of the Interior, 2011, USAJobs.com; Office of the Secretary of the Interior, "Auditor: Job Advertisement," U.S. Department of the Interior, 2011, USAJobs.com.

67 Subcommittee on Royalty Management, U.S. Department of the Interior, "Report to the Royalty Policy Committee: Mineral Revenue Collection from Federal and Indian Lands and the Outer Continental Shelf" (Office of Policy Analysis, U.S. Department of the Interior, 2007).
68 Ibid., 83, 86.
69 Ibid., 21, 26.
70 Ibid., 27.

A September 2008 GAO report further documented some of the difficulties MMS was having internally coordinating efforts with respect to certain aspects of its royalty collection processes.[71] For example, when discrepancies between company-reported oil and gas volumes and BLM or Offshore Energy measurements were uncovered, the affected companies would often need to submit corrected production statements. However, after receiving the updated information, those in Offshore Energy did "not relay this information to the royalty reporting section [Revenue Management] so that staff [could] check that the appropriate royalties were paid."[72] As a result, only through a reconciliation process several years later or in the case that an affected lease was selected for audit would Revenue Management be able to verify that the royalty payment was, in fact, correct or incorrect.[73] To mitigate these coordination problems, GAO suggested that it was "making several recommendations aimed at improving [MMS's] royalty IT system and royalty collection and verification processes."[74]

THE CREATION OF MMS AS BACKGROUND FOR ASSESSING ITS CAPTURE

Even so, the extent to which Offshore Energy and Revenue Management operated independently might be best revealed in their separation through Secretary Salazar's aforementioned Order 3299. A report submitted by Salazar to Congress on July 14, 2010, two months after the announcement, described both the rationale for as well as the plan to implement the secretary's decision to divide MMS into three organizations.[75] In planning for the transitions, the document highlighted the division between Offshore Energy and Revenue Management, noting that the "Office of Natural Resources Revenue can be transitioned most quickly and will begin operations on October 1, 2010, with the transfer of the largely intact Minerals Revenue Management function."[76]

However, the report explained that the "creation of the Bureau of Ocean Energy Management and the Bureau of Safety and Environmental Enforcement will be more complex. The two Bureaus will be created from a single bureau in which functions and process are tightly interconnected, making

---

[71] Government Accountability Office, "Mineral Revenues: Data Management Problems and Reliance on Self-Reported Data for Compliance Efforts Put MMS Royalty Collections at Risk" (GAO-08-893R, Government Accountability Office, 2008).

[72] Government Accountability Office, "Mineral Revenues," 5.

[73] Ibid., 10–11.

[74] Ibid., 5.

[75] Department of the Interior, "Reorganization of the Minerals Management Service."

[76] Ibid., 4.

the separation complicated and demanding."[77] The document called for six months of planning, followed by a phased implementation that only resulted in the actual separation of the two functions in October 2011, almost a year and a half after the plan was first introduced. Even then, it was recognized that the two organizations would need to work closely to "maintain a functioning and effective process."[78] In this way, the extent to which the evaluation, leasing, and regulatory functions, all housed in Offshore Energy, relied on each other presented a stark contrast to the independence maintained between Offshore Energy and Revenue Management.

In addition to further revealing the operational division between Offshore Energy and Revenue Management, the implementation plan has implications for evaluating the decision to reorganize as well. Given the impetus for the creation of MMS, the documented ease with which the Revenue Management function transitioned in contrast to the difficulties of dividing Offshore Energy is not surprising. MMS was created both because USGS's integrated structure did not allow it to develop sufficient expertise in revenue collection and because the sharp division between USGS and BLM caused infighting and neglect of their joint charge to manage offshore oil and gas production. Of course, MMS's organization was not without costs, as demonstrated by the December 2007 Subcommittee on Royalty Management and September 2008 GAO reports revealing that Revenue Management and Offshore Energy had difficulty harmonizing their activities.

Evaluating the order to divide MMS, which returned the offshore energy development functions to a structure that closely resembles the heavily criticized system prior to MMS's creation, implies that the benefits of doing so must be weighed against the previously demonstrated failings of that structure. More formally dividing the revenue collection and offshore operations functions by creating separate bureaus can expose offshore royalty collection to the same difficulties already evident with onshore royalty collection – as displayed through the interactions of MMS, BLM, and BIA. These problems may thus exacerbate the less extensive coordination issues already evident within MMS. As the December 2007 report suggested, despite the problems within MMS, relative to onshore royalty management, "Coordination of activities associated with managing offshore oil and gas leases is more straightforward because only a single bureau [MMS] is involved."[79] As a result, the Subcommittee as well as GAO recommended computer

[77] Ibid., 6
[78] Ibid., 11.
[79] Subcommittee on Royalty Management, "Report to the Royalty Policy Committee," 82.

system enhancements and more formal organizational structures to facilitate improved intra- and interagency coordination.[80]

Such a revelation also underscores the significance of carefully evaluating the extent to which the oil and gas industry captured MMS. In addition to the financial resources and employee dislocations that were necessary to implement the reorganization, the demonstrated problems in coordinating the activities of multiple bureaus accentuate the real importance that the benefits of increased independence, particularly in regulatory oversight. President Obama's announcement of the restructuring demonstrated the central role capture played in driving the reform. As suggested during his May 2010 press conference, following the first Inspector General report:

Secretary Salazar immediately took steps to clean up that corruption. But this oil spill has made clear that more reforms are needed. For years, there has been a scandalously close relationship between oil companies and the agency that regulates them. That's why we've decided to separate the people who permit the drilling from those who regulate and ensure the safety of the drilling.[81]

Given the costs, it seems that one should be reasonably confident of MMS's capture, that capture played an important role in the oil spill, and that the remedy will solve the problem. In the sections that follow, these issues are further examined.

CONGRESSIONAL OVERSIGHT AND MMS APPROPRIATIONS

The Department of the Interior's 1982 reorganization that created MMS appeared on the surface to temporarily divert political attention away from royalty management. In fact, Revenue Management was not the subject of a single oversight hearing independent of those associated with setting MMS's budget in 1983 and 1984. In contrast, Offshore Energy was the focus of at least twelve congressional hearings in which personnel from MMS appeared during that same two-year span. The issues associated with the hearings ranged from considering amendments to the Coastal Zone Management Act to ensure federal agencies acted in ways consistent with state coastal zone management plans, to the potential environmental impacts of possible offshore production in Georges Bank, located in the North Atlantic between Cape Cod and Nova Scotia.[82] In addition, during this same period,

---

[80] Ibid.; Government Accountability Office, "Mineral Revenues."

[81] Obama, "Remarks by the President on the Gulf Oil Spill."

[82] Committee on Commerce, Science, and Transportation, U.S. Senate, "Coastal Zone Management" (Hearing, 98th Congress, 1984); Subcommittee on Oversight and Investigations of the Committee on Interior and Insular Affairs, U.S. House of Representatives, "Lease

the House Committee on Merchant Marine and Fisheries held a series of hearings on offshore regulatory issues which included a review of procedures for emergency evacuations as well as a discussion of safety and training requirements for offshore drilling rigs.[83]

However, the apparent congressional focus on Offshore Energy veiled the investigations by GAO and OIG that were already in process at the time. By April 1985, when MMS appeared in the front of the House Committee on Government Operations, Revenue Management was already under intense scrutiny for its perceived inadequate performance in collecting royalties and disseminating them to states and Indian tribes.[84] In particular, a congressional inquiry had revealed numerous examples in which Revenue Management – which also maintained responsibility for collecting payments from oil and gas production on Indian lands and distributing those monies appropriately – either completely missed making payments to Indians or made them late and inaccurately. The evidence further revealed the extent to which MMS was unresponsive to BIA requests for individual account audits, a task that the Compliance group within Revenue Management was mandated to complete. In one case that later prompted affected Indians to camp outside of BIA's Anadarko, Oklahoma, office in protest, BIA had requested that Revenue Management perform reviews of eleven individual accounts based on landholder complaints. By the time of the hearing seventeen months later, only three reviews had been completed, revealing $59,000 in additional monies owed to the individual Indian landowners.[85] The remaining eight reviews were only initiated after the congressional investigation impelled MMS officials to do so. In its written response to a question about the delay, Revenue Management admitted that it was "an obvious case of something 'falling through the cracks.' The Anadarko request was lost in our Lakewood office for almost a year."[86]

By this time, these and other collection and dissemination problems identified by GAO and OIG had already led to numerous reforms within Revenue

Sale No. 82: The Federal and State Relationship Concerning Georges Bank" (Hearing, 98th Congress, 1984).

[83] Subcommittee on Panama Canal/Outer Continental Shelf of the Committee on Merchant Marine and Fisheries, U.S. House of Representatives, "Offshore Safety" (Hearing, 98th Congress, 1983); Subcommittee on Panama Canal/Outer Continental Shelf of the Committee on Merchant Marine and Fisheries, U.S. House of Representatives, "Offshore Installations Emergency Evacuation" (Hearing, 98th Congress, 1984).

[84] Subcommittee of the Committee on Government Operations, U.S. House of Representatives, "Problems Associated with the Department of the Interior's Distribution of Oil and Gas Royalty Payments to Indians" (Hearing, 99th Congress, 1985).

[85] Ibid., 116.

[86] Ibid., 117.

Table 10.2. *Subject matter of congressional hearings in which MMS personnel testified by function (1982–2009)*

Period	Evaluation	Leasing	Environment	Regulation	Revenue	Total
1982–1985	14	12	14	5	8	25
1986–1989	7	6	12	10	6	22
1990–1993	5	7	12	6	5	20
1994–1997	4	0	3	2	9	16
1998–2001	2	3	2	0	5	9
2002–2005	6	2	3	0	1	8
2006–2009	10	9	8	0	10	18

Notes: Does not include budget hearings. The sum of subject counts can exceed the total because hearings can involve multiple functions. Evaluation refers to identifying areas for oil and gas exploration whereas leasing refers to leasing properties to oil and gas producers. *Source*: Searches in LexisNexis Congressional database of congressional hearings. To categorize the subject matter of the hearings, each hearing's title and summary description were examined. In some cases where clarification was required, the testimony was reviewed as well.

Management.[87] The changes included moving the head of the Revenue Management group from Washington, D.C., to Lakewood, further centralizing the revenue functions in that office. In addition, two committees were established in response – one would include Indian representation and advise the secretary of the Interior on revenue improvement initiatives, and another would be created to improve coordination between MMS, BIA, and BLM for onshore royalty collection and distribution. The investigations also identified the need to acquire a new mainframe computer system as well as install remote terminals to provide Indian tribes and states with greater data access.

However, these investigations would turn out to represent only the beginning of a series of congressional inquiries into the activities of Revenue Management over the next twenty-five years. Although the actual volume of hearings focused on revenue collection was not noticeably different from the corresponding numbers associated with oversight of Offshore Energy, the tone of the inquiries was. For example, as Table 10.2 reflects, many hearings held between 1986 and 1993 emphasized environmental and regulatory issues related to oil and gas operations on the OCS. Yet much of the attention was driven by the Exxon Valdez oil spill in March 1989 – an accident in which an oil tanker as opposed to a platform or drill ship deposited more than 250,000 barrels of oil into the waters off the southern coast of

[87] Ibid., 84–85.

Alaska.[88] As a result, the Coast Guard and not MMS was the primary government agency with regulatory authority.[89] The Offshore Energy group did participate in the cleanup effort and received both regulatory authority to promulgate rules governing financial responsibility for oil spills as well as greater budgetary authority to conduct related research.[90] Even so, the hearings were not prompted by perceived faults in Offshore Energy's performance.

In contrast, in 1989, officials from Revenue Management again testified in front of Congress about additional allegations of deficiencies in the agency's efforts to collect royalties on behalf of Indian tribes and individuals.[91] Furthermore, in the previous year, MMS officials had appeared before the Senate Committee on Energy and Natural Resources to discuss the findings of several OIG audits of revenue collections from 1986 through 1988. To open that hearing, Subcommittee Chairman John Melcher declared, "As a result of the Linowes Commission recommendations in 1982, Congress passed... the Federal Oil and Gas Management Act... Unfortunately, progress in implementing those recommendations has been slow. To date, action by the Department [of the Interior] falls far short of adequately carrying out the requirements of the law."[92]

In addition to the individual hearings, even a cursory review of GAO reports over the period reveals the extent to which congressional criticism of MMS remained squarely focused on revenue collection relative to offshore energy management. During the four-year period from 1982 to 1985, royalties were the primary focus of three reports, offshore energy was the

[88] Samuel K. Skinner and William K. Reilly, "The Exxon Valdez Oil Spill" (The National Response Team, 1989).

[89] Skinner and Reilly, "The Exxon Valdez Oil Spill"; Subcommittee on Water, Power and Offshore Energy Resources of the Committee on Interior and Insular Affairs, U.S. House of Representatives, "Investigation of the Exxon Valdez Oil Spill, Prince William Sound, Alaska" (Hearing, 101st Congress, 1989).

[90] Committee on Energy and Natural Resources, U.S. Senate, "Gulf of Mexico Oil Spill Prevention and Response Act" (Hearing, 101st Congress, 1989); Minerals Management Service, "United States Department of the Interior Budget Justifications, F.Y. 1991" (U.S. Department of the Interior, 1990), 36–37; Minerals Management Service, "United States Department of the Interior Budget Justifications, F.Y. 1992" (U.S. Department of the Interior, 1991), 81–83; Minerals Management Service, "United States Department of the Interior Budget Justifications, F.Y. 1993" (U.S. Department of the Interior, 1992), 91–92.

[91] Special Committee on Investigations of the Select Committee on Indian Affairs, U.S. Senate, "Federal Government's Relationship with American Indians" (Hearing, 100th Congress, 1989).

[92] Subcommittee on Mineral Resources Development and Production of the Committee on Energy and Natural Resources, U.S. Senate, "Royalty Management Program" (Hearing, 100th Congress, 1988), 1–2.

subject of nine, and one covered both. In contrast, over the next twenty-four years ending in 2009, in addition to eight reports that included a discussion of both groups, Revenue Management was GAO's main target in thirty-four reports relative to only seven for Offshore Energy, almost a five-to-one ratio. Furthermore, the titles of the reports confirm GAO's dissatisfaction with the agency's revenue collection efforts. Examples include a 1992 report that GAO titled "Royalty Compliance: Improvements Made in Interior's Audit Strategy, But More Are Needed," as well as a 2007 report with the heading "Royalties Collection: Ongoing Problems with Interior's Efforts to Ensure a Fair Return for Taxpayers Require Attention."

Similar to the first hearing on Indian royalties in 1985, subsequent investigations were often accompanied by reform efforts by Revenue Management, including reorganizations. From 1992 through 2000, the group underwent two major and at least three minor reorganizations. In particular, with congressional approval in October 1992, Revenue Management, which had been previously organized around the functions Collections, Compliance, and Systems, completed the first of these major restructurings by dividing these work units.[93] Collections were folded into Operations and Compliance; some portions of Compliance moved to Audit; and Systems was divided into parts that were moved into each of the new functions, Audit, Operations, and Compliance.[94] Even so, by the spring of 1994, these three units were reorganized into two: Valuation and Operations as well as Compliance.[95] In addition, around the same time, Revenue Management opened offices in Oklahoma and New Mexico to manage Indian royalty issues.[96] Later, with the 1996 Appropriations Bill, Congress directed Revenue Management to centralize administrative support functions such as budget reporting in its Program Services Office.[97] In the following fiscal year, Revenue Management again revised its structure, centralizing Valuation and Operations with Compliance under one deputy director while at the same time combining two subdivisions and renaming another.[98] Finally, effective October 2000, Congress approved another major restructuring, which created the Revenue

[93] Minerals Management Service, "United States Department of the Interior Budget Justifications, F.Y. 1994," 7.

[94] Ibid., 108–109.

[95] Minerals Management Service, "United States Department of the Interior Budget Justifications, F.Y. 1996," 30.

[96] Ibid., 7.

[97] Minerals Management Service, "United States Department of the Interior Budget Justifications, F.Y. 1997" (U.S. Department of the Interior, 1996), 32, 139.

[98] Minerals Management Service, "United States Department of the Interior Budget Justifications, F.Y. 1998" (U.S. Department of the Interior, 1997), 119.

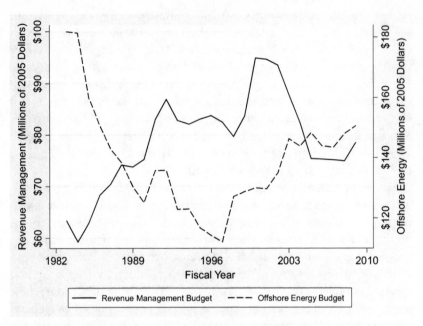

Figure 10.1. MMS's Offshore Energy and Revenue Management Funding Levels (1983–2009)
Notes: Actual budget amounts in millions of 2005 dollars. Does not include general administrative funding for tasks such as administrative support and executive direction.
Source: Minerals Management Service Budget Justifications for fiscal years 1985 through 2011.

and Operations as well as Compliance and Asset Management subactivities to better reflect "extensive changes to organizations and functional processes resulting from [Revenue Management's] program-wide reengineering effort that began in FY 1996."[99]

Somewhat counterintuitively, although Revenue Management was being scrutinized, this critical attention was not complemented by any overt actions by Congress or the Executive Office to discipline the group through budget cuts. In fact, Figure 10.1, which shows MMS's real budget by function over time, suggests that exactly the opposite was occurring during the period. From fiscal years 1983 through 1992, Revenue Management's real budget increased by 37 percent. Although it then stagnated and decreased somewhat through 1999, this was followed by another dramatic increase from 2000 through 2002. In all, from 1983 to 2002, MMS saw its appropriations associated with its Revenue Management group increase by almost 50 percent. Although this period was followed by a decline associated with

---

[99] Minerals Management Service, "United States Department of the Interior Budget Justifications, F.Y. 2002" (U.S. Department of the Interior, 2001), 22.

the completion of projects to develop computer systems to support both the redesign "of virtually every aspect of [Revenue Management] operations" as well as the newly formed RIK program, throughout the bulk of the period, Royalty Management enjoyed substantial budget growth.[100]

In direct contrast, during most of the same period, Offshore Energy's budget was moving in the opposite direction. With the exception of a brief period in 1991 and 1992 during which appropriations for MMS's Offshore Energy functions increased in response to heightened environmental concerns stemming from Exxon Valdez, the group's budget showed a steady decline through the mid-1990s. In total, the change amounted to a 38 percent decrease during the fifteen-year period ending in 1997. Furthermore, these reductions, although more concentrated in the Resource Evaluation and Leasing and Environmental programs within Offshore Energy, significantly affected the Regulatory program as well, which experienced a 24 percent drop in congressional appropriations during the same timeframe. These declines were also associated with reductions in headcount. Although Offshore Energy employed almost 1,100 individuals in 1983, by 1997, staffing had been reduced by 22 percent to 853.[101] Conversely, Revenue Management increased its personnel by 48 percent from 466 to 691 over the same interval.

Closer inspection of the changes in Revenue Management appropriations relative to those associated with Offshore Energy reveals further evidence that Congress did not view budgetary decisions as a tool to discipline the perceived inadequacies in the former group's performance. Table 10.3 shows a difference in means test for relative changes in current and next fiscal year budgets associated with the Revenue Management group compared with the Offshore Energy group. The row "Did Appear Before the Committee" references years in which MMS appeared before the House Committee on Oversight and Government Reform (formerly the Committee on Government Operations) in response to revenue management issues, and the row "Did Not Appear Before the Committee" references years in which the agency did not appear. As the table shows, in those years in which it did appear, Revenue Management enjoyed budget increases in that and the following year that were more than $9.3 million greater than the corresponding changes in appropriations targeted to Offshore Energy.

---

[100] Minerals Management Service, "United States Department of the Interior Budget Justification, F.Y. 2003" (U.S. Department of the Interior, 2002), 4; Minerals Management Service, "United States Department of the Interior Budget Justification, F.Y. 2004" (U.S. Department of the Interior, 2003), 219.

[101] Minerals Management Service, "United States Department of the Interior Budget Justifications, F.Y. 1985"; Minerals Management Service, "United States Department of the Interior Budget Justifications, F.Y. 1999" (U.S. Department of the Interior, 1998).

Table 10.3. *MMS relative budget changes and revenue management appearances before the House Committee on Oversight and Government Reform (1984–2009)*

Category	Observations	Relative budget change ($1,000)	Standard error	Statistic
Did appear before committee	6	9,352.23	3,800.20	
Did not appear before committee	20	484.28	1,823.02	
Combined	26	1,785.69	1,815.62	
Difference between did & did not		9,836.50	3,913.09	
t-statistic				2.5137
p value for H_a: Did ≠ Did not				0.0191
p value for H_a: Did > Did not				0.0095
p value for H_a: Did not > Did				0.9905

Notes: Relative budget change represents the difference between Revenue Management and Offshore Energy budget increases for any given year. Figures are in thousands of 2005 dollars. Did appear before committee represents budget years in which MMS personnel appeared before the House Committee on Oversight and Government Reform to discuss revenue management issues. The computation of Relative budget change includes both the budget in the year in which MMS personnel appeared as well as the budget in the subsequent year. 2006 committee appearances are not included as Did appear because these involved the leasing and revenue functions. However, their inclusion does not materially change the results. *Sources:* Minerals Management Service Budget Justifications for fiscal years 1985 through 2011 and searches in LexisNexis Congressional database of congressional hearings.

On the contrary, in those years in which MMS was not called by Oversight and Government Reform to testify regarding revenue problems, the relative increase in Revenue Management appropriations was not significantly different from zero. In other words, instead of lowering its budget in response to the problems it was having, Congress actually appears to have shifted more dollars to Revenue Management from Offshore Energy in an attempt to supply the revenue group with resources to deal with its problems. This observation is further bolstered by examining budget changes associated with the aforementioned major reorganizations of Revenue Management effective early in fiscal years 1993 and 2001. In the two fiscal years leading to the completion of each of these restructurings, Revenue Management's budget increased by an average of $3.3 million more than Offshore Energy's budget. In the years in between, the revenue group enjoyed relative increases averaging only $259,000 more than Offshore Energy.

Beyond reorienting MMS's budget between its two functions, during the 1990s Congress also made the decision to allow MMS to increase rental rates – or tax payments on nonproducing leases – by $2 per acre on each of its lease sales for the express purpose of offsetting the costs of developing a new computer system for its Offshore Energy group.[102] In addition to this increase not applying to royalty payments on properties actually producing oil and gas, the maximum aggregate amount that MMS could use was determined by Congress through the budgeting process.[103] Although the revenue offsets in budget years 1994 through 1996 were targeted specifically to the creation of this new system and related information management functions,[104] in 1997 Congress authorized MMS to use the rental increase to partially offset costs associated with running its core Resource Evaluation, Leasing and Environment, and Regulatory programs.[105] Not coincidentally, as shown in Figure 10.1, fiscal year 1997 also represented the beginning of a reversal in the previous downward trend in Offshore Energy's budget. Over the next twelve years, the group's real budget increased by 34 percent, ending in 2009 at the level it last achieved in 1986.[106] Furthermore, this growth was shared by all functions, ranging from a 50 percent budget increase for Leasing and Environment to 28 percent growth for the Regulatory program. Although the total number of personnel did not increase during this period, the relative changes in budgets did enable Offshore Energy to stem the previous decline, so that it ended in 2009 with roughly the same number of civil servants as it had in 1997.[107]

These observations are summarized in Table 10.4, which displays the results of another difference in means test of yearly changes in Revenue Management's budget relative to changes in Offshore Energy's budget before and after the congressional decision to allow MMS to use the additional rental

[102] Minerals Management Service, "United States Department of the Interior Budget Justifications, F.Y. 1996," 109.
[103] Subcommittee on Interior Appropriations of the Committee on Appropriations, U.S. House of Representatives, "Department of the Interior and Related Agencies Appropriations for 1996" (Hearing, 104th Congress, 1995), 508.
[104] Subcommittee on Interior Appropriations of the Committee on Appropriations, "Department of the Interior and Related Agencies Appropriations for 1996," 508–509.
[105] Minerals Management Service, "United States Department of the Interior Budget Justifications, F.Y. 1997," 107; Minerals Management Service, "United States Department of the Interior Budget Justifications, F.Y. 1998," 108.
[106] Minerals Management Service, "United States Department of the Interior Budget Justification, F.Y. 2011."
[107] Ibid.

Table 10.4. *MMS relative budget changes before and after the congressional decision to allow use of revenue receipts (1984–2009)*

Category	Observations	Relative budget change ($1,000)	Standard error	Statistic
Before congressional authorization	13	6,766.65	2,111.94	
After congressional authorization	13	3,195.28	2,267.16	
Combined	26	1,785.69	1,815.62	
Difference between before & after		9,961.92	3,098.43	
t-statistic				3.2152
p value for H_a: Before ≠ after				0.0037
p value for H_a: Before > after				0.0019
p value for H_a: After > before				0.9981

Notes: Relative budget change represents the difference between Revenue Management and Offshore Energy budget increases for any given year. Figures are in thousands of 2005 dollars. Before congressional authorization represents budget years prior to the 1997 decision by Congress to allow MMS to use a $2 per acre rental rate increase on its lease sales to partially fund the core functions of its Offshore Energy group. After congressional authorization represents budget years after the 1997 decision by Congress and includes fiscal year 1997. Tests substituting funding for each of Offshore Energy's core functions – Resource Evaluation, Leasing and Environmental, and Regulatory – for total Offshore Energy funding yield similar results. *Sources:* Minerals Management Service Budget Justifications for fiscal years 1985 through 2011.

receipts to offset its Offshore Energy budget. As demonstrated through the table, the difference between the two periods is quite dramatic. In the years before Congress's decision, Revenue Management enjoyed yearly budgetary increases which on average amounted to more than $6.7 million more than the changes to Offshore Energy's budget. In contrast, after Offshore Energy was allowed to offset its budget through the tax, the group's increases amounted to $3.2 million more per year than Revenue Management received. Thus, although not as large in absolute magnitude, the direction of the association between the two sets of budget changes completely reversed itself with the authorization decision. Not surprisingly, the difference in the relationship between the two periods is statistically significant at the 1 percent level, even using a two-sided test. In sum, the simple statistical analysis supports earlier observations that (a) budget changes for Revenue Management and Offshore Energy generally moved in different directions, (b) this relationship was moderated somewhat once Congress began to allow MMS to use rental receipts, and (c) the same congressional decision appears to have at least partially contributed to the general increases in Offshore Energy's funding beginning in the late 1990s.

CONNECTING REVENUE COLLECTION TO MMS'S CAPTURE

As described at the outset, numerous commentators have hypothesized that MMS's dual functions as revenue collector and regulator of offshore development led to its capture, a result exacerbated by the authority granted by Congress to Offshore Energy to offset its budget with a portion of those tax dollars it collected. However, when viewed within the context of the organizational development of MMS, such claims are less convincing. At least at the operational level, the vast separation between Revenue Management and Offshore Energy with regard to geography, functions, and systems complicates any claim that inspectors, for example, considered tax collection as they performed their jobs. Instead of operating as a single entity, MMS's dual structure reflected a desire to develop an independent and cohesive revenue management group in Colorado, where some of the function's most senior officials resided. Furthermore, the December 2007 Subcommittee on Royalty Management and September 2008 GAO reports document that – by not relaying production data received from oil and gas companies – Offshore Energy made auditing oil and gas tax submissions more difficult. Thus, instead of assisting tax collection as is claimed, if anything, Offshore Energy was actually impeding the Royalty Management group's ability to accomplish its mission.

Even so, this does not preclude the possibility that capture hampered decision making at MMS's highest levels, where simultaneous involvement in offshore management and revenue collection was more likely. Regardless, the evidence relied on by critics to allege capture of the regulatory arm of Offshore Energy through Revenue Management's pursuit of tax revenue is not focused on these employees. Rather, where the evidence implicates Offshore Energy, it is focused on both the inappropriate gifts from industry representatives to employees in the Lake Charles, Louisiana, office, as well as the allegations by Offshore Energy scientists that they did not exert enough influence over leasing decisions.[108] To the extent that unethical behavior was

---

[108] Eilperin, "U.S. Oil Drilling Regulator Ignored Experts' Red Flags"; Office of the Inspector General, "Investigative Report: Island Operating Company et al."; Urbina, "U.S. Said to Allow Drilling without Needed Permits."

uncovered at higher levels at MMS, it was associated with Royalty Management, and, in particular, a situation in which three employees orchestrated a contracting arrangement that awarded consulting work to two of them after they retired.[109] Furthermore, congressional decisions related to funding the agency, especially before Congress authorized MMS to offset its appropriations by increasing rental rates to oil and gas companies, highlight the extent to which gains to Revenue Management were offset by budget reductions for Offshore Energy. On balance, this might more plausibly suggest a competition between the two for resources rather than a joint effort to maximize revenue receipts.

The same appropriations data can also be used to analyze the extent to which the congressional decision to allow rental revenue offsets exacerbated conflict within MMS. The evidence that Offshore Energy in general and the Regulatory program in particular began to experience a reversal of their freefalling budgets once Congress allowed MMS's rental rate increase to broadly offset budgetary demands suggests that the effects of this change are complicated. Other factors, including increased political and industry interest in deep water drilling that occurred around the same time, as described in the next section might also have been important in bolstering Offshore Energy's funding. Regardless, a general consensus exists even among MMS's critics that the agency was severely understaffed.[110] Therefore, the increases in resources – which were strongly associated with the congressional authorization and which stemmed the massive reductions in Offshore Energy personnel through the mid-1990s – were a positive effect of what most regard as a development that precipitated MMS's failure. Given how operationally separated the revenue collection and offshore energy development groups were, the practical result of such an arrangement in a world of contracting appropriations might reasonably have outweighed any negative consequences associated with it.

Furthermore, the congressional approval only applied to rental receipts, which, as described, were industry payments on nonproducing leases. Even if Offshore Energy did consider oil and gas revenue receipts in its regulatory decision making, the rental increases it would not apply to producing leases that were the primary target of ongoing regulatory oversight, thus obscuring any link between lax oversight and revenue collection. In addition, in theory,

---

[109] Office of the Inspector General, "Investigative Report: Federal Business Solutions Contracts."

[110] Eilperin and Higham, "How the Minerals Management Service's Partnership with Industry Led to Failure"; Flournoy et al., "Regulatory Blowout"; National Commission on the BP Deepwater Horizon Oil Spill and Offshore Drilling, "Deep Water."

such an arrangement should have caused Offshore Energy to become a more – not less – stringent regulator. By denying lessees permits to explore for and produce oil and gas on then nonproducing leases, Offshore Energy would in effect be protecting its funding source because that revenue was only derived from leases not yet yielding oil and gas. However, if it acted as a lax regulator, readily approving permits to drill, Offshore Energy would be eliminating the revenue supply thought to be prompting it to be lax in the first place.

Moreover, Congress and not MMS set the gross level of the offset. As a result, the degree to which the agency would reap the benefits of the rental increase was not directly determined by its own leasing decisions. Because congressional budgetary decisions established the authorized offset in advance, where that level was set below the expected increase in rental receipts, MMS's leasing decisions on the margin would not affect its funding. In fact, this appears to have been the case. In fiscal year 1998, for example, MMS was expected to return $27 million in increased rental payments to the general Treasury,[111] indicating that the authorized offset was set at a level well below what the tax increase was expected to produce in additional revenue. Thus, not only did the congressional offset have a more complicated effect on Offshore Energy's incentives than is widely thought, the group's inability to control its funding level further contradicts the claim that the authorization compromised MMS's willingness to regulate adequately.

However, in considering congressional oversight of MMS over its almost thirty years, even the logic associated with the core argument that the competing revenue collection and regulatory missions caused MMS to neglect the latter is weakened. Recalling the patterns associated with oversight hearings and GAO reports, the vast majority of MMS's problems were connected to its function as an oil and gas revenue collector. Conversely, Offshore Energy received little critical attention from Congress throughout most of its existence. In fact, as described in the next section, until 2010, the group was widely regarded as successfully performing its functions as demonstrated through the numerous awards and general approval it received politically. Therefore, to the extent that MMS was struggling, it was struggling in the opposite way relative to the prediction of a theory that suggests that MMS's conflicting revenue and regulatory functions caused its capture. In such an account, MMS's subversion of its role as OCS steward to succeed as a

---

[111] Minerals Management Service, "United States Department of the Interior Budget Justifications, F.Y. 1999," 92.

revenue collector would be expected to show some outward signs that this was occurring. Stated differently, one should have expected to see indications that MMS's regulatory structure was being compromised to promote its efficient performances of its revenue function – not the reverse.

Combining these data points, the possibility that MMS's capture and failure were precipitated by its initial organizational structure, which linked offshore oversight and revenue, becomes less likely. This is not to say that such a hypothesis is completely without merit or impossible, given the reality of the environment surrounding MMS. Rather, the evidence demonstrates that it is prudent to remain guarded to assertions that the initial decision to consolidate offshore regulatory functions with revenue collection was a primary driver for MMS's capture, bound to eventually lead to something like the *Deepwater Horizon* disaster. Given that similar thinking triggered an organizational solution through Order 3299 that has been shown to have significant costs of its own, these results merely suggest that it can be important to consider the complete set of evidence before advancing with a radical policy shift such as the decision to eliminate MMS.

POLITICAL TRENDS, CHANGING TECHNOLOGY, AND BALANCING MULTIPLE OBJECTIVES AT MMS

At the same time it was experiencing changes to its budget structure, related political and environmental developments were simultaneously affecting the breadth of Offshore Energy's duties. As noted previously, although it did not directly involve OCS operations, the Exxon Valdez spill in 1989 still had important implications for MMS. In addition to prompting congressional hearings to review environmental and regulatory concerns, the Oil Pollution Act of 1990 bestowed additional responsibilities on MMS in connection with oil spill response planning and research while, at the same time, expanding Offshore Energy's ability to use penalties to enforce its regulations.[112] Furthermore, a series of moratoria issued through Congress and President George H. W. Bush in the wake of the spill substantially affected MMS operations. In his Statement on Outer Continental Shelf Oil and Gas Development in June 1990, President Bush communicated his intent to impose bans on drilling and development for the southwest coast of Florida, 99 percent of the California coast, and Oregon and Washington

---

[112] Minerals Management Service, "United States Department of the Interior Budget Justifications, F.Y. 1992," 31, 81–83, 91; Minerals Management Service, "United States Department of the Interior Budget Justifications, F.Y. 1994," 82–83.

waters until 2000 under the authority granted him through the OCSLA.[113] In addition, he declared a moratorium on development in the North Atlantic and authorized the buyback of leases already issued in Florida, prompting Offshore Energy to reacquire lands that it had already sold.

These moratoria were both supported and subsequently expanded by Congress. For example, the Department of the Interior and Related Agencies Appropriations Act passed in 1993 prohibited funds from being used to support leasing activities in additional areas in the eastern Gulf as well as the remainder of the Atlantic coast.[114] A subsequent Appropriations Act from 1997 further extended this prohibition to the North Aleutian Basin off the Alaska Peninsula.[115] President Clinton's June 1998 Memorandum for the Secretary of the Interior both extended George H. W. Bush's moratoria and added to the list other leasing areas already identified through congressional legislation.[116] In response to the moratoria and President Clinton's Executive Order 12,839, which directed agencies to eliminate 4 percent of their staff by 1995,[117] Offshore Energy closed its Atlantic office and scaled back operations in its Pacific and Alaska offices as well.[118]

Even so, the late 1980s and early 1990s appear to have marked the high point for political concern over environmental and regulatory issues in connection with OCS oil and gas development. More broadly, as part of his plan to produce a government that "works better, costs less, and gets results Americans care about,"[119] in 1993, President Clinton launched the National Partnership for Reinventing Government, an initiative emphasizing performance-based and other more innovative approaches to regulation. These efforts were reinforced in President Clinton's Executive Order 12,866, which explicitly established a role for market-based regulatory methods such as marketable permits, performance standards, and negotiated

---

[113] George H.W. Bush, "Statement on Outer Continental Shelf Oil and Gas Development" (The American Presidency Project, June 26, 1990).

[114] Department of the Interior and Related Agencies Appropriations Act, 1994, Pub. L. No. 103-138, §107 (1993).

[115] Department of the Interior and Related Agencies Appropriations Act, 1998, Pub. L. No. 105-83, §109 (1997).

[116] William J. Clinton, "Memorandum on Withdrawal of Certain Areas of the United States Outer Continental Shelf from Leasing Disposition" (The American Presidency Project, June 12, 1998).

[117] William J. Clinton, "Executive Order 12,839 – Reduction of 100,000 Federal Positions," *Federal Register* 58 (1993): 8515.

[118] Minerals Management Service, "United States Department of the Interior Budget Justifications, F.Y. 1996," 100.

[119] John Kamensky, "A Brief History," National Partnership for Reinventing Government .com, 1999, http://govinfo.library.unt.edu/npr/whoweare/history2.html.

rulemaking.[120] However, in addition to setting out a blueprint for regulatory innovation, President Clinton's program, which also aimed to consolidate and eliminate unnecessary government functions, targeted MMS as an agency initially subject to termination by October 1997.[121] As late as March 1995, the House Interior Appropriations Subcommittee was still considering the possibility that the functions of MMS would be dispersed throughout Interior, with oversight for state and Indian royalty collection in particular being outsourced to the beneficiaries themselves.[122] Even so, after a series of hearings during 1995 in which several observers noted the "irony" of the proposals, because they would in effect represent a return to the situation that prompted MMS's creation, Congress ultimately decided not to "devolve the functions of the MMS."[123]

In response to President Clinton's Reinventing Government program, MMS began to experiment with negotiated rulemaking almost immediately. In addition to forming a committee to study and propose revised gas valuation rules,[124] MMS organized negotiations between itself, local governments, and industry to reach compromises on contentious leasing issues on the Pacific OCS.[125] This foray into negotiated rulemaking was part of a broader plan by MMS to update its regulatory strategy in reaction to political and industry developments.

By the early 1990s, oil and gas operations in the Gulf as well as the Pacific OCS region were changing in two associated ways. The first shift reflected an increasing role for small development companies, referred to as independents by MMS and the industry, as integral players in bringing oil and gas to the market. During the seven years from 1985 to 1992, the number of operators producing in the Gulf roughly doubled from 64 to 133.[126] Independents often entered the market by purchasing already

---

[120] William J. Clinton, "Executive Order 12,866 – Regulatory Planning and Review," *Federal Register* 58 (1993): 51735–44.

[121] Bonora and Gallagher, "Retrospective."

[122] Subcommittee on Interior Appropriations of the Committee on Appropriations, "Department of the Interior and Related Agencies Appropriations for 1996," 500–501.

[123] Subcommittee on Energy and Mineral Resources of the Committee on Resources, U.S. House of Representatives, "Minerals Royalty Management" (Hearing, 104th Congress, 1995); Subcommittee on Energy and Mineral Resources of the Committee on Resources, U.S. House of Representatives, "MMS Devolution and OCS Royalty Stream Sales" (Hearing, 104th Congress, 1995b); Bonora and Gallagher, "Retrospective."

[124] Minerals Management Service, "United States Department of the Interior Budget Justifications, F.Y. 1996," 8; D. Cedar-Southworth, "Regulatory Reform – It's Working at MMS," *MMS Today* Summer (1996): 4–5.

[125] Minerals Management Service, "United States Department of the Interior Budget Justifications, F.Y. 1996," 11.

[126] Minerals Management Service, "United States Department of the Interior Budget Justifications, F.Y. 1994," 82.

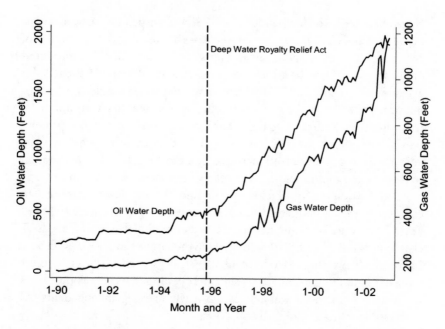

Figure 10.2. Average Water Depth of Oil and Gas Production in the Gulf of Mexico (January 1990–December 2002)

Notes: Oil Water Depth refers to the average weighted water depth of oil production in the Gulf during that month. Gas Water Depth is the same measure for gas. The average monthly water depth is computed as the average water depth of all producing wells weighted by each well's production in that month. *Source*: MMS's OGOR-A Well. Production data and BOEMRE's Offshore Statistics by Water Depth database.

producing oil and gas leases from large companies called majors with the hope that lower levels of overhead would enable them to operate these maturing properties more profitably. Largely as a result of the moratoria on drilling in the eastern Gulf as well as parts of Alaska issued by President H. W. Bush after Exxon Valdez,[127] majors were increasingly focusing their attention on more promising overseas markets, a move that intensified the influx of independents.[128]

However, soon after majors' interest in the shallow waters of the Gulf waned, these companies began to look to deep water production in waters greater than 200 meters as a potential source of new growth. Figure 10.2, which shows the average water depth of oil and gas production in the Gulf of Mexico weighted by total output, reflects this trend. As the figure suggests, instrumental in this growth was the Deep Water Royalty Relief Act, passed in

---

[127] Bush, "Statement on Outer Continental Shelf Oil and Gas Development."

[128] Minerals Management Service, "United States Department of the Interior Budget Justifications, F.Y. 1994," 82.

November 1995, which amended the OCSLA to suspend royalty payments on western and central Gulf deep water leases offered through the middle of November 2000 until significant amounts of oil and gas had been produced on those leases. Once the associated company applied for relief, the Act also extended to existing leases in which "new production would not be economic in the absence of the relief from the requirement to pay royalties."[129] In the five years leading up to the Act, the average water depth of oil production in the Gulf increased by less than four feet per month. In the five years after, the average water depth increased by almost eighteen feet per month, well over a four-fold increase. The relative numbers were even more dramatic for natural gas, for which the pace of monthly increases was more than eight times greater in the sixty months after the congressional legislation.

In response to the changing political and operational environment associated with Gulf oil and gas development in the early to mid-1990s, Offshore Energy made two changes to its regulatory strategy. First, it started to direct more of its attention toward overseeing the operations and developing rules to ensure the financial viability of the newly arriving independents. As described in its 1996 Budget Justification:

Significant resources will continue to be employed in the offshore inspection program with particular emphasis on small operators to ensure operations are conducted in a safe and environmentally sound manner. Many small operators are underfunded or understaffed, thus necessitating a higher level of inspection effort and monitoring of operations to ensure compliance with applicable safety and environmental regulations and requirements.[130]

The shift also extended to rule promulgation, where, for example, MMS updated its bonding rule to require supplemental protection to ensure that small companies would have sufficient resources to clear their sites at the end of leases.[131] As a complement to this approach, Offshore Energy began to also experiment with random sampling techniques to determine who to inspect as a mechanism to manage the increasing number of operators because staffing was declining at the same time.[132] A subsequent 1998 MMS commissioned study analyzing oil spill data to test whether independents actually did perform worse than majors did not find evidence to support this fear. However, importantly, the study reiterated that such a view was

[129] Outer Continental Shelf Deep Water Royalty Relief Act, Pub. L. No. 104-58, §302 (1995).
[130] Minerals Management Service, "United States Department of the Interior Budget Justifications, F.Y. 1996," 86.
[131] Minerals Management Service, "Bond Requirements for Offshore Oil and Gas Facilities to Increase" (Press Release No. 30040, September 8, 1993).
[132] Minerals Management Service, "United States Department of the Interior Budget Justifications, F.Y. 1994," 89.

common among industry observers, suggesting that there was "widespread concern that an expected increase in the independents' relative share of exploration and production (E&P) operations in the Gulf OCS region [would] be detrimental to worker safety or the marine environment."[133]

The second change involved an equally public decision by MMS to work with industry to jointly develop standards for deep water drilling and production. Fundamental to that effort was MMS's participation in the Deep-Star Research Project, which brought together sixteen oil and gas companies as well as forty vendors to develop technology and systems capable of extracting oil and gas in deep water.[134] Because the large oil and gas companies were those with the financial resources and capabilities to consider drilling in deep water, MMS's efforts to collaborate centered on its interactions with major producers. Still, the agency's shift to a more cooperative stance to develop standards and a regulatory infrastructure was a function of the nascence of deep water technology at the time. As described by Associate Director Carolita Kallaur at a 2001 talk at the Institute of Petroleum's International Conference on Deepwater Exploration and Production:

An HSE [health, safety, and environmental] lesson learned from our early experience with GOM [Gulf of Mexico] deepwater development is that there is tremendous value from collaboration between government, industry and the scientific community in the area of research and operational requirements. This is particularly true if it is found that the operating environment is totally different from what one is used to, and it is critical to be able to "think out of the box."[135]

Given that neither MMS nor its regulated entities knew how to conduct deep water operations, the agency determined that the best way to develop the capabilities was to work with industry in doing so. In response to the move to deep water and the increasing role for independents, the Regulatory program also developed a two-part formal inspector training program aimed at dealing with these changes.[136]

---

[133] Coastal Marine Institute, "Environmental and Safety Risks of an Expanding Role for Independents on the Gulf of Mexico OCS" (OCS Study MMS 98-0021, 1998), 35.

[134] OCS Policy Committee's Subcommittee on OCS Legislation, *The Outer Continental Shelf Oil and Gas Program – Moving beyond Conflict to Consensus* (Washington, D.C.: OCS Policy Committee, 1993), 65–66; Minerals Management Service, "United States Department of the Interior Budget Justifications, F.Y. 1997," 85.

[135] C. Kallaur, *The Deepwater Gulf of Mexico – Lessons Learned*, in *Proceedings of the Institute of Petroleum's International Conference on Deepwater Exploration and Production in Association with OGP* (Washington, D.C.: Bureau of Ocean Energy Management, Regulation and Enforcement, 2001).

[136] Minerals Management Service, "United States Department of the Interior Budget Justifications, F.Y. 1996," 92.

In some ways, the shift toward collaboration represented a new approach to regulation for Offshore Energy. Responding to a 1993 report submitted by the OCS Policy Committee – a group that included representation from coastal states, environmental groups, and industry – Secretary of the Interior Babbitt indicated in a letter to the Committee that one of its most important recommendations was "that the OCS program should be regenerated based on consensus."[137] Regardless, this was not the first time that the energy management function at MMS had used a collaborative approach to deal with emerging technologies. As early as the mid-1980s, MMS was cooperating with oil and gas companies to test and develop technologies to deal with the extreme conditions in the waters surrounding Alaska.[138] Furthermore, at that time, the Technology Assessment and Research Program element within Offshore Energy was even engaging industry to test platforms destined for deeper water around California and in the Aleutian area of southwest Alaska.[139]

As evidence of the broad support for its programs, Offshore Energy garnered several awards during the mid to late 1990s, including two Vice Presidential Hammer Awards, two Environmental Quality Awards, the Interior's Steve Kelman award for procurement franchising, and the Los Angeles Federal Executive Board's Heroes of Reinvention award for its collaborative approach toward oil and gas development in the Pacific OCS region.[140] In particular, MMS received its 1997 Hammer Award for its "several major reinvention streamline processes" and its efforts to "become customer focused."[141] One year earlier, MMS received one of two 1996 Federal Environmental Quality Awards given out by the Council on Environmental Quality for "its actions to integrate environmental values into its agency mission and its commitment to excellence in environmental decision making."[142]

Simultaneously, as shown in Figure 10.3, oil spills from OCS activities – as measured in barrels of crude oil, condensate, and other chemicals spilled as

---

[137] Minerals Management Service, "OCS Legislative Group Wades into Controversy; Finds Consensus Elusive but Possible" (Press Release No. 40065, September 21, 1994).

[138] Minerals Management Service, "United States Department of the Interior Budget Justifications, F.Y. 1985," 66.

[139] Ibid.

[140] Minerals Management Service, "United States Department of the Interior Budget Justifications, F.Y. 1996," 11; Bonora and Gallagher, "Retrospective."

[141] Hammer Awards, "The Minerals Management Service" (Department of the Interior/MMS, October 1, 1997).

[142] Office of Communications, "MMS Wins National Environmental Award" (Press Release, U.S. Department of the Interior, Minerals Management Service, 1996).

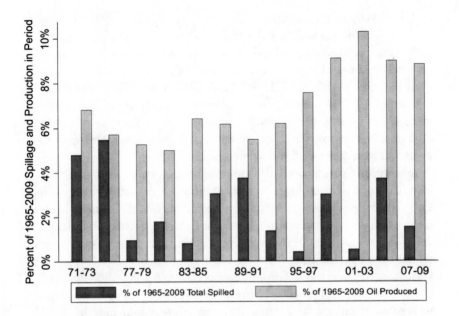

Figure 10.3. Percent of Total 1965–2009 OCS Barrels Spilled and Oil Produced in Successive Three Year Periods

Notes: For each three year period from 1965 through 2009, the vertical axis measures the percent of total barrels spilled as well as oil produced during that period relative to the entire 45 years. Barrels spilled is defined as total crude oil, condensate, and other chemicals spilled for spills of one or more barrels associated with OCS activities. Total oil production is defined as total federal OCS crude oil and condensate production in barrels. The periods 1965 to 1967 and 1968 to 1970 are removed to facilitate exposition as those periods were marked by relatively high spillage and would otherwise obscure diffrences in later periods. The period from 2004 to 2006 includes spills resulting from damage attributed to Hurricane Katrina. *Source*: BOEMRE spreadsheets titled Federal OCS Oil & Gas Production as a Percentage of Total U.S. Production: 1954–2010 and All Petroleum Spills ≥ 1 Barrel from OCS Oil & Gas Activities by Size Category and Year, 1964 to 2009.

a percentage of the total spilled during the entire period from 1965 to 2009 – were at an all-time low in the early to mid-1990s.[143] Relative to the six-year period from 1965 through 1970 when drilling and production resulted in almost 380,000 barrels being deposited into offshore waters, the period from 1992 to 1997 produced only 10,000 spilled barrels. Furthermore, except for a brief uptick between 2004 and 2006 associated with the damage to offshore platforms from Hurricane Katrina, spillage rates did not display

[143] Minerals Management Service, "United States Department of the Interior Budget Justifications, F.Y. 1996," 43.

any obvious upward trend prior to the *Deepwater Horizon* accident, despite climbing production and the move to deeper water. MMS's aforementioned 1998 commissioned study of independent oil and gas companies cogently summarized these observations, suggesting "it should be noted that the data available show a remarkable decline in accidents and oil spills over the past two decades."[144] In addition, in a question and answer session less than three weeks prior to the *Deepwater Horizon* explosion and fire, President Obama reiterated this view, suggesting "oil rigs today generally don't cause spills. They are technologically very advanced."[145]

In addition to legitimizing collaborative regulatory tactics through President Clinton's Reinventing Government initiative, executive policy during the presidency of George W. Bush further intensified the push to expand offshore oil and gas exploration. President Bush's efforts began in January 2001 with the creation of the controversial National Energy Policy Development Group, chaired by Vice President Dick Cheney. More commonly known as the Energy Task Force, the group was subsequently criticized for not adequately incorporating environmental groups' input in developing its recommendations for a national energy strategy four months later.[146] Furthermore, although President Bush's January 2007 Memorandum for the Secretary of the Interior made only minor alterations to existing moratoria to ensure its consistency with the Gulf of Mexico Security Act,[147] his 2008 Memorandum resulted in dramatic changes, opening up all areas of the OCS with the exception of those designated as marine sanctuaries.[148] In his accompanying remarks, President Bush noted, "One of the most important steps we can take to expand American oil production is to increase access to offshore exploration."[149] He further implored Congress to relax its restrictions on its appropriations bills. Only weeks before the *Deepwater Horizon* disaster, President Obama echoed President Bush's enthusiasm for

---

[144] Coastal Marine Institute, "Environmental and Safety Risks," 37.

[145] Barack Obama, "Remarks by the President in a Discussion on Jobs and the Economy in Charlotte, North Carolina" (The White House, Office of the Press Secretary, 2010).

[146] Michael Abramowitz and Steven Mufson, "Papers Detail Industry's Role in Cheney's Energy Report," *Washington Post* (July 18, 2007), http://www.washingtonpost.com/wp-dyn/content/article/2007/07/17/AR2007071701987.html; Eilperin and Higham, "How the Minerals Management Service's Partnership with Industry Led to Failure."

[147] George W. Bush, "Memorandum on Modification of the June 12, 1998 Withdrawal of Certain Areas of the United States Outer Continental Shelf from Leasing Disposition" (The American Presidency Project, January 9, 2007).

[148] George W. Bush, "Memorandum on Modification of the Withdrawal of Areas of the United States Outer Continental Shelf from Leasing Disposition" (The American Presidency Project, July 14, 2008).

[149] George W. Bush, "Remarks on Energy" (The American Presidency Project, July 14, 2008).

Table 10.5. *Summary of important statutes enacted pertaining to offshore energy or revenue management (1982–2010)*

Public law	Name of act	Year	Summary
97-451	Federal Oil and Gas Royalty Management Act	1983	Provided for accounting and auditing systems to determine oil and gas payments
99-272	Outer Continental Shelf Lands Act Amendments	1986	Established policy for providing information to coastal states related to development
101-380	Oil Pollution Act	1990	Established fund for oil pollution damages and provided for oil spill research
102-486	Energy Policy Act	1992	Required Interior to disburse monthly to states all mineral leasing payments
104-58	Deep Water Royalty Relief Act	1995	Provided royalty relief for offshore drilling in deep water of Gulf
104-185	Federal Oil and Gas Royalty Simplification and Fairness Act	1996	Established statute of limitations on royalty collections and appeal limits
109-58	Energy Policy Act	2005	Authorized Interior to develop alternative energy program on OCS
109-432	Gulf of Mexico Energy Security Act	2006	Required lease offerings for certain areas in Gulf previously under moratoria

Sources: Various Congressional Research Service summaries, Minerals Management Service Budget Justifications for fiscal years 1985 through 2011, and the public laws themselves.

further offshore drilling, removing only the Bristol Bay area from leasing consideration and proclaiming in an associated speech that "today we're announcing the expansion of offshore oil and gas exploration."[150]

Contrary to President George W. Bush's claim for the opposite, Congress appears to have supported this policy shift as well. Table 10.5 – which summarizes the important laws focused on either Offshore Energy or Revenue Management enacted during MMS's existence – provides some evidence. Beginning with the Deep Water Royalty Relief Act in 1995, the

[150] Barack Obama, "Memorandum on Withdrawal of Certain Areas of the United States Outer Continental Shelf from Leasing Disposition" (The American Presidency Project, March 31, 2010); Barack Obama, "Remarks of President Obama on Energy Security" (The American Presidency Project, March 31, 2010).

primary focus of each law Congress adopted for the subsequent fifteen years was on either encouraging offshore development or modifying royalty collection rules and operations. For example, although it represented a compromise by extending moratoria on waters near the Florida coast, the Gulf of Mexico Energy Security Act required Offshore Energy to offer within one year 8.3 million acres for leasing, 5.8 million of which were previously prohibited by either Congress or the president. With its emphasis on production relative to environmental preservation, this fifteen-year period stands in contrast with the first thirteen years of MMS's existence during which acts such as the 1986 OCSLA Amendments and the 1990 Oil Pollution Act revealed a congressional desire for more cautious development of oil and natural gas in offshore waters.

However, this evolution is perhaps most clearly demonstrated by recounting Table 10.2, which provides a tabulation of hearings in which MMS personnel appeared by the associated agency function or functions. As described, over the last twelve full years of MMS's existence prior to its disbanding in 2010, leasing issues were a focus in fourteen hearings and evaluation issues in eighteen hearings, whereas environment and regulation combined were subjects of only thirteen hearings. Yet even these numbers for environment and regulation are artificially inflated because hearings associated with laws to expand production still invited environmental groups to participate. Focusing specifically on regulation, one finds that the numbers are even more striking. Whereas over its first thirteen years, a total of twenty-two hearings involved an important discussion of offshore regulation, during MMS's subsequent fifteen years ending in 2009, only one hearing included any extended discussion of regulatory issues. Furthermore, even that case was fundamentally focused on a proposal to shift BLM's onshore regulatory responsibilities to the affected states and included very little mention of MMS's offshore regulatory program.[151]

Finally, evidence from public opinion surveys indicates that shifting congressional and presidential preferences over the period appear to have also reflected public sentiment on energy issues. Figure 10.4 shows Gallup Poll results over repeated samplings from September 1984 through May 2010 in which respondents were asked whether protection of the environment or economic growth should receive priority given that the other would suffer. The graph represents a ratio of the percentage that preferred environmental protection relative to the percentage that preferred growth. Although

---

[151] Subcommittee on Energy and Mineral Resources of the Committee on Resources, U.S. House of Representatives, "BLM Oil and Gas" (Hearing, 104th Congress, 1996).

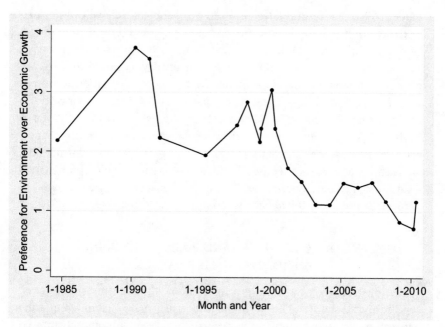

Figure 10.4. Gallup Opinion Poll Results Measuring Preference for Environmental Protection or Economic Growth (1984–2010)
Notes: Data from Gallup polls taken between 1984 and 2010 which asked "With which of these statements about the environment and the economy do you most agree – [ROTATED: protection of the environment should be given priority, even at the risk of curbing economic growth (or) economic growth should be given priority, even if the environment suffers to some extent?" Preference for Environment over Economic Growth is a ratio computed by dividing the percent of people that placed greater importance on environmental protection by the percent that preferred economic growth. *Source*: Gallup 2010. *Economy, Energy vs. Environment*. Poll. http://www.gallup.com/poll/137888/Energy-Environment.aspx.

the move toward greater interest in economic growth is not a continuous progression, the trend is evident. As the figure describes, although people preferred environmental protection to economic growth at almost a four-to-one ratio in 1991, the drift toward economic growth is accelerated beginning in 2000. By early 2009, the ratio dips below one, indicating for the first time in the poll's history that more people actually favored economic growth over environmental protection.

Even after the *Deepwater Horizon* spill, when people's relative concern shifted back toward the environment, the imbalance between the percentage that preferred the environment relative to the percentage that preferred economic growth was nowhere close to that displayed in the wake of Exxon

Valdez. Although Gallup later began to ask people specifically about prioritizing environmental protection or energy production, it only did so beginning in March 2001, and so the data are less instructive. Even so, except for a move back in 2007, these polls display a general shift toward greater emphasis on development relative to environmental protection as well. In the first year of the poll, 52 percent placed greater priority on the environment relative to 36 percent for energy production. By March 2010, only 43 percent favored environmental protection, whereas 50 percent placed precedence on developing energy supplies. Like the former poll, at the end of May 2010, after the oil spill, preference for the environment had again overtaken development, and the spread between the two was again 16 percentage points, as it had been when the poll was first taken in 2001.[152]

CONSIDERING POLITICAL AND PUBLIC PREFERENCES IN A THEORY OF MMS'S CAPTURE

As demonstrated by several authors in this book, the challenges in detecting capture are substantial. Thus it should not be surprising that differentiating between a productive cooperative regulatory relationship and a captured one is also difficult. It is certainly true that a fine line exists between collaboration and capture, and much research has attempted to detail that division, given the potential gains to both parties as well as to the public from cooperative regulatory structures.[153] Furthermore, even when a regulator appears to treat certain incumbent regulated entities preferentially, such evidence does not necessarily imply that the agency is captured by those same entities.[154] Rather, given a history of solid interactions with these firms, even

---

[152] Gallup, "Economy, Energy vs. Environment," 2010, http://www.gallup.com/poll/137888/Energy-Environment.aspx.

[153] Steven Kelman, *Regulating America, Regulating Sweden: A Comparative Study of Occupational Safety and Health Policy* (Cambridge, MA: MIT Press, 1981); Eugene Bardach and Robert A. Kagan, *Going by the Book: The Problem of Regulatory Unreasonableness* (Philadelphia, PA: Temple University Press, 1982); John T. Scholz, "Cooperation, Deterrence, and the Ecology of Regulatory Enforcement," *Law Society Review* 18 (2) (1984): 179–224; John T. Scholz, "Cooperative Regulatory Enforcement and the Politics of Administrative Effectiveness," *American Political Science Review* 85 (1) (1991): 115–36; Cary Coglianese, Richard Zeckhauser, and Edward Parson, "Seeking Truth for Power: Information Strategy and Regulatory Policymaking," *Minnesota Law Review* 89 (2004): 277–341. For a review of this literature, see Christopher Carrigan and Cary Coglianese, "The Politics of Regulation: From New Institutionalism to New Governance," *Annual Review of Political Science* 14 (2011): 107–29.

[154] Daniel P. Carpenter, "Protection without Capture: Product Approval by a Politically Responsive, Learning Regulator," *American Political Science Review* 98 (4) (2004): 613–31; Daniel P. Carpenter, Susan I. Moffitt, Colin D. Moore, Ryan T. Rynbrandt, Michael

a public-spirited regulator will favor them if they are attempting to maximize public welfare.

Faced with an influx of independents and congressional legislative action intent on stimulating deep water exploration, Offshore Energy's decision to focus more of its dwindling budgetary resources on the inexperienced actors while relaxing its oversight of those with whom it was most familiar represents in many ways a clear application of the aforementioned logic. Regardless of whether subsequent analysis indicated that newcomers were not more prone to spills, the choice is properly evaluated within the context of available data and the common perception that independents were not as safe when MMS made the decision. Furthermore, the circumstances under which it did so exactly mirror its decision to collaborate with established producers at least ten years earlier – an emerging technology in which all players had little knowledge of how to predict or overcome potential obstacles. Thus Offshore Energy's decision to center its inspection efforts on new industry players given the changing conditions of oil and gas production in the 1990s appears both consistent with its previous behavior when faced with untested technologies as well as plausible, even if it were a regulator whose intent was to maximize public welfare. In addition, it would explain why, in justifying its cooperative stance toward major producers, MMS pointed repeatedly to the industry's aforementioned excellent safety record with regard to oil spills and accidents.[155]

Regardless, as highlighted at the outset of this chapter, the 2008 and 2010 OIG memoranda – particularly the latter chronicling the activities of members of Offshore Energy's Lake Charles district office – provide reason to suspect that MMS was captured, at least in specific cases. Even setting aside these salient examples, it is hard to imagine that James Kwak's conception in this volume of "cultural capture" is not at all applicable to the interplay between at least some MMS inspectors and their industry counterparts. As Kwak describes, cultural capture is the condition whereby regulators

M. Ting, Ian Yohai, and Evan J. Zucker, "Early Entrant Protection in Approval Regulation: Theory and Evidence from FDA Drug Review," *Journal of Law, Economics, and Organization* 3 (2) (2009): 243–77.

[155] Minerals Management Service, "United States Department of the Interior Budget Justifications, F.Y. 1996," 43; Subcommittee on Interior Appropriations of the Committee on Appropriations, "Department of the Interior and Related Agencies Appropriations for 1996," 481; D. Francois and W. Bonora, "Agency Places a Premium on Safety," *MMS Today* Fall (1998): 1, 3–4; C. Quarterman, "Message from the Director," *MMS Today* Spring 2 (1998): 2, 5; P. Velez, "Safety and Environmental Protection: A Collaborative Approach," *MMS Today* Fall (1998): 5, 11; Bonora and Gallagher, "Retrospective," 9; Minerals Management Service, "United States Department of the Interior Budget Justification, F.Y. 2003," 108.

and regulated entities develop closely aligned understandings of the world, which encourages regulatory action that favors industry (Chapter 4). The fact that relationships between oil and gas workers and MMS employees "were formed well before they joined industry or government"[156] certainly implies that these individuals were likely to hold similar views of offshore operations and safety. This does not mean that there even needed to be any conscious intent that drove these beliefs. As acting Inspector General Kendall explained, "the MMS employees I have met who have come from industry are highly professional, extremely knowledgeable, and passionate about the job they do."[157] Still, the well-known centrifugal forces that can drive regulators in the field to empathize with their industry counterparts[158] would seem to be important factors in understanding the dynamics of the interplay between MMS and the oil and gas industry. In fact, Director Birnbaum's testimony at the National Commission on the BP Deepwater Horizon Oil Spill and Offshore Drilling hearings implies that a mutual understanding was inherent to the job. As she described, "the training necessary to understand the operations of oil and gas drilling rigs and platforms is not available in schools. It's something like being an auto mechanic. In order to understand how things work, you have to spend some time under the hood."[159] In a sense, part of the purpose of utilizing collaborative regulatory approaches is to facilitate such shared conceptions.

Ultimately, however, any discussion of the extent to which MMS's behavior reflected capture or collaboration cannot be divorced from the political and social circumstances in which it operated. As described, this history presents clear evidence that Offshore Energy's decision to cooperate with industry was not made on its own. Not only was the choice to proactively engage industry in developing deep water production standards a public one, the strategy was broadly supported, as evidenced through the variety of awards MMS received in the mid to late 1990s for its innovative regulatory methods. As MMS's experience with negotiated rulemaking suggests, in many cases, such efforts were even directly prompted by political policy choices. Furthermore, such prompting was not necessarily solely relegated

---

[156] Mary L. Kendall, "Testimony of Mary L. Kendall, Acting Inspector General for the Department of the Interior, before the Committee on Oversight and Government Reform" (U.S. House of Representatives, July 22, 2010).

[157] Mary L. Kendall, "Testimony of Mary L. Kendall."

[158] Herbert Kaufman, *The Forest Ranger* (Baltimore, MD: Johns Hopkins University Press, 1960); Peter Selznick, *TVA and the Grass Roots: A Study of Politics and Organization* (Berkeley, CA: University of California Press, 1984).

[159] S.E. Birnbaum, "Transcript of Testimony before the National Commission on the BP Deepwater Horizon Oil Spill and Offshore Drilling" (National Commission on the BP Deepwater Horizon Oil Spill and Offshore Drilling, 2010).

to the Executive Office or Congress. The OCS Policy Committee that, in 1993, stressed the need for MMS's strategy with regard to oil and gas development to be "regenerated based on consensus" incorporated the views of a broad set of interested parties.[160]

Beyond simply influencing MMS's choice of regulatory strategy, presidential and congressional policy decisions reveal that MMS followed its broad political mandate, even if one believes the group overemphasized expansion of offshore oil and gas production during its last fifteen years. As described, beginning by at least the mid-1990s, congressional and executive attention was focused on exploration, production, and revenue collection, with little regard for MMS's regulatory functions. Weakening presidential moratoria and a pattern of lawmaking after the Oil Pollution Act of 1990 that emphasized production provided clear direction to MMS on political priorities. Perhaps this is best exemplified through the Deep Water Royalty Relief Act, which permitted royalty relief with the explicit goal of encouraging deep water drilling, even when the technology was not available to support it safely.[161] As recounted in MMS's 2005 Budget Justification, this law "triggered record-breaking lease sales in 1997 and 1998 . . . and opened the door to increased deepwater production."[162]

Moreover, public opinion data appear consistent with presidential and congressional preferences as well. The Gallup poll results indicate that during the latter half of the 1990s and throughout the 2000s, public preferences also shifted toward favoring the expansion of production. In addition to being concordant with the actions of relevant political actors, this evidence further supports the notion of a more general desire to shift policy away from environmental protection. MMS Director Randall Luthi's comments connected to a controversial lease sale in Alaska's Chukchi Sea in 2008 show a clear awareness of this shift. He stated, "Our nation's demand for energy is increasing. Meeting that demand through carefully managed domestic production has to be a priority. Our first priority, though, is that all activity on the OCS be conducted safely and in an environmentally responsible manner."[163]

As a conceptual matter, capture theorists have historically asserted – in keeping with how the term is defined by Daniel Carpenter and David

---

[160] Minerals Management Service, "OCS Legislative Group Wades into Controversy."
[161] National Commission on the BP Deepwater Horizon Oil Spill and Offshore Drilling, "Deep Water."
[162] Minerals Management Service, "United States Department of the Interior Budget Justification, F.Y. 2005," 80.
[163] Randall Luthi, "Remarks Prepared for MMS Director Luthi, Chukchi Sea Sale 193, February 6, 2008" (Minerals Management Service, 2008).

Moss in the Introduction to this volume – that an agency is captured when it regulates for industry in opposition to the public interest.[164] To the extent that elected presidents and legislative mandates are assumed to reflect that interest, the activities of Offshore Energy do not appear to have satisfied the second part of the definition. Of course, this does not eliminate the possibility that politicians were the actors actually captured,[165] and MMS simply followed their lead. Even so, the fact that the public was also firmly behind the shift toward emphasizing energy development substantially limits the applicability of even this characterization of capture. Thus, to the extent that MMS was actually fulfilling its mandate and a broad view of the public interest, categorizing MMS's collaborative stance as capture requires a definition that emphasizes the notion that the agency's relationship with oil producers made it impossible for MMS to do what ought to have been the public preference. This seems to fall outside the common definition of what capture is.[166]

Possibly a more important implication of the shift in political and public preferences beginning in the early to mid-1990s is that it renders determining how it came to be and even whether MMS's behavior reflected capture less consequential. Facing a unified push for development and a broad array of mechanisms for politicians to influence oil and gas policy priorities, it is unclear how the actions of a regulatory agency not simultaneously asked to manage offshore development would have been substantially different. Even if such a regulator would have been able to resist – to some degree – the strong predilections of its political overseers and the public for cheap energy, the debate would then have likely centered on whether it was a rogue agency that needed to be corralled.

More fundamentally, to conclude that MMS was captured because it emphasized production over environmental protection and regulation requires the simultaneous acknowledgement that it was – in all practicality – fulfilling its mandate and supporting the public interest by doing so. To choose a path that limited drilling and emphasized safety, MMS would have needed to do so in the face of opposing statutory, political, industry, and public pressure. From this perspective, it is perhaps not as surprising or alarming that some scientists at MMS felt that environmental risks were not being given enough consideration.[167] In fulfilling its mandate to offer

---

[164] Huntington, "The Marasmus of the ICC"; Bernstein, *Regulating Business.*
[165] Stigler, "The Theory of Economic Regulation"; Peltzman, "Toward a More General Theory of Regulation."
[166] Levine and Forrence, "Regulatory Capture, Public Interest, and the Public Agenda."
[167] Eilperin, "U.S. Oil Drilling Regulator Ignored Experts' Red Flags;" Urbina, "U.S. Said to Allow Drilling without Needed Permits."

5.8 million previously prohibited acres of Gulf property for lease in one year as a result of the Gulf of Mexico Energy Security Act in 2006, it might be more surprising if environmental risks were actually being adequately considered. Thus it is not evident – even if one was able to reconstruct the world in such a way as to ensure MMS was not captured – that the agency would have made different choices. From this perspective, the question of whether, how, and to what extent MMS was captured through its organizational design or its collaborative stance with industry is relegated to a second-order issue.

EVALUATING THE REDESIGN OF FEDERAL OIL AND GAS FUNCTIONS

Recognizing the significance of political and public preferences in defining MMS's priorities does not imply that the activities outlined in the 2008 and 2010 OIG reports are in any way consistent with the notion of the public interest or inconsistent with most views of what a captured agency looks like. What it does suggest is that the blind application of the term *capture* to MMS may be too encompassing. Labeling an agency as captured implicitly assumes that the problems are pervasive enough that delineating between subpopulations within the agency is just not necessary. However, as this analysis of the organizational history of MMS has shown, distinguishing between various groups within the agency is as important in this context as it can be more generally.[168]

A closer evaluation of the evidence also appears to support the view that such captured behavior was less prevalent than a more cursory examination may suggest. In fact, the OIG report detailing the unethical behavior uncovered through its investigation of the Lakewood RIK Program suggested as much. As summarized by OIG, "Our investigation revealed that many RIK employees simply felt that federal government ethics standards and DOI policies were not applicable to them because of their 'unique' role in MMS."[169] In addition, the investigation revealed that these employees "took steps to keep their social contacts with industry representatives a closely held secret." When the investigators questioned one of the group members regarding why RIK employees attempted to keep their social activities from other MMS personnel, he responded, "They might have, you know, contacted the [Inspector General]."[170] These quotes indicate

---

[168] Graham T. Allison and Philip D. Zelikow, *Essence of Decision: Explaining the Cuban Missile Crisis*, 2nd ed. (New York: Addison Wesley Longman, 1999).

[169] Office of the Inspector General, "Investigative Report: MMS Oil Marketing Group," 5.

[170] Ibid., 6.

that the unethical behavior displayed by RIK employees was not necessarily reflective of MMS personnel more generally.

However, such evidence is not just confined to the RIK investigation. Although it did take issue with an MMS policy that required inspectors to contact some regulated entities prior to visiting their facilities, a subsequent September 2010 OIG report – investigating allegations that employees in the Lake Jackson, Texas, district office misused helicopters to attend lunches with industry personnel, rescinded notices of safety violations, and falsified inspection reports – did not reveal evidence of misconduct among inspection personnel.[171] Furthermore, a broader investigation commissioned by Secretary Salazar, while providing an extensive set of recommendations to improve regulatory operations, noted that the team performing the review "found the BOEMRE employees it interviewed to be a dedicated, enthusiastic cadre of professionals who want nothing more than to do their jobs effectively and efficiently."[172] Perhaps this is best summarized by the inspector general in his memo attached to the RIK investigation: "As you know, I have gone on the record to say that I believe that 99.9 percent of DOI employees are hard-working, ethical and well-intentioned. Unfortunately, from the cases highlighted here, the conduct of a few has cast a shadow on an entire bureau."[173] Given this evidence, it does not seem overly optimistic to suggest that the unethical behavior observed at MMS was just not symptomatic of the agency as a whole.

However, regardless of whether one believes that the evidence uncovered through the OIG investigations and interviews of some agency scientists is enough to demonstrate that MMS was broadly captured, it does not necessarily follow, of course, that the theories regarding how it became so are necessarily accurate. Furthermore, it also does not necessarily follow that capture can explain a significant portion of what might have led to the *Deepwater Horizon* disaster or that other factors are not more important. By incorporating an appreciation of the details surrounding MMS's organizational structure and political history, this chapter has attempted to provide evidence on each of these observations. First, an examination of MMS's organizational division between Revenue Management and Offshore Energy, as well as historical patterns of congressional oversight

---

[171] M.L. Kendall, "Report of Investigation for Alleged MMS Employee Misconduct – Lake Jackson District, PI-PI-10-0564-I" (Memorandum, U.S. Department of the Interior, 2010).

[172] M.L. Kendall, "Evaluation – Outer Continental Shelf (OCS) Oil and Gas operations, Report No. CR-EV-MMS-0015-2010" (Memorandum, U.S. Department of the Interior, 2010), 2.

[173] Devaney, "OIG Investigations of MMS Employees," 3.

and appropriations decision making related to the groups, has revealed inconsistencies with the hypothesis that MMS's revenue function led to the capture of its regulatory charge. Second, a review of important political developments as well as the political and public push for oil and gas development has underscored the important role of such influences on regulatory decision making at MMS. Third, these same patterns of congressional oversight as well as executive preferences and public opinion reveal that the question of MMS's capture might be less important in explaining the *Deepwater Horizon* tragedy than is widely believed. At a minimum, a review of the political and operational history of MMS has suggested that it is not unreasonable to think that there are other significant factors that might have been driving behavior at MMS as well.

Even so, these insights represent more than just an academic exercise, as the prevailing belief of MMS's capture as well as conclusions regarding the origin of the agency's compromised relationship with industry, in large part, drove the efforts to improve how the government manages offshore oil and gas operations. As a result, in addition to the diagnosis of capture itself, examining how an agency became captured is important because the perceived mechanisms can define, as they did in the case of MMS, how the subsequent reforms are structured. Yet, even to the extent that these conditions do help explain the existence of a partially compromised regulator, a fixation on remedying these facilitating circumstances can obscure the reasons why these conditions were imposed in the first place. Particularly when capture is not pervasive at the agency or is of a weak form – discussed by Daniel Carpenter and David Moss in the Introduction to this volume as capture that still promotes the public interest to a reasonable degree – the solution can impose offsetting costs that are as large or even larger.

Reorganizations, particularly those on the scale of what was implemented at Interior, cost money, take time, and impose dislocations on employees. In speculating on how the restructuring is likely to affect ongoing governmental oil and gas operations, it is instructive to recall the impetus for the creation of MMS in the first place. Instead of citing conflicts of interest as a reason to separate minerals management functions, GAO, as well as the Linowes Commission and Congress, pressed for the establishment of one agency to oversee "the entire mineral management area" given that the existing "division of function often caused problems of neglect, duplication, and turf wars."[174] Not only did having BLM conduct preleasing functions and sales while locating lease management at USGS create jurisdictional

---

[174] Commission on Fiscal Accountability of the Nation's Energy Resources, *Fiscal Accountability*; Committee on Appropriations, "Department of the Interior and Related Agencies Appropriation Bill, 1983"; Socolar, "Statement of Milton J. Socolar."

problems, it was also cited as a cause for Interior's inability to prevent oil companies from fraudulently removing oil without reporting it as production. As described by the Director of GAO's Energy and Minerals Division at a 1981 hearing before the House Committee on Interior and Insular Affairs, "The fragmentation of authority and accountability for implementing the mineral leasing laws contributes to the weakness of Federal minerals management. Such a weakening factor is central to any consideration of how to improve the revenue potential of Federal resources."[175] Thus, at the time, the fundamental question was not why the functions were combined, but rather why onshore development, leasing, and regulation were separately housed at BLM instead of MMS.[176]

Analogously, citing coordination problems between BLM, BIA, and MMS for onshore revenue collection as well as between MMS's Offshore Energy and Revenue Management groups for offshore collection, the December 2007 Subcommittee on Royalty Management report stressed the need for more – not less – intra– and inter bureau synchronization by creating cross organizational teams and syncing computer systems.[177] Moreover, given the extensive overlap associated with the functions that formed Offshore Energy, even Secretary Salazar's July 2010 implementation report recognized the inherent limitations in trying to create separate offshore planning and regulatory organizations. After the prolonged restructuring process was completed, the plan emphasized the need for the Bureau of Ocean Energy Management and the Bureau of Safety and Environmental Enforcement to maintain ongoing "close program coordination" to operate effectively, as "functions and process are tightly interconnected" between these components.[178] Thus, to the extent that the separation of offshore planning from oversight could, in theory, even partially insulate regulation from the political and public pressure to promote oil and gas production, the offsetting need to coordinate the associated functions makes that possibility both less feasible and less desirable.

Given that a closer investigation of the evidence has raised doubts about the role that capture played in the Gulf oil spill, the mechanisms

---

[175] J. Dexter Peach, "Statement of J. Dexter Peach, Director, Energy and Minerals Division, before the House Committee on Interior and Insular Affairs on Department of the Interior organizational Effectiveness for Management of Federal Energy and Mineral Resources" (U.S. House of Representatives, 1981), 6.

[176] General Accounting Office, "Interior's Minerals Management Programs Need Consolidation to Improve Accountability and Control" (GAO/EMD-82-104, General Accounting Office, 1982); Durant, *The Administrative Presidency Revisited.*

[177] Subcommittee on Royalty Management, "Report to the Royalty Policy Committee."

[178] Department of the Interior, "Reorganization of the Minerals Management Service," 6.

commonly cited that provided the impetus for capture, and even the extent to which MMS was captured, the reforms designed to address those perceived issues could be viewed with some skepticism. However, when the reforms return governmental oil and gas management to a structure that history has revealed to have substantial coordination costs and that demonstrated many similar outward signs of failure, the remedies risk causing more harm than good. To the degree that community ties between industry and Offshore Energy inspectors as well as MMS's collaborative style facilitated a common set of assumptions and prejudices surrounding oil and gas operations, there are few indications that separating offshore oversight from leasing and development decisions can, or was even intended to, deal with these deeper issues. As former MMS Director Birnbaum testified, there is "no silver bullet to eliminate the close connections between offshore inspectors and the employees of the industry they regulate. They will still live in the same communities."[179]

In his January 2011 State of the Union address, President Obama highlighted the redundancy associated with having twelve bureaus participate in managing exports, at least five for housing policy, and two for salmon conservation. Citing the need to get "rid of waste," the president promised a plan to "merge, consolidate, and reorganize" government to increase efficiency.[180] From this perspective, the breakup of MMS – based on uncertain evidence of how its capture by industry came to be or even the extent to which its capture led to failure – that may resurrect old problems of "neglect, duplication, and turf wars" and complicate implementation of energy policy could represent a step in the wrong direction.[181]

---

[179] Birnbaum, "Transcript of Testimony."
[180] Barack Obama, "Remarks by the President in State of the Union address" (The White House, Office of the Press Secretary, 2011).
[181] Committee on Appropriations, "Department of the Interior and Related Agencies Appropriation Bill, 1983," 40.

11

Reconsidering Agency Capture During Regulatory Policymaking[1]

Susan Webb Yackee[2]

This chapter, and the volume in which it resides, suggests the need to reconsider the theory of agency capture. Few constructs within the study of American politics and policymaking are more widely discussed than agency capture.[3] However, although scholars, politicians, and the media frequently employ the idea of agency capture, there is neither a clear definition of the construct[4] nor a common way to identify it.[5] In this chapter, I begin to address these shortcomings in three main ways. First, I define agency capture, which I suggest is the control of agency policy decision making by a subpopulation of individuals or organizations external to the agency.[6] Second, I put forward a two-prong test for identifying capture that separates the constructs of "influence" from "control." I argue that influence

[1] Previous versions of this chapter were presented at Duke University's interdisciplinary symposium on the "Crisis and the Challenges of Regulatory Design" (June 2011) and at the Midwest Political Science Association's annual conference (April 2011). I am grateful to the University of Southern California's Bedrosian Center on Governance and the Public Enterprise for funding parts of the data collection, and I acknowledge the late Deil Wright, the Earhart Foundation, Auburn University, and the Odum Institute for Research in Social Science at UNC-Chapel Hill for their support of the ASAP data collection.

[2] The University of Wisconsin at Madison, La Follette School of Public Affairs and Department of Political Science.

[3] Marver Bernstein, *Regulating Business by Independent Commission* (Princeton: Princeton University Press, 1955); George Stigler, "The Theory of Economic Regulation," *Bell Journal of Economics and Management Science* 2 (1971): 3–21; Paul Sabatier, "Social Movements and Regulatory Agencies: Toward a More Adequate – and Less Pessimistic – Theory of 'Clientele Capture'," *Policy Sciences* 6 (1975): 301–42.

[4] Kay Schlozman and John T. Tierney, *Organized Interests and American Democracy* (New York: Harper and Row, 1986).

[5] Daniel P. Carpenter, "Protection without Capture: Product Approval by a Politically Responsive, Learning Regulator," *American Political Science Review* 98 (2004): 613–31.

[6] As I discuss later, this definition holds both similarities and differences with the definition proposed in the introduction of this volume, as well as Carpenter's (Chapter 3) thought-provoking chapter.

is a necessary but not sufficient condition of capture. Third, I provide an empirical assessment of these constructs by applying them to a sample of rules from the U.S. Department of Transportation.

Tasked with filling in the details of congressionally passed statutes, public agencies routinely propose and promulgate legally binding rules and regulations. Although the scope and topics of rules vary dramatically, some of our key public policy battles have been fought and decided via rules. For instance, existing rules specify standards for automobile emissions, clean water, and workplace safety; moreover, forthcoming rules may set requirements for state health exchanges and capital bank standards. In short, rules matter, and so does "rulemaking," the political and policymaking process by which agency rules are formulated.[7]

The Administrative Procedure Act of 1946 (APA) guides federal agency rulemaking, and it typically unfolds across two stages. First, there is a *preproposal stage*, in which agency officials gather information and decide which stipulations and requirements to include in a draft rule (also called a Notice of Proposed Rulemaking, or NPRM). During a second stage, the *notice and comment period*, the APA requires that most NPRMs be opened for public comment. After considering any public feedback, agency officials often announce a legally binding Final Rule.

It is important to note that agency capture – as I define it – is not an argument particular to rulemaking. Yet, if capture exists, then one might expect to see it manifest during the rulemaking process because, as West[8] suggests, rulemaking is "the most important way in which the bureaucracy creates [regulatory] policy." As a result, rulemaking supplies an excellent test case for identifying agency capture. Moreover, this chapter does not assume

---

[7] Susan Webb Yackee, "Sweet-Talking the Fourth Branch: Assessing the Influence of Interest Group Comments on Federal Agency Rulemaking," *Journal of Public Administration Research and Theory* 26 (2006): 103–24; Susan Webb Yackee, "Assessing Inter-Institutional Attention to and Influence on Government Regulations," *British Journal of Political Science* 36 (2006): 723–44; Amy McKay and Susan Webb Yackee, "Interest Group Competition on Federal Agency Rules," *American Politics Research* 35 (2007): 336–57; William F. West, "Formal Procedures, Informal Procedures, Accountability, and Responsiveness in Bureaucratic Policymaking: An Institutional Policy Analysis," *Public Administration Review* 64 (2004): 66–80; William F. West, "Administrative Rule-Making: An Old and Emerging Literature," *Public Administration Review* 65 (2005): 655–68; Cornelius M. Kerwin and Scott R. Furlong, *Rulemaking: How Government Agencies Write Law and Make Policy*, 4th ed. (Washington, DC: CQ Press, 2010); Jason Webb Yackee and Susan Webb Yackee, "Is Agency Rulemaking 'Ossified'? Testing Congressional, Presidential, and Judicial Procedural Constraints," *Journal of Public Administration Research and Theory* 20 (2010): 261–82; Jason Webb Yackee and Susan Webb Yackee, "An Empirical Examination of Federal Regulatory Volume and Speed, 1950–1990," *George Washington Law Review* 80 (2012): 1414–92.

[8] West, "Administrative Rule-Making," 655.

the existence of agency capture and then seek remedies for its prevention; instead, it strives to put forward a reliable and generalizable method to identify agency capture during rulemaking.[9]

I assess capture during regulatory policymaking by focusing on thirty-six U.S. Department of Transportation (U.S. DOT) rules completed between 2002 and 2005. The most critical feature of these data is that each rule begins with an Advanced Notice of Proposed Rulemaking (ANPRM). An ANPRM is a government document that begins the preproposal stage for some rules. In an ANPRM, the agency indicates how it may regulate or deregulate on a topic and asks for public comment. In theory, the information generated in this first round of comments informs the NPRM. In accordance with the APA, the NPRM must then be open for a second public comment period before it can be finalized. Although all of the sample rules begin with ANPRMs, not all end as Final Rules; in fact, half of the rules are withdrawn by the agency before reaching Final Rule status.

I rely primarily on content analysis of government documents and a sample of the public comments taken from each stage of the rulemaking process to draw conclusions in this chapter. In the dataset, I coded information from the thirty-six U.S. DOT rules at each stage of the rulemaking process, for a total of fifty-nine points of evaluation. Additionally, for a subsample of nineteen U.S. DOT rules, I implemented a telephone survey of the public commenters. Finally, to assess implications generated through my analysis, I also used 2004 survey information drawn from agency heads in all fifty American states and across all policy areas.

These data provide several advantages. First, they allow me to study the full rulemaking process – from the preproposal stage through the notice and comment period – and evaluate how participation rates of different segments of the broader public, such as business or government interests, change across the different phases of rulemaking. Second, I am able to provide suggestive evidence regarding which segments or "subpopulations" are the most influential on policy outputs at various rulemaking stages. Third, by studying rules that are finalized, as well as rules that are withdrawn, these data are among the first to track the ability of subpopulations to halt the regulatory process. Fourth, I can assess influence tactics beyond the submission of comments, including the use of *ex parte* (i.e., "off the record") lobbying. Of course, these data do not hold all the answers we seek with regard to capture during rulemaking. One shortcoming is that

---

[9] See also the chapters by Carrigan (Chapter 10) and McCarty (5) in this volume for thought-provoking efforts to identify and understand the conditions associated with agency capture.

the study focuses on a relatively small number of rules drawn from nine agencies within one federal department (U.S. DOT). Moreover, if capture occurs either before the initiation or after the completion of rulemaking, then these data will be blind to its effects. Additionally, although the chapter breaks new ground by measuring multiple lobbying tactics – including *ex parte* lobbying – employed on a sample of agency rules, the chapter is limited in that I am not able to identify all of the potential influence mechanisms that may have been used by interested parties on these rules.[10]

The chapter proceeds as follows: First, I discuss the theoretical foundations of agency capture, and I put forward a two-prong test for identifying capture in the context of rulemaking. Second, I describe the data, variables, and methods employed. Third, I discuss the results. In particular, I uncover suggestive evidence that the participation and influence of state DOT agency officials – who are often important implementers of U.S. DOT policies – may deter agency capture. Finally, I conclude by suggesting potential pathways for future work.

THEORETICAL FOUNDATIONS AND A TWO-PRONG TEST

Images of the U.S. public bureaucracy are often curiously bifurcated. By one account, government agencies are made up of public servants who are among the best in the world and promote the public interest.[11] Here, bureaucrats strive to be nonpolitical actors[12] and are motivated primarily by their aspirations to serve citizens.[13] In contrast, the other image of the bureaucracy is much less sanguine and arguably more frequently employed. Here, narrow, self-serving interests capture government agencies with the result being inefficient, ineffective, or even undemocratic public

---

[10] In particular, I purposively focus on "inside lobbying" tactics over "outside lobbying" tactics, meaning that I study the methods used by interest groups to influence administrative officials directly, as opposed to more diffuse public campaigns meant to influence the general policymaking atmosphere or public opinion on the issue.

[11] Charles Goodsell, *The Case for Bureaucracy: A Public Administration Polemic*, 4th ed. (Washington, DC: CQ Press, 2003). Although the public's overall evaluations of U.S. bureaucratic performance vary markedly over time, the bureaucracy's macro-level approval often exceeds the approval of other representative institutions, such as the U.S. Congress [Susan Webb Yackee and David Lowery, "Understanding Public Support for the U.S. Bureaucracy: A Macro Politics View," *Public Management Review* 7 (2005): 515–36].

[12] Woodrow Wilson, "The Study of Administration," *Political Science Quarterly* 2 (1887): 197–222.

[13] James L. Perry and Lois R. Wise, "The Motivational Bases of Public Service," *Public Administration Review* 50 (1990): 367–73.

decisions.[14] In this section, I focus new attention on the latter description with the aim of better understanding the construct and its applicability to one of the main functions of the modern public bureaucracy: agency rule-making.

AGENCY CAPTURE

Agency capture is the control of agency policy decision making by a sub-population of individuals or organizations outside of the agency. Although in principle any subpopulation may capture agency decision making,[15] the vast majority of the literature concentrates on the potential for nefarious influence by business or economic interests on regulatory outputs to the detriment of the "public interest" or the "public good." Bernstein[16] begins much of the modern thinking; he theorized that over time, agencies "tend to relate their goals and objects to the demands of dominant interest groups in the economy." Similarly, Rourke[17] summarized capture as an over-reliance on an interest group by an agency, such that the group develops a veto power over the agency's actions. Stigler[18] and others[19] focused on how select interest groups attempt to capture "rents" by lobbying for additional government regulation. Bagley[20] suggested that capture is best understood as "shorthand for the phenomenon whereby regulated entities wield their superior organizational capabilities to secure favorable agency outcomes at the expense of the diffuse public."

Some recent scholarship suggests that concerns over agency capture remain relevant today. Barkow[21] wrote that agency capture may exist in the areas of banking, criminal justice, and consumer protection. Bagley[22] suggested that capture occurs at times within government agencies;

---

[14] Bernstein, *Regulating Business*; Stigler, "The Theory of Economic Regulation"; Theodore Lowi, *The End of Liberalism* (New York: Norton, 1979).

[15] James Q. Wilson, *The Politics of Regulation* (New York City: Basic Books, 1980).

[16] Bernstein, *Regulating Business*, 92.

[17] Francis E. Rourke, *Bureaucracy, Politics, and Public Policy*, 3rd ed. (Boston: Little, Brown and Company, 1984).

[18] Stigler, "The Theory of Economic Regulation."

[19] Richard A. Posner, "Theories of Economic Regulation," *Bell Journal of Economics and Management* 5 (1974): 335–58; Sam Peltzman, "Toward a More General Theory of Regulation," *Journal of Law and Economics* 19 (1976): 211–40.

[20] Nicolas Bagley, "Agency Hygiene," *Texas Law Review* 89 (2010): 1–14. See also Rachel E. Barkow, "Insulating Agencies: Avoiding Capture through Institutional Design," *Texas Law Review* 89 (2010): 15–79.

[21] Barkow, "Insulating Agencies."

[22] Bagley, "Agency Hygiene."

however, he cautioned that it can be subtle and difficult to detect. Nevertheless, both Barkow[23] and Bagley[24] concluded that elected officials ought to design public agencies and develop policy solutions so as to diminish agency capture in the modern bureaucracy.

However, a number of political scientists and public administration scholars call into question the widespread existence of agency capture,[25] as well as provide theoretical critiques against the concept. The most frequently cited challenge to the theory questions its black box treatment of political institutions. Moe,[26] for example, wrote, "[i]nstitutions are purposefully omitted from these [capture] models... The implicit claim is that institutions don't matter much." Hill[27] concluded that "capture, even among regulatory agencies, never has been as pervasive as was sometimes suggested." Wilson[28] argued that agency capture is much more difficult in the modern era due to diversity in organized interests, the lower cost of information, and access to the courts. Rourke[29] echoed this point, suggesting that agencies must satisfy the conflicting demands of a variety of groups.

Another challenge for much of the existing capture literature is the difficulty in clearly defining and in measuring the "public interest" or the "public good." Yet numerous scholars successfully employ proxies for this construct.[30] For instance, Berry[31] found that public participation – or the participation of a public interest representative – during regulatory development provides a critical hedge against agency capture. He suggested that the presence of such representatives reduces the likelihood of capture by

---

[23] Barkow, "Insulating Agencies."

[24] Bagley, "Agency Hygiene."

[25] Sabatier, "Social Movements and Regulatory Agencies"; Kenneth J. Meier and John P. Plumlee, "Regulatory Administration and Organizational Rigidity," *The Western Political Quarterly* 31 (1978): 80–95; William T. Gormley, "Alternative Models of the Regulatory Process: Public Utility Regulation in the States," *The Western Political Quarterly* 35 (1982): 297–317; William Berry, "An Alternative to the Capture Theory of Regulation: The Case of State Public Utility Commissions," *American Journal of Political Science* 28 (1984): 524–58.

[26] Terry M. Moe, "An Assessment of the Positive Theory of 'Congressional Dominance'," *Legislative Studies Quarterly* 12 (1987): 475–520.

[27] Larry B. Hill, "Who Governs the American Administrative State? A Bureaucratic-Centered Image of Governance," *Journal of Public Administration Research and Theory* 3 (1991): 261–94.

[28] James Q. Wilson, *Bureaucracy: What Government Agencies Do and Why They Do It* (New York: Basic Books, 1989).

[29] Francis E. Rourke, "American Bureaucracy in a Changing Political Setting," *Journal of Public Administration Research and Theory* 2 (1991): 111–30.

[30] See, for instance, Schwarcz' insightful chapter in this volume (Chapter 13) for a discussion of other political actors, such as advocacy leaders, representing the public interest.

[31] Berry, "An Alternative to the Capture Theory of Regulation."

business interests. Similarly, Sabatier[32] wrote that regulatory agencies promulgate more proconsumer policies when organized groups agitate for consumer interests, and Gormley[33] found that business interests are more influential in states where public interest advocates are inactive.

CAPTURE IN QUANTITATIVE RULEMAKING STUDIES

The quantitative rulemaking literature provides numerous accounts of who participates and who influences during rulemaking's notice and comment period, and it is through these accounts that our understanding of agency capture may be inferred. For instance, Golden[34] studied a sample of eleven rules and concluded that business interests submit the most comments on proposed regulations. However, she found little evidence of excessive business influence or what she refers to as "agency capture" in the data. In other work, Croley[35] and Kerwin and Furlong[36] also documented the dominance of business participation during the notice and comment period.[37] Furlong[38] collected opinions from bureaucrats in rulemaking, and he found that they believe themselves to be responsive – but not "captured" – by interest group participation.

In their survey effort, Furlong and Kerwin[39] found that businesses and trade associations are involved in rulemaking at a greater rate than public interest groups; however, businesses and government officials participate at about the same rate. My earlier research[40] provides evidence of subpopulation participation and influence during notice and comment rulemaking. Using content analysis on a sample of more than thirty rules, my coauthor and I found that business interests participate during the notice and

[32] Sabatier, "Social Movements and Regulatory Agencies."

[33] Gormley, "Alternative Models of the Regulatory Process."

[34] Marissa Martino Golden, "Interest Groups in the Rule-Making Process: Who Participates? Whose Voices Get Heard?" *Journal of Public Administration Research and Theory* 8 (1998): 245–70.

[35] Steven P. Croley, "Theories of Regulation: Incorporating the Administrative Process," *Columbia Law Review* 98: 1–168.

[36] Kerwin and Furlong, *Rulemaking*.

[37] However, see Mariano-Florentino Cuéllar, "Rethinking Regulatory Democracy," *Administrative Law Review* 57 (2005): 411–99.

[38] Scott R. Furlong, "Political Influence on the Bureaucracy: The Bureaucracy Speaks," *Journal of Public Administration Research and Theory* 8 (1998): 39–65.

[39] Scott R. Furlong and Cornelius M. Kerwin, "Interest Group Participation in Rulemaking: A Decade of Change," *Journal of Public Administration and Research* 15 (2005): 353–70.

[40] Jason Webb Yackee and Susan Webb Yackee, "A Bias toward Business? Assessing Interest Group Influence on the Bureaucracy," *Journal of Politics* 68 (2006): 128–39.

comment period at a higher rate than other commenter types and hold more influence over Final Rule content.

Other research suggests that interest group influence – and particularly business interest influence – may be more important during the preproposal stage than during the notice and comment period of rulemaking. For instance, Kamieniecki[41] concluded that the content of the proposed rule is "probably a better indicator of the amount of influence business has in the rulemaking process" than is business participation during the notice and comment process. My work with Naughton and others[42] demonstrates an agenda-setting and agency-blocking role for organized interests during the preproposal stage; however, we do not investigate subpopulation influence patterns. My recent research[43] finds that *ex parte* lobbying by interest groups during the preproposal stage holds influence over regulatory outputs. However, again, the focus is not on agency capture. Finally, others also suggested the need for greater study of the preproposal stage,[44] and at times, this work emphasizes the need for investigation into business influence patterns in particular.

TWO-PRONG TEST AND TESTABLE EXPECTATIONS

Despite years of scholarly discussion, ambiguity still surrounds the concept of agency capture. This ambiguity stems in large part from an unclear distinction between subpopulation *influence on* agency decision making and subpopulation *capture of* agency decision making in much of the literature.

---

[41] Sheldon Kamieniecki, *Corporate American and Environmental Policy: How Often Does Business Get Its Way?* (Stanford, CA: Stanford Law and Politics, 2006): 133.

[42] Keith Naughton, Celeste Schmid, Susan Webb Yackee, and Xueyong Zhan, "Understanding Commenter Preference during Agency Rule Development," *Journal of Policy Analysis and Management* 28 (2009): 258–77. See also David Nelson and Susan Webb Yackee, "Lobbying Coalitions and Government Policy Change," *Journal of Politics* 74: 339–53.

[43] Susan Webb Yackee, "The Politics of *Ex Parte* Lobbying: Pre-Proposal Agenda Building and Blocking during Agency Rulemaking," *Journal of Public Administration Research and Theory* 22 (2012): 373–93.

[44] John E. Chubb, *Interest Groups and the Bureaucracy: The Politics of Energy* (Stanford, CA: Stanford University Press, 1983); Wesley A. Magat, Alan J. Krupnick, and Winston Harrington, *Rules in the Making: A Statistical Analysis of Regulatory Agency Behavior* (Washington, D.C.: Resources for the Future, 1986); West, "Formal Procedures, Informal Procedures, Accountability, and Responsiveness"; West, "Administrative Rule-Making"; William F. West, "Inside the Black Box: The Development of Proposed Rules and the Limits of Procedural Controls," *Administration & Society* 41 (2009): 576–99; Wendy E. Wagner, "Administrative Law, Filter Failure, and Information Capture," *Duke Law Journal* 59 (2010): 1321–432; Sara R. Rinfret, "Behind the Shadows: Interests, Influence, and the U.S. Fish and Wildlife Service," *Human Dimensions of Wildlife* 16 (2011): 1–14.

Gormley[45] highlighted this ambiguity; he wrote that scholars too often confuse the concepts of influence and control when studying agency capture. Gormley[46] suggested that businesses may be quite influential without controlling the regulatory process or the decision making of agency officials. As a result, I define capture *as the control of agency policy decision making by a subpopulation of individuals or organizations external to the agency.* This definition fits with Carpenter's warning in 2004 and in his Chapter 3 contribution to this volume, both of which suggest that simply observing policy outcomes that appear to favor well-organized and wealthy interests is not evidence of agency capture. Therefore, if one uncovers evidence of policy influence by a subpopulation, then one must take the additional step of evaluating agency decision making to understand whether that subpopulation wields influence, or more powerfully, undue influence or even control over agency decision making.[47]

In short, I argue that influence is a necessary but not sufficient condition of agency capture. In light of this distinction, I separate out these constructs in a simple two-prong test. I ask: (1) does a set of a subpopulation of interests consistently hold greater influence over the writing of agency rules than other subpopulations? If yes, then the second prong of the test is activated: (2) does a subpopulation control agency decision making with regard to rulemaking? I argue that an affirmative response to both the first *and* second questions constitutes agency capture. I map this test onto rulemaking by deriving several testable expectations. If agency capture exists, then:

(a) I expect that a subpopulation of individuals or organizations – be it business interests or some other subpopulation – will stand out as the top lobbying participant during rulemaking. Here, lobbying represents the first step toward potential influence. I expect that a high

---

[45] Gormley, "Alternative Models of the Regulatory Process."

[46] Ibid.

[47] Before moving forward, it is worth briefly explicating how the definition of agency capture employed in this chapter relates to the construct as framed in this volume's introductory chapter, as well as Carpenter's contribution. The core idea in those important contributions is that capture pulls regulation away from the public interest. Moreover, there may be "strong capture," which moves regulation so far from the public interest that it is a net negative for society, or "weak capture," whereas the resulting regulation, despite interest group influence, still advances the public interest. My definition focuses less on the public interest (and thus does not make the distinction between strong and weak capture), and instead it equates capture with control. I go on to suggest that a single set of interests ought not to control the decision making of any public agency. Later in the chapter, however, I do bring back in the notion of the "public interest" by suggesting that so-called public interest groups and/or state and local government agencies may provide proxy measures for the construct.

level of participation will occur across the rulemaking process (i.e., during the preproposal stage and the notice and comment period). Participation domination will also carry across lobbying tactics: it will be evident during the submission of public comments to rules and will occur through other less discussed lobbying tactics, such as *ex parte* lobbying or indirect lobbying through legislators or the elected executive.

(b) I expect that a subpopulation will stand out as consistently influential across rules and agencies. Thus, if business or other interests have captured rulemaking, then they will be able to reliably move regulatory policy decision making in their preferred direction. If agency capture is a widespread phenomenon, then I expect to see these patterns across most rules, regardless of the agency; if agency capture is an agency-specific phenomenon, then I expect to see these patterns across the majority of rules promulgated by a particular agency. Again, if capture exists, then influence will likely occur across the different stages of the rulemaking process and across lobbying tactics.

(c) Assuming points (a) and (b) are satisfied, then in a captured agency, I expect to see agency decision making "controlled" by the subpopulation. Control may reveal itself empirically in several ways. For instance, I expect to see agency decision making gravitate toward the policy preferences of the subpopulation, even when technical information, data, or evidence points decision making in a different direction. I also expect to see agency decision making move toward the policy preferences of the subpopulation, even when the preferences of other political actors, such as Congress and the president, point agency rulemaking in a different direction. These patterns will occur across multiple agency rules, suggesting that agency capture is a broad theoretical construct that generalizes across agency decision making.

DATA AND VARIABLES

I provide one empirical application of the two-prong test in this chapter. To do so, I rely primarily on a dataset of thirty-six U.S. DOT rules. I focus on U.S. DOT because it is one of the top promulgators of rules at the federal level and regulates across a diversity of controversial policy topics. I began the study's data collection by completing fifteen background interviews in Washington, D.C., with the agency officials who worked on these rules. These interviews provided me context and insights into the rules' subject matter. I describe the data and variables next.

RULE SELECTION

To select the study rules, I first put together the population of U.S. DOT "completed actions" for the study's focus years, which span from 2002 to 2005. Here, "completed action" means that the agency either promulgated the rulemaking activity as a Final Rule or it was formally withdrawn. This stipulation allows me to study the politics of agenda setting and agenda blocking during rulemaking.[48] I then limited the selection to rules that began the preproposal stage with an ANPRM. As West[49] suggested, rules that begin with ANPRM procedures give scholars a way to study the often nontransparent participation of concerned parties during the preproposal stage. It is important to note that ANPRM procedures – although used at a greater rate than other more specialized procedural mechanisms – are not used for the majority of rules.[50] Nevertheless, as Naughton et al.[51] conclude in an analysis of ANPRM usage across the federal government, a "noteworthy" number of rules begin as ANPRMs, making studies utilizing ANPRMs an important "vehicle for understanding the broader phenomenon of [proposed] rule development."

These parameters yielded thirty-six study rules.[52] To capture the full rulemaking process – from the preproposal stage through the notice and comment period – I focused my analysis on each stage of rulemaking. Each stage represents the government agency's effort to solicit public comments, as well as make policy change, on one of these thirty-six rules. Within the preproposal stage of rulemaking, thirty-six rules took comments during an

---

[48] Kamieniecki, *Corporate American and Environmental Policy*; Naughton et al., "Understanding Commenter Preference."

[49] West, "Formal Procedures, Informal Procedures, Accountability, and Responsiveness."

[50] There has also been research into specialized procedural mechanisms employed during the preproposal stage, such as negotiated rulemaking [Cary Coglianese, "Assessing Consensus: The Promise and Performance of Negotiated Rulemaking," *Duke Law Journal* 46 (1997): 1255–349; Laura Langbein and Cornelius M. Kerwin, "Regulatory Negotiation versus Conventional Rule Making: Claims, Counterclaims, and Empirical Evidence," *Journal of Public Administration Research and Theory* 10 (2000): 599–632], which utilizes concerned parties to construct the preliminary rule. Despite great promise, negotiated rulemaking is infrequently used. Other work focuses on advisory groups [Steven J. Balla and John R. Wright, "Interest Groups, Advisory Committees, and Congressional Control of the Bureaucracy," *American Journal of Political Science* 45 (2001): 799–812], which, at times, aid in the development of rules. However, neither line of scholarship generalizes well to rules without these specialized mechanisms.

[51] Naughton et al., "Understanding Commenter Preference," 263.

[52] I initially identified thirty-eight candidate rules; however, despite significant efforts, I could not locate full rule docket information for two rules. Thus my study focuses on thirty-six rules.

ANPRM phase, whereas two rules also collected comments in a Supplemental Advanced Notice of Proposed Rulemaking (SANPRM).[53] Twenty rules were open for comments during an NPRM phase, whereas one rule also employed a Supplemental Notice of Proposed Rulemaking (SNPRM) to solicit public feedback. In the end, my study included fifty-nine total rule stages.

There were 2,857 public comments submitted across the fifty-nine stages. The range per rule was 3 to 387 comments, with an average of 48 comments. Several of the rules received fewer than fifteen comments. Although my past research focusing on public comments often studied rules garnering 200 or fewer comments,[54] there is no such restriction here. Instead, I used the following sampling rule to collect information on each rulemaking stage: randomly sample either 15 comments or 10 percent of the comments per stage, and use whichever number is larger. Using this sampling rule, 754 comments were selected for analysis. This represents about 26 percent of the total comments.

CONTENT ANALYSIS

The content analysis focuses on government documents and public comments. It was completed primarily by three doctoral students and took place in fall 2006 and spring 2007. The coders were provided coding instructions and coding rules. The team and I worked on the same rule stages for the first three months. During this time, we met frequently and adjudicated disagreements. After that point, the coders worked independently and met with me to discuss questions. Ultimately, 13 percent of the sample was jointly coded, and almost 12 percent was (blindly) double-coded to assess the inter-coder reliability of the independent work. I generated kappa scores on the key variables, and the scores all fell within acceptable bounds.[55]

In analyses that follow, I use the *stage change* dependent variable, which is generated by the content analysis and draws on variable construction techniques I have employed in other published work.[56] *Stage change* measures the change in direction, if any, of government regulations across rule

---

[53] Supplemental commenting periods are used on some rules to gather additional feedback from the public on new formulations of the government's draft regulatory policy.

[54] For example, Yackee, "Sweet-Talking the Fourth Branch"; Yackee, "Assessing Inter-Institutional Attention."

[55] The kappa score for the *stage change* variable was 1.0 and for the *commenter preference* variable was 0.786.

[56] Yackee, "Sweet-Talking the Fourth Branch"; Yackee, "Assessing Inter-Institutional Attention"; Naughton et al., "Understanding Commenter Preference."

stages. To generate the measure, coders read the preamble and text of the documents provided by the government at the beginning of a rule stage. These documents may have appeared in an ANPRM, SANPRM, or NPRM in the sample. Coders then read the preamble and text of the government documents issued at the end of that rule stage. Thus, if a rule proceeded from ANRPM   NPRM   Final Rule, then there were two separate *stage change* measures taken; if a rule proceeded from ANPRM   Withdrawal, then one *stage change* measure was taken. Using a three-point scale, coders evaluated whether each stage shifted the government's regulatory position toward more regulation ($+1$), stayed about the same (0), or less regulation (-1). The variable's average suggests more frequent shifts toward less regulation, with a mean of -0.339 and a range of -1 to $+1$.

Coders also developed the main independent variable, *commenter preference*, in the analyses. Here, coders used the same three-point scale to evaluate whether the sampled commenters wanted a shift away from the baseline (i.e., the government document that began that stage of the rulemaking process). Thus, when a commenter wanted a shift toward more regulation, a $+1$ was recorded; when the commenter desired no shift or wrote to express support for the baseline position, a 0 was recorded; and when a commenter wanted a move toward less regulation, a -1 was recorded. I then took the mean score across the stage to develop a measure of commenters' mean desires. The average for *commenter preference* is -0.201, with a range of -1 to 0.867.

In a separate set of analyses presented later, I use a *commenter success* score; this score draws on variable construction techniques I develop more fully elsewhere.[57] To generate this measure, I combine the *stage change* and the individual-level *commenter preference* measure. *Commenter success* is a dichotomous measure that scores a 1 whenever a rule shifts in the regulatory direction desired by the commenter and a 0 otherwise. For instance, when the commenter desires less regulation during a rule stage and the agency provides less regulation, then there is a match, and the *commenter success* scores a 1. However, when a commenter desires less regulation and the agency provides either more or the same level of government regulation as the baseline, then there is no match, scoring a 0. The variable mean is 0.615 with a standard deviation of 0.487.

I also place each commenter into one of three subpopulation groups: "business interests" (members or representatives of a trade association or individual business), "government interests" (state and local government

---

[57] Yackee, "The Politics of *Ex Parte* Lobbying"; Nelson and Yackee, "Lobbying Coalitions."

officials and members of Congress and federal agencies), and "nonbusiness/nongovernment" interests (citizens, public interest groups, academia, think tanks, professional associations, or unions).[58] This categorization draws on my earlier work.[59] Because of a high rate of involvement, some of the analyses presented here also break out participation by state-level department of transportation officials.

TELEPHONE SURVEY

I also draw conclusions from a telephone survey of public commenters drawn from a subsample of nineteen study rules. I chose the nineteen rules because – when looking at the sample – those rules all had "more recent" ANPRMs – meaning, they all had ANPRMs in 1999 or later. I employed this restriction to increase the probability of locating the survey subjects. In comparing the nineteen study rules where the telephone survey was implemented to the seventeen rules where the survey was not implemented, I found no systematic differences.[60]

The telephone survey was implemented by three graduate students and overseen by me during fall 2006 and spring 2007. Survey implementers attempted to contact the 230 commenters identified for the study and 133 respondents participated (a response rate of 58 percent). Comparisons made between the respondents and nonrespondents revealed few differences on key demographic factors, such as gender, or other comment-level characteristics, such as average comment length. There was a more measureable difference on commenter location: 23 percent of the respondents were from the Washington, D.C., area, whereas 36 percent of the nonrespondents were from D.C. The telephone survey queried respondents regarding topics connected to the specific study rules, including perceived comment influence and *ex parte* lobbying activity.[61] I also asked several more general

[58] Several of this volume's chapters, including the Introduction and Carpenter's important Chapter 3 contribution, focus on the "public interest." Reliable measurement of this construct has proven difficult given competing notions of what constitutes, or what ought to constitute, the public interest. However, the nonbusiness/nongovernment interests categorization used here may serve as a proxy measure for the public interest in these analyses.

[59] Yackee and Yackee, "A Bias toward Business?"

[60] I compared the averages for rule significance (measured via U.S. DOT's significance determination), rule complexity (measured via the length of the rule's abstract), and average length of the public comments.

[61] Elsewhere (Yackee, "The Politics of *Ex Parte* Lobbying") I make the argument that the ANPRM comment lists provide a mechanism to uncover *ex parte* lobbying trends during the preproposal stage of rulemaking. My argument draws on Chubb (*Interest Groups and*

questions about rulemaking, such as the level of influence of big businesses and corporations. Finally, the survey ended with demographic questions.

STATE ADMINISTRATORS SURVEY

To challenge implications generated by my analysis of the U.S. DOT rules, I also use data from the American State Administrators Project (ASAP), which secured survey data by mail from 940 agency heads in 2004. Responses were received from all fifty American states, and the agencies represented govern a broad range of subject matter, including state DOT agencies. The survey response rate was 28 percent.[62] In this chapter, I concentrate on responses by state agency heads to questions querying the degree of influence various actors held on the promulgation of rules and regulations, which I describe more fully later.

RESULTS

I apply the two-prong capture test using a variety of strategies, including descriptive statistics, correlation analysis, and regression analysis. In most cases, I am limited by small sample sizes from making broad generalizations. However, when appropriate, I present quantitative patterns, describe findings, and provide suggestive evidence and conclusions. I begin this section with some basic information about the data. I then discuss who participates and who influences this sample of rules. I conclude with a discussion of agency capture.

Table 11.1 provides information on the study rules, including the topic of the rule and the promulgating agency. The rule topics demonstrate that U.S. DOT agencies regulate or attempt to regulate across a wide variety of subject areas in this sample, including standards for school bus safety, English language requirements for flight attendants, and bridge inspection standards. Moreover, numerous agencies within U.S. DOT are active rule writers. In this study, nine agencies are represented: Federal Motor Carrier Safety Administration (FMCSA) was the largest rulemaking entity,

---

the Bureaucracy); however, Kerwin, Furlong, and West [Cornelius M. Kerwin, Scott R. Furlong, and William West, "Interest Groups, Rulemaking, and American Bureaucracy," in *The Oxford Handbook of American Bureaucracy*, ed. Robert Durant (Oxford: Oxford University Press, 2010), 590–611] also suggest that interest groups feel that they must put their views on the public record by commenting.

[62] Additional telephone follow-ups with survey nonrespondents completed by the ASAP survey administrators led them to conclude that the actual respondents to the questionnaire were representative of the universe of administrators to whom the ASAP surveys were sent.

Table 11.1. *Author's sample rules drawn from U.S. DOT*

#	Rule topic	DOT agency	ANPRM	SANPRM	NPRM	SNPRM	Final rule (FR) or withdrawn (W)
	Significant						
1	Airlines computer reservations system	OST	X	X	X		FR
2	Management systems pertaining to the National Park Service	FHWA	X		X		FR
3	Early warning defect reporting requirements	NHTSA	X		X		FR
4	Improve tire safety information	NHTSA	X		X		FR
5	Management systems pertaining to the Bureau of Indian Affairs	FHWA	X		X		FR
6	Training requirements for entry-level commercial motor vehicle operators	FMCSA	X		X		FR
7	Management systems pertaining to the Fish and Wildlife Service	FHWA	X		X		FR
8	Training requirements for longer combination vehicle operators	FMCSA	X		X		FR
9	National bridge inspection standard	FHWA	X		X		FR
10	Hazardous materials transport of infectious substances and microorganisms	RSPA	X		X		FR
11	Management systems pertaining to the Forest Service	FHWA	X		X		FR
	Nonsignificant						
12	Safety of uninspected passenger vessels	USCG	X		X		FR
13	Upgrade fuel integrity performance requirements	NHTSA	X		X		FR
14	Work zone safety and mobility	FHWA	X		X	X	FR
15	Development of standard for protection against shifting and falling cargo	FMCSA	X		X		FR
16	Adoption of latest IAEA standards	RSPA	X		X		FR
17	Incident reporting requirements and detailed hazardous materials incident report	RSPA	X		X		FR
18	Air carrier emergency telephone number requirements	RSPA	X		X		FR

(continued)

307

Table 11.1 (continued)

#	Rule topic	DOT agency	ANPRM	SANPRM	NPRM	SNPRM	Final rule (FR) or withdrawn (W)
Significant							
19	Domestic passenger manifest information	OST	X				W
20	English language requirement and qualifications of drivers	FMCSA	X				W
21	Emergency response plans for passenger vessels	USCG	X				W
22	Child restraint systems in airlines	FAA	X				W
23	Inspection, repair, and maintenance for intermodal container chassis and trailers	FMCSA	X				W
24	Interstate school bus safety	FMCSA	X				W
25	Flammability of interior materials on school buses	NHTSA	X				W
26	U.S.-flag vessels in the shipment of cargoes on ocean vessels	Maritime	X				W
27	Cargo tank rollover requirements for hazardous materials	RSPA	X				W
28	Commercial driver's license standards and biometric identifier	FMCSA	X				W
Nonsignificant							
29	Barges carrying bulk liquid hazardous material	USCG	X				W
30	Certification of size and weight enforcement for highways	FHWA	X				W
31	Sleeper berths on motor coaches	FMCSA	X	X			W
32	Out-of-service criteria	FMCSA	X				W
33	Highway bridge replacement and rehabilitation program	FHWA	X		X		W
34	Buy America requirements waivers for microcomputers	FTA	X				W
35	Flight attendant English language proficiency	FAA	X				W
36	Aircraft engines – fuel and induction systems	FAA	X		X		W

promulgating nine rules; Federal Highway Administration (FHWA) contributed eight rules, Research and Special Programs Administration (RSPA) wrote five rules, followed by National Highway Traffic Safety Administration (NHTSA; four rules), Federal Aviation Administration (FAA; three rules), U.S. Coast Guard (USCG; three rules),[63] Office of the Secretary (OST; two rules), Federal Transit Administration (FTA; one rule), and Maritime Administration (MARAD; one rule).

Table 11.1 also suggests diversity across the sample in terms of rule significance. Using U.S. DOT's significance determination, I classify both finalized and withdrawn rules. The classification, however, shows no clear trends. For instance, significant rules are neither finalized at a substantially higher rate than withdrawn rules, nor can withdrawn rules simply be classified as unimportant or trivial policy matters. Table 11.1 does make clear that a good number of rules with ANPRMs are withdrawn before finalization. As indicated in the final column, eighteen rules were ultimately finalized, whereas eighteen rules were withdrawn. Moreover, a high percentage of rules (83 percent) were withdrawn after receiving the ANPRM comments, whereas a lower percentage of rules (17 percent) were withdrawn after a later stage of rulemaking. These results imply that studying the politics of the preproposal stage may be just as important as the notice and comment period. If influence exists – indeed, if agency capture exists – then it may be directed toward stopping unwanted proposals early in the policy formation process.[64]

SUBPOPULATION PARTICIPATION

With these basic characteristics established, I now turn attention to the first set of testable expectations regarding the participation of subpopulations across rulemaking. My analysis here, as well as in the remainder of the chapter, focuses primarily on the three subpopulation groups of business interests, government interests, and nonbusiness/nongovernment interests. Figure 11.1 provides a bar chart capturing the participation rates of subpopulations across the sample rules.

The first column of data in Figure 11.1 displays the involvement of coded commenters during the preproposal stage of rulemaking. The figure clearly displays the prevalence of business participation: businesses interests

---

[63] USCG is now part of the U.S. Department of Homeland Security.
[64] Naughton et al., "Understanding Commenter Preference." See broadly John Kingdon, *Agendas, Alternatives, and Public Policies*, 2nd ed. (New York: Harper Collins, 1995); Frank Baumgartner and Bryan Jones, *Agendas and Instability in American Politics* (Chicago: University of Chicago Press, 1993).

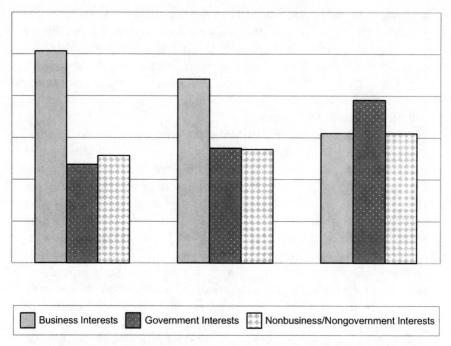

Business Interests ■ Government Interests ▨ Nonbusiness/Nongovernment Interests

Figure 11.1. Participation Across Rulemaking Stages and Lobbying Forms

make up more than 51 percent of total participants, followed by nonbusiness/nongovernment participants at 26 percent and government interests at 24 percent. Of the business interests, about one-third of the comments came from trade associations, whereas two-thirds came from individual businesses or corporations. For the nonbusiness/nongovernment participants, citizens are the largest participant type, with public interest groups representing only 4 percent of the preproposal commenters. The majority of comments from government interests came from state DOT officials. The second column in Figure 11.1 displays a similar pattern; however, although business interests remain the modal category, the relative participation of both nonbusiness/nongovernment and government officials increased during the notice and comment period. Most notably, the percentage of comments from public interest groups nearly doubles during this second stage of rulemaking; however, the relative size of their contribution remains small at only 7 percent.[65]

[65] Although the relative size of public interest group participation appears small, these findings are in keeping with what other scholars have uncovered during federal agency rulemaking. Writing almost fifteen years ago, Golden ("Interest Groups in the Rule-Making Process") found low levels of public interest group participation during the notice and

Column 3 in Figure 11.1 suggests a different conclusion with regard to subpopulation lobbying participation patterns. These data come from the telephone survey, which asked respondents: "Outside of your written comment, did you have any communications with federal Department of Transportation officials about this rule? Yes or No." Forty-nine of the 126 survey respondents who participated in this question answered yes, indicating that 38 percent of the respondents employed some form of *ex parte* lobbying.[66] Column 3 presents the subpopulation participation rates for those using *ex parte* lobbying.[67] The largest category here is government interests at 39 percent, with almost all of those *ex parte* contacts coming from state DOT officials. Business interests and nonbusiness/nongovernment interests both participate at the lower rate of 31 percent. The telephone survey also asked about indirect lobbying, which is operationalized on the survey as lobbying through elected legislators. The question was: "Did you contact any Members of Congress about this rule? Yes or No." Only 14 of the 129 (11 percent) respondents to this question answered in the affirmative. Six of the fourteen indirect lobbying participants came from business interests, whereas six came from nonbusiness/nongovernment interests. Only two government officials reported that they contacted a Member of Congress about the rule.

Overall, the results from Figure 11.1 suggest that business interests have an advantage within the primary form for providing feedback to agency officials – the submission of public comments – across both comment-gathering stages of rulemaking. This finding matches the general conclusion found in the literature.[68] It also provides renewed evidence in support of Furlong and Kerwin's[69] conclusion that "rulemaking actions typically increase the costs of doing business, and therefore one would expect increased participation by businesses or trade associations protecting their operations," and

---

comment period; notably, her data spanned several federal departments, including the Environmental Protection Agency, the U.S. Department of Housing and Urban Development, and U.S. DOT. Furlong and Kerwin ("Interest Group Participation in Rulemaking"), in their larger study of interest group participation in rulemaking, also uncovered low rates of formal comment submission by public interest groups.

[66] Survey respondents were asked to categorize their contacts, with the choice categories being phone call, e-mail, face-to-face meeting, or other (please specify). I suggest that these contacts may be conceptualized as *ex parte* communications. Only one respondent chose "other."

[67] I tend to concentrate on the occurrence of external contacts instead of perceived levels of *ex parte* influence during rulemaking because this concentration mitigates the potential survey response bias attached to revealing lobbying tactics, and more broadly, assessing the importance of lobbying tactics.

[68] Croley, "Theories of Regulation"; Yackee and Yackee, "A Bias toward Business?"; Kerwin and Furlong, *Rulemaking*.

[69] Furlong and Kerwin, "Interest Group Participation in Rulemaking," 361.

Wright's[70] suggestion that businesses and trade associations will be more active in agency lobbying due to superior information regarding administrative issues.

However, is this evidence of lobbying equal to domination by one subpopulation? Not necessarily. For instance, business interests do not appear to dominate participation across lobbying forms. Indeed, the evidence from the survey suggests that subnational officials frequently charged with implementing U.S. DOT's rules – state DOT officials – often provide agency officials informal feedback, and nonbusiness/nongovernment interests use indirect lobbying tactics at the same rate as businesses. Furthermore, when looking across this sample of rules, it is hard to conclude businesses dominate other subpopulation voices through the submission of public comments: approximately 50 percent of the comments sent to agencies come from nonbusiness interests.

Yet these aggregate-level descriptive statistics may obscure evidence of agency capture. For instance, business interests may dominate the dialogue surrounding particular rules, or the rule writing in particular government agencies may be plagued by a near monopoly on participation by business interests. To investigate these possibilities, Table 11.1 provides across rule, stage, and agency participation rates for business interests. The evidence is arrayed in the four columns tracking a rule's progress within rulemaking. Each cell is shaded depending on the percentage of coded comments in that stage coming from business interests. Cells in grayscale with diagonal lines have the most business participation at 75 percent or more; cells in grayscale indicate that 50–74 percent of the comments came from business interests; dotted cells represent business participation at the level of 25–49 percent; and cells with no shading suggest that businesses contributed 24 percent or less of the comments in that stage.

Several conflicting patterns emerge. On the one hand, business interests participate at a high rate (75 percent or higher) across numerous rule stages, and this high level of participation can be found across both finalized and withdrawn rules, significant and nonsignificant rules. On the other hand, there are more stages where business interests participate at a low rate (24 percent or lower) than at a high rate, and this low rate of business involvement also spans both termination events and rule significance types. Thus

---

[70] Jack Wright, *Interest Groups and Congress: Lobbying, Contributions, and Influence* (Boston: Allyn & Bacon, 1996). See also Christopher Jewell and Lisa Bero, "Public Participation and Claimsmaking: Evidence Utilization and Divergent Policy Frames in California's Ergonomics Rulemaking," *Journal of Public Administration Research and Theory* 17 (2007): 625–50.

there appears to be variation in business participation across rules. It is also notable that although individual rule stages or even entire rules may have high levels of business commenter participation, it is not clear that particular agencies consistently see high levels of business participation across rulemaking efforts. Of the three largest rule-writing agencies in the sample, both FMCSA and RSPA have rule stages that receive high levels of business participation but also rule stages that receive low levels of business participation. In addition, FHWA has the lowest level of business participation for an agency in the sample, with no stage at more than 50 percent business interest participation. In the end, these Table 11.1 findings suggest that business interest involvement is high across some rules; yet, businesses do not appear to dominate all subpopulation voices across multiple rules or across particular agencies. These conflicting results cut against my expectations regarding the first prong of the agency capture test.

SUBPOPULATION INFLUENCE

The second set of testable expectations points to sub-population influence during rulemaking. In this section, I start with several models focused on general commenter influence on rulemaking, and I then look for subpopulation differences in influence across rule stages.

Table 11.2 presents results of an analysis of commenter influence across the various stages of the rulemaking process.[71] The dependent variable is *stage change*, whereas the primary predictor variable is *commenter preference*, which represents the average regulatory direction sought by the coded commenters. The control variables include a measure of *congressional attention* to the rule, which is whether or not Congress passed legislation requiring the rule, and *presidential attention*, which is whether the president's Office of Management and Budget reviewed the proposed rule or not. The last two control measures are U.S. DOT's *rule significance* determination and a measure of *rule complexity*, which I operationalize as the length of the rule's abstract text in characters. I use regression analysis with robust standard errors clustered by agency; other clustering strategies, such as by rule, return the same results.[72] Finally, as I highlight later, the results, particularly

---

[71] The Model 2 results appear in my work already published with Naughton and others ("Understanding Commenter Preference"); however, the Model 1 and 3 results are new to this chapter.

[72] Given the ordered nature of the dependent variable, I also used ordered probit. Similar results were returned. I chose regression techniques over ordered probit given the small sample sizes, particularly in Model 3. Statistical significance in all chapter analyses is determined by two-tailed tests and $p \leq 0.10$.

Table 11.2. *Commenter influence across rule stages*

| | 1 | 2 | 3 |
	All rule stages	Pre-proposal stage	Notice and comment stage
Commenter	0.641	0.570	1.077
Preference	0.241	0.274	0.347
Congressional	0.126	0.221	−0.142
Attention	0.260	0.228	0.542
Presidential	−0.064	0.438	−1.104
Attention	0.156	0.241	0.277
Rule	−3.45E-04	−4.67E-04	−4.84E-04
Complexity	2.69E-04	2.50E-04	5.32E-04
Rule	−0.375	−0.578	0.363
Significance	0.156	0.275	0.413
Constant	0.255	0.149	0.753
	0.217	0.224	0.314
Observations	59	38	21
R-Squared	0.221	0.300	0.456

Notes: The dependent variable is *stage change*. OLS regression estimates are shown with clustered, robust standard errors below. $^*p \leq 0.10$, two-tailed tests employed.
Source: Author's datasets. See text for details.

from Model 3, must be considered suggestive in nature because of the small sample sizes.

Model 1 in Table 11.2 presents the results for *commenter preference* across all rule stages in the sample. The findings demonstrate a significant relationship between *commenter preference* and *stage change*, which implies that the mean regulatory direction sought within the public comments influences the direction of policy change during rulemaking. The predicted values of the dependent variable generated when other model variables are set to mean or median values find a pattern of responsiveness: when public commenters, on average, desire less government regulation, then agencies tend to respond by adjusting policies toward less government regulation. In a similar but more muted fashion, agencies move rules toward more government regulation when commenters are united for more government regulation. Models 2 and 3 break these results out for the preproposal stage and the notice and comment period. However, small sample sizes, especially in Model 3, and the requisite need to be parsimonious in the model specifications warrant caution in generalizing the results. However, despite these caveats, across both stages there is suggestive evidence of government responsiveness to the desires expressed in the public comments.

With this evidence suggesting the potential importance of commenters to policy change in hand, I now focus on subpopulation differences. Again, my efforts here prove difficult due to the data, which are rich in information, but are not as extensive as necessary to run multivariate models with the various subpopulation classifications across rule stages. Thus I turn to correlation analysis to look at potential patterns in subpopulation influence. I first look across rule stages at various levels of business interest participation and ask when commenters are most influential. To do so, I correlate *commenter preference* and *stage change* when business interests make up 75 percent or more of the public participants (twelve cases), 50–74 percent of the public participants (twenty-two cases), 25–45 percent (five cases), and 24 percent or lower (twenty cases).[73] When business participation is high, there is 0.73 correlation between *commenter preference* and *stage change*, and this relationship is statistically significant.[74] When businesses make up 50–74 percent of the public participants, the correlation remains significant but drops to 0.50. At business participation rates of 25–45 percent, the correlation is 0.34, and at 24 percent or lower, the relationship is –0.20; neither of these last two relationships is significant. Of course, these bivariate correlations must be treated with some care, given that they do not control for other rule-level factors likely to influence the relationship between commenter desires and rule change, such as rule salience and complexity and political oversight measures.

The evidence from this first set of correlations allows for the possibility of business influence across some sample rules, but is it evidence in support of the first prong of the capture test? Not necessarily: business interests are not consistently influential across rules or across agencies. Instead, the results suggest a responsive bureaucracy – as the proportion of business interest comments increases, so too does *commenter preference*.[75] These results correspond with Gormley's[76] finding that business interests are most successful

---

[73] These cases of high business participation span both significant and nonsignificant rules, as well as rule finalization and withdrawal patterns. See Table 11.1 for the illustration.

[74] It is noteworthy that business interests in the sample are not consistently asking for more or less government regulation in their lobbying. Although the mean preferences found in business interest comments suggest that they wish to move rules toward less regulation (–0.224), the 361 business interests in the sample span the entire range on the individual-level *commenter preference* variable, with 209 business interests desiring less government regulation during the stage, 24 requesting no regulatory change, and 128 desiring more regulation. Moreover, of the twelve rule stages for which business interests make up 75 percent or more of the public comment participants, four of the stages had the *commenter preference* variable tilted toward seeking more government regulation.

[75] See also Yackee and Yackee, "A Bias toward Business?"

[76] Gormley, "Alternative Models of the Regulatory Process."

Table 11.3. *Correlations across rule stages*

Commenter type	Preproposal stage	Notice and comment stage
Business interests	0.079	−0.236
Government interests	0.045	0.166
Nonbusiness/nongovernment interests	−0.137	0.084
Observations	457	250

Source: Author's datasets. See text for details.

in lobbying for policy change when their voices are largely uncontested by other interests in society.

A different way to think about subpopulation commenter influence entails moving away from the idea of average commenter success and instead focusing on the fulfillment of the individual desires of commenters. In these analyses, I use *commenter success*, which is a "match" score that returns a 1 if a rule change occurred in the direction desired by the commenter. I then correlate this variable with subpopulation type. Table 11.3 provides the findings broken out by rule phase.[77]

Table 11.3 suggests several findings. In particular, the correlation between *commenter success* and being a business interest commenter is positive, small, and significant (0.08) during the preproposal stage; however, it is negative and significant (−0.24) during the notice and comment period. This juxtaposition of influence is noteworthy, and on its face appears to suggest that although business interests are influential early in the regulatory process, they are less influential later.[78] Two facts, however, mitigate any strong conclusions with regard to these bivariate relationships. First, recall that numerous rules are withdrawn from consideration before reaching the notice and comment period in this sample. Thus, if business interests are successful in thwarting their least favorite regulatory initiatives early in the process, then one might expect that they would be on weaker footing with regard to rules that make it to the notice and comment period. Second,

[77] Again, it is important to note that these bivariate correlations do not acknowledge other commenter participation on a rule or control for contextual or political factors or lobbying tactics.

[78] This juxtaposition of influence intensifies when one looks at the correlation between *commenter success* and a comment coming from a business interest seeking less government regulation during a rule stage (as opposed to more government regulation or no regulatory shift). Businesses and trade associations seeking less regulation are more successful during the preproposal stage (0.18) and less successful at the notice and comment period (−0.29) than the overall results. Both correlations are statistically significant.

given that the sample rules all solicited comments during a preproposal stage, it may be that businesses were successful enough at this earlier stage of commenting that arguments for additional changes made later in the regulatory process were less persuasive.

Table 11.3 also suggests potential findings regarding the influence of government interests and nonbusiness/nongovernment interests on rule change. During the preproposal stage, there is no relationship between *commenter success* and a comment coming from a government interest, whereas there is a negative and significant (-0.14) relationship between *commenter success* and a comment coming from a nonbusiness/nongovernment interest. In contrast, during the notice and comment period, government interests appear better positioned to achieve *commenter success* with a positive and significant correlation (0.17), whereas the relationship for nonbusiness/nongovernment commenters is insignificant. These findings suggest that government interests may be, at times, influential during rule-making, while providing little evidence of nonbusiness/nongovernment influence.

When taken together, the results from this second set of correlations are mixed. However, in total, they do not suggest that any subpopulation consistently holds greater influence over the writing of agency rules than any other subpopulation. Although there appears to be some evidence of agenda-setting influence for business commenters – particularly when those business interests are advocating less government regulation early in the regulatory process – this influence may be partially offset by the influence of government officials during the notice and comment period, at least for those rules that are ultimately promulgated as legally binding Final Rules. Thus these analyses do not provide clear evidence in support of the first prong of the capture test.

Figure 11.2 displays information collected from the telephone survey on perceived commenter influence; this information, again, cuts against the expectation of agency capture. Respondents were asked: "Do you believe that your comment helped to influence the Department of Transportation's actions on this rule? Yes or No." A follow-up question asked all affirmative respondents: "On a scale of 1 to 5, with 1 being very little and 5 being a great deal, do you feel that this action affected this rule?" I then combined these questions into a six-point scale running from 0 to 5. Eighty-two of the 127 respondents (65 percent) answered that their comment had some effect, whereas on the six-point scale, the mean response across survey respondents was 1.83, which suggests a low level of influence. Figure 11.2 uses the six-point scale to display perceived influence patterns by subpopulation type.

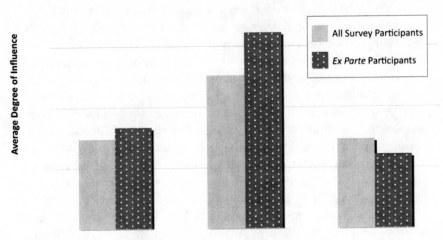

Figure 11.2. Perceived Comment Success

The figure clearly suggests that government interests – which in the case of the survey respondents are mostly state DOT officials – believe their comments to be the most influential of the subpopulations. Moreover, this finding holds if you look at all government respondents (column shown in grayscale) or only survey respondents who also employed *ex parte* lobbying tactics (column shown in black with dots). Business interests find themselves the next most influential, followed shortly by nonbusiness/nongovernment interests.

Survey respondents were also asked a more general question about business interest influence during rulemaking. The question was: "Do you feel that big businesses or corporations have an advantage during rulemaking? Yes or No." Ninety-two of the 127 respondents (72 percent) answered yes. The survey followed up with all affirmative respondents and asked: "Why?" Respondents' qualitative answers varied; however, two categories stood out. First, fifteen of the ninety-two respondents (16 percent) suggested that businesses have closer relationships with Members of Congress, and these relationships advantaged big businesses and corporations. Second, eighty-one of the ninety-two respondents (88 percent) mentioned resources, implying that big businesses and corporations had a resource advantage. One respondent stated, "it is easier for big business to get their voice heard," whereas another reasoned, "large businesses have more knowledge about the industry and the topic of the rule." However, there were those with a

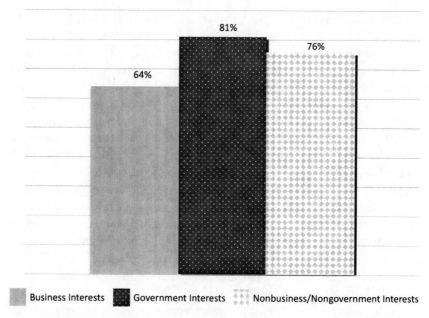

Figure 11.3. Big Business and Corporations Advantage During Rulemaking

different point of view, stating that "corporations or businesses do not have an advantage," whereas another respondent stated that businesses *should* influence DOT rules because they are likely to be most affected by them. Figure 11.3 breaks the findings down by subpopulation. Government interests were the most likely to agree that big businesses and corporations have an advantage during rulemaking at a rate of 81 percent. Nonbusiness/nongovernment interests were also high at 76 percent; business interests were lowest at 64 percent.

IS RULEMAKING CAPTURED?

Thus far, I have examined the testable expectations derived from the first prong of the agency capture test. I studied participation and influence patterns, reasoning that if broad and clear influence across rules or agencies by business interests could not be established, then there would be little need to activate the second prong of the test. In short, I asserted that influence was a necessary but not sufficient condition for agency capture. However, I do not find clear evidence of influence across rulemaking; indeed, the findings presented suggest a mixed picture of subpopulation participation and influence.

To summarize, businesses are the largest participants across the sample rules in these data, but as I showed earlier, business interest lobbying does not dominate across all sample rules, nor does it appear to dominate the rulemaking of particular agencies (at least the top three rule-writing agencies studied). In terms of influence, I completed two different assessments of potential business interest influence. Although suggestive in nature, the analyses put forward evidence that businesses are not consistently influential. Moreover, their preferences appear to be advanced more often when other business-related commenters also participate within a particular rule stage. Put in different words, business influence appears to decrease as other subpopulations' participation increases. The results also suggest that government interests may be a foil to business interests. I find, for instance, that government interests – which in the sample are largely state DOT officials – show up as the modal category of *ex parte* lobbying participants. Moreover, they perceive their comments to be the most successful of the subpopulation groups, and correlation analysis suggests that government interests may be well positioned to obtain their desired rule changes at certain times during rulemaking. In contrast, nonbusiness/nongovernment interests hold no clear advantage in participation or influence in these data.

Given these mixed results, I do not activate the second prong of the test. Stated differently, I do not look for evidence of subpopulation "control" over agency decision making in these data. Yet this decision may be shortsighted. Although Sabatier,[79] Gormley,[80] and particularly Berry[81] see the public or representatives of the public interest (operationalized most closely in this chapter as nonbusiness/nongovernment interest) as a critical bulwark against regulatory capture, I find no such discussion in the capture literature with regard to subnational government officials serving as a deterrent to capture. Indeed, the broader literature rarely studies the lobbying efforts of subnational officials on federal government policymaking,[82] and particularly the bureaucracy. However, it may be that business interests have also captured those subnational agency officials who lobby for policy change. If such a pattern of influence exists, then there would be a clear and convincing need to pursue the second prong of the capture test.

[79] Sabatier, "Social Movements and Regulatory Agencies."
[80] Gormley, "Alternative Models of the Regulatory Process."
[81] Berry, "An Alternative to the Capture Theory of Regulation."
[82] Donald H. Haider, *When Governments Come to Washington: Governors, Mayors, and Intergovernmental Lobbying* (New York: The Free Press, 1974); Anne Marie Cammisa, *Governments as Interest Groups: Intergovernmental Lobbying and the Federal System* (Westport, CT: Praeger, 1995).

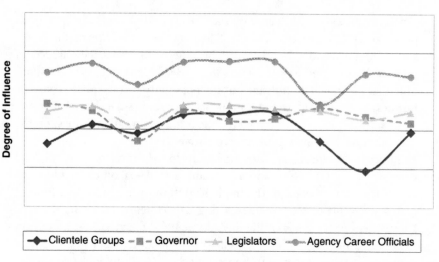

Figure 11.4. Influence Factors on State Rules and Regulations

I provide some leverage on this testable implication by utilizing a wholly separate dataset – in this case, data drawn from the American states – to perform several additional analyses. More specifically, I study the 2004 ASAP data, which queries state agency heads about the influence of clientele groups on the generation of their rules and regulations. Although clientele groups do not align perfectly to business interests, these data provide the opportunity to investigate whether select organized interests hold high levels of influence over state agency heads, especially state DOT officials. The survey question wording is: "In making various agency decisions it is usually possible to identify and weigh several major sources of influence. Among these are: (1) governor, (2) legislators, (3) state courts, (4) clientele groups, (5) professional associations and (6) agency career officials. Please indicate below (by circling) the degree of influence each source has on decisions your agency makes in the following decision areas." Agency heads were asked to respond about multiple decisions, including "Agency Rule/Regulations," on the following scale: 0, none; 1, slight; 2, moderate; and 3, high influence.

I present the results broken out by nine agency categories in Figure 11.4. Several patterns stand out. First, among transportation agencies, clientele group influence on agency rules and regulation registers closest to "slight" on the four-point scale and is, relatively speaking, much lower than the influence of state legislators, the governor, or career agency officials on rules. Second, when comparing clientele group influence across agency types, clientele group influence on state DOTs ranks near the bottom of all policy areas. Third, patterns in the 2004 data are not an aberration. ASAP survey administrators found consistent patterns on this same question in their other survey efforts (in 1978, 1984, 1988, 1994, and 1998).[83] I should note that these data do not rule out the possibility that clientele groups or business interests hold excessive influence over some state DOT agencies or some subnational officials. However, the findings do call into question the generalizability of this argument across state DOTs.

Subnational officials are often called on to help implement the federal rules issued by U.S. DOT, and as a result, state DOT officials hold critical information relevant to the implementation of federal policy. Indeed, many of the major federal rule-writing departments, including the U.S. Department of Interior and the Environmental Protection Agency, rely on their state government partners to help implement federal rules.[84] Thus it may come as little surprise to find state officials actively lobbying during rule formation. Indeed, these results correspond with Nugent's[85] findings, which suggest that state and local officials today use a strategy of constructive engagement with the federal government. Nugent[86] wrote that one way this constructive engagement occurs is through state officials participating in federal agency rule development. He reasoned that subnational officials often bring needed expertise and experience to federal policy implementation decision making. Given their access to technical information and data, subnational officials may provide a previously underappreciated deterrent to agency capture during regulatory policymaking.

CONCLUSION

In this chapter I set out to reconsider the agency capture thesis within the context of modern rulemaking. I define capture and put forward a

---

[83] See Cheryl M. Miller and Deil S. Wright, "Who's Minding Which Store? Institutional and Other Actors' Influence on Administrative Rulemaking in State Agencies, 1978–2004," *Public Administration Quarterly* 33 (2008): 397–428.

[84] Other research shows subnational officials moving beyond their role as implementers of federal regulatory policy to a position of regulatory innovator and policymaker on issues for which the federal government has either refused or failed to act [e.g., J.R. DeShazo and Jody Freeman, "Timing and Form of Federal Regulation: The Case of Climate Change," *University of Pennsylvania Law Review* 155 (2007): 1499–561].

[85] John D. Nugent, *Safeguarding Federalism: How States Protect Their Interests in National Policymaking* (Norman, OK: University of Oklahoma Press, 2009).

[86] Nugent, *Safeguarding Federalism.*

two-prong test for it. I apply the test to a dataset of thirty-six U.S. DOT rules with a focus on subpopulation differences in participation and influence. I find, in short, that business interests often participate at a high rate and hold influence over particular agency rules. However, this influence is not consistent across rulemakings or agencies. I also uncover evidence that the participation of subnational agency officials in rulemaking may provide a foil to business interests and thus may deter agency capture. In the end, I do not uncover evidence of wide-scale capture in these data.[87] It is especially noteworthy that this conclusion materializes from analysis of a sample of rules completed during a Republican administration, when one might expect business interests to be better positioned to obtain desired regulatory changes.

The data employed here – although rich in terms of knowledge about these thirty-six rules – are limited in several important ways and thus restrict the generalizability of the conclusions. I suggest three key limitations here. First, the rules all began with an ANPRM procedure, which limits the generalizability to federal rulemaking. Second, although nine agencies are included, all of these agencies reside within U.S. DOT, which may be less prone to agency capture than other agencies, particularly those with an express consumer-oriented mission.[88] Moreover, U.S. DOT may attract more subnational officials as lobbying participants than in some other agencies, given the tradition of state DOTs playing a role in implementing federal regulations. Third, as Golden[89] wrote, there is often variety in the messages sent by businesses within agency rulemaking. It may be that a more fine-grained treatment of variations in business interest lobbying is necessary to capture influence over agency decision making.

It is clear that more work is needed to fully understand the theory of agency capture and to appreciate its applicability (if at all) to federal agency rulemaking. Fruitful paths for future research may include a sample from across multiple federal departments, including independent agencies, and a more fine-grained collection of data on the lobbying desires of particular interests. Additionally, although I interviewed fifteen agency officials as part of the study, I did not collect information on the topic of agency capture

---

[87] Here is it worth stating the obvious: a more relaxed definition of capture – one in which influence and not control may identify the construct, or one that focuses on a particular rule or rules and not aggregate-level patterns across multiple rules – may return a different conclusion. Alternatively, a different conceptualization of capture, such as the one put forward by Kwak in his stimulating chapter (Chapter 4), may return different results.

[88] See Barkow, "Insulating Agencies."

[89] Golden, "Interest Groups in the Rule-Making Process."

(and in reviewing my lengthy transcripts from those interviews, the general topic never came up). Thus I was not able to evaluate whether regulatory officials actively or even strategically encourage the participation of some types of commenters over others. However, as Sabatier[90] broadly suggested, there is a tendency in the scholarly literature to see agency officials as passive actors, when in fact there are many cases in which their actions are key to understanding the politics of agency policymaking. Future work on agency capture ought to investigate this possibility during regulatory policymaking and integrate in agency officials' preferences, desires, and backgrounds.

By way of closing, I wish to reiterate the importance of clearly defining the construct of agency capture and putting forward new empirical assessments of its existence. In this book chapter, I have built on political science scholarship from three decades ago,[91] which suggests that any bias toward business and industry is exacerbated when other segments of society do not voice their concerns or advocate their preferences during regulatory decision making. Although this past scholarship uncovers the importance of citizen groups and public representatives generally, this chapter tentatively extends that focus to subnational government officials, suggesting that they, too, may play a role in countering business capture during agency rulemaking. The implications of the chapter for the design of regulatory policy and for leaders of regulatory agencies are two-fold. First, strategic agency officials may ensure greater legitimacy for their regulatory decisions when they actively encourage and engage segments of society beyond regulated entities. Indeed, even the appearance of a bias toward business during rulemaking may hold negative consequences for the agency by perpetuating the perception – if not the existence – of agency capture. Thus attempts to prevent or limit regulatory capture in practice may include reaching out directly to public interest groups and subnational officials to appraise them of future plans for agency policymaking and to encourage their participation via such traditional tools as public meetings and public commenting processes, as well as through new social media tools, including Wikis, Twitter, and Facebook. Second, although much has been said about the information asymmetries present between regulated entities and other "public" participants during rulemaking, agency officials may wish to use special administrative procedures (such as ANPRMs), activate *ex parte* or

---

[90] Sabatier, "Social Movements and Regulatory Agencies."
[91] Sabatier, "Social Movements and Regulatory Agencies"; Gormley, "Alternative Models of the Regulatory Process"; Berry, "An Alternative to the Capture Theory of Regulation."

"off the record" feedback networks, and use other regulatory design features to encourage the participation of knowledgeable subpopulations, such as state and local officials, during regulatory decision making. Doing so may provide their agencies with a competing source of high-quality information during administrative rulemaking.

12

Coalitions, Autonomy, and Regulatory Bargains in Public Health Law

Mariano-Florentino Cuéllar[1]

[W]e don't care about scientific things. We're talking dollars.[2]

In a country where approximately 450,000 people die prematurely because of tobacco and 47 million people are sickened by contaminated food each year,[3] few would dispute the relevance of public health law and policy to the overall well-being of Americans. The importance of public health looms large, even as the United States confronts a long list of structural problems ranging from reforming immigration to addressing education inequities or managing ongoing national security risks. Whether public organizations can successfully promote public health depends to a considerable degree, however, on a critical factor also shaping the nation's ability to address its other major challenges: the capacity of public organizations to execute

[1] Stanley Morrison Professor of Law, Stanford Law School; Director, Freeman Spogli Institute for International Studies. I am grateful for fine research assistance from Warner Sallman and Andy Parker and thoughtful feedback from Lawrence O. Gostin, Nathan Cortez, Jerry Mashaw, the editors of this volume, and an anonymous reviewer.
[2] "Small Processors Protest Inequities, Costs of HACCP Plan," *Food Chemical News* (June 5, 1995) (quoting meat processor criticizing new USDA rules requiring a once-daily test of production samples to assess potential pathogen contamination).
[3] Regarding foodborne illness, see Centers for Disease Control, "CDC Estimates of Foodborne Illness in the United States," February 2011, http://www.cdc.gov/foodborneburden/2011-foodborne-estimates.html (providing estimates indicating that roughly one in six Americans suffers from foodborne illness each year, of whom about 128,000 are hospitalized and 3,000 die from foodborne disease). On smoking's toll, see Centers for Disease Control, "Annual Smoking-Attributable Mortality, Years of Potential Life Lost, and Productivity Losses – United States 2000–2004," *Morbidity and Mortality Weekly Report* 57 (November 14, 2008), http://www.cdc.gov/mmwr/preview/mmwrhtml/mm5745a3.htm (also noting productivity losses attributable to cigarette smoking in the range of $100 billion per year). See also, California EPA, "Proposed Identification of Environmental Tobacco Smoke as a Toxic Air Contaminant," June 24, 2005, http://repositories.cdlib.org/tc/surveys/CALEPA2005C/.

intricate legal responsibilities without succumbing to "capture" by narrowly motivated private interests.[4]

Some actors undeniably engage with the regulatory process by crafting pointed strategies to weaken public health rules[5] or occasionally even dismissing scientific and health concerns in favor of "talking dollars."[6] In its strongest form, however, the capture thesis implies a strong claim about the efficacy of those efforts in a state that is institutionally complex and shaped by a variety of coalitions that emerge from pluralist politics. An environment in which public health officials are nonetheless all but certain victims of such capture would not only bode ill for the nation's capacity to perform a core activity of modern functioning nation-states; it would also make it difficult to expect much from bureaus working on energy policy, telecommunications, or other fields further from widespread public attention.[7]

This chapter analyzes three episodes involving the implementation of public health laws by federal government agencies in recent decades. It then connects these descriptions to a broader discussion of theories involving the so-called capture of regulatory agencies (or *regulatory capture*), as well as the evolution of the state and its laws in a democracy.[8] During the 1990s, the U.S. Department of Agriculture (USDA) sought to target foodborne pathogens through new regulatory rules, an effort that culminated with the implementation of a Hazard Analysis Critical Control Point (HACCP) framework along with a more demanding pathogen testing regime. Across town, the Food and Drug Administration (FDA) undertook an effort to assert jurisdiction over tobacco products, beginning with a major regulatory initiative in the mid-1990s. After the Supreme Court invalidated the

---

[4] In this context, the reference to capture is consistent with Carpenter's description of regulatory capture in this volume's chapter on "Detecting and Measuring Agency Capture."

[5] See Todd Lewan, "Industry Watch: Dark Secrets of Tobacco Company Exposed," *Tobacco Control* 7 (1998): 315. Strategies to undermine the legitimacy or substance of such regulation may reflect precisely the dynamic described by Carpenter in his chapter on the FDA in this volume (see Chapter 7).

[6] See *supra* note 2.

[7] Some scholars imply that the "capture" of regulatory agencies in such a fashion is common, even pervasive. See, for example, J.J. Laffont and Jean Tirole, "The Politics of Government Decision-Making: A Theory of Capture," *Quarterly Journal of Economics* 106 (1991): 1089; George Stigler, "The Theory of Economic Regulation," *Bell Journal of Economics and Management Science* 2 (1971): 3; Samuel Huntington, "The Marasmus of the ICC: The Commission, the Railroads, and the Public Interest," *The Yale Law Journal* 61 (1952): 467.

[8] As with other discussions of regulatory capture in this book, the core of the concept involves the degree of control that private interests exert over the regulatory process. If specific, narrow interests exert pervasive control over the state's regulatory functions, the legitimacy of the state itself is subject to question.

FDA regulation, the FDA and congressional allies sought statutory changes and eventually helped to enact the Family Smoking Prevention and Tobacco Control Act of 2009. Many of the epidemiological analyses informing public policy debates about tobacco and food safety, moreover, come from researchers at the Centers for Disease Control and Prevention (CDC), a once-small malaria control agency that has since grown into a sprawling organization capable of monitoring public health developments in far-flung corners of the world. The third story discusses the evolution of the CDC as its health surveillance capacity has grown and the under-appreciated role the agency plays in shaping public health responses – including some with considerable, quasi-regulatory implications for powerful economic actors in the American pluralist system of policymaking.

Two broad goals motivate my discussion of these case studies. The first is to provide some examples of how Americans today live and work in a public health context different from what existed fifty or even twenty years ago, and how agency-driven policy innovations played a major role in some of those changes. Although not always entirely successful in achieving their initial goals, political appointees and civil servants nonetheless marshaled technical information, acted as organizational entrepreneurs brokering new initiatives or areas of jurisdiction, and in some cases overcame significant resistance to break new ground in protecting public health. Each story reflects its own measure of political and legal dramas – conditions that hint at the messiness and subtlety of policymaking in our advanced industrialized democracy.[9] If that messiness sometimes produces statutes at war with themselves, such as the 1986 Immigration Reform and Control Act, or agency initiatives built to fail, such as Bureau of Alcohol, Tobacco, Firearms, and Explosives (ATF) supervision of gun dealers,[10] so too can the process yield dynamic agencies capable of protecting public health.

---

[9] Scholars in political science have sometimes described a policymaking involving competition among distinct organized interests as "pluralist." See, for example, Kenneth Prewitt, "Political Ideas and a Political Science for Policy," *Annals of the American Academy of Political and Social Science* 600 (2005): 14. Some conceptions of interest group pluralism could also be consistent with the idea that public organizations are "agents" implementing policies for "principals," such as lawmakers or, indeed, the organized interests themselves. The ideas associated with pluralism are certainly relevant to any system of governance that assigns such a prominent role to competing organized interests. My goal here is to show nonetheless why the conventional notion of pluralism needs to be balanced by an appreciation of the surprisingly important role that agencies themselves can play in shaping their political environment.

[10] On IRCA, see Mariano-Florentino Cuéllar, "The Political Economies of Immigration Law," *UC Irvine Law Review* 2 (2012): 101, and John Skrentny and Micah Gell-Redman, "Comprehensive Immigration Reform and the Dynamics of Statutory Entrenchment," *The Yale Law Journal Online* 120 (2011): 325. On ATF's problems, see Daniel C. Richman,

These examples complicate, at least in the public health context, the idea that agencies are largely powerless in overcoming external resistance to policy innovations capable of advancing social welfare. This conclusion matters not only for its analytical implications contravening some of the more aggressive versions of the now-commonplace "agency capture" theory.[11] It also matters because some capacity for policymaking *not* driven by private interests in the public sphere is an important – indeed, probably indispensable – component of the state's legitimacy and security. Little wonder that American courts confronting fundamental questions about the proper organization of administrative governance routinely emphasize the ideal of engaging actors outside government in the regulatory process without permitting wholesale delegations of state power to private actors.[12]

Second, I develop some preliminary ideas about how these agencies advanced significant public health efforts despite a political economy

---

"'Project Exile' and the Allocation of Federal Law Enforcement Authority," *Arizona Law Review* 43 (2001): 369.

[11] Some observers may even believe that a strong form of "regulatory capture" (e.g., involving sufficiently powerful influence by a narrow economic interest to render regulatory activity essentially injurious to the public interest) is pervasive. Even when scholars are not convinced that existing regulatory policies harm the public (relative to the absence of such regulations), they may nonetheless believe some form of regulatory capture to be the norm. For just one example of a recent claim by a scholar testifying before a congressional committee that agency capture is "pervasive," see "Testimony of Sidney A. Shapiro, Center for Progressive Reform, Before the Subcommittee on Administrative Oversight and the Courts, Committee on the Judiciary," U.S. Senate (August 3, 2010) (describing "agency capture" as one of "the most significant causes" of agencies' failure to achieve their statutory missions). See also Center for Progressive Reform, "Industry's 'Capture' of Federal Agencies Pervasive as Regulatory Failures Pile Up, Administrative Law Expert Tells Congressional Panel" (August 3, 2010), http://www.progressivereform.org/articles/Shapiro_AgencyCapture_NR_080310.pdf.

[12] See, for example, *A.L.A. Schechter Poultry Corp. v. United States*, 295 U.S. 495 (1935) (underscoring judicial concern over broad delegations of public authority to private parties); *Sangamon Valley Television Corp. v. United States*, 269 F.2d 221 (D.C. Cir. 1959) (*ex parte* contacts forbidden in a formal rulemaking proceeding where the FCC is deciding on the method through which valuable television licenses would be transferred). It is telling that even in the context of "informal" notice and comment rulemaking, a setting where agencies ordinarily have considerable flexibility to structure the process through which private interests are consulted in setting regulatory policy, courts have occasionally set limits on the extent of agency *ex parte* contact with private interests during rulemaking proceedings. See, for example, *Home Box Office v. FCC*, 567 F.2d 9 (D.C. Cir. 1977) (personal meetings, dinners, and Christmas turkeys provided by the president of a station with an interest in the outcome of the proceedings raised fundamental questions about the integrity of regulatory proceedings involving pay cable television rules). In some respects, this decision is an example of the role a court can assume in seeking to reduce the risk of many forms of corrosive regulatory capture. For additional insights on the judiciary's potential role in reducing risks of capture, see Elizabeth Magill's chapter on the judiciary in this volume (Chapter 14).

context that did not favor their work. Although these insights are necessarily tentative because of the comparison set and the scope of the project,
I gain some leverage from the similarities and differences in the cases discussed here. I also include occasional comparisons to other contexts such
as immigration and domestic security.

In comparison to immigration and domestic security agencies, for example, the public health agencies discussed here were able to leverage a lens of
scientific competence and technical expertise associated with public concerns over health. Even if one does not essentialize scientific expertise as a
quality relevant to public health but not public safety, it seems clear that a
reputation for scientific decisions is not something the perpetually controversial federal ATF can depend on in the same way that the FDA or the CDC
can.[13] The CDC's capacity to affect federal policy on consumer warnings
regarding aspirin, one of the country's most ubiquitous pharmaceutical
products, arises in no small measure from a reputation for competence and
technical efficacy respected both within the government and beyond it.[14]
Such reputational capital does not invariably deliver success to an agency,
and some agencies with public health responsibilities, such as USDA, have
less of it to deploy.[15] Yet all three of the agencies discussed here leveraged a
public health mission of considerable interest to private doctors and soccer
moms capable of offsetting, in contingent but nonetheless potentially significant ways, the concentrated interests conventionally presumed to capture
agencies.

Complementing their capacity to leverage concern over health, the agencies here appeared to benefit from broad statutory mandates allowing officials to craft initiatives they could promote with the larger public to shape
the nation's broader policy agenda. Although few statutes ever confer on

[13] On the Bureau of Alcohol, Tobacco, and Firearms, see Richman, *supra* note 10. Regarding
the challenges of immigration agencies in building legitimacy and a reputation for competence with the public, see Cuéllar, Political Economies, *supra* note 10. But note that in
certain circumstances, when lawmakers are divided and the relevant issue has relatively
low public salience, immigration authorities have also exercised a measure of flexibility
by issuing explicit policies governing enforcement discretion. Before the advent of legislative provisions governing Temporary Protected Status, for example, the Immigration and
Naturalization Service used extended voluntary departure where individuals subject to
removal faced removal to countries affected by a natural disaster or war. See Deborah Per-
luss & Joan F. Hartman, "Temporary Refuge: Emergence of a Customary Norm," *Virginia
Journal of International Law*, 26 (1986): 551.

[14] See *infra* notes 73–84, discussing the development of the Centers for Disease Control
(CDC).

[15] As used here, the term "reputational capital" refers to the reservoir of support among
opinion leaders and the public on which an agency may draw in explaining, justifying, and assembling coalitions in support of a particular policy intervention or innovation.

agencies the near-limitless authority they may occasionally crave, far-reaching statutory authority well suited to initial agency innovation without direct engagement from Congress is contained in the Food, Drug, and Cosmetic Act; the Federal Meat Inspection Act; and the Public Health Service Act. Even when agencies do not ultimately succeed in achieving all their public health goals under existing laws, expansive statutes that do not need to be reauthorized (reflecting in part lawmakers' decisions to delegate authority over areas perceived to involve intricate scientific judgment) often gave agencies a plausible legal basis to initiate action rather than simply reacting to Congress and the White House. Expansive legal authority also helped agencies tie new or continuing efforts to previously legitimized work and probably made it easier for agencies to forge alliances (though sometimes after the initial push for policy changes) with political appointees concerned about precedents and about the viability of agencies' legal positions.

With a capacity to leverage reputations for technical competence, concern over public health, alliances with political appointees, and broad legal authority, agencies broke new ground in protecting the public health. What the agencies did *not* do was achieve complete freedom from external constraints. Agencies must still operate in a context of representative democracy that forces them to make successful alliances with civil society and the public if they are to succeed in shaping politicians' incentives for interfering. Government lawyers square off in high-stakes litigation against well-financed adversaries contesting agency legal interpretations (the tobacco industry team that took on the FDA's interpretation of the Food, Drug, and Cosmetic Act included every living former FDA Chief Counsel). Although agencies with overlapping jurisdiction may occasionally compete in asserting regulatory authority, the fragmentation of agency jurisdiction can also increase the cost of policy change and give external actors multiple bites at the policymaking apple. What the long arc of public health law and policy offers, however, is a reminder that soccer moms and public health researchers can matter in the scheme of writing and implementing statutes, and that nothing in the end is a foregone conclusion in an institutionally rich, pluralist democracy.

ANALYTICAL FOUNDATIONS: INSTITUTIONAL CONSTRAINTS AND PARTIAL AUTONOMY

American public health depends not only on social behavior and market activity but also on the laws and institutions that structure those activities.[16]

---

[16] See generally Lawrence O. Gostin, Scott Burris, and Zita Lazzarini, "The Law and the Public's Health: A Study of Infectious Disease Law in the United States," *Columbia Law Review* 99 (1999): 1, 59, 64 (discussing a "behavioral model" of public health focusing

The probability of finding that a patty of ground beef grilled on the Fourth of July includes an undesired side order of deadly *Escherichia coli* 0157:H7 depends in no small measure on the successes and limitations of a system of governance linking lawmakers, agency and executive branch officials, civil society, and economic interests. And within that system, public health regulatory agencies face something of a paradox.

With one hand our laws entrust to agencies the power to protect public health and security. With another, though, laws embed those agencies in a political economy of constraints and influence routinely threatening to restrain, paralyze, or distort their ostensible mission.[17] Together, these dynamics can frustrate agencies' pursuit of a host of defensible public health measures ranging from stricter food defense standards to measures against the marketing of alcohol to minors. Indeed, because agencies face such constraints and the (economic and political) stakes are so high, some observers claim it is all but impossible for an agency to avoid being essentially "captured" by private interests with a stake in the agency's work. As one commentator recently put it, "[r]egulatory capture is the process by which the regulators of an industry come to view it through the eyes of its principal actors, and to equate the public interest with the financial stability of these actors."[18] Moreover, "[e]ven the regulator with the best intentions comes to see issues in much the same way as the corporate officers he deals with every day."[19] Problems may still arise when policymakers harbor starkly different views from those prevalent in the private sector, because agencies may lack the capacity to resist constraints imposed on them (whether directly or through legal or political institutions) by interested parties. If, even in a context as directly relevant to people's lives, agencies systematically are incapable of separating private interests from sensible public health goals, then the legitimacy of the nation-state itself is undermined.

To assess these arguments, one must first acknowledge that agencies operating in our system (and indeed, in virtually any legal and policy system) face a variety of political and legal constraints on their action. The term itself runs the risk of casting aside distinctions between senior political

---

   on behaviors that produce exposure to pathogens or illness and death, and an "ecological model . . . seeking the causes of disease in how society organizes itself").

[17]   In this context, "political economy" refers to the mix of institutions, actors, and incentives that combine to make particular policy outcomes more or less likely to emerge.

[18]   John Kay, "Better a Distant Judge than a Pliant Regulator," *Financial Times* (November 3, 2010): 13.

[19]   John Kay, "Better a Distant Judge."

appointees, career civil servants in prominent positions, and lower-level employees engaged in routine tasks.[20] Lawmakers and senior executive branch officials often seek to, and sometimes succeed in, controlling agencies or at least restricting their capacity to pursue new initiatives. Private actors can discourage agency action. And few if any agencies – even those with formal juridical independence from direct political control – can operate for long without depending on congressional appropriations, esteem from opinion leaders, or some outside measure of support. Given these relationships between public organizations (including public health agencies) and the outside world, whatever capacity for independent policy innovation agencies achieve is probably best understood as "partial" autonomy from external political or economic actors rather than absolute independence.

Partial autonomy is epitomized by a situation in which available evidence indicates that external parties do not design or uniformly support a major new agency policy. Instead, agency officials take the principal role in achieving significant legal or policy changes, despite the initial opposition or indifference from political leaders and interest group dynamics that do not – by themselves – explain the outcome. Agencies may be able to mobilize coalitions of support among sympathetic policymakers, opinion leaders, and civil society organizations. Such coalitions can allow an agency to make the most of scarce resources such as legal authority, budgets, and agency officials' capacity to bolster a bureau's reputation through persuasive communication with the larger public. Despite the fact that agencies are neither unitary actors nor impervious to opposition from inside government or beyond it, they can form coalitions and deploy their resources strategically to become powerful actors in law and policy – actors whose choices may shape some of the state's fundamental attributes.

At the same time, agencies are also themselves shaped by certain larger attributes of the state, including the details of the legal scheme implemented to govern administrative action. In particular, public health agencies' capacity for innovation implicates the management of a certain tension present in

---

[20] Although these distinctions are important to acknowledge and help explain some of the strategies pursued by individuals within public organizations, the idea that "agencies" as organizations are capable of driving policy may still be a useful metaphor in many cases. The concept is particularly apt when an agency's senior political leadership cements a motivated coalition of civil servants, overcomes potential opposition from agency rank-and-file employees, and is able to use reputational and bureaucratic resources throughout the agency to achieve policy changes such as expanded health surveillance activity or a new regulatory rule modifying food safety requirements.

the legal regimes governing many advanced industrialized democracies,[21] but captured by two doctrinal strands in American administrative law. One strand is prominent in the landmark *Schechter Poultry* decision, in which an expansive New Deal–era delegation of authority from lawmakers ran afoul not only because of the relatively unconstrained nature of the statutory scheme, but also because the authority ultimately was exercised by private actors with an economic stake in regulatory policy. Even long after *Schechter*'s overarching non-delegation holding has been eviscerated, existing doctrine continues to emphasize the importance of agency independence from private interests in decisions such as those governing agency *ex parte* communications or the requirement of reasoned decision making.[22] At the same time, however, public consultation and participation – including by private actors with economic stakes in a particular regulatory decision – remain a core elements of the administrative law framework governing agency action. The default expectation that prevails in federal and even state administrative law is that agencies need to be sensitive to external concerns.[23] Exceptions (e.g., those involving military or foreign affairs functions) are construed narrowly, and courts may withdraw deference to agency legal interpretations of the type that figure so prominently in agency policymaking innovations when regulators fail to comply with procedural rules requiring external consultation.[24]

As public agencies discharge their functions, it is easy to see how they end up facing considerable challenges in threading the needle between avoiding excessive external control of the kind posited by capture theory and

---

[21] Cf. Frank Johnson Goodnow, *Comparative Administrative Law* (Clark, NJ: The Lawbook Exchange, 2006).

[22] See *Action for Children's Television v. FCC*, 852 F.2d 1332 (D.C. Cir. 1988) (discussing *ex parte* communications); *Motor Vehicle Manufacturers Association v. State Farm Mutual Automobile Insurance Company*, 463 U.S. 29 (1983) (discussing the role of reasoned decision making by agencies in the context of determining whether a change in a regulatory rule was "arbitrary and capricious").

[23] See generally *Portland Cement Association v. Ruckelshaus*, 486 F.2d 375, 393 (D.C. Cir. 1973), cert. denied, 417 U.S. 921 (1974); see also Ronald M. Levin, "Nonlegislative Rules and the Administrative Open Mind," *Duke Law Journal* 41 (1992): 1497, 1501 n.19 (citing *Portland Cement Association v. Ruckelshaus*); Jerry L. Mashaw and David L. Harfst, "Regulation and Legal Culture: The Case of Motor Vehicle Safety," *The Yale Journal on Regulation* 4 (1987): 257, 282 (agencies must respond to all serious dimensions of the problem raised in comments). State administrative law provisions also sometimes emphasize the importance of obtaining input from diverse parties affected by the decision. See, for example, Michael Asimow and Marsha Cohen, *California Administrative Law* (Eagan, MN: West Group: 2002).

[24] See *United States v. Mead Data Corp.*, 533 U.S. 218 (2001).

engaging in sufficient public consultation.[25] At least in the public health context, however, the conventional regulatory capture concept may turn out to be a poor guide to how agencies manage these dilemmas. Agencies capable of making appeals to technical competence and scientific expertise – particularly on matters of relatively widespread public concern – may develop an enhanced capacity to manage relationships with organized interests, civil society, and the larger public from a position of strength relative to other agencies or organizations shaping the policy process.[26] Agencies may also benefit from a relatively simple-to-articulate connection of their mandate to domains of human health that, at least in principle, evoke universalistic, valence-oriented concerns rather than economically or culturally contested issues that permeate the jurisdiction of other agencies – even where in principle such agencies also have missions profoundly connected to human health.[27]

Historical examples offer at least a prima facie basis for presuming that certain significant past developments in public health fail to fit with the conventional regulatory capture story.[28]

Even beyond what is relevant to public health agencies, conventional capture theory does not devote much sustained attention to the nuances that might distinguish situations in which agencies legitimately seek public input. If anything, the following examples from the public health context show agencies fulfilling their legal responsibilities to incorporate external input while still (and largely independently) driving a process of policy

[25] Admittedly, defining precisely the normatively undesirable state of affairs described in this volume as "regulatory capture" is particularly challenging in light of statutory provisions and legal decisions requiring agencies to incorporate input from interested parties. Observers must make subtle distinctions to differentiate the phenomenon of "weak" regulatory capture described by Carpenter in the chapter on "Detecting and Measuring Capture" (see Chapter 3) from the routine incorporation of feedback from external interested parties that the law permits and sometimes even requires. That said, it is possible to raise questions about the allegedly pervasive nature of relatively strong forms of capture by identifying situations where private economic interests resisted, and ultimately sought to undermine without success, the policy innovations of public agencies.

[26] Cf. Daniel Carpenter, *Reputation and Power* (Princeton: Princeton University Press, 2010); Sheila Jasanoff, "Science's Influence," *Issues in Science and Technology* 27 (2010): 9.

[27] Hence a possible distinction between the EPA and ATF, on the one hand, and the CDC on the other.

[28] Cf. Centers for Disease Control and Prevention, "Ten Great Public Health Achievements – United States, 1900–1990," *Morbidity and Mortality Weekly Report* 48 (December 24, 1999): 1141.

innovation often pivoting on using their existing broad legal jurisdiction.[29] Indeed, public input probably helped the agencies anticipate and in some cases mollify opposition. At a minimum, these examples suggest that the legally regulated endeavor of obtaining broad public input can coexist with another dynamic – one rooted in legal and policy concerns about the value of independence – whereby public organizations resist control and develop significant public health reforms.

Given the questions raised by the preceding discussion of regulatory capture, we can proceed to take a closer look at certain features of the modern American public health system. The episodes that follow are worth discussing in particular because they represent significant changes in the public health system, implicating different agencies with distinct domains of jurisdiction and expertise. To shed further light on the relationship between these developments and the political–economic system that shapes much of American policymaking, we should focus particularly on three factors: (1) whether policy innovation was driven purely by external political or economic actors, (2) whether the agencies encountered conflict with private actors, and (3) what emerged from those conflicts, and in particular what tools agencies used to protect their legal jurisdiction and advance their policy commitments. Precisely how and with what consequences agencies have been able to overcome the impediments to significant policy innovation in the realm of public health are addressed in the case studies described next.

FOOD SAFETY AND THE RENEGOTIATION OF REGULATORY BARGAINS

Americans consume a staggering 233 lbs per capita of meat each year, creating an equally staggering challenge for regulators entrusted to keep that supply of meat relatively safe.[30] Accordingly, the officials who run the U.S. Department of Agriculture's Food Safety Inspection Service (FSIS) face the nearly impossible task of assuring the safety of the nation's supply of meat and poultry, as well as a number of specific products such as meat-topped pizza and processed egg products. Together with the FDA, which is

---

[29] See *supra* note 16. But see *Center for Auto Safety v. Peck*, 751 F.2d 1336, 1355 n.15 (D.C. Cir. 1985) ("An agency need not address every conceivable issue or alternative, no matter how remote or insignificant.").

[30] American Meat Institute, "Meat and Poultry Production and Consumption" (Fact Sheet, 2009).

responsible for protecting the other 80 percent or so of the food supply, the FSIS constitutes the core of the country's food safety capacity.

In contrast to the FDA, however, the FSIS until recently discharged its role in meat and poultry safety primarily through continuous inspection of carcasses. Federal meat inspection legislation dates from 1890, when lawmakers enacted a statute conferring on USDA the role of safeguarding that American meat exports met standards for import to the European market.[31] Protecting the food supply by examining carcasses was perhaps a plausible compromise then and in 1906, when the Federal Meat Inspection Act was passed. By the last quarter of the twenty-first century, however, the classic USDA inspection scheme – with carcass-level visual inspection as its linchpin – was highly problematic. Consumption of poultry products, which were cheaper and had lower fat compared with beef, had increased starkly since the middle of the twentieth century. Whereas processors had slaughtered just under 150 million chickens in the entire year of 1940, by the end of the 1980s the industry was slaughtering roughly 100 million chickens during a single week.[32] Meat consumption overall also swelled because of the expanding popularity of fast-food restaurants and the growing acceptance of processed and frozen foods using meat ingredients.[33] Congress and the agency worked in tandem between the 1960s and the 1980s to address the situation with several initiatives and legislative reforms, including establishing a voluntary "Total Quality Control" program giving inspectors access to more of an establishment's production records and explicit authority for FSIS to calibrate the frequency and thoroughness of inspections of a plant based on its history of sanitation violations.[34]

Even with these changes and a growing staff physically deployed at every establishment operating (as required by law), USDA inspection methods were increasingly difficult to adapt to faster, higher volume processing activities. Indeed, the primary mode of regulation presupposed by the statutory framework governing meat and poultry inspection – involving the continuous presence of FSIS inspectors at meat processing establishments – blurred

---

[31] "Pathogen Reduction: Hazard Analysis and Critical Control Point (HACCP) Systems," 60 Fed. Reg. 6775, 6775 (1995) (to be codified at 9 C.F.R. §§ 308, 310, 318, 320, 325, 326, 327, and 381) (proposed February 3, 1995).

[32] See James A. Albert, "A History of Attempts by the Department of Agriculture to Reduce Federal Inspection of Poultry Processing Plants – A Return to the Jungle," *Louisiana Law Review* 51 (1991): 1183, 1184.

[33] See, for example, "Pathogen Reduction," 60 Fed. Reg. at 6776–77.

[34] See "Pathogen Reduction."

the lines of responsibility between government and industry with respect to limiting safety problems.[35] Even more important, the central food safety concerns involved contamination by microscopic pathogens such as *Listeria*, *E. coli* O157:H7, and *Salmonella*. The relevance of laboratory testing raised further questions about an inspection and processing regime that did not allow products to be routinely held in abeyance while awaiting results.

Those questions became more prominent during the 1980s and early 1990s. A series of incidents occurred involving contaminated meat products, particularly involving the aggressive strain of *E. coli* 0157:H7. The National Academy of Sciences issued a report criticizing USDA's all but completely constrained capacity to address pathogen-related risks that did not involve obvious sanitation violations.[36] The highest profile incident involved contaminated meat made available by Jack-in-the-Box restaurants that killed several people and poisoned 500.[37] Although the Jack-in-the-Box *E. coli* outbreak in California, Idaho, Washington, and Nevada heightened public concern about food safety regulation, such concern did not coalesce around an explicit set of regulatory reforms or statutory changes. Early discussions about possible reforms nonetheless featured some private actors who voiced, at various points in the implementation process, cautious support for changes in meat inspection, joining consumer groups in raising questions about the viability of existing arrangements.[38]

The increasingly poor fit between its prevailing inspection methods and the agency's articulation of its organizational goals galvanized action at FSIS and culminated in what has come to be known as the Hazard Analysis and Critical Control Points (HACCP) rule. The HACCP rule is an elaborate new management-based regulatory regime that placed responsibility on food processors to identify critical control points that could be used to detect and reduce pathogen contamination. Companies would need to develop plans to respond if problems arose and were subject to testing and verification by

---

[35] See "Pathogen Reduction," 60 Fed. Reg., 6785.
[36] Some sanitation violations were indeed obvious, involving (for example) the reuse of spoiled pork or meats that had fallen to the floor of food processing facilities. The NAS report underscored, however, that a potentially vast problem involving pathogen contamination was largely beyond the purview of existing USDA regulatory rules. See, for example, National Academy of Sciences, *Meat and Poultry Inspection: The Scientific Basis of the Nation's Program, Committee on the Scientific Basis of the Nation's Meat and Poultry Inspection Program* (Washington, D.C.: National Academy Press, 1985).
[37] See, for example, "Bacterial Sickness Hits Dozens of Children," *Seattle Post-Intelligencer* (January 18, 1993): B-1.
[38] See, for example, William McAllister, "Recipe for Food Safety Starts from Scratch," *Washington Post* (February 15, 1996).

FSIS. Thus, instead of remaining an organization focused on inspecting meat carcasses, FSIS became at least partially geared to certifying and auditing private sector management plans implementing HACCP.[39]

When then-Assistant Secretary Michael Taylor and his staff set about transforming meat inspection, the agency could deploy broad but by no means unlimited legal authority.[40] In adapting early twentieth-century statutes to problems of pathogen contamination, the agency deployed novel legal arguments lashing up new private sector responsibilities for preventing contamination to established statutory and legal concepts such as "adulteration." The HACCP rule, for example, treated failure to comply with HACCP requirements (either arising from an unsatisfactory plan for a given establishment or from failure of an establishment to comply with the plan itself) as de facto adulteration.

Shepherding the rule through the regulatory process was not an easy task. The process through which USDA shepherded the new regulatory rule including HACCP and pathogen-testing requirements to completion illustrates both the opposition it engendered as well as some of the varied sources of political support on which the agency drew. After initially leveraging an early consensus including meat processors and some consumer groups regarding the value of HACCP, USDA officials increasingly encountered controversy over the precise content of the new regulatory rule.[41] The most intense controversy focused on whether the new rule should include demanding new standards governing the presence of pathogens in processing facilities.[42] Such pathogen standards constituted a considerable break from past practices for USDA, however, given the previously existing

---

[39] Because of the prominent role of plans developed by the private sector itself in the HACCP system, this approach incorporates elements that may be seen by some as cutting against state capacity and authority. Crucially, however, HACCP also incorporated a pathogen testing regime and other features designed to assess the efficacy of industry-generated plans.

[40] Taylor had earlier served as a lawyer representing the agricultural company Monsanto and, after leaving the USDA, became a senior official at the company. His career illustrates the complexities inherent in disentangling the consequences of the so-called revolving door between some public- and private-sector positions. When Taylor was later named to a new position in the FDA during the Obama administration, some food safety advocates lauded the appointment, whereas civil society groups promoting organic foods criticized it. See Gardiner Harris, "New Official Named with Portfolio to Unite Agencies and Improve Food Safety," *The New York Times* (January 14, 2010).

[41] See "HACCP 'Mega Reg.' Withdrawal Urged by Meat and Poultry Groups," *Food Chemical News* (August 28, 1995), available at 1995 WL 8215906.

[42] See, for example, "Industry Criticized by SFC for Efforts to Delay, Kill USDA HACCP," *Food Chemical News* (June 5, 1995), available at 1995 WL 8215430.

approach to meat safety inspection and the nature of the legal provisions governing USDA authority in this area.[43]

The controversy over the new pathogen-testing requirements had delayed the new regulatory rule for a considerable period. Even several years after the Jack-in-the-Box imbroglio that had galvanized public attention, USDA was still working on finalizing the new provisions. From the perspective of USDA's officials, regular testing for the presence of *E. coli* and *Salmonella* pathogens would play a critical role in validating the extent to which industry establishments were successfully carrying out their responsibilities under a HACCP regime. In particular, USDA officials determined that the situation warranted a regime linking the new HACCP requirements to testing for *E. coli* and *Salmonella*. To adapt the testing regime to the existing statute, USDA declared these pathogens "adulterants" – a term of art if there ever was one.[44] Although some consumer groups supported the more expansive approach USDA sought to take, the agency encountered swelling opposition from industry representatives eager to avoid a scenario subjecting their operations to strict pathogen standards.[45] As expectations built that USDA would finally issue the new regulatory rule bundling HACCP with the new pathogen standards, some lawmakers from the House Agriculture Committee sought to force the agency into a compromise with industry.[46]

Meanwhile, USDA was facing a leadership transition. Secretary Michael Espy had already departed, and incoming Secretary-Designate Dan Glickman had yet to be confirmed. The leadership of FSIS within USDA sought support from Glickman, however, and he signaled a willingness to back the agency's approach. So did the White House, where the staff of Vice President Gore among others had begun to follow the developments at USDA. By the

---

[43] Although that authority did provide, in USDA's analysis, sufficient legal justification for instituting the new pathogen-testing regime, there is little doubt that the agency would have designed the statute differently if it had been writing a new statute to govern the program at the time. Compare *supra* note 31 (USDA argument discussing the scope of statutory authority to implement HACCP under existing laws) with Denis R. Johnson and Jolyda O. Swaim, "The Food Safety and Inspection Service's Lack of Statutory Authority to Suspend Inspection for Failure to Comply with HACCP Regulations," *Journal of Food Law & Policy* 1 (2005): 337 (highlighting some of the limitations USDA faces in arguing that existing authority fully permits enforcement of HACCP regulations through suspension of inspections at food processing facilities).

[44] See *Supreme Beef Processors v. U.S. Department of Agriculture*, 275 F.3d 432 (5th Cir. 2001).

[45] See "Small Processors Protest Inequities, Costs of HACCP Plan," *Food Chemical News* (June 5, 1995), available at 1995 WL 8215441.

[46] See, for example, Dion Casey, "Agency Capture: The USDA's Struggle to Pass Food Safety Regulations," *Kansas Journal of Law & Public Policy* 7 (1998): 142; Robert Greene, "Compromise Reached on Meat Rules," *Tacoma Tribune* (July 19, 1995): A3.

time the new rule was ready, President Clinton announced it at the White House and took considerable ownership over a package of reforms that the agency had crafted over several years and drew ire from some lawmakers and industry representatives.[47]

USDA faced a variety of legal hurdles in implementing its new approach. One legal challenge insisted that the agency's preliminary determination that *E. coli* 0157:H7 was an adulterant, which the agency had initially announced informally rather than through a new regulatory rule, needed to follow a more formal regulatory process.[48] USDA prevailed by arguing that some aspects of its new approach were essentially changes in its enforcement strategy. Yet the agency faced further hurdles as it made headway in fashioning a new approach to meat and poultry inspection.

Eventually, USDA codified the amended HACCP rule in July 1996. For the first time, it required all slaughter and processing plants to adopt a series of process controls to mitigate or prevent food safety contamination risks. Each establishment was mandated to institute sanitation standard operating procedures. FSIS inspectors would hold establishments accountable in part by leveraging substantial recordkeeping requirements, shedding light on whether compliance problems existed. The establishment's overall HACCP plan needed to reflect analysis of internal activities to determine critical control points where contamination could occur. In addition, establishments needed to conduct generic *E. coli* testing and implement *Salmonella* performance standards to verify that process controls were working.

USDA's enforcement of the rule inaugurated a new chapter in the process, one that also provoked legal disputes. The agency was still hobbled by the lack of explicit enforcement provisions in the Federal Meat Inspection Act and the analogous statutory provisions governing poultry. In the absence of authority to levy fines or seize *Salmonella*-contaminated meat, USDA relied on a blunt feature of the early twentieth-century statutory scheme: no establishment could take to market meat and poultry products from an operation that did not have USDA inspectors present. Removing the inspectors would thus force the establishment to suspend operations.

Because USDA lawyers explicitly linked the removal of inspectors to HACCP violations, the agency became increasingly vulnerable to the charge that the statutory authority for inspectors did not allow them to be removed

---

[47] See "HACCP Negotiated Rulemaking Amendment Withdrawn in Compromise," *Food Chemical News* (July 24, 1995), available at 1995 WL 821585.

[48] See Casey, *supra* note 46, at n.140.

as a means of enforcing a regulatory rule comparable to the new HACCP rule. A few courts have been sympathetic to this argument, and one circuit's holding – that violation of *Salmonella* standards cannot be the basis for a per se conclusion that food is adulterated – raises doubts about whether USDA can enforce HACCP requirements simply by withdrawing inspectors.[49] Undaunted by the challenges to its preferred enforcement strategy, USDA has turned to its unquestioned authority to drastically ramp up testing for *E. coli* O157:H7 and conduct more intrusive and costly inspections if HACCP problems emerge.[50]

HACCP soon received a measure of attention from scholars and policymakers because of its focus on management and performance standards rather than, for example, deployment of technology-based regulation. The resulting flexibility appeals to some observers and at least a subset of the industry, because the structure of the rule offers the prospect of harnessing operators' private information to promote public health.[51] For present purposes, though, it is worth emphasizing that USDA's HACCP rule was starkly different from past regulation and raised compliance costs for the private sector. Indeed, at the time of its initial promulgation, the most logical comparison was not to technology-based environmental regulations but to the far less demanding regime USDA had maintained for most of its history.

The HACCP rule and its accompanying standards have created an important legacy. The evolution of foodborne illness patterns since HACCP was instituted suggests that, consistent with USDA's theoretical analysis and contemporaneous cost-benefit analyses, the rule has had a material effect on foodborne pathogens. In a two-year period following implementation of the rule, for example, the prevalence of *Salmonella* in all classes of raw meat products regulated by FSIS declined substantially and fell by as much as 50 percent in young chickens.[52] Subsequent research on *Salmonella* infection rates among the U.S. elderly indicates that the HACCP rule contributed to decreasing rates of infection.[53] In 2011, a meta-analysis of pathogen

---

[49] *Supreme Beef Processors v. U.S. Department of Agriculture*, 275 F.3d 432 .

[50] Cf. *Munsell v. Department of Agriculture*, 509 F.3d 572 (D.C. Cir. 2007).

[51] See, for example, Cary Coglianese and David Lazer, "Management-Based Regulation: Prescribing Private Management to Achieve Public Goals," *Law & Society Review* 37 (2003): 691.

[52] USDA FSIS, "Progress Report on Salmonella Testing of Raw Meat and Poultry Products, 1998–2000" (April 2000).

[53] Kenneth K.H. Chui, Patrick Webb, Robert M. Russell, and Elena N. Naumova, "Geographic Variations and Temporal Trends of Salmonella-Associated Hospitalization in the U.S. Elderly 1991–2004," *BMC Public Health* 9 (2009): 447.

contamination in slaughterhouses before and after HACCP supports the conclusion that the reforms reduced bacterial counts.[54] In succeeding years, the FDA implemented HACCP procedures similar to those implemented by USDA for seafood, fruit juices, and other foods.[55]

TOBACCO REGULATION AND THE INTERPLAY OF REGULATORY INNOVATION AND LEGISLATION

The history of public health regulation in the United States is in no small measure the history of the FDA, an agency with a vast statutory mandate to regulate medical devices, drugs, biologics, cosmetics, and food.[56] Yet for an agency whose mission is often described by lawmakers as protecting "the public health and safety of Americans," the regulatory elephant in the jurisdictional room was the agency's conspicuous failure to regulate the tobacco products that constitute the leading preventable cause of death in the United States.[57]

The FDA had occasionally considered regulating tobacco products in the long decades since passage of the Food, Drug, and Cosmetic Act (FDCA). Nonetheless, agency officials had conspicuously declined to do so for its entire history. The FDA's reluctance persisted over decades despite mounting evidence of tobacco's severely adverse health effects and a sensible argument that the provisions of the Food, Drug, and Cosmetic Act provided the agency residual power to regulate tobacco. Although the FDA had colorable legal arguments that tobacco could be regulated (e.g., as a drug delivery device), such a move would have exposed the agency to certain difficulties. Unlike drugs or medical devices – where the agency's longstanding goal was

---

[54] See Barbara Wilhelm, Andrijana Rajić, Judy D. Greig, Lisa Waddell, and Janet Harris, "The Effect of Hazard Analysis Critical Control Point Programs on Microbial Contamination of Carcasses in Abattoirs: A Systematic Review of Published Data," *Foodborne Pathogens and Disease* 8 (2011): 949. Although estimating the precise effect size of policy change is difficult in this context without random assignment, the results of this analysis and multiple additional studies in the decade and a half after HACCP was implemented are consistent with the arguments USDA advanced.

[55] See "New Rules Aim for Cleaner, Safer Seafood," *New Orleans Times-Picayune* (December 6, 1995).

[56] See Peter Barton Hutt, Richard A. Merrill, and Lewis A. Grossman, *Food and Drug Law: Cases and Materials 24–25*, 3rd ed. (New York: Foundation Press, 2007).

[57] See "Agriculture, Rural Development, Food and Drug Administration, and Related Agencies Appropriations Bill, 2006" (Senate Report No. 109-92), 109th Cong., 1st Session (2005) ("The Food and Drug Administration [FDA] is a scientific regulatory agency whose mission is to promote and protect the public health and safety of Americans.") See *supra* note 3 on tobacco's toll.

to allow only "safe and effective" products to reach the market, cigarettes and other tobacco products could not obviously be rendered safe and effective. Moreover, the vast tobacco industry, though not monolithic, had long waged aggressive efforts – particularly using litigation – against efforts to regulate tobacco.

FDA officials had periodically considered the possibility of regulating tobacco and confronted a two-fold problem. One was uncertainty about whether there was a legal basis to regulate tobacco, compounded by previous reluctance from policymakers to assert jurisdiction.[58] The other was whether the FDA could handle the political responses – including from those who questioned whether the agency had way too much to handle already, even without counting tobacco. Among the variety of obstacles the FDA and its parent agency (what is today the Department of Health and Human Services, or HHS) faced between the 1960s and 1980s was that lawmakers and presidential administrations were divided – to put it charitably – on the advisability of taking on this challenge. Contrary to some treatments of agency incentives from "public choice economics," agencies do not uniformly seek to expand their jurisdiction and indeed sometimes relish being able to tell the public that they lack authority. The Environmental Protection Agency (EPA), for example, repeatedly received rulemaking petitions advocating the regulation of greenhouse gases; the EPA's initial position was simply that it lacked jurisdiction, thereby side-stepping the complex practical and policy questions implicated in providing a substantive response.[59]

In addition, even after a surgeon general's seminal report released by Luther Terry in the 1960s, a measure of scientific uncertainty appeared to persist regarding the precise impact of cigarette smoking and tobacco in particular.[60] Scientists took decades, for example, to document the impact of second-hand smoke on health or to better understand the addictive properties of nicotine. The lack of credible findings on second-hand smoke and addiction underscored the idea that the problem of tobacco primarily involved individual responsibility, rather than severely time-inconsistent preferences or large negative externalities. In addition, prominent critics of

---

[58] For a comprehensive account, see Allan M. Brandt, *The Cigarette Century* (New York: Basic Book, 2009). See also David Kessler, *A Question of Intent: A Great American Battle with a Deadly Industry* (New York: PublicAffairs, 2001); "Developments in Policy: The FDA's Tobacco Regulations," *Yale Law and Policy Review* 15 (1996): 399, "Developments in Policy."

[59] *Massachusetts v. EPA*, 549 U.S. 497, 499 (2007).

[60] See Brandt, *The Cigarette Century.*

the FDA were emboldened by high-profile problems involving drug and food safety, such as the controversy over the FDA's regulation of generic drugs during the 1980s.[61]

As the FDA weathered those challenges, several local jurisdictions were stepping up efforts to curb smoking during the late 1980s, and civil society groups generated interest among the public by leveraging some nascent private lawsuits that were getting off the ground. Another key event in the story, however, was Reagan's Surgeon General C. Everett Koop's 1988 report on tobacco.[62] More than any other measure to stoke public attention on the issue, Koop's report galvanized interest with strong claims about the addictive properties of nicotine and the long-term health effects for smokers and nonsmokers affected by second-hand smoke. As Koop publicly reiterated the themes of his now-infamous report, his message increasingly undermined the idea that cigarettes primarily affected those who chose to smoke them. When President George H. W. Bush nominated David Kessler to the FDA Commissioner's Office in the wake of a generic drug scandal, the surgeon general's report had already stirred considerable interest among the public – and among employees of the FDA, who convinced Kessler that the agency could play a key role.

By the beginning of the following decade, the FDA's leadership decisively moved the agency in a different direction. Under the leadership of Commissioner David Kessler (and with the approval of HHS and the Clinton White House), the FDA began an elaborate effort to assert regulatory jurisdiction over tobacco products. In this effort, Kessler drew support from a variety of senior career FDA employees, some of whom had harbored an interest in regulating tobacco for some time. Kessler and his staff understood that they were taking on a major battle, one that would be waged within the administration, in Congress, and in the courts. The weight of the medical research on the effects of tobacco, however, had become all but overpowering to public health experts by the early 1990s. That evidence clearly indicated not only that tobacco products were addictive and deadly to their users, but also that their second-hand smoke could cause severe health problems to nonsmokers.

The agency prepared for a fight. Acknowledging that they were facing both legal and political constraints, Kessler's staff developed an elaborate regulatory rulemaking record documenting the effects of tobacco on health,

---

[61] See "The Generic Drug Scandal," *The New York Times* (October 2, 1989).

[62] C. Everett Koop, "Surgeon General's Report: The Health Effects of Involuntary Smoking" (U.S. Department of Health and Human Services, 1988).

the pharmacological properties of cigarettes and other tobacco products, and the basis for inferring that regulatory interventions would have an impact on market behavior.[63] Apart from the goal of asserting regulatory jurisdiction over tobacco under the FDCA, the FDA focused its regulatory strategy not on changing the entire public's tobacco-related behavior in the very short term. Instead, the focus was on reducing consumption of tobacco products by children and youth, and perhaps in the process, on reshaping what might be called the secular morality of cigarette use as well as their supply to minors.[64] Hence the FDA's proposed regulation limited tobacco companies' ability to advertise close to schools (something ultimately achieved through the states' tobacco settlement). Tobacco companies would be prohibited from penning marketing deals with athletic events. The FDA would oversee implementation of restrictions on access to minors. The significance of any specific regulatory requirement, however, paled in comparison with the fact that the FDA was asserting control over tobacco for the first time in its history.[65] Keenly aware of the significance of that historical milestone, Kessler and his allies within the FDA mobilized to garner administration support and ultimately secured the support of President Clinton and Vice President Gore.[66]

The tobacco companies mounted a severe attack on the legality of the FDA's new regulation that landed in the Supreme Court.[67] The industry's legal representatives hired virtually all living former FDA chief counsels to consult on the appeal. Attorneys for the tobacco companies essentially argued that the FDCA's terms did not obviously implicate jurisdiction over tobacco. Nor did the structure of the law, they argued, provide a good fit with tobacco – as these products were not under the proposed FDA rules going to be rendered "safe and effective." In addition, the tobacco industry argued that congressional practice following the enactment of the FDCA was relevant, wherein Congress had passed several statutes addressing tobacco marketing – thereby indicating that Congress had not (when passing the FDCA) contemplated that it would extend to tobacco.

---

[63] See generally David Kessler, *A Question of Intent.*

[64] Cf. Paul Verkuil, "A Leadership Case Study of Tobacco and Its Regulation," *Public Talk: The Online Journal of Discourse Leadership* 7 (1998).

[65] See generally Liza Goitein, Gregory S. Chernack, Goodwin Liu, and Melvin T. Davis, "The FDA's Tobacco Regulations," *Yale Law and Policy Review* 15 (1996): 399.

[66] See Verkuil, "A Leadership Case Study of Tobacco and Its Regulation."

[67] *Food and Drug Administration v. Brown & Williamson Tobacco Corp,* 529 US 120 (2000), 161.

The *Brown & Williamson* litigation is important for two reasons. First, event studies suggest that the litigation appears to have affected the valuation of tobacco companies, underscoring the economic stakes involved in the regulation of tobacco products.[68] Second, of course, the U.S. government lost in a five-to-four U.S. Supreme Court decision, shattering the FDA's effort to use the existing FDCA. The Clinton Administration and the FDA remained engaged, however, and growing public concern was arising from tobacco company documents made public by congressional investigations and the state lawsuits. The Supreme Court's decision thus moved the action from the courts to Capitol Hill.

Significantly, a bipartisan coalition of Hill lawmakers supporting tobacco regulation converged on a bill that, at core, codified the FDA tobacco rules and amended the FDCA to clarify that the agency had authority to implement the regulation. For the next ten years, as much of the tobacco industry sought to squelch Hill legislation, the FDA remained at the center of efforts to achieve tobacco regulation. FDA scientists, lawyers, doctors, and policy analysts worked on the legislation in the latter part of the Clinton Administration. Although the Bush Administration declined to support legislation to extend FDA jurisdiction to cover tobacco, the agency had already assembled the capacity to provide technical analysis on the issue and at key points provided informal technical assistance to lawmakers on Capitol Hill (particularly Congressman Henry Waxman and his allies in the House, and Senator Ted Kennedy and tobacco-regulation supporters in the Senate) before advocating for the bill more emphatically during the Obama Administration.[69] Over the decade during which success eluded supporters of the bill, the coalition supporting the bill changed and the content of the

---

[68] See Jeffrey R. Lax and Mathew D. McCubbins, "Courts, Congress, and Public Policy, Part I: The FDA, the Courts, and the Regulation of Tobacco," *Journal of Contemporary Legal Issues* 15 (2006): 163.

[69] See, for example, Drew Armstrong, "Two-Day Senate Committee Markup Expected for Bill to Regulate Tobacco," *CQ Today* (May 18, 2009), available at 2009 WLNR 9847532 (discussing FDA Commissioner Hamburg's support for the bill); Kessler, *A Question of Intent* (discussing the capacity the FDA assembled in the late 1990s to develop tobacco regulatory rules and analyze tobacco control policy). For a more general discussion of the FDA's capacity to particulate in legislative drafting, see Fran Hawthorne, *Inside the FDA: The Business and Politics Behind the Drugs We Take and the Food We Eat* (Hoboken, NJ: John Wiley, 2005), 211 (describing the work of the FDA's Office of Legislation). Although Hawthorne's account emphasizes the role of political appointees within the agency, she nonetheless provides a discussion of how some of the agency's internal structures are geared toward influencing the legislative process through monitoring developments, responding to questions, and providing technical assistance.

legislation changed. By the time lawmakers, FDA officials, and civil society groups had worked through the legislation, the bill expanded in scope to cover the listing of tobacco ingredients, bans on flavored cigarettes, and other matters that had remained beyond the purview of the 1996 regulatory rule. In other respects, the bill included classic compromises, such as the grandfathering of mentholated cigarettes to get around the ban on flavored cigarettes.[70]

When the Family Smoking Prevention and Tobacco Control Act was finally signed into law by President Obama in the summer of 2009, the resulting legislation represented the most significant change in federal public health policy in at least a generation. The Congressional Budget Office estimated that as early as 2019, the bill would result in an 11 percent decline among underage tobacco users, with additional declines among adult users over time.[71] Supporters had forestalled a last effort by supporters of tobacco companies that acknowledged the need for regulation but created a less-powerful agency separate from the FDA to administer limited regulations, one required the agency to publish an annual ranking of the safety of tobacco products.

Throughout the legislative effort to confer on the FDA explicit authority for regulating tobacco products, one tobacco company – Philip Morris – supported some form of tobacco regulation.[72] Its representatives occasionally held discussions with public health advocates and eventually even supported the FDA tobacco bill. It is difficult, however, to tell a story in which Philip Morris's preferred policy outcome involved FDA tobacco regulation. The tobacco giant had once opposed FDA regulation and fought new legal measures to restrict tobacco advertising. Its international sales were growing. The tobacco litigation had certainly demonstrated to the tobacco industry the potential impact of adverse publicity. Although it was a market leader in the United States and conceivably would not be as adversely affected by generally imposed further restrictions on marketing, it would now confront a regulator capable of undertaking additional initiatives to control tobacco and – eventually – requirements affecting the manufacture and sale of tobacco products throughout the country.

---

[70] See C. Stephen Readhead and Vanessa K. Burrows, "FDA Tobacco Regulation: The Family Smoking Prevention and Tobacco Control Act of 2009" (Congressional Research Service Report R40475, May 28, 2009).

[71] See Congressional Budget Office, Cost Estimate: H.R. 1256 – Family Smoking Prevention and Tobacco Control Act 6 (March 16, 2009).

[72] See Niv Elis, "FDA Regulates Tobacco, and Philip Morris Cheers," Forbes.Com (June 11, 2009). *See also infra* note 107.

BUILDING CAPACITY TO INFLUENCE REGULATION THROUGH PUBLIC HEALTH SURVEILLANCE

On April 17, 2009, public health specialists at the CDC confirmed a second case of infection with a threatening flu virus, one that came to be known as H1N1, that was different from any influenza virus known to exist in humans or animals. In the ensuing months, policymakers and the public across the world became deeply concerned about the spreading virus, and by mid-June 2009, the World Health Organization acknowledged that a global pandemic was underway.[73]

Not surprisingly, the CDC played a pivotal role in researching the virus and monitoring its spread. However, the sprawling agency also shaped a variety of policy responses affecting millions of people and having far-flung effects on private sector entities. In April 2009, the CDC urged travelers to postpone all nonessential travel to Mexico, where the outbreak had advanced further. The following month, the agency issued recommendations for clinicians prescribing antiviral medicines. It began working with manufacturers, distributors, and retailers of antivirals and respiratory protective equipment to assess the commercial supply chain and evaluate possible release of counter-measures from the Strategic National Stockpile.[74] In the CDC's use of expertise and legal authority to carry out such functions affecting private actors and the public during the H1N1 pandemic, we can begin to see the potentially far-reaching, quasi-regulatory consequences of an agency that is sometimes mistaken for a simple bureau charged with monitoring developments involving communicable disease.

For virtually its entire history, since the time when "CDC" referred to the "Communicable Disease Center" set up in humid Atlanta, Georgia, the CDC has played a vital role monitoring the spread of disease in the United States and designing strategies for prevention.[75] The CDC is rarely understood as a regulatory agency; most accounts of its work emphasize instead its role in research and monitoring. In contrast to the FDA or the EPA, the CDC would seem to have an exceedingly small footprint in terms of regulatory jurisdiction and capacity.

Such a depiction is misleading, though, for two reasons. First, Congress has vested the CDC with the capacity to regulate in areas such as disease

---

[73] See Centers for Disease Control and Prevention, "The 2009 H1N1 Pandemic: Summary Highlights, April 2009–April 2010" (June 16, 2010), 2, 4.

[74] See Centers for Disease Control and Prevention, "The 2009 H1N1 Pandemic," 6, 9.

[75] See Elizabeth Etheridge, *Sentinel for Health* (Berkeley and Los Angeles, CA: University of California Press, 1992), 155.

surveillance and quarantine.[76] Although the agency rarely uses such authority, its residual capacity to do so (and the sweeping nature of some of its
authority) makes the CDC an important player in regulatory policy. Second, the CDC is the quintessential example of a networked agency, whose
judgments are amplified through an elaborate web of formal and de facto
relationships with other agencies whose operational or regulatory decisions
(in areas ranging from biosecurity to occupational safety) turn heavily or
exclusively on CDC determinations. In a similar fashion, the CDC's decision to release information or issue a warning can directly influence market
behavior and shape the litigation environment. Viewed in this light, CDC
is a highly prominent actor in public health regulation. As the following
examples illustrate, it faces some of the same opportunities and dilemmas as other public health agencies whose decisions can heavily influence
industry.

Today the CDC sits at the center of an elaborate public health surveillance
infrastructure that, despite limitations, is among the best in the world.[77] As
much an innovation as the FDA's move to regulate tobacco or USDA's
launch of HACCP, this surveillance infrastructure is particularly important
for three reasons. First, as noted previously, public health surveillance turns
out to directly implicate regulatory or quasi-regulatory functions capable
of affecting private interests. Second, it requires externally supported organizational capacity and elaboration of legal authority, rather than simply
agency leaders' ideas for how to use guaranteed resources and relatively
unchanging legal authority. Finally, this system constitutes a hard-fought
achievement involving the development of considerable technical capacity and reputational capital – and requires ongoing maintenance from the
organization and its supporters (through, for example, budgets, promotion
paths, alliances with political appointees, and public outreach).

History is instructive in understanding these characteristics. Today the
CDC boasts a yearly budget of approximately $10 billion and more than
15,000 staff, with jobs ranging from engineers and behavioral scientists to
economists and biologists. It funds research, surveillance, and other efforts
for a variety of issues and diseases – including immunization, birth defects,

---

[76] See generally Lawrence O. Gostin, "Federal Executive Power and Communicable Disease
   Control: CDC Quarantine Regulations," *Hastings Center Report* 36 (2006): 10.
[77] See Julie E. Fischer, Eric Lief, and Vidal Seegobin, "U.S. Global Health Policy: Mapping
   the United States Government Engagement in Global Health" (August 2009), 38; Tiaji
   Salaam-Blyther, "Centers for Disease Control and Prevention Global Health Programs: FY
   2001–FY 2010" (Congressional Research Service, Report to Congress R40239, August 21,
   2009).

environmental health, and toxic substances.[78] This was not always the case.

The CDC was launched in 1946 under the umbrella of the Public Health Service (PHS), with only a few hundred employees. It had previously been the office of Malaria Control in War Areas, focusing on malaria eradication not in war zones but in areas of the southeastern United States that still struggled with the disease. As a result, most of the employees of the new CDC were engineers and entomologists.[79]

In its early years, the agency continued to prioritize the fight against malaria, assigning more than half its employees to this task. The CDC employed just a handful of medical officers for the first few years of its existence.[80] It grew initially by incorporating additional units of the PHS. It added the Venereal Disease Division of PHS in 1957and Tuberculosis Control in 1960, with the Immunization program following in 1963.[81] The CDC took over the Foreign Quarantine Service in 1967 and worked to redesign and update the department with an emphasis on surveillance. The CDC later brought on a nutrition program and the National Institute for Occupational Safety and Health. As the CDC grew, it tackled major infectious disease challenges involving measles, rubella, and family planning and pushed to increase its surveillance capabilities.[82]

Over time, and largely in response to the entrepreneurial efforts of Dr. Joseph Mountin and others in agency leadership positions, the new organization was charged with broadening its focus to the broad range of communicable diseases and to constantly adapt to best serve the public health interests of the United States. The CDC rapidly adjusted, bringing on scientists and working to train the public health officials of many foreign countries.[83] In the course of this growth, the agency received relatively little federal oversight as subcabinet officials focused relatively greater attention on the far better funded National Institutes of Health.[84]

---

[78] Centers for Disease Control and Prevention, "About CDC – State of CDC," May 19, 2010, www.cdc.gov/about/stateofcdc/html/budget-workforce.htm.

[79] Elizabeth W. Etheridge, "Fifty Years of History," *Journal of Environmental Health* 59 (1997): 16–18.

[80] Centers for Disease Control and Prevention, "About CDC – Our Story," January 11, 2010, www.cdc.gov/about/history/ourstory.htm.

[81] Beth E. Meyerson, Fred A. Martich, and Gerald P. Naehr, *Ready to Go: The History and Contributions of U.S. Public Health Advisors* (Research Triangle Park, NC: American Social Health Association, 2008).

[82] Etheridge, "Fifty Years of History," 16.

[83] Etheridge, "Fifty Years of History."

[84] Ibid.

This historical progression implicated a shared evolution in three domains that affected the agency's place in an American regulatory state often assumed to reflect instances of agency capture.[85] First, the agency's legal authority gave it the necessary power to gather health-related information and, increasingly, to make policy relevant recommendations capable of exerting powerful effects on private industry.[86] Such legal authority could enhance the agency's influence and bargaining position relative to other public organizations lacking the capacity to gather such data. Second, the agency's practical capacity to gather and analyze information changed over time, as new staff joined the agency and its relations with state health authorities grew closer.[87] Through early exchanges of information and relationships playing out largely outside public view, state agency reporting practices evolved partly in response to CDC specifications, and the CDC perfected reporting mechanisms such as FoodNet by adapting in part to the constraints and capacity of state and local reporting capacity.[88] Third, the CDC began to occasionally register in the public's broad perceptions of federal agency activity. Although controversy occasionally arose over CDC recommendations, most notably involving the swine flu outbreak in the late 1970s,[89] the agency's role generally bolstered a favorable reputation for technical competence.[90] The agency's reputation enhanced its ability to shape social behavior and to further affect other agencies through its recommendations. The existence of a latent degree of support among coalitions of civil society and the public can simultaneously help the agency maintain the resources to protect its practical capacity and retain legal

[85] See *supra* note 7 (discussing the putatively pervasive extent of capture).

[86] See generally Sarah A. Lister, "An Overview of the U.S. Public Health System in the Context of Emergency Preparedness" (Congressional Research Service, Report to Congress RL31719, March 17, 2005).

[87] See Etheridge, "Fifty Years of History," 16.

[88] See Centers for Disease Control and Prevention, "Public Health Preparedness: Mobilizing State by State" (CDC Report on the Public Health Emergency Preparedness Cooperative Agreement, February 2008); F. Douglas Scutchfield and C. William Keck, *Principles of Public Health Practice*, 2nd ed. (New York: Cengage Learning, 2003), 86 ("Among all federal health agencies, the CDC is undoubtedly the one most heavily invested in intergovernmental relationships with state and local public health organizations. Many of the CDC's initiatives in disease surveillance and control depend upon activities carried out by state public health agencies and their affiliated local health evidence departments.").

[89] See generally Richard E. Neustadt and Harvey V. Feinberg, *The Swine Flu Affair: Decision-Making on a Slippery Disease* (Washington, D.C.: National Institute of Medicine, 1978) (discussing the impact of perceived CDC over-reaction to the 1976 swine flu outbreak and subsequent consequences for the agency's capacity to shape policy).

[90] See Etheridge, *Sentinel for Health*, 122.

authority even if it wades into factually complex or politically contested territory.

That the modern CDC wades into such territory is plain from its recent history, and from the role it has come to occupy in American society. Over the last few decades, officials at the agency's Atlanta headquarters have routinely become involved in issues of considerable economic and political consequence. CDC officials establish occupational safety standards governing large tracts of American economic activity.[91] The CDC played an important role in early U.S. government deliberations regarding measures to address the spread of AIDS through the blood supply.[92] For instance, CDC researchers and policymakers expressed early concern about potential contamination and pressed for measures to reduce the risk of infection through the blood supply.[93] Because of the agency's unique level of capacity and resources relative to other domestic public health agencies, CDC officials use their domestic health surveillance capacity as well as links to other countries' public health authorities to collaborate with the World Health Organization in monitoring international developments. The CDC, for example, leveraged its surveillance role when supporting global efforts to eradicate smallpox during the 1960s and 1970s. Through a smallpox surveillance unit, the CDC could reduce delays in the cycle for perfecting vaccination techniques by rapidly analyzing regional disease prevalence data while perfecting vaccination techniques in Tonga, Brazil, and Central and West Africa.[94]

Another interesting example of how the CDC's role in health surveillance allows the agency to play a role in high-stakes issues involves the issue of Reye's syndrome and warnings for aspirin. In the late 1970s the CDC began to investigate the possibility that children with smallpox or other

---

[91] See the Occupational Safety and Health Act of 1970, Pub. L. 91-596, December 29, 1970, 84 Stat. 1590, 29 U.S.C. § 651; it created both NIOSH and the Occupational Safety and Health Administration (OSHA). Information pertaining to the specific responsibilities of NIOSH are found in Section 22 of the Occupational Safety and Health Act of 1970 (29 CFR § 671). In addition, the Federal Mine Safety and Health Amendments Act of 1977 delegated additional authority to NIOSH for coal mine health research. See David C. Vladeck, "The Failed Promise of Workplace Health Regulations," *West Virginia Law Review* 111 (2009): 15.

[92] See generally Lauren B. Leveton, Harold C. Sox., Jr., and Michael A. Stoto, eds., *HIV and the Blood Supply: An Analysis of Crisis Decision-Making* (Washington, D.C.: National Academies Press, 1995).

[93] See Leveton et al., *HIV and the Blood Supply*. The CDC, however, faced resistance from the FDA, which delayed implementation of the recommendation, resulting in delays before corrective action was taken.

[94] See Fischer et al., "U.S. Global Health Policy" (discussing the relationship of the CDC and the WHO as well as other organizations playing a role in promoting global public health).

infectious diseases could be at risk for Reye's syndrome if they consumed aspirin or related products.[95] The consequences could include mild but long-term brain damage. The CDC researched the issue intensely and, even in the absence of complete confidence, concluded that it was appropriate to publish research indicating the basis for the CDC's concern. Initially, the FDA agreed to a joint statement about the risks of aspirin for kids because of Reye's syndrome. Then the aspirin industry objected and pleaded for more time. CDC published its study despite such pressure. Although the White House reportedly interfered eventually, HHS political appointees apparently sided with CDC. Nonetheless, CDC launched a second study before warning labels were changed on aspirin. The conclusions of the second study were compelling, and warning labels were eventually added.[96]

The potential significance of this case study stems not only from the importance of Reye's syndrome. It is instead that CDC resisted pressure from the aspirin industry to slow down, when the FDA did not. Moreover, CDC was arguably in a precarious position following controversy over what was then perceived as an over-reaction to swine flu in the 1970s. This, in turn, says something about the CDC's capacity and its differences from other agencies.

The CDC's role in this episode almost certainly reflects a mix of distinctive factors and more general agency characteristics. For one, despite a record of collaboration with the FDA, the two agencies (like many agencies with related missions) probably sometimes compete (at the margin) for resources and influence. The Reye's syndrome problem implicated both infectious disease and pharmaceutical regulation, creating an opportunity for the CDC to show its relevance to pharmaceutical issues. Relative to other agencies moreover – such as FDA and National Institutes of Health – CDC appears to have had fewer officials with strong ties to pharmaceutical activity or (as with FDA) frequent direct dealings with industry. CDC also benefited (almost certainly) from support from HHS political appointees, who probably harbored a degree of reputational concern over a possible failure to share health information with the public (a concern that gave them different incentives relative to the White House, at least assuming the White House could subsequently downplay any role it had in slowing down

[95] See Etheridge, *Sentinel for Health*, 296 (discussing Reye's syndrome and the CDC role); Betty Anne Williams, "Administration Accused of Sidetracking Aspirin Campaign," *Associated Press* (November 29, 1983).
[96] Stephen B Soumerai, Dennis Ross-Degnan, and Jessica Spira Kahn, "Effects of Professional and Media Warnings about the Association between Aspirin Use in Children and Reye's Syndrome," *Milbank Quarterly* 70 (1992): 155.

the diffusion of information). The CDC's leadership may have perceived a remaining reservoir of credibility in the agency that could be enhanced if their move on Reye's syndrome succeeded, thereby enhancing the agency's reputation relative to where it stood after the swine flu controversy of the 1970s. Finally, agency leaders may have encountered an agency in which greater coherence existed between their own incentives and goals and those of individuals working directly on the research (such coherence would have strengthened the agency's overall resolve on the issue).

A somewhat similar dynamic – reflecting a relatively robust CDC role tempered by some external constraints – ensued as the CDC exercised surveillance and prevention functions associated with lead poisoning. Working with other federal agencies, the CDC played a leading role in sounding the alarm about lead poisoning. As it concluded further study of the health effects of lead exposure from the 1960s through 1970s, the CDC gradually lowered advisable levels of lead exposure. During the 1970s, the CDC played the leading role in organizing broad lead-screening efforts. These moves inspired aggressive detractors, including in some cases local municipalities and insurers. More recently, however, the CDC abandoned its goal of universal childhood lead screening. Reports of political interference with a CDC lead-related advisory committee in the last decade underscore the continuing political stakes involved in CDC determinations involving lead-related issues.[97]

In addressing high-stakes issues such as these, it is important to recognize that CDC does not always achieve implementation of its preferred recommendations. Even though it has engendered reputational capital and garnered an influential position shaping public health policy, some of the decisions in which the CDC is involved implicate multiple agencies with competing points of view and powerful external actors that may be able to affect other aspects of the policymaking process, even when they are less able to influence the relatively more insular CDC. The limits in the power of what is perhaps the world's most sophisticated health surveillance agency, however, also illustrate several important points connecting the CDC to broader discussions of agency autonomy and public health policy. First,

---

[97] See Barbara Bernay, "Round and Round It Goes: The Epidemiology of Childhood Lead Poisoning, 1950–1990," *Milbank Quarterly* 71 (1993): 10 (discussing the epidemiology and scope of the problem involving childhood lead poisoning); Gerald Markowitz and David Rosner, "Politicizing Science: The Case of the Bush Administration's Influence on the Lead Advisory Panel at the Centers for Disease Control," *Journal of Public Health Policy* 24 (2003): 105.

the agency's health surveillance capacity required a measure of autonomy to build and operate in its current form and appears to have evolved in no small measure through innovations from CDC officials rather than through externally imposed reforms originating with lawmakers or private interests. Second, the agency's health surveillance capacity shapes outcomes, and therefore its operation has high economic and political stakes. Third, although other agencies sometimes reject CDC recommendations, external actors have often played important roles in bolstering the agency's reputation and capacity.

Given these factors, it is a telling irony that the agency's health surveillance mission can appear to a variety of constituencies to be almost entirely apolitical. As a description of the agency's capacity to forge technical competence and resist routine partisan political interference, the term is apt. Where the description is less apt is in how it implicitly plays down the political–economic consequences of robust state capacity to monitor health-related developments. We can come full circle by discerning those consequences in the domains of food safety and tobacco regulation, where public sector officials with legal authority to monitor population health and a reputation for competence played important roles in creating the base of technical knowledge that facilitated the implementation of HACCP in the food safety domain and, eventually, the regulation of tobacco products.[98] As doctors and public health analysts generated and analyzed data with potentially stark consequences for lawmaking and regulation, then, it was among their most profound and under-appreciated political achievements to foment the narrative that their role was essentially apolitical.

IMPLICATIONS: COALITIONS, AUTONOMY, AND THE STATE

In a system epitomized by often-fragmented congressional coalitions, lawmakers with competing agendas, and multiple agency decision makers, the

---

[98] For one example of the CDC's continuing role in shaping tobacco policy, see "Tobacco Use: Targeting the Nation's Leading Killer; At a Glance 2010" (National Center for Chronic Disease Prevention and Health Promotion, Centers for Disease Control and Prevention, 2010), 2, http://www.cdc.gov/chronicdisease/resources/publications/aag/pdf/2010/tobacco_2010.pdf. The CDC's prominent role in food safety is discussed in, among other sources, U.S. Department of Health and Human Services, "Selected Federal Agencies with a Role in Food Safety," http://www.foodsafety.gov/about/federal/index.html (indicating that CDC "leads federal efforts to gather data on foodborne illnesses, investigate foodborne illnesses and outbreaks, and monitor the effectiveness of prevention and control efforts in reducing foodborne illnesses. CDC also plays a key role in building state and local health department epidemiology, laboratory, and environmental health capacity to support foodborne disease surveillance and outbreak response.").

political economy of lawmaking all but guarantees that no organized interest passively stands aside when threatened by new public health policies. That these efforts often succeed, or at least forestall more aggressive policies, is plain, for example, in the fate of initiatives such as ATF's efforts to improve its capacity to track the inventory of federally licensed dealers or take other measures to limit unlawful transfers of guns to prohibited purchasers.

In this vein, it is important to acknowledge that in two of the aforementioned cases, agency efforts to engage in regulatory innovation benefited from fragmentation among relevant private sector actors. The outbreak of health problems arising from the contaminated beef linked to Jack-in-the-Box catalyzed public concern about food safety, making regulatory changes more likely.[99] Not surprisingly, some of the industry responded by embracing in principle the idea of new process controls to be implemented by food processors themselves,[100] particularly if (as expected) those new standards reflected a philosophy of harnessing industry knowledge rather than imposing conventional command-and-control measures.[101] Moreover, the legislation ultimately conferring authority over tobacco to the FDA was not opposed by *one* critical private sector actor – the giant Philip Morris tobacco conglomerate.[102]

These episodes are telling, but before they are treated as sufficient cause to doubt the ultimate significance of what agencies achieved,[103] consider how these examples reveal as much about what private actors resisted from the regulatory process as they do about what private actors embraced. By and large, the meat industry representatives who had once supported the concept of HACCP parted company with USDA when the agency embraced relatively strict pathogen testing in addition to the overall framework for regulatory flexibility contained in the new 1996 regulatory rule.[104] The fierce litigation that ensued over salmonella standards in particular reflected deep-seated private resistance to the details of what USDA sought to achieve and highlight an important methodological limitation in capture-oriented

---

[99] Cf. Mariano-Florentino Cuéllar, "'Securing' the Nation: Law, Politics, and Organization at the Federal Security Agency, 1939–1953," *University of Chicago Law Review* 76 (2009): 587, 651 (discussing the impact of exogenous shocks on policymaking and government organization).

[100] See *supra* note 38 (discussing early industry support for some regulatory changes following the Jack-in-the-Box controversy).

[101] Cf. Coglianese and Lazer, "Management-Based Regulation," 691.

[102] See Michael Givel, "Philip Morris' FDA Gambit: Good for Public Health?" *Journal of Public Health Policy* 26 (2005): 450.

[103] For such a perspective, see Givel, "Philip Morris' FDA Gambit."

[104] See Richard Kluger, *Ashes to Ashes: America's Hundred-Year Cigarette War, the Public Health, and the Unabashed Triumph of Philip Morris* (New York: Knopf Doubleday, 1996).

accounts. Those accounts sometimes selectively emphasize the initial support in the industry, such as private actors' enthusiasm for HACCP requirements following the Jack-in-the-Box contamination incident. The HACCP story thus illustrates initial broad acceptance in the private sector for a general regulatory strategy that later produced considerable conflict.

At first glance, the trajectory of Philip Morris' support shows very nearly the opposite, with the preeminent American tobacco company initially joining its rivals in seeking to thwart FDA regulation by invoking limits of the then unamended Food, Drug, and Cosmetic Act.[105] Only later, after a considerable spike in public attention generated by the FDA's initially failed regulatory effort and tobacco lawsuits of nationwide scope,[106] did Philip Morris begin cautiously embracing the possibility of legislation providing the FDA with limited authority to regulate tobacco.[107] In both this case and the meat and poultry inspection scenario, however, the common theme is strong resistance from many elements of the relevant industries seeking to stymie regulatory efforts. What acceptance from private actors emerged, moreover, did so against a backdrop of broad public concern and capacity for agency action. Had these factors been absent in a counter-factual world, the resulting pluralist bargain over regulatory policy would have almost certainly been quite different. These characteristics of the tobacco and food safety stories described here underscore the risks of inferring capture simply from the presence of some private sector acceptance of regulatory measures.

If private actors are unlikely to passively stand aside when it becomes possible to change public health policy, the same is true of agencies. Through a combination of internal policy innovation, legal argument, and alliances

---

[105] See Kluger, *Ashes to Ashes*; see also Laurie Kellman, "Tobacco Bill Hits a Roadblock: Senate Refuses to Vote on It," *Chicago Sun-Times* (June 9, 1998).

[106] See Andrew L. Roth, Joshua Dunsby, and Lisa A. Bero, "Framing Processes in Public Commentary on U.S. Federal Tobacco Control Regulation," *Social Studies of Science* 33 (2003): 7, 13 (discussing how growing concern among the American public over youth access to tobacco provided an important political context for the development of the FDA youth access tobacco proposed regulatory rule).

[107] See Matthew R. Herington, "Tobacco Regulation in the United States: New Opportunities and Challenges," *Health Lawyer* 23 (2010): 13, 15 (discussing Philip Morris' support for the Family Smoking Prevention and Tobacco Control Act, as well as all tobacco companies' earlier opposition to the 1996 FDA proposed tobacco regulatory rule). The Family Smoking Prevention and Tobacco Control Act of 2009, though ultimately acceptable to Philip Morris, in part implemented the 1996 regulatory rule that the FDA had crafted to limit youth access to tobacco products and that Philip Morris had initially opposed. See, for example, 1999 WL 712548, "Brief for Respondents Philip Morris Incorporated and Lorrillard Tobacco Company" (September 10, 1999) [brief in *FDA v. Brown & Williamson*, 529 U.S. 120 (2000)].

with external political players and public constituencies, agencies have successfully changed the way millions of Americans get their food. Public officials have forged a new regulatory context for tobacco, contributing to changing social norms regarding the use of products that kill nearly half a million Americans a year. They have changed public health standards governing lead and medical practices concerning the use of a popular drug such as aspirin. Key to these developments is the fact that agencies are in a complex, evolving relationship with civil society, the private sector, and the more explicitly political components of government. Their capacity to pursue strategies to protect public health arises from the tensions and consequences associated with those relationships. Far from being merely passive objects of political control, agencies use their legal authority to shape their context. In the process, the coalitions of agency political appointees and career staff governing agencies can affect society by affecting its health and security.

Indeed, the preceding examples may reflect certain distinctive features of the public health context. Public health agencies tend to operate in a legal and policy space replete with participants from civil society and the private sector. The involvement of multiple political actors from civil society, the private sector, and government itself reflects the high stakes involved in public health decisions. Even crises far milder than the Great Influenza of 1918 can wreak havoc nationally and internationally. Public health decisions hold major financial stakes for vaccine providers, drug companies, insurers – and armies and families. In particular, concentrated costs can generate powerful incentives for corporations and other private interests in a pluralist, democratic system to thwart or water down reforms.

In the face of those efforts, public health agencies – though far from impervious to political conflict – also turned out to be far from powerless. In contrast to organizations responsible for a range of functions such as public housing or agriculture policy, public perceptions of an agency's reputation tend to favor a public organization's claims of expertise in this domain in ways that would surely trigger fits of envy among transportation or labor officials. The reservoir of trust can grow as agencies build personnel and capacity capable of validating preexisting public perceptions, or it can dissipate to some degree in the wake of heavily criticized choices, such as the CDC's response to the swine flu scare of the mid-1970s. In comparison to agencies with more conventional administrative functions, public health agencies appear to begin with a reservoir of legitimacy reflecting the public's broad association of modern health policy with scientific expertise.

Perhaps in part because of the technical uncertainty and perceptions regarding scientific expertise confronting lawmakers, many public health agencies also benefit from relatively supple legal authority. In a system where statutory change is difficult and plausible arguments about existing legal authority are one coin of the realm, a more flexible statute is worth its weight in gold. Even when agencies ultimately fail at convincing the courts, as did the FDA in pursuing tobacco regulation, their broad authority can give them crucial space to engineer the policy in question by validating their preparatory work and allowing agencies to bolster their reputations by arguing plausibly about the analogies and complementarities between new efforts to cover tobacco or food safety and existing efforts. Agencies such as ATF or the Internal Revenue Service wield limited authority by comparison or carry jurisdiction honeycombed with appropriations restrictions blocking even the gathering of information necessary to develop persuasive legal or policy arguments.[108] The result is a mismatch between the scope of certain agencies' legal jurisdiction and far narrower capacity to address policy problems in a meaningful way – an incongruity almost certainly sufficient to dilute an agency's reputation for competence even among constituencies supportive of its mission.

If broad delegations can conceivably play a role in public health innovation, conventional principal-agent models describing the agency as the "agent" of its political superiors seem to capture few of the relevant nuances. Not only do these examples cut against the idea of pervasive capture, but they also raise questions about the extent to which the process of agency innovation is usefully depicted by simple principal-agent models. One must distinguish between *discretion* and *autonomy*. The former is a central feature of many principal-agent models and akin, for example, to how agencies comparable to the USDA exercise authority under a preexisting regulatory regime. But the latter better describes the changes USDA undertook when implementing HACCP, as it worked to alter the legal and policy backdrop against which the rule would be considered.[109] Although discretion

---

[108] See, for example, Edward D. Kleinbard, "The Congress within the Congress: How Tax Expenditures Distort Our Budget and Our Political Process," *Ohio Northern University Law Review* 36 (2010): 1 (discussing the growth in the "congressional appetite for tax expenditures" specified explicitly by the legislature in statutes that effectively restrict agency discretion); William J. Vizzard, *Shots in the Dark: The Politics, Policy, and Symbolism of Gun Control* (Lanham, MD: Rowman & Littlefield, 2000) (discussing how congressional engagement, and particularly appropriations-related legislative restrictions, affect ATF operations).

[109] See, for example, Daniel Carpenter, *The Forging of Bureaucratic Autonomy* (Princeton: Princeton University Press, 2002) (discussing distinctions between autonomy and discretion).

implicates the authority that an organization receives under explicitly recognized institutional rules, autonomy refers to the organization's ability to influence its broader context. Accordingly, the central questions animating many (though admittedly not all) principal-agent models, such as how the principal might optimally allocate discretion to an agent, are distinct from the issues that arise in understanding autonomy. Conventional principal-agent models, for example, are rarely set up to consider how a public organization can fundamentally reshape the relationship to its principal, and its incentives, in a manner that neither the organization nor the principal first anticipated. Some observers may divine a democratic legitimacy problem in an agency's capacity to dissuade lawmakers from interfering with a new food safety rule or tobacco control effort. It is at least a partial rejoinder to emphasize that agencies are far from alone when appealing to the public – either directly or through trusted intermediaries such as civil society organizations and scientists. They are simply altering the costs and benefits of particular courses of action for representative politicians. Bureaus are doing so in a world where private actors and exogenous shocks also contribute to making the circumstances of lawmaking and legal interpretation a constantly moving target.

CONCLUSION

Broad social and economic developments heavily influence food safety, tobacco regulation, health surveillance, and other public health measures in advanced industrialized countries. Statutes and judicial decisions emerging in response to these forces also play a significant role, because formal rules governing matters such as agency jurisdiction help determine what public health problems are subject to a vigorous state response and what problems are left for another day.[110] Yet because virtually all such responses are implemented by organizations, developments in population-based health depend heavily and in underappreciated ways on how public organizations respond to their constraints and opportunities. Beyond agencies' role as implementers of legal authority, partially autonomous agencies working in concert with lawmakers and political officials have played critical roles in the development of public health law. Crucially, agencies have pursued both regulatory efforts as well as (through the work of the CDC) health-related surveillance activities with quasi-regulatory consequences by leveraging a mix of legal authority, agency capacity, and supportive external coalitions.

[110] See *FDA v. Brown & Williamson*, 529 US 120 (2000), 161.

Instead of reflecting a conventional principal-agent scenario, wherein legislative principals specify goals that public bureaus implement acting as "agents," public health often reflects a blurring in the roles of principal and agent. Lawmakers deeply identified with agencies' missions act to defend and expand the scope of the bureaus' responsibilities, while the FDA and other public health bureaus have played pivotal roles in drafting legislation. As they implement such legislation, public health agencies often forge reputations for competence and relative impartiality that can raise the political and economic costs of external interference with the agencies' work. Not only do some bureaus forge coalitions of external support, making it possible for them to play a preeminent role in the legislative process, but they achieve (at least in some cases) a capacity to alter for politicians the costs and benefits of direct interference with agency activities.

When those opportunities arise for food safety inspectors validating HACCP requirements, or for public health specialists pooling state-level data, it is not because of an arid statutory framework offering paper guarantees of independence. The political economy of legal and policy change plainly implicates lawmakers often (if not exclusively) concerned about reelection, executive branch officials making stark political trade-offs across issues, and a disaggregated public of people who rarely understand the stakes involved in complicated regulatory decisions to manage risk. In that environment, private actors forge coalitions, cultivate reputations, and deploy legal arguments to advance their agendas. Public health agencies play in the same space. On their often hard-fought efforts to forge capacity and create their own coalitions of support for policy innovations rests in large measure the contested legitimacy of the state.

SECTION IV

THE POSSIBILITY OF PREVENTING CAPTURE

The case studies in Section III suggest that capture is not ubiquitous and that it is (at least partially) preventable – and, in fact, already partly *prevented* within existing systems. Because undue influence can be exercised through many possible mechanisms, and because capture and efforts to prevent it have tended to co-evolve as in a centuries-old game of cat and mouse, new strategies for preventing capture are likely to take many forms. The authors in this section explore a range of efforts to mitigate special interest influence in the regulatory process and offer some important suggestions for building upon them.

First, in Chapter 13, Daniel Schwarcz examines state consumer empowerment programs that aim to bring the consumer perspective more fully into the process of regulatory decision making. Ultimately, Schwarcz finds considerable potential in several of these programs for increasing the influence of consumer interests as a productive, countervailing voice to business interests, which might otherwise be overrepresented in regulatory decisions. He concludes that employing the two most successful forms of consumer empowerment in combination could prove especially effective in protecting and advancing the public interest.

Exploring the role of the U.S. judiciary, Elizabeth Magill considers in Chapter 14 the powerful but limited ways in which judicial review can provide a bulwark against capture and redress against captured regulations. Magill argues that the courts have a unique ability to prevent capture by declaring an agency action legal or illegal, but are constrained by their passive stance as arbiters of only those cases brought before them.

Looking at the Office of Information and Regulatory Affairs (OIRA) in the Office of Management and Budget, Michael Livermore and Richard Revesz argue in Chapter 15 that OIRA stands as a safeguard against industry capture across executive agencies and that its activity should be expanded. In particular, the authors argue that OIRA should extend its role in conducting retrospective review, as planned, and should expand review of agency *inaction*, which could play an important role in preventing – or at least limiting – corrosive capture.

13

Preventing Capture Through Consumer Empowerment Programs

Some Evidence From Insurance Regulation

Daniel Schwarcz

INTRODUCTION

In many regulatory settings, consumers and citizens face a collective action problem in advocating for their preferred outcomes, whereas regulated entities can coordinate to overcome free rider problems.[1] The resulting imbalance in participation can, in some cases, produce outcomes that are "consistently or repeatedly directed away from the public interest toward the interest of the regulated industry by the intent and action of the industry itself."[2] In the classic story, such regulatory capture occurs through industry payment of rents to regulators, including explicit bribes, promises of future employment, or political contributions. However, more recent literature emphasizes that one-sided participation in regulation can also produce capture through cultural and behavioral forces.[3] Similarly, industry-dominated participation in regulatory processes may generate "information capture," by which industry exerts substantial control over regulatory outcomes by producing "uncontrolled and excessive" amounts of information.[4]

In recent years, academic interest in limiting these forms of regulatory capture has skyrocketed.[5] One approach to preventing capture that has

[1] George J. Stigler, "The Theory of Economic Regulation," *Bell Journal of Economics and Management Science* 2 (1971): 2.
[2] David Moss and Daniel Carpenter, "Introduction," in the current volume.
[3] James Kwak, "Cultural Capture and the Financial Crisis," Chapter 4 of the current volume; Brett McDonnell and Daniel Schwarcz, "Regulatory Contrarians," *North Carolina Law Review* 89 (2011): 1629.
[4] Wendy Wagner, "Administrative Law, Filter Failure, and Information Capture," *Duke Law Journal* 59 (2010): 1321.
[5] Geoffrey P. Miller and Gerald Rosenfeld, "Intellectual Hazard: How Conceptual Biases in Complex Organizations Contributed to the Crisis of 2008," *Harvard Journal of Law and Public Policy* 33 (2009): 807; Wagner, "Administrative Law, Filter Failure, and Information Capture"; Rachel Barkow, "Insulating Agencies: Avoiding Capture through Institutional

gained some traction in recent decades is the creation of consumer empowerment programs that directly enhance the capacity of consumer representatives to participate in regulatory processes. These programs come in
two basic varieties. First, proxy advocacy relies on independent government
entities that are tasked with representing the public interest in designated
regulatory proceedings. These programs became particularly prominent
in state regulation of utility rates during the 1970s and 1980s.[6] Second,
tripartite consumer empowerment programs seek to amplify the voice of
nongovernment public interest groups that would ordinarily be under-
represented in the regulatory fray.[7] Examples include statutorily required
consumer advisory panels for regulators and programs that reimburse consumer groups for the cost of participating in regulatory proceedings.

This chapter examines both types of consumer empowerment programs
in the context of insurance regulation. Insurance regulation is an important,
and heretofore largely neglected, setting in which consumer empowerment
programs have evolved to limit the perceived risk of regulatory capture.
Unlike virtually any other regulatory domain, dramatically different types
of consumer empowerment programs have been implemented in insurance
regulation in the last several decades. This allows for comparison of different consumer empowerment programs within similar regulatory contexts.
Additionally, insurance regulation is conducted primarily at the state level,
where regulatory capture can operate through distinctive mechanisms that
pose particularized opportunities and challenges.[8]

Three specific consumer empowerment programs have gained significant traction in insurance regulation. First, the Texas Office of Public
Insurance Counsel (OPIC) is a classic proxy advocate that is tasked with a
broad range of responsibilities in Texas insurance regulation. Second, the
California Public Participation Plan (CPPP) largely mirrors OPIC in its
scope, but is more consistent with the tripartism model. The CPPP reim-
burses designated public interest groups who make a "substantial contribution" to certain regulatory proceedings. Finally, the National Association of

---

Design," *Texas Law Review* 89 (2010): 15; Nicholas Bagley, "Agency Hygiene," *Texas Law
Review* 8 (2010): 1; McDonnell and Schwarcz, "Regulatory Contrarians."

[6] Guy L. Holburn and Pablo T. Spiller, "Interest Group Representation in Administrative
Institutions: The Impact of Consumer Advocates and Elected Commissioners on Regulatory Policy in the United States" (University of California Energy Institute, Energy Policy
and Economics Paper 002, 2002), http://escholarship.org/uc/item/5cg3d8q0.

[7] Ian Ayres and John Braithwaite, *Responsive Regulation* (New York: Oxford University Press,
1992).

[8] Richard C. Revesz, "Federalism and Environmental Regulation: A Public Choice Analysis,"
Harvard Law Review 115 (2001): 553.

Insurance Commissioners' (NAIC) Consumer Participation Program also fits the basic tripartism model, though less cleanly than does the CPPP. It provides approximately twenty-five selected consumer representatives with limited reimbursement of expenses, research assistance, free access to public documents, training, designated public fora to present on issues of their choosing, and privileged access to regulators.

This chapter compares and evaluates these three consumer empowerment programs. Integrating these case studies with preexisting literature, it also offers several tentative observations about when consumer empowerment programs might help offset, limit, or supplement industry influence in insurance regulation and similar regulatory settings, such as state securities and banking regulation. First, it suggests that proxy advocacy is most effective when there is a clear consumer position, new information is likely to influence regulatory results, and the involvement of nonindustry stakeholders is limited. These conditions are met in a broader set of circumstances than the current deployment of proxy advocacy might suggest. Second, it argues that tripartism may be more desirable than proxy advocacy when a clear consumer position is difficult to identify or the threat of political pressure is an important tool to influence results. However, in the absence of a robust network of public interest groups, effective tripartism may be difficult. Both for this reason and because proxy advocacy also enjoys some comparative advantages to tripartism, the chapter concludes by suggesting that it may sometimes be appropriate to deploy both forms of consumer empowerment.

Importantly, this chapter's focus is on the use of consumer empowerment programs to counteract industry influence in insurance regulation. Of course, not all industry influence of regulation amounts to capture.[9] But because other entries in this volume focus on diagnosing capture, this chapter sidesteps the question of when industry influence is indicative of capture. The chapter therefore does not consider the extent to which the underlying forms of insurance regulation discussed later are socially desirable, except insofar as that issue bears on the influence of consumer empowerment programs.

A BRIEF HISTORY OF CONSUMER EMPOWERMENT PROGRAMS

The public has long enjoyed the capacity to participate in regulatory rulemakings through notice and comment. In many cases, though, this

---

[9] Daniel Carpenter, "Protection without Capture," *American Political Science Review* 98 (2004): 613; Carpenter and Moss, "Introduction."

participation is dominated by regulated entities with similar, self-interested, perspectives.[10] Public involvement in regulatory processes other than rule-makings is often more limited. Even in proceedings that are ostensibly open to the public, such as certain rate-setting and licensing hearings, the public may lack the expertise to participate.[11] And for many types of regulatory activities, members of the public have few, if any, formal mechanisms of influence.

Seeking to enhance consumer and citizen influence over regulation, reformers in the 1970s proposed creating government entities that would operate as a proxy for the public in certain regulatory proceedings. These proxy advocates can take various forms, including (a) independent consumer counsels/advocates, (b) designated divisions within an attorney general office, or (c) specialized staff housed within a regulator.[12] Proxy advocacy became particularly prominent in state regulation of public utility rates during the 1970s and 1980s.[13]

Consistent evidence suggests that proxy advocacy in utilities regulation helps counteract industry influence. It results in a lower percentage of rate increase requests being granted, a decreased likelihood that utilities will seek to increase rates in the first place, and overall decreased rates.[14] The effects are strongest when proxy advocates are structured as an independent consumer counsel rather than as designated staff within a regulator or specialized division within an attorney general office.[15] However, findings are mixed about the extent to which these benefits are evenly distributed among consumers.[16] Proxy advocates wield their influence primarily by providing information and a consumer perspective to an Administrative Law Judge (ALJ) in technical rate-setting hearings, or negotiating settlements

---

[10] Jason Webb Yackee and Susan Webb Yackee, "A Bias toward Business? Assessing Interest Group Influence on the Bureaucracy," *Journal of Politics* 68 (2006): 128; Wagner, "Administrative Law, Filter Failure, and Information Capture"; Kimberly D. Krawiec, "Don't 'Screw Joe the Plumber': The Sausage-Making of Financial Reform," March 25, 2012, http://ssrn.com/abstract=1925431.

[11] Robert N. Mayer, Cathleen D. Zick, and John R. Burton, "Consumer Representation and Local Telephone Rates," *Journal of Consumer Affairs* 23 (1989): 267.

[12] Mayer et al., "Consumer Representation and Local Telephone Rates."

[13] Holburn and Spiller, "Interest Group Representation in Administrative Institutions."

[14] William Berry, "An Alternative to Capture Theory of Regulation: The Case of State Public Utility Commissions," *American Journal of Political Science* 28 (1984): 524; Holburn and Spiller, "Interest Group Representation in Administrative Institutions."

[15] Mayer et al., "Consumer Representation and Local Telephone Rates."

[16] William T. Gormley, "Alternative Models of the Regulatory Process: Public Utility Regulation in the States," *Western Political Quarterly* 35 (1982): 297; Holburn and Spiller, "Interest Group Representation in Administrative Institutions."

in connection with those hearings.[17] Unlike public interest groups, proxy advocates rarely emphasize the application of political pressure in describing their influence.[18]

In the 1980s and 1990s, tripartism emerged as an alternative form of consumer empowerment. Rather than creating a single government defender of the public interest, tripartism formally involves independent public interest groups in regulatory proceedings. Its developers, Ian Ayres and John Braithwaite, advance a quite specific vision of tripartism: empowered public interest groups – which they saddle with the unfortunate acronym "PIGs" – must be fully informed regarding regulatory issues, allowed to participate in the negotiation of regulatory outcomes, and permitted to challenge industry behavior through the same mechanisms as the regulator. Additionally, the role of empowered PIG must be contestable, such that alternative PIGs can become empowered. So conceived, tripartism can counteract regulatory capture through both economic and cultural forces, according to Ayres and Braithwaite. From an economic perspective, empowered PIGs can increase the cost to firms of securing regulatory compliance, effectively requiring industry to expend resources to capture two separate groups. Although PIGs may be subject to capture, this risk is limited both by their self-identification and the contestability of their position. From a sociological perspective, tripartism can promote a spirit of "regulatory communitarianism" among regulators, industry, and empowered PIGS, thus modifying "the deliberative habits and behavioral dispositions of actors" to promote mutually beneficial results.[19]

In recent years, lawmakers have experimented with cooperative and participatory approaches to regulation that fall loosely under the heading of "new governance" and have important similarities to tripartism. New governance emphasizes the capacity of flexible, participatory, and collaborative programs to displace traditional command and control regulation.[20] But while the involvement of public interest groups, concerned citizens, or other

---

[17] Holburn and Spiller, "Interest Group Representation in Administrative Institutions"; Stephen Littlechild, "Stipulated Settlements, the Consumer Advocate, and Utility Regulation in Florida," *Journal of Regulatory Economics* 35 (2009): 96.

[18] William T. Gormley, *The Politics of Public Utility Regulation* (Pittsburgh, PA: University of Pittsburgh Press, 1983).

[19] Ayres and Braithwaite, *Responsive Regulation*.

[20] Michael C. Dorf and Charles E. Sabel, "A Constitution of Democratic Experimentalism," *Columbia Law Review* 98 (1998): 267; Bradley C. Karkkainen, "'New Governance' in Legal Thought and in the World: Some Splitting as Antidote to Overzealous Lumping," *Minnesota Law Review* 89 (2004): 471; Orly Lobel, "The Renew Deal: The Fall of Regulation and the Rise of Governance in Contemporary Legal Thought," *Minnesota Law Review* 89 (2004): 342.

stakeholders is a feature of virtually all new governance experiments, these approaches vary significantly in the extent to which they seek to affirmatively empower public interest groups relative to other regulatory stakeholders and thus fit the definition of tripartism. At least some new governance scholars, however, do emphasize the need to promote "countervailing power," given the comparative ease with which organized powerful interests can participate in, and ultimately influence, certain new governance projects.[21]

Taken together, the tripartism and new governance literatures provide some limited guidance on how best to implement effective tripartism. For instance, Mark Seidenfeld[22] argues that empowered PIGs may be co-opted by other stakeholders if they are repeatedly involved in regulatory negotiations. He therefore suggests that government must "establish internal [PIG] mechanisms that ensure group leaders' accountability to putative beneficiaries of regulation.…"[23] Empirical studies of tripartite structures deployed outside of new governance contexts are limited. However, one detailed study of a program at the Consumer Safety Product Commission that reimbursed non-industry participation in notice and comment rulemaking offered mixed praise: although reimbursed involvement often meaningfully contributed to and influenced regulatory results, the program routinely failed to provide funding in the contexts where it would be most impactful.[24]

THREE CONSUMER EMPOWERMENT MODELS IN INSURANCE REGULATION

Although the political economy of insurance regulation is both complex and contingent, most observers agree that the insurance industry often enjoys substantial influence over regulatory outcomes.[25] In response, several insurance regulators (or quasi-regulators) have implemented consumer

---

[21] Archon Fung and Erik Wright, "Countervailing Power in Empowered Participatory Governance, in *Deepening Democracy: Institutional Innovations in Empowered Participatory Governance*, eds. Fung and Wright (New York: Verso, 2003).

[22] Mark Seidenfeld, "Empowering Stakeholders: Limits on Collaboration as Basis for Flexible Regulation," *William and Mary Law Review* 41 (2000): 411.

[23] Seidenfeld, "Empowering Stakeholders," 484–85.

[24] Carl Tobias, "Great Expectations and Mismatched Compensation: Government Sponsored Public Participation in Proceedings of the Consumer Product Safety Commission," *Washington University Law Quarterly* 64 (1986): 1101.

[25] Kenneth Meier, *The Political Economy of Regulation: The Case of Insurance* (Albany, New York: State University of New York Press, 1988); Susan Randall, "Insurance Regulation in the United States: Regulatory Federalism and the National Association of Insurance Commissioners," *Florida State University Law Review* 26 (1999): 625; Daniel Schwarcz,

empowerment programs designed to counteract insurer influence. Three of these have gained significant traction.[26] The first, the Texas Office of Public Insurance Counsel, is a classic proxy advocate that was originally modeled on proxy advocacy in public utilities regulation. The second, the California Public Participation Program, is an experiment in tripartism that comes relatively close to meeting the criteria developed by Ayres and Braithwaite. Finally, although the NAIC Consumer Participation Program is also an experiment in tripartism, it fits less neatly into the formal Ayres/Braithwaite framework. Table 13.4, at the conclusion of this subsection, summarizes some key features of each consumer empowerment program.

The Texas Office of Public Insurance Counsel

The Office of Public Insurance Counsel (OPIC) is an independent agency in Texas that is charged with representing Texas insurance consumers.[27] OPIC is formally independent of the Texas Department of Insurance (TDI) and has no regulatory authority. Its sixteen employees include attorneys, an economist, statisticians, researchers, and support staff. The Public Counsel, who directs OPIC, is appointed by the governor and confirmed by the Senate to a two-year term. The agency's funding, which amounts to slightly over a million dollars a year, comes directly from insurance companies, who pay

---

"Regulating Insurance Sales or Selling Insurance Regulation," *Minnesota Law Review* 94 (2009): 1707.

[26] The only other major consumer empowerment program in insurance is the Florida Insurance Consumer Advocate. This program was not studied because it is not independent, but reports directly to Florida's Chief Financial Officer. Other consumer-oriented insurance offices exist in various states, including Louisiana, Vermont, Maryland, New Jersey, and Ohio. However, all of these offices operate exclusively or almost exclusively to help resolve consumer complaints and do not therefore constitute "consumer empowerment programs" as that term is used herein. Finally, although Michigan briefly established by executive order the position of Automobile and Home Insurance Advocate, a new governor abolished that office three years after its creation.

[27] The statutory framework for OPIC is contained in Tex. Ins. Code Ann. § 501, et seq., available at http://codes.lp.findlaw.com/txstatutes/IN/5/A/501/C. The descriptive information about OPIC in this section is derived from (a) OPIC's self-evaluation reports, see, for example, Office of Public Insurance Counsel, "Sunset Self-Evaluation Report" (August 24, 2007), 3, http://www.opic.state.tx.us/docs/487_sunset_self_evaluation.pdf; (b) OPIC's operating budgets, Office of Public Insurance Counsel, "2010 Operating Budget" (December 2, 2009), §III.A, http://www.opic.state.tx.us/docs/612_opic_operating_budget_fy_2010 .pdf); (c) OPIC's strategic plans, OPIC, "Agency Strategic Plan for Fiscal Years 2011–2015" (June 30, 2010), 16, http://www.opic.state.tx.us/docs/657_2010_strategic_plan-sans_def .pdf; (d) OPIC's website, www.opic.state.tx.us.; and (e) OPIC's promotional materials (on file with author).

an annual assessment of approximately six cents for each policy in force during the calendar year.

Established in 1991, OPIC's original structure was similar to that of proxy advocates in utilities regulation. At that time, Texas utilized a strict version of rate regulation wherein TDI set a range of acceptable rates and companies wishing to deviate from this range were required to seek prior approval. OPIC's primary responsibility was to represent consumers in hearings setting benchmark rates and considering company requests for deviations. OPIC's role in other arenas was limited, although it did push some regulatory initiatives, such as banning the use of prior insurance as an underwriting guideline. Notably, Texas required homeowners insurers to use one of three state-promulgated insurance policies at the time of OPIC's establishment, thus limiting OPIC's involvement in form regulation.[28]

In 2003, however, Texas loosened its regulation of personal lines of insurance. First, with respect to core personal lines of coverage, it moved from a benchmark method of rate regulation to a file and use scheme. Under this approach, insurers are permitted to set their rates without prior approval from TDI and need only adjust if TDI affirmatively finds the rating plan to be "excessive, inadequate, or unfairly discriminatory."[29] Second, Texas substantially deregulated homeowners' policy forms in 2003. Carriers now have free rein to design their policy forms, although these forms cannot be used without TDI's prior approval. TDI is authorized to disapprove a policy form if it "violates any law . . . is unjust or deceptive, encourages misrepresentation, or violates public policy."[30]

These changes in regulation altered OPIC's primary responsibilities. Although OPIC continues to represent consumers in benchmark rate hearings (which persist in certain policy lines, such as credit and title insurance), its primary responsibility is now to review companies' rate and form filings. If it has concerns about these filings, it can request additional information from the insurer or file an objection to TDI. TDI is not required to hold a hearing in response to an OPIC objection, and any hearings it does hold must be within 30 days of the petition filing date. Throughout the filing process, OPIC may informally negotiate with the filing insurer and/or TDI to resolve its concerns.

---

[28] OPIC was nonetheless involved in evaluating proposals from industry to change the forms or use optional endorsements to change coverage.

[29] Tex. Ins. Code § 2251.051 (2010).

[30] Tex. Ins. Code § 2301.007 (2010).

OPIC also plays a role in TDI rulemaking and the provision of consumer information. OPIC evaluates rules before they are formally proposed and may informally submit comments to TDI. Once TDI publishes a rule for public comment, OPIC may participate in the same manner as any other stakeholder. Additionally, OPIC is statutorily empowered to recommend rule changes or legislative enactments. OPIC is also heavily involved in providing consumer information. In recent years, statutes have required OPIC to provide consumer report cards on Health Maintenance Organizations, a consumer bill of rights for personal lines of insurance, and a Web site that helps consumers understand the difference among different companies' policy forms.

Evaluations of OPIC's contributions to Texas insurance regulation are mixed. In 2008, a staff report to the Texas Sunset Advisory Commission – a legislative body that regularly reviews agencies to assess the continued need for their operations – recommended abolishing OPIC and replacing it with a consumer representative within TDI.[31] The report argued that OPIC's activities largely mirrored those of TDI, but were less effective because OPIC did not have any regulatory authority. It also suggested that OPIC was not regularly included in conversations and negotiations between TDI and insurers.

Various commentators, however, objected to this proposal.[32] Of particular note, TDI "strongly urge[d]" the legislature to maintain OPIC "as a separate state agency," arguing that "[a]s an independent consumer advocate, [it] has benefited Texans by providing perspectives and input that enriches the regulatory system." OPIC itself argued that "the most effective approach to providing consumer representation is to ensure that such representation is independent . . . [and] free from any limitations of the Commissioner's previous decisions and current views." Ultimately, the Commission soundly rejected the report's recommendation, concluding that "the independence provided by being a separate, stand-alone agency was important and outweighed any potential benefits of changing the Office's structure." The state legislature continued OPIC for two years, but asked the Commission

---

[31] Sunset Advisory Commission, "Final Report, Texas Department of Insurance & Office of Public Insurance Counsel" (July 2009), 110, http://www.sunset.state.tx.us/81streports/tdi/tdi_opic_fr.pdf.

[32] Comments submitted on OPIC in 2008 are available through the Sunset Commission's Web site (http://www.sunset.state.tx.us/81streports/tdi/responses/chart.htm). The 2010 testimony revisiting this issue is also available at http://www.sunset.state.tx.us/82ndreports/tdi/responses/chart.htm.

Table 13.1. *OPIC's recent activities*

	2007	2008	2009
Rate filings analyzed	761	805	706
Rate filings in which OPIC participated	32	32	52
Form filings analyzed	321	411	514
Form filings in which OPIC participated	24	15	36
Proposed rules analyzed	89	110	51
Proposed rules in which OPIC participated	16	35	16
Contested and industry-wide rate hearings	5	4	5

to revisit the issue at that time. In February, 2011 the Commission again concluded that "the state has a continuing need for" OPIC.

The regular activities of OPIC in the last three available years are documented in Table 13.1, which is based on OPIC's annual (and occasionally audited) performance measures.[33]

Notably, OPIC's participation need not be extensive to be counted as participation for purposes of these statistics. Participation includes any "participation in settlement negotiations or pre-hearing matters during the reporting period" as well as "discussions or negotiations prior to postings or hearings that may result in the agency's recommendation being incorporated into the proposal prior to publication, or which eliminates the need for a hearing."[34] The Sunset Report provides more detailed information on the scope of OPIC's participation. OPIC participated in thirty-two rate filings in 2007. Of these, it simply requested additional information in ten cases and filed formal objections to TDI in the other twenty-two cases. In half the cases in which OPIC formally objected, TDI did not take any action in response to OPIC's objection. OPIC enjoyed more success with respect to form filings in 2007, successfully negotiating, without resort to formal objection, settlements in twenty-two of the twenty-four form filings in which it participated. Finally, in the sixteen instances in which it participated in rule proposals, it informally worked on a rule four times, filed formal written comments four times, and testified at eight rulemaking hearings.

Recent OPIC promotional materials claim that the agency's nineteen most significant rate cases since 2009 have produced consumer savings of

[33] These statistics are derived from yearly "agency at a glance" summaries of OPIC available on the Sunset Commission's Web site, http://www.sunset.state.tx.us.

[34] This definition is not available online, but was provided in response to a public records request from the Automated Budget and Evaluation System of Texas.

$330 million, and $545 million if cases under appeal are included.[35] However, this statistic conflates various types of proceedings and credits OPIC alone for any savings arising from proceedings in which it participated. About $260 million (or $365 million if cases under appeal are included) of these savings stem from required, industry-wide rate hearings that would have occurred even without OPIC's involvement. Although OPIC's testimony and evidence may have increased the total amount of consumer savings, most of these savings would presumably have occurred even without OPIC's participation.

In most of the remaining cases, estimated savings are based on rate reductions or disallowances that occurred after OPIC objected to a filing. Collectively, these cases produced savings amounting to between $70 and $180 million. Of course, TDI might well have challenged these filings without OPIC's initial objection. However, OPIC deserves substantial credit for rate reductions in these cases given its role in initiating the challenge. Perhaps the most important case involves a long-standing dispute between TDI and State Farm Lloyds regarding the extent of a company overcharge of its policyholders. In calculating the amount of the alleged overcharge, TDI staff suggested that refunds should be paid through June 2006, whereas OPIC argued that this rebate period should extend through August 2008. The insurance commissioner ultimately adopted OPIC's suggestion, resulting in $110 million in additional projected policyholder refunds. As the Public Counsel credibly claimed in this case, "[t]his would not have occurred but for OPIC's role in this litigation."[36]

OPIC's own promotional materials also provide some information about its recent activities in form and rule regulation. Since 2009, OPIC claims credit for prompting change in eighty-seven policy forms. Examples include policies that required consumers to purchase uninsured/underinsured motorist (UIM) coverage and submit to mandatory binding arbitration. These claims are much less contestable than OPIC's purported savings to consumers, given the Sunset Report's finding that companies and TDI were willing to negotiate to resolve OPIC's concerns regarding policies in twenty-two of twenty-four cases. OPIC's impact on rulemaking is harder to quantify. Examples of rulemakings in which OPIC has been actively involved include disclosures regarding the scope of coverage and rules governing insurer underwriting. In at least one instance, OPIC seems to have

---

[35] These materials were distributed to various policymakers but do not appear to be available online. All such materials are available from the author on request.

[36] See "OPIC's Role in State Farm Case Results in $110 Million Dollar Increase in Ordered Refunds." http://www.opic.state.tx.us/homeowner.php.

been the driving force for a rule change that reduced the time within which health plans must respond to requests for verification of health coverage from 15 to 5 days.

Although OPIC has rarely invoked its authority to propose new rules, it has used this authority more frequently in recent years under the current Public Counsel. In the most important such instance, OPIC proposed and successfully lobbied for the prohibition of discretionary clauses in health, life, and disability insurance policies. These clauses purport to reserve to the insurer or plan administrator discretion whether or not to pay a claim, limiting any judicial review to a determination of whether that decision was arbitrary or capricious.[37] Additional recent rulemaking initiatives of OPIC include a rule intended to clarify consumer understanding of title insurance and a bulletin informing consumers that it is unlawful for insurers to require consumers to purchase specific amounts of UIM coverage.

California's Public Participation Program

In 1988, California approved by referendum Proposition 103, which broadly reformed the state's regulation of rates in personal lines of insurance, particularly auto insurance. Proposition 103 establishes a consumer empowerment program that has many features of tripartism. The California Public Participation Plan (CPPP) authorizes consumers and consumer organizations to "initiate or intervene in any proceeding permitted or established" by the insurance code governing rates, as well as to "challenge any action . . . and enforce any provision" of Proposition 103. Even more importantly, it provides for the reimbursement of such parties if they "make a substantial contribution to the adoption of any order, regulation or decision by the commissioner or a court."[38] Reimbursement includes "reasonable" attorney fees, witness fees, and costs, which have been interpreted to equal the rates that industry pays. In recent years, these rates range up to more than $500 an hour for certain attorneys and $300 an hour for certain actuaries. However, there is often a substantial time gap in the payment of this

---

[37] These clauses are commonly contained in employee-benefit plans. Caselaw suggests that a state ban on discretionary clauses in insurance policies is not preempted by ERISA. See *American Council of Life Insurers v. Ross*, 558 F.3d 600 (6th Cir. 2009).

[38] Cal. Ins. Code § 1861.05. Basic information about CPPP is available from CDI's Web site, http://www.insurance.ca.gov/0100-consumers/0300-public-programs/0300-public-participation/. A CDI informational report on the program is also available online: http://www.insurance.ca.gov/0250-insurers/0300-insurers/0200-bulletins/prop-103-recoup/report-on-intervenor-program.cfm.

compensation: intervenors typically receive compensation about two and a half years after they provide the underlying services.[39]

The CPPP process differs depending on whether it involves a specific company's rate filing or another regulatory matter. Companies seeking to change premiums for specified policy lines must first receive prior approval from the California Department of Insurance (CDI). To do so, they file an electronic rate change application, which is posted online. Potential intervenors can review these online applications and petition CDI for a hearing on any specific application. CDI must issue written findings if it declines a hearing request, and it cannot decline a request if the proposed rate change exceeds 7 percent for a personal line. After the underlying application is resolved, the intervenor can seek a reimbursement order from CDI by demonstrating that its participation "resulted in more relevant, credible, and non-frivolous information being available to the Commissioner."[40] Intervenors can seek reimbursement for participation in settlement negotiations, even in the absence of a formal hearing. Intervenors' costs are paid by the insurer seeking a rate increase. Interventions that do not involve specific rate filings typically occur in the same manner as ordinary participation in administrative processes: notice and comment rulemaking and judicial review. As above, however, intervenors can subsequently apply for compensation if they make a substantial contribution, although compensation is paid out of a specially designated fund to which all insurers contribute.

Table 13.2 reports basic information about the program's operation from 1993 to 2010, based on internal CDI records.[41] In examining these data, it is helpful to bear in mind that non-rate disputes frequently triggered interventions by multiple groups, whereas rate disputes often involved a single intervenor.

The years between 1996 and 2001 reflect compensation granted for actions filed during the time that Charles Quackenbush was commissioner

---

[39] These statistics as well as subsequent information in this section are derived from analysis of all documentation pertaining to requests for intervenor compensation in 2009 and 2010, including intervenors' requests for compensation, any motions in opposition filed by insurers, final decisions of CDI with respect to these requests, and any underlying ALJ decisions in such cases. These documents were acquired from CDI through the author's public records requests and are available from the author on request.

[40] California Department of Insurance, "Public Participation Plan." http://www.insurance. ca.gov/0100-consumers/0300-public-programs/0300-public-participation/.

[41] Information dating back to 2003 is available at http://www.insurance.ca.gov/0250-insurers/0300-insurers/0200-bulletins/prop-103-recoup/index.cfm. Information prior to that time was obtained from CDI through a public records request.

Table 13.2. *Historical experience of CPPP*

Year	Compensation grants	Compensation grants involving rate interventions	Total compensation awarded	Number of separate intervening parties	Number of separate parties in rate interventions
1993	17	4	$793,371.00	6	4
1994	8	3	$957,289.41	6	2
1995	17	6	$1,295,761.99	7	3
1996	17	6	$645,044.98	7	2
1997	10	0	$198,389.29	5	0
1998	8	2	$482,724.82	4	1
1999	5	3	$379,087.83	2	1
2000	3	2	$540,662.59	3	2
2001	2	0	$496,299.18	1	1
2002	3	0	$482,457.87	2	0
2003	9	4	$480,750.00	5	3
2004	9	4	$775,824.00	4	3
2005	6	1	$915,040.00	4	1
2006	18	8	$2,522,252.00	7	1
2007	10	4	$1,218,829.00	4	2
2008	7	3	$731,341.00	1	1
2009	5	5	$2,473,359.00	1	1
2010	6	5	$981,776.00	1	1

of CDI.[42] Consumer groups labeled Quackenbush "anticonsumer," and he eventually resigned in the face of allegations that he settled investigations of insurer misconduct on terms favorable to the industry in exchange for funding of his political advertisements. The data show that the number of intervenor proceedings, the total amount of compensation money granted, and the average amount of compensation money granted all dipped to their lowest point while Quackenbush-era interventions wended their way through the system.

As Table 13.2 shows, CPPP's success in inducing broad participation from public interest groups has been mixed. Until about 2004, a diverse range of organizations intervened in rulemaking and rate hearings, including organizations like the Southern Christian Leadership Conference, Public Advocates Group, Consumer Union, Voter Revolt, and a handful of private citizens and attorneys. In recent years, however, a single organization – Consumer Watchdog (CW) – has become the sole significant user of the

[42] Roughly speaking, actions filed during Quackenbush's tenure were compensated between the years of 1996 and 2001, even though his actual term ran from 1995 to 2000.

Table 13.3. *Rate proceedings in which compensation was awarded, 2009–2010*

Insurer	Hearing granted?	Requested rate change	Final rate	Difference
Allstate	Yes	12.20%	28.80%	41.00%
Allstate	Yes	7.10%	15.90%	8.80%
Fireman's	Settlement	5.60%	17.90%	12.30%
Geo Vera	Settlement	6.80%	0%	6.80%
Explorer	Yes	17.50%	15%	32.50%
Topa	Settlement	9.26%	6.90%	2.36%
Fireman's	Yes	24.70%	15.28%	9.42%
State Farm	No	3.20%	8%	4.80%
Progressive	No	6.49%	4.70%	1.79%
Mid-Century	No	1.50%	0.00%	1.50%

intervention process, particularly with respect to rate hearings. In fact, CW is the sole recipient of forty-two of the sixty-six awards made since 2003 and the only organization to receive any reimbursement since 2007. Notably, CW's founder and guiding force, Harvey Rosenfield, drafted Proposition 103, which initially established CPPP.

In the last two years, eleven requests for intervenor compensation were filed – ten for rate proceedings and one for administrative rulemaking. All of these requests were filed by CW, and all resulted in the payment of some compensation, which totaled $3,266,806. Table 13.3 summarizes CW's interventions in the ten rate hearings during this timeframe.

CW played an instrumental role in initiating challenges to the underlying rate filings in these cases. Eight of the ten proceedings began with CW's sole motion for a hearing in response to a proposed rate change, whereas only two were initiated by CDI. CDI typically granted the hearing request or the case settled before a hearing could be held. Even in the three most recent instances – in which CDI denied CW's hearing request – CW participated in extensive negotiations with CDI and the filing insurer, with CDI requesting CW's analysis of proposed rates and inviting it to participate in conference calls with the insurers. In these more recent cases, CDI agreed with some of CW's challenges, but bypassed formal hearings by directly ordering its preferred rate changes.

CW's role was even more significant when CDI granted its request for a hearing. In such cases, CW typically "propounded the bulk of formal discovery and informal requests for documentation."[43] These requests could

---

[43] "Decision Awarding Compensation to Foundation for Taxpayer and Consumers Rights Re: Fireman's Fund, PA-2007-00017" (CA Department of Insurance, April 6, 2008), 8.

produce as many as 10,500 pages of documents. CW was also substantially involved in the ultimate resolutions of these cases. CW participated in most settlement discussions. One typical case described how "between July 2007 and April 2008, the parties engaged in regular discussions, including at least five settlement conferences with [the insurer and CW's] actuaries."[44] Additionally, CW often took part in three-way negotiations with insurers and CDI. In some cases, CDI seemed to rely on CW to provide actuarial work and thorough critical analysis of an insurer's proposals.

CW's involvement was clearly responsible for producing decreased rates in at least some instances. For instance, in one intervention, CDI and insurer GeoVera attempted to stipulate a rate increase of 6.8 percent.[45] An ALJ blocked the proposed settlement after CW contested it. Ultimately, GeoVera entered a second settlement, this time agreeing to not raise its rate at all and to abandon its proprietary cost and replacement methodology. A few months later, a settlement was negotiated between CDI, CW, and insurer Topa. In its decision awarding CW compensation for that settlement, CDI noted that "virtually every issue raised in [CW's] petition was discussed with Topa either by the Department... or by both parties in subsequent negotiation proceedings."[46]

CW's impact on rate filings likely extends beyond the few cases in which it formally intervenes. Informal conversations with various members of both CW and CDI repeatedly suggested that the program has an important deterrent effect on rate filings. According to this theory, carriers initially seek lower rates or refrain from seeking rate increases because they want to avoid triggering a hearing or other type of public challenge. This hypothesis is consistent with empirical findings in the public utilities context that utilities are less likely to initiate rate reviews when monitored by a public consumer advocate.[47]

The impact of CPPP on rate filings is particularly notable because California has largely escaped many of the adverse consequences normally produced by regulatory efforts to suppress rates.[48] Most economic studies of such regulation are highly critical of the practice. Among other things,

---

[44] "Decision Awarding Compensation Re: Fireman's Fund, PA-2007-00017," 4.

[45] "Decision Awarding Compensation to Foundation for Taxpayer and Consumer Rights Re: GeoVera, PA-2007-00008" (CA Department of Insurance, September 15, 2009), 12.

[46] "Decision Awarding Compensation to Consumer Watchdog Re: Topa, PA-2008-00018" (CA Department of Insurance, January 7, 2010), 11.

[47] Holburn and Spiller, "Interest Group Representation in Administrative Institutions."

[48] To be clear, this research is generally focused on efforts to suppress rates through regulation rather than on regulation designed to regulate permissible risk classification practices by insurers. The two forms of rate regulation raise very different issues.

they find that price regulation tends to increase the size of involuntary markets, generate subsidies to more risky drivers, exacerbate moral hazard, and decrease the number of competing insurers.[49] Rate regulation often does not even accomplish its goal of suppressing rates in the long term, as firms are too reluctant to reduce rates when costs decrease and seek excessive rate increases when politically feasible.[50] In sharp contrast to these trends, automobile insurance premiums in California have increased at a slower rate since the passage of Proposition 103 than in any other state in the country, primarily as a result of decreases in amounts paid out in claims.[51] At the same time, insurer profits remain strong, numerous insurers compete for business, and remarkably few drivers resort to assigned risk pools. To be sure, interpretation of these outcomes is contestable.[52] But by limiting insurers' capacity to raise rates during politically favorable moments, the intervenor program may have contributed to California's comparatively favorable experience with rate regulation.

In addition to rate filings, CW participated in one rulemaking in the past two years: the promulgation of "Pay As You Drive" (PAYD) regulations, which allow premium rating based on verified driving data. CW's participation included repeated comments in response to proposed regulations, attendance at public hearings, drafting of proposed amendments, and meetings with CDI staff. Ultimately, CW enjoyed some limited success in shaping the final regulation: in response to CW concerns, complex "Price Per Mile" provisions were stripped out of the regulation and limitations were placed on allowable monitoring technology.[53] However, many of CW's most vigorous suggestions were not reflected in the final results. For instance, CW argued strenuously in favor of narrow mileage bands, which would allow consumers to reduce their premiums by changing their driving

[49] Sharon Tennyson, "Efficiency Consequences of Rate Regulation in Insurance Markets" (Networks Financial Institute, Policy Brief No. 2007-PB-03, 2007), 18, http://www
.networksfinancialinstitute.org/lists/publication%20library/attachments/15/2007-pb-03_
tennyson.pdf.

[50] Scott E. Harrington, "Effects of Prior Approval Rate Regulation of Auto Insurance," in *Deregulating Property-Liability Insurance: Restoring Competition and Increasing Market Efficiency*, ed. J. David Cummins (Washington, D.C.: Brookings Institution Press, 2002).

[51] Dwight Jaffee and Thomas Russell, "The Regulation of Automobile Insurance in California," in *Deregulating Property-Liability Insurance*.

[52] David Appel, "Comment on Chapter 5," in *Deregulation Property-Liability Insurance*; Harvey Rosenfield, "Auto Insurance: Crisis and Reform," *University of Memphis Law Review* 29 (1998): 69.

[53] "Decision Awarding Compensation to Consumer Watchdog Re: Pay As You Drive, REG-2008-00020" (California Department of Insurance, November 16, 2010), 3; "Consumer Watchdog's Request for Compensation Re: Pay As You Drive, REG-2008-00020, Exhibit B" (November 16, 2009), 1.

habits. Ultimately, though, CDI stripped out any provision limiting mileage bands. Similarly, CDI resisted CW's suggestions that variation in premiums solely reflect miles driven, which would have prevented insurers from favoring drivers who used electronic mileage verification systems. Tellingly, CW requested compensation for a post-promulgation editorial decrying the final regulations, claiming that it was a "final attempt to influence the Commissioner's actions."

CW has also participated in several important rulemakings prior to the previous two years. One of the most significant involved a prohibition on automobile insurers using ZIP codes to rate policyholders, a practice that some claim discriminates against low-income drivers. Although Proposition 103 prohibited rating on this basis, it was not until 2006 – under the leadership of a self-proclaimed consumer advocate commissioner – that CDI finalized regulations implementing this rule. At that time, insurers launched substantial legal and political challenges to the rule. Eight different intervenors, including CW, participated in the resulting court battle to defend CDI's implementing regulations.[54] In total, these organizations received approximately $3.5 million in reimbursement for their efforts.[55]

In virtually all facets of its involvement in California regulation, CW tends to adopt a very aggressive, advocacy-oriented stance. In rate hearings, it often argues in the alternative, advancing multiple competing rationales for a particular rate reduction. In one instance, it identified five distinct problems with the actuarial calculations supporting a single request for higher earthquake premiums. Notably, CDI endorsed none of CW's positions. Even when CDI opposes a particular rate change, CW will usually find a new and separate rationale for opposing the same change – perhaps ensuring that all bases are covered. Although these arguments occasionally succeed, CW's scattershot approach has its costs. ALJs often regard its positions with skepticism – and occasionally, with hostility. For example, one ALJ dismissed the organization's actuarial work as being "without merit," saying that its arguments were "deficient and not credible."[56] Another said that CW's testimony "at the least, is careless, and may be dodgier than that."[57]

---

[54] Ralph Vartabedian, "Good Driver? Bad Driver? Insurers May Wonder Too," *Los Angeles Times* (January 17, 2007), http://articles.latimes.com/2007/jan/17/autos/hy-wheels17.

[55] California Department of Insurance, "Informational Report on the CDI Intervenor Program," http://www.insurance.ca.gov/0250-insurers/0300-insurers/0200-bulletins/prop-103-recoup/report-on-intervenor-program.cfm.

[56] "Order Adopting Proposed Decision and Order Designating Portion as Precedential Re: Allstate, PA 2006-00004" (California Department of Insurance, July 8, 2008), 1.

[57] "Commissioner's Order Re: Fireman's Fund, PA 2007-00019," 49.

Currently, CW is waging a significant political campaign, along with numerous other interests, to extend prior approval rate regulation to California's health insurers. Some versions of a proposed bill would also extend the CPPP model to health insurance, thus allowing CW and other consumer groups to intervene in carriers' rate applications and subsequently apply for compensation. CW's advocacy for this legislation relies substantially on its experience in the CPPP. As CW states in one press release: implementing rate review along with a consumer intervention process would "save money on health insurance premiums" because "since 2003, our nonprofit organization has challenged the proposed rates of nearly 30 auto, home, and medical malpractice insurance companies in California, and these challenges have saved Californians over two billion dollars."[58]

The NAIC Consumer Participation Program

In 1992, the NAIC created a Consumer Participation Program to amplify the consumer perspective in all phases of NAIC activities and deliberations.[59] The NAIC is a voluntary association of state insurance regulators. Although it is not itself a regulator, the NAIC wields tremendous influence through activities such as drafting model laws and regulations, coordinating enforcement actions and investigations, and developing best practices.[60] Like the CPPP, the NAIC Program is fundamentally an experiment in tripartism: it empowers existing consumer organizations and individuals to participate in the NAIC's processes. In recent years, between twenty and thirty individuals have been selected to be consumer representatives by a board of commissioners and long-time consumer representatives.[61] These

---

[58] Doug Heller, "Intervenor System Has Worked to Save California Insurance Customers $2 Billion Since 2003," May 12, 2011, http://www.consumerwatchdog.org/blog/intervenor-system-has-worked-save-california-insurance-customers-2-billion-2003.

[59] Except where indicated otherwise, information in this section about the NAIC consumer representative program is drawn from (a) the NAIC Web site's description of the program, http://www.naic.org/consumer_participation.htm; (b) NAIC Resolution on Consumer Participation at the NAIC (on file with author); (c) NAIC Plan of Operation for the Consumer Participation Program (on file with author); (d) NAIC List of Funded and Unfunded Consumer Representatives, available at http://www.naic.org/consumer_participation.htm; and (e) NAIC Funded Consumer Representative Travel Expense Reimbursement Policy (on file with author).

[60] Schwarcz, "Regulating Insurance Sales or Selling Insurance Regulation."

[61] In prior years, the number of consumer representatives has been smaller, closer to between twelve to sixteen representatives [Elizabeth B. Goldsmith, "Consumer Empowerment: Public Policy and Insurance Regulation," *International Journal of Consumer Studies* 29 (2005): 86].

representatives are typically employees of public interest organizations or academics. Their tenure as consumer representatives ranges from a single year to more than a decade. The author is currently a consumer representative and has held that position for the last five years.

The Consumer Participation Program takes several approaches to empowering selected consumer representatives to participate in, and influence, NAIC activities. First, consumer representatives are reimbursed from the NAIC's operating budget for expenses (e.g., plane tickets and hotel rooms) they incur to participate in the NAIC's proceedings.[62] However, unlike CPPP, the program does not compensate consumer representatives for their time. Second, NAIC consumer representatives are provided a designated forum at each NAIC meeting to present on issues of their choosing. Third, consumer representatives enjoy privileged access to regulators: they use regulator facilities at meetings and frequently consult informally with regulators about NAIC issues outside of meetings. Finally, designated NAIC consumer representatives enjoy certain reputational benefits: they are more likely to be sought out by media, asked for their guidance by regulators, and offered opportunities to present at meetings.[63]

These approaches to empowering consumer representatives must be understood within the distinctive context of the NAIC's processes. The vast majority of the NAIC's work is conducted publicly through conference calls, email list-serves, and meetings that are run by regulators and their staff, but open to broad stakeholder participation. In this sense, at least, the NAIC operates within a new governance regulatory paradigm. The NAIC consumer participation program thus allows for the involvement of empowered consumers in virtually every facet of its operations, such as developing "charges" for committees and drafting model laws, white papers, bulletins, and consumer guides.[64]

Unlike in either CPPP or OPIC, the roles of NAIC consumer representatives are malleable and ambiguous. Aside from attending tri-annual meetings, little is affirmatively required of consumer representatives. Different consumer representatives focus on different issues, ranging from implementation of health insurance reform to the development of consumer disclosures. In some cases, individual representatives working on

---

[62] Several consumer representatives are unfunded, because their organizations have sufficient resources to pay for their expenses.

[63] Goldsmith, "Consumer Empowerment."

[64] Timothy Jost, "The National Association of Insurance Commissioners and Implementation of the Patient Protection and Affordable Care Act," *University of Pennsylvania Law Review* 159 (2011): 2043.

overlapping issues clash over their views about which policies best promote the consumer interest.[65] Since the passage of the Patient Protection and Affordable Care Act (ACA) – which delegates substantial responsibilities to the NAIC – the interests of consumer representatives have been skewed substantially toward health insurance: roughly seventeen out of twenty-seven consumer representatives currently focus predominantly on health insurance. By contrast, there is not a single consumer representative whose primary focus involves life insurance or solvency regulation.

The amorphous responsibilities of consumer representatives complicate evaluation of the NAIC consumer participation program.[66] The program has enjoyed some limited success cultivating the active engagement of consumer representatives in NAIC processes. On one hand, many consumer representatives spend a substantial percentage of their work time (often between 5 and 40 percent) on NAIC activities. Although they are tremendously outnumbered by industry representatives, they tend to be much more assertive in their participation, at least on certain issues: they literally sit in the front row of meetings and tend to offer their thoughts more frequently than industry representatives during meetings and conference calls. On the other hand, this participation only extends to a subset of the NAIC's activities, and industry representatives often dominate meetings involving low-profile regulatory issues.

When a sufficient number of consumer representatives have been actively engaged in specific NAIC issues and effectively coordinated their efforts, they have often enjoyed substantial influence in counteracting industry influence. This is clearest in the post-ACA health insurance domain. Perhaps the most notable example involves the NAIC's development of the Medical Loss Ratio (MLR) regulation.[67] Under the ACA, insurers are required to spend a set percentage of premiums improving policyholders' health. The ACA delegates to the NAIC the task of defining what expenditures qualify as meeting this requirement. Despite enormous industry pressure, the NAIC

---

[65] As one long-standing consumer representative, University of Georgia economics professor Brenda Cude, explained, "I've been forced to ask myself whether anyone can really represent the interests of all consumers. I've concluded the answer is usually no. More often, one must identify the population most at risk in a particular issue and speak on their behalf" (Goldsmith, "Consumer Empowerment").

[66] The observations in this paragraph are based entirely on the author's personal experiences participating in the Consumer Participation Program as well as informal discussions with other consumer representatives.

[67] Jost, "The National Association of Insurance Commissioners and Implementation of the Patient Protection and Affordable Care Act."

adopted a relatively strict approach that has infuriated various industry groups, particularly insurance agents. The NAIC consumer representatives undoubtedly played a substantial role in producing this result: the seventeen health representatives coordinated their efforts to leverage prominent media outlets, individually lobbied commissioners, submitted comments on work product, followed and participated in conference calls, testified in hearings, and provided technical expertise. Many health representatives effectively devoted all or most of their work time to these activities, as their job descriptions aligned precisely with their roles as NAIC consumer representatives. A recent article by Timothy Jost, law professor and NAIC consumer representative, describes this process in detail, as well as other areas in which consumer representatives influenced NAIC implementation of the ACA. These range from the development of standardized consumer disclosures to the drafting of model regulations for health insurance exchanges.[68]

By contrast, the program has struggled to counteract industry pressure when an issue is not policed by a sufficient number of qualified, interested consumer representatives (although it has done much good in these domains when industry resistance is limited). For instance, consumer representatives have enjoyed only limited success in advocating for enhanced transparency in property/casualty and life insurance contexts.[69] Examples include unsuccessful efforts to (a) make insurer-specific data regarding market conduct and claims handling available to the public; (b) make filings to the Interstate Insurance Product Regulation Commission public on submission to allow for public comment; and (c) collect and publish geo-coded, insurer-specific application, premium, exposure, and claims data, similar to the data required of mortgage holders by the Home Mortgage Disclosure Act. In each case, a small handful of consumer representatives devoted attention to the issue through both normal NAIC channels and the attempted application of political pressure through the media. For most (if not all) of these representatives, their efforts were tangential to their primary job responsibilities and thus the amount of time and effort they could devote

---

[68] Jost, "The National Association of Insurance Commisioners and Implementation of the Patient Protection and Affordable Care Act."

[69] For further detail on these issues, see "Emerging Issues in Insurance Regulation before the Senate Subcommittee on Securities, Insurance and Investment" (statement of Daniel Schwarcz, Associate Professor, University of Minnesota Law School, 2011), http://banking .senate.gov/public/index.cfm?FuseAction=Files.View&FileStore_id=32a9fa33-328f-4289-aeed-f95aeff7e5d3; Daniel Schwarcz, "Transparently Opaque: Understanding the Lack of Transparency in Insurance Consumer Protection," *UCLA Law Review* (January 2014), forthcoming.

to the issue was limited. Ultimately, each of these efforts floundered in the face of overwhelming industry opposition.[70]

Perhaps even more distressing than the numerous failed consumer representative initiatives is the near absence of any consumer participation involvement on a broad range of issues that the NAIC regularly encounters.[71] This is particularly notable in the realm of solvency regulation: although assuring insurers' solvency is undoubtedly the principal purpose of insurance regulation, consumer participants have virtually no collective expertise in this area, and the vast majority of meetings and initiatives in this domain involve essentially no participation from consumer representatives. The absence of meaningful consumer participation is also notable in various more obscure fields, such as crop insurance and risk retention groups. As one longtime consumer representative stated in a media report, "we just don't have the resources to put the full-court press on the regulators."[72]

PRELIMINARY THOUGHTS ON CONSUMER EMPOWERMENT PROGRAMS IN INSURANCE REGULATION

All consumer empowerment programs attempt to enhance the regulatory influence of consumers and thus to check industry sway over regulatory outcomes. But the means used by different programs vary, as do their prospects for success. The preceding case studies, when considered in light of preexisting research on similar programs, provide a starting point for thinking through these issues in insurance regulation.[73] They also may provide some guidance in regulatory domains, such as banking or securities, that resemble insurance in that they are conducted by states, involve technical regulatory matters, and concern powerful financial interests. Table 13.5, at the conclusion of this subsection, summarizes the key points.

---

[70] Schwarcz, "Transparently Opaque." Recently, NAIC consumer representatives adopted a new initiative to enhance the transparency of insurance policy terms in personal lines markets. Although still in its infancy, this effort seems to have gained some traction [Daniel Schwarcz, "Reevaluating Standardized Insurance Policies," *University of Chicago Law Review* 77 (2011): 1263].

[71] The observations in this paragraph are based entirely on the author's personal experiences participating in the Consumer Participation Program as well as informal discussions with other consumer representatives.

[72] Trevor Thomas, "Who's Watching the NAIC Henhouse," *National Underwriter Life & Health* (November 22, 2010).

[73] All information reviewed in this section is described previously either in the individual case studies or in the section describing the history of consumer empowerment programs.

Table 13.4. *Summary of consumer empowerment programs in insurance*

	Type of program	Funding amount	Funding source	Regulatory domain	Procedural rights
OPIC	Proxy advocate	About 1 million a year	6 cent assessment on policies	Rate and form filings Rulemakings Industry-wide rate hearings New initiatives Consumer Information	Cannot demand hearing Review rules before proposed Participate in industry-wide hearings Propose new initiatives
CPPP	Tripartism	Fees comparable to what industry pays, amounting to between 1 and 2 million a year	Payment from petitioning insurer in rate hearings Payment from fund contributed to by all insurers in non-rate interventions	Rate filings Rule makings	Can insist on hearing if rate request is larger than 7% Receive written explanation if no hearing is granted for requests less than 7%
NAIC Con. Part.	Tripartism	Reimbursement of expenses, amounting to about $100,000 a year	General NAIC Revenue	Crafting model laws Developing regulatory initiatives Coordinating regulatory activities	Designated forum to present issues Privileged access to regulators Reputational benefits

Table 13.5. *Summary of tentative thoughts on consumer empowerment programs*

Type of program	When to deploy	How to design
Proxy advocate	(1) Consumer perspective should be identifiable based on historical trends and industry views, even if contestable. (2) Consumer information and expertise should not be sufficiently presented by non-industry stakeholders.	(1) Should consider providing proxy advocates with procedural rights. (2) Proxy advocates should be independent government entities. (3) Should provide sufficient resources and select consumer-oriented individuals.
Tripartism	(1) No need for single consumer perspective or for absence of non-industry stakeholder participation. (2) Absence of robust number of willing potential PIGs raises effectiveness and efficiency concerns.	(1) Procedural rights are not necessary to ensure influence given capacity to exert influence through political/media channels. (2) Procedures to ensure contestability in future are essential. (3) Involvement of empowered PIGS in all facets of regulatory process and mechanisms to ensure accountability to PIG's constituents are important.

Deploying and Designing Proxy Advocates

Although proxy advocacy gained substantial traction in the 1970s and 1980s, its influence has since waned significantly. Part of the explanation for this may be that defining the mission of a proxy advocate is difficult given the conviction of many that there is no single, objective, consumer interest.[74] Alternatively, proxy advocacy may be objectionable to some because it supplants, or at least complicates, the mandate of the regulator, whose mission also encompasses representing consumers. These concerns are important. However, the experiences of OPIC and proxy advocates in the utilities arena suggest that this form of consumer empowerment is nonetheless an underexplored mechanism to counteract industry influence in insurance regulation and regulatory contexts that resemble it.

[74] Robert A. Dahl, *Dilemmas of Pluralist Democracy* (New Haven, CT: Yale University Press, 1983).

First, there is a broad range of regulatory issues in the insurance context on which a sufficiently clear "consumer position" exists to guide the efforts of a proxy advocate. To date, proxy advocacy has seemingly been premised on the notion that, to be effective, the advocate must be given a unidirectional mandate. Thus proxy advocacy in both utilities regulation and in the initial conception of OPIC has largely been designed solely to advocate for the suppression of rates in adversarial hearings. However, OPIC's evolution into a more multifaceted proxy advocate demonstrates that this implicit assumption is incorrect. In fact, proxy advocates in insurance regulation will often (though hardly always) be capable of meaningfully discerning a "consumer position." Consider, for instance, the initiatives of OPIC to ban discretionary clauses, decrease the time within which health insurers must certify coverage, and strike mandatory binding arbitration provisions in policies. Historical trends show that these positions are "consumer-oriented" and can expect industry resistance. To be clear, that does not mean that these positions are correct or even ultimately in the interests of consumers. Rather, it means that they represent part of a coherent and identifiable set of "consumer positions" that will tend to be under-represented in regulatory processes that do not substantially involve non-industry stakeholders.

This last point raises the second condition for proxy advocacy to represent a sensible strategy for counteracting industry influence: it must be the case that non-industry stakeholders would otherwise fail to effectively present these consumer positions to regulators. Proxy advocacy appears to influence regulatory results primarily by providing regulators with expertise and information from a consumer perspective, rather than by applying political pressure. As noted earlier, this is how proxy advocates in the utilities arena describe their influence compared with (nonempowered) public interest groups.[75] The information-without-pressure approach of proxy advocates is also reflected by OPIC's record. In contrast to CW, OPIC never publicly challenges TDI and often frames its successes as a product of cooperation with TDI, as in the cases of its campaign to ban discretionary clauses and its victory in extending the rebate period in the State Farm Lloyds case. Its lack of aggressive advocacy may also partially explain how OPIC involves itself in so many more proceedings than CW. In the last two years, OPIC was involved in twice the number of contested rate hearings as CW, "participated" in about eight times more rate reviews than did CW, and intervened in 100 times more rulemakings or policy form disputes than did CW. OPIC's limited appetite for aggressive advocacy is not surprising:

[75] Gormley, *The Politics of Public Utility Regulation.*

OPIC's Public Counsel is appointed by the same governor that appoints the head of TDI, and TDI strongly supported OPIC in the face of calls for its abolishment. To the extent that proxy advocates influence results primarily by providing information from a consumer perspective, they are only likely to counteract industry influence when other stakeholders, such as public interest groups or other government bodies, are not performing this role.

Even if these two conditions are met, proxy advocates nonetheless must be well structured to influence regulatory outcomes. The OPIC case study provides some limited guidance on this front. Perhaps most notably, it suggests that proxy advocates may be more likely to influence regulatory outcomes when they have procedural rights in the regulatory process. Without procedural rights, proxy advocates lack leverage with which to negotiate settlements with industry participants. It is therefore hardly surprising that OPIC rarely negotiates settlements on rates, given its inability to insist on a hearing when it objects to a rate filing. Encouraging negotiation is important, because recent research shows that negotiated settlements are a primary mechanism by which proxy advocates lower utility rates.[76] OPIC's lack of procedural authority may also have allowed TDI to dismiss OPIC objections to rate filings without sufficient consideration in 2007, when TDI did not respond to about half of OPIC's objections. Consistent with these observations, in the last several years, OPIC has repeatedly asked for the right to demand a hearing if it objects to a rate or form filing. In the rulemaking context, proxy advocates could be provided with procedural rights such as the ability to scrutinize draft rules before public exposure (as OPIC does) or the right to advise an ALJ regarding the advisability of a rule in a hybrid rulemaking.[77]

Preexisting literature on proxy advocacy provides additional guidance on the optimal design of proxy advocates. First, it suggests that proxy advocates should be structured as independent counsels, rather than as consumer representative divisions within a state attorney general office or specialized staff within the regulator itself.[78] This is consistent with Texas's own rejection of the Sunset Commission's proposal to abolish OPIC and create a consumer representative within TDI. Second, proxy advocates must employ individuals who have "a greater interest in consumer welfare than in any

---

[76] Littlechild, "Stipulated Settlements, the Consumer Advocate, and Utility Regulation in Florida."

[77] Wagner, "Administrative Law, Filter Failure, and Information Capture."

[78] Mayer et al., "Consumer Representation and Local Telephone Rates."

particular industry in which they participate" and be provided with "sufficient resources to look for agency transgressions."[79]

Deploying and Designing Tripartism

Tripartite consumer empowerment approaches may be appropriate in situations not conducive to proxy advocacy. First, unlike proxy advocates, tripartite schemes do not require the existence of an identifiable consumer perspective. Tripartite frameworks can empower multiple PIGs, each of which may have a particular perspective. This is illustrated by the NAIC consumer participation program, in which individual representatives often clash about how best to promote the consumer interest. Even if only one empowered PIG exists, as is currently the case in the CPPP, its status as a nongovernmental entity creates more leeway for it to embrace its own peculiar view of the consumer perspective. Thus, as described previously, CW advocated for its preferred regulations on the PAYD and ZIP-code rating issues even though it is not particularly clear that these views represented the natural "consumer positions."

Second, in contrast to proxy advocacy, tripartism may be capable of influencing results even if non-industry stakeholders already present "consumer positions" to regulators. This is because empowered PIGs are capable of influencing results not simply by providing regulators with additional information and perspective, but by marrying that information and perspective with the threat of political pressure through the use of media and public outreach. To be sure, even non-empowered public interest groups enjoy some capacity to set off "fire alarms" that prompt broad public scrutiny of agency behavior.[80] But empowered PIGS have a better capacity to leverage media sources than ordinary public interest groups given their enhanced access to information, richer perspective from direct participation in regulatory processes, and strengthened reputational capital. Even more importantly, empowered PIGs can leverage this threat during regulatory processes to exert pressure on regulators to fully consider their perspective and negotiate in good faith on that basis.

Both the CPPP and the NAIC Consumer Participation Program illustrate these points, as empowered PIGs in both programs couple their direct advocacy efforts with the threat of extending the regulatory or legislative fight into the public domain. Consider, in this vein, CW's op-ed lambasting

---

[79] Barkow, "Insulating Agencies," 63.
[80] Mathew D. McCubbins and Thomas Schwartz, "Congressional Oversight Overlooked: Police Patrols versus Fire Alarms," *American Journal of Political Science* 28 (1984): 165.

the final PAYD regulations, which drew heavily on CW's insurer-financed efforts to articulate and defend its position. Another example is CW's current efforts to expand prior approval rate review to the health insurance domain, which draws on CW's claimed successes in the property/casualty domain through the CPPP program. Similarly, consider the willingness of NAIC consumer participants to use the media to influence the MLR debate or advocate for increased transparency in property/casualty insurance markets.

This willingness of empowered PIGS to couple their information and advocacy efforts with political pressure is a function of several factors. Virtually all public interest groups are naturally adept at using media, as well as other public outreach tools, to convey their messages to the public. Moreover, their self-identity is devoted to their vision of consumer rights in a quite fundamental sense: the people who choose to work for CW or apply to be NAIC consumer representatives tend to be deeply devoted to their particular vision of consumer welfare. Finally, unlike proxy advocates, the existence of empowered PIGs is not jeopardized by the termination of public funding: such groups exist independently of tripartism-oriented consumer empowerment programs, and so, compared with proxy advocates, they are more likely to take political risks that could jeopardize the existence of those programs.

However, a key shortcoming of tripartism is that it requires a robust network of public interest groups with broad-ranging expertise and interests. Indeed, Ayres and Braithwaite explicitly acknowledge this point, but assume that "for most business regulatory statutes in a democracy, there will be an appropriate PIG" because "we think it is unlikely that statutes that threaten the interests of business would have been enacted in the absence of an interest group pushing for them."[81] Similarly, existing critiques of tripartism often focus on the profusion of different interest groups that may adopt "fringe" perspectives or embrace adversarialism.[82] However, the insurance case studies suggest that, in some regulatory settings, the problem with tripartism is precisely the opposite: that an insufficient number of expert PIGs will be available.

Consider the NAIC Consumer Participation Program. In fields such as health insurance, the influence of the program has been dramatic precisely because the program has harnessed the energy of a willing cadre of experts capable of devoting most or all of their time to their roles as NAIC consumer representatives. By contrast, the program's capacity to counteract industry

---

[81] Ayres and Braithwaite, *Responsive Regulation*, 59.
[82] Seidenfeld, "Empowering Stakeholders."

influence has been muted in other contexts, such as solvency regulation and the regulation of property/casualty and life insurance, where the program simply has not been able to maintain a critical mass of expert representatives. Of the few representatives who do operate in these domains, almost all are only able to devote a relatively small percentage of their time and efforts to NAIC activities, and most have a fairly narrow set of interests and expertise.

The CPPP illustrates a different risk of an insufficient network of PIGs in a tripartite scheme: inefficiency and contentiousness. Recall that when the CPPP was first established, it experienced robust participation from a variety of different groups. But as the program has aged, CW has come to dominate it. Although this hardly seems to have resulted in CW becoming captured by industry or regulator, it is nonetheless troubling. First, CW now enjoys a privileged position in California insurance regulation despite the fact that it often takes controversial positions on consumer issues. Second, CW's dominance of the intervenor program compromises the program's legitimacy, especially because CW's founder drafted the referendum creating the intervenor program in the first place. Third, CW's privileged position may incentivize it to devote excessive amounts of time and energy challenging industry, because doing so produces monetary payoffs whose appropriateness cannot be compared with other intervenors. As described previously, the rates of compensation paid to CW are substantial and paid in virtually every intervention. Not only might this result in higher expenses than necessary, but it also could undermine the capacity for the more collaborative forms of regulation emphasized in the new governance literature, as indicated by CW's aggressive style in advocating for consumers.

In settings where tripartite schemes are deployed, several design principles can be extracted from the case studies. First, tripartite design need not always meet the rigid constraints articulated by Ayres and Braithwaite. To be sure, certain elements appear to be a prerequisite to effective tripartism (or consumer empowerment of any type): representatives must have sufficient technical expertise and information to understand and evaluate regulatory issues. But while it might well be beneficial to allow empowered PIGs to challenge industry in the same way as regulators, this procedural right is not always necessary for empowered PIGs to successfully counter balance industry influence. Ayres and Braithwaite explain the importance of this procedural right as a mechanism to ensure that empowered PIGs have sufficient leverage during all earlier stages of the process. However, a reasonable (though admittedly imperfect) substitute for this leverage is the capacity of empowered PIGs to challenge industry behavior through political pressure and media scrutiny, as described above. This is most clearly suggested by the successes of the NAIC consumer participation program in the health insurance domain, where consumer representatives do not enjoy any procedural rights.

Second, tripartite schemes should be designed to promote contestability in the future, as well as the present. The evolution of CPPP demonstrates that contestability may be fragile, especially when one organization has a natural advantage. The CPPP design discourages contestability in several ways. Most notably, there is a substantial time gap between the expenditures required of intervenors and their ultimate compensation (about 2.5 years), and intervenor compensation cannot be ensured because it is dependent on an ex post assessment of whether the intervenor made a "substantial contribution." Additionally, the underlying regulatory process is complex and technical, thus strongly favoring repeat players. Taken together, these factors likely explain why new PIGs have not generally joined, or challenged, CW's status as the dominant user of CPPP. CPPP might be much more successful at promoting a contestable structure if, for instance, it allowed new organizations to make initial showings of their proposed contributions, provided them with some initial funding based on the likelihood that contribution would be substantial, and offered training and resources to groups interested in participating in the program.

Additional lessons for designing tripartite schemes can be extracted from the preexisting literature. For instance, consistent with the Ayres and Braithwaite framework, Jost[83] emphasizes that the NAIC consumer participation program was effective in the health arena because of the open and collaborative nature of NAIC processes, which allows consumer representatives to be involved at every stage of regulatory discussions and negotiations. And, as noted earlier, Seidenfeld[84] helpfully suggests that tripartite systems ought to include mechanisms that ensure that empowered PIGs are effectively representing their constituencies.

CONCLUSION

Different consumer empowerment mechanisms have distinct strengths and weaknesses in counteracting industry influence. When consumer interests are articulable and reasonably discernible, proxy advocates may be able to provide relevant information and perspective that would otherwise be underrepresented in the views of participating stakeholders. Empowered

---

[83] Jost, "The National Association of Insurance Commissioners and Implementation of the Patient Protection and Affordable Care Act."

[84] Seidenfeld, "Empowering Stakeholders."

PIGs, by contrast, are free to offer their own subjective set of consumer perspectives during the regulatory process, even when a single consumer position is not clear. PIGs can back up this perspective with the threat of political and media pressure. However, such tripartism may be ineffective, inefficient, or otherwise problematic in the absence of a robust network of public interest representatives.

At first blush, these preliminary observations may suggest that proxy advocacy and tripartism are mutually exclusive alternatives for counteracting excessive industry influence. However, many regulatory domains involve a range of issues, some more appropriate for proxy advocacy and some more appropriate for tripartite approaches. Employing both forms of consumer empowerment might consequently allow each mechanism to focus on its comparative advantage and safeguard against the limitations and blind spots of the other. This dual approach need not be costly. As the NAIC consumer participation program suggests, effective tripartism does not require substantial funding where a robust network of potential PIGs already exists. Simply by providing PIGs with improved access to information and regulators, some oversight over early regulatory proceedings, and better access to media, tripartism can enhance the capacity of concerned groups and individuals to counteract industry influence. Although the costs associated with proxy advocacy may be larger, OPIC illustrates that they are hardly exorbitant. To the extent that even this cost cannot be justified, proxy advocates might be permitted to directly solicit public contributions in the bills that private companies send to consumers, as is the case for some proxy advocates in the utilities domain. Consumers might even be defaulted into providing a small contribution (six cents a year in the case of OPIC) to fund these programs, but given the option of opting out of this default.

As emphasized at the start of this chapter, industry influence is not always harmful to the public interest. Nor is it always the case that industry influence is insufficiently counterbalanced by the influence of non-industry stakeholders. But well-designed consumer empowerment programs may be an effective option for responding to situations in which the regulated do indeed wield undue power over regulators at the public's expense.

14

Courts and Regulatory Capture

M. Elizabeth Magill[1]

Regulatory agencies have many supervisors. Congress gives them life, appropriates their money, and conducts oversight of their activities. The president appoints and can remove their senior officers, occasionally instructs them, and conducts review of many of their important actions before they take effect. Federal courts, too, supervise agencies. Statutes authorize federal courts to entertain complaints about agency action and, in the course of hearing those challenges, federal courts evaluate the legal validity of agency action. If a regulatory agency goes astray, each of these institutions has some ability to nudge it back to the proper path.

These supervisors have distinct tools at their disposal to supervise agencies. Congress, on paper, has nearly limitless authority over agencies, constrained only by the Constitution. Assuming the approval of the president, or a veto-proof majority, congressional power to legislate and appropriate can be deployed to control an agency in any number of ways. It can specifically tell an agency what to do, it can generally instruct an agency, it can prohibit future action, or it can reverse past action (or all four at once). The president, by contrast, has much more limited authority to initiate agency action or to alter the agenda of an agency, but there are many crucial "implementation" decisions that agencies make that are not clearly dictated by statute, and in that space, the president can seek to work his will through his appointments and his supervision. Compared with the institutions set forth in the first two articles of the Constitution, the federal courts identified in Article III seem to have the most limited authority to supervise agency action. They are purely reactive, permitted to intervene only when

[1] Dean and Richard E. Lang Professor, Stanford Law School. Thanks to Dan Carpenter, Jake Gersen, Stephen Griffin, Daryl Levinson, David Moss, Keith Werhan, anonymous reviewers, and participants in the Tobin Project *Preventing Capture* project for their comments. Nicole DeMoss and Sam Guthrie provided excellent research assistance. Errors are mine.

a challenger to agency action seeks to invoke the authority of the federal courts. Federal judges review a tiny slice of agency actions and they are not the authors of the playbook that guides their review – the judges are guided by statutes.

This chapter focuses on this third institution, the federal courts, and asks whether such courts prevent or facilitate regulatory capture and, if they do not presently act to prevent regulatory capture, asks whether judicial controls on administrative action can be redesigned to allow them to do so. These are not questions that should be answered in a vacuum, without attention to the available alternatives. Hence, as this chapter takes up these questions, it compares judicial supervision of agencies as a means to prevent regulatory capture to the supervisory capacities of the legislature and the executive.

THE BASICS OF JUDICIAL REVIEW

We should start first with a very basic outline of judicial review of administrative action. Courts are legally authorized to evaluate agency decisions in court. As a result of this formal authority, courts *might* be in a position to police regulatory capture. This judicial review is triggered only when a party who objects to agency action files suit claiming that some agency action is unlawful. Federal courts review the work of agencies pursuant to statutes, and there are many potentially relevant statutes in any given legal challenge to agency action, but the Administrative Procedure Act (APA) provides the basic framework for federal court review of agency action.[2]

That legal framework is organized into two major questions. The first question is whether judicial review of the agency action is even available. To those outside of law, this may come as a surprise, but it is important to understand that, even when a challenger appears and brings legal action against the agency, not all agency actions are reviewable in court. That is to say, in some cases a court will not even consider the parties' objections to the agency action, even if the objection that the agency ignored the law seems well founded based on the known facts.

Broadly speaking, the modern trend has been to expand the set of cases where judicial review is available, but, even so, judicial review is sometimes not available. It is not available in a variety of circumstances – a challenger may lack standing (he or she may not be injured in the right way by the

---

[2] Administrative Procedure Act, Pub. L. No. 79-404, 60 Stat. 237 (codified as amended in scattered sections of 5 U.S.C.).

agency action), he or she may come to court at the wrong time, or the agency-specific statute may make the particular decision not subject to review in court. In addition, some agency decisions are not reviewable in court because they are especially discretionary. This category is both important and hard to pin down, but, speaking generally, it means that parties are likely to have a difficult time challenging an agency's failure to act or an agency's general management of a regulatory program.

If judicial review *is* available, the second question is whether that review provides much of a constraint on agency action. Under administrative law, there are a series of different standards of review that apply in any given circumstance. Administrative lawyers call this area of the law "scope of review" doctrine, and these standards – for example, the "substantial evidence" test or the "arbitrary and capricious" test – dictate the intensity of the court's examination of agency action. The standards determine, that is, how skeptical or deferential the court will be of the agency's decision.

Which specific standard of review a court will apply depends on two factors. The first factor is what *procedure* the agency used when it made its decision. An agency might have completed an elaborate process, as agencies are generally required to do when they adopt general rules that are intended to constrain the actions of private parties. That process requires an agency to request comment on proposed agency action and consider and respond to those comments as it announces its final decision.[3] This may not sound particularly onerous, but it can be: a significant rulemaking can take an agency several years to complete.[4] In other cases, as when it announces how it will exercise its prosecutorial discretion, an agency is not required to provide notice, invite comment, and respond to those comments.[5] There is a similar range of agency process when it comes to adjudications, that is, decisions that determine the rights and duties of a single individual or entity (a corporation or union, for example). An adjudication may be elaborate, resembling a trial, with a judge, the presentation of evidence and witnesses,

---

[3] 5 U.S.C. § 553. This is commonly referred to as "notice and comment rulemaking" or informal rulemaking.

[4] Anne Joseph O'Connell, "Political Cycles of Rulemaking: An Empirical Portrait of the Modern Administrative State," *Virginia Law Review* 94 (2008): 889, 964 (finding that "the average duration of completed rulemakings for nine of the ten agencies [analyzed in the article] was under two years"); Sidney A. Shapiro and Randy Rabinowitz, "Voluntary Regulatory Compliance in Theory and Practice: The Case of OSHA," *Administrative Law Review* 52 (2000): 97, 98 (analyzing the Occupational Safety and Health Administration, which "has completed only a few rules in less than three years, and has taken between four and seven years to complete most rules").

[5] 5 U.S.C. § 553(b) (stating exceptions to the "notice and comment" rulemaking, including policy statements and interpretive rules).

and the requirement that the decision be based on the record compiled at the proceeding. An adjudication may, at the other end of the spectrum, be highly informal, involving no record or submissions by the parties about facts and law.[6]

The policymaking form the agency uses is only one factor that determines the appropriate scope of review standard that a court will apply. The second factor is the *character* of the decision that the agency made. An agency decision may rest on a finding of fact, such as the level of economic concentration in a particular industry. It may turn on an interpretation of law, such as the meaning of a key term in the relevant statute. Or it may rest heavily on a policy choice – a mix of fact, judgment, and law.

A court needs the answer to both of these questions in order to choose the proper scope of review standard to apply. There are different verbal formulations of the standards depending on whether an agency is making, for instance, a factual determination or a policy judgment. In the first case, the court will evaluate whether the agency's finding is supported by substantial evidence,[7] whereas in the second it will evaluate whether the agency's decision is arbitrary and capricious.[8] Likewise, there are different standards that apply depending on the procedure used. If an agency interprets the statute it administers in the course of promulgating a rule with the force and effect of law, then the court will be fairly deferential to the agency's interpretation,[9] but if the agency interprets the statute in the course of issuing a policy statement, the court will be less deferential to its interpretation.[10]

It is notoriously difficult to generalize about the consequences of judicial supervision of agencies. Its on-the-ground intensity can vary with context and, more than that, it is hard to know whether the distinctions that the legal doctrine makes, which could be characterized as very fine ones, have a significant effect on agency behavior. One generalization, however, is fair: judicial review of agency action will be quite a bit more skeptical of the government than the review a court conducts of routine legislative action of the same variety – legislatively crafted clean air standards would be treated quite differently by the courts than agency-crafted clean air standards.[11]

---

[6] 5 U.S.C. §§ 554, 556–58 (formal adjudication); 5 U.S.C. § 555 (informal adjudication).

[7] 5 U.S.C. § 706 (2)(E); *Universal Camera Corp. v. National Labor Relations Board*, 340 U.S. 474, 477 (1951).

[8] 5 U.S.C. § 706 (2)(A).

[9] *United States v. Mead Corp.*, 533 U.S. 218, 226–27 (2001); *Chevron U.S.A., Inc. v. Natural Resources Defense Council, Inc.*, 467 U.S. 837, 843–44 (1984).

[10] *United States v. Mead Corp.*, 533 U.S. 218, 231–34 (2001).

[11] *Motor Vehicle Manufacturers Association of the U.S., Inc. v. State Farm Mutual Automobile Insurance Company*, 463 U.S. 29, 44 n.9 (1983) (stating that the Court does not "view as

REGULATORY CAPTURE

Determining the role that judicial review does or could play in preventing or facilitating regulatory capture depends on when, and under what conditions, regulatory capture is likely to occur. The general idea of capture, as used in this volume, is easy to state: capture occurs when some special interest, typically an industry group, persuades government actors to exercise the coercive power of the state in ways that are not in the "public interest." That is, the interests of the industry group diverge from the public interest and the government chooses the former over the latter. The volume further distinguishes between "strong" and "weak" capture. In the first case, government adopts regulations that are so far away from what is in the public interest that it would be better not to have the policy at all. "Weak" capture, on the other hand, is a case in which the regulation does not, as the result of special interest influence, advance the public interest as much as it might, but it is on balance better to have the regulation than not.

A classic example of capture, provided in George Stigler's account, is when an industry group convinces government actors to adopt policies that erect barriers to entry in their industry.[12] For example, the present producers of coal have much to gain if they can persuade the government to adopt policies that inhibit competitors. They would favor government policies that make entry into the industry difficult – such as regulatory requirements for new entrants into their market from which existing players are shielded. In most careful versions of the account, it is important that the industry group is seeking a *private good* in the economic sense – one that is both excludable and rivalrous. This is important because it explains why the group can effectively organize to seek these goods in the first place. Members of such a group have much to gain that they will not have to share with anyone else, and for this reason they are able to overcome the typically powerful barriers to collective action.

How do we know when capture has occurred? That is a difficult question to answer. As Carpenter points out in this volume, the studies showing that legislative or regulatory outcomes coincide with the interests of industry fall (far) short of persuasively demonstrating "capture." Among other things, these studies do not identify the alternative policy that was not adopted that would have served the public interest, which is a very serious failing.

---

equivalent the presumption of constitutionality afforded legislation drafted by Congress and the presumption of regularity afforded an agency in fulfilling its statutory mandate").

[12] George J. Stigler, "The Theory of Economic Regulation," *Bell Journal of Economics and Management Science* 2 (1971): 3.

To know whether capture has occurred – either of the strong or the weak variety – we have to know what the public interest outcome would have been and compare that with the outcome adopted.

There are a variety of definitions of what counts as "public interest" regulation and, hence, identify what metric we should use to determine whether government policies are the product of capture.[13] Two measures are prominent. One measure posits that a government policy does not further the public interest when it is not, on net, welfare enhancing. Another posits that policy does not further the public interest where it is undemocratic – that is, where the policy departs from the preferences of the median voter.

The first definition of capture focuses on whether government action produces more benefits than costs. The many disputes over cost-benefit analysis demonstrate that it is hard to measure the costs and benefits of government intervention, but the example I have used might be considered an easy case of strong capture. The coal-industry preference for anticompetitive regulation will not be welfare enhancing because it will cost consumers more than the benefits it confers. In many cases, though, it will be much more difficult to determine – or, more precisely, it will be highly contested – whether a regulatory intervention is welfare enhancing.

The second measure focuses on whether government policies are consistent with a particular vision of democratic decision making. It assumes that government policies are in the public interest only to the extent that they accord with the views of the median voter. Some might argue that we should assume that the median voter will always prefer government action that is welfare enhancing, and thus these two measures are unlikely to produce different results. There are, however, several reasons why the median voter's preferences might not always favor what is, strictly speaking, welfare enhancing. The median voter may care more about distribution of benefits than overall welfare, and he or she may favor government intervention to respond to highly salient risks, such as the risk of cancer, even if the interventions cannot be justified as welfare enhancing.

The key difficulty with the median voter preference as a test of government policies is not one of measurement. The more difficult problem with

---

[13] See Steven P. Croley, *Regulation and Public Interests: The Possibility of Good Regulatory Government* (Princeton: Princeton University Press, 2008), 10–11, 254, 256 (stating that some measures of "socially beneficial regulation" include cost-benefit analysis, distributive consequences, expert opinion, and public support); Michael E. Levine and Jennifer L. Florence, "Regulatory Capture, Public Interest and the Public Agenda: Toward a Synthesis," *Journal of Law, Economics, and Organization* 6 (1990): 167 (discussing possible meanings and measures of "public" versus "private" interest and "special" versus "general" interest).

this measure is a theoretical one. It rests on a particular (and controversial) version of democratic decision making, one that ignores intensity of preference.[14] If we take a poll to determine the views of the median voter, and measure government action against those results, we ignore the obvious fact that those who have intense preferences have, and perhaps should have, more influence in shaping government policies. Mediating institutions stand between the voters' views about what government should do and what government does. Those institutions quite naturally, and in some cases are designed to, respond to those who are more engaged and interested in particular government policy outcomes.

It is not clear that we should take account of intensity of preference, however. That is because citizens exhibit intense preferences for different reasons, some of which we might reject. Some citizens' intense engagement is the result of especially deep ideological, religious, or substantive commitments that they want to see expressed in government policy. That is the sort of intensity of preference that most are talking about when they argue that intensity of preference is a valid consideration in evaluating whether government policy fairly "represents" the people's views. But some intense engagement is part of the logic of collective action that gives rise to the capture concern. Certain groups can overcome collective action problems *precisely because* they can obtain private goods – excludable, rivalrous – from the government, while the rest of us pay for that good.

I have focused for now on the difficulty of defining the "public interest" against which we are to measure government policies to test for capture, but there are other important difficulties. It is not clear, for instance, exactly what mechanism produces capture. One can construct an account of the mechanism for legislators. They seek reelection and thus need the resources for reelection. The focus of this chapter is regulatory capture, however, and the mechanism in that case is more difficult to identify. Some have suggested implicit bribes – the revolving door – as the mechanism by which regulators might be captured. Others suggest fear of retaliation by powerful interests. But it remains a bit murky how exactly regulators can be captured.[15]

Although defining the public interest and the mechanisms that produce regulatory capture remains difficult, this volume defines capture as

---

[14] For commentary about the role of intensity of preference in the legitimacy of government, see Wojciech Sadurski, "Legitimacy, Political Equality, and Majority Rule," *Ratio Juris* 21 (2008): 39; Sherman J. Clark, "A Populist Critique of Direct Democracy," *Harvard Law Review* 112 (1998): 434.

[15] See Croley, *Regulation and Public Interests*, 14–18; Rachel E. Barkow, "Insulating Agencies: Avoiding Capture through Institutional Design," *Texas Law Review* 89 (2010): 15, 21–24.

occurring when a special interest group succeeds in obtaining a regulatory outcome that is not in the "public interest" – either strongly or weakly inconsistent with that interest. As relevant, I discuss the different measures of public interest as well as the different mechanisms that might produce that capture. The case of interest is one in which the statute itself does not reflect capture, but the regulatory agency implements the statute in a way that produces policies that will benefit a particular group at the expense of the public.

JUDICIAL REVIEW AND REGULATORY CAPTURE

Does judicial review inhibit or facilitate capture? This part takes up that question. I first identify a basic characteristic of judicial review of agency action, the consequences of which will vary depending on the pattern of regulatory capture. I then identify those features of judicial supervision of agencies that might work to prevent capture and those that might facilitate capture. Along the way, I compare the institution of judicial review as a means to inhibit capture to the other available supervisors of agency action – the legislature and the executive.

Judicial Review as a Cost on Change

There is a fairly straightforward feature of judicial review of administrative action that is often ignored: judicial review of administrative action is conservative in the sense that it tends to protect the status quo. There are two reasons for this. First, judicial review is generally triggered by agency actions that depart from the status quo. In the typical case, that is, the legal challenge is to an agency action that proposes to alter preexisting rights and duties of regulated parties or beneficiaries. The Food and Drug Administration's rule requires new nutrition labels on food products; the Environmental Protection Agency's rule allows an increase in mercury emissions; the National Highway Traffic Safety Administration's rule requires passive restraints in cars; the Social Security Administration's rule alters the eligibility requirements for disability benefits. Each of these actions alters the status quo in some way, and a party who objected to them would be able to challenge the new rule in court.

By contrast, it is much more difficult to challenge agency inaction, or, put another way, agency behavior that leaves the status quo intact. It is, it is true, *possible* to challenge an agency's failure to take action. In *Massachusetts v. EPA*,[16] for example, states and environmentalists successfully challenged

---

[16]   549 U.S. 497 (2007).

the Environmental Protection Agency's (EPA's) failure to treat greenhouse gases as air pollutants under the Clean Air Act. Despite the result in *Massachuetts v. EPA*, challenging an agency's failure to act is systematically more difficult than challenging agency action that alters the status quo. A challenger to agency inaction must identify a discrete agency action that the agency failed to take, and he or she must identify an agency action that is not "committed to the agency's discretion."[17] These pockets of administrative law can impede parties' ability to challenge even an agency's failure to take a fairly specific action,[18] but they are an even stronger impediment to efforts to challenge an agency's general mismanagement of a regulatory program.[19]

The second reason that judicial review can be seen as a cost on change is that judicial review takes all comers. A poorly funded, disorganized group can challenge regulatory action. Precisely the same is true, however, for the well-funded and focused group. And parties do not bring a challenge in court unless, on balance, they prefer the status quo to what the agency has done. For these reasons, in the typical case, judicial review should be seen as a cost on change imposed by parties who, for one reason or another, prefer prior arrangements to the one the agency has or proposes to enact.

It is a straightforward insight that judicial review adds costs to agency-initiated change, but the hard question is whether these costs will generally inhibit capture or promote it. The answer to that question depends on the character of agency efforts to change the status quo. If the new agency action that is challenged reflects capture, then imposing judicial review as a cost on that change is a good thing, but if the policy reflects the public interest, then inhibiting that change does not police capture and could very well do the opposite by protecting pre-existing regulatory arrangements that reflect capture. There will not be a single answer to the question whether, as a general matter, agency policies that are challenged in court are the product of capture. The character of agency actions will no doubt vary across regulatory arenas, and across time. It is, however, important to keep in mind the general tendency of judicial review of administrative action to favor the status quo ante by allowing those who resist that change to make it more costly.

Judicial Review as a Brake on Capture

How does judicial supervision of agencies prevent capture? Imagine a world of political controls, where judicial review is rarely available and, in those

[17] 5 U.S.C. §701.
[18] See *Norton v. Southern Utah Wilderness Alliance*, 542 U.S. 55 (2004).
[19] See *Lujan v. National Wildlife Federation*, 487 U.S. 871 (1990).

rare cases where it is available, it is minimalist. Compare that with a second state of the world, judicial controls, where judicial review is often available and is probing when it is available. The latter is the world we live in and, as compared with political controls, there are several reasons to think that judicial controls make it more difficult for agencies to adopt policies that favor the private over the public interest.

There is the obvious point that judicial controls are – regardless of their content – an *additional* control. Judicial review is another potential veto point that is on top of and in addition to whatever political controls exist.[20] Capture is more likely to be detected when there are more controls and thus the addition of any control means that detection is more likely. Judicial controls, however, do more than provide a generic stop on the roadway between policy formulation and its ultimate implementation. They have a particular character that suggests that they may in some ways be superior to political controls in policing capture.

The *character* of political and judicial controls differs in ways that give judicial controls an edge in policing agency capture. If an agency has gone astray, there are multiple political controls available and their exercise requires political actors to take the initiative to exercise them. The president has the ability to fire senior officers (an authority that is sometimes constrained by statute),[21] the authority to "supervise" the implementation of policy (and the cajoling and pressure that that supervision might involve), and perhaps the authority to actually direct the reversal of the agency's position – although that is subject to dispute, at least in cases in which the statute delegates the choice to the agency.[22] The legislature can likewise cajole, pressure, shame, and otherwise jump and shout about the agency decision and the legislature has the authority, through the standard legislative process, to reverse agency policy by approving a statute that reverses the agency's

---

[20] I am admittedly assuming that if judges detect regulatory capture, they will try to do something about it, an assumption I cannot defend here.

[21] Barkow, "Insulating Agencies," 15, 27–30.

[22] The president's "directive" authority is a controversial topic. Some argue that unless Congress made explicit the President's authority, then he does not have it. See, for exmaple, Kevin M. Stack, "The president's Statutory Powers to Administer the Laws," *Columbia Law Review* 106 (2006): 263, 277 (stating that " ... delegations to executive officials alone – 'simple delegations' – should not be read to grant directive authority to the President"). On the other hand, some argue that it is reasonable to interpret a delegation of authority from Congress to an agency as including the president as one who may use that authority. See, for example, Elena Kagan, "Presidential Administration," *Harvard Law Review* 114 (2001): 2245, 2326–31. See generally Peter L. Strauss, "Overseer, or 'The Decider'? The President in Administrative Law," *George Washington Law Review* 75 (2007): 696.

decision. The exercise of any of these controls does not happen automatically, however. The president or Congress must *choose* to exercise that authority.

Whether and how political actors exercise their controls will depend on the costs and benefits of their exercise. Removing an agency head or passing new legislation will in the typical case be politically costly and thus the benefits must be substantial to justify the exercise. Other political controls, such as conducting aggressive oversight, will be less costly. The exact cost and benefit of the exercise of a political control will vary from one case to the next, depending on the political environment associated with the particular policy question. One feature that will remain constant, however, is that the forces that favor the agency policy, and the agency, will work to increase the political costs attendant to the exercise of political controls.

In contrast, judicial controls are simple. As just noted, there are a variety of political controls, they must be initiated by the political actors, their exercise will vary across cases depending on costs and benefits of their exercise, and supporters of agency policy are in a position to increase the (political) costs of reversal. Courts, in contrast, do not have a variety of controls available. A court does not pressure or cajole; it does not direct or remove. Courts have a single control – the formal authority to affirm the agency's choice as lawful, or to find that the choice was unlawful.[23] Nor is the exercise of that judicial control voluntary in the sense that it is for political controls. The judicial authority to review the legality of the agency's action is part and parcel of judicial review of administrative action. It is true that judicial examination of administrative action is reactive in the sense that a proper party must come before the court and raise a cognizable legal challenge. Even if those elements are satisfied, however, courts do not choose – or not – to exercise their authority in a particular case. Finally, the costs and benefits of exercising judicial controls will not be understood in terms of political costs and benefits, they will not vary much across cases, and the agency and the supporters of the agency policy do not have much capacity to increase the costs associated with the exercise of judicial controls.

Judicial controls may be simple, but they are powerful. In fact, these features make judicial controls in some ways superior to political controls as a mechanism for policing capture. Assume that an agency policy represents capture. If a proper party brings suit to set aside the agency action, judicial controls *will* be exercised one way or the other, their exercise will not be

---

[23] Ronald M. Levin, "'Vacation' at Sea: Judicial Remedies and Equitable Discretion in Administrative Law," *Duke Law Journal* 53 (2003): 291 (discussing the remedial options a court has in a successful challenge to administrative action).

inhibited by increasing political costs, and those who support the agency policy have few tools at their disposal to pressure the court. This is all true in any individual case, but if we consider the whole range of cases, judicial control has another feature that makes it superior to political controls. The likelihood of the exercise of political controls will vary widely depending on the nature of the underlying matter that the agency has taken on. Sometimes a politician will have an intense interest in intervening; other times, she will have no interest. Judicial controls, by contrast, operate with similar effectiveness across a range of cases. The political environment surrounding some cases of capture will make it impossible for political actors to exercise political controls and thus some cases of capture will escape reversal. Judicial controls do not suffer that fate.

Judicial review can also be seen to inhibit capture because, as Croley has argued, it levels the playing field between concentrated, well-funded interests and less well-funded interests.[24] To the extent that regulatory capture is most likely to occur in such circumstances, judicial controls will be superior to political controls in policing capture. It is true that it takes resources to file a lawsuit, especially one that has a plausible shot at reversing or significantly delaying an agency decision. But compare what it takes to do that to the resources it would take to influence outcomes in the legislature, the executive, or even at the agency as it formulates policy in the first instance. Influencing the legislature is a large-scale endeavor, requiring resources and savvy. Influencing the executive branch, such as getting the Office of Management and Budget interested in more closely supervising an agency decision, may require a similar level of resources. Influencing an agency's implementation of a statute in the first instance – before the matter gets to court – may be less resource-intensive than these two, but it is no small matter to get the agency's attention.

Relatively speaking, it does not take enormous resources to file a lawsuit. The relatively limited cost of filing a suit, however, is not the only factor that makes the judicial arena a distinctive and effective place to police agency behavior. The most striking consequence of filing a lawsuit is that the challenger receives what it is very hard to do – and very hard to do predictably – in other forums where regulatory decision making might be subject to review and revision: the legal challenger obtains the time and

---

[24] Croley, *Regulation and Public Interests*, 140–42 (stating that "[d]ifferences in economic or political-electoral resources therefore do not translate into different interest groups' relative ability to subject agency action to judicial review. Therefore, such disparities in interest group resources or political clout do not translate into equal disparities in regulatory influence in the way they may in the legislative arena").

attention of a decision maker who has the authority to, and will exercise his authority to decide the case that the challenger brought before the court. A government relations consultant who could guarantee something like that in the legislative arena – the legislature will listen to your objection, and it will decide whether your objection is valid within a certain time frame – would be considered a magician.

The reasons that courts may provide an effective response to capture so far focus on the existence and availability of a judicial forum and the remedies available there. But the *content* of that review also facilitates judicial controls on regulatory capture. If the court reviews the agency's decision – and sometimes it will not, as discussed shortly – the agency must defend its choice as supported by the record (in the case of a factual finding); as a permissible choice under the statute; and/or as well reasoned in light of the alternatives and the objections raised to the proposed course of action. That strips away a fair amount of complexity, but even so, it fairly illustrates an important feature of judicial controls that makes them distinctive. When courts review agency decisions, they apply a merits-based test. They ask: Is the decision well supported by the relevant facts, is it a reasonable interpretation of the statute, is it well explained, that is, reasoned? Under this form of review, a reason that sounds in "capture" will be quickly rejected by the court. An agency, that is, could not defend its decision by explaining that a "powerfully connected interest group sought this result." Given the nature of judicial controls, which agencies well understand, no agency would choose to defend its decision in that way, of course, but if discovery produced evidence that suggested to the court that the agency was captured by the regulated industry, the agency's decision would be reversed.[25] The doctrine thus allows courts to screen for cases of capture that come in the form of decisions unsupported by the facts, unreasonable in light of the statute, or poorly reasoned.

The last reason why judicial controls may be effective in policing regulatory capture, and more effective in doing so than political controls, is related to this feature of judicial controls – namely, the nature of what judges look for when they review agency decisions and (more generally) the nature of the federal judiciary. Imagine that it is true that regulatory capture is most likely to occur when an industry group persuades regulators to adopt policies that are not in the public interest. It is, as noted previously, not exactly clear what the mechanism is that produces this undue influence. Perhaps regulators hope to walk through the revolving door and obtain a job in

---

[25] An excellent example can be found in *American Horse Protection Association, Inc. v. Lyng*, 812 F.2d 1, 5–7 (D.C. Cir. 1987).

the industry; perhaps regulators fear retaliation by political actors that the interest group has the capacity to generate.

However it is that regulators are subject to capture, judges will not be vulnerable to it in the same way. Those who exercise political controls, by contrast, could be vulnerable. Federal judges are not generally planning to resign their post and seek another job and they are not (at least as a relative matter) that concerned about retaliation by politicians. That is to say, owing to the features of their positions, federal judges just do not think like regulators. Those who exercise political controls, on the other hand, might very well be subject to a similar pathology to that of the (captured) regulator. Elected officials may leave their posts and be interested in lucrative, post-official employment. Even if they are not likely to be interested in such an implicit bribe, political actors need to be re-elected, and they need the resources that the interest group can provide in order to succeed in that task. In short, the pathology that produces capture in the regulator could cause those exercising political controls to look the other way. The federal judge, as Macey has argued, is unlikely to do the same.[26]

Missing Capture

But not all the news is good. Judicial review of agency action could also fail to detect and prevent capture.

There are several large-scale structural features of judicial controls that weaken their capacity to police capture. One feature of judicial controls that is both obvious and worth emphasizing is that these controls are purely *reactive*. Judicial review is not available when no party challenges government action, even if it might otherwise be subject to challenge in court. A select group of agency decisions come before the courts and there is reason to fear that the cases that are not selected – that is, where there is no judicial review because no challenger steps forward – may coincide with a category of cases in which there are particular risks of regulatory capture. Most agency actions are not challenged in court at all.[27] That does not mean that agencies ignore what a court might say about action that is not challenged,

---

[26] Jonathan R. Macey, "Promoting Public-Regarding Legislation through Statutory Interpretation: An Interest Group Model," *Columbia Law Review* 85 (1986): 223, 263–64.

[27] Cary Coglianese points out that the Environmental Protection Agency (EPA), for example, issued 1,568 rules between 1987 and 1991, and yet the EPA was named in a lawsuit only 411 times – a 26 percent litigation rate. Cary Coglianese, "Assessing Consensus: The Promise and Performance of Negotiated Rulemaking," *Duke Law Journal* 46 (1997): 1255, 1296–301. Agencies take thousands of other actions that are not rulemakings, few of which are challenged.

because the agency operates in the shadow of judicial review even if it does not materialize in a particular case. Even so, there are many, many cases in which no party brings suit.

An optimistic view is that the absence of a challenger means that the agency's action is entirely unobjectionable. But the absence of a challenger might also mean something more disturbing: it may mean that those who captured the regulators chose wisely because no one will appear to object. A standard story in the literature of capture is that an intensely interested and organized interest group is able to persuade the regulator to provide private goods, while the dispersed and disorganized (and therefore disempowered) pay for those goods. If the dispersed and disorganized are unable to be a counterweight in the regulatory arena, they might not be able to bring suit (even though it is relatively cheap to do so) either. Coglianese's study of litigation challenges to the EPA's regulatory action could confirm this fear. He found that parties that have the most sustained and extensive involvement with EPA regulation are the ones that are the most likely to bring a legal challenge.[28] In other words, bit players or outsiders do not tend to sue to challenge agency action. If it is the case that those who most actively participate in the development of regulatory policy are generally the primary ones who bring suit to challenge that policy, that means that the participants can seek private benefits, not worrying about an outside objector coming along to upset the apple cart.

Other structural features of judicial control limit its capacity to police capture. Judicial review is only available ex post, not ex ante, and only to evaluate discrete decisions. Administrative law doctrine rules out challenges that allege systematic or programmatic illegality. Instead, a challenger has to focus on a discrete (and final) agency action.[29] Yet, capture can be exhibited systematically across a range of decisions within a program. That capture may be the product of malign personnel or may be facilitated by a highly discretionary regulatory program or statutory mandate. Those problems are best solved by systematic, ex ante action, and thus the tools available to the executive and Congress are – *if* they are exercised – superior to judicial controls. The president can supervise and replace personnel, the Congress and the executive can conduct across-the-board investigations of agency decision making, and both entities are in a position to work to prevent

---

[28] Cary Coglianese, "Litigating within Relationships: Disputes and Disturbance in the Regulatory Process," *Law and Society Review* 30 (1996): 735, 744 ("Organizations most active in rulemaking tend to be most active in litigation.").

[29] *Norton v. Southern Utah Wilderness Alliance*, 542 U.S. 55 (2004).

capture before it happens by constraining the range of available agency choices before the fact.[30] Courts cannot do anything similar.

These are large-scale structural features of judicial controls as compared with political controls, but consider now a closer-to-the-ground perspective on judicial review of agency action. There is reason to fear that, even from within the framework of judicial controls, judicial review is a thin shield against capture. Recall that, analytically, there are two large questions that organize the law of judicial review of administrative action. First, is review available? Second, if it is available, what is the content of that review and how skeptical is it of government action?

Judicial review is sometimes not available, and it is systematically less available in cases in which there may be a risk of regulatory capture. Even when a challenger appears to challenge an agency's action, the suit might complain about matters that are not "reviewable" in the language of administrative law or the challenger may not be the right party to bring suit. If either of these barriers is present in a particular case, a court will not evaluate the challenger's objection to the agency's decision.

A challenger must complain about agency action that is actually subject to review in court. Although modern courts have expressed a "presumption" in favor of review,[31] categories of unreviewable agency action remain. Statutes sometimes identify whole swaths of agency decisions that cannot be challenged by anyone in court – these statutes are said to "preclude" judicial review.[32] Preclusion of judicial review, however, is not a large problem for objectors to regulatory capture because Congress has generally not chosen to preclude review in the regulatory arena. Statutes preclude review most often in cases involving national security, immigration, foreign affairs, and Veterans affairs.[33]

The larger issue is that, even where a statute does not explicitly preclude judicial review, courts will not review an action that is, in the language of the relevant statute, "committed to agency discretion by law."[34] In this category, there are several types of agency activity that will be difficult to

---

[30] Joseph O'Connell, "Political Cycles of Rulemaking," 889, 918–20; M. Elizabeth Magill, "The First Word," *William and Mary Bill of Rights Journal* 16 (2007): 27, 30–35.

[31] *Citizens to Preserve Overton Park, Inc. v. Volpe*, 401 U.S. 402, 410 (1971) (stating the rebuttable presumption of judicial review of agency action); *Abbott Labs. v. Gardner*, 387 U.S. 136 (1967), which established this presumption.

[32] 5 U.S.C. § 701(a)(1).

[33] See Ronald M. Levin, "Understanding Unreviewability in Administrative Law," *Minnesota Law Review* 74 (1990): 689, 739–40 (discussing an apparent hierarchy the Court uses regarding preclusion).

[34] 5 U.S.C. § 701(a)(2).

challenge in court. The most controversial among commentators is agency *inaction*.[35] Although *Massachusetts v. EPA*[36] evidences some movement by the courts in this area, in the typical case it will remain difficult to attack an agency's failure to regulate and it has always been, and remains, very difficult to attack an agency's failure to bring an enforcement action.[37] Critics of this feature of judicial review doctrine complain that it allows an agency to favor industry through inaction, while the courts sit idly by. Although perhaps problematic for other reasons, this feature of doctrine does not mean that strong forms of regulatory capture will escape judicial review. Such strong regulatory capture is likely to require the government to *act*. In the classic formulation, for example, the agency exhibits capture when it regulates to establish barriers to entry in a market or otherwise disadvantages competitors to the industry group that sought the private good.[38] Such agency behavior will constitute *action*, and should in the normal case be subject to judicial review.

Other agency behavior that is insulated from judicial review as "committed to agency discretion" poses more of a threat of capture. It is exceedingly difficult to attack an agency's general administration of a program, including its pattern of enforcement decisions.[39] By devising a particular pattern of enforcement, however, an agency might very well exhibit regulatory capture in either its strong or weak forms. Consider agencies that are authorized to engage in various forms of economic regulation – antitrust, consumer fraud, securities regulation. These agencies might have general rules that are

[35] *Heckler v. Chaney*, 470 U.S. 821, 832–38 (1985) (stating that "an agency's decision not to take enforcement action should be presumed immune from judicial review under § 701(a)(2)" of the APA and that "[t]he general exception to reviewability provided by § 702(a)(2) for action 'committed to agency discretion' remains a narrow one...but within that exception are included agency refusals to institute investigative or enforcement proceedings, unless Congress has indicated otherwise"); Eric Biber, "Two Sides of the Same Coin: Judicial Review of Administrative Agency Action and Inaction," *Virginia Environmental Law Journal* 26 (2008): 461.

[36] 549 U.S. 497 (2007).

[37] For a discussion of *Massachusetts v. EPA*, see Ronald A. Cass, "*Massachusetts v. EPA*: The Inconvenient Truth about Precedent," *Virginia Law Review* 93 (2007): 75, 80–81. For an attempt to clarify the status of judicial review of action/inaction, see Biber, "Two Sides of the Same Coin." See also Daniel T. Deacon, "Deregulation through Nonenforcement," *New York University Law Review* 85 (2010): 795, 802–04 (discussing *Chaney*'s holding that "an agency's decision not to prosecute or enforce...is a decision generally committed to an agency's absolute discretion" has not been widely adopted in the context of agency refusal to promulgate rules, as exhibited by the *Massachusetts v. EPA* decision).

[38] Stigler, "The Theory of Economic Regulation," 3, 4–5.

[39] *Heckler v. Chaney*, 470 U.S. 821, 832–33 (1985) (stating that "an agency's decision not to take enforcement action should be presumed immune from judicial review under § 701(a)(2)" of the APA); Deacon, "Deregulation through Nonenforcement," 795, 804.

even-handed, but they might choose to pursue enforcement action selectively – in one segment of a market but not in another, against newcomers but not incumbents. An agency could thereby advantage a class of competitors within a market. That pattern of agency decisions would be extremely difficult, if not impossible, to challenge in court. Courts would treat a pattern of behavior that arguably represents capture as "committed to agency discretion."

Courts are thus sometimes not available to evaluate particular agency decisions, but even if the action is reviewable, there is another barrier: the courts must determine *which* parties can challenge agency action. Not just any party can come into federal court to complain about agency action. Courts must be satisfied that some source of law, most often a statute, authorizes the party to bring the challenge *and* that the party's standing is consistent with the Constitution's requirement that federal courts entertain only cases or controversies. The law of standing is devilishly complicated, but, as described later, in some ways it operates to fence out those who might challenge regulatory capture in the courts.

Statutes that govern agency decision making often provide that agency actions can be challenged in court by so-called "aggrieved" parties.[40] This is a term of art, and its meaning has changed over time to include two groups of challengers. It includes so-called regulatory competitors.[41] A regulatory competitor is not directly subject to the agency's regulatory action, but its competitive position is affected by the agency action. Thus, if a rate-making agency makes a decision that sets a favorable rate for a regulated party, but hurts that party's competitor, the competitor counts as an aggrieved party. Aggrieved parties also, in principle, include those individuals who are supposed to benefit from regulation, such as consumers, workers, drivers, and those who care about the environment.[42] Since the early 1970s, there has been another model of statutory standing, the so-called citizen suit

---

[40] 5 U.S.C. § 702. For example, 47 U.S.C. § 402(b)(6), the Federal Communications Commission, allows "any other person who is aggrieved or whose interests are adversely affected by any order of the Commission" to seek an appeal. Similarly, the Occupational Safety and Health Act of 1970 allows for "person[s] adversely affected or aggrieved" to obtain judicial review (29 U.S.C. § 660).

[41] *National Credit Union Administration v. First National Bank and Trust Company*, 522 U.S. 479, 492 (1998); *Association of Data Processing Service Organizations, Inc. v. Camp*, 397 U.S. 150, 152 (1970).

[42] *Lujan v. Defenders of Wildlife*, 504 U.S. 555, 562–63 (1992) (stating that "the desire to use or observe an animal species, even for purely esthetic purposes, is undeniably a cognizable interest for the purpose of standing"); *Sierra Club v. Morton*, 405 U.S. 727, 734 (1972); *Animal Legal Defense Fund v. Glickman*, 154 F.3d 426, 437 (D.C. Cir. 1998) (en banc) (there is a "myriad [of] cases recognizing individual plaintiffs' injury in fact based on affronts to

provision.[43] Instead of identifying a limited class of people, such as those who are aggrieved by agency action, who can challenge government action, these statutes authorize "any person" to challenge agency action. These provisions were intended to, and do, extend standing as far as is possible under Article III of the Constitution. It is here that some who would challenge regulatory capture might run into trouble.

Constitutional standing doctrine requires that challengers demonstrate an alleged injury from the government action, and, more than that, that the injury is traceable to the government's action, and that it can be redressed by judicial intervention.[44] The idea is that only those with this sort of an injury can make out a case or controversy that federal courts under the Constitution are authorized to hear. The way courts have defined "injury" has evolved over time. Today, it is clear that competitive injury counts to establish standing. It is also the case that injury to aesthetic and ideological interests *can* count to establish standing.

Despite this evolution in the law, however, at least as compared with the regulated parties, certain types of parties will have difficulty establishing standing. Examples of the types of parties that cannot establish standing illustrate the difficulties. It is clear that a citizen or voter who is disturbed by the direction of government policy cannot, on that basis, establish standing. Nor can a taxpayer (outside of limited area not relevant here) – qua taxpayer – establish standing. These two categories cover many parties who might otherwise wish to challenge government regulation. Others, like consumers and those who represent aesthetic interests, may under certain circumstances be able to establish standing, but they will face difficulties. The injury they complain of may not be specific enough to them, or may be speculative, and, more than that, they may have difficulty showing so-called causation and redressability because there are likely to be many different causes of their injury and there may be very limited ways judicial intervention can cure that injury.

---

their aesthetic interests in observing animals living in humane habitats, or in using pristine environmental areas that have not been despoiled").

[43] The first citizen suit provision was contained in the Clean Air Act of 1970, Pub. L. No. 91-604, 84 Stat. 1676 (codified as amended in scattered sections of 42 U.S.C.). There are also similar provisions in a number of statutes, including the Endangered Species Act of 1973 (16 U.S.C. § 1540(g)); the Surface Mining Control and Reclamation Act of 1977 (30 U.S.C. § 1234–1328); and the Emergency Planning and Community Right-to-Know Act (EPCRA) (scattered sections of 42 U.S.C.).

[44] *Lujan v. Defenders of Wildlife*, 504 U.S. 555, 568–71 (1992) (discussing the requirement of redressability, specifically that even if a decision were made in the environmental group's favor, the injury complained of would not be redressed).

The consequences of these limits on standing depend on the pattern of capture. If capture occurs when (in the simple case) there are two present economic actors and one is advantaged over the other, the disadvantaged economic actor can challenge the action as a competitor. But if capture occurs in other types of cases, establishing standing will be more difficult. For instance, in the case in which an agency erects a barrier to entry for new entrants in a market, one injured party is a future competitor who will not now exist. The present-day proxy for that future competitor will be a present consumer, but that consumer, qua consumer, will have a difficult time establishing standing. A court would be likely to consider the injury, loss of competition that would otherwise exist in a future market, speculative. Another case in which capture can occur is when the agency fails to regulate with the rigor that it should because it has been captured by the industry. Here the present regulatory beneficiaries are the obvious challengers, but they will systematically have a difficult time establishing standing.[45] Together, these limits on standing may mean that a court will not even have the opportunity to catch regulatory capture in its net.

Even if judicial review is available and the right sort of party has brought suit, that does not mean that the court will be able to invalidate agency action that is the product of capture. The fundamental problem is that judicial evaluations of the legality of agency action are simply not designed to screen for the possibility of regulatory capture. It is true, as noted already, that a court will inquire into the merits of the agency's decision, and that an agency cannot defend its action on the grounds that concentrated interests lobbied hard for it. But no (competent) agency will provide such an explanation.

Regulatory capture occurs when an industry group succeeds in persuading the agency to deliver regulation that is not in the "public interest" – that is, regulation that is not welfare enhancing or is not in accord with the preferences of the median voter. Assuming the agency does not confess that it was captured, how will judges be able to detect whether that has occurred? Judicial examination of agency action does not elicit information that would allow a judge to comprehensively evaluate the net welfare

---

[45] *Ibid.*, 561–62; *Block v. Community Nutrition Institute*, 467 U.S. 340, 346–47 (1984); Karl S. Coplan, "Ideological Plaintiffs, Administrative Lawmaking, Standing, and the Petition Clause," *Maine Law Review* 61 (2009): 377, 404–08; Glen Staszewski," The Federal Inaction Commission," *Emory Law Journal* 59 (2009): 369, 370–71 ("Simply put, regulated entities have access to legal relief when they challenge unduly aggressive agency action, whereas regulatory beneficiaries do not have access to legal relief when they allege that an agency has failed to implement its statutory mandate.").

effects of the policy or its correspondence to the median voter's views. Under the doctrine, courts ask whether a factual determination is well supported, whether an exercise of discretion is reasoned, or whether an interpretation of the statute is reasonable. They also ask whether the agency followed the proper procedures. The agency's response to these questions does not supply the information that the judge would need to make the determination about the welfare effects of the policy and it certainly does not supply information about the median voter's views. Nor is it easy to see how the agency's answers to these questions bear a *reliable* and *predictable* connection to the existence or nonexistence of regulatory capture. An agency could answer all of these questions to the satisfaction of a court, and it could have followed all of the needed procedures, and it could still be delivering private benefits; conversely, an agency could flunk these tests and not be captured, but rather be incompetent.

Even if courts obtained the needed information in the course of evaluating the agency action, judges are not trained to make the kind of determinations that would be necessary to deciding whether an agency action represents capture. Nor are they inclined to do so. Judicial review of agency action is merits-based in the sense that a bald assertion by the agency that it delivered rents would doom the agency action. It is true that that may rule out a very small number of cases in which capture has occurred, but those may also be cases in which the agency is just incompetent. For the vast majority of cases, judicial review does not screen for regulatory capture.

REVISING JUDICIAL REVIEW

The analysis of the last section does not produce an easy answer to the question whether judicial review works to prevent capture. In some ways it does, in some ways it does not, and much depends on the causes and pattern of regulatory capture in the real world. A final question, however, is whether judicial review can be revised to bolster its capacity to detect and invalidate regulatory capture. Unfortunately, this chapter cannot fully explore this question, but it identifies some of the possibilities for reform and identifies some constraints on broader reforms.

The last section identified five ways in which judicial controls on administration may not, or do not, successfully police regulatory capture. Judicial review is status quo protecting; judicial review is reactive; judicial review is only available ex post and with respect to discrete decisions; judicial review is systematically less available in cases in which capture may be a real risk; and judicial review is not designed to screen for the subtle cases of regulatory capture, whether capture is defined as non-welfare-enhancing regulation or regulation that departs from the median voter.

Some of these aspects of judicial review could be revised, and others are close to hard-wired and cannot be remedied without a dramatic restructuring of judicial controls. One could tinker with the several judicial doctrines that inhibit judicial review. It is quite possible, for instance, to imagine that more parties, including taxpayers or ideological plaintiffs, could have standing to challenge government action. It is also imaginable that a broader range of agency actions and behaviors – including failures to take action, patterns of enforcement, or systematic management of programs – could be subject to judicial review as opposed to being unreviewable. These changes might be vigorously resisted by many courts and scholars of administrative law, but they are certainly conceivable revisions to existing doctrines.

Several of the features identified earlier, however, are not so amenable to revision. Without a fundamental rethinking of federal courts, it is not possible to imagine them as anything other than *reactive*. That is, it would take a substantial conceptual shift in our constitutional design to imagine federal courts that could proceed without a challenger appearing before them and raising objections to government behavior. This means that courts will inevitably see only a small slice of agency decisions, and therefore it is possible that the selected cases will not include the worst forms of regulatory capture. Second, it is hard to understand how judicial doctrines could be revised to catch subtle cases of regulatory capture. Courts will be fine at catching those cases in which there is some smoking gun evidence of capture, but in the absence of that, it seems quite inconsistent with basic conceptions of judicial function to imagine federal judges sitting in judgment of whether regulation enhances social welfare or comports with the views of the median voter. Finally, even if judicial review can be expanded to encompass challenges to systematic program mismanagement and failures to act, the tools available to judges will remain narrow. Their job is to resolve the particular case brought before them, not to conduct an overall investigation of the agency, to replace its personnel, or to revise its statutory mandate. Those are tools available only to the executive and the legislature and there will be cases in which those are the best, if not the only, tools to inhibit regulatory capture.

* * *

Courts can undoubtedly play some role in inhibiting capture. They have some advantages over the controls political actors have available to them. In particular, courts have a narrow but unique power to declare agency action legal or illegal. It is a power that courts, if a proper case is brought to them, will exercise, and it is a power that supporters of the agency action have little power to resist. In certain cases, then, courts will be best situated to and most likely to police agency capture. But courts are far from the perfect policemen when it comes to agency capture. The narrowness of judicial authority and the unique role of judges in our constitutional system is in some cases an advantage, but is a disadvantage in others. In some ways, the more extreme the capture, the less useful the judicial controls. If what is needed is systematic, across-the-board investigation and revision of an agency's agenda, then the executive or the Congress is far better suited to respond.

15

Can Executive Review Help Prevent Capture?

Michael A. Livermore and Richard L. Revesz[1]

INTRODUCTION

Centralized review of federal regulations has become a core institution in the contemporary administrative state. Presidents of both political parties have embraced it, with relatively few changes since President Reagan put in place the basic architecture in 1981. Although the institution of centralized review continues to receive criticism from some quarters,[2] there is broad consensus that it is likely to remain a persistent feature of the administrative state for the foreseeable future.

Since its inception, centralized review has been closely linked with theories of agency capture. Many of its most prominent defenders have grounded the legitimacy of regulatory review in fears that unchecked agencies will be systematically biased in the exercise of their powers, including by accommodating powerful special interests to the detriment of general social welfare. According to this line of thinking, centralized review facilitates presidential control over agencies, which helps to ensure that administrative action is responsive to the broad national constituency represented by the president rather than to parochial special interests.

There are two important problems with this account. First, the background assumption of the conventional account – that the president responds to a national, rather than parochial, constituency – is overly simplistic. Presidents respond to a range of incentives that may not be well aligned with the broad national interest. More important, the Office of

---

[1] This chapter is adapted from Michael A. Livermore and Richard L. Revesz, "Regulatory Review, Capture, and Agency Inaction," *Georgetown Law Journal* 101 (2013): 1337.

[2] See, for example, OMB Watch, "The Obama Approach to Public Protection: The Regulatory Process" (Report, 2011); Amy Sinden, Rena Steinzor, Shana Jones, and James Goodwin, "Obama's Regulators: A First-Year Report Card 28–30" (Center for Progressive Reform White Paper No. 1001, January 2010).

Information and Regulatory Affairs (OIRA), which is charged with carrying out centralized review, is not the functional equivalent of the president. Even if increased presidential control is desirable, it is not obvious that OIRA review always achieves this goal.

This does not mean, however, that OIRA cannot and does not play an important role in mitigating the threat of agency capture, but it does so for four reasons unrelated to proximity to the president. First, because OIRA is a generalist institution, it is more difficult to capture than a single-issue agency. By creating a generalist body like OIRA to oversee agency decisions, the institutional structure of centralized review can reduce the potential influence of special interest actors on regulation. Second, OIRA often plays a coordinating role, bringing together different agencies, which are each likely to be influenced by different interest groups. Because this coordination function requires interest groups to capture multiple agencies involved in decision making, it reduces the ability of any one interest group to dictate decisions, by raising the cost of capture. Third, cost-benefit analysis, which is the standard used to conduct regulatory review, is a professionally accepted methodology that is available for public scrutiny. It therefore acts as a check against capture by raising the risk of detection for agencies tempted to massage the economic analysis in response to interest group pressure. Finally, there is a tradition of appointing relatively independent individuals without strong connections to special interest groups to run OIRA, which helps reduce the threat of capture.

Two steps can be taken to expand this anti-capture role. First, retrospective review can require interest groups to continually reinvest in capture to ensure their preferred regulations are not amended or rescinded, which in turn decreases the return on investment of capture and acts as a disincentive to agency capture. A recent retrospective review process initiated by the Obama Administration, however, has focused too much on cost cutting, rather than net-benefit maximization, creating the risk of antiregulatory bias. This process should be reformed to be more balanced, examining how agencies can increase benefits as well as reduce costs. Second, OIRA should expand its review of agency inaction. In large part, OIRA has focused its review on agency action, examining major rules that are proposed by agencies before they are finalized. There has been significantly less review of agency inaction – that is, of the cases where net benefits could be generated through rulemakings in new areas. This bias has historical roots in the original conception of OIRA as a check against overzealous regulators. However, because an agency's failure to act can be as detrimental to social well-being as overactivity – and can just as easily result from agency capture – it is important that OIRA establish an institutional mechanism to ward against both kinds of failure.

This chapter proceeds in three parts. The first part provides a brief overview of the thirty-year history of OIRA oversight of agency rulemaking, discussing and criticizing traditional capture-related justifications for OIRA review. The second part examines the features of OIRA that suggest it can reduce capture risks, focusing on its role as a generalist body, its coordinating function, the nature of cost-benefit analysis, and the tradition of drawing OIRA directors from the academic community rather than from interest groups. The final part of this chapter discusses steps that can be taken to improve regulatory review with an anti-capture role in mind.

TRADITIONAL ACCOUNTS OF REGULATORY REVIEW AND CAPTURE

Brief History

As U.S. regulatory agencies gained new powers over large portions of the economy through statutes meant to address environmental, public health, and workplace risks, presidents engaged in a series of increasingly strenuous efforts to exert centralized executive control over administrative decision making. President Richard Nixon initiated a requirement of interagency comment for certain types of rules,[3] and President Gerald Ford created the Council on Wage and Price Stability, which exercised increased central control over agency rulemaking.[4] President Jimmy Carter went even further with Executive Order 12,044,[5] which required the newly created Regulatory Analysis Review Group to perform an economic analysis for any major regulation, defined as one with a likely impact of more than $100 million.[6] President Ronald Reagan, with his Executive Order 12,291,[7] placed

---

[3] President Nixon initiated a "Quality of Life Review," which required the Environmental Protection Agency and the Occupational Health and Safety Agency to engage in an interagency consultation process and provide an estimate of the costs of proposed regulation along with a set of alternatives. Thomas O. McGarity, *Reinventing Rationality: The Role of Regulatory Analysis in the Federal Bureaucracy* (New York: Cambridge University Press, 1991), 18.

[4] Curtis W. Copeland, "The Role of the Office of Information and Regulatory Affairs in Federal Rulemaking," *Fordham Urban Law Journal* 33 (2006): 1257, 1264.

[5] Exec. Order No. 12,044, 3 C.F.R. 152 (1979).

[6] Exec. Order No. 12,044, 3 C.F.R. 152 §3.

[7] Exec. Order No. 12,291, 3 C.F.R. 127 (1981), reprinted in 5 U.S.C. § 601 (1988), revoked by Exec. Order No. 12,866, 3 C.F.R. 638 (1993), reprinted in 5 U.S.C. §601 (2000).

centralized review and cost-benefit analysis at the heart of regulatory decision making.

Reagan's Executive Order 12,291 created what has become the persistent architecture of regulatory review at the federal level. Utilizing OIRA, a newly created entity within the Office of Management and Budget (OMB), the Executive Order required agencies to conduct cost-benefit analysis of proposed major rules, adopt only those rules with positive net benefits, and submit their analyses to OIRA for review. If OIRA found that a rule was not properly justified, the rule could be sent back to the agency for further analysis.[8] Despite some pushback from Congress, review continued apace during the presidencies of Reagan and George H. W. Bush.

After the election of Bill Clinton, many protection-oriented groups were looking for a radical departure on regulatory issues. Indeed, many commentators believed that the election of a Democratic president would result in an overhaul of the process of regulatory review.[9] That is not what happened. Instead, Clinton issued Executive Order 12,866, which replaced and updated Executive Order 12,291 but maintained the same architecture of regulatory review based on cost-benefit analysis.[10] Executive Order 12,866 did include several important reforms, such as transparency requirements, an emphasis on the importance of unquantified costs and benefits, and a place for distributional analysis.[11] However, on the whole, it represented a continuity of approach, rather than a break from the past. The Clinton order was carried over by the Administration of George W. Bush, which implemented a robust practice of regulatory review and cost-benefit analysis.

The Obama Administration, in keeping with three decades of presidential tradition, has maintained this tradition. Through its choice of appointments – most importantly of Cass Sunstein as the head of OIRA – the administration has signaled a commitment to cost-benefit analysis.[12] Soon after taking office, Obama issued a memorandum to the heads of executive departments and agencies stating that "centralized review is both legitimate and appropriate as a means of promoting regulatory goals."[13] The clearest endorsement of regulatory review by the Obama Administration came on

---

[8]   Exec. Order No. 12,291, 3 C.F.R. 127 § 3(f)(1).

[9]   Richard H. Pildes and Cass R. Sunstein, "Reinventing the Regulatory State," *The University of Chicago Law Review* 62 (1995): 1, 5–6.

[10] Exec. Order No. 12,866, 3 C.F.R. 638 (1994), reprinted in 5 U.S.C. § 601 (2000).

[11] Exec. Order No. 12,866 §§ 1(a), 1(b)(5), 6(b)(4).

[12] Michael A. Livermore and Richard L. Revesz, "Retaking Rationality Two Years Later," *Houston Law Review* 48 (2011): 1, 12–19.

[13] "Memorandum on Regulatory Review," *Daily Compilation of Presidential Documents* (January 30, 2009): 287.

January 18, 2011, when the president issued Executive Order 13,563, which "is supplemental to and reaffirms the principles, structures, and definitions governing contemporary regulatory review" from the Clinton order.[14] Obama's order has left the same structure of review in place with some minor – but important – improvements, such as greater emphasis on distributional analysis, enhanced transparency in enforcement actions, and a renewed focus on retrospective analysis (which is discussed in more detail in the third part of this chapter).[15]

As OIRA's role in regulatory review has gained a seemingly permanent place in the architecture of administrative decision making, it has drawn its share of detractors. Over the past thirty years, opponents of regulatory review have engaged in a (perhaps quixotic) campaign to reduce the influence of OIRA. Citing a range of concerns, including delay,[16] political meddling,[17] and solicitousness to industry,[18] commentators and advocacy organizations have argued that OIRA plays a pernicious role in the regulatory system that undermines the legitimacy and effectiveness of government action.[19] The proposed solution is a radical rethinking of OIRA's role that essentially strips the office of genuine oversight authority.[20]

At the same time, a group of staunch defenders has arisen who provide support for OIRA and the practice of executive review of agency action. Representing diverse points on the political spectrum, commentators and former executive officials from both parties have argued that OIRA plays a productive, even essential, role in the administrative process. Drawing from both personal experience and academic literature, OIRA's defenders have provided a range of rationales for why the growth of regulatory review over the past several decades represents an important and positive development in administrative decision making.

[14] Exec. Order No. 13,563, § 1(a), 76 Fed. Reg. 3821, 3821 (January 21, 2011).

[15] Michael A. Livermore, "A Brief Comment on Humanizing Cost-Benefit Analysis," *European Journal of Risk Regulation* 2 (2011): 13.

[16] Sidney A. Shapiro and Ronald F. Wright, "The Future of the Administrative Presidency: Turning Administrative Law Inside-Out," *University of Miami Law Review* 65 (2011): 577, 613.

[17] Peter L. Strauss, "The Place of Agencies in Government: Separation of Powers and the Fourth Branch," *Columbia Law Review* 84 (1984): 573, 664–65.

[18] Lisa Schultz Bressman and Michael P. Vandenbergh, "Inside the Administrative State: A Critical Look at the Practice of Presidential Control," *Michigan Law Review* 105 (2006): 47, 49–50, 75.

[19] See Mark Seidenfeld, "A Big Picture Approach to Presidential Influence on Agency Policy-Making," *Iowa Law Review* 80 (1994): 1.

[20] See generally Center for Progressive Reform, "A Return to Common Sense: Protecting Health, Safety, and the Environment through 'Pragmatic Regulatory Impact Analysis'" (2009).

Capture and Presidential Power

The threat of capture has played an important role in justifying OIRA's oversight authority. The explanations of regulation given by Stigler,[21] Posner,[22] Pelzman,[23] and Becker,[24] among others, promoted the idea that government institutions – including both legislatures and regulatory agencies – respond primarily to demand for regulation from regulated industries themselves, which seek ways to restrict competition from new firms or otherwise transfer wealth from consumers to producers. Proponents of the "economic theory of regulation" helped formalize the model of government decision makers – and especially agencies – as primarily responsive to pressure from outside interest groups. With their examples of blatant government failure, these scholars also helped contribute to both popular and expert concerns that agencies could not be trusted to protect the public welfare against rapacious private interest.

Concerns related to the influence of well-organized special interests over regulatory decisions have come to be roughly grouped together under the rubric of capture. As has been discussed elsewhere in this volume, finding a useful definition for capture has been a consistent problem. In the worst cases, the term is "sometimes little more than an insult" applied to a policy choice that someone dislikes.[25] Political aims can fall out of line with the public good for a variety of reasons having nothing to do with organized special interest power. Similarly, the mere influence of organized interests is not always normatively undesirable: there are many reasons why the regulated community, for example, should be a welcome contributor to deliberation over public policy, including providing information that regulators need and helping to facilitate voluntary compliance.

There have been several recent attempts to specify the term more carefully. Bagley referred to capture "as shorthand for the phenomenon whereby regulated entities wield their superior organizational capacities to secure

---

[21] George J Stigler, "The Theory of Economic Regulation," *Bell Journal of Economics* 2 (1971): 3.

[22] Richard A. Posner, "Theories of Economic Regulation," *Bell Journal of Economics* 5 (1974): 335.

[23] Sam Peltzman, "Toward a More General Theory of Regulation," *Journal of Law and Economics* 19 (1976): 211.

[24] Gary S. Becker, "A Theory of Competition among Pressure Groups for Political Influence," *Quarterly Journal of Economics* 98 (1983): 371.

[25] Lawrence G. Baxter, "'Capture'" in Financial Regulation: Can We Channel It Toward the Common Good?" *Cornell Journal of Law & Public Policy* 21 (2011): 175, 178.

favorable agency outcomes at the expense of the diffuse public."[26] In Chapter 11 of this volume, Susan Webb Yackee defines capture as "control of agency policy decision making by a subpopulation of individuals or organizations external to the agency," and in the Introduction to this volume, Daniel Carpenter and David Moss define capture as "the result or process by which regulation, in law or application, is consistently or repeatedly directed away from the public interest and toward the interests of the regulated industry, by the intent and action of the industry itself."

Taking a relatively broad view, then, capture can be understood to occur when organized groups successfully act to vindicate their interests through government policy at the expense of the public interest. Agency capture is a special case in which regulators within the bureaucracy have been influenced by organized special interest groups to adopt policies that are out of line with the broad public interest. Of course, there remains the considerable problem of generating an acceptable account of the public good. Nevertheless, although everyone may not agree exactly on what the public interest entails, there is broad consensus on some very bad outcomes that most people (if not everyone) would prefer to avoid, such as massive oil spills, worldwide financial crises, or direct wealth transfers from relatively poor consumers to well-off and well-connected capital owners. How much one is willing to pay to avoid those risks, and how best to reduce them, are of course questions of value and policy on which reasonable people are likely to disagree. The most egregious cases, however, in which very little is done to address a large risk, or much is done to address risks of small magnitude, are likely to be widely recognizable.

Organized special interest groups are the cause of regulatory capture. Traditionally, regulated industry was viewed as the most likely culprit: these actors have the incentive, the know-how, and the lowest barriers to over-coming collective action problems to organize well-funded special interest groups. For Stigler and his contemporaries, industry sought regulation to protect itself from competition. More recently, the possibility that industry would use its influence to avoid regulation has also been recognized – Carpenter and Moss refer to this possibility in the Introduction to this volume as "corrosive capture." During the late 1970s and early 1980s, groups representing broad, diffuse interests – such as environmental preservation and consumer protection – came to be seen as threats as well. Writing in the 1970s, Weidenbaum, a conservative economist and the first head of

[26] Nicholas Bagley, "Agency Hygiene," *Texas Law Review See Also* 89 (2010): 1, 2. See Rachel E. Barkow, "Insulating Agencies: Avoiding Capture through Institutional Design," *Texas Law Review* 89 (2010): 15.

President Reagan's Council of Economic Advisors, crystallized the view in which "the villain . . . has become a self-styled representative of the Public Interest, who has succeeded so frequently in identifying his or her personal prejudices with the national well-being."[27] The apogee of the public interest capture theory is perhaps the "bootleggers and Baptists" coalition,[28] in which protection-oriented groups and regulated industry team up against consumers and new market entrants by erecting regulatory barriers. Borrowing from classic capture theory, the idea is that public interest groups could work in tandem with incumbent market actors to erect regulatory protections that are relatively easier for existing firms to comply with and that therefore serve as a barrier to entry for new firms.[29]

The story is augmented by theories on why agencies are such easy prey for "self-styled" public interest advocacy organizations. Most influential has been the self-aggrandizement hypothesis, championed by Niskanen, in which bureaucrats seek to increase the budgets and mandates of their agencies, ultimately leading to inefficiently high levels of regulation.[30]

Additional theories have been forwarded for why both career staff and political appointees end up identifying with the agency's mission, leading to overly zealous agency action. According to one line of reasoning, agencies such as the Environmental Protection Agency (EPA) and the Occupational Health and Safety Administration attract career employees whose personal policy preferences track the agency's mission[31] and who may use their positions of authority to promote their own, perhaps idiosyncratic, views of the public interest. These career employees in turn influence political appointees, who may end up "go[ing] native"[32] or "succumb[ing] to the pressures of the entrenched ideologues to sustain the preexisting mission of

---

[27] See, for example, Murray L. Weidenbaum, "The High Cost of Governmental Regulation," *Challenge* (November–December 1979): 32–39.

[28] Bruce Yandle, "Bootleggers and Baptists – The Education of a Regulatory Economist," *Regulation* (May/June 1983): 12; Bruce Yandle, "Bootleggers and Baptists in Retrospect: The Marriage of High-Flown Values and Narrow Interests Continues to Thrive," *Regulation* 22 (3) (Fall 1999): 5.

[29] Lloyd N. Cutler and David R. Johnson, "Regulation and the Political Process," *Yale Law Journal* 84 (1975): 1395, 1396.

[30] William A. Niskanen, *Bureaucracy and Representative Government* (Chicago: Aldine, Atherton, 1971), 38.

[31] See, for example, David B. Spence, "Administrative Law and Agency Policy-Making: Rethinking the Positive Theory of Political Control," *Yale Journal on Regulation* 14 (1997): 407, 424.

[32] E. Donald Elliott, "TQM-ing OMB: Or Why Regulatory Review under Executive Order 12,291 Works Poorly and What President Clinton Should Do about It," *Law and Contemporary Problems* 57 (1994): 167, 176.

the agency even when it deviates from the administration's agenda."[33] Agencies, then, are susceptible to the influence of public interest organizations that push them in the direction they are already inclined to go.

If agencies are subject to capture from interest groups on both sides of the political spectrum, defenders of greater presidential authority of all political stripes can claim that increased White House control over the regulatory process will improve outcomes. Indeed, the standard defense of OIRA authority starts with the notion that the president is uniquely situated to remedy the particular failures of capture and narrow-sightedness that hamper agency decision making. In their important defense of OIRA, former OIRA Administrators Christopher DeMuth and Judge Douglas Ginsburg argued that "because the President is responsible to a national constituency, he (or she) will be less sensitive to the kinds of special-interest pressure that might dominate the agencies."[34] As stated by now-Justice Elena Kagan in her defense of presidential power over administrative agencies, "[t]ake the President out of the equation and what remains are individuals and entities with a far more tenuous connection to national majoritarian preferences and interests."[35]

Under this line of thinking, OIRA mitigates capture by facilitating the exercise of presidential power. DeMuth and Ginsburg argued that OIRA will implement the president's will "in a way that the heads of the program agencies cannot be counted upon to do."[36] In support of this claim, they introduce several pieces of evidence. They note that "with centralized review [the president] has to control only one rather than many agency heads."[37] As the number of agencies grows, it becomes more costly for the president to monitor their activities and ensure their loyalty. Far easier for the president to identify a single, central agent and focus monitoring resources on ensuring its compliance.

They also argued that the director of OMB "invariably has a closer working relationship with the President than has the head of any regulatory agency."[38] Because OIRA is subject to OMB oversight, this is thought to

---

[33] Bruce Ackerman, "The New Separation of Powers," *Harvard Law Review* 113 (2000): 633, 698.

[34] Christopher C. DeMuth and Douglas H. Ginsburg, "White House Review of Agency Rulemaking," *Harvard Law Review* 99 (1986): 1075, 1082.

[35] Elena Kagan, "Presidential Administration," *Harvard Law Review* 114 (2001): 2245, 2336.

[36] Christopher C. DeMuth and Douglas H. Ginsburg, "Rationalism in Regulation," *Michigan Law Review* 108 (2010): 877, 904.

[37] Ibid., 903.

[38] Ibid., 904.

create a relatively close relationship between the president and the regulatory review process. On the other hand, the authors claim that agency heads often have "neither a tie of personal loyalty nor a regular relationship with the President," with opportunities for contact potentially limited to "ceremonial occasion[s], such as . . . attendance at the White House Christmas party."[39] Although the president will seek to appoint agency heads that "share his policy perspective," he may have few "particular idea[s]" about how a particular agency should exercise its authority other than "a [general] sense that the agencies have been 'too lax' or 'too aggressive' during the preceding administrations."[40]

Contrasting the limited contact of the president with the stew of pressures faced by agency heads, DeMuth and Ginsburg concluded that "the president has much less control over agency heads than he does over OIRA." Because of the variety of ways that interest groups can pressure agencies, "the president is just one, and often not the most influential, of the agency's constituencies."[41] As a result of the comparatively closer relationship between the president and OIRA, the argument goes, the process of centralized review can reduce the impact of agency capture by pushing agencies to adopt policies that are more palatable to the president and to his national constituency.

Problems in the Presidential Power Justification

There are two broad problems with the presidential power anti-capture justification for OIRA. First, the president's responsiveness to a national constituency is not always altogether clear. In recent years, the Electoral College has delivered a president who lost the popular vote,[42] and in the twentieth century alone, seven presidential elections were settled with a plurality winner.[43] National elections are subject to a variety of distortions, including private expenditures,[44] the vagaries of the primary process,[45] and

---

[39] Ibid., 905.
[40] Ibid., 904.
[41] Ibid., 906.
[42] See Federal Election Commission, "2000 Presidential Popular Vote Summary" (January 2001).
[43] Wilson (1912, 1916), Truman (1948), Kennedy (1960), Nixon (1968), Clinton (1992, 1996).
[44] See generally Daniel Hays Lowenstein, "On Campaign Finance Reform: The Root of All Evil Is Deeply Rooted," *Hofstra Law Review* 18 (1989): 301.
[45] See generally Anthony Busch and William G. Mayer, *The Front-Loading Problem in Presidential Nominations* (Washington, D.C.: Brookings Institution, 2004).

a lack of participation by eligible American voters. Debate tends to focus on highly salient, emotionally laden issues[46] and the personality and character traits of the candidates,[47] rather than on specific policy proposals. Broad macroeconomic factors are strongly correlated with election outcomes,[48] indicating that the actual content of a candidate's proposals may have little effect on voters' choices.

Once elected, the president must secure his agenda and ensure reelection; both goals may cause the president's interest to diverge from that of a national constituency. The president's policy preferences may represent his electoral constituency rather than his entire constituency because the winner-take-all Electoral College system gives the president an incentive to pursue policies favored in the swing states needed for reelection.[49] The president may also direct regulatory policy to curry favor with certain legislators needed to advance his legislative agenda by promising regulatory concessions to a legislator in return for his support on a piece of legislation or appointment.[50] Finally, the president may be more beholden to his political party than a broader national constituency and may support regulations that tend to favor his party.[51]

The second, and more important, problem is that the administrator of OIRA has no stronger claim to directly represent a national constituency than the head of any other agency.[52] Indeed, at least in the appointment process, the link between national electorate and the head of OIRA is similar to that of other agency heads: they are all nominated by the president and confirmed by the Senate. During times of divided government, the president does not have full control over the person chosen to run OIRA and must negotiate with members of the opposition party to fill the

---

[46] Cf. D. Sunshine Hillygus and Todd G. Shields, *The Persuadable Voter: Wedge Issues in Presidential Campaigns* (Princeton: Princeton University Press, 2008), 13–14.

[47] See generally Oksana Malanchuk, Arthur H. Miller, and Martin P. Wattenberg, "Schematic Assessments of Presidential Candidates," *American Political Science Review* 80 (1986): 521.

[48] See Michael S. Lewis-Beck, William G. Jacoby, Helmut Norpoth, and Herbert F. Weisberg, *The American Voter Revisited* (Ann Arbor, MI: The University of Michigan Press, 2008), 365–93.

[49] See Cynthia R. Farina, "Faith, Hope, and Rationality or Public Choice and the Perils of Occam's Razor," *Florida State University Law Review* 28 (2000): 109, 128–29; see also Jide Nzelibe, "The Fable of the Nationalist President and the Parochial Congress," *UCLA Law Review* 53 (2006): 1217, 1231–42.

[50] Nolan M. McCarty, "Presidential Pork: Executive Veto Power and Distributive Politics," *American Political Science Review* 94 (2000): 117, 118.

[51] Cf. Steven D. Levitt and James M. Snyder, Jr., "Political Parties and the Distribution of Federal Outlays," *American Journal of Political Science* 39 (1995): 958.

[52] Nicholas Bagley and Richard L. Revesz, "Centralized Oversight of the Regulatory State," *Columbia Law Review* 106 (2006): 1260.

position. It is not clear that it would be wise to devote greater presidential cognitive resources to selecting and monitoring the OIRA administrator than the head of any other agency. OIRA is a small office, employing only a couple of dozen professional staff and operating under a budget that is a rounding error of the federal budget. Administrative agencies are vast bureaucracies, employing tens of thousands of people, with sprawling offices, satellite branches across the country, and far larger budgets. OIRA's main role is in formally reviewing agency regulatory decisions, a process that typically spans only a few months, plus some informal inputs here and there during the rulemaking process. Agencies are responsible for the all-important task of crafting rulemaking agendas. They collect and analyze the data supporting their proposals and develop records that can run into the thousands of pages. They decide which congressional deadlines to meet and which to ignore and whether a court mandamus order will be followed or put off until another day. Outside the rulemaking context, they decide how and against whom enforcement actions will be carried out, who will get permits on what timescale, and how grants will be allocated – all decisions that are essentially unreviewable. It may be the case that OIRA is easier to monitor than agencies, if only because it has such a larger range of activities that are carried out. However, this comparative advantage is relatively insignificant, because the total amount of time the president has for monitoring either agencies or OIRA is extremely small.

Proximity is another argument offered in favor of a tighter president-OIRA connection. According to this logic, the Executive Office of the President (EOP), which houses OIRA, is more likely to understand and carry out the president's will because it is located close to the White House and is populated with various political appointees. High-level political advisors to the president are nearby, along with staff at the White House coordinating offices, such as the Domestic Policy Council and Council of Economic Advisors, which interact with the president on a more regular basis. The OMB director – often closely consulting with the president, especially during the budget cycle – plays a supervisory role over OIRA, potentially communicating information and perspectives from the president.

This argument is difficult to evaluate, in part because it relies on a cultural dynamic that would be hard for an outsider to directly observe and also because officials within the EOP have an incentive to overstate their relationship with the president. To the degree that EOP officials are widely perceived as genuinely faithful agents of the president, it will be easier for them to exert influence over various actors in the executive branch.

First-hand reports from inside the EOP that confirm a close relationship with the president, then, provide only moderately useful evidence.

Potential cultural influences at play within OIRA could also pull the administrator away from presidential preferences. A number of commentators have raised concerns about agency heads going "native"[53] in response to interaction with civil servants within their departments. There are indeed a wide number of mechanisms that career personnel have at their disposal to influence political appointees at the agency, including controlling the flow of information, arranging meetings, or prompting actions by outside interest groups. Gaining the trust and loyalty of career staff is also essential for the success of the political appointees: those appointees whose views more closely align with the staff may find their projects running more smoothly, on faster timelines, and with fewer bureaucratic hassles. This creates a subtle incentive to consider the views of staff when forming policy preferences. Daily contact with the staff – who are extremely knowledgeable about their subject areas, are often very dedicated public servants, and have become experts at interacting with (sometimes inexperienced) politically appointed supervisors – may also engender trust and a greater willingness to consider staff opinions.

All of these mechanisms could be expected to work within OIRA as well, notwithstanding its location within the EOP. The flow of information from and to the OIRA administrator will be determined in large part by the staff at OIRA. The administrator, tasked with the Herculean challenge of overseeing the rulemaking activities of the entire federal government, must rely on the staff if he or she is to be successful, which creates a need to establish bonds of loyalty and trust. Many of the career personnel at OIRA have held their positions for substantial periods of time – sometimes decades – and they are all experts in the regulatory process and agency decision making, in addition to working with OIRA administrators of different political stripes. Just as the daily interactions with an expert staff and the need to achieve loyalty may tilt agency heads in favor of the views of career staff, the OIRA administrators may find themselves subject to the same dynamic.

An additional argument that OIRA better represents the president is that its relative insulation from the daily scrum of agency decision making will make it easier for the OIRA administrator to represent presidential preferences, free from the influence of outside interests. Agencies are constantly interacting with interest groups, members of Congress, media figures, and

---

[53] E. Donald Elliott, "TQM-ing OMB," 176.

even concerned members of the broader public. Although the OIRA administrator sometimes must appear before Congress and may take meetings with some interest groups, there is much less robust interaction with outside parties. If the OIRA administrator comes into office with preferences that are closer to the president, there are fewer built-in avenues for outside influences to pull or push those preferences in any direction.

At the same time, however, the rulemaking process, and the larger institutional contexts of agencies, with their multiple masters, overseers, and constituencies, may make it *easier* for agencies to represent the broader national interests and therefore (presumably) presidential priorities, especially as the views of the public evolve as a result of new information and changing circumstances. If OIRA is too insulated from the broader world, it could fail to keep pace with the national conversation. Soliciting the views of a broad array of actors, engaging in the national debate over regulatory issues, and being subject to criticism in media and scrutiny in the public eye may make agencies more likely to make decisions that favor the broadest possible constituency. Even assuming that OIRA is more insulated than typical agencies (which itself is debatable), it is not clear that this will always work in an anti-capture direction.

As Croley has persuasively argued, the structure of the rulemaking process may also facilitate agency independence from special interest influence,[54] making it more likely that an agency's decision will reflect national preferences. The open structure of the notice and comment process, for example, would seem to advantage public interest groups and the public vis-à-vis the legislative process by lowering the cost of information gathering and reducing the benefits associated with larger lobbying budgets. Furthermore, there are procedural mechanisms that facilitate more even-handed participation. Any person can petition an agency for an action or comment on a proposed rulemaking, and "[u]nlike campaign dollars, the arguments and information that make up rulemaking comments are not fungible, and redundant comments are virtually worthless."[55] In the administrative process, there is a very fast rate of diminishing returns to investment, reducing the value of big lobbying budgets. This reality levels the field for relatively underfunded groups, because a single, well-reasoned set of comments can have influence that is very large compared with its cost of production.

---

[54] Steven P. Croley, "Public Interested Regulation," *Florida State University Law Review* 28 (2000): 7, 33–49.
[55] Croley, "Public Interested Regulation," 36.

The relative advantages of the administrative process over the legislative process do not mean that it is perfect, or free from capture risks. Concentrated well-funded interests hold many advantages against public interest groups. However, it does indicate that if OIRA is as susceptible to political influence as agencies (through presidential or congressional mechanisms of control) but less exposed to the administrative process, that may increase the risk of capture for OIRA. In that case, its relative insulation would be a hindrance from a capture perspective, rather than an advantage.

The traditional argument that OIRA oversight mitigates the threat of agency capture by increasing presidential control, then, has serious flaws. Most important, it is not clear the OIRA is a better proxy for the president than the political appointees within agencies. In addition, the president cannot be counted on to simply represent a broad national constituency in all cases.

INSTITUTIONAL FEATURES OF OIRA THAT FACILITATE AN ANTI-CAPTURE ROLE

OIRA, however, has several institutional features that suggest that it can play an anti-capture role. First, because OIRA is structured as a generalist body, capturing it is more difficult and is therefore less likely to occur than at single-mission agencies. Second, the process of OIRA review typically involves coordinating the interests of multiple agencies, each with different perspectives; this coordination can blunt the capture-induced bias of any particular agency. Third, OIRA review focuses on the use of cost-benefit analysis, which requires the weighing of all relevant competing considerations, thereby providing some check against the possibility that particular considerations would be left out of an agency's decision-making process as a result of capture. Finally, a tradition has developed of appointing OIRA administrators from a pool of individuals who are relatively independent and do not have strong ties to particular interest groups. This tradition would be costly to reverse and helps insulate OIRA from outsized influence of particular interest groups.

Benefits of a Generalist Perspective

One of the core features of OIRA is that, as compared with the various regulatory agencies, it is a generalist institution. The benefits of capturing a generalist institution are comparatively less than those of capturing a specialized institution, because they are diluted by the wide range of matters that are of no concern to a particular special interest group.[56] For example, labor unions may be concerned about how regulatory review will influence safety standards promulgated by the Occupational Safety and Health Administration and so could seek to influence the appointment of the OIRA administrator or otherwise build connections to the office. However, OIRA also deals with many other issues. As a result, from the unions' perspective, their hard fought influence is almost entirely wasted because of the large number of rules that are not important to them.[57]

At the same time that any one group will be interested only in a small portion of OIRA's portfolio, there will be many other groups seeking OIRA's attention. Because of the broad array of issues that OIRA must deal with, attempts to influence the institution will be spread among many different interests. Whereas repeat players will participate in many rulemakings before an agency, the regulatory review process will involve a different set of actors each time. Groups that are repeat players when acting before an agency are thrown in with a larger number of other repeat players during the regulatory review process. Each group then lacks the ability to exert the kind of sustained and continual pressure that is associated with the highest risk of capture.

The incentives to influence OIRA, then, are diffuse and diluted. Although for any particular rule, there may be powerful and concentrated interests before an agency, any incentive to capture OIRA in general will be diffused across many different interests, leading to familiar collective action problems.[58] Interest groups will withhold resources and energy assuming that they can free ride on the efforts of others. Because OIRA deals with such varying issues, each individual interest group will have an incentive to shift the costs of capturing the office to other groups. Although this phenomenon may also exist at agencies, because, for example, EPA regulates entirely different industries under its air quality program and its toxic site cleanup program, the scale of the problem at OIRA is substantially enlarged.

---

[56] See Richard L. Revesz, "Specialized Courts and the Administrative Lawmaking System," *University of Pennsylvania Law Review* 138 (1990): 1111, 1150; Michael E. Levine and Jennifer L. Forrence, "Capture, Public Interest, and the Public Agenda: Toward a Synthesis," *The Journal of Law, Economics, & Organization* 6 (1990): 167, 184.

[57] See Jonathan R. Macey, "Organizational Design and Political Control of Administrative Agencies," *Journal of Law, Economics, & Organization* 8 (1992): 93, 99. It is worth noting that there is some specialization even within OIRA, so that a desk officer will deal with only a handful of agencies. Nevertheless, capture of even the more specialized personnel in OIRA is relatively more costly, and the benefits of generalization are even more clear for the OIRA Administrator.

[58] Mancur Olson, *The Logic of Collective Action*, rev. ed. (Cambridge, MA: Harvard University Press, 1971), 2, 48, 53.

Disparate interests and free-rider problems stand in the way of having different groups form coalitions to control OIRA. In addition, because OIRA must deal with a large range of interests over time, each of which at any given moment might want to influence it, any attempt to capture the institution would be diluted with many similar attempts coming from other directions at different times.[59]

The anti-capture potential of a generalist institution resembles in some ways the arguments made in favor of presidential power over agencies. Drawing on the logic of *Federalist 10*, defenders of greater presidential power argue that the national constituency will reduce the influence of any particular interest group: "[e]xtend the sphere, and you take in a greater variety of parties and interests."[60] The same basic logic applies for OIRA, but not because of an assumed OIRA-president nexus. Justifying regulatory review based on the generalist design of the review office, rather than institutional features of the presidency, avoids the necessity of grounding the review on the arguably weak claim that OIRA is a better proxy for the president than the political appointees at agencies.

The most obvious way in which a generalist regulatory review agency can help reduce capture risks is by identifying cases in which proposed rules favor a specific interest group at the expense of the public. Because rulemaking takes place in the shadow of review, flagrant attempts to privilege private interests through rulemaking may also simply be avoided altogether as a result of the prospect that such attempts would be identified as such during the review process. Especially over a large number of rules, a reviewing body that is not captured should be able to identify agency tendencies to favor particular interests groups and focus its reviewing efforts accordingly to help rebalance the rulemaking process.

Broad jurisdiction is not necessarily a panacea. When agencies are given several different goals, they can sometimes skew too heavily in favor of one or another, a risk that is especially grave if there are powerful and well-organized interests promoting particular priorities but not others.[61] Congress also sometimes gives agencies mandates that are seemingly contradictory. Agencies carrying out disparate tasks – such as promoting an

---

[59] See Richard L. Revesz, "Federalism and Environmental Regulation: A Public Choice Analysis," *Harvard Law Review* 115 (2001): 533, 561.

[60] James Madison, *The Federalist*, no. 10, ed. Clinton Rossiter (New York: New American Library, 1961), 82–84.

[61] See generally Eric Biber, "Too Many Things to Do: How to Deal with the Dysfunctions of Multiple-Goal Agencies," *Harvard Environmental Law Review* 33 (2009): 1; J.R. DeShazo and Jody Freeman, "Public Agencies as Lobbyists," *Columbia Law Review* 105 (2005): 2217, 2220.

activity while also issuing safety regulations – may have a tendency to "prioritize one task at the expense of the other,"[62] especially when there is consistent pressure to produce results in one area.

These concerns may not by overly troublesome for OIRA. Its priority should be clear: maximizing the net benefits of regulation. If it wishes to conduct more than perfunctory review, OIRA has relatively little discretion to shift resources away from review, given the deadlines it faces under governing executive orders and the political pressure to conduct review in a timely fashion.[63] OIRA is a generalist because of its broad jurisdiction over many subjects, not because multiple missions have been combined into a single agency.

Coordinating Agencies

OIRA review typically involves coordinating the interests of multiple agencies. As part of its review process, OIRA circulates proposed rules and the accompanying regulatory impact statements to other agencies and solicits their feedback on regulatory proposals. This practice provides an important opportunity for each agency to weigh in and express concerns about the regulatory actions being contemplated by other agencies.[64] Agency coordination, in addition,[65] can also have a significant capture-related benefit. Because these agencies each have different perspectives, and likely favor differing interests, parties that otherwise might have been excluded will now have the opportunity to weigh in during the rulemaking process. Coordination can thus blunt the capture-induced bias of any one particular agency.

If, as a general matter, there is no agency that can entirely avoid some degree of capture, the coordinating process, which expands the range of interests that are potentially involved in a regulatory process, should have beneficial effects on capture risks. This dynamic works in a similar fashion to generalization: because different agencies work on a large range of subject matters, it would be difficult for any one interest group to capture all of the agencies that might wish to weigh in on a rule. To the extent that most major interest groups will have some agency to which they can express concern

---

[62] Bagley, "Agency Hygiene," 10.

[63] Under Executive Order 12,866, OIRA is generally required to complete its review within 90 days after an agency formally submits a draft regulation. See Exec. Order No. 12,866, 3 C.F.R. 638 (1994), reprinted in 5 U.S.C. § 601 (2000).

[64] Jody Freeman and Jim Rossi, "Agency Coordination in Shared Regulatory Space," *Harvard Law Review* 25 (2012): 1131, 1180.

[65] See Peter L. Strauss and Cass R. Sunstein, "The Role of the President in Informal Rulemaking," *Administrative Law Review* 38 (1986): 181, 189–90.

over a proposed rule, this coordinating function will reduce the influence of any particular interest group. Although some may be concerned that environmentalists have captured EPA, any rules proposed by EPA will also be examined by the Department of Energy, the Department of Transportation, and the Small Business Administration – agencies with which environmentalists are not thought to have overly close connections. Similarly, a regulator such as the Federal Energy Regulatory Commission, with a less protection-oriented culture, can be shifted in a more environmentally friendly direction when influenced by agencies such as EPA and their related interest groups. The result of coordination should often be some degree of "policy mediation, in which agencies introduce to other agencies a set of interest that they may otherwise ignore, or treat only lightly."[66]

To be sure, OIRA's coordination role is not as developed as it could be. OIRA can use, and has at times used, its coordinating role to centralize power rather than to rationalize policies across agencies. Sometimes, goals such as checking agency action and reducing regulatory burdens have trumped goals such as harmonization or standardization.[67] Experience with several different administrations suggests that the strength of the coordination function of OIRA is largely dependent on how strongly the political leadership in the White House values that function.

There are also other substantive areas in which OIRA could play a role in harmonizing agency policy but has failed to so.[68] Examples include the methodologies for incorporating distributional considerations into regulatory impact analysis and for valuing the benefits of mortality risk reduction. Since the Clinton Executive Order, there has been specific presidential authorization for agencies to examine the distributional effects of rulemakings, but agency efforts to do so have been scattered and ad hoc, and OIRA has offered scant guidance on the question. Although potentially politically fraught, such an effort could help decrease the appearance of regulatory inconsistency among agencies and allow for comparison of the risk reduction achieved by regulation across agencies.

Despite these shortcomings, agency coordination during the OIRA review process provides a meaningful opportunity to involve parties and interests that otherwise might have been excluded. Bringing together different agencies with different perspectives can minimize the disproportionate influence

---

[66] DeShazo and Freeman, "Public Agencies as Lobbyists," 2299.

[67] See Bagley and Revesz, "Centralized Oversight of the Regulatory State," 1264–65.

[68] See Letter from Michael A. Livermore et al., Institute for Policy Integrity, New York University School of Law, to Cass Sunstein, Administrator, Office of Information and Regulatory Affairs (May 11, 2012), in the author's possession.

of any one interest group. When performed in this manner, coordination can have an important and significant role in minimizing the potential for capture in the rulemaking process.

Cost-Benefit Analysis

At the heart of OIRA's review of agency decision making is the cost-benefit standard, which requires, to the extent possible, that agencies identify and quantify the benefits and costs of proposed rulemakings. This methodology has three important features that have the potential to reduce agency capture: it is comprehensive, requiring the examination of a wide range of regulatory effects; it is standardized and supported by a set of professional norms; and it is improves transparency by publishing for public scrutiny agency estimates of regulatory effects. OIRA facilitates the potential for the cost-benefit analysis requirement to reduce the threat of agency capture by ensuring that agencies comply with the requirement, by establishing and enforcing uniform and rigorous methodological standards, and by helping to ensure basic transparency in the process of review.

The basic idea of cost-benefit analysis is simple: the promulgating agency must identify the problem, identify alternative policies for addressing the problem, assess the costs and benefits of each alternative, and select the policy that best achieves its goals.[69] Cost-benefit analysis is meant to be comprehensive, examining the wide range of impacts from a rule on individual well-being and measuring the value of those impacts based on the preferences of the affected parties.[70] In theory, no regulatory effects are excluded from the calculus. In practice, although resource constraints mean that analysis only extends so far, at least all of the most important categories of effects should be considered.

Although some agencies may be inclined to carry out this analysis, others may not. By itself, an executive order is not necessarily sufficient to force agencies to undergo analytic exercises that they are disinclined to carry out. A stark example is Executive Order 13,132 on federalism, signed by President Clinton, which requires agencies to conduct a rigorous consultation process with states for all regulations "that have federalism implications."[71]

---

[69] See Robert W. Hahn and Cass R. Sunstein, "A New Executive Order for Improving Federal Regulation? Deeper and Wider Cost-Benefit Analysis," *University of Pennsylvania Law Review* 150 (2002): 1489, 1498–99.

[70] See generally U.S. Environmental Protection Agency, "Guidelines for Preparing Economic Analyses" (2010).

[71] Exec. Order 13,132, 64 Fed. Reg. 43,255 (August 10, 1999).

This order has, for the most part, been "blithely ignored," in part because there was no White House office ensuring that agencies complied.[72]

OIRA's role in regulatory review ensures that the cost-benefit analysis requirement is taken seriously by the agencies. The process of review set out in the Reagan Order, and carried through in each successive executive order, creates a clear role for OIRA prior to publication of rulemakings. The vigilance of OIRA has helped ensure that agencies take the cost-benefit analysis directive seriously or risk having their regulations delayed during the process of review. As comparison with the federalism order illustrates, OIRA's role in simply ensuring agency compliance with the cost-benefit analysis requirement has likely been extremely important.

The methodology developed to carry out the cost-benefit analysis directive is, given the detail and scale of many agency rulemakings, quite complex. Agencies employ a large array of experts in a range of fields – including toxicology, risk analysis, engineering, and economics – each with a set of professional norms, to carry out this analysis. As the practice of cost-benefit analysis has developed over the decades, it has become relatively standardized, with a common set of methodologies and approaches that are relied on and that change only slowly through the gradual accumulation of evidence or theoretical innovation. The standardization of the practice of cost-benefit analysis, although far from complete, constrains agencies in the types of analytic choices – in terms of data, models, or assumptions – that can go into the analysis. Although agencies may have some incentives to tweak analysis to arrive at favorable results, there is limited scope for them to do so while using a methodology with relatively clear and well-known parameters.[73]

Cost-benefit analysis is also a relatively transparent process. Although the practice has come under some criticism for its technical nature, which some commentators see as excluding average citizens from decision-making processes, the regulatory impact analyses produced by agencies in support of rulemakings are part of the public record and freely available for any citizen to access. Although there may be only a limited number of people with the expertise to fully digest these documents, interested parties, civil society actors, media outlets, and other institutional actors outside of the government all have the opportunity to examine, comment on, and criticize how well agencies counted costs and benefits. As with other information disclosure requirements – such as the environmental impact statement requirement of the National Environmental Policy Act – there is always the

[72] Catherine M. Sharkey, "Federalism Accountability: 'Agency-Forcing' Measures," *Duke Law Journal* 58 (2009): 2125, 2164, 2177.

[73] Michael A. Livermore, "Cost-Benefit Analysis and Agency Independence," forthcoming.

risk that too much disclosure will trigger information overload.[74] However, at the very least, cost-benefit analysis places information in the public domain, where it can be subjected to some degree of scrutiny.

An additional capture-related criticism of cost-benefit analysis is that, because it is a highly technical exercise, carried out by experts and laden with complex jargon and sophisticated methodology, it obscures the value choices made by agencies in an aura of scientific certainty that is both inaccurate and impedes broad-based inclusion in the regulatory process.[75] According to this argument, regulatory impact statements that can easily run hundreds of pages may do more to alienate the public than facilitate participation.

Information overload is certainly a valid concern, but this critique of cost-benefit analysis can easily be overdrawn, and the appropriate remedy is to improve the communication of results rather than to scale back the analysis. Agencies must communicate with multiple different audiences – Congress, interest groups, and affected individuals – often through intermediary institutions such as trade associations, advocacy organizations, and most importantly the media. Certainly, complex cost-benefit analysis is not the optimal communications medium for all of these audiences, and agencies should include easily understood distillations of results in impact analyses[76] and should continue developing techniques to encourage participation. Complex supporting documents can be extremely important transparency tools, but must be augmented by broader communications strategies. In other contexts, OIRA encourages agencies to distinguish between "summary disclosure" and "full disclosure," where the first is "clear, salient information at or near the time that relevant decisions are made" and the latter is "a wide range of information [that] . . . include[s] far more detail."[77] Summary disclosure should be based on "explicitly" identified goals, should be "simple and specific, and should avoid undue detail or excessive complexity," should "be accurate and in plain language," should include "meaningful" ratings or scales, and also be tested for "how people react to a given

---

[74] See Wendy E. Wagner, "Administrative Law, Filter Failure, and Information Capture," *Duke Law Journal* 59 (2010): 1321, 1393.

[75] See Sidney A. Shapiro and Christopher H. Schroeder, "Beyond Cost-Benefit Analysis: A Pragmatic Reorientation," *Harvard Environmental Law Review* 31 (2008): 433, 436.

[76] See Office of Information and Regulatory Affairs, "Regulatory Impact Analysis: A Primer" (2011).

[77] Memorandum from Cass R. Sunstein, Administrator, Office of Information and Regulatory Affairs, for the Heads of Executive Departments and Agencies (June 18, 2010), 3, 6.

piece of information."[78] A similar distinction can and should be made with respect to regulatory impact analysis, in which summary disclosure is used to communicate impacts to a broad audience, and full disclosure is used to facilitate deep participation by intermediary groups including journalists, outside experts, and affected interests.

Appointment of OIRA Administrators

Since Congress created the position of OIRA Administrator in 1980,[79] presidents have tended to nominate to this position relatively independent figures, rather than individuals with close ties to interest groups. This tradition would presumably be costly to depart from, especially because the administrator position is subject to Senate confirmation. If a new president appointed, for example, the head of a trade association representing polluters or the head of an ideological group, there might well be serious political fallout. This appointment practice, which developed over three decades, helps – at least to some degree – insulate OIRA from interest group influence.

Since 1980, there have been eleven OIRA Administrators. By and large these administrators share an educational background in law or economic policy and careers in academia or generalized administrative law practices prior to joining OIRA. Many former administrators enter or reenter academia after leaving OIRA. This trend, which stands in stark contrast to the revolving door between industry and heads of regulatory agencies, bolsters the claim that OIRA administrators tend to be independent.

Of the eleven OIRA administrators, five were trained in economics or public policy. James Miller III received a PhD in economics from the University of Virginia. Wendy Gramm received a PhD in economics from Northwestern University. James MacRae, Jr., holds a Masters in Sociology from Duke University and a Masters in Public Policy from Harvard University. John Graham received a Masters in Public Policy from Duke University and a PhD in Urban and Public Affairs from Carnegie Mellon University. Susan Dudley studied economics as an undergraduate and holds a Masters from the MIT School of Management. Six were trained as lawyers. Christopher DeMuth and Douglas Ginsburg received law degrees from the University of Chicago. S. Jay Plager received law degrees from the University of Florida College of Law and Columbia Law School. Sally Katzen received a law

---

[78] Memorandum from Sunstein (2010), 3–5.
[79] Paperwork Reduction Act of 1980, Pub. L. No. 96-511, 94 Stat. 2812 (December 11, 1980).

degree from the University of Michigan. John Spotila received a law degree from Yale Law School. Cass Sunstein holds a law degree from Harvard Law School.

These appointees had generalized expertise in administrative law and regulation and tended to join OIRA from academia, think tanks, or the legal profession, rather than from the ranks of industry or particular interest groups. James Miller III was a scholar and then codirector of the Center for the Study of Government Regulation at the American Enterprise Institute. Douglas Ginsburg was a professor at Harvard Law School. Wendy Gramm taught economics at Texas A&M. S. Jay Plager taught law at the University of Florida and the University of Illinois College of Law and was Dean of the Indiana University School of Law. John Graham was a professor of Policy and Decision Sciences at the Harvard University School of Public Health. Cass Sunstein is one of the most important legal academics of his generation, with a distinguished career at University of Chicago School of Law and Harvard Law School.

Administrators with prior careers in the private sector have tended to focus on administrative law and regulation generally rather than on a particular area or industry. Christopher DeMuth worked at Sidley Austin, a law firm based in Chicago, and at Harvard's Kennedy School of Government. Sally Katzen was a partner at what is now WilmerHale, a D.C. law firm where she had a general administrative law practice. Two served in government prior to joining OIRA. John Spotila served in the Small Business Administration. Susan Dudley served in career positions at several government agencies before leaving to teach at George Mason University and direct the Regulatory Studies Program at its Mercatus Center.

After leaving OIRA, many administrators have gone on to join academia or serve in the nonprofit sector at think tanks. James Miller III eventually ran the Office of Management and Budget before leaving government. Since then he has served as a fellow at the Citizens for a Sound Economy Foundation, the Center for Study of Public Choice at George Mason University, and the Hoover Institution. He has also served as an advisor to several companies, government bodies, and law firms. Christopher DeMuth joined the American Enterprise Institute after leaving OIRA, retiring as its president in 2007. James MacRae III served in the U.S. Department of Health and Human Services for over a decade after serving as acting administrator. Sally Katzen held other positions at the OMB before joining academia as a visiting professor at several law schools. John Graham was dean of the RAND Graduate School in California and is now dean of the Indiana University School of Public and Environmental Affairs. Susan Dudley is a professor at the George Washington University Trachtenberg School of Public Policy and Public Administration.

Two administrators were appointed to the federal judiciary. Douglas Ginsburg was appointed to a seat on the D.C. Circuit Court of Appeals after serving as OIRA Administrator. S. Jay Plager was appointed to a seat on the U.S. Court of Appeals for the Federal Circuit.

Wendy Gramm and John Spotila are exceptions to this general rule, as both spent significant time in the private sector after leaving OIRA. Gramm headed the Commodity Futures Trading Commission and served on the Enron Board of Directors during its collapse, before joining George Mason University's Mercatus Center as a senior scholar. Spotila served as the president and COO of GTSI Corp., an information technology provider, and is now the CEO of R3i Solutions, a government-contracting firm.

Rather than appointing individuals with clear connections to the regulated parties or other interest groups, presidents have by and large chosen individuals from the academic arena, who have based their careers on scholarship and general expertise on the regulatory system, for the position of OIRA administrator. This, of course, does not mean that OIRA administrators are mere technocrats, free of political views or policy commitments, or that presidents do not seek to appoint administrators with similar views of the regulatory process. Of course, many OIRA administrators do have quite clear and well-established views that can be gleaned from their writing and public statements. However, the generalist nature of the position makes it difficult for any one interest group to exert very strong influence on the nomination process, and the requirement for someone with broad knowledge of the regulatory system tends to exclude the kinds of specialized appointments that are often associated with interest groups. As a consequence, a tradition of appointing relatively independent voices to the position of OIRA administration has developed that would likely be difficult to break.

NEXT STEPS

Retrospective Review

In 2011, President Obama issued Executive Order 13,563, supplementing President Clinton's Executive Order 12,866.[80] Among other things, the order required agencies to submit plans to OIRA within 120 days detailing

---

[80] 76 Fed. Reg. 3,821 (January 21, 2011).

how the agency would periodically review its regulations and determine which could be made "more effective or less burdensome."[81] The order does not detail what agencies are required to do with those plans or specify a role for OIRA beyond serving as a repository for those plans. Cass Sunstein, the OIRA administrator at the time this order was signed, issued a memorandum to agencies and departments that encouraged agencies to publish their plans online, solicit public comment, and finalize plans within eighty days of initial publication.[82] The plans submitted by agencies vary greatly in terms of the details offered and number of potential regulations targeted.[83]

Transparent, robust retrospective review can raise the cost of capture to interest groups in two important ways. First, retrospective review helps ensure that regulations initially passed through capture face a threat of future review. By forcing interest groups to reinvest in capture at each interval of retrospective review, the present value of capture to interest groups decreases. Rather than a one-time investment that leads to persistent benefits with relatively small monitoring costs, interest groups would be faced with the prospect of (potentially) making substantial, continual investments over time to protect whatever favorable regulatory treatment they were able to extract during the bargaining process over the initial rule. This possibility could substantially reduce the incentive to invest in capture, so long as the risk of retrospective analysis is sufficiently high.

Second, a robust practice of retrospective review means that regulations are more likely to be reviewed by agencies under different and potentially less favorable administrations later on. Political control of the White House tends to shift over time, and although there is some overlap within the coalitions that make up contemporary political parties, there are also substantial differences. A robust practice of retrospective review facilitates oversight by both political parties. For special interest groups to enjoy durable results, they could not limit their investment to a single party but would have to ensure against reviews by both parties. Especially for groups seeking treatment that conflicts with the core ideologies of either party, this prospect could be especially daunting. The risk of having the efforts of capture

---

[81] 76 Fed. Reg. 3,821 § 6.

[82] Memorandum from Cass R. Sunstein, Administrator, Office of Information and Regulatory Affairs, for the Heads of Executive Departments and Agencies (April 25, 2011). The memorandum also encouraged agencies to consider ways to institute empirical testing of the effects of their rules both prospectively and retrospectively.

[83] "Regulation Reform," WhiteHouse.gov, http://www.whitehouse.gov/21stcenturygov/actions/21st-century-regulatory-system.

overturned by a subsequent administration may deter investment in capture ex ante.

Based on the experience of previous attempts at retrospective review, OIRA can play an important role in ensuring that the process maximizes its anti-capture potential. As with the cost-benefit analysis requirement, agencies are more likely to engage in rigorous and sustained retrospective analysis if OIRA uses its position to encourage agencies to do so. Past efforts to require retrospective review, including one stated in the Clinton Order, have languished or been largely ignored by agencies. A substantial push by OIRA, however, improves the chances that agencies will actually carry out the new retrospective review requirements.

In addition, OIRA can provide guidance to agencies to standardize the retrospective review process. A 1997 Government Accountability Office study of agency retrospective review found that "the units of analysis that agencies used in their reviews, and the scope of individual reviews, varied widely."[84] As discussed previously, an established process makes deviations owing to capture by interest groups more likely to be noticed, and OIRA could improve the value and credibility of retrospective reviews by issuing guidelines for the reviews, as it did with Circular A-4 for agency cost-benefit analyses. A systematic approach to retrospective review by agencies would ensure that the regulations targeted for review are likely to be those of economic significance for which there is real opportunity for efficiency gains.[85]

OIRA can also facilitate the disclosure to the public about the scope, nature, and progress of retrospective reviews. The same 1997 GAO study noted that agencies did not adequately notify the public when reviews were initiated or what the results of reviews were.[86] OIRA's involvement in previous attempts at retrospective review suffered the same problems.[87] Transparent retrospective review also mitigates the risk that the review

---

[84] Government Accountability Office, "Reexamining Regulations: Opportunities Exist to Improve Effectiveness and Transparency of Retrospective Reviews" (GAO-07-791, 2007), 17.

[85] Government Accountability Office, "Assessing the Impacts of EPA's Regulations Through Retrospective Studies" (GAO-/RCED-99-250, 1999), 17 (criticizing EPA's "ad hoc approach" to retrospective review – less than 5 percent of the economically significant rules promulgated over the seven-year study period were reviewed – because it offered "no assurance that economically significant regulations will be subjected to review").

[86] Government Accountability Office, "Reexamining Regulations," 50–51.

[87] Richard L. Revesz and Michael A. Livermore, *Retaking Rationality: How Cost-Benefit Analysis Can Better Protect the Environment and Our Health* (New York: Oxford University Press, 2008), 155–56 (describing earlier attempts by OIRA to coordinate the review and elimination of inefficient regulations through the use of a "hit list" of regulations that was not publicized or tracked).

process itself might be captured by industry groups seeking a chance to initiate challenges to regulations they previously failed to prevent or pressure agencies to drop a review already initiated. To avoid this threat, OIRA should take on an information gathering and publishing role.

Unfortunately, throughout the Order's early implementation, much of the focus from agencies and OIRA has been on "small-bore red tape-snipping"[88] with very little emphasis on expanding rules where they have proven effective or testing agencies' ex ante predictions of regulatory costs and benefits against ex post data. This emphasis on cost-cutting threatens to undermine the ability of retrospective review to serve a balanced, anti-capture purpose.

In a second order, President Obama moved retrospective review even further in an antiregulatory direction. Executive Order 13,610 states that, when "implementing and improving their retrospective review plans . . . agencies shall give priority . . . to those initiatives that will produce significant quantifiable monetary savings or significant quantifiable reductions in paperwork."[89] No similar language is included requesting that agencies emphasize rules that would increase regulatory benefits at low cost. This language places a permanent tilt in the process of regulatory review away from net benefits maximization and toward simple cost-reduction, a move that may result in a long-term antiregulatory bias within regulatory review. If this occurs, it will represent a major lost opportunity to use this tool to protect administrative agencies against capture. Indeed, by providing regulated industry with an additional opportunity to seek less stringent regulation, without providing protection-oriented groups with a similar opportunity to increase regulatory benefits, the retrospective review process may ultimately increase the susceptibility of the administrative state to capture.

Agency Inaction

Because both over- and under-activity can have detrimental effects on social well-being, it is important for OIRA to engage in review of both agency action and agency *in*action. The current system of regulatory review, in which OIRA review is triggered only when proposed rules are sent to the

---

[88] Michael A. Livermore and Jason A. Schwartz, "Unbalanced Retrospective Regulatory Review," RegBlog, July 12, 2012, https://www.law.upenn.edu/blogs/regblog/2012/07/12-livermore-schwartz-review.html.

[89] Exec. Order 13,610, 77 Fed. Reg. 28,469 § 3 (May 10, 2012).

White House, is inadequate to the task; therefore, reforms should be considered to expand OIRA's review powers to cases in which agencies fail to act.

Since the time of the Reagan Order, when Niskanen's self-aggrandizing bureaucrat hypothesis held broad sway in the White House, OIRA review had tended to focus on ensuring that regulatory costs did not exceed benefits. It is agency action that is typically subject to review, to ensure that overzealous regulators do not generate overly burdensome requirements for businesses. In general, the lion's share of OIRA's regulatory review resources are devoted to this checking function that is meant to rein in costly rules.

This institutional arrangement would be well justified if agencies had a systematic tendency to overregulate or provide inefficiently high levels of protection against environmental, public health, or safety risks. However, in fact, there are a variety of reasons to expect that agencies would be just as likely to suffer from a bias toward inaction, rather than overactivity. When agencies act, they face a wide range of potential criticisms from powerful interest groups, as well as review in court, the executive, and from Congress.[90] The failure to act, although it may generate some complaints, is not accompanied by the same level of scrutiny.[91] This fact alone would tend to drive risk-averse agency officials toward delay and ossification.[92] A host of other factors, from a desire to please regulated industry with lax standards, to an internal ideological commitment to a light government touch, might push agencies away from aggressively carrying out their mandate.[93]

To deal with the reality that agencies can err by regulating too little as well as too much, OIRA review of inaction is appropriate. There is some precedent for this type of review. Under Administrator John Graham, OIRA instituted a limited practice of issuing "prompt letters" to agencies concerning areas in which additional rules could be useful. These prompt letters represented an important innovation in regulatory review: it was the first time that OIRA took a proactive role in prodding agencies forward.[94] Graham's prompt letters were an important step in balancing the function of review to recognize that agencies could also, for a range of reasons, fail to take

---

[90] See Daryl J. Levinson, "Empire-Building Government in Constitutional Law," *Harvard Law Review* 118 (2005): 915, 932–43.

[91] Glen Staszewski, "The Federal Inaction Commission," *Emory Law Journal* 59 (2009): 369, 375–82.

[92] Michael A. Livermore, "Reviving Environmental Protection: Preference-Directed Regulation and Regulatory Ossification," *Virginia Environmental Law Journal* 25 (2007): 311.

[93] See Michael A. Livermore, "Cause or Cure? Cost-Benefit Analysis and Regulatory Gridlock," *New York University Environmental Law Journal* 17 (2008): 107, 119–20.

[94] Bagley and Revesz, "Centralized Oversight of the Regulatory State," 1277–80.

useful steps in providing cost-beneficial public protections. Prompt letters are an insufficient solution to the problem of agency inaction, however, because most of OIRA's resources are dedicated to keeping up with its regulatory review duties. As a result, prompt letters have tended to be issued only in an ad hoc fashion.

One difficulty in structuring review of inaction is that there are a potentially limitless number of "inactions" that could be the subject of review. There need to be some mechanisms to cabin that review and channel it in a direction that will ultimately be useful in the administrative process. One potential mechanism that could help give OIRA a more proactive role toward agencies would be through OIRA review of petitions for rulemaking. All agencies have some process where individuals or groups can petition that agency for a rulemaking. Under the Administrative Procedure Act, agencies are required to respond to these petitions and there must be some reasoned explanation if the petition is denied – although courts are highly deferential with respect to both the timeline and the standard of review of petition denials. Even given judicial deference to agencies in this area, petitions have had an important action-forcing effect on agencies: the most famous example is *Massachusetts v. EPA*,[95] in which the Supreme Court found that the EPA had not provided appropriate justification for its decision not to regulate greenhouse gases emission from motor vehicles under the Clean Air Act.[96]

Each year in an annual report to Congress, OIRA compiles a list of the regulations that were adopted in the past year, aggregates costs and benefits, and makes recommendations to agencies regarding improvements in their process of regulatory decision making. This annual review provides a procedural opportunity for OIRA to collect information about petitions that are currently pending before agencies and, when appropriate, examine petitions that are either languishing or that have been denied without adequate justification. Through this review mechanism, OIRA can use information generated by private actors to identify areas in which action is needed but agencies have failed to move forward. In this way, some OIRA review of agency inaction will help balance the existing structure of regulatory review, which focuses almost exclusively on agency action.

Complete review of agency inaction is implausible. There are a potentially limitless number of potential regulations that agencies could adopt but do not. At the same time, OIRA's exclusive focus on agency action tends

---

[95] *Massachusetts v. EPA*, 549 U.S. 497 (2007).

[96] See generally Jody Freeman and Adrian Vermeule, "*Massachusetts v. EPA*: From Politics to Expertise," *Supreme Court Review* 2007: 51.

to tilt the institution of centralized regulatory review in an antiregulatory direction; it checks agency action but does not spur agencies forward. This system would make sense if there were good reason to believe that agencies are more inclined toward overregulation than under-regulation, but there is not. In fact, the variety of motivations and influences affecting administrative agencies are just as likely to produce too little regulation or ineffective tools to meet legitimate goals. A more balanced OIRA review will be better structured to overcome the range of obstacles that can undermine efficient decision making by administrative agencies.

CONCLUSION

Despite the shortcomings of the traditional justification for OIRA's anti-capture role, this chapter has nonetheless argued that OIRA plays an important anti-capture role for other reasons having to do with four important institutional features of the office. First, the generalist nature of OIRA's mandate and activities reduces the potential influence of special interest actors on regulation. Second, the coordinating role OIRA plays during the regulatory review process brings together different agencies, each of which will likely to be influenced by different interest groups, thereby reducing the ability of any one group to capture the multiagency process. Third, because cost-benefit analysis must be done according to an accepted methodology, is conducted in a relatively transparent manner, and is standardized across agencies through the OIRA review process, it acts as a check against capture. The nature of cost-benefit analysis raises the risk of detection of regulations unduly influenced by interest group pressure. Finally, the tradition of appointing relatively independent OIRA administrators helps ensure that OIRA is not subject to the policy priors of an administrator who came from an interest group, which is one source of interest group pressure that may influence other agencies.

In addition to offering a new defense for OIRA's anti-capture role, this chapter noted two opportunities for OIRA to expand that role. First, a greater role for retrospective review, recently initiated by the Obama Administration, may help augment OIRA's anti-capture role. Second, more robust OIRA review of agency inaction is needed to balance OIRA's role by addressing both over- and under-regulation by agencies.

Conclusion

A Focus on Evidence and Prevention

David A. Moss and Daniel Carpenter

Capture varies in both degree and kind, across regulations and agencies. This simple statement is as important as it is obvious, ultimately setting the stage for a new focus on the *prevention* of regulatory capture.

In tackling this variation head on, the study of capture is turning a corner. An early focus on models of regulatory decision making is increasingly giving way to fine-grained empirical work on special interest influence in the regulatory process. To be sure, weakness on the evidentiary front has long been an open secret in the field. Already in 1974 Richard Posner observed that "empirical research [on capture] has not been systematic."[1] As late as 2006, Ernesto Dal Bó declared in a review essay that "empirical evidence on the causes and consequences of regulatory capture is scarce."[2] Although Dal Bó's observation is still broadly correct today, it is becoming ever less so. A more detailed picture of the phenomenon is beginning to emerge, and many students of capture – including the authors of this volume – are rethinking their approach, asking not just what causes capture and what problems it creates, but what accounts for its relative strength or weakness in real-world situations.

The essential variance of regulatory capture cries out for explanation, and it points to *capture prevention* as an empirical topic every bit as important as capture itself. One reason is that the older, more extreme diagnoses no longer have compelling evidence behind them. The latest empirical work is revealing a portrait far more nuanced than the stark black and white sketches of earlier times (covered in Sections I and II of this volume). Capture, we learn, is neither absolute nor uni-dimensional. The old rendition of

[1] Richard A. Posner, "Theories of Economic Regulation," *Bell Journal of Economics and Management Science* 5 (2) (Autumn 1974): 353.

[2] Ernesto Dal Bó, "Regulatory Capture: A Review," *Oxford Review of Economic Policy* 22 (2) (2006): 220.

capture – in which powerful incumbent firms inevitably buy (or otherwise influence) regulators to build barriers to entry in their industries, and always eviscerate the public interest in the bargain – continues to enchant many onlookers in both academic and policy circles, but is increasingly difficult to reconcile with the world as it is. Particularly with the rise of health, safety, and environmental regulation, industry-specific regulators have become far less common, and industry pressure to *reduce* the scope of regulation (*corrosive capture*) is probably now considerably more common than industry efforts to expand it. Entry barriers are by no means the only goal of industry interests when it comes to regulation, and most likely not the principal one. In some cases, influence over regulators may still be explicitly purchased, but such illegal activity is likely more the exception than the rule in the United States. Implicit quid pro quos are almost certainly more typical, whether through campaign contributions or the revolving door, and industry may find even implicit deals unnecessary when broader influence can be exercised, indirectly, through *cultural capture.*

Simply put, regulatory capture is not an all-or-nothing affair. The old Stiglerian notion of a fully captured regulator is most likely a rarity, if it exists at all. In fact, in recent years, the most searching analyses have cast doubt on some of the most celebrated cases of Stiglerian capture. Much of the evidence used in the older literature – including selective examination of the historical record and simple correlations between measures of special interest and regulatory outcomes – no longer suffices for rigorous analysis or understanding.

In a world where capture varies, it seems very likely that some regulatory systems and agencies have done a better job than others at resisting it. Put differently, the prospect of *preventing* or *limiting* capture becomes a distinct possibility and creates an exciting new frontier in social scientific research (as explored in Sections III and IV of our volume). Such research can and should begin with the relative successes of the past, for the prevention of capture actually has deep roots in regulatory practice. In Molière's classic comedy *The Bourgeois Gentleman*, the central character Monsieur Jourdain is delighted to discover that he has been speaking prose all of his life, and without knowing it. Countless scholars and policymakers, it turns out, have been living in a similar state of blissful ignorance of an unrecognized capacity. Preventing capture is something our regulatory system has been doing all along, at least to a degree, without almost anyone recognizing it. In fact, this may be the most important finding to arise from this volume. Many regulatory bodies have developed surprisingly strong immune systems, apparently capable of keeping the worst forms of capture at bay.

Our regulatory system has thus been speaking prose – and perhaps even a little poetry – without us knowing it. Past claims of capture, meanwhile, have often been greatly exaggerated, as if no regulatory defense mechanisms existed at all.

Yet these defense mechanisms are widespread. Some, ranging from judicial review to the role of the media in informing the public and holding policymakers accountable, are built deeply into the institutions of American democracy. Others, such as the rules of administrative procedure (particularly the public notice and comment period), are the products of congressional action, whereas still others, such as standardized cost-benefit analysis run through the Office of Information and Regulatory Affairs (OIRA), hail from the executive branch. A quick list of some additional capture-prevention strategies at the agency level, which emerged across the chapters of this volume, include:

- Involvement of subnational officials in federal notice and comment (Yackee, Chapter 11);
- Creation of consumer empowerment programs tied to regulators (Schwarcz, Chapter 13)
- Cultivation of diverse and independent experts (Kwak, Cuéllar, McCarty, Chapters 4, 12, and 5, respectively)
- Institutionalization of "devil's advocates" within agencies (Kwak, Chapter 4)
- Expanded review by OIRA to include agency *inaction* as well as action (Livermore/Revesz, Chapter 15)

We review all of these strategies, as well as a number of others, in greater detail in the pages that follow. The point here is simply that there are many capture-prevention mechanisms already at work – and many others, including those proposed in this volume, that merit careful attention. To a significant extent, therefore, capture appears to be a treatable condition.

Until fairly recently, however, one rather radical treatment – deregulation – was the remedy of choice. Many saw it as the only remedy. If capture was absolute and deeply destructive of the public interest, then eliminating the offending regulation seemed like the appropriate response. Yet as we have seen throughout this volume, capture is almost always a matter of degree. While the presence of undue special interest influence in the policymaking process means that the resulting regulation will be suboptimal from a public interest perspective, it does not imply that the regulation will necessarily harm the public interest, on net. We stress this point by distinguishing between *strong* and *weak* capture; the former is associated with regulation that actually harms the public interest, whereas the latter produces regulation that is less public serving than it could be, but not harmful, on net. Although most – and perhaps all – regulatory systems are subject to some undue influence and are thus weakly captured, only *strong* capture – which we suspect is far less common – creates a situation in which outright elimination of the regulatory regime is justified.

Because we define weak versus strong capture relative to the *net benefit* of the captured regulation (a binary distinction that has obvious policy relevance), this distinction does not perfectly track the *degree* to which undue influence bends regulation from the public interest – that is, whether capture is *pervasive* or *limited* in an empirical sense.[3] As we previewed in our Introduction, capture can in theory be empirically pervasive but still weak if the social benefits of the captured regulation continue to outweigh its costs, and it can also be empirically limited but strong if the captured regulation ends up harming the public interest overall. In practice, however, these two dimensions of capture – strong/weak and pervasive/limited – are likely to be linked, and a finding of pervasive capture may be suggestive of strong capture, and limited of weak, even if the association is clearly far from perfect. What we can say, based on our review of both the literature and the empirical studies in this volume, is the following: although capture can (and does) take a range of forms, credible evidence of strong and/or pervasive capture is difficult to find, and we suspect that cases of both are quite rare.

It is worth pausing here and reflecting on the implications of even this *minimal* conclusion. If, as we claim (and as many of our chapters have plausibly suggested), most agencies and regulations suffer at most only from weak capture, then like Molière's Monsieur Jourdain, policymakers must have been doing something right (or avoiding doing something wrong) all along. To the extent that strong capture exists, the policy implications

---

[3] The distinction between strong/weak and pervasive/limited can be represented in terms of variables in a simple linear welfare equation. Suppose that we can observe the benefits of a regulation B, its costs K, and the reduction in benefits (or addition to costs) due to capture, C. For the purposes of the sketch here, we can assume all these variables to be continuous and non-negatively valued (≥ 0). When capture is more empirically pervasive, C will correspondingly take larger values, and C will take lower values when capture is limited. Yet whether capture is strong or weak depends on how much capture disrupts the net welfare delivered by the regulation. A policy is considered desirable if $B - K \geq \eta$, where η is a cutoff value (≥ 0) that settles the choice between favoring a regulatory policy or something else. Yet strong capture would, by definition, reverse the inequality, such that $B - K - C < \eta$, with the critical "cutoff" value between weak and strong capture being simply $C' = B - (\eta + K)$. When C is so pervasive as to be above this level, capture is strong; when C is sufficiently limited to rest below this level, it is weak.

are obvious: either resolve the capture problem or remove the regulation.[4] However, if weak capture is the reigning pattern, then the range of suitable reforms should extend far beyond simple deregulation, and – importantly – any reforms undertaken must account for the fact that the present structure has resisted capture, at least to a degree and potentially rather robustly.

The empirical turn in capture research that has brought us to this point has thus opened the door to new thinking on the prevention of capture and how this might be accomplished. At the same time, it has invited new perspectives on capture itself, and how it functions in practice, and it is to those new perspectives that we now turn.

NEW PERSPECTIVES ON REGULATORY CAPTURE

As William Novak suggests in his historical essay in this volume, special interest influence has been a perennial problem of American democracy. It has literally always been with us, and each attempt to address one manifestation of the problem has inevitably created others, whether in the form of legislative corruption or regulatory capture or private coercion. More often than not, it has been a story of two steps forward and one step back. The independent regulatory commission played a significant role in reducing the impact of legislative corruption, but also became subject to special interest influence itself. The "discovery" of capture in the early 1970s, in other words, did not represent the identification of a dangerous new ailment of American democracy, which had the potential to be cured, but rather the *rediscovery* of a chronic disease that was far from fatal but still required ongoing management to limit its adverse effects.

Given this history, it should be no surprise that capture itself has continued to evolve. As Daniel Carpenter suggests in Chapter 7 on the Food and Drug Administration, for example, *corrosive* or *deregulatory* capture, in which firms seek to avoid regulation or press for its elimination, may

---

[4] We remind the reader here that resolving the problem could involve a kind of "blow it up and start over again" solution, as the Department of Interior did with the Minerals Management Service after the *Deepwater Horizon* tragedy, or as France has recently done with its national medical products regulator (replacing the Agence française de sécurité sanitaire des produits de santé with a new regulator) in the wake of the Mediator scandal there. Martine Lochouarn, "France Launches New Drug Regulatory Agency," *Lancet* 379 (9832) (June 9, 2012): 2136, accessed December 21, 2012, http://www.thelancet.com/journals/lancet/article/PIIS0140–6736%2812%2960927–1/fulltext. The key is that in the case of *strong corrosive capture*, the solution may require the abandonment of an existing regulatory structure followed by its replacement with one that is expected to be more effective.

today be even more common than the more traditional notion of capture, in which incumbent firms actively pursue regulatory barriers to entry. Mariano-Florentino Cuéllar reinforces this observation in Chapter 12, noting how frequently business interests find themselves fighting regulation – trying to prevent or dismantle it – rather than trying to build it. Richard Posner takes a similar observation still further, arguing in Chapter 2 that because regulation has changed so fundamentally since the 1970s, particularly as a result of the movement for deregulation and the rise of non-industry-specific regulation, the term *capture* is itself no longer meaningful or relevant. Today, he suggests, firms regularly aim to weaken regulation to reduce the costs of compliance, rather than to grab hold of regulation (i.e., capture it) as an anticompetitive weapon. Although we agree with Judge Posner about the changes in the regulatory landscape – with corrosive capture largely replacing entry-barrier capture over the past several decades – we favor a broader definition of capture and therefore find the term still relevant.

Another variation on the traditional conception of capture is *cultural capture*, which James Kwak unpacks in Chapter 4. Here, as Kwak explains, the problem is not that regulators are lured into favoring special interests at the expense of the public interest, intentionally and knowingly, but rather that they are so persuaded by the special interests' worldview that they come to believe they can best serve the public interest by advancing the agenda of the special interests. Although this reflects corruption of a very different sort, if it can be called corruption at all, it is nonetheless a potentially powerful way in which special interests undercut the public interest and is thus highly deserving of further attention.

Luigi Zingales in Chapter 6 comes at a similar problem in a different way by focusing on academic economists and whether they are themselves subject to capture by special interests. If so, then reliance on their ostensibly neutral expertise could again end up shaping regulatory decisions in ways that mimic more traditional capture, even in cases in which the regulators remain entirely uncorrupted. Zingales's analysis gestures to a broader mechanism of regulatory capture – indirect capture of regulatory agencies by means of the capture of the professions on which those agencies rely for information, expertise, and even appointments. For this reason, Zingales's inquiry points to fundamental connections between conflict of interest, on the one hand, and regulatory capture, on the other.[5]

---

[5] Lawrence Lessig, "Democracy after Citizens' United," *Boston Review*; Dennis F. Thompson, "Understanding Financial Conflicts of Interest," *New England Journal of Medicine* 329 (8) (August 19, 1993): 573–576.

A NEW EMPIRICAL APPROACH TO DIAGNOSING CAPTURE

The studies in this volume are theoretically informed – they ask questions about the existence of weak versus strong capture, they ask about the kind of capture at work (anticompetitive versus corrosive), and they invoke mechanisms such as quid-pro-quo capture and cultural capture. Yet what most distinguishes them from an earlier generation of capture scholarship is their deep empirical focus. We will return to the issue of prevention in the next section, but first we review the new empirical approach to diagnosing capture.

While some degree of capture may well be inevitable, several chapters in Sections III and IV of the volume suggest that claims about the extent and effects of special interest influence in the regulatory process are often overstated. Because regulatory decisions will always favor one interest or another, it is all too easy to conclude – without much evidence – that the party that benefits must have captured the regulation. Indeed, several chapters show that initial inferences about regulatory capture can prove mistaken or exaggerated when assessed forthrightly against the historical record. David Moss and Jonathan B.L. Decker examine in Chapter 8 a case that has been regarded as a classic historical example of capture – the broadcast spectrum restrictions of the Federal Radio Commission (FRC) – and show that the evidence for capture of the FRC in this episode from 1927 is essentially zero. The FRC's refusal to expand the broadcast spectrum in 1927 is commonly attributed to the quiet influence of incumbent broadcasters seeking to restrict the space available to their competitors. However, not only is there no evidence of broadcasters having tried to exert inappropriate influence in this case, but such an effort would hardly have been necessary given that *every* major interest group, from listeners to manufacturers, supported the FRC's decision as a way of keeping costs down and maximizing the quality of existing radio broadcasts. Christopher Carrigan, meanwhile, examines in Chapter 10 the Minerals Management Service (MMS), which is widely regarded along with financial agencies as emblematic of capture today. He shows that although special interest influence did buffet the MMS, a pro-industry influence also came from voters and elected legislators who wired the agency with potentially incompatible aims. And in a methodologically sophisticated analysis of responses to mining accidents, Sanford Gordon and Catherine Hafer show in Chapter 9 that at the Mine Safety and Health Administration, political appointees made a measurable impact on regulator actions over and above the influence of industry. Even accounting for strategic behavior, Gordon and Hafer demonstrate that changes in political leadership and the public salience of mine safety combine to shape enforcement in ways that transcend the interests and influence of the industry. To understand how regulation of mine safety works, they persuasively show that more sophisticated analysis is required.

A key insight regarding the tendency to overdiagnose capture also comes from Nolan McCarty's analysis in Chapter 5 of policy complexity. In complex regulatory settings, McCarty shows, politics and decision making may seem to favor industry even when regulators are pursuing the public interest, because of their need to obtain specialized information from business. McCarty argues that although certain complex situations force regulators to rely on industry in ways that industry can use to its favor, such results may in some cases be best for the public relative to the alternatives of banning the activities or not regulating them at all.[6] Combined with previous research showing that industry and large-firm advantages can occur in regulation without capture,[7] McCarty's theoretical contribution suggests that an inference of capture cannot be premised only on agency design or on observed industry or firm advantages, particularly in a context of regulatory complexity. Analysts must also examine the process by which the politics of attempted capture translates into regulatory results.

STRATEGIES AND MECHANISMS FOR PREVENTING CAPTURE

All of these insights – and many others from this volume and beyond – reinforce our belief that close empirical work will continue to foster a richer, more nuanced, and more expansive understanding of regulation and regulatory capture. Such work is especially important from a policy

---

[6] It is worth keeping in mind that, as with all general models, McCarty's analysis focuses upon a certain kind of complexity. Not every complex situation creates these constraints, and there are cases – such as in American pharmaceutical regulation – where the informational benefits of regulation overcome these problems. See, for example, Daniel Carpenter, "Reputation, Information and Confidence – The Political Economy of Pharmaceutical Regulation," in Daniel Farber and Anne Joseph O'Connell, eds., *Public Choice and Public Law* (Northampton, MA: Edward Elgar, 2009). As a consequence, it is important not to view complexity as an inescapable "institutions trap" from which society – in all cases – can escape only by resorting to the extremes of outright bans on the one hand or no regulation (laissez-faire) on the other.

[7] Carpenter, "Protection without Capture: Product Approval by a Politically Responsive, Learning Regulator," *American Political Science Review* 98 (4) (2004): 513–31. A similar conclusion is reached in a game-theoretic model applied to "approval regulation" contexts such as licensing and permitting, or the review of new drugs and medical devices at the FDA; Carpenter and Michael M. Ting, "Regulatory Errors with Endogenous Agendas," *American Journal of Political Science* 51 (4) (October 2007): 835–53.

standpoint because it allows for new possibilities in the critical area of prevention. The fact that some agencies appear more or less captured than others – a fact that Mariano-Florentino Cuéllar highlights in Chapter 12 – is fundamental to this project. Variation across agencies provides both a compelling reason to believe that capture *can* potentially be prevented and, at the same time, a source of strategies, ideas, and proposals for prevention.

Today, deregulation (or lack of regulation) is often seen as the best antidote to regulatory capture. Sometimes this may be right. But there is a danger of throwing the baby out with the bathwater. The more we understand the nature of special interest influence over regulation, the more we should be able to devise a *spectrum* of remedies to reduce the scope of regulatory capture – remedies including, but not limited to, deregulation.

Although research on strategies for preventing capture remains at an early stage, there have been some notable contributions over the past several decades, which we review here in combination with contributions from this volume.

Dividing Power. In the 1990s, a number of scholars began to focus on the division of power across multiple regulators (or, more specifically, the division of responsibility for oversight of a particular industry across multiple regulators) as a means of preventing capture. One prominent argument was that competition among regulators could reduce the likelihood of collusion between individual regulators and a regulated industry by driving up the costs. As the game theorists Jean-Jacques Laffont and David Martimort explained, "Separation of regulators divides the information at their disposal and thus limits their discretion in engaging in socially wasteful activities. . . . As a result, the transaction costs of collusive activities increase and preventing collusion becomes easier. . . . The separation of regulators may be an optimal organizational response to the threat of capture."[8] The political scientist Terry Moe has observed, meanwhile, that the "American separation of powers system virtually guarantees that the losers, opposing interest groups, will have enough power to participate in some fashion as well."[9]

Although these are powerful arguments, here too the essays in our volume can render a more nuanced understanding, one that has policy relevance and that also lays the groundwork for further research. McCarty's analysis

---

[8] Jean-Jacques Laffont and David Martimort, "Separation of Regulators against Collusive Behavior," *RAND Journal of Economics* 30 (2) (Summer 1999): 233, 257.

[9] Terry M. Moe, "The Politics of Structural Choice: Toward a Theory of Public Bureaucracy," in Oliver E. Williamson, ed., *Organization Theory: From Chester Barnard to the Present and Beyond*, expanded ed. (New York: Oxford University Press, 1995), 147.

in Chapter 5 suggests that in highly complex industries – with finance as the exemplar – the problem is sometimes *not* that a monopoly on information leads self-interested regulators to collude, but that ambiguous information and a lack of expertise combine to prevent even the most benevolent regulator from creating policies that advance public welfare. If McCarty is right, it seems unlikely that dividing that information among multiple regulatory agencies would address the underlying problem. Indeed, such division may even exacerbate it by decreasing capacity and therefore increasing the agencies' dependence on industry insiders. As with other cases of "observational equivalence" among capture theories (and between capture and noncapture theories), casual analysts might find it difficult to determine whether a Laffont-Tirole collusion model or a McCarty capture-by-complexity model is at work in a particular case. Yet the two mechanisms would likely call for very different policy responses. This underscores once more the importance of carefully diagnosing the causes of capture, and evaluating alternatives, before advocating reform.

Administrative Procedure. In 1987, Mathew McCubbins, Roger Noll, and Barry Weingast hypothesized that administrative procedure was introduced and employed with strategic ends in mind, precisely so that elected lawmakers could control unelected bureaucrats and, in turn, prevent "agency officials [from allowing] the bureau to be 'captured' by selling out to an external group."[10]

More recently, in a 2008 volume based on a series of case studies, Steven Croley refocused attention on administrative procedure as a powerful device for preventing capture, but suggested an almost opposite logic from Mc-Cubbins, Noll, and Weingast. Instead of subjecting regulators to greater oversight and control by legislators, administrative procedure (according to Croley) effectively gives regulators greater autonomy from legislators and ends up leveling the playing field across interests, weak and strong, by requiring greater openness (public notice) and broader input (public comment). "[W]hile it is true that notice-and-comment rulemaking enables regulated interest groups and Congress to monitor agencies more easily," Croley wrote, "the rulemaking process also allows other types of groups – public-interest law firms, the media, the public, government watchdog groups – to keep abreast of agency action more easily as well. Relative to these groups, Congress and regulated parties would certainly have a comparative

---

[10] Mathew D. McCubbins, Roger G. Noll, and Barry R. Weingast, "Administrative Procedures as Instruments of Political Control," *Journal of Law, Economics, & Organization* 3 (2) (Autumn 1987): 247.

advantage at monitoring agencies, if agency rulemaking processes were not standardized."[11]

Media Coverage and Journalistic Scrutiny. In recent years, the media has also been held up as a potential bulwark against capture, including legislative capture – again on the basis of detailed empirical work. Moss and Mary Oey showed that in each of three major cases in which weak interests prevailed over better organized ones, significant legislative movement followed the appearance of relevant horror stories in the press, which presumably alerted the public to an underlying problem. In 1980, for example, Superfund was enacted over the vehement objections of the chemical industry after revelations about Love Canal exploded in the national media.[12] Alexander Dyck, Moss, and Zingales, meanwhile, showed that lawmakers during the Progressive period were more likely to alter their normal voting patterns after a piece of muckraking journalism appeared on the issue in question. More generally, they argued that "profit-maximizing media firms can play an important role in reducing the power vested interests have on policymaking.... By informing voters, media help make elected representatives more sensitive to the interests of their constituencies and less prone to being captured by special interests."[13]

Chapters in this volume extend this logic by pointing to the importance of public debate and media coverage in plausibly reducing or preventing capture. The various regulatory initiatives covered by Cuéllar had the property of being intensively followed by general media interests and by consumer and health specialists. Gordon and Hafer find that mine safety regulators are more aggressive in the aftermath of highly publicized disasters. And both Cuéllar and Carpenter point to the legitimacy of existing regulatory arrangements (the reputations and acknowledged expertise of an implementing agency), which means in part that the media organizations responsible for shaping an agency's reputation can affect administrative behavior.[14]

---

[11] Steven P. Croley, *Regulation and Public Interests: The Possibility of Good Regulatory Government* (Princeton: Princeton University Press, 2008), 143–44. An earlier empirical demonstration of this pluralist outcome appears in Steven Balla, "Administrative Procedures and Political Control of the Bureaucracy," *American Political Science Review* 92 (1998): 663–73.

[12] David Moss and Mary Oey, "The Paranoid Style in the Study of American Politics," in *Government and Markets: Toward a New Theory of Regulation*, eds. Edward Balleisen and David Moss (Cambridge: Cambridge University Press, 2010).

[13] Alexander Dyck, David A. Moss, and Luigi Zingales, "Media versus Special Interests" (NBER Working Paper Series, No. 14360, September 2008), 31.

[14] There is growing evidence for a more general association between media coverage and agency behavior; Daniel Carpenter, "Groups, the Media, Agency Waiting Costs and FDA Drug Approval," *American Journal of Political Science* 46 (3) (July 2002): 490–505; Sanford

Consumer Empowerment and the Promise of Diffuse Interests. Daniel Schwarcz focuses in Chapter 13 on the potential for consumer empowerment in regulatory processes, whether through dedicated governmental entities designed to reflect consumer interests or through formal empowerment of independent groups representing consumer interests, and how this too might constitute a valuable counterweight to concentrated industrial interests in some circumstances. Schwarz's analysis of consumer empowerment programs suggests particular conditions for their effectiveness, including a unity of purpose and focus among consumer representatives, and a combination of legitimacy and expertise among consumer organizations.

An especially striking claim about diffuse interests, including consumers, comes from the political scientist Gunnar Trumbull, who argues that diffuse interests typically exercise a great deal of influence and ultimately play a powerful role in preventing capture by concentrated interests. This represents a sharp departure from traditional capture theory, which portrays diffuse interests as inevitably too weak to stand up to those concentrated interests. As Trumbull shows – once again through a series of detailed case studies, particularly involving consumer groups – diffuse interests are actually far more capable of organizing than is commonly believed. He argues further that these diffuse interests prove influential because of their considerable legitimacy.[15] If so, then an important challenge in contemplating how best to prevent capture will involve determining the conditions under which diffuse interests are (and are not) able to organize effectively, because they apparently stand as a strong potential counterweight to narrower interests, including industrial lobbies.

Diverse and Independent Expertise. Several of the studies in this volume invoke the issue of expertise and the opportunities for reducing the risk of capture by diversifying the sources of expertise in regulatory decision making. In her close study of rulemaking at the U.S. Department of Transportation, for example, Susan Webb Yackee stresses in Chapter 11 the importance of engaging with a diversity of interests and experts, beyond the regulated industry itself. In particular, she emphasizes (as a result of her empirical analysis) the highly constructive role of subnational officials in the public comment period, which "may provide a foil to business interests and thus may deter agency capture." Similarly, in Chapter 4 on cultural capture, James Kwak highlights the potential value of academic advisory boards that

---

Gordon, "Politicizing Agency Spending: Lessons from a Bush-Era Scandal," *American Political Science Review* 105 (4) (November 2011): 717–34.

[15] Gunnar Trumbull, *Strength in Numbers: The Political Power of Weak Interests* (Cambridge, MA: Harvard University Press, 2012).

some agencies convene to review data and methodologies. According to Kwak, "the external academic community might do a better job of ensuring that agencies consider a diversity of relevant opinion and research." Looking across regulators, Mariano-Florentino Cuéllar examines in Chapter 12 three public health agencies (U.S. Department of Agriculture, Food and Drug Administration, and Centers for Disease Control and Prevention) and asks why they have been able to achieve at least a degree of independence from the industries they regulate, especially as compared with an agency such as the Bureau of Alcohol, Tobacco, Firearms and Explosives, which has been far less independent relative to gun dealers. With respect to expertise, Cuéllar observes that the more independent agencies had succeeded in developing their own "scientific expertise and technical competence," which heightened agency legitimacy and autonomy. Along much the same lines, McCarty suggests in Chapter 5 that "Government agencies that regulate complex domains need to develop career paths and educational opportunities for . . . key personnel that are more autonomous from the regulated industry."

Diverse Viewpoints and Interests. Even beyond the question of expertise, several authors stress the value of exposing the rulemaking process to diverse perspectives and ideas. Cuéllar, for example, highlights the importance of regulators forging linkages and alliances with a broad range of interests and authorities, which diversify information sources and empower and insulate the agencies vis-à-vis any particular interest. And Kwak recommends a variety of strategies for injecting greater diversity into the process, including "[n]egotiated rulemaking, in which competing interest groups are invited to the agency's table to negotiate proposed rules," efforts to "increase the set of backgrounds from which regulators are drawn, thereby requiring a diversity of viewpoints," and even the institutionalization of "independent 'devil's advocates' within agencies to represent contrarian viewpoints."

Judicial Review of Regulatory Decisions. Elizabeth Magill, meanwhile, highlights in Chapter 14 the power of judicial review to invalidate captured decisions after the fact. Although recognizing that this mechanism is far from perfect (because it only kicks in after a regulation is in place, and because a party with standing has to take the initiative before any review can occur), she nonetheless sees it as an important mechanism for limiting capture and calls for its expansion. In particular, judicial review helps to level the playing field, allowing weak as well as strong to be heard, and is often effective in detecting cases in which the logical or evidentiary foundation for a particular regulatory action is weak. In most cases, moreover, judges (as compared to regulators) may be less liable to being captured themselves, because of lifetime tenure and greater independence from political actors.

Executive Review of Regulations Based on Cost-Benefit Analysis. Michael Livermore and Richard Revesz remind us in Chapter 15 that the Office of Information and Regulatory Affairs (OIRA) inside the Office of Management and Budget already plays an important role in limiting capture. This is not because the office is an extension of the president (as is commonly argued), but rather principally, in their view, because OIRA creates an additional external check on agency behavior and decisions through standardized cost-benefit analysis. Livermore and Revesz suggest that OIRA is itself quite difficult to capture, because it is a "general institution" rather than a "single-issue" institution, and that it reduces the risk of regulatory capture by increasing the diversity of agency perspectives represented in the rulemaking process. These authors propose that OIRA encourage agencies to conduct vigorous retrospective review, a process that can dramatically expand the investments that firms must make to successfully capture a regulation. Given their assessment of its effectiveness, Livermore and Revesz call for an expanded role for OIRA – including more robust OIRA review of agency *inaction* – to further limit possibilities for regulatory capture in all of its forms.[16]

LOOKING AHEAD

Although the proposals outlined in these pages are by no means exhaustive, they do provide an indication of the types of remedies that may be most promising in combating regulatory capture going forward. The empirical work on which they are based, moreover, suggests that many institutional protections against special interest influence are already in place and that at least in some cases these mechanisms may be considerably more effective than is commonly assumed, particularly against conventional forms of capture.

Ultimately, we believe that the increasingly empirical approach to capture that has been taking hold in recent years – and that we hope is exemplified in this volume – promises not only a more realistic picture of the problem, but also the possibility of more finely tuned remedies. Ideally, this shift toward the empirical in the study of capture presages a new orientation

---

[16] President Obama's first director of OIRA, Cass Sunstein (now at Harvard Law School), has offered similar general arguments about the promise of cost-benefit analysis to avoid both particularistic and populist errors, although his focus has not been placed on capture per se; see Sunstein, "Empirically Informed Regulation," *University of Chicago Law Review* 78 (2011): 1349.

toward government failure more generally, focused not just on whether failures exist, but also on how they play out in practice and how (and under what conditions) they can be prevented or minimized.[17] Surely, there would be little satisfaction with cardiologists if they could tell us only that heart failure exists, without having much to say about how to prevent it or limit its effects, short of killing the patient. Political economists should face the same challenge vis-à-vis government failure: they should feel the need to identify a range of preventive measures and remedies and the conditions under which each would be most effective. With respect to capture in particular, deregulation may be a valuable remedy in some cases, but it can hardly be the right remedy in all cases. A deeper and more detailed understanding of capture is required, and it is our hope that this volume constitutes at least a helpful step in the right direction.

---

[17] See especially David Moss, "Reversing the Null: Regulation, Deregulation, and the Power of Ideas," in Gerald Rosenfeld, Jay W. Lorsch, and Rakesh Khurana, eds., *Challenges to Business in the Twenty-First Century* (Cambridge, MA: American Academy of Arts and Sciences, 2011), 35–49.

Afterword

Senator Sheldon Whitehouse (D–RI)
Jim Leach, Professor, University of Iowa Law School; former
Republican Chairman of the House Committee on Banking and
Financial Services

For the most part, our country's regulatory framework serves the public interest well. It helps keep Americans safe from pollutants, personal injury, and other harms and supports the orderly operation of a dynamic economy. Yet the threat of regulatory capture is ever present. When powerful interests gain excessive influence over regulatory agencies, the integrity of the regulatory process is compromised, and catastrophic consequences can unfold.

The concept of regulatory capture is well established in economic, regulatory, and administrative law theory, appearing in the research of Nobel Laureate George Stigler, the writings of President Woodrow Wilson, and contemporary commentary by conservative as well as liberal columnists. Continued research and public attention to the issue are critical as the world becomes increasingly developed and interdependent. To that end, this volume represents an important step toward a better understanding of what regulatory capture is and points to ways it may be constrained.

Highlighted in the chapters are a variety of opinions about the causes and nature of regulatory capture within government agencies. As legislators (one former), we add an emphasis on the challenges of crafting statutory approaches that enable effective regulation and are conducive to regular oversight to ensure that regulations work as intended. We begin with seven key propositions about regulatory capture. We then touch on the implication of regulatory failures during recent financial crises and note several potential remedies to the capture issues involved.

The first widely accepted proposition is that the threat of regulatory capture is real and its consequences frequently substantial. As Woodrow Wilson explained more than one hundred years ago, "[i]f the government is to tell big business men how to run their business, then don't you see that big business men have to get closer to the government even than they are now? Don't you see that they must capture the government, in order not to be restrained too much by it?"[1] Regulatory agencies, like many other institutions making high-stakes decisions, by their very nature are vulnerable to capture. Marver Bernstein, the first dean of Princeton's Woodrow Wilson School of Public and International Affairs, wrote fifty-eight years ago that regulators tend over time to "become more concerned with the general health of the industry" and that they try "to prevent changes which will adversely affect" the industry.[2] Today, conservative columnist George Will annually identifies these corrupt relationships, such as the Louisiana Board of Embalmers and Funeral Directors, which Will argues "has become yet another example of 'regulatory capture,' controlled by the funeral industry it ostensibly regulates."[3]

Thus, from Wilson to Bernstein to the present day, the threat of regulatory capture has been broadly recognized. This volume takes the next major step forward by illuminating the contours of this threat and, perhaps most importantly, turning attention toward the question of prevention.

This volume not only demonstrates that regulatory capture is a real threat, but also identifies forms of capture that have not been recognized in the earlier literature, such as "cultural capture" and "capture through complexity." James Kwak and Nolan McCarty detail the risks of regulatory capture in the financial sector arising from the oft-mentioned problem of a "well-oiled revolving door," but they also trace new pathways through which this closeness can lead to capture, deemed "cultural capture," which comes about when regulators "share strong social ties to the industry and are more sympathetic on average to the industry's interests and viewpoints."[4] Christopher Carrigan likewise documents the types of unethical relationships that regulated industries have a strong incentive to develop. He notes that the unethical activity of employees of the Department of Interior's Minerals Management Service (MMS) before the BP oil spill was "clearly wrong and, if it promotes agency actions that favor the regulated industry, can be associated with capture."[5]

---

[1] Woodrow Wilson, *The New Freedom* (1912), 102.

[2] Marver H. Bernstein, *Regulating Business by Independent Commission* (Princeton, NJ: Princeton University Press, 1955), 87.

[3] George F. Will, "Will Supreme Court Answer Monks' Prayers?," *Washington Post*, November 14, 2012; see also George F. Will, "In Arizona, Nibbling Away at Free Enterprise," *Washington Post*, September 23, 2011.

[4] Kwak, Chapter 4, 91–93; McCarty, Chapter 5, 102.

[5] Carrigan, Chapter 10, 240.

Second, regulated entities have a strong incentive to gain influence over the drafting and enforcement of regulations. As Daniel Carpenter notes, for example, the Food and Drug Administration regulates industries that represent nearly a trillion dollar market.[6] Most companies, if given the option, would choose to spend a few million dollars to stop or mitigate rules that would cost them billions more. The bank robber Willie Sutton is said to have once explained that he robbed banks "because that's where the money is." When it comes to why regulated entities seek influence with regulators, a similar answer might be given. Today's financial markets, for example, are very different from those in our grandparents' era. The notional value of derivative products alone is greater than the gross domestic product of the United States.

Given the high stakes of regulation – the gains or losses caused by regulatory action or inaction – it is no surprise that tremendous efforts are undertaken every year to influence regulatory decisions. The same incentive is at work when powerful interests spend millions of dollars to lobby Congress. In the Eisenhower era, Senator Everett Dirksen is rumored once to have commented that "a billion here, a billion there, and pretty soon you're talking real money." With regard to drugs, derivatives, and other massive industries, it would appear that a trillion here and a trillion there can be the stakes of regulatory capture. In one sense it is impressive how much money is spread throughout the political process; yet these money flows are trivial compared with the potential benefits particular interests might receive with well-placed political "investments." This cost-benefit advantage to vested interests is particularly stark in the regulatory capture area, where so much decision making and oversight are outside of public view.

Third, regulated entities often have substantial organizational and resource advantages in the regulatory process, especially compared with the diffuse public interest. James Kwak highlights this point. Industry groups have extraordinary resources and can focus with great precision on a narrow group of regulators. In contrast, the public interest tends to be represented by broad-based groups that advocate on a number of issues and "likely lack the organizational infrastructure and staying power to knock on regulators' doors month-in, month-out on issue after issue."[7] Intensity of interest matters in the regulatory as well as the political world. And industry interest in regulatory decision making is difficult to match. As Luigi Zingales points out, industry's resource advantages help to grease the revolving door

---

[6] Carpenter, Chapter 7, 152.
[7] Kwak, Chapter 4, 106.

between regulatory positions and well-paid private sector jobs in the regulated industry, serving as both a cause and a symptom of regulatory capture.[8]

Fourth, some regulatory processes are more easily manipulated by special interests than others. McCarty demonstrates, for example, that agencies that rely on industry for funds, information, or expertise can be particularly susceptible to excessive industry influence.[9] This is particularly the case in high finance, where governmental overseers frequently lack relevant experience to keep up with fast-changing markets and product offerings. On the flip side, as Mariano-Florentino Cuellar argues in this volume, public health agencies seem to be less susceptible to capture. They are able to achieve some degree of independence from the industries they regulate, in large part because of their success in building in-house expertise.[10] Understanding this range of susceptibility to capture is integral to developing better and smarter regulation.

Fifth, regulatory capture is often difficult to detect. With respect to the revolving door between industry and government, Zingales explains that "this form of regulatory capture does not require an explicit quid pro quo between regulators and regulated, where a job is offered in exchange for a favorable decision."[11] The implicit prospect of a high-paying industry job may subtly influence a regulator to favor industry in a way that Zingales describes as "much more legitimate, and thus pervasive." Carpenter's chapter on detecting and measuring capture responds to this threat with a new set of tools for scholars and regulators to determine where industry influence has risen to the level of regulatory capture.[12] This can be quite difficult, as capture can be present even in regulations that never result in conspicuous failures. Prevention may be most effective and do the most good then when capture is detected *before* a catastrophe or when it is still in a mild form.

Sixth, regulatory capture can cause great damage. Although the cost of regulation can often seem high, the cost of inadequate regulation can be even greater. The failures at the MMS before the BP oil spill, of banking and housing regulators before the global financial crisis, and of the Mine Safety and Health Administration in the lead-up to the Sago Mine disaster reveal the enormous damage ineffectively regulated industries can cause. Incidents like these bring about human, environmental, and economic loss

---

[8] Zingales, Chapter 6, 127.
[9] McCarty, Chapter 5, 120.
[10] Cuellar, Chapter 12, 325.
[11] Zingales, Chapter 6, 127.
[12] Carpenter, Chapter 3.

and undermine public confidence in government. However, not all damage caused by failed regulations is due to capture. That is why it is so important to distinguish when capture is occurring from when it is not, so that reforms can target the real problem.

Seventh, congressional oversight and legislation are key to preventing and combating regulatory capture, so it is critical that Congress overcome barriers to effective action in this area. Members of Congress tend to focus on regulatory issues only within the jurisdictions of their committees, so there is an absence of meaningful, comprehensive oversight of regulatory capture as a general threat. Gaps or overlaps in committee jurisdictions can lead to oversight failures. Furthermore, congressional oversight is generally reactive rather than proactive, with hearings or investigations often only held after rather than before a disaster has occurred.

Yet with so much law made through regulation, and so much influence brought to bear on regulators, Congress has a responsibility to pursue regulatory capture as a systemic risk across all agencies. It must go beyond just investigating past failures. Hearings should periodically be held that focus on how to search for and identify regulatory capture across the entirety of the federal government. The need to give continual attention to the integrity and independence of regulatory institutions is a social imperative.

Regulatory authority, like all governmental power, is divided within and between federal, state, county, and city agencies. Accordingly, Congress must be vigilantly aware of the strengths and weaknesses of regulation at the state and community levels, particularly if that regulation affects national liabilities. For instance, during the savings and loan crisis of the 1970s and 1980s, cozy regulation of state-chartered savings and loans in a handful of states compounded the massive losses that had accumulated in a federal insurance fund. In the more recent financial crisis, lax state regulation of mortgage brokers allowed mortgage fraud to infect bundled products sold across the world. The federal government eventually found itself responsible for bailing out many of these bundled mortgage offerings as well as a state-regulated insurance company for losses embedded in a London subsidiary.

In the development and execution of laws, as of regulations, word-smithing nuances and manners of application can affect the bottom line of business. Accordingly, in many parts of American commerce, most notably finance, regulatory arbitrage can be an understandable but sometimes mis-chievous business option. Corporations have a natural preference to seek state and local jurisdictions where taxes are lowest and establish charters where the regulatory burden is least. Conversely, regulators in different institutions and jurisdictions sometimes compete for authority in ways that are most attuned to the regulated rather than the public.

These concerns make it easier to understand the regulatory failures in the lead-up to the financial crisis. To that end, Kwak explains that in the years preceding the 2007–2009 financial crisis, "several signs of traditional capture were present"[13] – for example, the Securities and Exchange Commission allowed investment banks to increase their leverage while foregoing comprehensive oversight.[14] In housing, Fannie Mae and Freddie Mac were ineffectually regulated by an agency largely unknown to the public, the Office of Federal Housing Enterprise Oversight. The agency was hamstrung by statutory restrictions, limitations placed on manpower, lack of expertise, and inattentive, industry-conflicted legislative oversight.

Washington's commercial banking regulators – the Federal Reserve, the Treasury, and the Federal Deposit Insurance Corporation – were more knowledgeable, experienced, and laden with greater regulatory discretion than the housing regulators. Nevertheless, their actions taken together had an industry-accommodating ideological bent that allowed our largest commercial and investment banks to leverage excessively their capital. High-risk strategies involving off-balance sheet investments and investments in derivatives became the norm in the first decade of the twenty-first century with disastrous consequences. There are many interrelated causes of the recent financial crisis, but the governmental intervention that followed could in large part have been constrained, perhaps avoided, if traditional leverage ratios applied to community banks had been maintained for money center institutions.

The full scope and form of regulatory capture involved in the financial crisis have yet to be fully documented, but this episode in the economic history of our country underscores the need for more independent regulatory processes and more vigorous congressional oversight. The American taxpayer has compelling reason to demand that systemically consequential institutions operate in the future with more prudence, fewer conflicts, and less leverage.

There will never be a silver bullet to completely prevent regulatory capture. There are too many aspects of human nature involved, and with such rapid commercial and technological change, governmental policy makers will always be a step behind the sophistication of American industry. Nonetheless, a variety of approaches have been suggested to constrain and

---

[13] Kwak, Chapter 4, 93.
[14] Kwak, Chapter 4, 72.

at least put a spotlight on the problem. For instance, contributors to this volume Michael Livermore and Richard Revesz recommend a centralized review of all regulations by an independent government body that they believe would not face the same pressures that specialized agencies experience from regulated industries,[15] Kwak proposes the appointment of an official public advocate who would represent the public interest during the regulatory process,[16] and Daniel Schwarcz suggests creating "consumer empowerment programs" to counteract industry influence over regulation.[17] In addition, Senator Whitehouse has pressed for the creation of an inspector general for regulatory capture.

Specific remedies aside, it is past time to acknowledge that regulatory capture has been observed too long and addressed too little. Scholars and advocates must together spread the word and engage voters and the media to be alert to the capture of regulatory agencies and to the possibility of prevention. Congress and the Executive Branch must at last pay adequate attention to this recurring infection in the body politic. The great challenge that these policy makers face is to infuse a public interest perspective into the regulatory decision-making process, because ultimately, the principal oversight that matters is of the public over its government.

[15] Livermore and Revesz, Chapter 15, 429.
[16] Kwak, Chapter 4, 96.
[17] Schwarcz, Chapter 13, 395–96.

Index

academia and academics, 125. *See also*
  economists' capture
  academic advisory boards, 463
  business interests influence on, 133, 138,
    139, 142, 146
  careers outside of, 125, 131
  contemporary capture scholarship, 5, 6
  cultural capture and, 97
  information needs and, 141
  limits of capture in, 125
  OIRA administrators and, 443, 444
  pro-business bias in tenure, 138
  publication process in, 132, 133
Act for the Protection of the Lives of Miners
    in the Territories (1891), 215
Adams, Charles Francis, 42, 43, 44
administrative law, 334, 405, 412, 442, 443,
    453. *See also* cost-benefit analysis;
    judicial review; notice and comment
  administrative law doctrine, 411
  interest groups taking advantage of, 75, 77
  OIRA administrators and, 443
  preventing capture and, 460
  rate of diminishing returns to investment,
    433
Administrative Law Judge (ALJ), 368
Administrative Procedure Act (1946), 293,
    399, 449
adulteration
  new legal concepts in, 340, 341, 342
Advanced Notice of Proposed Rulemaking
    (ANPRM), 302, 303
  defined, 294
adversarialism, 132, 236, 393
  as capture prevention, 246
  contentiousness and, 331

advertising and advertisements
  in pharmaceutical industry, 156, 158
  in radio industry, 182, 183, 201, 203, 204
  tobacco industry and, 348
advocacy. *See also* proxy advocacy
  focus on degree of capture, 21
  patient advocacy, 170
agency action, 118, 413, 438. *See also* agency
    inaction; by specific agency; judicial
    review
  across-the-board investigations of, 412
  adaptiveness in, 337, 340, 351, 352
  agency responsiveness to public
    comment, 314
  conditional forbearance and, 209
  Congress and president as supervisors of,
    397, 404, 406, 407
  influence capture model for, 118
  legal challenges to, 404, 405
  media coverage and, 211, 225, 236, 458
  OIRA review of, 421
  overzealous action by career employees,
    427
  political and legal constraints on, 333
  political principals and, 211
  principal-agent relationships and, 208,
    209
  public interest and, 334
  public salience and, 226
  regulatory delay and, 218
  responsiveness to industry interests, 209
  unreviewable agency action, 412
agency authority, 215, 260, 331, 471
  of FDA, 170
  of FRC, 183
  of OIRA, 425

475

CPSIA information can be obtained at www.ICGtesting.com
Printed in the USA
LVOW13*1605030114

367841LV00003B/8/P